M000287754

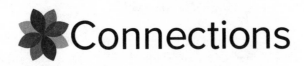Connections

Editorial Board

General Editors

JOEL B. GREEN (The United Methodist Church), Professor of New Testament Interpretation and Associate Dean for the Center for Advanced Theological Studies, Fuller Theological Seminary, Pasadena, CA

THOMAS G. LONG (Presbyterian Church (U.S.A.)), Bandy Professor Emeritus of Preaching at Candler School of Theology, Emory University, Atlanta, GA

LUKE A. POWERY (Progressive National Baptist Convention), Dean of Duke University Chapel and Associate Professor of Homiletics at Duke Divinity School, Durham, NC

CYNTHIA L. RIGBY (Presbyterian Church (U.S.A.)), W. C. Brown Professor of Theology, Austin Presbyterian Theological Seminary, Austin, TX

CAROLYN J. SHARP (The Episcopal Church), Professor of Homiletics, Yale Divinity School, New Haven, CT

Volume Editors

ERIC D. BARRETO (Cooperative Baptist Fellowship), Frederick and Margaret L. Weyerhaeuser Associate Professor of New Testament, Princeton Theological Seminary, Princeton, NJ

GREGORY CUÉLLAR (Baptist), Associate Professor of Old Testament, Austin Presbyterian Theological Seminary, Austin, TX

WILLIAM GREENWAY (Presbyterian Church (U.S.A.)), Professor of Philosophical Theology, Austin Presbyterian Theological Seminary, Austin, TX

CAROLYN B. HELSEL (Presbyterian Church (U.S.A.)), Assistant Professor of Homiletics, Austin Presbyterian Theological Seminary, Austin, TX

JENNIFER L. LORD (Presbyterian Church (U.S.A.)), Dorothy B. Vickery Professor of Homiletics and Liturgical Studies, Austin Presbyterian Theological Seminary, Austin, TX

SONG-MI SUZIE PARK (The United Methodist Church), Associate Professor of Old Testament, Austin Presbyterian Theological Seminary, Austin, TX

ZAIDA MALDONADO PÉREZ (The United Church of Christ), Professor Emeritus of Church History and Theology, Asbury Theological Seminary, Florida Dunnam Campus, Orlando, FL

EMERSON B. POWERY (The Episcopal Church), Professor of Biblical Studies, Messiah College, Mechanicsburg, PA

WYNDY CORBIN REUSCHLING (The United Methodist Church), Professor of Ethics and Theology, Ashland Theological Seminary, Ashland, OH

DAVID J. SCHLAFER (The Episcopal Church), Independent Consultant in Preaching and Assisting Priest, Episcopal Church of the Redeemer, Bethesda, MD

ANGELA SIMS (National Baptist Convention), President of Colgate Rochester Crozer Divinity School, Rochester, NY

DAVID F. WHITE (The United Methodist Church), C. Ellis and Nancy Gribble Nelson Professor of Christian Education, Professor in Methodist Studies, Austin Presbyterian Theological Seminary, Austin, TX

Psalms Editor

KIMBERLY BRACKEN LONG (Presbyterian Church (U.S.A.)), Editor, *Call to Worship: Liturgy, Music, Preaching, and the Arts*, Louisville, KY

Sidebar Editor

RACHEL TOOMBS (The Episcopal Church), Baylor University, Holy Spirit Episcopal Church, Waco, TX

Project Manager

JOAN MURCHISON, Austin Presbyterian Theological Seminary, Austin, TX

Project Compiler

PAMELA J. JARVIS, Austin Presbyterian Theological Seminary, Austin, TX

Year B, Volume 2
_____
Lent through Pentecost

Connections

A Lectionary Commentary for Preaching and Worship

Joel B. Green
Thomas G. Long
Luke A. Powery
Cynthia L. Rigby
Carolyn J. Sharp
General Editors

WESTMINSTER
JOHN KNOX PRESS
LOUISVILLE · KENTUCKY

© 2020 Westminster John Knox Press

First edition
Published by Westminster John Knox Press
Louisville, Kentucky

20 21 22 23 24 25 26 27 28 29—10 9 8 7 6 5 4 3 2 1

All rights reserved. No part of this book may be reproduced or transmitted in any form or by any means, electronic or mechanical, including photocopying, recording, or by any information storage or retrieval system, without permission in writing from the publisher. For information, address Westminster John Knox Press, 100 Witherspoon Street, Louisville, KY 40202-1396. Or contact us online at www.wjkbooks.com.

Unless otherwise indicated, Scripture quotations are from the New Revised Standard Version of the Bible, copyright © 1989 by the Division of Christian Education of the National Council of the Churches of Christ in the U.S.A., and are used by permission. Scripture quotations marked CEB are from the Common English Bible, © 2011 Common English Bible, and are used by permission. Scripture quotations marked NIV are from *The Holy Bible, New International Version.* Copyright © 1973, 1978, 1984, 2011 by Biblica, Inc.® Used by permission. All rights reserved worldwide. Scripture quotations marked TNIV are from *The Holy Bible, Today's New International Version.* Copyright © 2001, 2005 International Bible Society. Used by permission of International Bible Society®. All rights reserved worldwide.

Book and cover design by Allison Taylor

Library of Congress Cataloging-in-Publication Data
Names: Long, Thomas G., 1946– editor.
Title: Connections : a lectionary commentary for preaching and worship / Joel B. Green, Thomas G. Long,
    Luke A. Powery, Cynthia L. Rigby, Carolyn J. Sharp, general editors.
Description: Louisville, Kentucky : Westminster John Knox Press, 2018– |
    Includes index. |
Identifiers: LCCN 2018006372 (print) | LCCN 2018012579 (ebook) | ISBN 9781611648874 (ebk.) |
    ISBN 9780664262433 (volume 1 : hbk. : alk. paper)
Subjects: LCSH: Lectionary preaching. | Bible—Meditations. | Common
    lectionary (1992) | Lectionaries.
Classification: LCC BV4235.L43 (ebook) | LCC BV4235.L43 C66 2018 (print) |
    DDC 251/.6—dc23
LC record available at https://lccn.loc.gov/2018006372

Connections: Year B, Volume 2
ISBN: 9780664262419 (hardback)
ISBN: 9780664264833 (paperback)
ISBN: 9781646980130(ebook)

PRINTED IN THE UNITED STATES OF AMERICA
♾ The paper used in this publication meets the minimum requirements of the American National Standard
for Information Sciences—Permanence of Paper for Printed Library Materials, ANSI Z39.48-1992.

Most Westminster John Knox Press books are available at special quantity discounts when purchased in bulk by corporations, organizations, and special-interest groups. For more information, please e-mail SpecialSales@wjkbooks.com.

Contents

Second Sunday of Easter

Third Sunday of Easter

Fourth Sunday of Easter

Fifth Sunday of Easter

Sixth Sunday of Easter

Ascension of the Lord

Seventh Sunday of Easter

Day of Pentecost

Sidebars

Publisher's Note

"The preaching of the Word of God is the Word of God," says the Second Helvetic Confession. While that might sound like an exalted estimation of the homiletical task, it comes with an implicit warning: "A lot is riding on this business of preaching. Get it right!"

Believing that much does indeed depend on the church's proclamation, we offer Connections: A Lectionary Commentary for Preaching and Worship. Connections embodies two complementary convictions about the study of Scripture in preparation for preaching and worship. First, to best understand an individual passage of Scripture, we should put it in conversation with the rest of the Bible. Second, since all truth is God's truth, we should bring as many "lenses" as possible to the study of Scripture, drawn from as many sources as we can find. Our prayer is that this unique combination of approaches will illumine your study and preparation, facilitating the weekly task of bringing the Word of God to the people of God.

We at Westminster John Knox Press want to thank the superb editorial team that came together to make Connections possible. At the heart of that team are our general editors: Joel B. Green, Thomas G. Long, Luke A. Powery, Cynthia L. Rigby, and Carolyn J. Sharp. These five gifted scholars and preachers have poured countless hours into brainstorming, planning, reading, editing, and supporting the project. Their passion for authentic preaching and transformative worship shows up on every page. They pushed the writers and their fellow editors, they pushed us at the press, and most especially they pushed themselves to focus always on what you, the users of this resource, genuinely need. We are grateful to Kimberley Bracken Long for her innovative vision of what commentary on the Psalm readings could accomplish, and for recruiting a talented group of liturgists and preachers to implement that vision. Rachel Toombs did an exceptional job of identifying the sidebars that accompany each worship day's commentaries. At the forefront of the work have been the members of our editorial board, who helped us identify writers, assign passages, and most especially carefully edit each commentary. They have cheerfully allowed the project to intrude on their schedules in order to make possible this contribution to the life of the church. Most especially we thank our writers, drawn from a broad diversity of backgrounds, vocations, and perspectives. The distinctive character of our commentaries required much from our writers. Their passion for the preaching ministry of the church proved them worthy of the challenge.

A project of this size does not come together without the work of excellent support staff. Above all we are indebted to project manager Joan Murchison. Joan's fingerprints are all over the book you hold in your hands; her gentle, yet unconquerable, persistence always kept it moving forward in good shape and on time. We also wish to thank Pamela Jarvis, who skillfully compiled the dozens of separate commentaries and sidebars into this single volume.

Finally, our sincere thanks to the administration, faculty, and staff of Austin Presbyterian Theological Seminary, our institutional partner in producing Connections. President Theodore J. Wardlaw and Dean David H. Jensen have been steadfast friends of the project, enthusiastically agreeing to our partnership, carefully overseeing their faculty and staff's work on it, graciously hosting our meetings, and enthusiastically using their platform to promote Connections among their students, alumni, and friends.

It is with much joy that we commend Connections to you, our readers. May God use this resource to deepen and enrich your ministry of preaching and worship.

WESTMINSTER JOHN KNOX PRESS

Introducing Connections

Connections is a resource designed to help preachers generate sermons that are theologically deeper, liturgically richer, and culturally more pertinent. Based on the Revised Common Lectionary (RCL), which has wide ecumenical use, the hundreds of essays on the full array of biblical passages in the three-year cycle can be used effectively by preachers who follow the RCL, by those who follow other lectionaries, and by nonlectionary preachers alike.

The essential idea of Connections is that biblical texts display their power most fully when they are allowed to interact with a number of contexts, that is, when many connections are made between a biblical text and realities outside that text. Like the two poles of a battery, when the pole of the biblical text is connected to a different pole (another aspect of Scripture or a dimension of life outside Scripture), creative sparks fly and energy surges from pole to pole.

Two major interpretive essays, called Commentary 1 and Commentary 2, address every scriptural reading in the RCL. Commentary 1 explores preaching connections between a lectionary reading and other texts and themes within Scripture, and Commentary 2 makes preaching connections between the lectionary texts and themes in the larger culture outside of Scripture. These essays have been written by pastors, biblical scholars, theologians, and others, all of whom have a commitment to lively biblical preaching.

The writers of Commentary 1 surveyed five possible connections for their texts: the immediate literary context (the passages right around the text), the larger literary context (for example, the cycle of David stories or the Passion Narrative), the thematic context (such as other feeding stories, other parables, or other passages on the theme of hope), the lectionary context (the other readings for the day in the RCL), and the canonical context (other places in the whole of the Bible that display harmony, or perhaps tension, with the text at hand).

The writers of Commentary 2 surveyed six possible connections for their texts: the liturgical context (such as Advent or Easter), the ecclesial context (the life and mission of the church), the social and ethical context (justice and social responsibility), the cultural context (such as art, music, and literature), the larger expanse of human knowledge (such as science, history, and psychology), and the personal context (the life and faith of individuals).

In each essay, the writers selected from this array of possible connections, emphasizing those connections they saw as most promising for preaching. It is important to note that, even though Commentary 1 makes connections inside the Bible and Commentary 2 makes connections outside the Bible, this does not represent a division between "what the text *meant* in biblical times versus what the text *means* now." *Every* connection made with the text, whether that connection is made within the Bible or out in the larger culture, is seen as generative for preaching, and each author provokes the imagination of the preacher to see in these connections preaching possibilities for today. Connections is not a substitute for traditional scriptural commentaries, concordances, Bible dictionaries, and other interpretive tools. Rather, Connections begins with solid biblical scholarship, then goes on to focus on the act of preaching and on the ultimate goal of allowing the biblical text to come alive in the sermon.

Connections addresses every biblical text in the RCL, and it takes seriously the architecture of the RCL. During the seasons of the Christian year (Advent through Epiphany and Lent through Pentecost), the RCL provides three readings and a psalm for each Sunday and feast day: (1) a first reading, usually from the Old Testament; (2) a psalm, chosen to respond to the first reading; (3) a second reading, usually from one of the New Testament epistles; and (4) a Gospel reading. The first and second readings are chosen as complements to the Gospel reading for the day.

During the time between Pentecost and Advent, however, the RCL includes an additional first reading for every Sunday. There is the usual complementary reading, chosen in relation to the Gospel reading, but there is also a "semicontinuous" reading. These semicontinuous first readings move through the books of the Old Testament more or less continuously in narrative sequence, offering the stories of the patriarchs (Year A), the kings of Israel (Year B), and the prophets (Year C). Connections covers both the complementary and the semicontinuous readings.

The architects of the RCL understand the psalms and canticles to be prayers, and they selected the psalms for each Sunday and feast as prayerful responses to the first reading for the day. Thus, the Connections essays on the psalms are different from the other essays, and they have two goals, one homiletical and the other liturgical. First, they comment on ways the psalm might offer insight into preaching the first reading. Second, they describe how the tone and content of the psalm or canticle might inform the day's worship, suggesting ways the psalm or canticle may be read, sung, or prayed.

Preachers will find in Connections many ideas and approaches to sustain lively and provocative preaching for years to come. But beyond the deep reservoir of preaching connections found in these pages, preachers will also find here a habit of mind, a way of thinking about biblical preaching. Being guided by the essays in Connections to see many connections between biblical texts and their various contexts, preachers will be stimulated to make other connections for themselves. Connections is an abundant collection of creative preaching ideas, and it is also a spur to continued creativity.

JOEL B. GREEN
THOMAS G. LONG
LUKE A. POWERY
CYNTHIA L. RIGBY
CAROLYN J. SHARP
General Editors

Introducing the Revised Common Lectionary

To derive the greatest benefit from Connections, it will help to understand the structure and purpose of the Revised Common Lectionary (RCL), around which this resource is built. The RCL is a three-year guide to Scripture readings for the Christian Sunday gathering for worship. "Lectionary" simply means a selection of texts for reading and preaching. The RCL is an adaptation of the Roman Lectionary (of 1969, slightly revised in 1981), which itself was a reworking of the medieval Western-church one-year cycle of readings. The RCL resulted from six years of consultations that included representatives from nineteen churches or denominational agencies. Every preacher uses a lectionary—whether it comes from a specific denomination or is the preacher's own choice—but the RCL is unique in that it positions the preacher's homiletical work within a web of specific, ongoing connections.

The RCL has its roots in Jewish lectionary systems and early Christian ways of reading texts to illumine the biblical meaning of a feast day or time in the church calendar. Among our earliest lectionaries are the lists of readings for Holy Week and Easter in fourth-century Jerusalem.

One of the RCL's central connections is intertextuality; multiple texts are listed for each day. This lectionary's way of reading Scripture is based on Scripture's own pattern: texts interpreting texts. In the RCL, every Sunday of the year and each special or festival day is assigned a group of texts, normally three readings and a psalm. For most of the year, the first reading is an Old Testament text, followed by a psalm, a reading from one of the epistles, and a reading from one of the Gospel accounts.

The RCL's three-year cycle centers Year A in Matthew, Year B in Mark, and Year C in Luke. It is less clear how the Gospel according to John fits in, but when preachers learn about the RCL's arrangement of the Gospels, it makes sense. John gets a place of privilege because John's Gospel account, with its high Christology, is assigned for the great feasts. Texts from John's account are also assigned for Lent, Sundays of Easter, and summer Sundays. The second-century bishop Irenaeus's insistence on four Gospels is evident in this lectionary system: John and the Synoptics are in conversation with each other. However, because the RCL pattern contains variations, an extended introduction to the RCL can help the preacher learn the reasons for texts being set next to other texts.

The Gospel reading governs each day's selections. Even though the ancient order of reading texts in the Sunday gathering positions the Gospel reading last, the preacher should know that the RCL receives the Gospel reading as the hermeneutical key.

At certain times in the calendar year, the connections between the texts are less obvious. The RCL offers two tracks for readings in the time after Pentecost (Ordinary Time/standard Sundays): the complementary and the semicontinuous. Complementary texts relate to the church year and its seasons; semicontinuous emphasis is on preaching through a biblical book. Both approaches are historic ways of choosing texts for Sunday. This commentary series includes both the complementary and the semicontinuous readings.

In the complementary track, the Old Testament reading provides an intentional tension, a deeper understanding, or a background reference for another text of the day. The Psalm is the congregation's response to the first reading, following its themes. The Epistle functions as the horizon of the church: we learn about the faith and struggles of early Christian communities. The Gospel tells us where we are in the church's time and is enlivened, as are all the texts, by these intertextual interactions. Because the semicontinuous track prioritizes the narratives of specific books, the intertextual connections are not as apparent. Connections still exist, however. Year A pairs Matthew's account with Old Testament readings from the first five books; Year B pairs Mark's account with stories of anointed kings; Year C pairs Luke's account with the prophetic books.

Historically, lectionaries came into being because they were the church's beloved texts, like the scriptural canon. Choices had to be made regarding readings in the assembly, given the limit of fifty-two Sundays and a handful of festival days. The RCL presupposes that everyone (preachers and congregants) can read these texts—even along with the daily RCL readings that are paired with the Sunday readings.

Another central connection found in the RCL is the connection between texts and church seasons or the church's year. The complementary texts make these connections most clear. The intention of the RCL is that the texts of each Sunday or feast day bring biblical meaning to where we are in time. The texts at Christmas announce the incarnation. Texts in Lent renew us to follow Christ, and texts for the fifty days of Easter proclaim God's power over death and sin and our new life in Christ. The entire church's year is a hermeneutical key for using the RCL.

Let it be clear that the connection to the church year is a connection for present-tense proclamation. We read, not to recall history, but to know how those events are true for us today. Now is the time of the Spirit of the risen Christ; now we beseech God in the face of sin and death; now we live baptized into Jesus' life and ministry. To read texts in time does not mean we remind ourselves of Jesus' biography for half of the year and then the mission of the church for the other half. Rather, we follow each Gospel's narrative order to be brought again to the meaning of Jesus' death and resurrection and his risen presence in our midst. The RCL positions the texts as our lens on our life and the life of the world in our time: who we are in Christ now, for the sake of the world.

The RCL intends to be a way of reading texts to bring us again to faith, for these texts to be how we see our lives and our gospel witness in the world. Through these connections, the preacher can find faithful, relevant ways to preach year after year.

JENNIFER L. LORD
Connections Editorial Board Member

Connections

Ash Wednesday

Joel 2:1–2, 12–17
Psalm 51:1–17
2 Corinthians 5:20b–6:10

Matthew 6:1–6, 16–21
Isaiah 58:1–12

Joel 2:1–2, 12–17

¹Blow the trumpet in Zion;
   sound the alarm on my holy mountain!
Let all the inhabitants of the land tremble,
   for the day of the LORD is coming, it is near—
²a day of darkness and gloom,
   a day of clouds and thick darkness!
Like blackness spread upon the mountains
   a great and powerful army comes;
their like has never been from of old,
   nor will be again after them
   in ages to come.
. . . .
¹²Yet even now, says the LORD,
   return to me with all your heart,
with fasting, with weeping, and with mourning;
   ¹³rend your hearts and not your clothing.
Return to the LORD, your God,
   for he is gracious and merciful,
slow to anger, and abounding in steadfast love,
   and relents from punishing.
¹⁴Who knows whether he will not turn and relent,
   and leave a blessing behind him,
a grain offering and a drink offering
   for the LORD, your God?

¹⁵Blow the trumpet in Zion;
   sanctify a fast;
call a solemn assembly;
   ¹⁶gather the people.
Sanctify the congregation;
   assemble the aged;
gather the children,
   even infants at the breast.
Let the bridegroom leave his room,
   and the bride her canopy.

¹⁷Between the vestibule and the altar
   let the priests, the ministers of the LORD, weep.
Let them say, "Spare your people, O LORD,
   and do not make your heritage a mockery,
   a byword among the nations.
Why should it be said among the peoples,
   'Where is their God?'"

Commentary 1: Connecting the Reading with Scripture

Joel 2 is set against a chilling description of crisis in Israel. An unprecedented locust plague has struck the land (1:4), laying waste to fields and orchards, depriving the Israelites of food, and robbing them of produce for sacrificial offerings. The destruction is total. With storehouses depleted and granaries empty, joy and gladness fade from the temple (1:16) and the people are left to mourn (1:8, 13). Whether the locust plague is to be understood as an actual event or an extended metaphor for Israel being invaded by a foreign army (see 1:6) is a matter that is left unsettled.

In either case, the trauma pictured in chapter 1 is but a prelude to a greater problem addressed in chapter 2: the coming of the Day of the Lord. The Day of the Lord refers to a future time when God will decisively intervene in history to right wrongs and restore justice. While not necessarily signaling the end of the world, this is a day of reckoning in which God's enemies are condemned and God's people are vindicated. But the coming of this day is not always good news for Israel; if faithless and recalcitrant, Israel itself will face judgment.

With this latter possibility in view, Joel calls Israel to attention. The blowing of a trumpet (2:1) serves to warn Israel that the approaching Day of the Lord will be one of doom and darkness (2:2). The following verses (vv. 3–11), excluded from the lectionary reading, describe in some detail what this day will be like. It will be a time of cosmic and ecological upheaval. Fires will rage (v. 3), armies will ravage (v. 4), the heavens and earth will tremble (v. 10), and even the sun and moon will cease to shine. It will be a "terrible," or fear-filled, day (v. 11).

Though imminent, God's judgment is not inevitable. The prophet calls the people to return to the Lord with fasting, weeping, and mourning (v. 12), behaviors associated with humility and repentance. In the Old Testament, acts of penitence can be initiated by individuals, but here the process is clearly communal. The whole congregation is called to assemble, young and old alike (v. 16). So urgent is the task that even a soon-to-be bride and bridegroom should interrupt their nuptials to take part (v. 16). The goal is clear: by rending their hearts (v. 13), Israel hopes that God might "have a change of heart" (v. 14, my trans.), relenting from bringing judgment against the people.

Importantly, the motivation for the people's repentance is not the threat of "fire and brimstone." Rather, it is the promise of God's compassion. In verse 13, the prophet quotes God's self-revelation at Sinai (Exod. 34:6), a text loaded with evocative imagery that describes God's loving nature. The term translated as "merciful" (*rakhum*) is derived from the Hebrew word for "womb" (*rekhem*), suggesting a feminine metaphor that underscores God's motherly love for Israel. The phrase "slow to anger," which more woodenly means "long of nose," is related to a Hebrew idiom that describes anger in terms of one's nose burning. If the nose is a wick that ignites God's anger, then affirming that God is long of nose is another way of saying that God does not have a quick temper. The word "steadfast love" (*hesed*) connotes tenacious loyalty within a covenant relationship, and "relents from punishing" carries with it a willingness to forgive. Taken together, the portrait of God given in Joel 2:13 stands in sharp contrast to popular (mis)conceptions about the God of the Old Testament as an angry, vengeful deity.

If verse 13 offers a rationale for why the people should repent, then verse 17 offers a rationale for why God should forgive. Not only is forgiveness consistent with God's character, it is also vital to God's international reputation. If God were to fail to show mercy to God's own people, the nations would mock God's heritage (Israel) and would derisively jeer: "Where is their God?" Thus, while the experience of forgiveness is highly personal, it also has a public dimension insofar as it bears witness to the world about God's gracious disposition and fidelity.

Starting with Joel 2:18 (absent from the lectionary selection), the language abruptly shifts from the actions required of Israel to the promises offered by God. In response to Israel's repentance, God will remove the locust plague (v. 20), allow agricultural abundance to return (vv. 19, 24), and repay Israel for all that was lost (v. 25). The section concludes with an

God Invites Us to Peace

"We pray you in Christ's stead to be reconciled to God"; that is, to be friends with him, no longer to stand in terms of distance; for every habitual sinner, every one that provokes Him to anger by his iniquity, is his enemy: not that every sinner hates God by a direct hate; but as obedience is love, so disobedience is enmity or hatred by interpretation . . . and therefore the reconciling of these [wicked works], is to represent them "holy and unblamable and unreprovable in his sight." Pardon of sins is the least part of this reconciliation; our sins and our sinfulness too must be taken away; that is, our old guilt, and the remnant affections, must be taken off before we are friends of God. And therefore we find this reconciliation pressed on our parts; we are reconciled to God, not God to us. For although the term be relative, and so signifies both parts; as conjunction, and friendship, and society, and union do: yet it pleased the Spirit of God by this expression to signify our duty expressly, and to leave the other to be supposed; because if our parts be done, whatsoever is on God's part can never fail. And secondly, although this reconciliation begins on God's part, and He first invites us to peace, and gave His Son a sacrifice; yet God's love is very revocable till we are reconciled by obedience and conformity.

Jeremy Taylor, *The Doctrine and Presence of Repentance*, vol. 10 of *The Whole Works of the Right Rev. Jeremy Taylor, D.D.* (London, 1828), 71.

affirmation of God's presence with and commitment to Israel (v. 27), as well as the promise that God's spirit would be poured out on all flesh, whether young or old, male or female, slave or free (vv. 28–29). The promise of God pouring out the spirit on all flesh is cited later by Peter in Acts 2.

Between the promises laid out in verses 18–20 and 24–29, there is a series of imperatives directed at the land (v. 21), the animals (v. 22), and the children of Zion (v. 23). Though different in their formulations, the dual refrains of "do not fear" (vv. 21, 22) and "be glad and rejoice" (vv. 21, 23) bind this minisection together. The picture offered is of all creation joining in fearless praise of a God who has freely forgiven. Though the Day of the Lord is one of doom and darkness, the reality of God's compassion points to the possibility of peace and harmony.

Two of the lectionary texts paired with Joel 2 echo the sentiment behind the prophet's call to "rend your hearts and not your clothing" (v. 13). In Psalm 51, a penitential psalm, the worshiper beseeches God for mercy with striking candor. In acknowledging that burnt offerings do not automatically wash away his sins, the psalmist affirms that the sacrifice acceptable to God "is a broken spirit; a broken and contrite heart" (Ps. 51:17). Similarly, in Isaiah 58 the prophet calls

for a different type of religious fast, one that consists not of outward displays of mourning (Isa. 58:5), but rather of loosening the bonds of injustice, freeing the oppressed, and caring for the hungry and homeless (vv. 6–7, 10). Neither Psalm 51 nor Isaiah 58 implies that outward religious expressions are meaningless or unnecessary, but both underscore that the most meaningful external actions are those that manifest an internal change of attitude. A similar dynamic is true of Ash Wednesday: the imposition of ashes on the forehead is meant to make visible a believer's repentant heart.

When heard in a broader canonical context, Joel's appeal to God's self-revelation at Sinai (Joel 2:13) comes into sharper focus. As a paradigmatic expression of God's merciful character, Exodus 34:6 is cited in various biblical contexts. In Psalm 86, an individual prayer for help, the psalmist prays Exodus 34:6 back to God (Ps. 86:15) in the hope of urging God to be who God promised to be in a moment of anguish and despair. In Psalm 145, the psalmist prays the same words, but this time as part of a longer litany of unfettered praise. In Jonah 4:2, the prophet cites Exodus 34:6 as the reason he originally resists his call to go to Nineveh, the capital of Assyria, Israel's archenemy. Jonah, like Joel, knows that the Lord's compassion and readiness to forgive extend to all who would sincerely repent. For Jonah, the Lord's compassion and readiness to forgive are an astonishing truth that challenges his narrow view of divine mercy; for Joel, God's compassionate and forgiving nature is cause for hope in the midst of doom and darkness.

RYAN P. BONFIGLIO

Commentary 2: Connecting the Reading with the World

The question "Where is God?" is a real concern. A great calamity is about to befall God's chosen. An army of locusts is about to descend, bringing a day of darkness and gloom. The prophet Joel fears that God's supposedly chosen people might question God's promise. He fears that in the midst of hopelessness, they may question the God of providence, the God of deliverance. Joel fears reality might contradict the theology that promises God's presence. So the prophet promises that this day of destruction can be avoided, but only if God's people repent and return to the Almighty, for God is gracious and compassionate, slow to anger, and abounding in love. Hope is provided in God's covenant with God's people, a hope that even now, when all seems lost, promises the people will be spared. Theologians such as Jürgen Moltmann, in his classic book *Theology of Hope*, have been influenced by passages such as this.[1] Both Joel and Moltmann base their faith on a God who keeps God's promises in shielding the faithful from such holocausts.

Remembering that we are but dust and that to dust we will return, our salvation from the destruction we are told we deserve leads many to a Lenten period of abstention and self-restraint in hope that God's anger toward us would relent. In spite of our inevitable death, a God of covenant and promise safeguards a future that has meaning and purpose, providing a sense of security and tranquility in the midst of invading armies bent on our destruction. However, what do you do when the God of liberations fails to liberate? When, regardless of our repentance, abstention, or self-restraint, we are still devoured by the vicissitudes of life? When God's promises fall short, theology must explain why the faithful, in spite of their fidelity to the Almighty, nonetheless perish. How do we understand God's promises this side of the Holocaust?

Maybe once God had made promises to the Jews, but did God's mind change? Has the Christian creation of salvation history provided a new chosen: Europeans? Are God's kept promises now exclusively for this new chosen people? Originally, God's promises to the Hebrews were achieved through the massacre of indigenous peoples in the land of Canaan. So, when God promised Euroamericans their own promised land, manifest destiny required the genocide of Native people. The indigenous peoples of Canaan and the United States were deemed to stand outside of salvation history; thus, their eradication was believed to be God's will. The new chosen becomes the invading army that brings a day of darkness and gloom to those deemed outside of the promise. So, when God's chosen (Jews) face persecution and death at the hands of another chosen (Christians), does it mean God chose others to be the new chosen people? Are Euroamerican Christians right when they write themselves into the historical narrative as the New Jerusalem or the New Israel?

Joel may promise deliverance, but even after repentance, destructive armies still descend. To protect God from a guilty verdict for failing to keep God's original promises would require victims to bear responsibility for their predicament, for their own slaughter. My fear about this form of reasoning is that it absolves Eurocentric Christians from complicity with the Holocaust (and all other colonial massacres) by shifting the blame to the Jew (or the colonized) for lacking

---

1. See Jürgen Moltmann's *Theology of Hope: On the Ground and the Implications of a Christian Eschatology* (Minneapolis: Fortress, 1993) and his *Ethics of Hope* (Minneapolis: Fortress, 2012).

faith in the "true" God. The hearers of Joel's words might very well have rent their garments and hearts. If the army of doom failed to appear, praise God. If destruction came regardless of the prayers offered, then the slaughtered were nonetheless blamed for their unfaithfulness.

The horrors of concentration camps, where Jews were literally reduced to dust in the crematoria, bear a terrible witness to the failure of God's promises to materialize. A God of promise becomes theodicy's answer as long as the promise of redemption is continuously delayed. What good is promise if such promises fail to be realized during our existential reality? Divine promises delayed beyond our lives are unfulfilled promises, obscuring a God who falls short. God would be more just if unsatisfied promises were never made. The problem of linking an eschatology to ethics is that praxis can be ignored as the focus remains on some futuristic utopian hope for which the victims of Christianity wait, long after their bones are literally reduced to ashes by ovens. Hope in some pie in the sky becomes the ultimate opiate numbing the pain of the oppressed by securing the oppressor's grip on a reality beneficial to the dominant Euro-Christian culture at the expense of others.

Hope can be sustained and maintained through faith, a belief that imposes meaning on a lineal progression of history. Hope can be embraced as long as we proclaim knowing how history ends. Because we accept without question an eschatological hope, our focus on a glorious future obscures the repressive reality of the present. What if there is no rhyme or reason to the movement of time?

For those of us who think in Spanish, we recognize that hope (*esperanza*) is derived from the word *esperando*, waiting. To hope in Spanish connotes a sense of waiting. *Esperar*, to wait, does not ensure that what we are waiting for will end up being good or bad. In a real sense, waiting can lead to nothingness. We

who are familiar with deprivation, or grew up in marginalized communities, are used to this. To wait can encompass the eventual arrival of the invading army. Waiting for salvation from invading armies may end with death. Waiting for our prayers and rituals to work can become tiresome. Hence hope, in Spanish, contains this element of the hopeless.

To join white Christians who appropriate passages such as these in Joel so as to embrace the hope of a God of promises would be to suffer from the curse of Eurocentric privilege, which can lead to an overacceptance of the present, an acceptance based on a life filled with God; but what happens when life is cut short? When life is relegated to genocidal oppression, suffering, deprivation, and, yes, hopelessness? Because a life in abundance is denied to those falling short of the white ideal, hope of promises yet fulfilled is problematic for them, and all who are massacred by those who rely on the divine forgiveness of sins that promises hope for eternal life. Belief in a future holds little for those on the margins.

What we notice is that hope in promises that forestall our return to dust, as expressed by the dominant Christian culture, more often than not has led to a false comfort in the present, not in future possibilities. If we are going to insist on hope, let it not be the utopian hope found in "no place" (the English rendition for the Latin word *utopia*). Any hope proclaimed must be tied to a real space and to the now. Because too many bodies of the innocent have piled up to the heavens, the hope of future promises is obscured by the tang of rotting flesh ensnared in the nostrils of God. We should be repulsed by Eurocentric futuristic fantasies based on religious ideologies constructed to provide peace in the midst of massacres caused by invading armies. Instead, we should claim a hope for those on the margins that is not based on unanswerable questions.

MIGUEL A. DE LA TORRE

Psalm 51:1–17

[1]Have mercy on me, O God,
  according to your steadfast love;
according to your abundant mercy
  blot out my transgressions.
[2]Wash me thoroughly from my iniquity,
  and cleanse me from my sin.

[3]For I know my transgressions,
  and my sin is ever before me.
[4]Against you, you alone, have I sinned,
  and done what is evil in your sight,
so that you are justified in your sentence
  and blameless when you pass judgment.
[5]Indeed, I was born guilty,
  a sinner when my mother conceived me.

[6]You desire truth in the inward being;
  therefore teach me wisdom in my secret heart.
[7]Purge me with hyssop, and I shall be clean;
  wash me, and I shall be whiter than snow.
[8]Let me hear joy and gladness;
  let the bones that you have crushed rejoice.
[9]Hide your face from my sins,
  and blot out all my iniquities.

[10]Create in me a clean heart, O God,
  and put a new and right spirit within me.
[11]Do not cast me away from your presence,
  and do not take your holy spirit from me.
[12]Restore to me the joy of your salvation,
  and sustain in me a willing spirit.

[13]Then I will teach transgressors your ways,
  and sinners will return to you.
[14]Deliver me from bloodshed, O God,
  O God of my salvation,
  and my tongue will sing aloud of your deliverance.

[15]O Lord, open my lips,
  and my mouth will declare your praise.
[16]For you have no delight in sacrifice;
  if I were to give a burnt offering, you would not be pleased.
[17]The sacrifice acceptable to God is a broken spirit;
  a broken and contrite heart, O God, you will not despise.

Connecting the Psalm with Scripture and Worship

Psalm 51 is the psalm appointed for Ash Wednesday in all three years of the lectionary cycle, always as a response to the Old Testament text from Joel. The Joel passage begins, "Blow the trumpet in Zion; sound the alarm on my holy mountain!" (Joel 2:1a). In the twenty-first-century church, trumpets are usually associated with Easter, not Ash Wednesday, and with celebration, not penitence, but here in Joel the trumpets are sounding an alarm (vv. 1–2), an alarm so important that all must hear it and respond: the aged, the infants, even the newlyweds in their wedding tent (v. 16). The Day of the Lord is coming, and it does not look good. The call is to "return to the LORD, your God," and to "rend your hearts and not your clothing" (v. 13). The response of the psalm is the quintessential plea of Ash Wednesday: "Create in me a clean heart" (Ps. 51:10).

The heart, to the ancient Hebrew population, meant much more than the seat of emotion or even the physiological heart. For the Hebrew people, the heart was considered the core of their humanity—the center of the will and of the intellect, a representation of who they were in their very beings. To pray for a clean heart was to pray to be recreated; even more than a prayer of penitence, it was a plea to be made a completely new and better person.

This psalm is attributed to David in response to the whole affair with Bathsheba and Uriah, but it is probably even more powerful outside of that context. The psalm stands on its own as a plea for a new beginning, a true repentance, a chance to start again. It is more than a prayer for mercy, though it certainly is that (vv. 1, 9, 11, 14). The psalmist does not deny the sin; to the contrary, we read, "For I know my transgressions, and my sin is ever before me" (v. 3). Nor is punishment questioned: "so that you are justified in your sentence and blameless when you pass judgment" (v. 4). Throughout the psalm there are an expression of confidence in God's mercy and forgiveness (vv. 1, 7, 9) and a pledge to live an exemplary new life: "Then I will teach transgressors your ways, and sinners will return to you" (v. 13) and "my tongue will sing aloud of your deliverance" (v. 14).

The trumpet turns up again in the Gospel reading from Matthew, but this time we are told not to use it. Matthew 6:2 exhorts, "Do not sound a trumpet before you"; rather, give alms and pray in secret. The people are to turn to God in private, even in secret, so that the turning is known only to God. This direct and individual relationship is echoed in verse 4 of Psalm 51, "against you, you alone, have I sinned." This might suggest a homiletical direction a bit different from the typical Ash Wednesday sermon. Certainly, all the texts call for turning away from sin and back to a godly life, but in the Matthew text, the epistle, and the psalm, there is a contrast between an outer, more public life, and an inner life in relationship to and with God (Matt. 6:4, 6, 18, 20; 2 Cor. 6:8–10).

Happily for worship planners, the liturgical possibilities for Psalm 51 practically leap from the page. The text itself can provide a call to worship using verses 10–13 or a confession using verses 1–4. The psalm has been set as a sung confession, and as a Kyrie. Even better might be to sing a metrical or responsive version of the psalm in response to the Joel reading. There are literally hundreds to choose among, ranging from texts by Isaac Watts and Charles Wesley to more recent works, such as David Gambrell's hymn, "Have Mercy, God, upon My Life" and Michael Morgan's setting of Psalm 51 found in the *Psalter for Christian Worship*. Many of these resources appear not only in English but in Spanish, Korean, Xhosa, and other languages.

There is a variety of anthems that the choir could offer. For example, "The Morning Trumpet," arranged by Timothy Paul Banks, is a choral piece from *The Sacred Harp* and uses a hand drum in place of a trumpet to call the world to be delivered from sin. Another accessible choice would be "Create within Me a Clean Heart," written by Alison Adam of the Iona Community and suitable for choirs of all levels. It can be done with a handbell ostinato, or the choir could hum or sing on "oo" while Psalm 51 is read above the choral parts. After the conclusion of the reading, the choir sings in English or in Latin. Larger choirs might sing "Create in Me" by Michael Larkin, a beautiful choral piece that highlights verses 10–12 of Psalm 51; the motet "Create in Me a Clean Heart (Schaffe in mir, Gott)" by Johannes Brahms is a standard setting of Psalm 51 that is well known in the choral repertoire. Another choral choice would be "Thou Knowest, Lord" from the *Requiem* by Bob Chilcott. This piece reflects on the essence of Psalm 51, making it a good choice for Ash Wednesday.

Psalm 51 is surely the perfect beginning for the journey through Lent and speaks to and for every one of us in a way that is both exquisitely simple and deeply profound.

DAVID A. VANDERMEER

2 Corinthians 5:20b–6:10

^{5:20b}We entreat you on behalf of Christ, be reconciled to God. ²¹For our sake he made him to be sin who knew no sin, so that in him we might become the righteousness of God.

^{6:1}As we work together with him, we urge you also not to accept the grace of God in vain. ²For he says,

> "At an acceptable time I have listened to you,
>   and on a day of salvation I have helped you."

See, now is the acceptable time; see, now is the day of salvation! ³We are putting no obstacle in anyone's way, so that no fault may be found with our ministry, ⁴but as servants of God we have commended ourselves in every way: through great endurance, in afflictions, hardships, calamities, ⁵beatings, imprisonments, riots, labors, sleepless nights, hunger; ⁶by purity, knowledge, patience, kindness, holiness of spirit, genuine love, ⁷truthful speech, and the power of God; with the weapons of righteousness for the right hand and for the left; ⁸in honor and dishonor, in ill repute and good repute. We are treated as impostors, and yet are true; ⁹as unknown, and yet are well known; as dying, and see—we are alive; as punished, and yet not killed; ¹⁰as sorrowful, yet always rejoicing; as poor, yet making many rich; as having nothing, and yet possessing everything.

Commentary 1: Connecting the Reading with Scripture

Ash Wednesday marks the beginning of the season of Lent, a period of forty days in which Christians reflect on Jesus' life, ministry, suffering, death, and resurrection. As we remember that his death on the cross freed us from sin and death, the hope is that we are also compelled to the act of repentance. Ash Wednesday sets in motion a spirit of deep-seated contemplation and sorrow as we think about the sacrificial act of Jesus on the cross. The season also prompts gratefulness tempered with repentance, lest we boast as we, in our sinfulness, ponder God's unmerited gift of Jesus. Many Christians honor this time of reflection and seek a renewed relationship with God through the acts of fasting and prayer. The lectionary text for this day highlights the importance of establishing and maintaining a good relationship with God and others despite the trials and tribulations we may experience. The sacrificial work of Jesus makes this relationship possible. This focal text for Ash Wednesday highlights

the importance of remembrance, repentance, and reconciliation.

The designated passage for today begins with a strong exhortation to "be reconciled to God." A look at the broader literary context, particularly the previous chapter, is warranted in order to understand both the historical context and the author's instruction. To be reconciled to God means to be put in right relationship with God. Sinful beings are unable to do this on their own. Because of God's unconditional love for us, God sent Christ to aid in this effort (2 Cor. 5:18). We are able to be in relationship with God, to approach God with our prayers, solely due to God's grace. For this reason, a proper response is not only repentance, but also to offer this "ministry of reconciliation" to others (5:18) as "ambassadors for Christ" (5:20).

The community in Corinth is undergoing persecution and suffering, but they are encouraged not to "lose heart" (4:16). The psalmist says, "Weeping may endure for a night, but joy cometh in the morning" (Ps. 30:5 KJV). In the same way, Paul urges the hearers of this text to remain steadfast and faithful in the midst of their suffering. They are able to do this because God is with them and will welcome them into God's "heavenly dwelling," as "guaranteed" by the Spirit God has given them (2 Cor. 5:2, 5). He supports his exhortation by reminding them about the suffering they knew they would incur in their earthly bodies (5:1–4); but they should not fret, because God has already prepared them to handle it (5:5). Thus, they shall "always be confident" (5:6). As they suffer, they should act accordingly as faithful Christians, not only because their "aim" is to please God, but also because everyone eventually will have to "appear before the judgment seat of Christ" and deal with the consequences of their actions (5:9–10). They are, therefore, without excuse, and have been forewarned.

Paul has provided the community of believers with a great incentive to offer reconciliation to those who persecute them (5:18–20): salvation. Just as Christ suffered in order to bring them back into right relationship with God (5:20), so too must they extend reconciliation to others as they suffer (6:4–5). Not only is their offering of reconciliation to be nondiscriminatory, as was the sacrificial act of Jesus; they are also not to retaliate. "Through great endurance, in afflictions, hardships," and with the "power of God; with the weapons of righteousness for the right hand and for the left" (6:4–7), they shall receive salvation, which is "now" (6:2). In other words, salvation is already and not yet. This ambivalent state is further expounded as the author says they are "dying . . . [and yet] are alive; . . . punished, and yet not killed; . . . sorrowful, yet always rejoicing; . . . having nothing, and yet possessing everything" (6:9–10). As they remain faithful through their suffering, while offering reconciliation to their persecutors, they have also already obtained salvation, the benefits of which they will experience in full when they are "at home with the Lord" (5:8).

As we usher in this season of Lent, however, a word of caution is in order. As we embark on the liturgical part of the year when we focus on the promise of salvation due to the sacrificial work of Jesus Christ, we must also temper the

message of being like Christ in our suffering. The text provides a warning regarding what we do—how we respond—when we suffer by reminding us that each of us will face judgment for our actions "whether good or evil" (5:10). What are the implications of this message for those who seek to defend or protect themselves when they suffer abuse or harm? Would they no longer be in accordance with what Paul suggests here? Will punishment be the consequence for those who seek to protect their bodies, which the author refers to as "the temple of the living God" (6:16)?

What about the temporal issue of when salvation will come? The text says that "if anyone is in Christ, there is a new creation: everything old has passed away; see, everything has become new!" (5:17). But when? A person who is suffering *in the now*, in the body that is "away from the Lord," is still experiencing pain and trauma (5:6). What has been made new? How has their reality changed? Is it theologically sound and pastorally beneficial to preach a message of endurance because of *future* salvation to someone who is *presently* undergoing distress? What are the ethical implications of this message to endure suffering and, at the same time, offer reconciliation to those bent on harm, instead of eliminating various forms of interlocking oppressions, which they have the power and the means to do?

Ash Wednesday, also known as the Day of Ashes, is symbolized by the rubbing of ash on the believer, most often in the form of a cross on either the back of the hand or the forehead. The forehead is the most noticeable location for the ashes, and the most popular. Believers who wear these ashes are not only signifying Christ's salvific work for themselves, but also readily identifying themselves as followers of Jesus Christ to those who see the ashes on them. The symbol of the ashes is like a blinking light that causes others to zero in on Christians to see how they comport themselves through suffering. Will they behave in a Christlike fashion in the midst of tribulation? If one falls short of this behavior, one's Christian status may be called into question. Perhaps this is what Paul was trying to prevent: a negative portrayal of Christians by others. Although the text does not state that believers bore the symbol of Christ's death on their foreheads in ash, the marks (both physical and emotional) that they bore during their suffering functioned as their Christian identification—especially when they did not seek vengeance.

As we reflect on Jesus' death on the cross and the benefit of being reconciled to God because of it, let us also humble ourselves and repent for our sins. Paul reminds us that we do not have to go through this process of remembrance, repentance, and the ministry of reconciliation alone, as indicated by the use of the plural pronoun "we": "As *we* work together with [God]" (6:1). On this Ash Wednesday and throughout the rest of the Lenten season, let us set our individual and communal intention on reconciliation to God and to each other.

SHANELL T. SMITH

Commentary 2: Connecting the Reading with the World

This stirring passage from Corinthians begins with the call to be reconciled to God, yet it is difficult to imagine how we could be reconciled to God without first acting on the injunction in Matthew 5:23–24 to be reconciled with others before approaching God. Seeking reconciliation with family, friends, or community members can be challenging, but in many situations, we have the ability to address the issue directly and suggest options for change. Addressing the large-scale social issues that fracture and polarize our societies, however, seems a daunting task. We often feel that our efforts are inadequate and can have little impact on the situation.

It is instructive for Christians to remember that as our faith spread over the centuries, it often traveled hand in hand with European colonialism. Although it is difficult to acknowledge, the spread of Christianity was deeply enmeshed in the economic and political aims of the conquerors. More troubling still, Christian theology was used to justify genocide, the destruction of languages and cultures, the appropriation of land and resources, and the enslavement of human beings. While we rightly celebrate our sacred traditions, we must also acknowledge that we have inherited the legacy of many centuries of violence.

The Rev. Dr. Martin Luther King Jr. often asserted that eleven o'clock on Sunday morning is the most segregated hour for Christians in the United States. More than fifty years later, this is still the case. Despite our moral and ethical commitments, we Christians have not learned to transcend the racial tensions of the society at large. King articulated his vision of building the Beloved Community—a just and equitable society in which all share in the wealth of the earth, racism and discrimination have been abolished, and conflicts are resolved nonviolently—in a process of reconciliation. Although it may be painful, educating ourselves and accepting our history is a necessary step on the road to developing mutual compassion for and with others, which itself is a precursor to true reconciliation.

In what ways have Christians led prophetic efforts to undo the harms of colonization and dismantle entrenched racism?

The liberation theology movement that emerged in Latin America in the 1960s is known for its insistence that God is on the side of the poor. As theologians, pastors, and activists brought this movement to life, they struggled against the political, socioeconomic, and cultural systems that trampled on the rights of vulnerable people, but they also turned a critical eye toward their own churches. In what ways had their churches sided with the wealthy and powerful, conspiring to ignore the needs of those who were hurting? Perhaps more insidiously, in what ways had the churches justified their actions using distorted theology?

In Brazil, the Roman Catholic bishop Pedro Casaldáliga spent the decade of the 1970s working with the landless peasants and the indigenous peoples in the interior of the country. Although he had long known of the role his church had played in the conquest of the Americas, he became conscientized to its ongoing neglect of indigenous communities. Bishop Casaldáliga worked with a team of collaborators to compose a liturgy of repentance, the *Missa da terra sem males* (Mass of the Land without Evil). This liturgy is a Catholic mass with an extended penitential rite that explicitly names the harms the church has perpetrated against the indigenous peoples, asks for forgiveness, and pledges to walk in solidarity with these communities in the future. The following year, Casaldáliga wrote a similar liturgy, the *Missa dos Quilombos*, addressed to Afro-Brazilians. These extraordinary liturgies are public statements that model a three-part process of reconciliation: acknowledging the harms committed, seeking forgiveness, and proposing concrete actions toward healing.[1]

In 1985, a group of South African theologians issued the Kairos Document criticizing apartheid and the failure of the church to denounce it. The authors believed that God stood with the politically oppressed and that the churches shirked their moral responsibilities when they advocated a superficial reconciliation. Reconciliation, they insisted, requires repentance and justice. Drawing on this history, Kairos Palestine is a Christian Palestinian movement that advocates for ending the Israeli occupation and calls on all Christians everywhere to engage in nonviolent resistance against injustice and apartheid and to work for a just peace.[2]

In the United States, the Society of Friends (Quakers) sponsors the Toward Right Relationship with Native Peoples Project, which creates educational resources and offers presentations in educational, church, and civic settings. Paula Palmer, the project's director, researched the Quaker Native American day schools and boarding schools to uncover the church's role in the forced assimilation of Native children and produced a video and presentation on this topic for use with congregations.

In the 2008 documentary *Traces of the Trade: A Story from the Deep North,* filmmaker Katrina Browne tells the story of her New England ancestors, a wealthy and powerful slave-trading family. Ten descendants of the family travel to Rhode Island, Ghana, and Cuba, retracing the steps of the Triangle Trade and reflecting on the healing and transformation still needed. The Unitarian Universalist Association created an extensive discussion guide for use with congregations.

A different, but no less important, vision of reconciliation emerges in the theological exploration of moral injury, especially as it pertains to military veterans. Moral injury is the harm done to one's conscience or moral sensibilities when a person violates core moral beliefs or ethical codes of conduct. For example, in the context of war, soldiers might be directly involved in killing or harming others. As a result, they may judge their own behavior negatively and feel unable to regard themselves as decent human beings, which can cause depression and lead to suicide.

For those experiencing moral injury, learning to trust themselves and others is an important aspect of healing. The Soul Repair Center emphasizes the importance of community in this process and offers training to congregations to help them support veterans struggling with moral injury.[3] Through outreach efforts, preaching, and ritual action, churches can play a role in helping individuals suffering moral injury to be restored and reconnected to the community, to themselves, and to God.

In this Ash Wednesday reading, Paul entreats us to be reconciled to God. The Lenten season gives us an opportunity to reflect on our lives, to evaluate how we are doing, and to work toward reconciliation. For some, this might be a time to reflect on personal spirituality; for others, an opportunity to strengthen interpersonal relationships; and for still others, an opportunity to contribute their efforts to large-scale social

1. The original Portuguese texts of these liturgies can be found on the Servicios Koinonia website: http://www.servicioskoinonia.org/Casaldaliga /poesia/index.html. Cónrado Berning's 1979 documentary on the premiere of *Missa da terra sem males* is available on YouTube at https://www .youtube.com/watch?v=pBNqtK-VF5g, as are other performances of both liturgies.

2. The Kairos Document is available on the South African History Online website: https://www.sahistory.org.za/archive/challenge-church -theological-comment-political-crisis-south-africa-kairos-document-1985. Information about Kairos Palestine can be found on their website: https://www.kairospalestine.ps.

3. The Soul Repair Center is a project of Brite Divinity School. More information is available at https://www.brite.edu/programs/soul-repair/.

activism to uproot racism, sexism, economic exploitation, or environmental destruction.

In each of these scenarios, reconciliation is long and hard work, but the passage assures us that God has promised to listen and help us. We may be asked to put aside mistaken notions and acknowledge our own failings. We may be asked to make compromises. We may be asked to embark on a long journey toward healing.

Despite these challenges, Paul reminds us: now is the acceptable time!

ANN HIDALGO

Matthew 6:1–6, 16–21

¹"Beware of practicing your piety before others in order to be seen by them; for then you have no reward from your Father in heaven.

²"So whenever you give alms, do not sound a trumpet before you, as the hypocrites do in the synagogues and in the streets, so that they may be praised by others. Truly I tell you, they have received their reward. ³But when you give alms, do not let your left hand know what your right hand is doing, ⁴so that your alms may be done in secret; and your Father who sees in secret will reward you.

⁵"And whenever you pray, do not be like the hypocrites; for they love to stand and pray in the synagogues and at the street corners, so that they may be seen by others. Truly I tell you, they have received their reward. ⁶But whenever you pray, go into your room and shut the door and pray to your Father who is in secret; and your Father who sees in secret will reward you. . . .

¹⁶"And whenever you fast, do not look dismal, like the hypocrites, for they disfigure their faces so as to show others that they are fasting. Truly I tell you, they have received their reward. ¹⁷But when you fast, put oil on your head and wash your face, ¹⁸so that your fasting may be seen not by others but by your Father who is in secret; and your Father who sees in secret will reward you.

¹⁹"Do not store up for yourselves treasures on earth, where moth and rust consume and where thieves break in and steal; ²⁰but store up for yourselves treasures in heaven, where neither moth nor rust consumes and where thieves do not break in and steal. ²¹For where your treasure is, there your heart will be also."

Commentary 1: Connecting the Reading with Scripture

Our Gospel lesson today consists of three sections that follow the same outline, its pattern predicted by 6:1, warning against using one's religious practices to impress other people. These sections, which deal with almsgiving, prayer, and fasting, tell readers that when they engage in these activities, they should not do so in a way that calls attention to themselves. If they do, then that attention will be their only reward. Instead, they should do it anonymously, with the result that God the Father who sees in secret will reward them. The KJV says that reward will be given "openly," but that word is not in the oldest manuscripts; it is now generally assumed that the reward will be given when the kingdom of God (or, as Matthew has it, the kingdom of heaven) comes and the rewarded one will have eternal life.

These three sections have as their source what scholars call M, meaning the source on which

Matthew draws for his Gospel that is neither Mark nor the ancient source Q. There is no reason to suppose that it does not derive from actual teaching of Jesus and the expansion of it in the community from which the evangelist comes. These sections are interrupted in 6:7–15 by the insertion of the Q material containing the Lord's Prayer, which thus becomes the center of the Sermon on the Mount. This important insertion is left out of our reading for today, undoubtedly because of the occasion of this reading. Our Gospel and the other lections are to be read on Ash Wednesday, one of the few midweek services in the calendar commented on in this series. This holy day is focused on penitence, as is the section from M into which the evangelist has inserted the Lord's Prayer material. As important as the Lord's Prayer is, it interrupts the penitential flow of the M material and would thus distract from concentration on this day's theme.

15

Each of these three sections offers a vigorous statement involving hyperbole and caricature. The persons who do what the reader is told not to do are called hypocrites, a Greek word that had as one of its original meanings an actor on a stage. Thus, the whole performance is exaggerated. All three of the sections share one basic message: the activity is not about the person playacting; it is about God—and to behave otherwise is damnable.

While the three sections share a common message, how that works can be seen by examining them separately to see how each reaches a common goal. The first section, on almsgiving, describes the effort to call attention to one's donations as like having a horn blown to call attention to the achievement. While many fund-raising activities today seem to use similar techniques to encourage gift-giving, sounding a trumpet in a synagogue or even the street is not something that was actually done; it is instead a hyperbolic analogy to ways attention was called to the donor. The reward of hypocrites was to have people admire their great generosity, as though they bought admiration with their gifts. That is all it bought. The description of the proper alternative also involves exaggeration for emphasis: one's hands are not conscious, so one could not know what the other was doing.

The section on prayer (vv. 5–6) condemns hypocrites who stand and say prayers ostentatiously in a synagogue or on a street corner. This seems not to refer to officiants at liturgy but to individuals who want to appear pious. This discussion of prayer seems to suggest that only private prayer can be sincere, that one needs to go into a private space to do it; the real distinction, however, is between opposite motivations for saying prayers: showing off versus relating to the Holy One. As Eugene Boring has said, "One can also ostentatiously call attention to going to the inner room to pray."[1]

The next verse, which is not in our lection, seems at first to follow the pattern of the sections of our passage, calling on readers not to do something in the way others (in this case, Gentiles) do. However, this is just a way of preparing for the introduction of the Lord's Prayer.

This material resumes and is completed in verses 16–18. The issue here is fasting. Originally the Jews had only one fixed fast day, the Day of Atonement (Yom Kippur). Other fasts may have been added to their liturgical calendar by Matthew's time; in addition, the believer could fast voluntarily, and Mondays and Thursdays were considered good days for doing so. These could be days of "sackcloth and ashes," which could add to people's efforts to prove how holy they were by excessive fasting. Matthew summarizes this playacting as "disfiguring their faces," which he contrasts with the sprucing up done by those who are fasting for God, rather than for show.

Our lection ends with a contrast between storing treasure on earth and storing it up in heaven: the contrast between showing off or doing things hypocritically and devoting ourselves to the service of God. The latter is required to enter the kingdom of heaven.

Something of the significance of our reading can be understood when it is seen in context in Matthew's Gospel. Matthew starts with narratives about Jesus' infancy and ends with an account of his crucifixion and resurrection. In between are five sections, beginning with a biographical section that is essentially based on Mark's account and ending with speech based on material from Q and M. All this was edited by Matthew for his own purposes. Since early days in the church's history, a comparison has been made between the Pentateuch—the five books of Law (Torah) in the Old Testament—and these five parts of Matthew. Yet Matthew's emphasis is not on the teaching but on the narrative, with the speeches related to the theme of the narratives. For instance, the initial part from which our reading comes has to do with the beginning of Jesus' life and ministry. It ends with Jesus' calling the Twelve and beginning his ministry in Galilee. The Sermon on the Mount is the introduction (theirs and ours) to the teaching of Jesus; there has been no teaching before this.

The Sermon begins with the Beatitudes, which elucidate the traits that will enable disciples to be a part of kingdom of heaven. Jesus then compares the disciples to salt, light, and

---

1. "Matthew," in *The New Interpreter's Bible* (Nashville: Abingdon, 1995), 8:201.

a city on a hill. He continues what he has to say about living in the eschatological community by showing how it is a greater righteousness than that of the Law, offering illustrations in relation to anger, adultery, and divorce, and then in relation to swearing, revenge, and one's attitude toward enemies. This is followed by today's Gospel reading about not showing off in almsgiving, praying, and fasting; this material is intersected by the model of prayer in the Lord's Prayer, the center of the Sermon. Jesus then continues with other statements about life in the kingdom, culminating with the Golden Rule, and then concludes with warnings about the dangers of not living according to the view of life in the kingdom that been described in the Sermon. Thus, the newly called disciples have been well instructed in the life to which they—and we—are called.

O. C. EDWARDS JR.

Commentary 2: Connecting the Reading with the World

In today's readings from Matthew we are presented with three spiritual disciplines: giving, praying, and fasting. The act of giving presupposes that the giver has resources that can improve the recipient's present condition. This brings into view a range of activities—from the small acts of kindness of giving food, clothing, or money to the poor and destitute to providing an endowment so that a school, library, or hospital may be established and maintained. The act of giving may also serve to point us to those places where our social and economic structures are broken or inadequate and in need of repair.

Conventional wisdom says that giving someone fish will provide food for a day but teaching that person to fish will provide food for a lifetime. In this proverbial statement, one finds a view of giving that goes beyond a charitable and short-term commitment. Rather, one is challenged to move beyond passive acceptance and maintenance of the status quo, to seek ways to cultivate wholesome living, to enhance a community's life, and to optimize human potential.

Preachers can draw on the teachings of Jesus to represent giving as doing righteousness, acting rightly, and making things right (Matt. 6:3; 7:21; 25:37–40). The focus of giving cannot be the giver but rather the work of righteousness that is divinely inspired, enabled, and sustained. Jesus steers us away from giving that is energized by self-congratulation or the adulation of others. Genuine giving is an unrelenting commitment to righteousness and to the perennial work of making things right in the world. The person who seeks recognition for his or her gift celebrates human endeavor and diverts attention from the divine work of the giver of all good gifts. In a world where others are dependent on the kindness of patrons, it is easy to forget that the earth is the Lord's (Ps. 24:1). Above all else, giving is a response to God, a celebration of God's blessings, and an act of honor and thanksgiving. From this perspective, we serve as instruments of God's generosity, benevolence, and providential care in the world. Giving is living out one's sense of identity, calling, and relationship in community to the giver of all good gifts.

The second spiritual practice, praying, may be viewed as recognition and acknowledgment that one is invited into relationship with God in every moment of life. Praying provides multiple ways to sense that divine invitation and to engage the relationship through gratitude for divine favor, sorrow at one's neglect or falling short, and supplication for help in one's life. When we pray, we may learn something about how we are connected to the Divine and to all of God's creation. We may learn that as we draw nearer to God through prayer, we also draw nearer to our fellow human beings through our love and service. We may also learn that our self-aggrandizement, pride, and self-centeredness are antithetical to our desire to be in relationship with God.

Preachers can show how genuine prayer enables one to be seen by God, whereas the hypocrites pray to be seen by others. God sees us in the totality of our beings, including our failures and successes, our grief and joy, our fears and hopes. In prayer, we may encounter God as the One who sees our misery (Gen. 16:10–13), hears the cries of those who are oppressed or enslaved (Exod. 3:7), and draws near to us. We acknowledge God as the center and sole focus of our prayer as we seek to discern how God is working in our lives and in the world. In prayer, we acknowledge God's initiative and self-revelation in secret spaces where God is glorified and away from those spaces that offer self-promotion or public display of our piety (Matt. 6:6).

Preachers may observe that when prayer seeks to go beyond the bounds of personal piety, we may be afforded the opportunity to transcend our own images of God, and our preconceived theological postulations. We may find that prayer transports us to spaces where we fully experience love, forgiveness, healing, acceptance, joy, and life in ways that go beyond our understanding and our cognition. Prayer that is designed to display one's piety so that others may revere the supplicant or be impressed is unable to channel God's work of revealing, inspiring, touching, and transforming.

Prayer that calls us into relationship with God is prayer that is orchestrated by God and whose content moves us beyond the need for "empty phrases" or "many words" (Matt. 6:7). In reflecting on the teaching of Jesus, we are invited to reexamine our practices and understandings of prayer; we are also called to embrace prayer that changes our perception, attitude, and behavior. Such changes may bring new ways of being in God's presence, addressing divine mystery, touching and handling things unseen. We embrace the transformations that are possible as we also are embraced by divine presence, ineffable mystery, overflowing love, transfiguring light, healing, and abundant mercy. Not only are we invited to discern how God is at work in our lives and in the world, but we are also invited to participate in God's work. Through prayer we learn and experience the role, value, and efficacy of prayer.

The third spiritual discipline in today's reading is fasting. In this practice, one goes without some measure of food or drink for a certain period. Traditionally, fasting has been linked with other practices such as abstinence from other activities, including sexual intimacy. It is not difficult to see that this demand on the physical body may send the message that the body needs to be subdued if we are to embark on a spiritual pilgrimage. The view of the body as a burden for the journey, the dwelling place of vices, disposable for the good of the soul, can lead to extreme practices such as self-flagellation.

However, one may also adopt a perspective that draws no distinction between the physical and spiritual. An individual does not come before God as differentiated and disconnected components but as a whole and unified being. One stands before God not as mind, spirit, soul, or body but, rather, as the totality of our thoughts, emotions, experiences, our weaknesses and strengths, our vices and virtues, our aversions and delights. Fasting may help us recognize and confront the challenges that we face in the totality of our being and enable us to acknowledge the assaults on our dignity and humanity from insults, addictions, stress, injury, or trauma, among other things. Further, because we cannot go for long periods without food, fasting may remind us of the contours and parameters of our human experience. We confront our limits and boundaries, and become more acutely aware of our finitude and our mortality.

These three spiritual practices have ancient roots across a range of religious traditions, and in every expression the practice calls attention away from the visible to the invisible, the mortal to the immortal, or the human to the Divine. In Matthew's Gospel, we are presented with an earthly and heavenly orientation (6:19–21), and these three spiritual practices enable the right orientation toward God. The earthly is transient, destructible, and insecure and includes our self-centered projects and our pride. The heavenly is permanent, indestructible, and secure, and includes our devotion to God and the correct orientation of our hearts. The spiritual practices of giving, praying, and fasting are matters that focus one's heart on the kingdom of heaven and its righteousness. "For where your treasure is, there your heart will be also" (6:21).

LINCOLN E. GALLOWAY

Ash Wednesday

Isaiah 58:1–12

¹Shout out, do not hold back!
　　Lift up your voice like a trumpet!
Announce to my people their rebellion,
　　to the house of Jacob their sins.
²Yet day after day they seek me
　　and delight to know my ways,
as if they were a nation that practiced righteousness
　　and did not forsake the ordinance of their God;
they ask of me righteous judgments,
　　they delight to draw near to God.
³"Why do we fast, but you do not see?
　　Why humble ourselves, but you do not notice?"
Look, you serve your own interest on your fast day,
　　and oppress all your workers.
⁴Look, you fast only to quarrel and to fight
　　and to strike with a wicked fist.
Such fasting as you do today
　　will not make your voice heard on high.
⁵Is such the fast that I choose,
　　a day to humble oneself?
Is it to bow down the head like a bulrush,
　　and to lie in sackcloth and ashes?
Will you call this a fast,
　　a day acceptable to the LORD?

⁶Is not this the fast that I choose:
　　to loose the bonds of injustice,
　　to undo the thongs of the yoke,
to let the oppressed go free,
　　and to break every yoke?
⁷Is it not to share your bread with the hungry,
　　and bring the homeless poor into your house;
when you see the naked, to cover them,
　　and not to hide yourself from your own kin?
⁸Then your light shall break forth like the dawn,
　　and your healing shall spring up quickly;
your vindicator shall go before you,
　　the glory of the LORD shall be your rear guard.
⁹Then you shall call, and the LORD will answer;
　　you shall cry for help, and he will say, Here I am.

If you remove the yoke from among you,
　　the pointing of the finger, the speaking of evil,
¹⁰if you offer your food to the hungry
　　and satisfy the needs of the afflicted,
then your light shall rise in the darkness
　　and your gloom be like the noonday.

> ¹¹The LORD will guide you continually,
>   and satisfy your needs in parched places,
>   and make your bones strong;
> and you shall be like a watered garden,
>   like a spring of water,
>   whose waters never fail.
> ¹²Your ancient ruins shall be rebuilt;
>   you shall raise up the foundations of many generations;
> you shall be called the repairer of the breach,
>   the restorer of streets to live in.

Commentary 1: Connecting the Reading with Scripture

Isaiah 56–66 are set in the Judean homeland, the Persian province of Yehud, to which the Babylonian exiles have returned. In the wake of the return, tensions develop between returning exiles—many of whom represent and therefore have the support of the Persian Empire—and the people who were not exiled and so remained in Judah after the Babylonians conquered Judah in 587 BCE. Chapters 56–59 reflect the acrimonious conflict among various factions within the house of Israel. The material is driven by wrenching questions: Who is a true Israelite? How will the community determine membership? Will these membership standards be more inclusive or more exclusive, so as to preserve one community's particular traditions? What constitutes righteous behavior and practice? Which values represent the core of Israelite identity?

The messages of consolation and hope in Isaiah 40–55, set in the Babylonian exile, give way in Isaiah 56–59 to oracles of judgment. The accusations of injustice echo those of the preexilic prophets. Isaiah 58:1–8 in particular reintroduces themes and tropes from the first chapter of Isaiah (Isa. 1:10–20). In both texts (Isa. 1 and Isa. 58), the prophet rhetorically creates a disjunction between the ritual activities that the people perform and the oppressive social, economic, and legal practices that they sanction. That said, the passage concludes with promises of salvation that recall Isaiah 40–55. Here, however, the promises pertain to only one group within Israel.

The writers of the Hebrew Bible depict their God in different ways and often those depictions stand in direct opposition to one another. Some texts portray a God of order, while others insist on a God who disrupts order for the sake of redemption. In some texts, we see a God who works with the powerful and is affiliated with the temple and the monarchy; in other parts of the canon, we hear about a God who sides with the oppressed and the marginalized, who wants to roam wild in the wilderness and chafes at the prospect of living in "a house" (i.e., a temple). The prophets, who prefer traditions associated with the liberation from Egypt, the Mosaic covenant, and economic and social justice, see cult-related practices such as fasting as attempts to manipulate or domesticate YHWH. The friction between these two testimonies is particularly heated in Isaiah 58:1–12.

Chapter 58 begins with God commanding the prophet to announce judgment against God's people with a voice like a *shopar*, a ram's horn that was blown for a number of different reasons, including to inaugurate a fast but also to announce the beginning of a battle. Despite the bellowing warning, the people are delighted with themselves. The Hebrew word *khpts*, which means "delight, pleasure, desire," appears three times in verses 2–3. In verse 2, the prophet says, "Day after day they ... *delight* to know my [God's] ways," as if they were a righteous nation and did not forsake the justice of their god; "they *delight* to draw near to God." In verse 3, the people ask why God is not impressed with their fasting, and the prophet responds by repeating the word "delight," but this time without God as the object: "on the fast day, you seek *delight* and oppress your laborers" (my trans.). The implication is that the delight they seek has nothing to do with God. Their search for pleasure is intimately tied to the oppression of their workers; they are able to pile up material delights because they pay cheap wages. Their self-interest is disguised as piety, and that is nowhere more evident than on the day of the fast.

Fasting served a number of purposes in the ancient world: to prepare themselves to encounter YHWH, to express grief, or to assuage an angry god. The prophet Isaiah rails against ritual acts of fasting, because to him they suggest YHWH can be mollified and manipulated. Further, he insists that YHWH cares about those who are truly hungry—rather than those who are hungry by choice—and is not impressed by the elites' attempts to symbolically express their humility. YHWH demands that humility and solidarity with the poor, who are always hungry, be enacted—not symbolically but materially and actually. The elites' decision to fast, to refuse the food they have in abundance, while the hungry remain underfed, represents an egregious affront to these hungry people.

In short, YHWH says to the fasters, fasting designed to draw attention to you and your performance of humility will not draw my favor (Isa. 58:4–5).

In verses 6–7, there is a shift from accusation to plaintive admonition in the form of a series of questions. Isaiah urges the people to remember what they know deep in their bones, namely, that YHWH chooses to loose the bonds of justice, break every yoke, feed the hungry, shelter the homeless, and clothe the naked.

Once the people reorient themselves to their god and to their neighbors, "then," YHWH promises, "your light will break forth like the dawn" (v. 8). The language here recalls images in Second Isaiah, where Israel is called "a light to the nations" (42:6; 49:6), and anticipates Isaiah 60:1, in which Israel is invited, "Arise, shine; for your light has come."

If the people will do what God commands (58:6–7), "Then you shall call, and the Lord will answer; you shall cry for help, and he will say, 'Here I am'" (v. 9). The words of hope here allude to the well-known response of Isaiah ("Here I am," *hinneni*) to God's question, "Whom shall I send?" (6:8). Here the roles of the caller and the responder are reversed; "you" (probably prophets working in the mode of Isaiah) will call, and God will respond—faithfully—as Isaiah did: "Here I am" (*hinneni*).

The images of hope in the final verses in this passage may be an attempt not merely to console the ones who consider themselves righteous but also to address the division in the community. While the rhetoric in verses 1–5, and to some degree in verses 6–7, could be seen as exacerbating the internal rift, the tone and imagery in the second part of the passage provide some hope for reconciliation.

Those who practice what we might call a "justice fast" live out their commitment to justice and serve to model something for the rest of the community. The images of restoration depict the people living in a state of *shalom* in such a way as to provide sustenance and succor to others. In the language of Isaiah, they will be like a light in the darkness (v. 10)—not only to the nations (42:6; 49:6), but to their own kin, from whom they have become estranged. They will be "like a watered garden" (58:11; see Jer. 31:12), a place that will grow fruit and provide sustenance, and "like a spring of water" (58:11; see Isa. 41:18), a vital and consistent source of life. They will be called "the repairer of the breach, the restorer of streets to live in" (58:12), because they will have attended to the fissures and fractures in the community. Their role is not only to judge the hypocrites among them but also to model something more satisfying to those people who have not yet learned to find their delight in YHWH. The final verses suggest that the deep fulfillment—the lasting delight—they will gain from living in accordance with YHWH's justice will not only serve the poor and the oppressed; it will also serve to ease the strife within the community.

AMY ERICKSON

Commentary 2: Connecting the Reading with the World

There may be times when a preacher's voice is like a soft, cool breeze on a blistering hot day, but there are also times when it should be raised up "like a trumpet" shouting out the word of the Lord to a numb people. Like music, not all sermons are in a soft register; sometimes the gospel needs to be a loud blast of truth! This is what Isaiah calls out from preachers, if we are willing to tell the truth in another righteous register. If a preacher cannot tell the truth on Ash Wednesday, when we remember that we are dust and to dust we will return, then when can we tell the truth out loud?

The words of this pericope ring out with a variety of possibilities for preachers. It is Ash Wednesday, the beginning of the Lenten journey. Not only do the faithful often have ashes imposed on their foreheads as symbolic of repentance, but they may "impose" different spiritual practices on their lives to foster self-reflection during this liturgical season. In general, one might hear some aim to "give up" something during Lent—chocolate, Facebook, watching TV, or a beloved habit or activity. Lent is often portrayed as a liturgical time of "giving up," when people give up something as a sign of giving themselves up to God. One prominent spiritual discipline used to give up is fasting.

The spiritual practice of fasting, mentioned in Isaiah, is a popular practice during this season. It is a fast diet, a worship diet, where one abstains from food in an attempt to improve one's own spiritual life before God and remember one's humanity and mortality, and whose daily bread sustains us. It is no surprise that this text is used to begin Lent on Ash Wednesday.

Israel engages in this type of fast as good religious people do. They abstain from food and wear sackcloth and ashes as a sign of mourning and penance. They are liturgically literate and ritually right. They want to draw closer to God, and this is the way they know how to do it. This is how they have worshiped for years, but they seem to move further from God as they dive deeper into themselves and deeper into their own worship pattern. They cannot figure out why their fasting will not work this time: "Why do we fast, but you do not see? Why humble ourselves, but you do not notice?" (Isa. 58:3).

Israel cannot figure out what is wrong with their fast diet until God speaks: "Look, you serve your own interest on your fast day, and oppress all your workers. Look, you fast only to quarrel and to fight and to strike with a wicked fist. . . . Is such the fast that I choose, a day to humble oneself?" (58:3–5). The preacher might explore how God brings a serious liturgical critique against Israel because their fast diet is an abstention, not just from food, but from others. They delight in God but despise God's people. They abstain from loving their neighbor and feed on a worship diet full of their "own interest."

A ritual ethic has become disconnected from a righteous ethic in life. Their fasting leads them toward ethical negligence, because religious ritual without a social outlook can become only self-serving. Israel reveals how tempting it is to believe that performing holy acts like fasting or the imposition of ashes makes us holy. This prophetic text raises a cautionary note about our religious practices and how God requires more than right ritual practice.

Another avenue for consideration as a preacher might be to problematize the usual idea of "giving up" something during the season of Lent. What Isaiah reveals is less an emphasis on "giving up" and more on "giving to" others and definitely not "giving up" on love of neighbor. In fact, the preacher might explore how the liturgy and its associated practices are connected to the liturgy after the liturgy, that is, living in the world. How is worship linked to social witness?

This is the challenge God offers when God refashions the meaning of fasting to include such things as letting the oppressed go free and sharing bread with the hungry (vv. 6–7). How does one live out Lent in the world? Why do we fast? This is an important question. Is it to be drawn more into oneself or to be drawn out toward others? Isaiah emphasizes the latter (vv. 3–4). In some way, Israel's story and liturgical approach may have become a congregation's practical theology of worship: believers may think that a particular spiritual practice encompasses the totality of what it means to worship God, and that it is all about "self-maximization"[1] and our "own interest." Preachers could explore a church's worship diet—whether it is deficient, thin on God's love for the least of these (Matt. 25:31–46), or more robust and integrated.

For Isaiah, it is clear that fasting, worship, is service, the church doing the mission of God in the world. If Christian worship services become severed from service in the world, then we lose liturgical integrity because our creeds do not match our deeds. God's fast challenges believers to see worship as ethics, fasting as action. Worship as a verb. If there is any abstention in this form of fasting, it is the abstaining from indifference and inactivity and egotism, because right worship is righteous living committed to others, especially the least of these. In his sermon "Three Dimensions of a Complete Life," the Rev. Dr. Martin Luther King Jr. preached, "Life's most persistent and urgent question is, what are you doing for others?"[2] Preachers should ask their congregations: What are *we* doing for others?

This becomes a critical socioethical question for Christians, because God redefines fasting by moving beyond the practice itself to include the freedom of and provision for other people, such as sharing bread with the hungry and clothes with the naked. In God's own words through the prophet, God calls for worship as service in the world, in which one's lip service matches one's life service, reframing fasting, therefore worship, as a way of life, not a particular day or a singular practice. God-centered worship will lead to a deeper sense of community in which people work toward the flourishing of all people.

The rich opportunity for preachers on this day is to lift up how loving God is connected to loving one's neighbors, how our healing is linked with the healing of others, because we are part of the interconnected web of humanity and all of us are truly dust. When the breach of brokenness in a society is bridged and healed, the light of God shines on all. Where there is reconciliation, God is and God's light shines. This is God's promise to us—that when we work to repair the breach between us and our neighbors by repairing the divide between our worship practices and mission in the world, God is present, restoring what was damaged and ravaged to create an eternal communal harmony where all are made whole in the process. We may ask, "Why do we fast, but you do not see?" basically asking God, "Where are you?" Look where the ruins are rebuilt and breaches bridged; there we will find God saying, "Here I am."

LUKE A. POWERY

1. Christian Scharen, *Faith as a Way of Life: A Vision for Pastoral Leadership* (Grand Rapids: Eerdmans, 2008), 27–40.
2. Martin Luther King Jr., "Three Dimensions of a Complete Life," https://kinginstitute.stanford.edu/king-papers/publications/knock-midnight-inspiration-great-sermons-reverend-martin-luther-king-jr-6.

First Sunday in Lent

Genesis 9:8–17
Psalm 25:1–10

1 Peter 3:18–22
Mark 1:9–15

Genesis 9:8–17

⁸Then God said to Noah and to his sons with him, ⁹"As for me, I am establishing my covenant with you and your descendants after you, ¹⁰and with every living creature that is with you, the birds, the domestic animals, and every animal of the earth with you, as many as came out of the ark. ¹¹I establish my covenant with you, that never again shall all flesh be cut off by the waters of a flood, and never again shall there be a flood to destroy the earth." ¹²God said, "This is the sign of the covenant that I make between me and you and every living creature that is with you, for all future generations: ¹³I have set my bow in the clouds, and it shall be a sign of the covenant between me and the earth. ¹⁴When I bring clouds over the earth and the bow is seen in the clouds, ¹⁵I will remember my covenant that is between me and you and every living creature of all flesh; and the waters shall never again become a flood to destroy all flesh. ¹⁶When the bow is in the clouds, I will see it and remember the everlasting covenant between God and every living creature of all flesh that is on the earth." ¹⁷God said to Noah, "This is the sign of the covenant that I have established between me and all flesh that is on the earth."

Commentary 1: Connecting the Reading with Scripture

Genesis 9:8–17 marks the conclusion of the flood story. After three chapters and many days of deluge and destruction, the rain ceases and the water begins to abate (Gen. 8:2). Eventually, Noah, his family, and the animals disembark (8:18–19). Noah's first act on dry ground is to build an altar to the Lord so he can offer a sacrifice (8:20). Smelling the pleasing odor of the burnt offering, God vows never to destroy God's creatures again (8:21–22) and blesses Noah and his family (9:1–7).

In the scene that immediately follows (9:8–17), God ratifies God's promise through the making of a covenant. Though biblical covenants can take various forms, their primary function is to serve as a formal commitment between two parties. Covenants establish, or recognize, a relationship. In the case of Genesis 9, that relationship is between God and all of creation, including Noah and his family (vv. 9–10). In contrast to God's covenant with Moses, the covenant with Noah is one-sided.

The promise never again to bring destruction does not hinge on certain stipulations being followed, nor is there any mention of blessing for obedience or curses for disobedience. Rather, the integrity of the covenant rests solely on God's fidelity.

After describing the substance of the covenant (vv. 8–11), this passage shifts to the question of the sign of the covenant (vv. 12–17): the setting of God's bow in the clouds. Traditionally interpreted as a rainbow, God's bow (*qeshet*) is arguably the most iconic element of the flood story. That the sign of the covenant is a rainbow and not a cloudless sky is instructive. Though breathtaking and beautiful, a rainbow is a meteorological phenomenon that emerges only in the midst of, or just after, a rainstorm. Given the circumstances, the rainbow is an apt symbol of this covenant. In Genesis 9, God is not promising the complete absence of loss and destruction in the future. Rather, Genesis 9 promises life after loss, hope after destruction. A similar theme reverberates throughout the New Testament. Especially as we enter the season of Lent, we are mindful that the promise of the gospel is not life without death, but resurrection from the dead.

There is another possible interpretation of the sign of the covenant. While many translations render the Hebrew word *qeshet* as "rainbow" (e.g., NIV, NCV, NKJV, NLT, *The Message*), in the Old Testament this term more typically refers to an archer's bow. Used by warriors and hunters, the *qeshet* is a deadly weapon. In ancient art, a drawn bow is often found in the hands of Ashur and Ahura Mazda, the chief deities of the Neo-Assyrians and Persians, respectively. Some Old Testament texts depict the Lord in the mode of a divine archer, with a drawn bow position (Zech. 9:13–14), yet in Genesis 9 one does not find God's bow in use. Rather, it is hung in the clouds, undrawn (the curve of a rainbow approximating the shape of an undrawn bow). Understood in this fashion, the sign of the covenant is an image of demilitarization. When God sees the divine bow in the sky, God calls to mind God's promise never to take up that weapon against creation again (Gen. 9:16).

While the waters of the flood are sometimes thought to anticipate the waters of baptism (see 1 Pet. 3:18–22, another lectionary text for this Sunday), Genesis 6–9 never describes the flood's purpose in terms of washing away sin. In fact, as a comparison of Genesis 6:5 and 8:21 reveals, the human heart is just as inclined to evil after the flood as it was before. If understood as a form of cleansing, the flood has not worked. The story of the flood, much like the story of the entire Bible, is not primarily about how humanity's heart changes for the good after encountering God. Rather, it is a story about how God covenants to remain with God's people despite the inclination of their hearts to evil.

The covenant described in Genesis 9:8–17 is rooted solely in the gracious and unmerited action of God. In 8:1, we learn that God "remembers" Noah and all the rest who were in the ark. While we think of human remembering as a mental process that entails calling to mind something from the past, divine remembering is of a different sort. It is about attention and

intervention. It bespeaks God's commitment to be in relation with sinful humanity, to deliver out of destruction those who are not yet inclined to do good, and to suffer with, and sometimes because of, a broken world. That God is a God who remembers is the only thing that ultimately holds back the waters of the flood, and it is the only thing that makes new life possible.

The story of the flood is situated within the broader context of the primeval history (Gen. 1–11). These chapters trace the drama of God's involvement with a world marred by the intrusion of sin. In this context, the flood can be seen as a type of undoing of God's initial act of creation (1:1–2:4a). As the flood narrative unfolds, clouds hide the light of the sun (reversing days one and four), plant and animal life is destroyed (reversing days five and six), the dry ground disappears (reversing day three), and, as the rain descends and seas rise, the distinction between the waters above and the waters beneath is effaced (reversing day two). At the height of the flood the earth is once again a "formless void" (1:2).

In the midst of such chaos, God once again sends a wind (*ruach*)—a word in Hebrew that can also mean spirit—to bring life and order (8:1; cf. Gen. 1:2). From here, creation begins afresh. The sun shines through the clouds, the waters are separated, dry ground emerges, and plant and animal life returns. Likewise, humanity is commissioned to be fruitful, multiply, and fill the earth (9:1, 7; see 1:28). While the first creation account ends with God at rest (i.e., the Sabbath), the story of re-creation in Genesis 6–9 ends with God's bow at rest in the clouds. Adding to this parallel is the fact that Sabbath keeping is referred to as a "perpetual covenant" (*berit 'olam*) in Exodus 31:16. The same Hebrew phrase is used in Genesis 9:16 to describe the nature of God's covenant with Noah (NRSV "everlasting covenant").

Just as core themes in the flood story reach back to the opening chapters of Genesis, so they also reach forward to the closing chapters of the book of Revelation. Within its description of a new heaven and a new earth, Revelation 21:1 notes that "the sea was no more." This reference draws on a widely held symbolic association between the primordial forces of chaos on the one hand and the sea and floods on the other (e.g., Jonah 2:1–6; Ps. 74:13–15). In the vision of Revelation 21, the one who makes all things new ultimately overcomes death and chaos, such that "mourning and crying and pain will be no more" (Rev. 21:4). Read in light of Revelation 21, the covenant God makes in Genesis 9:8–17, never to bring destruction on creation again, is a foretaste of this final act of restoration. Put differently, Genesis 9 captures in miniature what is writ large across the canon: through the promise of God's covenant, the sea and the flood—and all that they symbolize—will not have the final say.

RYAN P. BONFIGLIO

Commentary 2: Connecting the Reading with the World

The world was inundated. Life as previously known had ceased, as the corpses of animals and humans floated on the still waters surrounding a microcosm of a world that now was contained in an ark. In the midst of the apocalypse, hope and grace were the promises made by God to the remnant after this global catastrophe. After the destruction of the earth through water, the occupants of the ark must wait for the land to be dry again in order to disembark. A new earth awaited them, and all creatures, as on the first day of creation, were called to be fruitful and multiply so as to fill the earth again. Among the first acts of Noah was offering his deity several clean animals as sacrifices. As the sweet savory fragrance of the burnt offerings reached God's nostrils, the Almighty was so pleased that God swore never again to destroy the earth by water. While God makes a covenant never to curse the earth again and never to strike down every creature due to the evil found in the hearts of humans, the new creation has not brought forth newly contrite human hearts. Evil tendencies continue to flourish in a postdeluge world.

Humans did not change, but maybe the God who never changes changed. Humans will ceaselessly continue to partake in evil; but God makes a covenant nonetheless. In this new world order, humans need not fear extinction. They can rely on a new relationship with a deity who will be more patient and merciful. The covenant God makes with Noah and his descendants is the first legal agreement made between humans and their God. Unlike the future covenants God would make with Abraham (Gen. 12:1–3) and with Moses at Mount Sinai (Exod. 19–24), this covenant with Noah is not exclusively for the people of Israel. It is a covenant made with all humanity and, just as important, all of creation. The well-being of humans will forever be intertwined with the well-being of the planet and all the forms of life it contains.

The covenant will be known by God's war bow set on the clouds, what we call today a rainbow. God will see the rainbow whenever it rains and remember the covenant and thus not destroy the earth by flood. We too will see God's war bow and be comforted by God's promise. Even though the bow is an instrument of war, the unstrung bow in the sky testifies to God's pledge never to make war on humans again. However, before we get too comfortable with God's promise, some, including the author of 2 Peter 3:5–7, insist that the promise was limited to a watery destruction, leaving open the possibility of a fiery apocalypse on the day of judgment.

Although speculation about God destroying the earth in some future apocalypse may sell books and novels, the real question we should be wrestling with is whether God can be trusted to keep God's promises. After all, God promised to make the people of the covenants with Abraham and Moses a chosen people who would not be abandoned. Yet in a post-Holocaust world we cannot ignore God's absence. God's promise to God's chosen people becomes problematic with the overwhelming proof of the abandonment of some six million people with whom God entered into covenant. So before we place too much hope in the covenant made with Noah, in the shadow of Auschwitz we must ponder what happens to a hope and grace based on God's promises when God fails to keep those promises.

Hope cannot be reduced to wishful thinking; rather, it is an expected joy that God's will shall come about, according to God's purposes. This is a hope based on Noah's God, a God who is faithful to God's covenant with humanity and thereby becomes a God of the future, a God who remains a step ahead of humanity, making all things new. Covenant promises work if a salvation history (spiritual or secular) is adopted. Modernity has taught us that we, as a species, are moving toward utopia, say, by means of capitalism (a rising tide will raise all ships) or communism (the eventual withering away of the state). Both share a salvation history. Hope exists that the future, thanks to God or science or human ingenuity, will be more forward thinking and more egalitarian than the past. However, what if there is no salvation history? What if the premodern view (history made by God) and modern view (history made by the human subject) are both wrong? What if the historical dialectic that moves history in an upward spiral is but an optimistic construct forced on a very select history?

Dark ages of ignorance can follow spans of enlightenment, creating at times downward spirals, at other times upward spirals, yet at other times unrelated and unconnected events—in other words, a nonlinear disjointed, multidimensional passage of time. What exists is a permanent historical discontinuity, where history is not defined through triumphant metanarratives, but instead is a kaleidoscope comprised of contradictory and complex untold stories and struggles of the very least among us, who remain unnamed. History is full of stories of evil vanquishing good, brutality crushing peace. The world is not getting better for the globally marginalized. Due to the widening wealth gap, many are experiencing an economic situation that is getting worse. Billions are born into poverty and die because of its consequences, so that a privileged chosen can enjoy first-world status. The marginalized offer up their lives as living sacrifices, so that an elite can be saved and live well.

Hope in God's covenants can be sustained if it remains a product of salvation history. We can therefore optimistically believe that the arc of history bends toward justice; but if the past and present are reliable guides, the existence of such an arc is a faith statement assumed without proof. All too often, hope becomes an excuse not to deal with the reality of injustice. For those struggling to survive, destitution and death await. The reality of reading our daily newspapers confirms that for many on the margins of society, there is no hope.

The oppressed of the world occupy the space of Holy Saturday, the day after Friday's crucifixion and not yet the Easter Sunday of resurrection. This is a space where some faint anticipation of Sunday's good news is easily drowned out by the reality and consequences of Friday's violence and brutality. It is a space where hopelessness becomes the companion of used and abused people. The virtue or audacity of hope become a class privilege experienced by those protected from the realities of Friday or the "opium" that is used to numb that same reality until Sunday rolls around.

Regardless of the optimism professed in rainbows in the sky, the disenfranchised, their children, and their children's children will more than likely continue to live in an ever-expanding poverty. The situation remains hopeless. Covenants that the world will not be destroyed again— rainbows supposed to signify to the drowning marginalized that they will not perish—become a cruel imposition for those whose life, a world unto itself, continues to be destroyed, whether from rising waters or some other threat.

What then is the word to preach in the hopeless bleakness faced by the majority of the world's marginalized? We struggle for justice, not because we hope that in the end it will all work out, or so that we can obtain some heavenly reward. We struggle for justice because it defines our faith and our humanity.

MIGUEL A. DE LA TORRE

Psalm 25:1–10

¹To you, O LORD, I lift up my soul.
²O my God, in you I trust;
    do not let me be put to shame;
    do not let my enemies exult over me.
³Do not let those who wait for you be put to shame;
    let them be ashamed who are wantonly treacherous.

⁴Make me to know your ways, O LORD;
    teach me your paths.
⁵Lead me in your truth, and teach me,
    for you are the God of my salvation;
    for you I wait all day long.

⁶Be mindful of your mercy, O LORD, and of your steadfast love,
    for they have been from of old.
⁷Do not remember the sins of my youth or my transgressions;
    according to your steadfast love remember me,
    for your goodness' sake, O LORD!

⁸Good and upright is the LORD;
    therefore he instructs sinners in the way.
⁹He leads the humble in what is right,
    and teaches the humble his way.
¹⁰All the paths of the LORD are steadfast love and faithfulness,
    for those who keep his covenant and his decrees.

Connecting the Psalm with Scripture and Worship

Because Psalm 25 is an acrostic poem in Hebrew, it is often suggested that it is rather disjointed in its English translation—a bit staccato rather than legato—lacking narrative flow. It is nevertheless poetic in its structure and compelling in its meaning. Although it is written in the first person singular, it is not so much a personal prayer as a generic plea for learning: "make me to know" (Ps. 25:4), "teach" or "teaches" (vv. 4, 5, 9), "instructs" (v. 8). It is a prayer for learning that can come only from God, spoken to the God whom the psalmist completely trusts.

The attitude of prayer begins in the first verses, "To you, O LORD, I lift up my soul. O my God, in you I trust." Throughout the psalm, the writer is asking not for changes in personal circumstances, but rather changes in self, making it particularly appropriate for the beginning of the Lenten season. This reading for the First Sunday in Lent ends with verse 10, "All the paths of the LORD are steadfast love and faithfulness, for those who keep God's covenant and God's decrees." This ties in beautifully with the reading from Genesis 9:8–17, the story of God's covenant after the flood. Unfortunately, the flood story is often reserved for the children's Sunday school, despite its vital importance in a world where steadfastness and trust are rare, and in some cases unknown.

The bow, unstrung, hanging up in the clouds, is not really for us, but rather is intended as a sign to God, to indicate the end of retribution, and specifically to ask God to "be mindful of your mercy, O LORD, and of your steadfast love, for they have been from of old" (v. 6). In the twenty-first-century world it might be as important to assure adults as it is to assure

Come to the Immortality of Baptism

The beloved generates love, and the light immaterial the light inaccessible. "This is my beloved Son," He who, being manifested on earth and yet unseparated from the Father's bosom, was manifested, and yet did not appear. For the appearing is a different thing, since in appearance the baptizer here is superior to the baptized. For this reason did the Father send down the Holy Spirit from heaven upon Him who was baptized. For as in the ark of Noah the love of God toward man is signified by the dove, so also now the Spirit, descending in the form of a dove, bearing as it were the fruit of the olive, rested on Him to whom the witness was borne. For what reason? That the faithfulness of the Father's voice might be made known, and that the prophetic utterance of a long time past might be ratified. And what utterance is this? "The voice of the Lord (is) on the waters, the God of glory thundered; the Lord (is) upon many waters." And what voice? "This is my beloved Son, in whom I am well pleased." This is He who is named the son of Joseph, and (who is) according to the divine essence my Only-begotten. "This is my beloved Son"—He who is hungry, and yet maintains myriads; who is weary, and yet gives rest to the weary; who has not where to lay His head, and yet bears up all things in His hand; who suffers, and yet heals sufferings; who is smitten, and yet confers liberty on the world; who is pierced in the side, and yet repairs the side of Adam.

But give me now your best attention, I pray you, for I wish to go back to the fountain of life, and to view the fountain that gushes with healing. The Father of immortality sent the immortal Son and Word into the world, who came to man in order to wash him with water and the Spirit; and He, begetting us again to incorruption of soul and body, breathed into us the breath (spirit) of life, and endued us with an incorruptible panoply. If, therefore, man has become immortal, he will also be God. And if he is made God by water and the Holy Spirit after the regeneration of the laver he is found to be also joint-heir with Christ after the resurrection from the dead. Wherefore I preach to this effect: Come, all you kindreds of the nations, to the immortality of the baptism. I bring good tidings of life to you who tarry in the darkness of ignorance. Come into liberty from slavery, into a kingdom from tyranny, into incorruption from corruption. And how, says one, shall we come? How? By water and the Holy Ghost. This is the water in conjunction with the Spirit, by which paradise is watered, by which the earth is enriched, by which plants grow, by which animals multiply, and (to sum up the whole in a single word) by which man is begotten again and endued with life, in which also Christ was baptized, and in which the Spirit descended in the form of a dove.

Hippolytus of Rome, "The Discourse on the Holy Theophany,"*Ante-Nicene Fathers*, vol. 5, ed. Alexander Roberts, James Donaldson, and A. Cleveland Coxe (Buffalo, NY: Christian Literature Publishing, 1886), 236–37.

young people that they are beloved children of God, and that nothing they could ever say or do can change that.

So this prayer from the psalmist to the God of Noah is to a God who instructs, and leads, and teaches (vv. 8–9). It is also to a God who is notably nonaggressive. In this psalm, unlike many other psalms, the writer does not ask that his enemies be injured or done away with, but only that they be ashamed, even those who are "wantonly treacherous." This seems very different from the world of "an eye for an eye" or from today's world, where some are taught that

if a person accidentally bumps into you, the best response is to turn around and knock them over! It could well be that the treacherous enemies the psalmist has in mind are really enemies within, perhaps more likely to have power over us than any external enemy could possibly have.

The writer of the psalm is asking to be taught—taught the ways of the Lord, taught the paths of God, taught God's truth, God's mercy, and God's steadfast love. The writer is asking to be made new, just as God made creation new in the flood, and just as all who follow Jesus are made new in the waters of baptism (cf. Mark 1:9–15).

Both the Old Testament reading and the Gospel passages for the First Sunday in Lent are also connected through the biblical number forty. Noah experienced forty days of rain, the Lord's path for the Hebrew people took them forty years through the wilderness, and this week's Gospel text includes Jesus spending forty days in the wilderness. In like fashion, we begin the forty days of the season of Lent.

From a liturgical perspective, two of the most helpful phrases in the psalm are to "wait for [the Lord]" (Ps. 25:3) and "for you I wait all day long" (v. 5). This waiting motif is incorporated into many hymns, such as "Wait for the Lord"; "For You, My God, I Wait"; "For You, O Lord, My Soul in Stillness Waits"; "I Waited Patiently for God"; and "If Thou But Trust in God to Guide Thee." Waiting is a frustrating activity for many people, and the idea of "waiting for the Lord" might be interesting to explore. Other hymns based on the psalm include "Lord, to You My Soul Is Lifted," a twentieth-century text set to a Renaissance tune, and "Lead Me, Guide Me," an African American gospel song.

As with most psalms, the text itself can easily become a liturgical element. Verses 1–2 or 8–10 make excellent opening sentences, and verses 6–7 can be used as a part of a confession sequence. It would also work well to use any of the verses related to teaching as a part of a prayer for illumination. There are also many anthems related to this psalm. "I Waited for the Lord," from the cantata *Hymn of Praise* by Felix Mendelssohn, is scored for two solo sopranos and four-part choir. "Teach Me, O Lord" by David Hurd is accessible for choirs of all levels. As the piece closes, each singer moves independently at will from note to note in an undulating pattern. This continues until the final chord from the organ. One can easily imagine that this effect musically illustrates the up-and-down flow of the Lenten journey.

This psalm has two major themes, both vitally important as we move through Lent. To ask to be taught by God, and to wait patiently for that teaching, suggest a path that all of us might well choose to follow.

DAVID A. VANDERMEER

1 Peter 3:18–22

¹⁸For Christ also suffered for sins once for all, the righteous for the unrighteous, in order to bring you to God. He was put to death in the flesh, but made alive in the spirit, ¹⁹in which also he went and made a proclamation to the spirits in prison, ²⁰who in former times did not obey, when God waited patiently in the days of Noah, during the building of the ark, in which a few, that is, eight persons, were saved through water. ²¹And baptism, which this prefigured, now saves you—not as a removal of dirt from the body, but as an appeal to God for a good conscience, through the resurrection of Jesus Christ, ²²who has gone into heaven and is at the right hand of God, with angels, authorities, and powers made subject to him.

Commentary 1: Connecting the Reading with Scripture

On this First Sunday in Lent, we continue our time of reflection on Jesus' life, ministry, and especially his suffering and death. Jesus' resurrection is omitted here. During the Lenten season, oftentimes we as Christians are uncomfortable spending time with Jesus in the trauma and pain of his suffering. Instead, we want to tread ever so lightly over this sad time and jump to the joy of Easter Sunday. The lectionary text for this day compels us to reside in this place of discomfort, not only with regard to Jesus' pain, but also with regard to the pain of the early church and ultimately our own pain.

Jesus' death on a cross was God's unmerited gift of grace to us; this sacrificial act helped reconcile us to God (1 Pet. 3:18). Because of this, Christians also look inward to reflect on their sinful nature and are led to repentance. During the Lenten season of forty days, which signifies both the number of years the Israelites spent in the wilderness (Num. 33:38; Deut. 1:3) and the number of days Jesus fasted in the wilderness during his time of temptation by Satan (Matt. 4:1–11; Mark 1:12–13; Luke 4:1–13), Christians should observe a heightened period of spiritual discipline and focus.

The author of 1 Peter places special emphasis on Jesus' suffering, which Christians are to emulate. His readers (specifically, enslaved believers) are to suffer "because Christ also suffered for [them], leaving [them] an example, so that [they] should follow in his steps" (1 Pet. 2:21). Written for Christians in the five Roman provinces of Asia (1:1), who are facing tribulation (1:6; 2:12, 19–20; 3:14–17; 4:1, 4, 12–19; 5:9–10), they are told to expect to suffer as Christ did (2:21–24; 3:17–18; 4:1–2, 12–14). In fact, the author describes their suffering as a calling for which they will receive a reward (3:9), to which I will refer below. It is said of Jesus that "when he was abused, he did not return abuse; when he suffered, he did not threaten" (2:23). Similarly, enslaved believers are not to retaliate. They are not to "repay evil for evil or abuse for abuse"; rather, they are to "repay with a blessing" (3:9). In so doing, they will have God's approval (2:20).

In addition to returning violence or hatred with a blessing, this early Christian community is advised to rejoice despite, and in the midst of, suffering (1:3–9). The irony here is that the text does not mention Jesus' expressing joy about his suffering and imminent death. If they are to follow in Christ's example, then perhaps they should ask God to "remove this cup from them" (Luke 22:42). Only an author writing decades after Jesus' death—with a firm belief in the salvific and eternal value of this death for all believers—could tell his audience to rejoice. He knew the benefits that Christians are afforded because of it.

After describing how Christ suffered because of our sins, "the righteous for the unrighteous, in order to bring [us] to God" (1 Pet. 3:18), he then describes Jesus' transition from "death in the flesh" to being "alive in the spirit" (3:18). The author's intent is not to move the believers' focus from the cross to the resurrection, but rather to remind them of what Jesus' death granted, that is, salvation. This is the blessing they may inherit (3:9). This salvation is Christians' "inheritance that is imperishable, undefiled, and unfading, kept in heaven for [us]," which the author describes at the outset of the text (1:3–4). This is not an Easter moment. Although the resurrection made salvation possible, the author uses it as motivation for Christians as they suffer, those who are "being protected by the power of God through faith for a salvation ready to be revealed in the last time" (1:5).

Jesus' salvific work on the cross made salvation available to all believers, which they access through baptism (3:21). This focus on baptism is one of the reasons some scholars have suggested that 1 Peter may have originated as a baptismal homily (3:21; cf. 2:2). According to the author, baptism is what "now saves" them (3:21). The author does not include any details as to *how* believers are baptized—such as through immersion or the sprinkling of water—nor does the author explicitly state *when* this baptism must take place (whether the person baptized is an adult or an infant). Instead, he describes the benefits of baptism. Christians are made clean, "not as a removal of dirt from the body, but as an appeal to God for a good conscience," which has been made available through Christ's resurrection (3:21). This "good conscience" may refer to the instruction to "sanctify Christ as Lord" in their hearts (3:15), as well as the urge to do everything "with gentleness and reverence," so that when they "are maligned, those who abuse [them] for [their] good conduct in Christ may be put to shame" (3:16).

What are the implications of rejoicing in one's suffering for contemporary Christians? Are we supposed to "turn the other cheek" when we are persecuted, even if unjustly, like the first-century audience? What is the "living hope" that we receive through baptism, "through the resurrection of Jesus" (1:3)? Perhaps it is the hope of salvation spoken to the early church. Nevertheless, the inquiry of the psalmist remains: "How long, O Lord?" (Ps. 13:1). How much are we expected to suffer "for the Lord's sake" (1 Pet. 2:13), especially since Jesus has made the ultimate sacrifice?

One might surmise that perhaps the early church had similar concerns. Suffer. Because of. Rejoice. In spite of. Really? I assume that enslaved believers must have asked themselves these questions. Later in the text, the author claims that "the end of all things is near" (4:7). Thus, suffering for being a Christian during that time may have been understood as a short-term plight. It may have been a bit easier to hear the instruction: "Live for the rest of your earthly life no longer by human desires [such as retribution?] but by the will of God" (4:2). Maybe it was commendable, a yearning even, to suffer as a Christian in order to "bear [God's] name" (4:16). Nevertheless, for me, the biblical author's response is theologically, socially, and ethically inadequate.

Like Christians during the Lenten season, the author of this text focuses on Jesus' sufferings. Although many Christians, as well as the author, believe Jesus to be preexistent (1:20), it is Jesus' earthly ordeal that gives us pause. His suffering is what compels believers to set time apart for spiritual reflection, to evaluate our relationship with God through Jesus Christ, and to reflect on our own character and behavior, especially when our faith is "tested by fire" (1:7). Jesus' suffering, which led to his death and his resurrection, provided us with the gift of salvation.

It may be difficult to rejoice and say, "God is good," while going through trials and tribulation, but it is indeed a blessed assurance to know what God has in store for us. As the author states: "Although [we] have not seen him, [we] love him; and even though [we] do not see him now, [we] believe in him and rejoice with an indescribable and glorious joy, for [we] are receiving the outcome of [our] faith, the salvation of [our] souls" (1:8–9).

SHANELL T. SMITH

Commentary 2: Connecting the Reading with the World

The season of Lent provides an opportunity for us to pause and reflect on the role of faith in our lives. We are prompted to think deeply about the ways in which our beliefs lead us to engage with the world around us and to evaluate how we are living out our Christian values. Despite the peculiar theological connection this text draws between the flood and baptism, it provides a starting point for considering the idea of salvation, as well as the language we use to describe it.

The work of womanist theologians invites us to consider the ways traditional theological language about salvation has been used to put oppressed members of our society, specifically African American women, at risk. In one of the foundational texts of womanist theology, *Sisters in the Wilderness: The Challenge of Womanist God-Talk*, Delores Williams warns against the tendency in Christian theology to overemphasize the language of surrogacy—the idea that the suffering of one allows for the redemption of many (as in 1 Pet. 3:18). According to Williams, excessive veneration of the suffering and death of Jesus on the cross both displaces attention from Jesus' life and ministry and risks validating suffering for its own sake. For this reason, Williams consistently attempts to redirect attention from the veneration of the death of Jesus to the life-giving character of Jesus' ministry.

Williams's specific objection to the use of surrogacy language in relation to African American women is both historical and contemporary. In the past, enslaved African American women nursed and cared for children who were not their own, while today marginalized women are pressured into accepting caring roles for the benefit of others, due to limited opportunities and the need for income. Williams argues that both surrogacy language and the exhortation to "take up your cross" have been used to justify the subjection of African American women and other oppressed peoples.

This problem, for Williams, can be addressed by reversing our theological priorities. She controversially claims: "Humankind is, then, redeemed through Jesus' *ministerial* vision of life and not through his death. There is nothing divine in the blood of the cross."[1] The resurrection, for Williams, stands at the core of our faith, not because Jesus died a painful and violent death, but because life—and, more precisely, Jesus' vision of life lived to the fullest—triumphed over death.

Keeping in mind this valuable critique, we might also note that the first phrase of this passage tells us that salvation is offered "for all" (3:18). Perhaps the generosity of this offer challenges our sensibilities. For example, are there individuals or groups of people whom we consider to be outside the reach of God's grace? Alternatively, are there actions, thoughts, or feelings for which we cannot forgive ourselves? Have we extrapolated from these concerns that salvation is not available to them or to us?

In East Los Angeles during the late 1980s, Jesuit priest Greg Boyle began working with former gang members in a job training program intended to offer high-risk youth an alternative to gang life. Over time, this effort evolved into Homeboy Industries, a program for gang intervention serving nearly 9,000 people each year through a supportive community, education and job-training opportunities, and a variety of other services to help participants redirect their lives.

Each participant works with a case manager to plan a program that may include academic classes (reading and writing, high school diploma or equivalent credential, or college readiness), life-skills training (parenting classes, anger management), recovery support groups, legal assistance, and tattoo removal, among other offerings. Participants begin their job training with basic building maintenance and can progress into working in a variety of fields, including the on-site bakery and restaurant, farmers' market, silkscreen and embroidery, electronics

---

1. Delores S. Williams, *Sisters in the Wilderness: The Challenge of Womanist God-Talk* (Maryknoll, NY: Orbis, 1993), 167. On womanist theology, see also Stephanie Y. Mitchem, *Introducing Womanist Theology* (Maryknoll, NY: Orbis, 2002).

recycling, and solar-panel-installation training. Using this holistic model of recovery, participants are empowered to change their lives and to contribute to the well-being of their families and communities.

In his powerful and poignant book *Tattoos on the Heart: The Power of Boundless Compassion*, Boyle weaves together vignettes drawn from his interactions with the "homies" and a beautifully inclusive theological vision rooted in the expansive reach of God's love, which Boyle describes as *no matter whatness*. At the heart of this theology is the assurance that God loves each of us intensely—no matter what. We do not have to earn this love. God will never take it away from us. We are precious to God just as we are. Although circumstances we witness and experience in our daily lives might lead us to the conclusion that some lives matter more than others, Boyle insists that God plays by different rules. If we can imagine anyone standing outside the embrace of God's love, then our vision of God is simply too small and too limiting.

This is a crucial message for the homies, who as gang members and convicted felons have been among the most reviled members of our society, and who now, in order to summon the strength and resilience needed to pursue the difficult path of recovery, need so desperately to know that they are precious and loved.

It is not only the homies who long to hear this message. Boyle explains in the book's introduction that his purpose in writing is not only to evoke compassion by putting a human face on gang members, but also for us "to recognize our own wounds in the broken lives and daunting struggles of the men and women in these parables."[2] Although we may not share the homies' experiences, each of us has suffered and can benefit from the assurance that we are loved despite our wounds and failings. Boyle's narratives coax us to admit that although we may give intellectual assent to the notion that God loves us, we, like the homies, sometimes feel unworthy of this love.

It is precisely from these broken, wounded places in our own hearts, Boyle tells us, that we can reach out to connect with the brokenness and woundedness of others. This connection becomes a virtuous circle: acknowledging our own wounds allows us to recognize that we share experiences of suffering in common with others; these shared experiences become the basis of compassion; compassion enables us to expand our sense of kinship and encourages us to build community; and living in community creates a space in which we can accept our wounds and both give and receive support for healing.

Boyle reminds us that "the desire of God's heart is immeasurably larger than our imaginations can conjure." In his characteristic storytelling tone, he continues: "It is precisely because we have such an overactive disapproval gland ourselves that we tend to create God in our own image. It is truly hard for us to see the truth that disapproval does not seem to be part of God's DNA. God is just too busy loving us to have any time left for disappointment."[3]

As part of our Lenten practices, may we be attuned to God's abundant love and grace. May we strive to refine the language we use for the sacred so as not to harm the most vulnerable among us. May we extend compassion to those who have been excluded, remembering that God loves us all. No matter what.

ANN HIDALGO

2. Gregory Boyle, *Tattoos on the Heart: The Power of Boundless Compassion* (New York: Free Press, 2010), xv.
3. Boyle, *Tattoos on the Heart*, 27.

Mark 1:9–15

[9]In those days Jesus came from Nazareth of Galilee and was baptized by John in the Jordan. [10]And just as he was coming up out of the water, he saw the heavens torn apart and the Spirit descending like a dove on him. [11]And a voice came from heaven, "You are my Son, the Beloved; with you I am well pleased."

[12]And the Spirit immediately drove him out into the wilderness. [13]He was in the wilderness forty days, tempted by Satan; and he was with the wild beasts; and the angels waited on him.

[14]Now after John was arrested, Jesus came to Galilee, proclaiming the good news of God, [15]and saying, "The time is fulfilled, and the kingdom of God has come near; repent, and believe in the good news."

Commentary 1: Connecting the Reading with Scripture

To understand anything in the Gospel according to Mark, it helps to remember several things. The first is that the literary genre of gospel was invented by Mark. Various literary forms have been compared to it, but none is precisely like Mark's Gospel, which offers a narrative argument for the identification of Jesus as the Son whom God the Father has sent into the world to reclaim it. So Mark had to figure out how to do what he felt called to do. His education was limited, and he did not know how to write in a polished literary manner. Indeed, he seems to have been someone more aware of how to do public speaking than of how to write elegant prose. Many scholars have talked about his oral style, pointing out that this applies to the Gospel as a whole as well as its general prose style. Some confirmation of that is found in the way some public speakers have memorized the entire Gospel and recite it as a single performance—a little long for a speech today but not for speeches through most of Western history.

The next thing to be remembered is that Mark's Gospel begins with Jesus' baptism. While Matthew and Luke begin with stories of Jesus' birth and infancy, and John begins with a theological prologue, our reading begins with Mark 1:9, and the first eight verses of Mark exist

to prepare the way for our story. The first verse seems to be a title for the Gospel, designed to lead into the beginning of the story. It is followed by a reference to the Hebrew Scriptures.[1] Verse 1 has already identified the genre of the work, giving it the name still used for the genre Mark invented: "Gospel" (*euangelion*)—making him the first evangelist, although Mark probably just means "good news," rather than the genre of his work. Most translations of this verse end it by describing Jesus the Christ as "the Son of God." While that final phrase does not appear there in all early manuscripts, it appears often enough in the rest of the Gospel as to leave no doubt that Mark accepted that title of Jesus as genuine and appropriate. Yet that identification of Jesus appears to be treated as inside information; it may have been shared by Mark and his readers, but was not common knowledge during Jesus' life.

Then verses 2–8 introduce the reader to John the Baptist and his ministry; this section ends with John identifying his main significance as being to prepare for the greater one who was to come. Yet John was important in his own right: verse 5 tells of the crowds he attracted from Judea and Jerusalem. An important detail easily missed is in the description of John's clothing,

---

1. Mark claims that he is quoting Isaiah, but his first verse is from Malachi.

an apparent allusion to what 2 Kings 1:8 has to say about that of Elijah, whom Malachi 3:1 identifies as the messenger to be sent to prepare the way of the Lord. That Mark accepted that identification of John with Elijah is made clear in Mark 9:13.

All of this has set the stage for the three events in our reading for the day: Jesus' baptism with its heavenly voice, his temptation in the wilderness, and the beginning of his ministry in Galilee. John's baptism is for "repentance for the forgiveness of sins" (1:4). Many through the ages have wondered why the Son of God would need or want such forgiveness. A number of interpreters, the other Gospel writers among them, have suggested possible reasons. Matthew 3:14, for instance, has John say that it would be more appropriate for Jesus to baptize him; Mark had already taken care of that by having John say that one greater than he was to come and that while he baptized with water, the one to come would baptize with the Holy Spirit (Mark 1:8). Such lacks of explanation, such as this one about Jesus' decision to be baptized by John, are common in Mark; he gives only information that helps him make the points he intends to make.

The point that Mark wishes to make here is, of course, the theophany that occurs when Jesus is coming up out of the water. The significance of the event is indicated by the way the heavens do not just "open," as earlier translations had it, but are "torn open" (NIV) or "torn apart" (NRSV). Another difference between Mark and the other Synoptics is that for Mark, the descent of Spirit is *like* that of a dove, while for the others it comes *as* a dove. For them it lands on Jesus, but for Mark the Spirit descends *into* Jesus (Gk. *eis*).

Another difference between the way Mark treats this event and the ways Matthew and Luke do is that in Mark, only Jesus is aware of the voice from heaven proclaiming him to be God's beloved Son. This is consistent with the way Mark limits to himself and his readers those who understand that Jesus is the Son of God. During Jesus' ministry, not even the disciples have a full appreciation of who their leader is.

This is what scholars call "the messianic secret," a theme that is more central to Mark than it is to Matthew and Luke.

All of this has generated much discussion concerning whether Jesus was aware of his identity before this event. Is he then driven into the wilderness to reflect on the implications of his calling? This is just another one of our questions that Mark does not answer.

Mark does say, however, that while Jesus is in the desert, he is tempted by Satan— although "tested" may be a better description of what happens. "Tempted" suggests a desire to do the proffered thing. Mark does not specify what the temptations are; he simply says that the entire forty days are a time of testing. There is a lack of specificity about the testing; Mark says only that it is done by Satan, that it takes place in a wilderness in which there are also wild animals, and that angels "waited on him" (1:13). While it is impossible to know what Mark means by this setting, a history-of-religion approach could understand it as an environment of great uncertainty and indefiniteness, where Jesus is to decide what he will make of the world.

This is very different from the three specific temptations that Matthew and Luke have drawn, according to many scholars, from the ancient source known as Q. Incidentally, this reference to the temptation is probably the reason that our pericope was chosen as the Gospel for the First Sunday in Lent for Year B. The importance of that connection is borne out by the fact that the accounts of the temptation in Matthew and Luke appear on this Sunday in Years A and C. While it is generally not a good idea to compare the acts and attitudes of parishioners to those of Jesus because of differences in role and capacity, doing so seems indicated here. This then would be a good time for the preacher to quote Hebrews 4:15, observing that Jesus is "one who in every respect has been tested as we are, yet without sin."

The final verses of our Mark reading announce the moment toward which everything so far has been leading: the beginning of Jesus' ministry.

O. C. EDWARDS JR.

Commentary 2: Connecting the Reading with the World

In today's readings from Mark's Gospel, we are invited to witness and be transformed by the drama at the intersection of two different spheres. The first sphere is represented by tangible and concrete entities such as Nazareth of Galilee, the river Jordan, the wilderness, and wild beasts. The second points us to supernatural figures and events that include the image of the heavens torn apart, the Spirit, a voice from heaven, Satan, angels, and the kingdom of God. From both spheres we find images and metaphors for the life and witness of the faith community.

As Jesus is ascending from beneath the water and the Spirit is descending on him, the event of Jesus' baptism is transcribed for us on a vertical axis with water below and the heavens above, the baptized body below and the divine Spirit above, the natural elements below and the supernatural above. In this moment, the river Jordan, a natural source of life-giving water, has become the realm of the extraordinary and supernatural.

The river Jordan holds religious significance as a place that the children of Israel crossed to enter the promised land. As Joshua led the people to cross the Jordan "and the feet of the priests bearing the ark were dipped in the edge of the water, the waters flowing from above stood still," and the people crossed over on dry ground (Josh. 3:14–17). Many centuries had gone by when enslaved people on plantations in the United States lifted their voices to pay homage to a river forever transformed by the power of the supernatural. They visualized a new reality that was full of promise when they sang, "Roll, Jordan, roll."[2] The Jordan had become a symbol of freedom, hope, and renewal. As one spiritual declares, "Deep river, my home is over Jordan. Deep river, Lord. I want to cross over into campground."

For the enslaved in the cotton fields of the South, when the opportunity came to break free of their shackles and when the promise of freedom was realized through uprisings, rebellions, or the Underground Railroad, every water

crossing was their Jordan, and they could sing words of encouragement: "Wade in the water! God's gonna trouble the water!" For those seeking freedom from slavery, water was more than a metaphor; it was their salvation. Water symbolized life-giving energy and also the sphere where God acts to bring about liberation and deliverance, healing, and wholeness. Those seeking healing could identify with the many blind, lame, and paralyzed persons lying in the porticoes waiting for the moment when the pool is stirred up (John 5:1–9).

The image of "the heavens torn apart" suggests a *kairos* moment that points to the inbreaking of the divine into the human sphere, the colliding of the supernatural and the natural, and the point at which heaven touches earth. Such moments mark beginnings and inaugurate a new identity, relationship, or vocation. In this passage it is the occasion of a baptism, and for faith communities there are other rituals such as confirmation, consecration, or ordination that mark a new sense of identity or a call to leadership, ministry, and service. In each case, we are reminded that our call is attributable to a work from above and an awesome and timeless moment of divine activity breaking into our ordinary spaces and our human sphere.

The image of "heavens torn apart" provides an awesome divine drama and choreography designed to reveal, affirm, and declare Jesus' identity. The voice from heaven announces it: "You are my Son, the Beloved; with you I am well pleased" (Mark 1:10). It is so because the heavens declare it and the Spirit bears witness to it. In the same way, our call stories and rituals of baptism, confirmation, consecration, and ordination remind us of our identity. We belong to the realms of body and spirit, the earthly and heavenly, the natural and the supernatural.

A new image comes into view of the Spirit descending like a dove upon Jesus. It does not just touch Jesus and anoint him with a heavenly benediction; it stays with him. The Spirit hovers, surrounds and envelops him, enters and

---

2. "Roll, Jordan, Roll" and other spirituals discussed in this essay may be found in Bruno Chenu, *The Trouble I've Seen: The Big Book of Negro Spirituals* (Valley Forge, PA: Judson, 2003).

abides with him, uplifts and sustains him. Our images of the Spirit's work also influence our spiritual journeys and our common life together from our call stories, our leadership, our proclamation, and our worship.

The image of a dove evokes a sense of beauty, grace, gentleness, peace, and serenity. There is also the image of the Spirit driving Jesus into the wilderness to begin his ministry in complete reliance on the Divine. One hymn writer invokes the Spirit in this way: "Spirit, Spirit of gentleness, blow through the wilderness, calling and free."[3] A spiritual reflects the human response to the Spirit's prompting: "I'm gonna sing when the Spirit says sing."

The Spirit's freedom, gentleness, invitation, guidance, and persuasion are all reflected in the life and witness of our congregations. Enabled by the Spirit of gentleness, our worship is introspective or contemplative, designed around moments of meditation, silence, and reflection. Enabled by the same Spirit, we open ourselves to a mighty rushing wind that removes barriers to communication, calls forth prophetic speech, and creates melodies and rhythms for shouting and dancing. Enabled by the same Spirit, we are equipped for works of justice that bind us together across cultural differences.

Finally, the divine drama moves to the wilderness. In faith communities, the image of the wilderness functions to convey loss, temptation, barrenness, grief, desolation, brokenness, and alienation in one's spiritual journey. We focus on those parts of our lives that seem to be arid, uncultivated, and lacking vitality and energy.

We are reminded that God led the children to Israel from bondage by way of the wilderness and provided them with water and their daily bread. We also recall that it was the Spirit that drove Jesus into the wilderness so that he too might focus and learn to rely exclusively on divine guidance, strength, and provision.

The wilderness experience may also be seen positively as a place away from life's indulgences, a place of simplicity, retreat, and renewal. As we live with sparseness and scarcity, away from distractions and modern amenities, we learn to rely on God's providential care. One hears anew the call to be good stewards of God's creation, and we lament our own participation in systems and structures that are oppressive and destructive. In the wilderness, we may see and marvel at heavens that are torn apart, valleys that are exalted, mountains that are brought low, and crooked paths that are made straight. In the wilderness, we learn how to traverse the paths of righteousness and how to participate in the work of divine liberation from all that would enslave and oppress us.

In the wilderness, we feel the gentle breeze and the mighty rushing wind of the Spirit, reminding us that the Spirit is not ours to contain, restrain, or domesticate. In the wilderness, we may learn again how to be attentive so that our lives may be open and receptive to the angels sent to minister to us. In the wilderness, we may be affirmed, filled with the Spirit, and we may hear anew the good news that heaven has touched earth and God has come near.

LINCOLN E. GALLOWAY

---

3. "Spirit, Spirit of Gentleness," by James K. Manley, in *The New Century Hymnal* (Cleveland: Pilgrim, 1995), #286.

Second Sunday in Lent

Genesis 17:1–7, 15–16
Psalm 22:23–31
Romans 4:13–25

Mark 8:31–38
Mark 9:2–9

Genesis 17:1–7, 15–16

¹When Abram was ninety-nine years old, the LORD appeared to Abram, and said to him, "I am God Almighty; walk before me, and be blameless. ²And I will make my covenant between me and you, and will make you exceedingly numerous." ³Then Abram fell on his face; and God said to him, ⁴"As for me, this is my covenant with you: You shall be the ancestor of a multitude of nations. ⁵No longer shall your name be Abram, but your name shall be Abraham; for I have made you the ancestor of a multitude of nations. ⁶I will make you exceedingly fruitful; and I will make nations of you, and kings shall come from you. ⁷I will establish my covenant between me and you, and your offspring after you throughout their generations, for an everlasting covenant, to be God to you and to your offspring after you." . . .

¹⁵God said to Abraham, "As for Sarai your wife, you shall not call her Sarai, but Sarah shall be her name. ¹⁶I will bless her, and moreover I will give you a son by her. I will bless her, and she shall give rise to nations; kings of peoples shall come from her."

Commentary 1: Connecting the Reading with Scripture

As Genesis 17 begins, the pressing question Abraham and Sarah face is whether God will fulfill the promise to give them an heir. God originally made this promise some twenty-five years earlier, when God first called Abraham and Sarah to depart from Haran (Gen. 12:1–3). Since that time, the couple has remained childless. With Abraham (age ninety-nine) and Sarah (age ninety) advanced in years, having a child was, biologically speaking, implausible.

In response, God intervenes in Genesis 17 by making a covenant. As a formal commitment, this covenant ratifies what God had already promised. In doing so, it also makes the substance of the promise more specific. God covenants to make Abraham not just a "great nation" (12:2) but "the ancestor of a multitude of nations" (17:4). Lest Abraham misunderstand what is being promised, God, with painstaking repetition, affirms that Abraham will be made "exceedingly numerous" (17:2), "exceedingly fruitful" (17:6), and the father of a "multitude

of nations" (17:5). Further, God clarifies that the promise at play is not bound by time. It is an "everlasting covenant" (17:7) that extends not only to Abraham but to his offspring.

Though not included in the lectionary reading, the verses that immediately follow (17:8–14) fill out the nature of this covenant in two important ways. First, these verses reiterate that God's promise to Abraham is one not just of progeny but also of land. The land in question is that of Canaan, in which Abraham currently dwells as an "alien" (*ger*, v. 8). Second, these verses reveal that the sign of the covenant is circumcision (vv. 10–11). This ceremonial act functions as a concrete embodiment of trust in God's promises and entrance into the covenant.

As the lectionary reading resumes (17:15–16), it is clear that Sarah has not been excluded from God's promises. Still speaking to Abraham, God affirms that Sarah also will be blessed and that she too "shall give rise to nations" (v. 16). That Abraham will be given a son through Sarah

39

clarifies the issue underlying the drama of Genesis 16. There, Sarah and Abraham attempt to circumvent the problem of barrenness (which, in the Old Testament, is always described in reference to the would-be mother) by means of obtaining a surrogate wife (Hagar) for Abraham. While the practice of having an heir through a surrogate is not unprecedented in the ancient world, in this context it reflects wavering faith in God's promise of progeny.

The momentous nature of God's promise to Abraham and Sarah is reflected in the fact that both individuals are renamed in Genesis 17. In the ancient world, the giving of a new name was meant to signify a new status or stage in a relationship. The man who has been referred to as Abram since Genesis 11:26 is renamed Abraham (17:5). The two names are lexically related; the former means "exalted father," while the latter means "father of a multitude." God's promise is thus inscribed in the patriarch's new name. To Abraham's wife is given the name Sarah (17:15). A variant of her former name (Sarai), Sarah means "princess," perhaps in reference to God's promise that "kings of peoples shall come from her" (17:16). The theme of renaming appears again in the ancestral narratives as Jacob, meaning "supplanter," becomes Israel, "the one who strives with God" (32:28).

The account of God's covenant with Abraham in Genesis 17 runs closely parallel with the account of the covenant in Genesis 15. Both affirm and make more specific the promises made in Genesis 12. In both cases, the covenant depends completely on God's promise, with no requirement placed on Abraham. In Genesis 17:1, Abraham is called to walk before God and be blameless, but this is best understood not as a condition that must be met in order to receive the promise, but as a consequence of or response to Abraham's prior calling.

Similarly, in Genesis 15:6 it is said that Abraham believed the Lord and "the LORD reckoned it to him as righteousness." This phrase can be interpreted as implying that Abraham's belief (the "it") is a precondition of his being declared righteous. This interpretation seems to underlie Paul's argument in Romans 4:13–25, another lectionary reading for this Sunday. However, the wording of Genesis 15:6 in Hebrew is more ambiguous. Though appearing in most English translations, "the LORD" is not found at the beginning of this phrase, making it less clear who is reckoning what and to whom. If the subject of "reckoned" is Abraham, then it is Abraham who is reckoning the promise (the "it") to God (the "him") as a reliable and sure manifestation of God's righteousness. This latter interpretation suggests that the promise hinges on God's faithfulness, not Abraham's faith. A similar translation issue is at play in the New Testament, where it is debated whether the phrase *pistis Christou* (e.g., Rom. 3:21–22) is best translated as "faith in Christ" or "the faithfulness of Christ."

Questions about the faith of the ancestors pervade the broader context of Genesis 12–50. It is common to think of Abraham and the other ancestors as models of faith for both Israel and the church today. On closer inspection, these characters often waver in their faith, doubting the surety of God's promises in the face of obstacles and threats. This is certainly the case with Abraham. In the verse that immediately follows the end of the lectionary reading, Abraham falls to the ground and laughs, cynically wondering, "Can a child be born to a man who is a hundred years old? Can Sarah, who is ninety years old, bear a child?" (Gen. 17:17). Despite the covenant affirmation, Abraham still struggles to believe in God's promise. The same is true of Sarah. In Genesis 18, three strangers visit the tent of Abraham and Sarah. One of the strangers says to Abraham, "I will surely return to you in due season, and your wife Sarah shall have a son" (18:10). Sarah overhears the conversation and, like Abraham before her, laughs and wonders in disbelief, "Shall I indeed bear a child, now that I am old?" (18:13).

Though the faith of the ancestors often wavers (for good reason), the message of the ancestral narratives (Gen. 12–50) is that God is steadfast in God's promises. Ultimately, Sarah conceives and bears Abraham a son, Isaac. In Hebrew, Isaac means "he [God] laughs," and thus the name of the child of promise juxtaposes God's laughter with the laughter of Abraham and Sarah. Having seen and experienced the long-awaited fulfillment of God's promise, Sarah testifies that "God has brought laughter for me; everyone who hears will laugh with me" (21:6). The laughter of Sarah's disbelief has been transformed into the laughter of joy, not only for her but for all those who witness what God has done.

This theme of wavering faith is echoed in the Gospel reading for this Sunday (Mark 8:31–38). After Jesus' first passion prediction (v. 31), Peter rebukes Jesus and seeks to prevent him from going to Jerusalem (v. 32). Peter knows that Jesus is the Messiah (v. 29), but struggles to grasp how the promises of the gospel could be actualized through a messiah who will suffer and die. Like Abraham and Sarah, Peter sets his mind on earthly things (the problem of barrenness; the problem of the passion) rather than the things of God (the promise of an heir; the promise of resurrection). For both the disciples of Jesus and the ancestors of old, following God entails trusting in God's faithfulness, even when God's promises have not yet been fulfilled.

RYAN P. BONFIGLIO

Commentary 2: Connecting the Reading with the World

God has a sense of humor. God makes the promise of childbearing to a woman who is barren and advanced in years. Hearing the absurdity that the elderly ninety-year-old Sarah would soon give birth to a promised child causes Abram to laugh, saying to himself, "Will a son be born to a man a hundred years old?" (Gen. 17:17 NIV). No doubt God joined in the laughter, explaining why this future child was named Isaac, the Hebrew word for laughter. As funny as the thought of an elderly couple producing a child may be, it nonetheless points to the character of the God whom this couple worshiped. The God of Abram and Sarai is truly almighty.

"I am El Shaddai," God says to Abram (v. 1). The divine name is probably best translated as "God, the one of the mountains"; this may be a reference to a future Sinai or the name of some Canaanite mountain deity. The passage of time obscures the name's original meaning with a new definition: "God Almighty." This Shaddai calls Abram to "walk before me faithfully and be blameless" (v. 1 NIV). To walk before God does not mean God is following Abram. Rather, it means to walk in the ways of God—that is, to act justly, love tenderly, and walk humbly with one's God (Mic. 6:8). Abram is instructed not only to do justice but, as the father of future nations, to teach the world justice by the way he walks. El Shaddai calls for the praxis of walking justly, not merely talking about justice. Sadly, thus far Abram has failed, as seen when he pimped his wife in Egypt (Gen. 12:10–20); he will do so again in Gerar (20:1–3).

The ninety-nine-year-old Abram already has a son, Ishmael, through whom the covenant can be fulfilled. After all, Ishmael came forth from Abram's loins, even though he was not Sarai's child. Sarai, hoping to fulfill God's promise, offered up her slave girl Hagar to be sexually used by Abram (16:1–4)—what today we can call rape. God, however, would fulfill God's promise not through Ishmael but through a child to be born to Sarai. Thus, the promise is really with Sarai, not Abram. He already has a male child and, after Sarai's death, will have six more boys with Keturah (25:1–2). Abram's seed does not carry the promise; Sarai's womb does.

Her role in birthing a nation requires her name to be changed to Sarah. Unfortunately, her call to birth nations is given with neither her consent nor her presence. Sarai's name in Hebrew may mean princess, queen, or woman of noble or royal birth; nevertheless, she, like all other women in Genesis, was seen and treated as an object. The women of Genesis are understood to be property—possessions owned by men. Their identities are defined by their sexual relationships with men, either as married women, virgin daughters, barren wives, widows, concubines, or sex slaves. We see their status codified in the Ten Commandments: "You shall not covet your neighbor's house; you shall not covet your neighbor's wife, or male or female slave, or ox, or donkey" (Exod. 20:17). Like a house, slave, ox, or donkey, the wife is just another object owned that other men should not covet. Any woman, as is the case with Sarai, can be offered up as ransom to save the life of her owner, Abram. Her body is simply acted upon.

Abram's name is also changed to Abraham, a variant spelling of the same name. With the rejection of Ishmael, enmity is established between Hagar's child and Sarah's child—an antagonism that still exists today between some of Hagar's descendants (Muslims) and some of the descendants of Sarah (Jews). The men of the story enter into a covenant with their God even though the promise is kept through the women. Circumcision, a cut upon the male body, outwardly signifies this new covenant, which establishes a "chosen people" with a special relationship with God, with the promises of one day occupying a promised land.

Circumcision was not a new practice; it was customary among western Semites and Egyptians as an initiation ritual and occasionally used for hygienic reasons. Non-Semitic Philistines, Babylonians, and Assyrians did not participate in this ritual. To enter into covenant with God required cutting off the foreskin of one's penis, leaving us to wonder whether those without anything to circumcise (i.e., women) could ever enter into covenant with God. Not only were the "chosen" called to be circumcised, but, according to a later tradition, even the angels were supposedly already born circumcised (*Jubilees* 15:25–27); we might wonder, then, further whether female angels existed, in the minds of ancient Jewish thinkers.

However, physical circumcision (alone) proves to provide a false sense of salvation. The Hebrew text calls for more than an outward sign of belonging. As important as physical circumcision was, El Shaddai also called for an inward circumcision. Moses called the people to circumcise their hearts (Deut. 10:16). Jeremiah condemned those circumcised only in the flesh while housing uncircumcised hearts (Jer. 9:25–26). John the Baptist would eventually make a similar argument: those claiming Abraham as father fell short of salvation, for God could raise up from the stones new children of Abraham (Matt. 3:9).

Circumcision signified Jewish identity. During the first century of the Christian church, the ritual of circumcision became a focal point of disputes about what it means to be a Christian. As uncircumcised Gentiles chose to become followers of Jesus, church leaders wrestled with how to be inclusive of non-Jews. Some argued that Gentiles must first convert to Judaism before they could become Christians. Acts 15:1–6 records the controversy that unfolded at Antioch. "Unless you are circumcised in the tradition of Moses, you cannot be saved," cried out the guardians of the faith.

The controversy was eventually settled, with the church deciding against requiring the act of circumcision for Gentiles. Gentiles could become Christians without first becoming Jews. The sign of the covenant with Abraham made in Genesis 17 was no longer required to become part of God's chosen.

Yet the controversy still rages today. While the controversy no longer centers on a physical cut, those within communities of color are often called to cut off the foreskin of their identity and culture to enter into covenant with white Christians. Before those who are not white can be considered Christian, they are expected to convert to Eurocentrism. To be a Christian, one must first adopt Eurocentric liturgy, theology, philosophy, hermeneutics, politics, and of course ecclesiology. Three-hundred-year-old German hymns are quickly translated into native tongues, because white Christian leaders assume indigenous people lack the sophistication to worship the Almighty in their own languages. One's faith must be described and understood in the symbols of the dominant culture, using Eurocentric philosophical and theological language, the same language that for centuries justified the oppression of those seen as primitive, falling short of the white ideal.

To become white first, before one can become Christian, is a death-causing self-mutilation deemed necessary by the gatekeepers of Eurocentric Christianity. The God presented to "uncircumcised" communities of color is all too often wrapped within Eurocentric cultural structures. Christian thought assumes the superiority of Eurocentric paradigms and methodologies, even when they directly contradict the cultures and identities of believers of color.

However, there is good news to preach! Those outside of the covenant, those who are uncircumcised, can now enter into the presence of El Shaddai, insisting on their right to enter into covenant without cutting off one's foreskin, one's culture, or one's identity. We get to perceive the Divine through our own eyes. To do otherwise becomes blasphemous.

MIGUEL A. DE LA TORRE

Psalm 22:23–31

²³You who fear the LORD, praise him!
  All you offspring of Jacob, glorify him;
  stand in awe of him, all you offspring of Israel!
²⁴For he did not despise or abhor
  the affliction of the afflicted;
he did not hide his face from me,
  but heard when I cried to him.

²⁵From you comes my praise in the great congregation;
  my vows I will pay before those who fear him.
²⁶The poor shall eat and be satisfied;
  those who seek him shall praise the LORD.
  May your hearts live forever!

²⁷All the ends of the earth shall remember
  and turn to the LORD;
and all the families of the nations
  shall worship before him.
²⁸For dominion belongs to the LORD,
  and he rules over the nations.

²⁹To him, indeed, shall all who sleep in the earth bow down;
  before him shall bow all who go down to the dust,
  and I shall live for him.
³⁰Posterity will serve him;
  future generations will be told about the Lord,
³¹and proclaim his deliverance to a people yet unborn,
  saying that he has done it.

Connecting the Psalm with Scripture and Worship

Psalm 22, for good reason, is categorized as the lament of an individual. It is a prayer for help, the first line of which is quoted by Jesus on the cross (Matt. 27:46; Mark 15:34), so it is no wonder that it appears in Year B for the Second Sunday in Lent, and on Good Friday in all three years. James Mays notes that there are thirteen Old Testament quotations or allusions in the Passion Narrative, eight of which come from the Psalms.[1] Of these eight, five are from Psalm 22, more evidence that its importance in the season of Lent can hardly be overstated. The link between the prayers of Jesus and the psalms is direct, but care must be taken not to think of the psalm only in a christological context.

The portion of the psalm appearing in this week's texts does not include the anguished cry for help, but rather the hymn of praise in verses 23–31. This hymn is really in two parts, the first being an expression of gratitude in the first person: "he did not hide his face from me, but heard when I cried to him" (Ps. 22:24b). The psalm ends, though, by extending the reach of the praise: "All the ends of the earth shall remember . . ." (v. 27a); "To him, indeed, shall all who sleep in the earth bow down" (v. 29a);

---

1. James L. Mays, *Psalms*, Interpretation: A Bible Commentary for Teaching and Preaching (Louisville, KY: Westminster John Knox, 1994), 105.

"future generations will be told about the Lord, and proclaim his deliverance to a people yet unborn" (vv. 30–31). The movement in this psalm from individual affliction to individual salvation, and then to universal praise, both from those long dead and those not yet born, is perfectly placed as we move through Lent.

The last five verses of Psalm 22 also connect God's response to the psalmist's suffering with the coming of the kingdom. In verse 27 we hear "all the ends of the earth shall remember and turn to the LORD; and all the families of the nations shall worship before him." The sovereignty of the Lord is declared: "For dominion belongs to the LORD, and he rules over the nations" (v. 28).

This broad scope provides a direct connection and a wonderful response to the Genesis text, where Abram and Sarai become Abraham and Sarah and are told, "You shall be the ancestor of a multitude of nations" (Gen. 17:4), and "she shall give rise to nations; kings of peoples shall come from her" (v. 16). Similarly, the Romans text quotes the Genesis text and cites Abraham's faith: "Hoping against hope, he believed he would become 'the father of many nations,' according to what was said, 'So numerous shall your descendants be'" (Rom. 4:18).

In the Gospel text from Mark, Jesus is explaining to the disciples what is for them a difficult lesson: "The Son of Man must undergo great suffering, and be rejected by the elders, the chief priests, and the scribes, and be killed, and after three days rise again" (Mark 8:31). Peter's reaction to these words, and Jesus' reaction to Peter, are well known and often quoted, but the link between the Mark text and the psalm comes near the end of both. Beginning in Mark 8:34 we read these words (again well known): "If any want to become my followers, let them deny themselves and take up their cross and follow me." This strong call for individuals to "turn to the Lord" parallels the much broader call in verse 27 of the psalm noted above, where it is applied to the whole world.

This psalm was written to be liturgy and is wonderfully suited for that purpose. Verses 23 and 24 would make excellent opening sentences, as would verses 27 and 28. Alternately, the movement in the psalm from individual to communal could be emphasized, while reinforcing the character of praise that results from God's help. One example might be the following responsive reading:

Reader 1: I sing praises to the Lord.
Reader 2: Those who seek the Lord shall offer praise.
Reader 1: The Lord did not despise my affliction.
Reader 2: All the families of the nations shall worship the Lord.
Reader 1: The Lord did not hide from me, but heard my cries.
Reader 2: All the ends of the earth shall remember and turn to the Lord.

As noted above, the entire section of the psalm could be read in response to the Genesis text, or as the first text ahead of the reading from Romans, where it is quoted. Unfortunately, many of the metrical versions of Psalm 22 found in hymnals and other resources emphasize the early verses of the psalm, rather than the section in today's lectionary. There are two metric settings in *Psalms for All Seasons*, 22F and 22G, that use the text directly, but they are not set to particularly familiar tunes. The most readily available hymn referencing Psalm 22 is "The God of Abraham Praise," found in many hymnals. The majority of anthems based on Psalm 22 focus on the early part of the psalm, though a few exceptions exist. "From the End of the Earth" by Alan Hovhaness is a gorgeous choral setting; its text echoes verses 27 and 28 of the psalm and is also related to the Genesis text. The composer links it to Psalm 61, but it serves equally well for Psalm 22.

In some ways this is a psalm of movement, or maybe even a psalm of growth. The path from individual to universal, to all the nations, to the ends of the earth, and the path from lament to trust and praise is a path for all of us to follow in this season of spiritual growth.

DAVID A. VANDERMEER

Romans 4:13–25

[13]For the promise that he would inherit the world did not come to Abraham or to his descendants through the law but through the righteousness of faith. [14]If it is the adherents of the law who are to be the heirs, faith is null and the promise is void. [15]For the law brings wrath; but where there is no law, neither is there violation.

[16]For this reason it depends on faith, in order that the promise may rest on grace and be guaranteed to all his descendants, not only to the adherents of the law but also to those who share the faith of Abraham (for he is the father of all of us, [17]as it is written, "I have made you the father of many nations")—in the presence of the God in whom he believed, who gives life to the dead and calls into existence the things that do not exist. [18]Hoping against hope, he believed that he would become "the father of many nations," according to what was said, "So numerous shall your descendants be." [19]He did not weaken in faith when he considered his own body, which was already as good as dead (for he was about a hundred years old), or when he considered the barrenness of Sarah's womb. [20]No distrust made him waver concerning the promise of God, but he grew strong in his faith as he gave glory to God, [21]being fully convinced that God was able to do what he had promised. [22]Therefore his faith "was reckoned to him as righteousness." [23]Now the words, "it was reckoned to him," were written not for his sake alone, [24]but for ours also. It will be reckoned to us who believe in him who raised Jesus our Lord from the dead, [25]who was handed over to death for our trespasses and was raised for our justification.

Commentary 1: Connecting the Reading with Scripture

On this Second Sunday in Lent, our hearts and minds continue to contemplate and reflect on Jesus' saving work on the cross. We give thanks for the unmerited gift of salvation his death and resurrection granted us, and we emphasize our need for repentance because of our unworthiness of such a precious gift. The lectionary texts for today, however, remind us that righteousness is not something that sinful beings could ever attain on their own. We cannot gain it by doing certain practices; we cannot work for it. Rather, we can access it only through faith. Because of this, God's gift of salvation through Jesus' sacrifice is not contingent on any laws or regulations, but rather is made available to *anyone* who believes. This is instructional for churches who seek to burden believers with provisional membership and acceptance.

The apostle Paul writes to the Gentile Christian church in Rome, which is in the center of empire (1:5). He has never visited this church, but has plans to do so (Rom. 15:22–23). Since he has never visited this community, the rhetorical questions he states at the start of chapter 6 seem to suggest that one of the goals of his writing is to correct misunderstandings regarding his teaching. For example, a main concern for Paul is to explicate how righteousness, that is, being in a right relationship with God, is obtained. This is a primary concern of Paul, because some Jews argued that in order for Gentiles to attain salvation, they must be circumcised (e.g., Acts 15:1).

Paul is adamantly against this view. Using the example of Abraham and the death of Jesus in relation to the law, he sets out to correct this misunderstanding of his gospel message, which he says "is the power of God for salvation to everyone who has faith, to the Jew first and also to the Greek" (1:16). It is given to the Jews first because God's promise to the Jewish people is in fulfillment of the Jewish Scriptures. However, this led to the problem of human arrogance, which Paul asserts both the Jews and the Gentiles exhibit. The Jews boasted about having the covenant that included God's blessings (9:1–5), and the Gentiles are without excuse in terms of their own behavior because, "what can be known about God is plain to them, because God has shown it to them" (1:19–21). Additionally, Paul later questions Gentile boasting *after* they became believers (e.g., 11:18). Paul asserts that despite the order regarding the distribution of salvation, it is for everyone who believes, as illustrated by Abraham's example.

The passage for today opens with Paul reminding the early church that God's promise to Abraham had nothing to do with his adherence to the law, but rather "through the righteousness of faith" (4:13). He explains that if God's promise of salvation was given only to those who adhered to the law, then "faith is null and the promise is void" (4:14). Because God's salvation is a gift, humans cannot *work* for it. It has nothing to do with the law (even Abraham received God's promise prior to his circumcision). Paul, having an overly positive reading of the Abraham saga (since Abraham questioned God throughout the process—e.g., Gen. 18), asserts that it had everything to do with Abraham's faith (Rom. 4:16). Abraham was promised that he would be the "father of many nations" (4:17) and—despite his age and the barrenness of his wife, Sarah (4:19)—his faith remained unwavering (4:20). In fact, Paul says that his faith increased because he was "fully convinced that God was able to do what he had promised" (4:20–21)!

God's Divine Light and Love

For all is within man, that can be either good or evil to him: God within him, is his divine life, his divine light, his divine love; Satan within him is his life of self, of earthly wisdom, of diabolical falseness, wrath, pride, and vanity of every kind. There is no middle way between these two; he that is not under the power of the one, is under the power of the other. And the reason is, man was created in and under the power of the divine life; so far therefore as he loses or turns from this life of God, so far he falls under the power of self, of Satan, and worldly wisdom. When St. Peter, full of *human* good love towards Christ, advised him to avoid his sufferings, Christ rejects him with a *Get thee behind me Satan*, and only gave this reason for it, for thou *savorest not the things that be of God, but the things that be of men.* A plain proof, that whatever is not of and from the holy Spirit of God in us, however plausible it may outwardly seem to men, to their wisdom and human goodness, is yet in itself nothing else but the power of Satan in us.

William Law, *An Humble, Earnest, and Affectionate Address to Clergy* (Pittsburgh: Cramer, Spear and Eichbaum, 1816), 29–30.

This is righteousness. It is having faith in God and God's ability to fulfill God's promises. It is about God's integrity and our own.

Paul then uses the example of Abraham to instruct his Gentile audience. Righteousness "will be reckoned to [those] who believe in him who raised Jesus our Lord from the dead" (4:24). Like Abraham, if we Christians believe in the salvific work of Jesus on the cross, and the power of his resurrection, we will be considered righteous (4:25). It is about having faith in God because God is faithful to us. Certainly, God's faithfulness is problematized and questioned when equated with God's justice. When "bad things happen to good people," we frail humans are confused and troubled. There is evil in the world; however, God is all-powerful. How do we make sense of this? The process of trying to comprehend and reconcile the problem of evil with the presence of God is known as the problem of theodicy. Perhaps Paul is unable to sense this same tension because of his heavy leaning in the direction of God's sovereignty (e.g., 9:18).

Although in the passage for today Paul focuses on the importance of having faith in

Jesus' death and resurrection, which afford us salvation, let us not gloss over the suffering that Jesus endured to make salvation available to us. It came at a cost. This is the season in which we set aside time intentionally to reflect on Jesus' life, his ministry of reconciliation when he walked the earth, and the pain, humiliation, and suffering he experienced as the Son of God. Let us not forget Jesus' humanity.

One of the other lectionary passages, Mark 8:31–38, seems to capture this forgetfulness, and Peter (and others) refuse to accept this type of suffering Messiah. Let us recall Jesus' emotional prayer in Gethsemane in which he said, "My Father, if it is possible, let this cup pass from me; yet not what I want but what you want" (Matt. 26:39). Let us remember Jesus' distorted face when he cried out to his Father from the cross, "My God, my God, why have you forsaken me?" (Matt. 27:46). Let us never forget that he bled, suffocated, and died. For us.

Jesus' sacrifice was God's unmerited gift to us. His death and resurrection made salvation available to us. His work alone is what healed our broken relationship with God. Salvation is waiting for us. What Paul tells us is that there is only one way to access it: through faith. This is the proper response as Christians to God's righteousness. This response of faith is not simply an individual one, but also a communal one. How is the Christian church responding in faith to God's gift of salvation? What *works* has the church allowed to take faith's place, instead of allowing these works to be an extension of its faith?

As a community of believers during these days of Lent, let us work on our spiritual discipline, let us enhance our prayer life, and let us bear witness to the sacrificial life of Jesus. On this Second Sunday in Lent, let us reflect on the significance of Jesus' death on the cross and his resurrection, such that it revealed God's gift of grace and salvation to believers. Let us remember that this gift is undeserved, and is indicative of God's righteousness (Rom. 1:17). Let us remember that because of God's promise to us, our proper response as Christians is faith. Let us be grateful that God's promise of salvation through the work of Jesus has nothing to do with us, and everything to do with God's righteousness. Let us remember that like Abraham, who had faith in God's promises *prior* to his circumcision, we cannot work for salvation. Let us remember that the promise of salvation "depends on faith, in order that the promise may rest on grace and be guaranteed to all . . . who share the faith of Abraham" (4:16).

SHANELL T. SMITH

Commentary 2: Connecting the Reading with the World

We might struggle with Paul's words in this passage as we look back over two thousand years of Christianity and consider this history in relation to the world today. While we might appreciate, from a theological perspective, Paul's invocation of the promises made to Abraham to be the father of many nations with innumerable descendants, we might nevertheless be uncomfortable with this language when putting our faith in conversation with our understanding of history, geopolitics, or ecology.

Postcolonial critics—who study the legacy of colonialism and its impact on the lives of colonized people—point out that the promises to Abraham and the Great Commission to make disciples of all nations (Matt. 28:19) have been misused to justify the project of colonial domination.[1] Much of the European colonization of the Americas, Asia, and Africa was enacted ostensibly under the framework of spreading the gospel. Without doubting the sincerity and dedication of many generations of missionary workers, we can acknowledge that missionary efforts often functioned hand in hand with political and economic projects bent on extracting wealth from the colonies and

---

1. See Leela Gandhi, *Postcolonial Theory: A Critical Introduction* (New York: Columbia University Press, 1998); Kwok Pui-lan, *Postcolonial Imagination and Feminist Theology* (Louisville, KY: Westminster John Knox, 2005).

imposing Euroamerican values and norms. By undermining local cultures and wisdom traditions and by extracting resources and talent, colonial practices laid the groundwork for current geopolitical inequities among nations.

Ecologists, likewise, look with suspicion at the biblical mandates to be fruitful and multiply (or, as Paul writes in this passage, to have numerous descendants), to fill the earth and subdue it, and to have dominion over all of creation. While the biblical writers saw these actions as expressions of hope for the future and proof of divine favor, it is helpful to remember that they wrote in a context dramatically different from ours. The current state of the planet would have been unimaginable to them, but we know today that an ever-increasing population is unsustainable. Romans 8:22, a favorite passage of ecologically concerned theologians, tells us that all of creation is groaning. We humans have become so numerous that we have overwhelmed the self-correcting functions of the ecosystem. The planet cannot maintain its well-being in the face of the destruction of nature caused by our work and our play.

In *Ecowomanism: African American Women and Earth-Honoring Faiths*, Melanie Harris demonstrates the practice of writing an eco-autobiography.[2] In doing so, she traces back through generations the relationships that her ancestors had with the earth and evaluates how these relationships influence her own thinking and behavior. Her reflections range from the simple beauty of singing and praying while watering the flowers in her mother's garden to the determination of her paternal grandparents, who left Mississippi's fertile land and culture of white supremacy to work the inhospitable land of the first black agricultural community in Colorado. For Harris, recovering and claiming her relationship with the earth is both empowering and an act of political resistance.

Like Harris, we might explore our eco-autobiographies, looking for examples within our family histories of relationships with the earth that inspire us to tread more lovingly on sacred ground. Can we imagine ways to simplify our lifestyles and alleviate the burdens that we

place on our collective home? Can we consider our role in producing the global imbalance between those who consume the most resources and those who suffer the most harm from pollution, deforestation, and climate change? Perhaps most pertinently, are we able to find wisdom in the Christian tradition to guide us?

These postcolonial and ecological critiques surface important issues that provide a healthy corrective to a faith that would ignore the expanding ripple effects of our actions. At its core, however, this passage is an exhortation to be strong in our faith, remembering Abraham as a model of one who trusted in God despite the obstacles.

In addition to Abraham and other biblical role models, we can identify historical and contemporary figures who inspire us by their courageous and compassionate faith. Some names are widely familiar: Mother Teresa of Calcutta, Martin Luther King Jr., Óscar Romero, Dorothy Day, Dietrich Bonhoeffer, Sojourner Truth, Martin Luther, Hildegard of Bingen. Others are perhaps less familiar: Helen Prejean (an opponent of the death penalty in the US), George "Tink" Tinker (a scholar of Native American liberation theology), Ruth Manorama (a social activist in Bangalore, India, who advocates for the rights of domestic workers), Nyambura J. Njoroge (an advocate for gender justice and for people with HIV/AIDS in sub-Saharan Africa).

We might also consider doing some research in our hometowns or in our denominational histories to uncover people of faith who sacrificed personal comfort, reputation, or well-being in order to demonstrate their love for others and their commitment to building a more just and equitable world.

Oftentimes, however, the people who have the strongest influence on our personal faith journeys are those closest to us—a family member, a friend, a teacher, a pastor. As children, we learn by watching those around us, and it is likely that each of us can identify someone whose faith shaped us profoundly. As we reflect on the people who most influenced our faith, we might think of a grandmother whose constancy in prayer provided her with a deep well of strength with which to face life's challenges,

---

2. Melanie L. Harris, *Ecowomanism: African American Women and Earth-Honoring Faiths* (Maryknoll, NY: Orbis, 2017).

or a friend who is able to handle even the most difficult circumstances with grace, a kind word, and a sense of humor.

Many Latino/a/x theologians in the United States and Canada emphasize *lo cotidiano,* "the everyday," as an important ground for theological reflection. Theologian Carmen Nanko-Fernández describes *lo cotidiano* as a source of divine revelation that provides the content for theologizing while highlighting the context from which theology is articulated.[3] Focusing on *lo cotidiano* invites us to attend to the people and circumstances in our immediate sphere and helps us to avoid thinking about faith only in the abstract. It is in ordinary living—through our bodies and senses, our work and play, our struggles and celebrations—that we experience God's presence. Because our daily lives occur in particular contexts, they are enmeshed with our identities (age, gender, sexual orientation, race, ethnicity, socioeconomic status, citizenship, education, etc.). These characteristics, and the

intersections among them, influence the ways in which we interact with others and the ways in which we perceive and respond to God.

This emphasis on *lo cotidiano* encourages us to recognize the ways in which we are shaped by our past and by those around us today. It helps us appreciate our communities and the many individuals who handed down our faith and who continue to inspire us by embodying the best of our traditions. It also calls on us to live our faith wisely and boldly, noting the ways we influence those with whom we interact.

During the season of Lent, let us pause to consider our place on this interconnected planet and the ways in which our choices and actions affect others. As we reflect on our lives, let us give thanks for all the people, both near and far, who have inspired and encouraged our journey of faith. May we strive to live in such a way that our faith is known through our actions, and may that faith be a blessing to others.

ANN HIDALGO

---

3. Carmen M. Nanko-Fernández, "Lo Cotidiano as Locus Theologicus," in *The Wiley Blackwell Companion to Latino/a Theology,* ed. Orlando O. Espín (Hoboken, NJ: John Wiley & Sons, 2015), 15–16.

Mark 8:31–38

³¹Then he began to teach them that the Son of Man must undergo great suffering, and be rejected by the elders, the chief priests, and the scribes, and be killed, and after three days rise again. ³²He said all this quite openly. And Peter took him aside and began to rebuke him. ³³But turning and looking at his disciples, he rebuked Peter and said, "Get behind me, Satan! For you are setting your mind not on divine things but on human things."

³⁴He called the crowd with his disciples, and said to them, "If any want to become my followers, let them deny themselves and take up their cross and follow me. ³⁵For those who want to save their life will lose it, and those who lose their life for my sake, and for the sake of the gospel, will save it. ³⁶For what will it profit them to gain the whole world and forfeit their life? ³⁷Indeed, what can they give in return for their life? ³⁸Those who are ashamed of me and of my words in this adulterous and sinful generation, of them the Son of Man will also be ashamed when he comes in the glory of his Father with the holy angels."

Commentary 1: Connecting the Reading with Scripture

Two important steps in preparing a sermon for today are to consider its place in the liturgical calendar and to take into account the significance of the location of our pericope in Mark's Gospel. What better time to reflect on Jesus' telling his disciples to take up their cross and follow him than in Lent? Reflection on that will follow below, but preachers need to keep this in mind through all their preparation. They and their congregations need to deal with the realization that this Gospel applies to them.

The significance of our reading's location in Mark's Gospel has been recognized for some time. Relevant themes are well spelled out, for instance, in D. E. Nineham's 1963 commentary: "The Gospel divides fairly sharply into two parts, each with its own clearly marked characteristics. Down to 8:26 the emphasis falls very largely on the miraculous deeds of Jesus, and such teaching as is recorded is mostly (a) directed to the crowd, (b) couched in parables, and (c) concerned with the coming of God's kingdom."[1] Very little is said, however, about the identity of Jesus that enables him to do all that.

That all changes with today's Gospel lesson. In the second part of Mark, miracles are mentioned much less frequently, and the content is mostly Jesus' teaching, a good deal of which explains his messiahship, which will not involve a parade of its glory but will instead show that its way is the way of the cross. This teaching is not to the crowd; Jesus seems to have given up on them and directs his efforts to explain his identity to his disciples, and even they—or maybe especially they—have trouble getting the point.

The transition to the second section begins in the story of Jesus' healing of a blind man in Bethsaida (Mark 8:22–26). There are two remarkable aspects to this story: it is the first time Jesus is reported to have healed a blind person, and Jesus has to do it in two steps. It could be that Mark intended this as a symbol of the second section: the disciples are treated as not seeing who Jesus really is, and they need instruction in stages, a process not complete until the resurrection. The next step is an illustration of their need for enlightenment. Jesus asks them who people think he is; the range of

---

1. D. E. Nineham, *The Gospel of St. Mark* (New York: Seabury, 1967), 37.

responses is familiar. However, when Jesus asks who they think he is, and Peter says he is the Christ,[2] we feel that the disciples are having a breakthrough—until we read what follows in the beginning of our lection.

The shift is abrupt: When Peter says that Jesus is the Messiah, there is an upbeat feeling in the passage—but then Jesus announces that he will be crucified. That makes us go back and look at his response to Peter's confession. First, Jesus said that they should not tell anyone that he is Messiah; then he talked about himself not as the Messiah but as the Son of Man. It will become apparent over time that Jesus is giving a qualified acceptance of the title of Messiah, a "yes, but" response. He is the Messiah, but this does not mean what they think it means.

The preacher's consideration of how the title Messiah applies to Jesus should start with a reminder of what the term meant before it was applied to him. The basic meaning of the word is "anointed," meaning that someone is set aside for a particular role. The three offices for which it is used in the Old Testament are prophet, priest, and king. Later generations of Christians would recognize that Jesus was in some sense anointed for all three roles.

In the meantime, Jesus refers to himself as Son of Man. In the Hebrew Scriptures this term has a variety of meanings, ranging from "a man" (e.g., Ezek. 2:1) to "a divine being" (e.g., Dan. 7:13). Scholars disagree about both the earlier meaning of the term and Jesus' use of it. Here it will be assumed that most of the time, including in Mark 8:31, it is just a self-reference, where in other instances, Jesus uses it to predict his suffering and to speak of his exaltation.

He calls himself Son of Man in this, the first of three passion predictions. There are slight differences among them, but they are essentially the same (see 9:31; 10:33–34). These predictions do not foretell the sort of glory and glamor of messiahship that Peter has expected, though they predict Jesus' resurrection after his crucifixion. By calling Jesus the Messiah, Peter means something different than Jesus' understanding of his mission. This seems true of the

other disciples as well. Immediately after Jesus' third passion prediction (10:35–45)—the one offering extensive detail about the suffering that awaits Jesus—James and John come to ask a favor of him, that when he comes into his kingdom, he will allow them to be his second and third in command; and before the resurrection Peter denies him three times (14:66–72).

It will take the resurrection for the disciples to understand what messiahship—and discipleship—truly mean. Yet even this we know only by implication, since our oldest manuscripts of Mark end at 16:8, with the women leaving the empty tomb in fear. Even Jesus had not been wildly in favor of a suffering Messiah, praying in Gethsemane that if it were possible, the Father would remove that cup from him (14:36).

Yet Jesus certainly knew what was at stake, predicting it three times and telling the crowd with his disciples what being his followers would entail: it would involve their taking up their crosses and following him. Doing so would be necessary for them; in fact, it would be more valuable to them than the whole world. What is sauce for the Savior is sauce for the saved. "God so loved the world that he gave his only Son, so that everyone who believes in him may not perish but may have eternal life" (John 3:16). God created human beings so they could spend eternity with God, sharing the divine life. To do that, we must become as much like God as is humanly possible. If God could love us so much that God would give the Son for our creation and sanctification, then such self-giving has to be the best possible way for us to exist, the greatest blessing that could possibly be bestowed on us.

Some Christians seem to believe that heaven is a reward for a virtuous life, and they think that is a good deal for them to make. They think they can earn heaven. There may be a sense in which that is so, but living a virtuous life for the reward will mean that they will not receive it. They have to learn that life is not about them, but is about God and God's creation. They must love others enough to be willing to die for them, or they cannot receive eternal life. In fact, much of what makes heaven heavenly is that it is filled

---

2. Mark uses the Greek term "Christ" rather than the Hebrew "Messiah" used in the NRSV.

with such transformed lovely beings; becoming one of them is the most precious experience anyone can have. That is why those who would save their life must lose it. That is why all of us need to take up our crosses and follow Jesus.

O. C. EDWARDS JR.

Commentary 2: Connecting the Reading with the World

At the beginning of the Gospel, Mark introduces the reader to Jesus, the Son of God (Mark 1:1). In today's reading, Jesus is presented as the Son of Man. Both "Son of God" and "Son of Man" are used as titles for Jesus in our Christian proclamation, hymnody, and prayers, without a great deal of debate or reference to their origins, biblical or extrabiblical traditions, or theological significance. Readers and hearers of the Gospel in the twenty-first century may readily identify with Jesus, the Son of Man who speaks to the realities of our human experience when he points to his own impending suffering, rejection, and death. We can reflect on our own experiences of pain and suffering, our finitude, and our understanding of our mortality. However, the words of Jesus have less resonance when he points beyond our human experience to signal his own rising from the dead.

We do not know the underlying reason for Peter's rebuke of Jesus. Perhaps he was struck with terror when the Son of Man described his ministry in terms of a harsh and dangerous undertaking that would include death. Perhaps he was incensed that the Son of Man would speak in what he considered to be naive and possibly reckless terms of his rising from the dead. Peter may have wondered whether Jesus was taking threats to his life seriously (3:6) or whether their dying with him would also lead to rising with him. Surely, a more strategic approach of Jesus to impending danger could include hiring a security team or perhaps arming his disciples and deterring any potential threat to their lives with a display of weaponry, a strong show of force, and a willingness to fight rather than a willingness to die. Clearly, Peter was moved to express his strong disapproval of Jesus' pronouncement.

Mark's Gospel introduces us to Satan as the one who tempts Jesus while he is in the wilderness for forty days (1:13). We are not presented with the temptations that Jesus experienced, nor are we shown the content of Peter's rebuke. We know only that Jesus considered Peter's rebuke to be satanic, as Peter's rebuke is met by Jesus' rebuke: "Get behind me, Satan!" (8:33).

Jesus' response to Peter seems to circumscribe three spheres of engagement or influence, namely, the (i) human, (ii) satanic, and (iii) divine. Like the Son of Man, humans face temptations and are incessantly assailed by the satanic, which seeks to infect, corrupt, and destroy humankind. The Son of Man stands with us in the human sphere and points us to the Divine, where humanity can be redeemed, restored, and made whole. Like Peter, we are challenged to set our minds on divine things (8:33) so that we may encounter the Divine and be transformed. From the beginning of Jesus' ministry, he is focused and shaped by divine things. The Spirit drives him into the wilderness, and soon after, he begins to proclaim the good news of the kingdom of God (1:14–15). He calls disciples (1:16–20), is followed by crowds (3:7), and speaks openly to them about his own path (8:32).

Seeking a divine encounter and setting one's mind on divine things will require obedience to God alone. In the life of Jesus, it is a life of teaching, miraculous acts of healing, feeding the crowds, and bringing peace and calm to the sea. Yet the call to the divine life is not about walking on water, as it were. The Son of Man indicates that to set one's mind on divine things and perform the work that one is called to do will bring opposition, and lead to suffering, rejection, and even death.

This is the path that Jesus announces for himself, and now he presents the challenge to his disciples and would-be followers within the crowd: "If any want to become my followers, let them deny themselves and take up their cross and follow me" (8:34). The stark reality is that this offer of discipleship comes just as Jesus has declared openly that he is on a journey toward suffering and death. The disciples hear a call to set their minds on divine things, to come and die, and thus to make the greatest possible investment in the kingdom of God.

To follow Jesus is to respond to the good news that God has come near by setting one's mind on divine things and also by relinquishing ownership of one's aspirations, future, and life. This form of discipleship would mean denying oneself the likelihood of a long and prosperous life, getting married and having a family, a home, and profession, among other things. As difficult as these choices must have been, they pale in comparison to the challenge of taking up one's cross, the symbol of death by crucifixion. It is difficult to imagine that anyone could equate setting their mind on divine things with a willing acceptance of a horrific and torturous death.

For today's reader of Mark's Gospel, there is much that is outside of our daily experience. The preacher may find paintings or images to help the hearers visualize the cosmic drama that is unfolding (v. 38). We may find ourselves transfixed or energized by images of the cleansing of the world from all that infects, contaminates, or destroys the human realm. We witness the portrayal of the destruction of all that is sinful or satanic, and the final victory of good over evil. Finally, we embrace not only the visual depictions but also the reality of a divine realm that evokes our veneration of the Son of Man, who stands in its midst "in the glory of his Father with the holy angels" (8:38).

However, we do not just stand before the drama. We are participants in the work of cleansing the world from all forms of pollutants within educational, governmental, corporate, environmental, and societal structures and institutions. In contexts in which health care is available, one can embrace longevity as a wonderful gift from God, and where wealth and prosperity are broadly viewed as markers of divine favor and overflowing blessings, Jesus' probing question still demands honest engagement: What profit would it be to gain the whole world and forfeit one's life?

In the midst of this drama, we are confronted with a cross, and the choice to die so that we may live. We seek to discern where the drama ends and reality begins and what are the metaphors that are actualized in our lives. In our context, the cross is not a feared tool for executions in our political and judicial system. For many, the cross is a treasured icon to be worn as an accessory, painted on sacred objects, marking the graves of loved ones, or adorning the steeple of a place of worship. Even so, taking up one's cross has deep resonance for those who are answering the call of discipleship.

Today's reader of the Gospel is also on the road with the Son of Man, hearing him speak, responding with a measure of incredulity to his pronouncements of rejection, suffering, and death. We are confronted with hard choices and temptations that may place us on the side of Satan. Ultimately, we discern in the Son of Man that God has come near, and we are invited to listen to the divine voice, to acknowledge the way of the cross, and to set our minds on divine things.

LINCOLN E. GALLOWAY

Mark 9:2–9

²Six days later, Jesus took with him Peter and James and John, and led them up a high mountain apart, by themselves. And he was transfigured before them, ³and his clothes became dazzling white, such as no one on earth could bleach them. ⁴And there appeared to them Elijah with Moses, who were talking with Jesus. ⁵Then Peter said to Jesus, "Rabbi, it is good for us to be here; let us make three dwellings, one for you, one for Moses, and one for Elijah." ⁶He did not know what to say, for they were terrified. ⁷Then a cloud overshadowed them, and from the cloud there came a voice, "This is my Son, the Beloved; listen to him!" ⁸Suddenly when they looked around, they saw no one with them any more, but only Jesus.

⁹As they were coming down the mountain, he ordered them to tell no one about what they had seen, until after the Son of Man had risen from the dead.

Commentary 1: Connecting the Reading with Scripture

The transfiguration in the book of Mark appears at the midway point of the book and at a turning point in the trajectory of Jesus' mission. The story sits between his ministry of healing the sick and the possessed in Galilee and his fated march to Jerusalem, where the narrative of the passion will radically redefine what it means for God to claim him as God's Son. The transfiguration story functions in a way that is consistent with the Gospel's narrative aims, namely, to highlight the ways the disciples' expectations of messiahship are in conflict with the divine plan. Mark has the disciples express a Christology of glory so that he can refute it by contrasting it with one that is centered on the Messiah's suffering and vulnerability—a cross-informed Christology that is haltingly revealed over the course of the Gospel. That said, the transfiguration is a fabulously strange text.

The story begins "six days later," with Jesus taking Peter, James, and John up a high mountain (Mark 9:2). In the ancient world, mountains are places where the gods reside. In the Hebrew Bible, God's abode (the temple) sits atop Mount Zion, and of course Mount Sinai is the place from which God speaks directly to the people of Israel and reveals God's almighty, thundering self, along with the "ten words" intended to shape their life as a newly formed

people together. In the wake of this event, Israel tells Moses that it would be better for him to mediate any future communications from God, in order to spare them the terror of a direct divine encounter (Exod. 20:19). By beginning with Jesus and his three disciples ascending a high mountain, Mark may be setting up the reader familiar with the Greek Old Testament to anticipate an impressive divine display, complete with thunder, lightning, and earth shaking (see also 1 Kgs. 19).

However, what happens on the mountain in Mark is puzzling; the story both affirms and overturns the Jewish reader's expectations. Jesus does appear in ways that suggest his divinity (he is "transfigured"), but rather than speaking in thunderclaps and making the mountain smoke (see Exod. 20:18), he radiates light. Actually, his clothes turn dazzling white "such as no one on earth could bleach them" (Mark 9:3).

In the Septuagint, the verb "to bleach, whiten" (*leukainō*) refers metaphorically to the purging of sin, in which bloodred sins are made whiter than snow (Ps. 51:7; Isa. 1:18). Perhaps the image suggests that Jesus is sinless. Perhaps the dazzling white clothes are meant to evoke God's glory (Heb. *kabod*), which shines from beneath a cover of cloud (Exod. 16:10; Num. 14:10b; Ps. 63:2) in order to mark Jesus' divinity. Maybe the shining clothes are intended to remind readers of Moses' face, which shines, and so must be veiled, after a divine encounter (Exod. 34:29, 30, 35), in order to highlight Jesus' special relationship with God. The text here is strikingly open, drawing the reader into engagement with the mystery of this divine encounter.

The image of Jesus' shining clothes also alludes to Greek epiphany stories. In such stories, some gods, such as Demeter, Aphrodite, and Apollo, disguise themselves as humans in order to move freely among humans, but their divine glory cannot be completely contained or restrained. It is as if there is some sort of glitch in the system; radiant light suddenly starts to shine forth from their divine bodies, shattering the illusion of a human appearance. The allusions to epiphany stories from Greek myths suggest that although Jesus looks like a human being most of the time, he is also divine. However, his divinity is selectively and temporarily revealed to particular individuals, in this case the three disciples. It is as though Jesus' divinity spills over.[1] This private, almost accidental, display of divinity is consistent with the slow revealing of Jesus' true and counterintuitive mission as the Son of God that we see in the book of Mark.

Also puzzling is the rather mundane-sounding announcement that Elijah and Moses were present. Mark simply notes that they appeared, "talking with Jesus" (Mark 9:4). Obviously, these two figures are pillars of the Hebrew Bible; they were particularly revered not only as God's messengers but as prophets with mysterious endings—Elijah, who was taken up in a whirlwind (2 Kgs. 2:11–12), and Moses, whose burial place is unknown (Deut. 34:5–7). Here they stand, centuries later, on this unnamed mountain, not calling attention to themselves or to Jesus, but merely talking with the suddenly shining Jesus—about what, we can only guess.

Like Israel in Exodus 20:18 (see also Exod. 34:40), the disciples are terrified (Mark 9:6). Mark reports that Peter does not know what to say but wonders if it might make sense, given the allusions, to build a tabernacle or a tent, something to materialize his desire to worship Jesus along with these two long-dead Jewish

holy men (v. 5). Although preachers often ridicule Peter for his suggestion, his is a wholly appropriate response to an epiphany. Indeed, Jesus does not rebuke him.

Before anyone can say or do anything else, a cloud casts a shadow over them, and out of the cloud a voice says: "This is my Son, the Beloved; listen to him" (v. 7). The designation of the Son as "beloved" is poignant. In the binding of Isaac (the *aqedah*), the repeated language of "your son, your beloved son" (LXX Gen. 22:2, 12, 16) emphasizes the terrible sacrifice God asks Abraham to make in the name of obedience to God. Following as it does Jesus' own foretelling of his death in Mark 8:31–9:1, the voice foreshadows Mark's conviction that God's salvific plan depends on the sacrifice of Jesus.

This announcement of Jesus' unique status (as God's beloved Son) is the second of three in Mark. The first comes at his baptism (Mark 1:11), while the third comes at his death (15:39). However, this is the only time the voice from heaven commands the gathered disciples to "listen to him." As in English, the Greek word translated "listen" in the imperative shades into more insistent meanings such as "hear," "heed," and "obey." Perhaps resonant here is the Shema ("Hear [or listen], O Israel," Deut. 6:4) or commands to listen to divinely appointed prophets (Deut. 18:15). Even so, the question remains: what might it mean to obey this one who occasionally shines but who, most of the time, walks around like one of us? That is the invitation to the reader of Mark.

"Suddenly," in good Markan fashion, the curtain closes on the scene, and everything is as it was. The disciples saw "no one with them anymore, but only Jesus" (Mark 9:8). "Only Jesus" may simply mean that Elijah and Moses have disappeared and Jesus now stands alone, but it may also imply that without his gleaming clothes, Jesus now appears in the form with which they are familiar: he is "only Jesus" again. The fully human Jesus now stands before them. The glimpse of terrifying holiness is now a memory.

The transfiguration invites preachers to explore the allusions in the text not as a means to make definitive faith claims or to nail down

---

1. Candida R. Moss, "The Transfiguration: An Exercise in Markan Accommodation," *Biblical Interpretation* 12 (2004): 69–89.

the plain meaning of the story, but to appreciate the way Mark relishes the puzzles and the mysteries that he poignantly but playfully presents. In other words, the opportunity here is not to demythologize the text but to remythologize it, and in so doing to open the text to a variety of interpretive possibilities.

AMY ERICKSON

Commentary 2: Connecting the Reading with the World

Lent is a time when we see God in a different light, a light that transfigures Jesus before the very eyes of some of his disciples. Lent presents a different Jesus, an other Jesus. He transfigures, metamorphizes, changes his form, to indicate that he is *other* and not one of the disciples or us. This holy and wholly other God, however, is not the God the disciples thought he was. Lent reveals this about Jesus; thus, the transfiguration is fitting for this liturgical season. This God in Christ is one who endures a wilderness, great suffering, and death on a cross. The transfiguration occurs in the context of predictions of Jesus' death and resurrection. His trajectory is one of suffering.

This should not necessarily be surprising, because Jesus is *other*. So the inevitable happens. This is what often happens to the other: they suffer and are eventually destroyed. In some cases, the other is branded, whipped, imprisoned, encaged, and thrown in border detention centers, because difference is frequently demonized. The other is disregarded and discarded. Though Mark presents a scene of glory, preachers should remind hearers that the transfiguration occurs amid the prediction of Jesus' suffering and death. His gaze is turned toward Jerusalem, the place of his death, a reminder that he did not come to make disciples successful. Discipleship is not dazzling work; it is about following Jesus, the other, in his life of suffering and death. To be honest, discipleship is a death sentence. This is not obviously the Jesus the disciples bargained for, because who would expect or want their Messiah to die? As other, this is inevitable for Jesus, and preachers can paint a picture of how the other, those who are deemed different, often suffer in society.

One example of this is Sam Hose, a black farm laborer in Georgia. He was charged with killing his white employer over a dispute about wages. Because of it, Sam experienced his own kind of bloody crucifixion on April 23, 1899. In the Springfield (MA) *Weekly Republican*, it was described in the following way:

> Before the torch was applied to the pyre, the [N]egro was deprived of his ears, fingers, and genital parts of his body. He pleaded pitifully for his life while the mutilation was going on, but stood the ordeal of fire with surprising fortitude. Before the body was cool, it was cut to pieces, the bones were crushed into small bits, and even the tree upon which the wretch met his fate was torn up and disposed of as "souvenirs." The [N]egro's heart was cut into several pieces, as was also his liver. Those unable to obtain the ghastly relics direct paid their more fortunate possessors extravagant sums for them. Small pieces of bones went for 25 cents, and a bit of liver crisply cooked sold for 10 cents.[2]

As a black other, Sam Hose endured a brutal death, which is what happened to Jesus. Sam was not just wounded; he was obliterated. What happens to the other is not usually pretty. The other can easily be torn out of the pages of humanity because they play loud music in their SUV or wear a hoodie or are simply in the wrong place at the wrong time. The other is often the object of violence, perpetuating a direct assault on otherness, because they are merely different. This kind of treatment of the other demonstrates a change from whatever might be the norm.

Even though Jesus' transfiguration occurs in "dazzling white" and there is glory, the glory of otherness, there is still too much uncertainty about what the other means to the disciples,

2. See M. Shawn Copeland, *Enfleshing Freedom: Body, Race, and Being* (Minneapolis: Fortress, 2009), 119.

which leads to their particular reaction. Lent is a good season to call Christians to repentance for the way we turn the glory of the other into a gory reality for them and by doing so, miss the presence of God in front of our faces. The disciples respond normatively to the other Jesus. "They were terrified" (Mark 9:6). Fear is a typical response to the other and to what one does not understand fully.

Fear, even from disciples, can lead to attempts to control that which is other. Peter wishes to extend common hospitality when he offers to make dwellings for Jesus, Moses, and Elijah. In many ways, this could be a way to control that which they did not understand, to enclose or place boundaries around the other, who is Jesus in this case. One could view this as an attempt to domesticate Jesus and create the parameters of his dwelling and activity because of fear. They fear the transfiguration, the change, the difference, the otherness, dazzling on the face of Jesus even when it is God. Otherness is often scary and the disciples' reaction to Jesus' metamorphosis may reveal how uncomfortable we all are with the other, including when we encounter change.

At one juncture in the life of church music, there were the so-called worship wars. During those battles, Christians wrestled with each other about what kind of music and instrumentation would be appropriate for worship services. There may not have been blood spilled, but there was definitely linguistic violence toward each other. There was a more traditional seminary professor who referred to praise songs as "7–Eleven songs," because they had seven words that were repeated eleven times. He claimed that they were so simplistic that even his dog could sing them. This liturgical musical genre was "other" to him; thus he felt as if he could denigrate it and, by doing so, implicitly dismiss the worship life of thousands of Christians from around the world. Underneath this liturgical elitism was perhaps a fear that the God

he knew had transfigured in front of him and was different and other, now.

People struggle with difference and change, even while otherness dazzles on the face of God in Jesus. This represents how otherness is the glory of God on earth, even if it strikes fear in people, including in Jesus' disciples. Jesus is transfigured in front of the disciples to show that otherness, change, and difference are the will of God and a crucial aspect of the family of God. The voice from the cloud affirms this: "This is my Son, the Beloved; listen to him!" The other is a loved child of God. The other and holy Other have something to offer us. Disciples can learn from the other, if they listen. After listening, learning, and loving, perhaps disciples will invoke these words and become like the Statue of Liberty in the 1883 poem "The New Colossus":

> Not like the brazen giant of Greek fame,
> With conquering limbs astride from land to
>   land;
> Here at our sea-washed, sunset gates shall
>   stand
> A mighty woman with a torch, whose flame
> Is the imprisoned lightning, and her name
> Mother of Exiles. From her beacon-hand
> Glows world-wide welcome; her mild eyes
>   command
> The air-bridged harbor that twin cities frame.
> "Keep, ancient lands, your storied pomp!"
>   cries she
> With silent lips. "Give me your tired, your
>   poor,
> Your huddled masses yearning to breathe free,
> The wretched refuse of your teeming shore.
> Send these, the homeless, tempest-tost to me,
> I lift my lamp beside the golden door!"[3]

In other words, give us the other. Give me Jesus. During Lent, we see an other Jesus. Let the other Jesus come, because Jesus others himself, revealing that the other may be the very person who can save you. The other may be God in your midst.

LUKE A. POWERY

---

3. Emma Lazarus, "The New Colossus," https://www.nps.gov/stli/learn/historyculture/colossus.htm.

Third Sunday in Lent

Exodus 20:1–17
Psalm 19

1 Corinthians 1:18–25
John 2:13–22

Exodus 20:1–17

¹Then God spoke all these words:

²I am the LORD your God, who brought you out of the land of Egypt, out of the house of slavery; ³you shall have no other gods before me.

⁴You shall not make for yourself an idol, whether in the form of anything that is in heaven above, or that is on the earth beneath, or that is in the water under the earth. ⁵You shall not bow down to them or worship them; for I the LORD your God am a jealous God, punishing children for the iniquity of parents, to the third and the fourth generation of those who reject me, ⁶but showing steadfast love to the thousandth generation of those who love me and keep my commandments.

⁷You shall not make wrongful use of the name of the LORD your God, for the LORD will not acquit anyone who misuses his name.

⁸Remember the sabbath day, and keep it holy. ⁹Six days you shall labor and do all your work. ¹⁰But the seventh day is a sabbath to the LORD your God; you shall not do any work—you, your son or your daughter, your male or female slave, your livestock, or the alien resident in your towns. ¹¹For in six days the LORD made heaven and earth, the sea, and all that is in them, but rested the seventh day; therefore the LORD blessed the sabbath day and consecrated it.

¹²Honor your father and your mother, so that your days may be long in the land that the LORD your God is giving you.

¹³You shall not murder.

¹⁴You shall not commit adultery.

¹⁵You shall not steal.

¹⁶You shall not bear false witness against your neighbor.

¹⁷You shall not covet your neighbor's house; you shall not covet your neighbor's wife, or male or female slave, or ox, or donkey, or anything that belongs to your neighbor.

Commentary 1: Connecting the Reading with Scripture

Exodus 20:1–17 lists the Ten Commandments that God gave to the Israelite people. This passage is arguably the most well-known legal pericope in the Bible. The Hebrew text refers to them as "words," and this is the basis for the term Decalogue ("ten words") that is sometimes used in relation to the commandments. They are called the "ten words" in Exodus 34:28 and Deuteronomy 4:13; 10:4. The scene takes place at Mount Sinai (known as Mount Horeb elsewhere in the Hebrew Bible) early in the Israelites' forty-year sojourn in the wilderness on their way to the promised land. The mountain is described as a foreboding and dangerous place, not unlike a fiery, rumbling volcano accompanied by lightning, thunder, and smoke, and the people are urged to keep a safe distance from it (Exod. 19:16–23).

Representations of the scene in art and film commonly depict Moses alone on Mount Sinai communing with God as the Ten Commandments are given, but that does not match the description given in the book of Exodus. The previous chapter ends with Moses descending the mountain to return to the people at God's request (19:24–25), and immediately after the commandments are given, the Israelites fearfully ask him to serve as an intermediary between themselves and the Deity (20:18–21). Only at that point does Moses return to God's presence; so while the Decalogue is delivered, Moses and the people are together at the foot of the mountain.

Many laws and regulations are given to the Israelites throughout the rest of Exodus and the books that follow it, but these are the only words God speaks to the people. The remainder of the legal corpus is mediated through Moses, as the Deity communicates directly with him, and Moses then relays the laws to the Israelites. The Decalogue is also mentioned in Deuteronomy 5:6–21, where Moses is on the plains of Moab and reminds the people about the laws they received at Sinai (here referred to as Horeb) when they began their wandering in the wilderness. The Ten Commandments he recites to them on this occasion do not match up perfectly with the ones that are given in Exodus 20, though they are nearly parallel.

The most significant difference between the two passages is found in the reason why the Israelites should observe the Sabbath day remembrance. According to Exodus, the Sabbath observance recalls God's rest on the seventh day after the world had been created (Exod. 20:11); but in Deuteronomy the Sabbath observance will help the people recall how God rescued them after their enslavement in Egypt (Deut. 5:15). The Exodus passage is often referred to as the Priestly account of the Ten Commandments, because God rests after creation in the Priestly version of creation (Gen. 2:2), and Sabbath observance is something that would have been of particular interest in priestly circles. The preacher might note the discrepancy between the Exodus and Deuteronomy versions of the Ten Commandments and ask the congregation to reflect on what motivates them to observe the Sabbath—that is, to come to church—or what motivates the people of God in their actions generally.

Another discrepancy between the two lists is seen in the last commandment, where a slightly different order of what one should not covet is presented, and the Deuteronomy passage adds some things not in the Exodus text. In Exodus 20:17 the order is your neighbor's house, wife, male or female slave, ox, donkey, or anything that belongs to your neighbor. According to Deuteronomy 5:21 you should not covet your neighbor's wife, house, field, male or female slave, ox, donkey, or anything that belongs to your neighbor. In Exodus the neighbor's wife is part of what is in his house, but in Deuteronomy she is listed first before the house and therefore is not part of the household possessions. The different versions are probably due to the different contexts in which they developed and to which they attempted to respond.

This scene is closely tied to the theme of covenant. The giving of the Ten Commandments and the rest of the law establishes a special bond between God and the Israelites that will remain unbroken as long as they follow that law. Prior to this, circumcision was the sign of the covenant (Gen. 17:9–14), but over time observance of the law came to be seen as the primary means of maintaining the covenantal relationship. This is subtly hinted at immediately after this passage when Moses tells the Israelites that they should not sin (Exod. 20:20). The first reference to sin since their escape from Egypt comes immediately after God begins to deliver to the people the laws and statutes they are expected to obey.

This establishes a central theme that runs throughout the rest of the Deuteronomistic History that is recounted in the books of Joshua, Judges, 1 and 2 Samuel, and 1 and 2 Kings and describes the Israelites' entry into the promised land, the rise of kingship, and the ultimate destruction of Jerusalem at the hands of the Babylonians. According to that history, the people prosper when they follow the law, but when they violate it and sin, they are punished with hardship and oppression. This law-based understanding of the covenant has its origin in this passage with the giving of the Ten Commandments. A sermon on this passage might call attention to discrepancy between behavior and outcome (bad things sometimes happen to good people, and vice versa) in our daily lives.

The Sermon on the Mount, found in Matthew 5–7, is one of the ways the first Gospel tries to present Jesus as a second Moses. This is done through both its location and its content. The setting on a mountain recalls Mount Sinai, and the law is a topic that features prominently in Jesus' words. Early in the sermon, in a section known as "the six antitheses," Jesus explains the difference between the law as it has been understood in the past and his new vision of it. Three of the six laws he cites have a direct connection with the Ten Commandments: those that forbid murder (Matt. 5:20–26), adultery (Matt. 5:27–30), and making false statements (Matt. 5:33–37). In each case Jesus does not simply reiterate the law, but urges his listeners to avoid doing the things that are the root causes of these offenses. For example, he says that it is not enough to refrain from committing adultery, but one must also not give in to the temptation to lust that is the first step toward adultery. This is an example of how Jesus fulfills the law (Matt. 5:17).

Some of the Ten Commandments are mentioned elsewhere in the New Testament. The Synoptic Gospels describe a scene in which a man comes to Jesus and asks him what he must do to attain eternal life. Jesus first tells him he must follow the law, and he specifically mentions about half of the Ten Commandments. When the man responds that he has done this, Jesus then instructs him to sell his possessions and give the money to the poor (Matt. 19:16–22; Mark 10:17–22; Luke 18:18–25). Similarly, in his letter to the Romans, Paul says that the commandments against adultery, murder, stealing, and coveting may be summed up in the charge to love your neighbor as yourself. Their references to the Ten Commandments indicate that the New Testament authors believed they encapsulated the law given to Moses and also affirmed these laws as essential to the faith.

JOHN KALTNER

Commentary 2: Connecting the Reading with the World

Exodus 20, the reading for the Third Sunday in Lent, initially seems straightforward: God speaks the Decalogue, otherwise known as the Ten Commandments or Ten Words—a set of laws that also appears in a nearly identical form in Deuteronomy 5:6–21. The end. However, a close reading of the Ten Commandments reveals that each commandment or word speaks to our communion with God and our sense of community with each other. Though the laws are too often relegated to what God demands of us in our hearts, they together convey how God wants us to live together in loving ways.

Because of the fame of this passage, a word of caution about anti-Judaism and Christian views of legalism is needed. To be sure, there are moves within Christian legalism that would denounce the "dispensation of the law" outright as passé, now that Christ has come. The contemporary reality of Christian legalism, however, betrays us on two counts. First, it denies the Jewish roots of Christian belief, practices, and personalities (including Jesus!), while at the same time it ignores the legalistic views present-day Christian churches hold in their polities, Books of Order, Books of Discipline, bylaws, and constitutions.

Indeed, it is not clear which group—the various Jewish or Christian sects—is the more legalistic. A possible sermon topic therefore is to discuss and talk about the long history and terrible effects of anti-Judaism in the church.

This text moreover gives the preacher the opportunity to raise the civic context of laws. Because of separation of church and state protections, many preachers avoid the semblance of speaking of politics and religion. Granted, every civic and communal arrangement needs some guiding rules of interaction and engagement that conveys the idea of living in good community. Laws are a necessary part of the contract of the body politic.

In speaking about the United States in particular, we should acknowledge that there are some who believe that the founding of the United States is based on its identity as a "Christian" nation. The Ten Commandments as an icon loom large in American understandings of law and order. The architecture of the Supreme Court Building cannot escape this interpretation. However, because of this vision, religion and politics are, at points, irresponsibly colluded. People often misconstrue the presence of

Moses and the depiction of the Bill of Rights articles 1–10 (in Roman numerals) as a sign that these Ten Commandments are at the basis of American jurisprudence.

This text gives the preacher the opportunity to explore the matters of law and faith. Can faithfulness be legislated by law and order? What is the interrelationship, if any? This is a line of queries that weaves through both Hebrew and Christian Scriptures, especially in the epistles and their admonishments to "obey those who have rule over you for they are ordained by God" (Rom. 13:1–7).

Moreover, what happens when the laws legislated by humankind are distributed in ways that disenfranchise and dehumanize its citizens? The rights of minorities and the marginalized are frequently denied with laws used as a weapon to enforce injustice. Which law should we, the people of God, obey? What should we do in the face of unjust human laws that contravene the just laws demanded by God? This is one of the questions at the heart of the civil rights movement and other movements for equality, justice, and freedom. As Martin Luther King Jr. asserted in the face of "legal" hypocrisy: "All we say to America is to be true to what you said on paper."[1]

Within this reality, marginalized groups are either told to obey or find destructive ways to teach themselves to conform to the rules and laws of the status quo. In her 1993 book *Righteous Discontent*, Evelyn Brooks Higginbotham introduced an important phrase into the sociopolitical lexicon, "respectability politics": the set of beliefs holding that conformity to socially acceptable or mainstream standards of appearance and behavior will protect a member of a marginalized or minority group from prejudices and systematic injustices. However, the path to the peace sought in the kin-dom of God is not the absence of conflict but the holy disruption of laws and practices that prevent all of humanity from realizing its full and authentic identity as "children of God."

There is another significant observation that must be made from this text from Exodus. The precedent is set here for a new arrangement of how God will communicate with humanity. The theatrics and pyrotechnics of God speaking directly was perhaps over the top. How do we get the word of God to people who are terrified by God's voice and presence directly? The people understand that they need an intermediary, and they ask Moses to stand in that place. How does one stand as human being (finite and limited) on behalf of God (infinite and limitless)? Further, with what authority does one "infected with the same disease get to speak to others about the cure"?[2] Exodus 20:18–21 establishes and affirms that the authority for speaking on God's behalf is set into motion by the people's acknowledgment that listening directly to the voice of God, to be directly in the presence of God, is going to lead to their death. They ask (command?) Moses to seek a different arrangement, to speak to them on God's behalf. It is here that the concept of humans speaking the word of God is initiated. Everyone who ever has or ever will preach is a part of this permission granted by the faith community.

Speaking on God's behalf is only half of the responsibility Moses is thrust into here. Moses draws toward the thick darkness where God is (v. 21). Here a second striking aspect of Moses' responsibility is birthed. Moses is not only to speak to the people for God; he also enters the space into which the congregation will not go. Moses draws close to the "thick darkness" where God is. Moses is pulled away from the cries and concerns of the people to face God on their behalf. Throughout his life of leadership, Moses faces God on the people's behalf, pleading their case and appealing for mercy. In a culture that privileges whiteness, as in the United States, the symbolic understandings of white/dark are used to reinforce the preference for the white (light/bright); thus the conclusion of this Exodus 20 scene is worth pondering. As the people leave "at a distance," Moses returns to the darkness ("thick cloud") where God is.

Too often we limit the presence of God to our bright days of promise and times of happiness. This is not the reality for the community or the leader's life. Away from the bright

---

1. Martin Luther King Jr., "Letter from the Birmingham Jail," April 16, 1963.
2. Gardner Taylor, *How Shall They Preach?* 1975–1976 Yale Lyman Beecher Lectures (Elgin, IL: Progressive Baptist Press, 1977).

spotlight of leadership, the leader must be willing to face the God who is present and powerful inside the darkness—the abyss, the uncertain, the painful, the fuzzy, the foggy, and beg and barter with God for the salvation and sustenance of the people.

Affirm some of the aspects of God that go beyond mere algorithms calculated by strict adherence to laws to the mystery of a daring encounter. God is awesome but the encounter with God is also "awe-filled." Awful. Fear inducing. Worshipful. Moses is willing to return again and again to that awful place with God and to bring that encounter with God to the people who have asked him to function in this way.

GARY V. SIMPSON

Psalm 19

¹The heavens are telling the glory of God;
    and the firmament proclaims his handiwork.
²Day to day pours forth speech,
    and night to night declares knowledge.
³There is no speech, nor are there words;
    their voice is not heard;
⁴yet their voice goes out through all the earth,
    and their words to the end of the world.

In the heavens he has set a tent for the sun,
⁵which comes out like a bridegroom from his wedding canopy,
    and like a strong man runs its course with joy.
⁶Its rising is from the end of the heavens,
    and its circuit to the end of them;
    and nothing is hid from its heat.

⁷The law of the LORD is perfect,
    reviving the soul;
the decrees of the LORD are sure,
    making wise the simple;
⁸the precepts of the LORD are right,
    rejoicing the heart;
the commandment of the LORD is clear,
    enlightening the eyes;
⁹the fear of the LORD is pure,
    enduring forever;
the ordinances of the LORD are true
    and righteous altogether.
¹⁰More to be desired are they than gold,
    even much fine gold;
sweeter also than honey,
    and drippings of the honeycomb.

¹¹Moreover by them is your servant warned;
    in keeping them there is great reward.
¹²But who can detect their errors?
    Clear me from hidden faults.
¹³Keep back your servant also from the insolent;
    do not let them have dominion over me.
Then I shall be blameless,
    and innocent of great transgression.

¹⁴Let the words of my mouth and the meditation of my heart
    be acceptable to you,
    O LORD, my rock and my redeemer.

Connecting the Psalm with Scripture and Worship

The opening verses of Psalm 19 are well known, often captured in songs of praise, whether the soaring phrases of Joseph Haydn's *Creation* oratorio or Marty Haugen's uplifting melody in "Canticle of the Sun." Celebrating the wonder of creation and the majesty of the Creator, the psalmist begins by declaring, "The heavens are telling the glory of God / and the firmament proclaims his handiwork" (Ps. 19:1). Much of the music, prayers, and art based on Psalm 19 never move beyond the first six verses, including Haydn's magisterial composition. However, to consider Psalm 19 as only a celebration of God's hand in creation is to miss the richness of what this psalm may offer to preachers and liturgists.

The temptation, even among scholars, is to break Psalm 19 into two distinct psalms—the first proclaiming the glory of God in creation (vv. 1–6) and the second declaring the holiness of God's law (vv. 7–14). Yet, when taken together, Psalm 19 proclaims a God of all creation who cares so much about human creatures that God offers guidance and instruction, even redemption.

Psalm 19 may best be understood as a unity in three parts, each section building on the previous. In the first section, verses 1–6, creation is lauded for the way it puts on full display the wonder and majesty of God. However, the psalmist is interested in more than just the beauty of creation; in verses 2–4 the psalmist asserts that creation itself "declares knowledge" and "pours forth speech," even if it is not perceptible to human ears. Then, there is a somewhat abrupt shift into the second section beginning at verse 7. In an instant the psalmist moves from the cosmic to the particular, focusing on the instruction God offers human beings (vv. 7–10). Much like creation, God's law (or *torah*) is to be praised and, like creation, stands as evidence of God's glory and care. Finally, in verses 11–14, the psalmist responds to the gift and demand of God's *torah*, admitting that while keeping the law of the Lord is not easy (vv. 12–13a), through God's redemption and

grace, the psalmist is able to follow the *torah* in thought, word, and deed (v. 14).

The rich language and imagery of Psalm 19 may serve to enliven the first reading for the day, Exodus 20:1–17, the giving of the Ten Commandments. These verses from Exodus can come across a bit sterile, a cold recitation of the law God is now placing on the newly freed Israelite people. It does not help that this inventory of God's instructions has often been memorialized on statues and posters, numbered one to ten, like a holy to-do list. As if delivered by a teacher on the first day of school, this inventory of "thou shalts" and "thou shalt nots" can feel like a precautionary set of rules to keep a rogue class in line. While not completely off base (indeed, the Israelites did prove to require plenty of parameters and corrections along the way), Psalm 19 invites us to hear the often-recited and replicated rules of Exodus 20 in a new way.

First, Psalm 19 reminds us that the law is not meant to be restricting or stifling, but life-giving. As verse 7a declares, "The law of the LORD is perfect, reviving the soul." Biblical scholar J. Clinton McCann suggests that a better translation might be, "The instruction of the LORD is all-encompassing, restoring life."[1] God's *torah* is not intended to limit God's people, but to free them toward fullness of life! The psalmist insists that the "precepts of the LORD are right, rejoicing the heart; the commandment of the LORD is clear, enlightening the eyes" (v. 8). God's law allows God's people to flourish as a community and in the land that the Lord intends to give them. The law does not foreclose options for the people, but instead, like the sun that marches across the sky (vv. 4b–6), the law illumines life God intends for God's beloved creatures.

Second, Psalm 19 encourages readers to conceive of the giving of God's *torah* as gift. God gives the law not because the people are bad, but because God is good. The "perfect" or "all-encompassing" law of God is not an expression of God's frustration, but of God's care. The Lord of the cosmos, whose glory is declared in the heavens, cares enough about human beings to

---

1. J. Clinton McCann Jr., "Psalms," in the *New Interpreter's Bible* (Nashville: Abingdon, 1996), 4:752.

give them guidance as to how to live faithfully together as they navigate their freedom from slavery in Egypt and anticipate the new land that God has promised. As the psalmist notes, such a gift is more desirable that decadent food or great wealth (v. 10).

God's *torah* is a life-giving gift that invites both healthy relationship among the people (Exod. 20:12–17), as well as an enduring relationship with God (Exod. 20:1–11). In spite of the "errors" and "faults" that are bound to happen (Ps. 19:12) when following God's law, the gift of God's *torah* ultimately leads the psalmist to find closer relationship with God, "my rock and my redeemer" (v. 14)—a God who cares enough to gift beloved human creatures with instruction and grace to follow.

While it is valuable to consider Psalm 19 as a unity, parts of the psalm might be a rich addition to the worship liturgy. The first part of the psalm (vv. 1–6), which praises God as creator and the creation as evidence of God's glory, might be a powerful call to worship. The remainder of the psalm (vv. 7–14) might be a powerful prayer for illumination, either read by the preacher or read responsively with the congregation.

Psalm 19, a psalm that praises God as Creator, Redeemer, and *Torah*-giver, invites preachers, teachers, and liturgists to break through the layers of dust that have accumulated on the often-referenced list of laws in Exodus 20 and rediscover the life-giving gift of God's empowering grace shining through.

KIMBERLY R. WAGNER

1 Corinthians 1:18–25

[18]For the message about the cross is foolishness to those who are perishing, but to us who are being saved it is the power of God. [19]For it is written,

> "I will destroy the wisdom of the wise,
>   and the discernment of the discerning I will thwart."

[20]Where is the one who is wise? Where is the scribe? Where is the debater of this age? Has not God made foolish the wisdom of the world? [21]For since, in the wisdom of God, the world did not know God through wisdom, God decided, through the foolishness of our proclamation, to save those who believe. [22]For Jews demand signs and Greeks desire wisdom, [23]but we proclaim Christ crucified, a stumbling block to Jews and foolishness to Gentiles, [24]but to those who are the called, both Jews and Greeks, Christ the power of God and the wisdom of God. [25]For God's foolishness is wiser than human wisdom, and God's weakness is stronger than human strength.

Commentary 1: Connecting the Reading with Scripture

This reading from 1 Corinthians is excellent preparation for the events of Good Friday. Paul says straightforwardly that it seems foolish to say that the crucifixion is a demonstration of the power of God. We sometimes forget how strange it is to claim that the humiliating death of Jesus is good news. Knowing how outlandish it sounds in his world, Paul still directs the Corinthians' attention to the cross as the guide for how to live the Christian life.

The Corinthian church was experiencing all kinds of internal disputes, disputes about leaders, ethics, the nature of the resurrection, and especially about what it means to be spiritual. First Corinthians 1–4 is devoted to redefining spirituality. Many of the Corinthians' other problems grow out of their misunderstanding of spirituality. They have brought into the church the ideas about spirituality they had held before their conversion. In Greco-Roman religions (particularly those known as mystery religions), an experience of a god gave a person a variety of gifts. They believed that contact with the power of a god made people more impressive and successful and gave them wisdom to help them get ahead. All of these results were directed toward enhancing the life of the individual who experienced the god's presence. The Corinthian church members think that the presence of the Spirit in their lives should do the same things for them.

Paul rejects this notion, arguing that the gift of the Spirit is not about gaining advantages for oneself. He points to the crucifixion as the event that shows the way of life the Spirit enables. This contradicts the cultural expectations of his day. He gives a list of experts on the way things should be: the wise, scholars, and those adept in demonstrating what others should think and do. They are all confounded when they see the cross. They cannot see how dying on a cross can be a demonstration of God's power. As they see things, wisdom and contact with a god bring strength and a powerful personality; they bring financial gain and personal independence. If this is what Gentiles expect, Paul says that Jews expect a mighty sign that shows the power of God in action. No. Everyone gets a crucifixion.

Paul says nonbelievers miss the meaning of the cross because they belong to "this age" and seek the wisdom of "the world" (1 Cor. 1:20). These brief expressions designate the cross as an end-time event that initiates what Paul else-where calls a "new creation" (2 Cor. 5:17). This new creation has different values. The membership of the Corinthian church demonstrates just how different its values are. In 1:26–28 Paul tells them to look at who is in their church. He says there are not many well-educated, wealthy, or from good families. No one would have thought that God would choose to live among and within a group like that, but it is that motley crew that can perceive acts of God and demonstrate what God wants for the world.

The cross seems like foolishness because it asserts that self-giving love is strength. In Greco-Roman culture, gaining honor and status were of crucial importance. Humility was not a virtue. It was a sign of weakness and dishonor. Crucifixion was the epitome of dishonor. It was designed to humiliate the person killed. It was a demonstration of their complete lack of power and dignity. To proclaim it as a demonstration of God's power makes no sense. To say such a thing about how God works does seem like a scandal (1 Cor. 1:23). It simply violates what everyone knows crucifixion means.

To see the cross as God's wisdom and power requires people to reject the ways they have understood and evaluated everything. The Corinthians can see the cross as wisdom and power only if they adopt the new creation's values and norms. It is the same with us. In our world, where financial success and personal advancement are central goals, it is hard to argue that a crucifixion demonstrates wisdom and power, because it is hard to maintain the idea that self-giving love is superior to personal success. Indeed, the Corinthian letters are evidence of just how hard it is.

Throughout chapters 1–2, Paul contrasts his preaching of the cross and powerful oratory, because groups in Corinthians were arguing about who should be leaders based on how impressive they seemed. In our passage he rejects what is normally seen as wisdom, before contrasting his preaching with "persuasive words of wisdom," a reference to powerful oratorical performance (2:4). One reason the Corinthians have divisions is because they evaluate leaders according to the values of the world, not according to the standard of the cross.

Their inability to make the self-giving love of the cross their central value shows itself in many ways in this letter. It is seen in the ways they exercise spiritual gifts, in how they conduct the Lord's Supper, in the legal cases they bring against one another, and in the ways they demand to exercise their rights to the detriment of others. They still think God's presence should make them impressive and allow them to dominate others. Paul rejects this by naming the cross as the standard for the Christian life.

Paul certainly believes in the saving significance of the cross. He affirms that function of Christ's death in many places, but that is not the central idea he has in mind in 1 Corinthians 1–4. Here the cross serves as an exemplar for the Christian life. He wants the Corinthians to see it as the pattern for the way believers are to act in relation to one another. Similarly, he tells the members of the Philippian church to put the good of others ahead of their own good because that is what Christ did for them (Phil. 2:3–11). Christ's self-giving love shown in privileging the good of others is a—really *the*—guide for how to be spiritual and for how to live the whole Christian life. This remains a demanding standard that calls us to be willing to accept personal and financial disadvantages for the good of others. Whether it is decisions at church, or business dealings, or tax policy, the standard remains the same.

This Sunday's Old Testament reading is the Ten Words or Ten Commandments. While the commandments may, at first, seem a strange pairing, there is an important connection. Much of the Ten Words teaches people to live in relation to one another in ways that recognize the full dignity and worth of each person. That is a significant part of learning to live in accord with the exemplar of the cross. When we recognize the value of other people, we are better able to relate to them through self-giving love.

This week's Gospel reading has Jesus utter words that no one understands. After disrupting some operations at the temple and being challenged for it, Jesus says that if they destroy the temple, it will be raised in three days. The disciples, to say nothing of his antagonists, have no idea what he means. John comments that after he was raised, they understood. In various places John regularly notes that the full meaning of what Jesus said could be understood only after his resurrection. As in 1 Corinthians, John recognizes that the full meaning of Christ's death and resurrection can be understood only after the new creation has broken in.

It is no less difficult to preach about the centrality of self-giving love in our culture than it was in Paul's. Yet adopting that way of life is essential to what it means to follow Jesus.

JERRY L. SUMNEY

Commentary 2: Connecting the Reading with the World

Following a formal introduction (1 Cor. 1:1–9), Paul's letter to the Corinthians begins with a plea for unity (1:10–17). Paul's congregants in Corinth are quarreling from opposing sides, and he urges them at the outset of his letter to find common ground. In a world rife with division, the contemporary pastor will surely identify with Paul's letter to a divided community. Our churches are fraught with political, theological, economic, and social divisions, and too many pastors find themselves in the midst of a delicate juggling act every Sunday morning as they set about the task of preaching to a discordant audience.

The epistle lesson for the Third Sunday in Lent follows Paul's initial acknowledgment of the conflict in Corinth and seems to place further focus on the inharmonious nature of the Corinthian church. Specifically, Paul's rhetoric makes use of common dualities that tempt us to foreground contention in our interpretations of the text (i.e., death vs. salvation, foolishness vs. wisdom, Greek vs. Jew, us vs. them). The juxtapositions in this lectionary passage, however, are deceptive. Just like the stories that fill our airways and news feeds, they lure us into their conflictual nature and prevent us from recognizing Paul's underlying message to the Corinthians.

The opening words of this week's lectionary lesson provide an alternative focus for our attention: the message of the cross (v. 18). What happens if we set aside the seductive comparisons and focus instead on the crucifixion of Christ? In other words, what happens if we set aside our contemporary divisions and read this text at the foot of the cross? I suggest a few implications.

An emphasis on the cross draws us into the season of Lent. Paul reminds us that as Christians we cannot shy away from the cross. We cannot have Easter without the crucifixion. An

Easter that overlooks the crucified Christ is a whitewashed Easter that ignores the pain and suffering that continues in today's world. Bringing forward the cross reminds us that we must be able to identify the crucified Christ: "For I decided to know nothing among you except Jesus Christ, and him crucified" (2:2). In the midst of conflict, Paul sets aside Jesus' resurrection in favor of his death. The cross, for Paul, is the unifying factor; to be in agreement is to know the crucified Christ.

A focus on Jesus' crucifixion also encourages us to reckon with those who are suffering in our context. Who are the crucified among us? The same forces of imperialism, indifference, hatred, and violence that crucified Jesus live on in our context. On our Lenten journey to the cross, we would do well to draw our attention to any of these diabolical forces as well as their victims, the crucified, in our world.

In the United States, for example, at the southern border, immigrant families in search of security and sustenance are judged as criminals and incarcerated unjustly. In cities throughout the world, the unemployed and low-wage workers bear the scars of an economic system that repeatedly lashes them. In schools around the country, students carry bulletproof backpacks, afraid of another outbreak of mass violence and in hopes of preventing the piercing of their bodies. People already writhing in economic pain in Flint, Michigan, and other places throughout the world quench their thirst on the poisonous water offered them by systemic mismanagement and greed. At a rate far higher than the general population, persons of color breathe their last breath after brief encounters with the local law enforcement charged with protecting them. It is not difficult to find the crucified among us; we need only to be willing to look.

An emphasis on the cross also has implications for the mission of the church. As Paul sees it, the central role of a Christian is to proclaim the story of the cross, to profess a crucified Christ. Paul has already declared this as his central purpose. He tells the Corinthians that Christ sent him to proclaim the gospel, locating its message in the power of the cross (1:17). Paul does not stop there. He names the Corinthians as participants in the proclamation of the cross. He writes, "But we proclaim Christ crucified, a stumbling block to Jews and foolishness to Gentiles" (v. 23). It is worth reminding the church that the call to proclaim the message of the cross is not merely the work of the apostle; it is also the central task of the church.

The NRSV translates the Greek word *kēryssō* as "proclaim," a common translation, but the verb carries with it so much more. To proclaim something is to make it known publicly, to announce it for all the world to hear, to shout it aloud, to scream it from the rooftops. Like the fanfare of a trumpet call, the Corinthians are called to broadcast Christ's crucifixion. In a world that prefers to hear the resounding "hallelujahs" of resurrection, Paul reminds us that it is equally important, if not more important, for Christians to name the suffering in our world. Members of the church are called to join their voices one to another crying out in anguish and proclaiming loudly for all to hear, "These are the crucified among us!"

The apocalyptic imagery in this passage further points to our active participation in the work of ushering into existence the coming kingdom of God through our proclamation of the cross. Paul's dualistic language of "the saved" vs. "the perishing" serves to set us within this eschatological context (v. 18). It is through two comparisons that Paul emphasizes our participation in God's work. He writes, "For Jews demand signs and Greeks desire wisdom, but we proclaim Christ crucified" (vv. 22–23a).

While a sign is a common eschatological expectation in Jewish apocalyptic literature, wisdom is a popular trope in Hellenistic philosophy and is considered something that might be achieved. By putting proclamation in contrast with these common images, Paul acknowledges the active role of the Corinthian church in the salvific work of God. In contrast to those who wait for a sign or who seek to master wisdom, Paul encourages the Corinthians to participate continuously in the message of the cross. It is not something they can wait for; it is not something they can earn. The Corinthians are expected to do more than count the days until the coming kingdom of God; they are expected to participate in its inbreaking.

The preacher who challenges the church to point out the crucified among us might also offer a word of caution. In 2018, at the ripe age of fifteen, Swedish activist Greta Thunberg began her work of drawing attention to the crucified in our world—specifically, the environment. From her work in organizing strikes to her chilling testimony at the 2018 UN Climate Change Conference, Thunberg has repeatedly raised her voice in protest. She laments humanity's participation in the crucifixion of our planet, and she refuses to be silenced by those who attempt to stand in her way. Thunberg also knows the risk. World leaders and politicians have ridiculed her prestige and mischaracterized her volume and passion as an anger-management problem and the rantings of a disrespectful youth. Not everyone is comfortable being made aware of their participation in crucifixion. Maybe Paul was on to something when he linked our proclamation of the cross with foolishness (v. 21). It might seem to some a fool's errand to run around pointing out the atrocities in our world. As Paul reminds, however, this supposed fool's errand is exactly what the people of God are called to do (v. 18).

ANNA M. V. BOWDEN

John 2:13–22

¹³The Passover of the Jews was near, and Jesus went up to Jerusalem. ¹⁴In the temple he found people selling cattle, sheep, and doves, and the money changers seated at their tables. ¹⁵Making a whip of cords, he drove all of them out of the temple, both the sheep and the cattle. He also poured out the coins of the money changers and overturned their tables. ¹⁶He told those who were selling the doves, "Take these things out of here! Stop making my Father's house a marketplace!" ¹⁷His disciples remembered that it was written, "Zeal for your house will consume me." ¹⁸The Jews then said to him, "What sign can you show us for doing this?" ¹⁹Jesus answered them, "Destroy this temple, and in three days I will raise it up." ²⁰The Jews then said, "This temple has been under construction for forty-six years, and will you raise it up in three days?" ²¹But he was speaking of the temple of his body. ²²After he was raised from the dead, his disciples remembered that he had said this; and they believed the scripture and the word that Jesus had spoken.

Commentary 1: Connecting the Reading with Scripture

In the Synoptic Gospels, Jesus' action at the temple takes place in the final week of his life leading up to the Passover (Mark 11:15–19). The Johannine version, however, adds a layer of complexity to the interpretive task, for here the event appears not at the end of Jesus' ministry, but its beginning. While all four evangelists interpret Jesus' action as an indictment of the temple leadership of his day, John goes further. Jesus' response to the demand for a sign to justify his expulsion of the money changers and sellers points forward to his death and resurrection, while also dropping a hint of his messianic identity.

Ancient literary standards do not require biographies to adhere to strict chronology. John's relocation of Jesus' temple action to a much earlier point in his narrative signifies a theological impetus rather than incompetent historical recounting. The historicity of this event is not in question, but its meaning needs explanation. A solo protest that is too small even to attract the Roman guards will not stop all commercial activities within the temple precincts. Business will resume the following day, if not sooner. Rather, Jesus' action is symbolic, exposing the spiritual corruption of the temple when its power brokers have "[made his] Father's house into a marketplace" (John 2:16).

Although Jesus overturns the money changers' tables and drives out the animals, his furor is secondarily against the merchants and primarily against those who allow them to set up shop in the first place. In Jesus' view, the buying and selling are an affront to God's honor. The Jewish leaders have deviated from the true worship of God for the sake of political and economic expediency.

Both the section that precedes this story and the one that follows reinterpret the Jewish institutions of Jesus' day. It is ironic that Jesus uses the water for the rites of purification and changes it into 120 gallons of fine wine, thereby demonstrating the abundance that the Messiah brings (2:1–10). Later, Jesus takes issue with the inability of Nicodemus, a Pharisee of considerable standing, to grasp the necessity of spiritual rebirth from above (3:1–12). In all three stories—the wedding at Cana, the temple action, and the conversation with Nicodemus—particular theological understanding evinced by some sects of Judaism needs recalibration in light of Jesus' arrival. "The law indeed was given through Moses; grace and truth came through

The Word from the Cross

"Christ sent me to preach the gospel, and now with eloquent wisdom, lest the cross of Christ be emptied of its power. . . . For the word of the cross is folly to those who are perishing, but to us who are being saved it is the power of God . . ."

The *word from the cross* is the gospel of Paul—the message he announced to Jews and pagans. It is a plain witness, without a trace of grandiloquence, without any effort to convince on the grounds of reason. It derives its entire force from that *which* it proclaims. And that is the cross of Christ, that is, the death of Christ on the cross, and the crucified Christ himself. Christ is God's power and God's wisdom not only as one sent by God, as God's Son who is himself God, but as the Crucified One. For the death on the cross is the salvific solution invented by God's unfathomable wisdom. In order to show that human power and human wisdom are incapable of achieving salvation, he gives salvific power to what appears to human estimation to be weak and foolish, to him who wishes to be nothing on his own, but allows the power of God alone to work in him, who has "emptied himself" and "become obedient to death on the cross."

Edith Stein, *The Science of the Cross,* trans. Josephine **Koeppel** (Washington, DC: Institute of Carmelite Studies, 2002), 20.

Jesus Christ" (1:17). A new era of salvation has dawned, and God's people must recognize that the Word has become flesh and is now "tabernacling" among them (1:14).

The disciples connect Jesus' action with the words of the righteous sufferer in Psalm 69: "Zeal for your house will consume me" (2:17; Ps. 69:9; 68:10 LXX). In John's rendition, the tense of the verb has been changed from the aorist ("has consumed") to the future ("will consume), foreshadowing Jesus' death. His fervor for God's honor will ultimately destroy his life.

Jesus' authority for what he has done is challenged by other religious leaders who demand a supernatural sign of divine endorsement (2:18). Jesus retorts, however, that he *is* the sign. Three days after his death, his body will arise as the purified temple to replace the current temple, rendered unclean by its leaders and destined for destruction (2:19, 21). In Jewish messianic thought, a new temple is expected to be built by God or by the Messiah. Jesus' identification with the new temple underscores his messianic status, but this truth is completely lost to his challengers, who puzzle over the possibility of building in three days a temple that has been under construction for decades (2:20). Moreover, by claiming to be God's eschatological temple, Jesus implies that he is the embodiment of God's presence, an assertion that will lead

to either an insight into his divine origin or a charge of blasphemy.

By positioning this account early in Jesus' public ministry, John sets in motion an escalating conflict between Jesus and the temple authorities. Throughout the narrative, Jesus faces hostility in Jerusalem. He is called a sinner and a Samaritan (9:16, 24), and is accused of blasphemy and demon possession (7:20; 8:48, 52; 10:20, 33). Multiple attempts have been made to arrest, stone, or kill him (7:1, 25, 30, 32, 44–45; 8:59; 10:31, 39; 11:49–57). In the end, those in power succeed in seeking his death (18:28–19:16), but the seed of rejection has already been sown back in chapter 2.

Another important use of a literary time stamp is that of the Passover, a feast that commemorates the sparing of the Israelites when God destroyed the firstborn of the Egyptians (Exod. 12:1–29). Each year, the observance of Passover rekindled the flame of messianic hopes among the Jewish groups. Unlike the Synoptics, where Jesus' temple action and his crucifixion take place over a single Passover, the Gospel of John makes reference to three Passovers. At the first Passover, Jesus alludes to his death by means of the temple imagery (2:13–22). Near the second Passover, Jesus feeds the five thousand, launches into a discourse declaring himself to be the bread of life, and exhorts his hearers to eat his flesh and drink his blood (6:1–59)—an invitation reminiscent of the Last Supper in the Synoptics (Mark 14:22–25 and par.). At the final Passover, Jesus dies on the cross as the sacrificial lamb while actual lambs are being slaughtered for sacrifice (18:28, 39; 19:14). As the reader approaches each Passover, a backward glance at the temple action serves as a reminder that Jesus' death comes as no surprise to him. The crucifixion is not his enemies' victory, but Jesus' hour of glorification as appointed by the Father.

That God is worthy of all glory and honor is a theme that weaves through the four lectionary texts for this week. Psalm 19 affirms the power and wisdom of God through the praise of creation and the law. The latter is represented by the Ten Commandments in Exodus 20, which demand of God's people an undivided loyalty, for YHWH is a holy and jealous God, who shows steadfast love to the obedient and punishes the disobedient. In 1 Corinthians 1, Paul attests to God's wisdom and power as well, seeing them in the plan of salvation that defies all human expectations, calling for Israel's Messiah to die and then be raised to life again by the power of God.

Jesus' temple action in John 2 reiterates these themes in ironic terms. Of all places, with its feasts, rituals, and holy boundaries, the temple ought to exemplify the most reverent and dedicated worship of God. To the contrary, its leadership fails so miserably in their responsibility that the whole establishment is slated for destruction. Yet God will not abandon the faithful. Through the body of the risen Christ, God will once again institute a spiritual and eschatological temple, giving God's people the assurance of divine presence forever (cf. Rev. 21:22).

Jesus' indictment of the religious leadership of his day should give the leaders of today's denominations and congregations pause. Have power and personal gain threatened to detract the church from its raison d'être? Do those who hold important responsibilities lead with integrity? Do the church's witness and worship honor or dishonor God? In this season of Lent, is there room for self-reflection and humility? Where does one seek hope and divine presence in a world torn by strife and distrust? Are they found in Gothic cathedrals and multimillion-dollar structures (the modern equivalent of the grandiose temple in Jerusalem), or in the risen Jesus, God's eschatological temple, where the soul finds its ultimate rest?

DIANE G. CHEN

Commentary 2: Connecting the Reading with the World

If we are going to let it get through to us properly, the Lenten season will drive us to posit certain questions to ourselves about our own doing and thinking: What are we up to, and why? Whom do we credit, and why? What have we normalized, and why? As ever, Jesus flips the script on what we have gotten used to and what we have come to view as essential.

John's Gospel gives us a Jesus who busts things up from the get-go, as early as the second chapter. Within a few verses of turning water into wine at a wedding in Cana, Jesus goes and causes a disturbance in Jerusalem. Where others see a functional, sustaining economy at the Jerusalem temple, with sacrificial cattle, sheep, and doves for sale, Jesus sees a meaning crisis and does something about it. "Take these things out of here! Stop making my Father's house a marketplace!" Jesus cries out as he scatters money, overturns tables, and strikes livestock with an improvised whip made of cords.

Many of us are prone to try to side with Jesus, even at his most dramatic, as we contemplate such scenes; but agreeing with him too quickly might distract us from registering the difficult ethical pinch he puts us in. Is it really the case that a space set aside for worship is not to involve marketing at all? By calling for the immediate cessation of sales in the temple, Jesus is calling into question one of the central means by which this sacred structure and the temple cult within it could be kept up. Houses of worship, after all, do not grow on trees. Realism says so. Perhaps we can get a sense of Jesus' hard sell if we think of the question that makes the record skip in our own world whenever a new idea appears among us. We are welcome to want to wish marketing away, but *how are you going to pay for it?* In these times of declining membership, this is a particularly relevant question for the preacher and the people of God.

Not long ago, the fire that consumed most of the Notre Dame Cathedral in Paris focused the minds of millions in the direction of this kind of question. What seemed like a unique monument of Western civilization suddenly appeared fragile and its reconstruction a crushingly expensive prospect. The news left us to mull a little harder over what we really deem sacred and necessary. Regardless of where one stood in relation to Roman Catholic tradition, it was universally understood as a loss of something crucial.

Like other ancient structures established as testaments to the transcendent, Notre Dame represents a centuries-long effort in beauty alongside all manner of ethical complications. Jews were expelled from France in the early years of its construction, for instance. Needless to say, the faith tradition it represents in the minds of the watching world often fails, catastrophically, to live up to the moral witness of Jesus and other prophets.

One can mourn the loss and celebrate the outpouring of concern and offers of financial assistance, while also wishing our country's culture extended similar energy toward drinking water in Flint, historically black churches burned down in Louisiana, and the frail infrastructure within which economically deprived Americans have access to the goods and services they need to live. Why the fuss over a building when people are dying for lack of resources? Our relationship to bricks and mortar, as our passage reminds us, is endlessly complicated.

Is there a place for gift shops and collection plates in maintaining what we think of as beautiful and holy? One would hope so, but, same as it ever was, Jesus gives us the gift of a question mark to place next to whatever it is we are thinking of as a big, loving deal. As they take in the sight of Jesus knocking over tables and imposing an order amid the moral chaos of a temple reduced to a commodity, the disciples, we are told, recall a line from a psalm that provides context for his unconventional behavior: "Zeal for your house will consume me."

Bad manners? Yes, but his zeal is righteous. That is how and why Jesus is right, and the maintainers of status quo decorum are wrong. Zeal of one kind or another, after all, is perhaps the engine of human survival. The question of what we are zealous for, in the details and the minute particulars of our budget, our bandwidth, and our everyday decisions, is one our reading brings into focus. Where our zeal is, there will our hearts be also. What we do with our zeal is what we will have done with our lives. Our zeal costs us dearly.

It certainly cost Jesus, but weirdly, it is along the broad trajectory of his teachings, his death, and his resurrection that the largely burned-down Cathedral of Notre Dame almost immediately found willing corporate sponsors, with Apple, Gucci, L'Oreal, and other moneyed interests pledging to restore it. How shall we characterize this largesse in light of our text? What would the peasant artisan-activist Jesus make of this turn of events? Would he recognize in it any sign of the coming reign of God on which he banked his life? It is hard to say.

We do have a clue in Jesus' back-and-forth with those asking for an explanation for behaving like a vandal. "Destroy the whole thing," Jesus, ever one for an enigmatic saying, says, "and I will raise it up in three days." His interlocutors push back with dismay over how he could be expected to accomplish such a thing when the last rebuilding of the temple took forty-six years. According to John's Gospel, Jesus' disciples came to believe Jesus had his own resurrection in mind, but we can zoom out even further to consider the zeal that the witness of Jesus and other prophets put in motion, the righteous zealotry of right relationship between people and things, what some figures refer to as Beloved Community. The conviviality toward self, neighbor, and enemy that Jesus commands is a church not made with hands, an impregnable movement, a more lasting structure than market forces can facilitate or imagine.

As we ought to be when we are contemplating the actions, the incarceration, and the execution of Jesus of Nazareth in our own context, we are awash in paradox. What does the witness of Jesus have to do with an outpouring of corporate love for a cathedral in Paris? An awful lot. Jesus' clearing of the temple proposed a new normal, a normal *so new* that we have to strive to pick up anew the teaching he set down—in speech and action—so long ago. In order to sustain itself, the Roman Empire had to pretend, at least on paper, to follow his lead. When the Notre Dame Cathedral burned down, few moneyed entities could afford to be seen standing idly by as this storied testament to a communal movement of lonely Jewish revolutionaries lay in ruins.

The good news of Beloved Community to which Jesus commissioned his friends to bear witness has a longer reach than any one building. In a deep sense, all governments, institutions, corporations, and other organizers of human resources, in the final analysis, take their measure by it. So it is with ourselves. We each have zeal, of one kind or another, but in which directions are we employing it? What contexts do we find to live out our excitement? What do we get worked up about? May we follow Jesus' zealous lead in quiet and risky ways in the worship that is our everyday saying and doing.

DAVID DARK

Fourth Sunday in Lent

Numbers 21:4–9
Psalm 107:1–3, 17–22

Ephesians 2:1–10
John 3:14–21

Numbers 21:4–9

⁴From Mount Hor they set out by the way to the Red Sea, to go around the land of Edom; but the people became impatient on the way. ⁵The people spoke against God and against Moses, "Why have you brought us up out of Egypt to die in the wilderness? For there is no food and no water, and we detest this miserable food." ⁶Then the LORD sent poisonous serpents among the people, and they bit the people, so that many Israelites died. ⁷The people came to Moses and said, "We have sinned by speaking against the LORD and against you; pray to the LORD to take away the serpents from us." So Moses prayed for the people. ⁸And the LORD said to Moses, "Make a poisonous serpent, and set it on a pole; and everyone who is bitten shall look at it and live." ⁹So Moses made a serpent of bronze, and put it upon a pole; and whenever a serpent bit someone, that person would look at the serpent of bronze and live.

Commentary 1: Connecting the Reading with Scripture

This passage from Numbers 21:4–9 is part of a lengthy account in Numbers 11–25 that describes various episodes that occurred as the Israelites journeyed through the wilderness toward the promised land of Canaan. It begins with the people at Mount Hor, which is west of the southern end of the Dead Sea and is the place where Moses' brother Aaron has just died (Num. 20:22–29). As they head east to go around the land of Edom, on the southeast shore of the Dead Sea, the Israelites speak against Moses and God, and begin to complain about the lack of food and water. The timing of their complaint is somewhat odd, because just prior to this God had responded favorably to the people's request for protection and allowed them to defeat a group of Canaanites that had attacked them and taken some of them as prisoners (21:1–3).

The grumbling of the Israelites in this story is one of a number of passages in Numbers 11–25 that describe rebellion and complaints by groups and individuals as the people make their forty-year journey, a long-winded trek that served as punishment for another instance of complaining

(chap. 14). The pattern is established in the opening verses when the Israelites complain about their situation, which causes the Lord to send fire against them. This leads them to cry out to Moses, who then successfully intercedes with the Deity on their behalf (11:1–3).

In the next chapter, Moses' siblings Aaron and Miriam speak out against Moses' marriage to a Cushite woman and claim they are on equal footing with him as God's spokespersons. This results in Miriam's being temporarily punished by God with leprosy. Soon after this, a team of scouts sent by Moses to survey the land brings back a false report that causes the people to lose heart and complain about their situation. Only Moses' intercession on their behalf prevents God from destroying the Israelites (Num. 14). A sermon on this passage might highlight the theme of complaint and ask the congregation to consider the role it plays in their lives.

Further rebellion is reported in the story about Korah, Dathan, and Abiram, who are swallowed up by the ground after they complain and question the authority of Moses and Aaron (Num. 16). In these traditions, Moses

The Remedy for This Evil

Why need we enlarge on the pleasures of the belly? For we may almost say that there are as may varieties of pleasure as there are of gentle flavours which are presented to the belly, and which excite the outward sense. Was it not then, with great propriety that pleasure, which is derived from many varied sources, was presented to an animal endowed with varied faculties? On this account, too, that part in us which is analogous to the people, and which acts the part of a multitude, when it seeks "the houses in Egypt," that is to say, in its corporeal habitation, becomes entangled in pleasures which bring on death; not that death which is a separation of soul and body, but that which is the destruction of the soul by vice. . . .

How, then, can there be any remedy for this evil? When another serpent is created, the enemy of the serpent which came to Eve, namely, the word of temperance: for temperance is opposite to pleasure, which is a varied evil, being a varied virtue, and one ready to repel its enemy pleasure. Accordingly, God commands Moses to make the serpent according to temperance; and he says, "Make thyself a serpent, and set it up for a sign." Do you see that Moses makes this serpent for no one else but for himself? for God commands him, "Make it for thyself," in order that you may know that temperance is not the gift of every one, but only of that man who loves God. And we must consider why Moses makes a brazen serpent, when no command was given to him respecting the material of which it was to be formed. May it not have been for this reason? In the first place, the graces of God are immaterial, being themselves only ideas, and destitute of any distinctive quality; but the graces of mortal men are only beheld in connection with matter. In the second place, not only does Moses love the incorporeal virtues, but our own souls, not being able to put off their bodies, do likewise aim at corporeal virtue, and reason, in accordance with temperance, is likened to the strong and solid substance of brass, inasmuch as it is form and not easily cut through. And perhaps brass may also have been selected inasmuch as temperance in the man who loves God is a most honourable thing, and like gold; though it has only a secondary place in a man who has received wisdom and improved in it. "And whomsoever the one serpent bites, if he looks upon the brazen serpent shall live:" in which Moses speaks truly, for if the mind that has been bitten by pleasure, that is by the serpent which was sent to Eve, shall have strength to behold the beauty of temperance, that is to say, the serpent made by Moses in a manner affecting the soul, and to behold God himself through the medium of the serpent, it shall live. Only let it see and contemplate it intellectually.

Philo of Alexandria, *On the Allegories of the Sacred Laws*, in *The Works of Philo Judœs*, trans. C. D. Yonge (London: George Bell and Sons, 1890), 99–100.

tempers the divine wrath by convincing God either not to harm the people or to punish only the guilty parties, even sometimes shaming God by declaring that destruction would make God look bad to the other nations. The story of the bronze serpent continues this pattern of Moses acting as an intermediary between the complaining Israelites and their God, who wants to put them in their place. These complaint stories are also related to the theme of the people's disobedience and inability to remain faithful to God that dominates the books of Deuteronomy through 2 Kings—books that follow Numbers

and recount the history of Israel from the entry into the land until the end of the kingdom when the Babylonians invaded in 587 BCE.

Serpents are mentioned in other biblical passages, with the most well known being the snake in the garden of Eden that tempts Adam and Eve and becomes the enemy of humanity (Gen. 3:1–7, 11–15). Like the serpents in Numbers, which will be used to both hurt and to heal, the snake in the garden is ambivalent in terms of its relationship to the well-being of human beings.

Snakes play a role in two other traditions associated with Moses, and both feature a staff reminiscent of the pole in the story in Numbers 21. When Moses encounters God at the burning bush, the Deity tries to convince him to go to Pharaoh and demand the Israelites' release by temporarily changing his staff into a snake that writhes on the ground (Exod. 4:1–5). When Moses and Aaron come before the Egyptian ruler a few chapters later, Aaron throws his staff down before Pharaoh, and it becomes a snake. When Egyptian sorcerers duplicate this feat, Aaron's staff/snake swallows up theirs (Exod. 7:8–13). Unlike the snakes in these other passages, the snakes in the Numbers 21 story are described as poisonous (Num. 21:6, 8). The Hebrew word (*saraf*) can also mean "fiery" or "burning," so there is some ambiguity as to their exact nature. The same term in found in the story of Isaiah's call to be a prophet, when a group of six-winged seraphs proclaim God's holiness in the temple and one of them touches the prophet's mouth with a live coal to remove his sin (Isa. 6:1–7). The plural form of the Hebrew word (*serafim*) is the origin of the term "seraphim," which describes a category of angelic beings.

There are specific references to the episode involving Moses and the serpents elsewhere in the Bible. A passage in Deuteronomy refers to God as the one "who led you through the great and terrible wilderness, an arid wasteland with poisonous snakes and scorpions" (Deut. 8:15). The Hebrew word translated "poisonous" in this verse is *saraf*, as in Numbers 21. King Hezekiah of Judah is lauded for his efforts to instill proper worship, including his destruction of the bronze serpent from Moses' time, because it had become an illegal object of worship (2 Kgs. 18:4). In this verse the serpent's name Nehushtan means "made of bronze," and it derives from the Hebrew word for bronze (*nekhoshet*), which is a word play in Numbers 21, due to its similarity to the word for serpent (*nakhash*). Here

the serpent is associated with improper cultic practices; so it is viewed more negatively than in Numbers 21, where it is an object that heals and saves.

That healing quality is highlighted in the New Testament's sole reference to Moses and the bronze serpent in a conversation Jesus has with a Jewish leader named Nicodemus, recorded only in John's Gospel (John 3:14–15). Here the Gospel reinterprets the scene in the wilderness so that the serpent represents Jesus and the pole on which it is placed represents the cross on which Jesus will die. Whereas in Numbers 21 a person who had been bitten by a poisonous snake needed only to look upon the bronze serpent to be healed, it is now faith in Jesus that is required, and it will lead to the reward of everlasting life for the person who believes.

In each passage, both the danger people find themselves in and the means by which they are healed are connected to what has been lifted up before them. The preacher might explore this theme with the congregation by asking them to reflect on the things in their lives that both harm and heal them. In the wilderness tradition, the life-threatening effects of the bites they have received are neutralized by their gazing upon an image of the snakes responsible for their condition.

Similarly, in John's Gospel the pain caused by human mortality and most evident in the reality of death is removed by Jesus when he defeats death and makes eternal life possible for all who believe in him. In this way, John's Gospel presents Jesus in the double role of both Moses and the bronze serpent. Like Moses, he serves as an intermediary between God and the people, and like the serpent, he provides the means by which human beings are able to overcome that which threatens them.

JOHN KALTNER

Commentary 2: Connecting the Reading with the World

Lent is the season of self-denial. Since Ash Wednesday the people have been encouraged to deny the urges, delights, and delicacies that make life good and pleasurable. Some set up

elaborate and ambitious lists of the things they are giving up for the Lenten season—like our New Year's resolutions. We begin these seasons with good intentions. About this time in the journey, the challenges of personal sacrifice are heightened, and the resolutions soon become daily reminders of how difficult it is to be human. We are face to face with the possibilities and confirmations of failure at the most intimate places of life. Some have slipped up; others have resigned themselves to the fact that sacrifice is too hard and unnecessary. About this time in the Lenten season, a certain resentment of both God and the clergy grows; are they not the ones who have insisted that to be faithful is to give up their favorite things?

Most people want change. No one wants *to change.* The sin of nostalgia takes over, memories are cluttered, and people start to remember "the better days" that have now passed—and, in fact, never were. They believe that where they once were, both in time and in place, was so much better than the present hardships. We never seem to recognize that new life and the change that comes with it do not come easily. Living in the transition between what was and what will be is uncomfortable territory. Yet life is one long transition.

The text from Numbers serves as a reminder of how quickly the challenges of sacrifice and change are turned into fault finding in leadership. Who exactly is responsible for the rough and tough places along our journey? The wandering children of Israel, as they usually do, place the blame at the feet of God and Moses: "Why have you brought us out here?" Their blame offers a possible topic of discussion at the pulpit: Whom do we unfairly (and fairly) blame for the difficulties in our lives? How do we responsibly separate the difficulties caused by our actions from those that stem from a larger system of injustice?

In a pivotal scene in *The Wizard of Oz,* Dorothy and her compatriots return to the Emerald City after successfully vanquishing the wicked witch. When the wizard tells them to come back the next day, the ever curious and wandering Toto ends up at a curtain and manages to pull it back to expose the frantic wizard pulling the levers that create the smoke and mirrors producing the ominous image of the "great and powerful Oz." The people are paying attention

to those behind the curtains, the smocks, the vestments, and the ecclesial mystique as never before. But those with smocks and vestments are not needed to produce an image of God. God shows up profoundly, on God's own, irrespective of our attempts to make God appear.

At this particular time in history we have uncovered and exposed years of sexual misconduct, abuse, and violence perpetrated by clergy. These heinous and egregious acts make the cries for justice and restoration more pronounced. It is not rare to hear these stories of pain and violation followed by the resolve: "That's why I am leaving God." The impulse to implicate God by equating the behaviors of faith leaders with God's action, though understandable, does not acknowledge that God is indeed present in the very cries for justice and accountability.

God continues to show up and be present in the community despite the tragic, traumatic, and trifling behaviors of people who are supposed to "represent" the Divine. Given the truth of these realities, communities of believers are called to create appropriate, life-giving, and healthy distance between God and religious leadership and to hold clerics and institutions accountable for their behaviors in community. Indeed, how to do so—creating appropriate distance while holding those in leadership accountable—is an important topic for a sermon.

This text from Numbers is the last of the murmurings that have accompanied the former slaves, now freed from Egypt. The people's railings are not without warrant. They are worried about their very survival. There is no water or edible food. These questions are still significant in the present day. In urban centers in the United States where poor and black communities are concentrated, there are food deserts where affordable, fresh, and nutritious food is scarce.[1] "How are we going to feed our people?" is a legitimate question in the wilderness.

In April 2014, the governmental authorities in Flint, Michigan, switched the drinking water source to the Flint River. As a result of that decision to save money, black and poor neighborhoods have toxic levels of lead in the drinking water. The outcry from the community in this

---

1. For an effective strategic addressing of this issue, see the Campaign Against Hunger New York City at www.tcahnyc.org.

case is warranted. Is it not appropriate to cry out when life-giving necessities are denied?

Indeed, there is a key difference between Flint and the situation described in Numbers. In Numbers, God has repeatedly saved and provided for the wandering Israelites. Unlike today, God's actions to correct situations of need have been direct, clearly evident, and nearly immediate. This is why God's first reaction to another instance of complaining is fierce anger. Indeed, God summons the serpents to come and kill the murmurers with their poisonous bites. As with many prophets, Moses is both chided for the bad behavior of the people and yet asked to pray for them to God, who tells Moses to have the people look upon a serpent on a pole.

The serpent symbolized both poison and healing (from poison) in many ancient cultures, which is in part why the caduceus, with its entwined snakes, is the symbol for the practice of medicine. For our purposes, this passage presents an opportunity for speaking of healing and health. Perhaps this is a perfect Sunday to remind people to see about their own advocacy in their preventive health care and/or encourage ministries to invest in preventive health care. It might also be the appropriate time to discuss the need for everyone to have access to affordable health care.

What are the symbols and icons that give one life? We all have them.

The people remind Moses of his responsibility to take their hurts and concerns before God: "Pray to the Lord to take the snakes away from us" (Num. 21:7). Gary Gunderson offers a significant reorientation of understanding health, health care, and wellness. The normal conversation on these matters is dominated by the language of "risk factors." Gunderson proposes that instead of speaking of risk factors, we should frame the conversation in terms of what are the "life-giving factors" for wellness.[2]

Instead of making a pronouncement of words, God calls Moses to construct something the people can see and experience. The bites of seraph serpents have been the cause of death. Moses is told to place the image of the snake on a pole so that the people may look and live. God makes the image of fear and death into an icon of life. This is a radical reorientation to the places and objects that induce pain.

What things do we need to place before the people, in order that that they might be spared from premature and unnecessary death?

GARY V. SIMPSON

---

2. Gary Gunderson, with Larry Pray, *Leading Causes of Life: Five Fundamentals to Change the Way You Live* (Nashville: Abingdon, 2009).

Psalm 107:1–3, 17–22

¹O give thanks to the LORD, for he is good;
    for his steadfast love endures forever.
²Let the redeemed of the LORD say so,
    those he redeemed from trouble
³and gathered in from the lands,
    from the east and from the west,
    from the north and from the south.

. . . .

¹⁷Some were sick through their sinful ways,
    and because of their iniquities endured affliction;
¹⁸they loathed any kind of food,
    and they drew near to the gates of death.
¹⁹Then they cried to the LORD in their trouble,
    and he saved them from their distress;
²⁰he sent out his word and healed them,
    and delivered them from destruction.
²¹Let them thank the LORD for his steadfast love,
    for his wonderful works to humankind.
²²And let them offer thanksgiving sacrifices,
    and tell of his deeds with songs of joy.

Connecting the Psalm with Scripture and Worship

Psalm 107 immediately announces itself as a psalm of thanksgiving: "O give thanks to the LORD, for he is good; for his steadfast love endures forever" (Ps. 107:1). Yet these words of thanksgiving are not called forth from those who have lived a life of blameless ease; instead, the psalmist summons "the redeemed of the LORD . . . , those he redeemed from trouble" (v. 2). In short, the *hesed* or steadfast love of the Lord has not been encountered in the midst of comfort and prosperity, but amid experiences of deep trouble and pain.

Having invited God's people to tell the truth about God's redemption and love from all the corners of the earth (v. 3), the psalm then continues with four episodes describing times when Israel found themselves in "trouble" and yet experienced the steadfast love of the Lord. Two episodes describe instances of existential and natural chaos (vv. 4–9, 23–32), while the other two episodes detail times of trouble caused by disobedience and sin against God (vv. 10–16, 17–22).[1] Returning to the thesis statement laid out in verse 1, each stanza ends with an invitation to give thanks to God for God's steadfast love. The psalm ends with a proclamation praising all that God has done (vv. 33–42) and a final challenge to "all those who are wise" to "consider the steadfast love of the LORD" (v. 43).

The architects of the lectionary invite us to focus on the opening verses of the psalm and the third of four historical episodes. In this stanza, some of Israel are "sick through their sinful ways" (v. 17). Whether suffering physical or spiritual illness, the psalmist confesses that it is the "iniquities" of the people that have led to their "affliction" and brought them "near to the gates of death" (vv. 17–18). Yet the afflicted

---

1. Jorge Mejía, "Some Observations on Psalms 107," *Biblical Theology Bulletin* 5 (1975): 58, 66.

"cried to the LORD in their trouble, and [God] saved them from their distress" (v. 19).

While not explicitly named as such, this stanza of Psalm 107 could easily be conceived as a poetic retelling of the story from Numbers 21:4–9, the first lectionary reading for the day. This short, somewhat odd story in Numbers takes place during a time of transition, as the Israelites are on the move, as well as on the cusp of ushering in the new generation that will claim the promised land. Yet some things never change—specifically, the Israelites' desert grumbling. They complain against Moses and God about the wilderness conditions, even making the absurd statement that they have "no food and no water" while in the same breath they whine that "we detest this miserable food" (Num. 21:5). In response to their faithless murmuring, the Lord sends poisonous snakes to bite the people, but as in the psalm, when the people confess their sin to Moses and Moses calls to God, God offers a remedy—a bronze serpent to be placed in the camp that, if looked upon, would allow those bitten by the poisonous snakes to live. This six-verse story in the midst of the Israelites' journey from Mount Hor toward the Transjordan can feel out of place. Yet, in the light of Psalm 107, this story from Numbers 21 might be placed in the larger arc of God's redemptive work, revealing the nature of God's steadfast love and calling for human confession and response.

Psalm 107 imagines all stories of Israelite disobedience and struggle as an opportunity to apprehend God's nature more fully. Though the Israelites grumbled against God in the wilderness, God ultimately offered healing and forgiveness. As the psalmist writes, God "saved them from their distress; he sent out his word and healed them, and delivered them from destruction" (Ps. 107:19b–20). A key part of God's steadfast love is healing and forgiveness. In a story filled with odd complaints and poisonous snakes, Psalm 107 encourages preachers to consider how the nature of God is revealed in the text—as a God who grieves over faithlessness, but whose steadfast love ultimately offers redemption, healing, and forgiveness.

Psalm 107 also invites preachers and teachers to recognize the importance of the voice of the people. As in Numbers 21, throughout the psalm, God's steadfast love (*hesed*) is catalyzed by the cry of the people (Ps. 107:19). Both Numbers 21 and Psalm 107 embolden people to trust in God's love and cry out when in distress. In both texts, God does not ignore the voices of the people, but receives their cries and responds in mercy.

However, this is not the only summons offered for people to raise their voices. As mentioned earlier, each historical stanza of Psalm 107 ends with a call for people to raise their voices in thanks and praise. In the pericope for the day, the people are called both to "thank the LORD for his steadfast love, for his wonderful works to humankind" (v. 21) as well as "tell of [God's] deeds with songs of joy" (v. 22b). Psalm 107 guides faithful people toward a response to the snake-filled story of Numbers 21: to cry out to God when in distress, to offer praise for God's faithful love, and to testify to the ways we have experienced God's mercy at work.

Psalm 107 may find a rich place in worship as a response to the good news proclaimed in the sermon. The congregation might enact the praise and testimony to which they are called through the reading or singing of the psalm communally or responsively. Psalm 107 especially lends itself to antiphonal singing, with the first verse of the psalm sung as the repeated refrain.

Psalm 107 richly illumines the story of Moses and the bronze serpent in Numbers 21, for it invites praise and thanksgiving, while taking seriously the trouble of the world as well as human complicity in such trouble. Not in spite of, but through such trouble, the faithful are reassured of the mercy and steadfast love of the Lord, as well as the power of their own voices to cry, praise, and testify.

KIMBERLY R. WAGNER

Ephesians 2:1–10

¹You were dead through the trespasses and sins ²in which you once lived, following the course of this world, following the ruler of the power of the air, the spirit that is now at work among those who are disobedient. ³All of us once lived among them in the passions of our flesh, following the desires of flesh and senses, and we were by nature children of wrath, like everyone else. ⁴But God, who is rich in mercy, out of the great love with which he loved us ⁵even when we were dead through our trespasses, made us alive together with Christ—by grace you have been saved— ⁶and raised us up with him and seated us with him in the heavenly places in Christ Jesus, ⁷so that in the ages to come he might show the immeasurable riches of his grace in kindness toward us in Christ Jesus. ⁸For by grace you have been saved through faith, and this is not your own doing; it is the gift of God— ⁹not the result of works, so that no one may boast. ¹⁰For we are what he has made us, created in Christ Jesus for good works, which God prepared beforehand to be our way of life.

Commentary 1: Connecting the Reading with Scripture

Today's epistle reading celebrates the magnitude of God's love, mercy, and grace. It follows a prayer that focuses on the great things God has done for Christ. That prayer ends by saying that God has enthroned Christ above all powers and given him authority over all things. Our passage picks up this theme, now turning to the great things God does for believers through Christ.

We cannot comprehend the enormity of what God has done for us without recognizing the depth of our need. The first three verses of our reading describe our dire situation. These verses say "you" (i.e., Gentiles) were dead, a rather startling image, because of sins. These are not just occasional mistakes. Ephesians is talking about an orientation of life. They "lived" in sins. They lived in conformity with the values of "this world." By doing so, the writer says, they were living the way the ruler of demons directed them. He says this spirit still determines the life orientation of unbelievers.

This grim assessment does not describe just Gentiles, because "we all," Jews and Gentiles, were in this position. All lived in accord with our fleshly desires and thoughts. The designations of "flesh" and "thoughts" do not describe parts of human nature but indicate that the whole person was controlled by these desires. Even worse, this is who we are "by nature" (Eph. 2:3). This is not a statement about predestination, because we are all in this category.

Many in our churches find it difficult to think of themselves in these terms. They grew up in the church and have always been decent people. This description comes from a faithful Jewish believer who has lived a good life, yet he recognizes that we are all trapped in the political, social, and cultural structures that cause us to sin. We turn our backs on what God wants for the world when we buy groceries that were picked by people who live in conditions we would find unacceptable for our children or when we buy cell phones made with dangerous metals that unprotected children retrieve from piles of old phones. Much of our participation in common economic life implicates us in injustice that opposes the will of God. These are the kinds of behaviors Ephesians sees as governed by the "ruler of the power of the air" (v. 2). Like the first readers of Ephesians, we are captured by this sin and at the same time are willing and often unwitting participants in it.

Ephesians identifies a powerful response to this dire circumstance: God's love and mercy.

Verse 4 is an acclamation of the character of God. God's response to the willful disobedience of humanity should be wrath: "we were children of wrath" (v. 3). Instead, God's response to human sinfulness is that God loves us. This dramatic turn is shocking. It is not at all what is warranted. The reason God loves is that God has mercy as a part of the core of God's nature: God is "rich in mercy." God's willingness and ability to save is grounded in the mercy and love that are essential elements of God's nature. All that follows in verses 5–10 is an explanation of how God shows that love.

Verse 5 returns to the image of verse 1: we were dead. God's response is that God makes believers alive together with Christ. Ephesians describes this further as being raised together with Christ and being enthroned with Christ in the heavens. Believers are brought into the gifts God has given Christ. While the thanksgiving of 1:15–23 celebrates the things God has done for Christ, our passage makes believers participants in those gifts. Because they have identified themselves with Christ, they now share in what Christ has been given.

In the midst of this listing of ways believers share in the resurrection and exaltation of Christ, the writer breaks off to interject the reminder that "you have been saved by grace" (v. 5). Salvation is often talked about as something to be experienced in the future or something granted in the past, but here the writer uses the perfect tense ("have been"). In Greek, this tense designates something that happened in the past and continues to have consequences in the present. Interpreters often note that Ephesians talks of possessing salvation in the present more than other Pauline texts. In our verses believers are already raised and seated in the heavens.

The undisputed Pauline letters always reserve that possession of resurrection and exaltation for the future. Claiming those things as present, however, helps this author extol God's love. Since it is obvious that they are not literally enthroned, the author still reserves blessings for the future as well. Believers experience the life God gives in Christ now and will have it more fully in the future. The author claims the blessings now to provide readers assurance and to help them maintain the perspective on all things that possessing these blessings should give them.

Verse 7 continues the focus on the amazing abundance of God's grace. In Romans Paul says that the salvation that comes through Christ's death is a demonstration of God's justice and mercy (Rom. 3:25–26). Ephesians here narrows the focus, saying only that God has given all these things to believers to demonstrate the riches of God's grace in kindness. Ephesians says God saves through Christ because it is God's nature to love deeply, even those who have turned away.

Verses 5–7 describe the whole process of salvation as accomplished by God alone. After repeating this proclamation, verses 8–10 provide one explanation for what that means: we are saved by grace through faith and not by works. This contrast is different from what we find in the undisputed Paulines. While Paul contrasts faith with "works of the law," Ephesians contrasts faith with works in a more general way. Ephesians sets the contrast in these starker terms to keep the focus on the love and grace of God. The salvation that raises believers from the dead is solely the product of the creating activity of God.

While salvation comes solely through the grace of God, this does not mean there is nothing for the recipients to do. Rather, God prepared in advance a life of doing good works. Such a life is part of accepting the gift of salvation. These good works are what God created the saved to do. Doing good works is to determine the orientation of believers' lives. Ephesians uses the same verb here and in verse 2 (*peripateō*). In verse 2, those who were dead in sin "lived," conducted their lives, according to the standards of the world; in verse 10 those made alive "live," conduct their lives, according to God's expectation that they do good works. Salvation has changed the orientation of their lives. This new orientation is part of the salvation they have already received.

All of the readings for this week celebrate God's saving love and mercy. The Numbers passage, like the epistle, first describes the sinful people and then tells of the mercy and salvation God provides. The Gospel reading draws on this story from the wilderness to interpret the coming death of Jesus as an expression of God's love and mercy. Like our epistle text, the psalm today is a celebration of God's salvation that has already been experienced. It calls the saved not only to thank God but also to tell others about God's saving activity for them. This week's texts urge us to see the death and resurrection of Jesus as an expression of God's enormous love for humanity.

JERRY L. SUMNEY

Commentary 2: Connecting the Reading with the World

At first glance, this text appears a little out of place as the epistle reading for the Fourth Sunday in Lent. It begins with a description of the Ephesian church prior to its experience of Christ, before it relates God's transformative, life-giving work. The epistle underscores the benevolent nature of God and stresses that salvation is made possible only through God's merciful acts of grace. In short, it explains that salvation is a gift from God, not something achievable through one's own doing. So, what is this reading doing in the Lenten cycle of the Revised Common Lectionary? Reformation Sunday seems a better fit for a text discussing the relationship between faith, grace, and works, and Easter seems a better fit for a text centered on the Ephesians' deliverance from death to life.

Lent is usually thought of as a season of penitence. It is the time of the year we stop to reflect on the ways we fail to follow the life God desires for us. In preparation for the paschal season, we use the seven weeks leading up to Easter as a time to journey with Jesus to the cross. Through careful introspection and spiritual reflection, we search deep within ourselves to identify where we fall short in life, to name what is wrong in our world, and to recognize our complicity in it. As the author of our epistle unfolds for the Ephesians in verses 1–3, the world is a place fraught with pursuits contrary to the good works God prepared to be our way of life. Like the earliest Christians, we too live in a world designed to serve the people in power and dominated by systems of oppression that seek to elevate wealth, suppress minority voices, and enforce the status quo.

Within this season, however, there is light amid the darkness. Laetare Sunday, the fourth Sunday in the season of Lent, serves as a moment within our journey when we pause to rejoice, to celebrate, to look ahead in anticipation of the resurrection of Jesus. It might help to think of this Sunday as the Sunday when we briefly look up. In other words, we have spent the past three weeks with our heads down, looking at the road, making note of every bump and wrong turn along the way. This week we stop and take a moment to look up and remind ourselves of where we are going. Then, only after this brief glance forward, we resume our journey with the reassurance that what is necessary has already been accomplished. We put our heads back down and resume our inner journey to the cross.

This passage from Ephesians is perfect for Laetare Sunday. It reminds us that this journey to the cross, this season of penance, is followed by a journey out of the grave. Following a description of the Ephesians' death in verses 1–3, the author abruptly transitions to a description of their salvation from God. He writes, "*But God* [italics mine], who is rich in mercy, out of the great love with which he loved us even when we were dead through our trespasses, made us alive together with Christ—by grace you have been saved" (vv. 4–5). Grace follows transgression; life follows death. Just as the author of this epistle finds the Ephesians at their weakest, he reminds them "But God . . . !"

Another facet of this text that a preacher might wish to bring forward on Sunday morning is confession. Confession is a practice in identifying both our participation and our complicity in the ailments of our world. Confession names our wrongdoing and works to move us toward reconciliation with God and with one another. It is an exercise in self-examination, and for some it is even an act of preparation for the Table.

This week's epistle reading has something important to say about the nature of confession. The passage begins with a personal address. The author speaks directly to the Ephesian church, employing the plural pronoun "you" in the opening verses of the chapter (vv. 1–2). In the third verse, however, the author shifts to the first-person plural: "All of us once lived among them in the passions of our flesh, following the desires of flesh and senses, and we were by nature children of wrath, like everyone else" (v. 3). With the slip of a pronoun, the author quickly drops his accusing finger and joins the Ephesians in their journey from death to life. His accusatory description of the Ephesians' life prior to Christ has morphed into a communal confession.

There is something beautiful about a community coming together to share its struggles and failures. During the season of Lent many churches take up the practice of corporate confession as a part of their Sunday liturgy. I wonder what might transpire on Sunday morning if a church bravely gathered together during the weeks of Lent to write collectively as a community the following Sunday's prayer of confession. They might focus, for example, on their participation in larger systemic sins, such as racism, gender disparity, and economic inequality. It is often easier to admit we are wrong when we can stand alongside others and confess our transgressions side by side. There is something unique about the way a communal confession allows us to look around and recognize that we are not alone, that others alongside us have contributed to the ills of the world and that others alongside us are also committed to their repair. Some transgressions are larger than any individual. Repentance, therefore, often requires committed partnership; it requires community.

Outside of the liturgical context of this pericope, there are two points of contact between the text and our world that a pastor might wish to bring forward. The first connection concerns allegiance. Throughout this week's passage the author draws a sharp division between two realms, the realm of this world and the realm of God. The realm of this world is characterized by death, disobedience, oppressive powers, and an enslavement to earthly desires, whereas the realm of God is characterized by immeasurable grace and the good works of God as demonstrated in the life of Christ Jesus. An important concern for the author of Ephesians regards allegiance. Where does your allegiance lie, and in whom do you put your trust?

A pastor might wish to draw out some of the ways contemporary Christians negotiate their own allegiances to competing realms. What are these different realms that claim and divide our allegiance? How do we faithfully live in this world while remaining unwavering in our obedience to the inbreaking kingdom of God?

The second point of connection regards works. The author of Ephesians stresses that our salvation is not earned by our works but is a gift from God given by grace through faith. This is a commonly cited passage from Ephesians. What often gets overlooked in this passage is that we are called to participate with Christ in the good works of God (v. 10). While our gift of grace is not transactional, it is also not terminal. Grace is not the end of the story. Grace compels us to participate in the transformative works of Christ Jesus. Works, therefore, shift in meaning from an avenue for earning salvation to an opportunity for being an expression of Christ in the world. The preacher here finds reason to invite congregants to experience the joy of a free gift *and* the joyful opportunity to respond to that gift by emulating the life of Christ.

ANNA M. V. BOWDEN

John 3:14–21

¹⁴"And just as Moses lifted up the serpent in the wilderness, so must the Son of Man be lifted up, ¹⁵that whoever believes in him may have eternal life.

¹⁶"For God so loved the world that he gave his only Son, so that everyone who believes in him may not perish but may have eternal life.

¹⁷"Indeed, God did not send the Son into the world to condemn the world, but in order that the world might be saved through him. ¹⁸Those who believe in him are not condemned; but those who do not believe are condemned already, because they have not believed in the name of the only Son of God. ¹⁹And this is the judgment, that the light has come into the world, and people loved darkness rather than light because their deeds were evil. ²⁰For all who do evil hate the light and do not come to the light, so that their deeds may not be exposed. ²¹But those who do what is true come to the light, so that it may be clearly seen that their deeds have been done in God."

Commentary 1: Connecting the Reading with Scripture

With the commemoration of Jesus' death and resurrection looming in the near horizon, this passage from John 3:14–21 is a fitting selection for the Lenten season. Working in tandem with the other lectionary readings, this text succinctly proclaims God's gift of salvation, with the most famous verse in the Bible—John 3:16—as its focal point.

These verses are located at the end of Jesus' conversation with Nicodemus, who struggles to grasp the notion that one must be born from above (or born of water and Spirit) in order to enter the kingdom of God (John 3:3, 5). If Nicodemus thinks that only proselytes require spiritual rebirth—whereas the Jewish people do not, for they are already God's people—then he is understandably mystified by Jesus' statements. Here Jesus challenges Nicodemus to embrace the love of God that is expansive and radical: God loves not just Israel but also the world. Furthermore, God's love is the epitome of sacrificial love, for the divine Son is given to death for the world's salvation.

Using a double entendre implicit in the Greek verb *hypsoō*, which means "to lift up" and "to praise," John underscores that Jesus' crucifixion is at the same time his glorification. As Jesus

is hoisted up on a Roman cross, he is enthroned as king and Messiah. In John, Jesus' resurrection and ascension constitute the Son's return to the Father after having completed that which he has been sent to do (19:30).

Jesus uses an incident in Numbers 21 to emphasize the salvific efficacy of his crucifixion. In the wilderness, the Israelites complained about the lack of food and water, and God punished them by sending poisonous snakes to bite them. Many died and the people repented. God then instructed Moses to make a bronze serpent and attach it to the top of a pole, so that anyone who looked up at it would not die.

The point is not to compare Jesus to a poisonous snake, but since the bronze serpent, which is later called the Nehustan, functioned as a sign of God's healing, how much more indispensable will be the role of the Son of Man in God's saving agenda. God's plan necessitates that Jesus must, like the Nehushtan, be lifted up in crucifixion. Paradoxically, this shameful and gruesome death is the very means of his glorification, because through dying Jesus offers eternal life to all who believe (3:14–15; cf. 12:23–24). An additional parallel may be found in Jesus' identification with the Isaianic Servant of YHWH, who "poured out himself to death" (Isa. 53:12), yet "shall be exalted and lifted up" (Isa. 52:13).

Twice more in John's narrative, Jesus is said to be lifted up in reference to his crucifixion and subsequent glorification. In 8:28, the lifting up of Jesus will reveal his divine identity—"you will realize that I am he" (cf. Exod. 3:14)—and vindicate his claim to be sent from above (6:46; 8:23, 42). Then in 12:32, after having been lifted up, Jesus "will draw all people to [him]self." Since gathering is an image of salvation for Israel (Jer. 31:7–9; 32:37), Jesus hereby expands that idea of gathering only the children of Israel to include those of other nations.

Whereas the bronze serpent was intended to spare some disobedient Israelites, salvation through the death of God's Son is offered to everyone in the world who believes (John 3:16). Despite the familiarity with this verse, the word "so" in "God so loved the world" is often misconstrued. The Greek adverb *houtōs* stresses the manner of divine love rather than its quantity. The giving of God's Son refers to *the way* God showed his love for the world, rather than *how much* God loved the world. The extent of divine love is implicit in its sacrificial nature. Any attempt to quantify that love will inevitably fall short.

Jesus' mission is primarily to save and not to condemn (3:17). Throughout John, Jesus repeatedly offers life, couched in metaphors such as water, bread, and light (4:14; 6:51; 8:12). Those who refuse this gift stand self-condemned (3:18), even though the Father has given the Son the prerogative to cast judgment (5:21–22, 26–27). Those who accept Jesus come to the light and receive eternal life. Conversely, those who reject him prefer to remain in darkness, which leads to death. Here lies the irony: people who are sinful naively think that they will be safer if they hide in darkness, when it is actually by coming to Jesus—the light that overcomes darkness (1:4–5)—that they will truly be saved and safe (3:19–21).

The author consistently presents two mutually exclusive and opposing outcomes when it comes to one's response to Jesus. The dualisms in this passage can be found elsewhere in John's narrative. There are only two options or loci of identification: light versus darkness (1:5; 8:12; 12:35, 46), belief versus unbelief (6:35–40;

14:10–12), life versus death (5:24, 29; 10:28). One resides in one realm or in the other. In this choice of eternal consequence, there can be no compromise.

The Old Testament reading for this Sunday (Num. 21:4–9) provides the historical background to Jesus' being lifted up in 3:14. This story also illustrates the pattern evident in the divine-human relationship: people sin, God judges, people repent, God saves. In its entirety, Psalm 107 presents multiple scenarios in which this pattern repeats itself. The verses selected for today's reading speak of sin and iniquities resulting in sickness and affliction, but when people cry out to God, God heals, delivers, redeems, and saves, because God's love is steadfast and enduring.

In Ephesians 2, when Paul describes the readers' prior condition as being "dead through the trespasses and sins" (Eph. 2:1, 5), he refers to all Christians, whether Jewish or Gentile, as objects of God's mercy, beneficiaries of God's grace, and recipients of God's salvation through Jesus Christ. In agreement with John 3:16, Paul affirms the universality of God's gift of salvation.

Taken together, these four lectionary texts show the expanding scope of salvation as God's timeline progresses through the history of Israel to Jesus and the early church. The divine design is for salvation to move from a particular group to the nations. Although the cycle of sin, judgment, repentance, and salvation is played out again and again in Israel's history, these smaller cycles lead up to the coming of Jesus, in whose death and resurrection God deals with sin once and for all, so that those who repent, believe in Jesus, and come to the light will also receive eternal life once and for all.

Does Nicodemus finally grasp Jesus' point? The answer is not found in chapter 3, but in Nicodemus's subsequent appearances in the narrative. In chapter 7, he calls for his fellow Pharisees to give Jesus a fair hearing before judging him, and is taunted by his peers as a result (7:50–52). More telling is the account of Nicodemus joining Joseph of Arimathea as the two bold disciples ask Pilate for Jesus' body and then honor the Messiah with a burial fit for a king (19:38–42). This religious leader has made the transition from darkness to light.

The same challenge is issued at this season of Lent to all who ponder the saving act of God: "Everyone who believes in [God's Son] may not perish but may have eternal life" (3:16b). Even though Jesus has already come, the final judgment lies yet in the future. Since there is still time, is God's church faithful and effective in preaching the good news?

DIANE G. CHEN

Commentary 2: Connecting the Reading with the World

The frequency with which John 3:16 is cited on billboards, posters held aloft at sporting events, baseball caps, bumper stickers, and T-shirts can distract us from its power. Pulling it out of context and isolating it can make it appear like a kind of formula for the afterlife. When we receive its illuminating strangeness in the context of a rare and somewhat philosophical exchange, we see it as an initiation into mystery, calling readers toward introspection and a deeper leveling with self and others.

Under the cover of darkness, Nicodemus has come to praise Jesus, at which point they engage in a conversation about the nature of conversion. Nicodemus is largely persuaded by Jesus' signs, but Jesus has pressed him to think through what it means to be born anew, to be born of God's spirit. Just as Moses lifted up a bronze serpent to complaining and snake-bitten Israelites for healing and deliverance, Jesus now appears as a living sign of eternal life, a public demonstration of what an imperishable existence looks like. A wise preacher would do well to think about how we, as the people of God, reflect Jesus, the living sign of eternal life, and how we fail to do so.

Jesus' explanation of what he is up to is attentive to process. If Nicodemus was hoping to fit Jesus into any preconceived program, he is bound to be frustrated. Jesus will not let him leave with a teaching or a sign that can be filed away. He is instead inviting to a lifelong movement of righteousness, even as his enigmatic sayings reflect the understanding that nobody can force-feed a realization. Being born anew is a process rather than a program, and true conversion, Jesus seems to say, is a long acquaintance with what is real, a process involving shade and illumination, darkness and light, denial and acceptance. As readers of John's Gospel, we are told that, in Jesus, light has indeed come into the world, but we are also invited to grapple with how to maneuver our way into its presence in a consistent and lasting way in spite of all the darkness.

There is a moment within the popular lore of *Star Wars*, specifically *The Empire Strikes Back*, when young Luke Skywalker is trying to complete his training as a Jedi. He jogs through a swamp with Yoda on his back, urging him to feel the power of the Force running through him, while worrying aloud that he will not be able to rightly discern good from evil (the dark side of the Force from the light) when it counts. When they pause to rest, Luke senses something amiss:

> "There's something not right. . . . I feel cold."
> Yoda gestures in the direction of a cave: "That place is strong with the dark side of the Force. A domain of evil it is. . . . And you must go."
> "What's in there?"
> "Only what you take with you."[1]

Consider the power of that line: Only what you take with you.

Nicodemus knows something is up with Jesus, and he has come to him with compliments. Jesus, though, is more than just another commendable teacher. What is needed for Nicodemus to proceed is a full immersion in a whole new way of thinking, seeing, and being, but Jesus cannot take the next step for him or anyone else. He can pull out the poetry. He can speak of wind and water and being born

---

1. *The Empire Strikes Back*, episode V of *Star Wars*, produced by Lucasfilms, 1980.

a second time, but the question of what to *do* with and about Jesus is a life's work, a journey into the eternal now. That deep engagement with the transforming power of God, which will look a little different for everyone, will also be a matter of what hopes and fears we bring to the table. Because it is a process, what we find *in* Jesus, his person and his teachings, will have a lot to do with our own context. We will see, at least initially, whatever it is we are already up to.

As Jesus explains to Nicodemus, someone might conclude that Jesus was sent to condemn us. Jesus might seem to condemn the world as it is, certainly, but also our own process. To do so would be to perceive Jesus' mission wrongly. God has not sent Jesus to condemn us, but to save us through him. The realization of God's life abundant made known in an encounter in Jesus might trigger our sense of shame, scarcity, and anxiety at first blush, but it is, through and through, abundant life nonetheless. Our defensive response does not change the fact that Jesus comes to save, rescuing us from every form of perishing.

Nevertheless there is judgment, and it arises in the fact that Jesus is a bearer of a light brought into the world that, as light does, exposes the deeds of those who prefer darkness. Light cannot *not* do that. To the extent that we do and speak truly, light makes these words and deeds even clearer. Alternately, our habits of denial are unmasked and made evident in a deep encounter with Jesus. If sin is active flight from a lived realization of available data, light will, by being light, make us more aware of sin. Light clarifies. What will we see when we move toward it? Only what we take with us. Yoda knows the score.

Is this not a trustworthy principle? Is it not the case that, when we open a Bible, read a poem, look at a screen, or listen to a song, we will bring what we are going through? "Only what you take with you" is an awfully helpful line for naming the risk and reception of media intake. I may try to avoid a realization, but there is a sense in which I often only access it more deeply when I try to escape it by reaching for my phone. The unconscious will have its way anyway. That cave, that hole, that dark and brooding abyss, is before us, in one way or another, at all times, and, as Jesus understood, it is something of a mirror. There is no getting away from yourself. Projection is, it turns out, nonoptional. Carl Jung could even spin it positively: "The cave you fear to enter holds that treasure that you seek."

Taken all by its lonesome, John 3:16 can appear before us with the broadband simplicity of a sales pitch: Believe in Jesus, have eternal life. A generalization might indeed serve as an entry point, but the imperishable life to which Jesus calls is an immersion in nuance and specificity, a deepening engagement with reality, rather than a flight from it. Taken in context, Jesus' words are an ethical summons to deep mindfulness of self and others, deep acquaintance with our inner situation. "This is the judgment," Jesus says. We are likely to feel stuck there from time to time, but the goal is more soul, more light, more profound acknowledgment of where we are and are not yet. To believe in Jesus is to begin to step away from condemnation (whether administered from within or without).

To encounter the Jesus of John's Gospel is to begin opening the book of what happened to us. The truth of our own experience will come out eventually, and it is as if Jesus is giving Nicodemus advance warning of the difficulties and the joys involved. The perceived threat and the power of God's judgment can leave us standing and stuck on the threshold of deeper awareness for an awfully long time, but there is information in the specifics of our fears and a loving, imperishable future in the life God gives us.

DAVID DARK

Fifth Sunday in Lent

Jeremiah 31:31–34
Psalm 51:1–12 or Psalm 119:9–16

Hebrews 5:5–10
John 12:20–33

Jeremiah 31:31–34

³¹The days are surely coming, says the LORD, when I will make a new covenant with the house of Israel and the house of Judah. ³²It will not be like the covenant that I made with their ancestors when I took them by the hand to bring them out of the land of Egypt—a covenant that they broke, though I was their husband, says the LORD. ³³But this is the covenant that I will make with the house of Israel after those days, says the LORD: I will put my law within them, and I will write it on their hearts; and I will be their God, and they shall be my people. ³⁴No longer shall they teach one another, or say to each other, "Know the LORD," for they shall all know me, from the least of them to the greatest, says the LORD; for I will forgive their iniquity, and remember their sin no more.

Commentary 1: Connecting the Reading with Scripture

Jeremiah 31:31–34 is part of the Book of Consolation (Jer. 30–33), a section of Jeremiah in which Israel's restoration after the Babylonian exile is a central theme. The focus of these verses is on how the covenant will be reimagined in the future age as something written on the people's hearts. This is the second of three eschatological statements in this chapter that begin with the words, "The days are surely coming, says the LORD . . . ," and describe a new reality for the people (see Jer. 31:27–30, 38–40). In each case, something important is restored—first the kingdom, then the people, and finally the city. The section that addresses the covenant is in the key middle position and is the longest of the three. Between the second and third statements is a divine oracle in which God guarantees the ongoing existence of Israel (vv. 34–37).

References to both the heart and the covenant are also made in the following chapter in a passage that describes the Deity's concern for Jerusalem despite the Babylonian invasion. "They shall be my people, and I will be their God. I will give them one heart and one way, that they may fear me for all time. . . . I will put the fear of me in their hearts, so that they may not turn from me" (32:38–40).

These promises concerning the heart in Jeremiah take on additional valence once we realize that the heart had outsized meaning in the worldview of the ancient writers. Today the heart is typically seen merely as the center of emotions, but in the Hebrew Bible the heart was also viewed as the place of intellectual, ethical, and moral activity (e.g., Jer. 17:10; Ps. 20:4). Considering that the ancients viewed emotion as intertwined with rational, intellectual, and ethical thought as well as actions and activity, the heart was central to the behavior and the mentality of a person.

The distinction between ancient and modern understandings of the heart is something a homilist might unpack for the congregation. This enlarged vision of the heart is why in some places in Jeremiah it has a more negative meaning as the location where sin and evil—that is, wrong moral activity and thought—reside. This is evident in a passage that speaks of the Israelites' hardened hearts that need to be circumcised, a ritual closely identified with the covenant (Jer. 4:3–4; cf. 17:1).

Not only are the promises by God to Jeremiah all-inclusive and universal—"all" shall know God (31:34)—but they also reflect a transition from one understanding of the divine-human relationship to another. The covenant, according to Jeremiah 31, will no longer be expressed solely through external means like sacrifice and circumcision, but will be experienced within the depths of a person. This shift is a response to the changed circumstances of a community that has left its homeland and has lost the temple as the focal point of its ritual life. Because the covenant will be written on their hearts, it will not be identified with a particular place and will be with the people wherever they may be.

The description of God's putting the law within the people and writing it on their hearts (v. 33) has some connection with what took place with the previous covenant, which was external in nature. After Moses communes with God on Mount Sinai, he returns to the Israelites and puts in writing the law he has received (Exod. 24:4a). Soon after this, Moses is summoned back up the mount and informed that the Deity has written the law on stone tablets. "The LORD said to Moses, . . . 'I will give you the tablets of stone, with the law and the commandment, which I have written for their instruction'" (Exod. 24:12). Later on, just prior to the golden calf episode, a more detailed account of God's scribal activity is provided. "Then Moses turned and went down from the mountain, carrying the two tablets of the covenant in his hands. . . . The tablets were the work of God, and the writing was the writing of God, engraved upon the tablets" (Exod. 32:15–16; cf. 31:18).

Through Jeremiah God now promises that the holy law that was earlier written and passed along through an intermediary, the great Moses, will now be directly inscribed by God in the very center, the very heart, of the person who will have direct and innate access.

Elements of Jeremiah are noted in the New Testament, including the idea of a new covenant. Hebrews 8, for example, begins with a reference to Jesus as a different type of high priest, who has rendered the older understanding of that office obsolete and unnecessary. The author maintains that this priestly role of Jesus is tied to the notion of covenant, which has also been modified (Heb. 8:1–6), and then goes on to quote Jeremiah 31:31–34 as scriptural support for this new perspective (Heb. 8:8–12). The writer also twice offers a negative assessment of the prior covenant, once at Hebrews 8:7, before the citation of the Jeremiah passage and once after it: "In speaking of 'a new covenant,' he has made the first one obsolete. And what is obsolete and growing old will soon disappear" (Heb. 8:13). This somewhat critical view of the previous covenant is not explicitly put forward in the Jeremiah text, and it is likely meant to serve the christological agenda of the author of Hebrews, who believes that in Jesus a new relationship between God and humanity has become possible (Heb. 9:15; 10:11–16).

Paul draws on imagery found in Jeremiah 31 to explain how it is that some people act in accordance with the law even though they are not familiar with it: "When Gentiles, who do not possess the law, do instinctively what the law requires, these, though not having the law, are a law to themselves. They show that what the law requires is written on their hearts, to which their own conscience also bears witness" (Rom. 2:14–15a). In another of his letters, Paul makes use of the image of a new covenant when he recounts Jesus' words to his disciples at the Last Supper (1 Cor. 11:25). The three Synoptic Gospels, all composed after Paul wrote 1 Corinthians, record Jesus' words in a similar fashion, but some of the oldest manuscripts do not use the word "new" in reference to the covenant. "Then he took a cup, and after giving thanks he gave it to them, saying, 'Drink from it, all of you; for this is my blood of the (new) covenant, which is poured out for many for the forgiveness of sins'" (Matt. 26:27–28; cf. Mark 14:24; Luke 22:20).

It is unclear if these New Testament authors were dependent on the Jeremiah passage in their own writings, but it is beyond doubt that certain elements of that text are echoed in the Gospels and other early Christian literature. The time of Jesus was not the future age Jeremiah had in mind when he spoke to his contemporaries who were experiencing the trauma and uncertainty of the Babylonian invasion of Judah. Nonetheless, his imagery and language express hope and restoration that can speak to people in all times and places. The homilist might ask the congregation to reflect on how the concept of a new covenant addresses the fears and uncertainties of their own lives.

JOHN KALTNER

Commentary 2: Connecting the Reading with the World

A time is coming. What is the vision of the future? If one followed the vision of some filmmakers, we would conclude that apocalyptic cataclysm and dystopia are inevitable. It appears that we are pointed headlong into a dismal and hopeless future brought on by the global consequences of human greed and avarice.

However, the vision and hopeful promise of a new covenant are yet ahead of us. In today's text from Jeremiah, we must be careful not to take the Christian default position, that whenever the word "new" is used, we make it a reference to Christ and the New Testament. Always defaulting to this position is at the very heart of Christian supersessionism. "New" need not be thought of as substitutionary. New could be the result of a God who is great enough to adapt and, dare it be said, "evolve"? Hence, a possible topic for a sermon is to think about the ways in which God is always evolving and adapting, and the ways in which the people of God are required to do the same.

A quote attributed to the late great physicist Stephen Hawking asserts that "intelligence is the ability to adapt to change."[1] With rest on the Sabbath, could it be that God models the expectation of human rest from labor? Could it be that in speaking of a "new covenant" God is again modeling for the human family the power of adaptive intelligence? At its heart, preaching is about helping people make authentic, ethical responses to inevitable change.

In Jeremiah we see God adapting to the realities of the relationship with the people of Israel and Judah. The covenants grounded in fear and obedience are simply not working. The people continue to fall short (betray). God presses into the future. "The days are coming . . . ," and God in this decision models the moral integrity we are to manifest as human beings. As a song made popular by the jazz artist George Benson states:

Mysteries do unfold. . . .
Nothing and no one goes unchanged.[2]

The idea of "intelligence" as adaption to change has moral implications and consequences. Martin King asserted that human beings have "a moral responsibility to be intelligent."[3] In King's view, this intelligence would lead the human family to the right understanding of love and justice distributed and dispensed in society without prejudice or preference. Imagine the implications of calling hearers to that moral responsibility in a world filled with deliberate and intentional misinformation and "fake news." This calls the listeners to seek and search for the truth.

What if those days are still yet coming? At this moment in the liturgical calendar we are getting yet closer to the glories of resurrection morning. There is still much terrain we must traipse through. The drudgery often causes us to look back over the journey and imagine (whether in reality or not) that things were better "back then." This is the idolatry of nostalgia—the dangers of which offers another topic worthy of address at the pulpit—that creates in us an unquenchable desire to return to something that may not have truly been and to glorify the players and actors of a former time. We bestow on them a heroism, if not superhuman character, that separates the former time and their successes from our present time and its perceived failures.

The other sin that betrays us is the sin of being stuck in the present. (Dis)Satisfied with what is. Exactly the way it is. This is the season. Everything before this is irrelevant. This is the sin of pronounced contemporality, which at its heart is a vacillating moodiness depending on how the current happenings affect us.

Wise preachers would do well to remind their congregations that both of these postures—overindulgent nostalgia and being fearfully stuck in

---

1. See Valerie Strauss, "Stephen Hawking famously said, 'Intelligence is the ability to adapt to change.' But did he really say it?," *Washington Post*, March 29, 2018, https://www.washingtonpost.com/news/answer-sheet/wp/2018/03/29/stephen-hawking-famously-said-intelligence-is-the-ability-to-adapt-to-change-but-did-he-really-say-it/.

2. Benard Ighner, "Everything Must Change," Universal Music Publishing Group, 1977.

3. Martin Luther King Jr., "The Danger of Misguided Goodness," in Clayborne Carson, Susan Carson, Susan Englander, Troy Jackson, and Gerald L. Smith, eds., *The Papers of Martin Luther King, Jr.*, vol. 6: *Advocate of the Social Gospel, September 1948–March 1963* (Oakland: University of California Press, 2007), 584.

the present—fail us. We are not fulfilled complete until we move, as Tom Long articulates it, "from memory to hope."[4] The stories we have told, the encounters we have had, should urge us on through the challenges of today and the false worship of the past to a compelling vision for the robust promise of the future with God. Indeed, as Jeremiah reminds us, a new time is coming, and with it a changed covenant. It is through this change that "they shall all know me" (Jer. 31:34).

How miserably we have failed this vision. Perhaps we are not yet there in that we spend our time in the faith(s) trying to teach each other how to be in the right relationship with God. We are called to move from catechesis to knowing. This will have a profound effect on our relationships, not only with God but also with each other.

The process and accumulation of "knowing" the teaching can become a god with its own worship. Perhaps the new (non)religionists have a point. "I am spiritual but not religious." They offer a critique of the incessant "teachings" and posturing we inflict on one another as if the teachings can get us to relationship with God on their own rote memorization.

This text moves us from mere catechism to another form of belonging and its validation. Rather, the new covenant is based on relationship with God and the communal relational power of forgiveness (31:34). As Jeremiah states, "I will be their God" is at the center of this new covenant of forgiveness. Not only will God forgive sins, but God is willing to alter the very heart of the people, so that sin will be intuitively recognized and rejected by them. Sin will be forgotten.

This kind of forgiveness and righteousness that emerges from sin being forgotten is evident in some of the modern practices in Africa. Beginning in Uganda in 1977 and most famously exhibited in South Africa in 1995, many countries established what would be known as Truth and Reconciliation Commissions. These commissions were intended to reveal and uncover the past doings of governments in order to establish restorative justice for the peoples who had been harmed by governmental practices. At the center of this type of restorative justice is the correct balance of memory and forgiveness.

In speaking of restorative justice, "from the least of them to the greatest" conveys the determined justice of God. How often are poor and disenfranchised people forced to have justice delayed or denied because they do not have resources? In 2015, Kalif Browder committed suicide in a New York City jail after spending years in pretrial detention and solitary confinement, all because his family was too poor to post the $3,000 bail. Such tragedies and trauma will be avoided because God knows the urgency of those who have nothing or no one to advocate on their behalf. What work should the followers of Jesus be doing in a country that has built the most complex and far-reaching prison-industrial complex in the world? A faithful people is a justice-seeking people. Starting with the least. Relentlessly so.

The writer is clear that this work is still ahead of us. This is the second of three successive sections that begin with the phrase "The days are surely coming . . ." (Jer. 31:27–30; 31:31–36; 31:38–40).

God is determined and resolved to see this to fruition: "I will be their God and they will be my people."

GARY V. SIMPSON

---

4. Thomas G. Long, *Preaching from Memory to Hope* (Louisville, KY: Westminster John Knox, 2009).

Fifth Sunday in Lent

Psalm 51:1–12

[1]Have mercy on me, O God,
  according to your steadfast love;
according to your abundant mercy
  blot out my transgressions.
[2]Wash me thoroughly from my iniquity,
  and cleanse me from my sin.

[3]For I know my transgressions,
  and my sin is ever before me.
[4]Against you, you alone, have I sinned,
  and done what is evil in your sight,
so that you are justified in your sentence
  and blameless when you pass judgment.
[5]Indeed, I was born guilty,
  a sinner when my mother conceived me.

[6]You desire truth in the inward being;
  therefore teach me wisdom in my secret heart.
[7]Purge me with hyssop, and I shall be clean;
  wash me, and I shall be whiter than snow.
[8]Let me hear joy and gladness;
  let the bones that you have crushed rejoice.
[9]Hide your face from my sins,
  and blot out all my iniquities.

[10]Create in me a clean heart, O God,
  and put a new and right spirit within me.
[11]Do not cast me away from your presence,
  and do not take your holy spirit from me.
[12]Restore to me the joy of your salvation,
  and sustain in me a willing spirit.

Psalm 119:9–16

[9]How can young people keep their way pure?
  By guarding it according to your word.
[10]With my whole heart I seek you;
  do not let me stray from your commandments.
[11]I treasure your word in my heart,
  so that I may not sin against you.
[12]Blessed are you, O LORD;
  teach me your statutes.
[13]With my lips I declare
  all the ordinances of your mouth.
[14]I delight in the way of your decrees
  as much as in all riches.

¹⁵I will meditate on your precepts,
and fix my eyes on your ways.
¹⁶I will delight in your statutes;
I will not forget your word.

Connecting the Psalm with Scripture and Worship

In *The Biblical Psalms in Christian Worship*, John Witvliet writes, "The biblical Psalms are the foundational mentor and guide in th[e] vocabulary and grammar for worship."¹ There are few better mentors for the grammar of confession than Psalm 51, especially as the faith community marches along the penitent and introspective byways of Lent. In Psalm 51, the psalmist models the journey and vocabulary of honest confession, petition for God's forgiveness, and both a plea for and declaration of trust in God's transforming power. Psalm 51 stands as a prime model of the work of a prayer of confession and might even be prayed collectively or responsively as such. Among the seven Penitential Psalms (Pss. 6, 32, 38, 51, 102, 130, and 143), Psalm 51 is arguably the most well known and certainly appears the most in the lectionary, due in large part to its rich and dramatic language, as well as the way it recognizes both the individual (Ps. 51:3–4) and the communal/societal (v. 5) nature of sin.

Yet Psalm 51:1–12 speaks as much to the nature and work of God as it does to the reality of human sinfulness. From the beginning, the psalmist seeks God's "steadfast love" and "abundant mercy" (v. 1), implicitly trusting that those are a central part of God's character. Even more, the psalmist is clear that it is God's action, not their own, that will lead to forgiveness and re-creation. Beginning in verse 6, the psalmist uses a string of imperatives, imploring God to offer forgiveness and renewal. Though the psalmist takes responsibility for their transgressions and acknowledges their sin (v. 3), the psalmist also recognizes that it is God and God alone who can "pass judgment" (v. 4), "teach . . . wisdom" (v. 6), "purge . . . with hyssop" (v. 7), "blot out all . . . iniquities" (v. 9), and ultimately "create

. . . a clean heart" in the psalmist (v. 10) in order to "restore" the psalmist to the "joy of [God's] salvation" (v. 12).

This redemption and re-creation are not something the psalmist can do for themselves. In fact, in verse 10, when the psalmist pleads, "Create in me a clean heart, O God," the Hebrew word for "create" (*bara'*) is used in the Hebrew Bible only to refer to God's creative activity (such as in the opening chapters of Genesis). God alone can forgive. God alone can *create* (*bara'*) a new reality for the psalmist as they seek forgiveness, fuller communion with God, and walking in God's ways.

God's forgiving, creative, and re-creating spirit on full display in Psalm 51 carries lectionary preachers and teachers to the heart of the Jeremiah text, the first reading for the Fifth Sunday in Lent. Jeremiah 31:31–34 describes the new reality God intends to make with the covenant people. Unlike the old covenant, "a covenant they broke" (Jer. 31:32), this new covenant is a personal one, written on the hearts of the beloved people. This new covenant first requires God's forgiveness for a people who, as the psalmist might say, were "born guilty" (Ps. 51:5). God promises to "forgive their iniquity, and remember their sin no more" (Jer. 31:34). As in Psalm 51, God's forgiveness is intimately connected to God's creative work, as God casts an eschatological vision of this new community shaped by a new covenant. As God declares through the voice of Jeremiah, "I will put my law within them, and I will write it on their hearts" (Jer. 31:33).

God anticipates that this new covenant, with instructions sealed in the hearts of the people, will lead to a deeper communion between God and God's people. Not only does God

---

1. John D. Witvliet, *The Biblical Psalms in Christian Worship: A Brief Introduction and Guide to Resources* (Grand Rapids: Eerdmans, 2007), 12.

An Exchange of Hearts

One day, in the fervor of [Catherine of Sienna's] prayer, she said with the Prophet: "Create within me O God a new heart," etc. And supplicated our Lord to condescend to take away her own heart and her own will. It seemed to her that her Spouse presented himself to her, opened her left side, took out her heart and carried it with him, so that in reality she no longer perceived it in her breast. This vision was striking and her attendant symptoms agreed with it so well, that when she spoke of it to her Confessor, she assured him that she really had *no heart*. Her Confessor began to laugh, and rebuked her for saying any thing of the kind, but she only renewed her assurance. "Really, Father," she said to him, "as far as I can judge of what I experience in my person, it seems to me that I have no heart. The Lord appeared to me, opened my left side, drew out my heart, and went away." And, as her Confessor declared to her that it would be impossible to live without any heart, she answered that nothing was impossible with God, and that she had a heart no longer. Some days later, she was in the Chapel of the Church of the Friar Preachers, in which the *Sisters of Penance* of St. Dominic assemble: she remained there alone so as to continue her prayer, and was disposing herself to return home, when on a sudden she saw herself environed with a light from Heaven, and amid this light, the Saviour appeared to her, bearing in his sacred hands a Heart of vermillion hue and radiating fire. Deeply affected with this presence and splendor, she prostrated herself on the ground. Our Lord approached, opened anew her left side, placed in it the Heart which he bore, and said to her: "Daughter, the other day I took thy heart, to-day I give thee mine, and this will henceforward serve thee." After these words he closed her breast; but, as a token of the miracle, he left there a cicatrice that her companions have frequently assured me they had seen, and when I questioned her pointedly on this subject, she avowed to me that the incident was true, and that from that period she had adopted the custom of saying: "My God, I recommend to thee my Heart."

. . . After that wonderful exchange of hearts, Catherine appeared to herself to have undergone an amazing exchange: "Father," she said to her Confessor, "do you not perceive that I am no longer the same: I am completely changed: Oh! Did you but know what I experience! *No,*—certainly, if it were comprehended what passes within my soul, there would be no harshness nor pride that could resist it. All that I can say falls short of reality." She sought however to give an idea: "My soul," said she, "is so inebriated with joy and delight, that I am astonished that it remains in my body. Its ardor is so great, that external fire is as naught in comparison with it; it seems that I should find refreshment in *that*. And this ardor operates in me such a renovation of purity and humility, that I feel as though I had returned to my fourth year of age. The love of the neighbor also augments in me to such a degree, that it would be my great pleasure to die for any one."

Raymond of Capua, *Life of Saint Catherine of Sienna*, ed. Etienne Cartier (Philadelphia: P. F. Cunningham, 1860), 124–26.

anticipate, "I will be their God, and they shall be my people" (v. 33), but also this new covenant will lead people to a deeper knowledge of the Lord (vv. 33b–34). Through God's act of forgiveness and re-creation, the people will be freed to be in fuller relationship with God and more faithful followers of God's instruction.

In Jeremiah 31:31–34, the Lord casts a relationally rich, yet somewhat vague eschatological vision for how this new people might live in communion with God and God's instruction. However, the psalmist of Psalm 119—the alternative psalm for this Fifth Sunday in Lent—might offer a more concrete picture of the kind of faithful life lived in response to God's law being inscribed in one's heart. Psalm 119, the longest psalm in the Psalter, is probably best considered a "*torah* psalm," as for twenty-two eight-line stanzas this acrostic poem again and again praises God's instruction and stands as a repetitive and artistic shrine to God's revelation. All but four verses of the psalm contain some synonym for *torah* (including terms such as "word," "commandment," "statute," and "precept").

This deluge of praise for God's instruction, with repeated synonyms and stanzas organized in alphabetical order (according to the Hebrew alphabet) may come across as tedious. However, as biblical scholar J. Clinton McCann argues, this avalanche of Hebrew poetry is intended to be consuming and even overwhelming: "As a literary artist, the psalmist intended the structure of the poem to reinforce its theological content. In short, *torah*—God's revelatory instruction—is pervasive and all-encompassing. It applies to everything from A to Z, or in Hebrew, *Aleph* to *Taw*."[2] While the Mosaic and oral tradition is clearly of value to the psalmist, the psalmist is also open to the ongoing instruction and revelation of the Lord. The psalmist of Psalm 119 begs for God to continue to teach them all the instruction God might have (Ps. 119:12, 26).

As if already participating in the future reality projected in Jeremiah 31, the psalmist of Psalm 119 is committed to and insistent on pursuing, keeping, and following the ever-unfolding instructions of God. In the lectionary selection for the day, the second stanza of the acrostic poem (Ps. 119:9–16), the psalmist describes seeking God with their "whole heart" (v. 10), and begging God to "teach me your statutes"

(v. 12), in order that they may "declare all the ordinances of your mouth" (v. 13).

The psalmist is not self-righteous with regard to their knowledge of the Lord. Throughout the psalm, the psalmist names suffering, scorn, affliction, persecution, and even the temptation toward sin (v. 10b). While the psalmist is all too aware of their lived reality, they seek to lean into an eschatological future where the fullness of the revelation of God reigns and is known by the people. Like the people of the new covenant of Jeremiah 31, the psalmist celebrates the gift of God's *torah* and longs to be closer to God by knowing, deeply and well, the boundless revelation of God.

If Psalm 51 is a model for confession, Psalm 119 is a model for meditation. This psalm invites congregations to meditate on God's word and anticipate God's ongoing revelation. With its repetitive content, the psalm might be prayed or chanted by the community multiple times throughout the service. For example, Psalm 119:9–16 might be offered as both a prayer for illumination before the reading of the text and as a petition to God after the sermon. With Psalm 119 bookending the reading of Scripture, the text might serve to summon congregations to both a meditative posture toward Scripture and a longing for the Word.

KIMBERLY R. WAGNER

---

2. J. Clinton McCann, "Psalms," in *New Interpreter's Bible* (Nashville: Abingdon, 1996), 4:1166.

Hebrews 5:5–10

⁵So also Christ did not glorify himself in becoming a high priest, but was appointed by the one who said to him,

> "You are my Son,
>   today I have begotten you";

⁶as he says also in another place,

> "You are a priest forever,
>   according to the order of Melchizedek."

⁷In the days of his flesh, Jesus offered up prayers and supplications, with loud cries and tears, to the one who was able to save him from death, and he was heard because of his reverent submission. ⁸Although he was a Son, he learned obedience through what he suffered; ⁹and having been made perfect, he became the source of eternal salvation for all who obey him, ¹⁰having been designated by God a high priest according to the order of Melchizedek.

Commentary 1: Connecting the Reading with Scripture

This reading assures believers of their salvation by identifying Christ as the ultimate high priest. It is the final part of a section of Hebrews (Heb. 4:14–5:10) that links the discussion of Christ as the Son of God, a central theme of the first part of this book, with the discussion of Christ as the uniquely qualified and effective high priest. This latter theme will occupy all of 7:1–10:18. Following a warning about coming judgment (4:11–13), 4:14–5:10 encourages readers to enter the presence of God boldly because Christ is their high priest. After asserting that Christ is a sympathetic high priest (4:14–16), the author describes the function, personal qualities, and qualifications a high priest needs, especially noting that a high priest must be appointed by God (5:1–4). This leads to our reading, 5:5–10, which shows that Christ fulfills those qualifications better than anyone else could.

The "So also" (NRSV) that begins verse 5 connects it directly with the expectation that a high priest must be chosen by God. As Aaron was appointed by God (5:4), "so also" Christ did not assume the office on his own, but was appointed by God. The two psalm quotations

in verses 5–6 support this claim. Verse 5 quotes Psalm 2:7 to identify Jesus as God's Son. Many in the church used this enthronement psalm to identify Jesus as God's Son. Since much of the first three and a half chapters of Hebrews is devoted to establishing this identity for Jesus, the use of this psalm is no surprise. What is surprising is that Hebrews links this citation with Psalm 110:4. While New Testament writers quote the first verse of Psalm 110 more often than any other text of the Hebrew Bible, this is the only citation of verse 4 in all early church writings. Hebrews uses this text to assign Christ a priestly office and to link this role to his identity as Son of God. Indeed, Hebrews will argue that his identity as Son is part of what makes him the ideal high priest.

Hebrews is also the only early-church writing that connects Melchizedek's priesthood with Christ. In fact, no other New Testament book mentions Melchizedek, a figure that is briefly described in Genesis. Readers will not know the full significance of this identification with Melchizedek until chapter 7. Here the specific point is that Christ is appointed by God to be a priest forever.

Verses 7–8 argue that being sympathetic, rather than harsh, with those who need forgiveness is an essential quality for a high priest. Christ is sympathetic because he learned what it was like to be human in "the days of his flesh" (v. 7; see also 2:17–18), an expression that emphasizes human weakness and suffering. While experiencing what it is like to be human, the author says, Christ prayed, crying loudly and shedding tears. Since God is described as the one who "is able to save him from death," these prayers seem to be associated with the passion. While Hebrews shows no familiarity with the Gospels' versions of the Gethsemane story, these prayers would include those in the Garden, but also other prayers during the passion. Their fervency shows that Christ's suffering and his desire to be saved from it were genuine.

Hebrews says that those prayers were heard because of Christ's piety. This seems strange, because God, who is called the one who is "able to save" him, does not save him. So, being heard as a righteous person does not mean that suffering is taken away. The act of God that vindicates Christ's suffering comes only after his death. This is important, because the original readers of Hebrews are experiencing persecution, and their prayers have not brought relief. They may be wondering if God hears, or is able to help, or even whether they have offended God. Hebrews makes the experience of Jesus a pattern for how God responds when the righteous suffer. It assures them that persecution is not a sign of God's displeasure or lack of concern. God fully vindicates the faithful, but that may come only after death.

Verse 8 gives Christ's suffering another meaning: he learned through it. A well-known Greek saying spoke of learning through suffering (Aeschylus, *Agamemnon*). Like our "school of hard knocks," the suffering this maxim referred to was a result of doing wrong. Jesus, however, suffers for doing right. Even being a faithful Son does not exempt him from learning through suffering. While not said explicitly, what he seems to have learned was the full meaning of obedience or the full meaning of being human. This learning is a part of what qualifies him to be a sympathetic high priest and the source of eternal salvation. Because he suffered, he can

sympathize with those who suffer. The importance of empathy offers then a possible point of discussion in the pulpit. The eternal salvation he gives stands in contrast to the temporary suffering the readers are experiencing (v. 9). God, the text implies, may want readers to learn through their suffering, an idea that is both instructive and dangerous, as it can be utilized to dismiss and explain away hardship.

While the image is strange, Christ is both the priest and the sacrifice. He is the one appointed to approach God and the gift that is offered. Hebrews says Christ is the source of salvation for "those who obey him." This obedience is not to be contrasted with faith. Hebrews has already argued that obedience is a part of faith. This way of describing the saved encourages readers to remain faithful despite persecution and so contributes to that central goal of the whole book.

Verse 10 returns to the claim that God has appointed Christ to a priesthood like that of Melchizedek. The author will explain the significance of this claim only after a series of exhortations calling readers to move past simple teachings so they can more fully appreciate the salvation God has given them.

Christ's death serves three crucial purposes in this text. First, believers can trust Christ, the sympathetic high priest, to be compassionate with them in their weakness, because he knows what it is like to suffer. This high priest is sympathetic, even to the point of giving his life for our sin, rather than requiring the sinner to offer a gift. Second, Hebrews asserts, though it does not explain fully, that Christ's faithful offering, that is, his death, makes him the source of salvation. Finally, Christ's suffering gives readers an exemplar to imitate. He is the pattern they are to follow, because his experience shows that God vindicates righteous suffering. His experience promises that God is with us when we are suffering. The pattern of his life also assures us that the absence of an immediate rescue is no sign that God has abandoned us.

Interpreting the death of Jesus as salvific because it leads to his exaltation to the office of high priest coordinates nicely with this week's Gospel reading. In John 12 Jesus speaks of his crucifixion as his being glorified. John does not say how the crucifixion brings glory rather than shame, but Hebrews provides one possibility: it is the way Christ becomes high priest. In addition, while Hebrews speaks of Jesus identifying with those who suffer because they remain faithful, John has Jesus call believers to imitate him by being willing to suffer for their faith. Both encourage believers to be faithful in the midst of suffering, with the assurance that Christ fully understands that experience and that God will vindicate their faithfulness.

JERRY L. SUMNEY

Commentary 2: Connecting the Reading with the World

On occasion the lectionary deals the pastor a real doozy of a text. This week's epistle reading is one of those moments. From supersessionist theology to substitutionary atonement, it has all the things that make a good pastor squirm. So, how might a preacher tasked with preaching the epistle on Sunday morning approach such an undertaking? I propose two trajectories.

One approach to a difficult text is to redeem the text. For example, a pastor might attempt to read a familiar text in a new way, to reconsider something typical that allows something more redemptive to emerge. In the epistle lesson for this week, I suggest there is something redemptive about the act of prayer.

The author of Hebrews is committed to two agendas: establishing Jesus as the ultimate high priest and delegitimizing the sacrificial priesthood. Both are present in this week's lectionary reading. The passage begins by citing Psalms 2:7 and 110:4 as proof texts, or arguments from Scripture, that Jesus is a high priest. Hebrews argues that Jesus, lacking the appropriate genealogy for the position of high priest, is a priest according to the order of Melchizedek (Heb. 5:5–6). Having established Jesus' appointment as divinely ordained, the author then turns to rendering the sacrificial priesthood obsolete. It is within this context that the text mentions prayer.

Hebrews describes, "In the days of his flesh, Jesus offered up prayers and supplications, with loud cries and tears, to the one who was able to save him from death, and he was heard because of his reverent submission" (v. 7). Given the reference to Jesus' death, it is often assumed that the prayers mentioned in verse 7 refer to the final words Jesus uttered from the cross, "My God, my God, why have you forsaken me?" (Matt. 27:46; Mark 15:34). Interpreters often assume that this passage about prayer from Hebrews means that Jesus was praying for himself, but if we look closely at the text, this interpretation does not really make sense. If Jesus' prayer was a request for God to relieve him of his impending death, what does it mean that Jesus' prayers were heard by God? After all, Jesus was not rescued from death; he was not spared pain and suffering.

The Greek does not clarify for whom Jesus was offering prayers. It is not clear for whom Jesus was making supplication. Is it possible that interpreters wrongly assume a parallel to Jesus' final words? Is it possible that Jesus is not making supplication for his own pain and suffering, but instead offering prayers for others? There is something familiar about a Jesus who speaks up on behalf of others. The Gospels are full of examples of a Jesus who raises his voice in the interests of the downtrodden. A pastor might ask the congregation to imagine what it would look like for Christians to offer prayers and supplications on behalf of those who are suffering in our world. What might we cry aloud? Who in our contexts are in need of our tears? Jesus models that not only may we pray for those around us, even in the midst of our own struggles, but that our own suffering and prayer might serve to illuminate that of others.

Reading Jesus' prayers and supplications as on behalf of others not only models a less narcissistic form of prayer for the modern Christian; it also provides an alternative to substitutionary atonement. In this reading of Hebrews, Jesus does not offer up his body as a sacrifice for our sins; he reverently bears our scars. He offers up to God in supplication our deepest wounds. It is our pain Jesus takes to the cross, not our transgressions.

In contrast to an approach that attempts to redeem a difficult text, another course of action for the preacher is to confront the text, to tackle it head on, to push back against its theology. It is good for pastors to recognize problematic passages in the biblical canon, because it helps point to areas in need of growth within the Christian tradition. Confronting the text recognizes that these texts impact and shape our theology, and acknowledges that it is important to know what is damaging about our history, in order to avoid further damage in the future and perhaps to set right any damage of the past. A sermon on this passage from Hebrews might, therefore, lean in the direction of dissent. I note two particular dangers.

First, this week's epistle is dangerous because it is supersessionist in nature. Hebrews as a whole seeks to replace, or supersede, one theology with another—to replace the theology of the Jews with the theology of Jesus. Throughout the document the author repeatedly reinterprets the Scriptures of Israel as pointing to Jesus. Both of the psalms cited in this week's text are an example. The author uses the psalms to make an argument from Scripture that Jesus is a high priest. In other words, the author appropriates Jewish Scriptures for Christian advantage. Christians would do well to remember that Jewish theology does not recognize the foretelling of Jesus in the Jewish canon. We need to be more careful in our interpretations of Scripture not to deny the Jewish community of its own interpretation of its Scripture.

One danger of replacement theology is that it can create a sense of superiority. In other words, it risks encouraging Christians to think of Jewish traditions as obsolete and monolithic. To question the ongoing force of temple sacrifice and the Levitical priesthood is also part of Jewish tradition. Jewish tradition is arguing with itself. Hebrews is part of that argument. Another danger is that it can lead to religious misunderstanding. What is seen as transformation or positive change in one tradition might be interpreted as an aberration or regression in another. If Christians are not intentional with the careful interpretations of sensitive texts, they risk reading the Jewish tradition through a Christian lens and therefore misunderstanding the Jewish religion as a whole.

Finally, recognizing the anti-Semitic tendencies of this text is particularly important in our modern context. With the emergence of mass shootings and an increase in hate crimes on religious and ethnic minorities in our world, we would do well to recognize the role of our Scriptures and our interpretation of these Scriptures in the development of anti-Jewish sentiments. In addition to naming some of the larger instances of anti-Semitism, such as the shooting at Tree of Life Synagogue, a pastor might wish to include local instances of anti-Semitism in a sermon on Hebrews. A pastor might also seek to build relationships between the church and the local Jewish community. As faithful Christians, we must resist supersessionist theology and actively seek to encourage religious pluralism in the communities around our churches.

Second, domineering language is another danger of this week's lectionary text. Language built around systems of domination and oppression is dangerous in any religious setting. Phrases like "reverent submission" (v. 7), "he learned obedience through what he suffered" (v. 8), and "eternal salvation for all who obey" (v. 9) risk ideologies that engender violence under the guise of Christian theology. Preachers do well to lead their congregations in ruminating on the dangers of such language.

Preaching against the text requires a studied, skilled, and brave pulpiteer. The goal of any sermon is not to strip validity from a beloved text, but to demonstrate where grace may be found, even when tradition has unwittingly erred. Speaking against the Christian canon is not to abandon Christian tradition; it is to raise one voice of our tradition to confront another. This is how traditions survive; this is how Scripture finds new voice.

ANNA M. V. BOWDEN

John 12:20–33

²⁰Now among those who went up to worship at the festival were some Greeks. ²¹They came to Philip, who was from Bethsaida in Galilee, and said to him, "Sir, we wish to see Jesus." ²²Philip went and told Andrew; then Andrew and Philip went and told Jesus. ²³Jesus answered them, "The hour has come for the Son of Man to be glorified. ²⁴Very truly, I tell you, unless a grain of wheat falls into the earth and dies, it remains just a single grain; but if it dies, it bears much fruit. ²⁵Those who love their life lose it, and those who hate their life in this world will keep it for eternal life. ²⁶Whoever serves me must follow me, and where I am, there will my servant be also. Whoever serves me, the Father will honor.

²⁷"Now my soul is troubled. And what should I say—'Father, save me from this hour'? No, it is for this reason that I have come to this hour. ²⁸Father, glorify your name." Then a voice came from heaven, "I have glorified it, and I will glorify it again." ²⁹The crowd standing there heard it and said that it was thunder. Others said, "An angel has spoken to him." ³⁰Jesus answered, "This voice has come for your sake, not for mine. ³¹Now is the judgment of this world; now the ruler of this world will be driven out. ³²And I, when I am lifted up from the earth, will draw all people to myself." ³³He said this to indicate the kind of death he was to die.

Commentary 1: Connecting the Reading with Scripture

In the preceding week, for the Fourth Sunday in Lent, the reading from John 3 focuses on God's love for the world and the universality of God's salvation (John 3:16). This theme is further developed in this week's reading, emphasizing the fruitfulness of Jesus' sacrifice as one death for the eternal salvation of many.

The setting of John 12 is the Passover festival, the third in the Johannine narrative (see 2:13, 23; 6:4; 11:55; 12:1). As is known, the Passover celebrates the death of all of the firstborn, which God, in the form of the destroyer, afflicted on the Egyptians in the book of Exodus. Passover commemorates God's passing over the Israelites during this final plague. As the celebrants commemorate in gratitude God's deliverance of Israel in the past, they also look forward in anticipation of God's final salvation. This time, though, salvation is not just for Israel but for the world. Israel's Messiah is in fact "the Savior of the world" (4:42).

This pericope follows Jesus' triumphal entry into Jerusalem. Given that the raising of Lazarus in chapter 11 has generated much interest in

Jesus, the crowd welcomes him enthusiastically, much to the chagrin of the Pharisees (12:12–18). Frustrated, they complain to one another, "Look, the *world* has gone after him!" (12:19).

Even though the Pharisees' observation is somewhat hyperbolic, "the world" indeed shows up next when some Greeks who have come to Jerusalem to celebrate the Passover find Philip and Andrew, and express their desire to see Jesus (12:20–21). While some interpreters assume these to be Diaspora Jews, it seems likely that they are Gentile God-fearers (see Acts 16:14; 17:4; 18:7). They seek out this pair of Jesus' disciples who bear Greek names and are from Bethsaida (1:44), a bilingual town inhabited by both Jews and Gentiles. The readers are not told whether the Greeks end up seeing Jesus, but their appearance triggers a pivotal declaration from Jesus: "The hour has come for the Son of Man to be glorified" (12:23). In short, Jesus' death is imminent.

"The hour" is a prominent motif in John to signal the timing of Jesus' death, which is determined by God alone. Until this time, the hour is said to be coming or to have not yet come (2:4; 4:21, 23; 5:25, 28; cf. 7:6, 8). There have been failed attempts to arrest or kill Jesus, because again his hour has not yet come (7.30; 8:20). Now the hour has finally arrived, and this note is repeatedly sounded as Jesus moves toward his crucifixion (12:23, 27; 13:1; 16:32; 17:1).

Jesus' death is the culmination of the work that the Father has sent the Son to do. Even so, the resoluteness with which Jesus goes to the cross is not without struggle. Verse 27 represents the Johannine rendition of Jesus' prayer at Gethsemane in the Synoptic Gospels (Mark 14:32–36 and par.). Here Jesus describes his soul as troubled (*tarassō*, to cause severe sorrow or pain). The English translation weakens the force of the Greek verb in expressing the depth of Jesus' emotion. The same verb is used to describe his response upon seeing how people wept when Lazarus died (11:33). Jesus asks not to be spared but to glorify the Father's name by his death. Because the Father and the Son are one, both are glorified, as Jesus' death is the very means of God's salvation (12:28). God will raise Jesus and vindicate him, and the world will come to know and glorify God through accepting this salvific gift.

One death brings life to many who believe. This is the meaning of the agricultural metaphor used by Jesus in 12:24. It is not that a grain actually "dies," but it must be placed in the soil ("falls into the earth") in order to germinate and grow into a new stalk of wheat that yields many more grains. The image of the grain "dying" correlates with Jesus' impending death and introduces the irony inherent in the plan of salvation. Life does not end with death but emerges by way of death. If this is the self-giving path of Jesus, so it will be for his followers. As the Son does his Father's bidding, even to the point of death, Jesus' servants must relinquish the life that the world offers them in order to gain the life that is imperishable and honored by God (12:25–26).

Who are those who will make it to the end? Will the Greeks who ask to see Jesus be among them? Despite the crowd's enthusiasm when Jesus arrives in Jerusalem, they show little understanding of the paradoxical nature of Jesus' sacrifice. The people remain obtuse, unable to discern God's affirmation of Jesus'

words by mistaking it for thunder or an angelic utterance (12:29–30). Their unbelief will result in judgment (12:31).

Human unbelief cannot lessen the power of divine initiative. Jesus claims, "And I, when I am lifted up from the earth, will draw all people to myself" (12:32). As explained in the lectionary reading on John 3:14–21 for the Fourth Sunday in Lent, the verb *hypsoō* ("to lift up") is a double entendre to signify both Jesus' death by crucifixion and his glorification. In John, crucifixion, resurrection, and exaltation constitute one event that reveals Jesus' true status and divine identity (8:32). Jesus dies to give life to the world, but he also draws the world—all people—to himself.

While people have to believe that Jesus' sacrificial death is the means of salvation, their faith is enabled only by a draw or a pull from Jesus himself. Hence Jesus refers to his disciples as those whom the Father has given to him (17:11, 24). No one can snatch these sheep from the shepherd's hand (10:27–28). This flock includes not only Israel, but also "other sheep," like the Gentiles who ask to see Jesus. If they listen to the shepherd's voice, the good shepherd will lay down his life for them and bring them into the sheepfold as well (10:15–16).

The twin themes of divine initiative and human response come to the fore as this text is read alongside the other selections for this Sunday. On the one hand, there is no salvation apart from God's initiative. In Jeremiah 31, the renewed covenant is predicated upon God's forgiving, teaching, and helping Israel to become the people whom God intends them to be. Even as David, penitent from his sin of adultery, expresses a deep desire to seek after God in Psalm 51, it is God who forgives his sins, teaches him wisdom, creates in him a clean heart, and puts a right spirit in him. On the other hand, those who earnestly seek after God will remain pure. The alternate reading from Psalm 119 stresses the psalmist's love for God's statutes and the need to meditate on them. In Hebrews 5, Jesus is put forth as the model of total submission, as a result of which God bestows on him the honor of an eternal priesthood in the order of Melchizedek. In John 12, those who believe in Jesus must follow his example of obedience, even if it means losing everything, including this earthly life, for the assurance of life eternal.

On this final Sunday of Lent, it is fitting to ponder the grandeur of God's plan of salvation that undergirds the terrible suffering and injustice endured by Jesus. The reminder that God's love is wide and God's reach is broad, drawing all people to Jesus, encourages and challenges Christians of all generations to persevere in faithfulness. God's promise of a glorious future will not disappoint.

DIANE G. CHEN

Commentary 2: Connecting the Reading with the World

While John's Gospel is often portrayed as representing Jesus in more cosmic, otherworldly terms than the Synoptic Gospels, certain passages have Jesus discerning the misconceptions of hearers and onlookers, and addressing them in an impromptu fashion. The monologues can distract us from noting how concerned he is with correcting misimpressions. Just before we are told that Greeks have traveled to Jerusalem for the express purpose of beholding and perhaps getting in on his act, Jesus has made sure that the "triumph" part of his triumphal entry is clear. As is the case in other Gospels, as he enters Jerusalem, the crowds gather branches and begin to declare him a king. In John's account, however, Jesus has gone and procured a donkey, as if in response to their misplaced enthusiasm for monarchical might. He hopes to better communicate the call of downward mobility, humility on humility, and the nature of the countercultural triumph he has in mind.

This increased popular buzz surrounding Jesus, moreover, is itself a sign of the paradoxical glory he is entering. Philip has been approached by a company of Greeks desirous to see Jesus, Philip tells Andrew, and they have now notified Jesus together. Jesus accepts it as an omen. The hour of glorification is at hand, but it is a dark glory. He will be magnified through public martyrdom. Unless a grain of wheat is crushed and buried deep within the earth, it remains alone, but if it dies, it bears much fruit. There is a principle here that he invites his hearers to recognize as essential to real human thriving. As it is with him, so it shall be with his followers. It is by holding too tightly to our lives that we lose them, and it is by letting go of our lives that we enter into life most profoundly. Self-giving love, Jesus seems to say, is the currency of the life to come.

These are difficult sayings. As a philosophy of living, it is about as contrary to our age of "Hurry up and matter" as it gets, but the anonymous Greeks of John's Gospel are not alone in suspecting there is something to it. Jesus is testifying to a convincing but scandalously new social reality. New then and new now. It is as if Jesus is introducing us to a form of outlawed awareness in advance of getting charged for it.

W. H. Auden once remarked that Jesus' conception of glory differed so radically from anything that has ever passed commonsense knowledge that it rendered his witness peculiarly persuasive: "I believe because He fulfills none of my dreams, because He is in every respect the opposite of what He would be if I could have made Him in my own image." No other figure in lore, literature, or history struck him as quite so offensive. What is more, he made Auden anxious, defensive, and even angry. As Auden testified, Jesus manages to "arouse *all* sides of my being to cry 'Crucify him!'"[1]

Does Jesus strike us as a tough act to swallow? If he does not, it could be that we have reduced him to the size of our own imaginations, transmogrifying his righteous witness into a kind of ghost friend who forgives our sins but will not pull us out of our comfort zones. If Auden's standard is to be credited, we might even say that if we do not hate Jesus a little, we have yet to love him a lot or to begin to understand him. Have we received his witness deeply enough to be offended by it? Have we thought through the call of self-denial he answered and invites his

---

1. *The Complete Works of W. H. Auden: Prose*, vol. 2, *1939–1948*, ed. Edward Mendelson (Princeton: Princeton University Press, 2002), 197.

hearers to take up? Have we truly understood his call? Are we really among his hearers?

In an exceedingly helpful turn, John's Gospel reminds us that Jesus' vocation to laying down his life in a posture of nonresistance, even at the moment of arrest leading up to his torture and execution, did not sit well with Jesus either: "Now my soul is troubled. And what should I say—'Father deliver me from this hour'? No" (John 12:27). He is resolved, but he is not called to pretend to be happy about it. Neither are we. Observational candor and honest confusion before God and others is not part of the deal. Transparency is.

To hold out your own troubled soul with open hands, to say what you see, and then to let the chips fall is perhaps vocation enough. As Irenaeus of Lyon instructs, the glory of God is a human being fully alive (*Against Heresies* 4.20). What inspiration and courage may we draw from Jesus' honesty concerning his own anxiety in the face of death? Moreover, what questions are raised with Jesus' anxiety and nonresistance? When and to what things should we acquiesce, and when and about what things should we resist and fight? There is, in fact, a cycle of self-justification and accusation that the Jesus of John's Gospel would have us believe is brought to an end by Jesus' glorified witness: "Now is the judgment of this world; now the ruler of this world will be driven out."

We need not look far into our news cycles, our neighborhoods, or our national and international norms to conclude, a couple of millennia later, that the power of denial and accusation has not, in fact, been driven out. Nevertheless, Jesus' obedience to God in his confrontation with armed force has set in motion a different order, a new way to be human, which calls into question all claims to authority.

In Oscar Wilde's play *Salome*, Herod has received word from a witness that there is a man out there who has been raising people from the dead. Understandably, this poses a threat to Herod's job security, and he puts his worry into words: "I do not wish him to do that. I forbid Him to do that. I allow no man to raise the dead. This man must be found and told that I forbid Him to raise the dead. Where is this man at present?"

"He is in every place, my lord," the witness explains, "but it is hard to find Him."[2]

This exchange offers us an indication of what God's judgment of this world in Jesus looks like. A confused ruler has just been confronted by an elusive, paradoxically risen, and alarmingly ubiquitous peasant defying the well-established rules of the game. A different form of judgment is now in effect. Herod is terribly displeased by all this, because this judgment against "the ruler of this world" is bad news for anyone whose power depends on lethal force. He does not want dead people coming back. That ruins the whole point of his illustrious career.

It means that history is not written only by winners, and that might does not, in the final analysis, make right. The "silenced" are not, it turns out, ultimately silenced. The might come back with an authoritative, more genuinely liberating word than brute force can know or understand. Victory over death deprives power of its primary means of persuasion. There are, it turns out, no closed books. Now is the judgment of this world.

When Jesus' triumph is normative, history is no longer just the memory of states, and politics as usual will not hold. Does this disturb our business as usual? Are we open to rethink in the direction of Jesus' victory over death-dealing culture, all that degrades and denies true human flourishing? If we are, we are perhaps among those who are drawn to the strange glory of Jesus made known in his exaltation by God.

DAVID DARK

---

2. Oscar Wilde, "Salome: A Tragedy in One Act" (London, John Lane, 1907), https://www.gutenberg.org/files/42704/42704-h/42704-h.htm.

Liturgy of the Palms

Psalm 118:1–2, 19–29　　　　　　　　　John 12:12–16
Mark 11:1–11

Psalm 118:1–2, 19–29

[1]O give thanks to the LORD, for he is good;
　　his steadfast love endures forever!

[2]Let Israel say,
　　"His steadfast love endures forever."

. . . .

[19]Open to me the gates of righteousness,
　　that I may enter through them
　　and give thanks to the LORD.

[20]This is the gate of the LORD;
　　the righteous shall enter through it.

[21]I thank you that you have answered me
　　and have become my salvation.
[22]The stone that the builders rejected
　　has become the chief cornerstone.
[23]This is the LORD's doing;
　　it is marvelous in our eyes.
[24]This is the day that the LORD has made;
　　let us rejoice and be glad in it.
[25]Save us, we beseech you, O LORD!
　　O LORD, we beseech you, give us success!

[26]Blessed is the one who comes in the name of the LORD.
　　We bless you from the house of the LORD.
[27]The LORD is God,
　　and he has given us light.
Bind the festal procession with branches,
　　up to the horns of the altar.

[28]You are my God, and I will give thanks to you;
　　you are my God, I will extol you.

[29]O give thanks to the LORD, for he is good,
　　for his steadfast love endures forever.

Connecting the Psalm with Scripture and Worship

Ordinarily, the Revised Common Lectionary appoints a psalm or a portion of a psalm to complement or respond to the first reading of the day, which, for most of the year, is a reading from the Old Testament. However, on Palm Sunday the lectionary appoints only two readings: the passage from one of the Gospels that tells the story of Jesus' entry into Jerusalem and Psalm 118:1–2, 19–29. The psalm has been chosen to respond to the entry story.

That He Should Come to Us

Our Evangelist has no word to speak about the march of the procession down into the valley, and up the other side, and through the gate, and into the narrow streets of the city that was "moved" as they passed through it. His language sounds as if he considered that our Lord's object in entering Jerusalem at all was principally to enter the Temple. He "looked round on all things" that were there. Can we fancy the keen observance, the recognition of the hidden bad and good, the blazing indignation, and yet dewy pity, in those eyes? His visitation of the Temple was its inspection by its Lord. And it was an inspection in order to cleanse. To-day He looked; to-morrow He wielded the whip of small cord. His chastisement is never precipitate. Perfect knowledge wields His scourge, and pronounces condemnation.

Brethren, Jesus Christ comes to us as a congregation, to the church to which we belong, and to us individually, with the same inspection. He whose eyes are a flame of fire says to His churches to-day, "I know thy works." What would He think if He came to us and tested us? . . .

We need nothing more, we should desire nothing more earnestly, than that He would come to us: "Search me, O Christ, and know me. And see if there be any wicked way in me, and lead me in the way everlasting." Jesus Christ is the King of England as truly as of Zion; and He is your King and mine. He comes to each of us, patient, meek, loving; ready to bless and cleanse. Dear brother, do you open your heart to Him? Do you acknowledge Him as your King? Do you count it your highest honour if He will use you and your possessions, and condescend to say that He has need of such poor creatures as we are? Do you cast your garments in the way, and say: "Ride on, great Prince"? Do you submit yourself to His inspection, to His cleansing?

Remember, He came once on "a colt, the foal of an ass, meek, and having salvation." He will come "on the white horse, in righteousness to judge and to make war," and with power to destroy.

Oh! I beseech you, welcome Him as He comes in gentle love, that when He comes in judicial majesty you may be among the "armies of heaven that follow after," and from immortal tongues utter rapturous and undying hosannas.

Alexander MacLaren, *The Gospel according to St. Mark, Chapters IX to XVI* (London: Hodder and Stoughton, 1906), 117–18.

The church gathers on Palm Sunday to celebrate Jesus' entry into Jerusalem. In each of the four Gospels we hear the crowd proclaim, "Blessed is the one [or "the king" (Luke 19:38)] who comes in the name of the Lord" (Mark 11:9b). Jesus rides into the city on the back of a colt (Mark 11:7) as many people follow, shouting, "Hosanna! Blessed is the coming kingdom." Psalm 118:26 reverberates as well with the shout of the crowd: "Blessed is the one who comes in the name of the LORD." No doubt, this proclamation of the king's entry was key in the choosing the psalm response for Palm Sunday.

Psalm 118 is a song of thanksgiving. The psalm begins and ends with the same words, "O give thanks to the LORD, for he is good; his steadfast love endures forever!" (Ps. 118:1, 29). The psalmist expresses gratitude for the never-ending love of the Lord. While the voice of the psalm seems to be that of an individual, praise is offered for the Lord's faithfulness to the whole community. God has acted. Salvation is known. "This is the LORD's doing" (v. 23). Offering thanksgiving in the place of worship is a fitting response of the individual and the community as well.

Psalm 118 is a psalm about movement, which makes it a perfect choice to accompany the Gospel stories of Jesus' processional entry into Jerusalem. Verse 19 declares, "Open to me the gates of righteousness, that I may *enter* through them and give thanks to the LORD." The psalmist begs for entry into the temple. Verses 19–27 describe movement: "that I may enter" (v. 19), "the righteous shall enter" (v. 20), "blessed is the one who comes" (v. 26), and "bind the festal procession" (v. 27). Perhaps these verses were used to accompany a liturgical procession as the people approached the entry way of the temple. The psalmist pleads for the gates to be opened so that entry is possible (v. 19). The gates open, and the righteous enter (v. 20), moving in a festal procession toward the altar.

Sixteen verses—a sizable portion of Psalm 118—are omitted from the lection for the Liturgy of the Palms/Palm Sunday. However, these omitted verses give the reason for giving thanks and the celebratory atmosphere heard in verses 19–29. Out of distress the psalmist called to the Lord for help (v. 5), and the Lord answered the psalmist's plea. The Lord is on the side of the psalmist, and refuge is found in the Lord (vv. 7–9). Furthermore, even when enemies surrounded the one asking for assistance, the Lord helped and enabled the psalmist to "cut them off" (vv. 10–14). The life of the psalmist is spared, and victory is known. Suffering is over (v. 5). The Lord is on the side of the one calling out for help. Strength and might and salvation are known because of the steadfast love of the Lord. There is much to celebrate. There is much for which to be thankful. Praise is the appropriate response.

Psalm 118 has been part of Palm Sunday observances at least since Egeria's pilgrimage in the fourth century, when the procession of the faithful made its way from the Mount of Olives down into Jerusalem proclaiming, "Blessed is the one who comes in the name of the Lord." Today, a worshiping body might gather at the front doors of the church building or in an open courtyard to sing or to hear or to read the psalm and to hear the proclamation of the Jerusalem entry before processing into the worship space.

A congregation may sing Argentinean minister and hymn writer Pablo Sosa's setting of Psalm 118, "Este es el día," with an English translation by Mary Louise Bringle ("This Is the Day").[1] The hymn might be sung in its entirety, or the sung refrain might be interspersed with a reading of the psalm verses by the gathered community or a choir of young voices. Both Sosa's version and Bringle's translation are faithful to the psalm text and sung to a singable, lilting tune.

ERIC T. MYERS

---

1. Pablo Sosa, "Este es el día," ©1983 GIA Publications, Inc., English trans. ©2006 GIA Publications, Inc. All rights reserved.

Mark 11:1–11

¹When they were approaching Jerusalem, at Bethphage and Bethany, near the Mount of Olives, he sent two of his disciples ²and said to them, "Go into the village ahead of you, and immediately as you enter it, you will find tied there a colt that has never been ridden; untie it and bring it. ³If anyone says to you, 'Why are you doing this?' just say this, 'The Lord needs it and will send it back here immediately.'" ⁴They went away and found a colt tied near a door, outside in the street. As they were untying it, ⁵some of the bystanders said to them, "What are you doing, untying the colt?" ⁶They told them what Jesus had said; and they allowed them to take it. ⁷Then they brought the colt to Jesus and threw their cloaks on it; and he sat on it. ⁸Many people spread their cloaks on the road, and others spread leafy branches that they had cut in the fields. ⁹Then those who went ahead and those who followed were shouting,

"Hosanna!
     Blessed is the one who comes in the name of the Lord!
     ¹⁰Blessed is the coming kingdom of our ancestor David!
Hosanna in the highest heaven!"

¹¹Then he entered Jerusalem and went into the temple; and when he had looked around at everything, as it was already late, he went out to Bethany with the twelve.

Commentary 1: Connecting the Reading with Scripture

By the time Jesus arrives at the outskirts of Jerusalem for his triumphal entry into the city, readers of Mark are prepared for hints of a royal inauguration. The Gospel opens by connecting Jesus to the kingdom or reign (*basileia*) of God (Mark 1:1–15). Mark calls this "good news" (*euangelion*, 1:1), a term used in the first century to announce the birth of an emperor or his ascent to the throne. In the OT, in its verbal form, "good news" announces return from exile and the restoration of God's rule (e.g., Isa. 52:7). Jesus' first words in Mark make explicit these imperial intimations: "The time is fulfilled, and the kingdom of God has come near" (1:15a). God is in charge, and God's chosen king has arrived.

Mark's account of the triumphal entry suggests, however, that the "many people" who correctly acclaim Jesus as "the one who comes in the name of the Lord" (11:9) may still have something to learn about the sort of king who is

in their midst. Like Peter at Caesarea Philippi, they are right to identify Jesus with messianic hopes, but they do not yet comprehend the sort of Messiah he is. Apparently, the ways of God can be difficult to understand.

Together with other pilgrims, Jesus is on the way to Jerusalem for the Passover. After passing through Jericho, they stop near Bethphage and Bethany. Although the precise location of Bethphage is uncertain, Bethany lies near the ridge of the Mount of Olives, a convenient rest stop less than two miles from Jerusalem (John 11:18). It is the home base to which Jesus will return during the weeklong Passover festivities (Mark 11:11–12; 14:3).

Events in Bethany around Passover play a key role in all four Gospel accounts. In John, Bethany is the home of Mary, Martha, and their brother Lazarus, whom Jesus raised from the dead (John 11:1–44). As a result of this "sign," the Jewish authorities plot the murder of both

Jesus and Lazarus (John 11:53; 12:10–11). In Luke, the village is the site of the ascension (Luke 24:50–51). In Mark as well as in Matthew, Bethany is home to Simon the leper, at whose table Jesus dines when a woman interrupts the meal to anoint Jesus' head with expensive ointment (Mark 14:3–9; cf. Matt. 26:6–13). Her ministrations mirror the anointing of a king (see 1 Sam. 10:1; 2 Kgs. 9:3), but Jesus explains them as preparation for his burial (Mark 14:8; Matt. 26:12), a sign of things to come.

Also in Mark, the arrival at Bethany places Jesus and his disciples right at the cusp of the passion that Jesus has predicted three times—with increasingly horrifying detail—since Peter's confession at Caesarea Philippi (Mark 8:31; 9:31; 10:33–34). The last of these predictions occurred recently, in narrative time, "on the road, going up to Jerusalem" (10:32). So far, the disciples have failed to grasp the gravity of Jesus' predictions, arguing repeatedly among themselves about the potential for greatness and glory (9:33–34; 10:35–37, 41). For their part, the people traveling with Jesus recognize only the celebratory and triumphant arrival of their Messiah. Mark's readers, however, cannot help but see the deepening pall cast over Jesus' approach to Jerusalem by the shadow of the cross that will meet him there.

Jesus sends two of his disciples into the village to procure a colt (Mark 11:2; Luke 19:30; cf. Matt. 21:2; John 12:14), a reminder of their earlier, two-by-two mission (Mark 6:7). His explicit instructions include words to say if anybody questions them, which in fact "some of the bystanders" do (11:5). Events turn out exactly as Jesus predicts, suggesting that his words are trustworthy and true, an oblique reminder of those three predictions of the passion as well as the promise that God will raise Jesus from the dead.

The disciples throw (*epiballō*) cloaks (*himation*) onto the colt before Jesus is seated on it, while many people spread their own cloaks "on the road" (*eis tēn hodon*; Mark 11:7–8; cf. Matt. 21:7–8; Luke 19:35–36). Their actions evoke the impromptu scene of a royal procession (see 2 Kgs. 9:13). They also suggest a verbal link to Jesus' earlier encounter with Bartimaeus, the man

who was blind and seated at the outskirts of Jericho when Jesus and the crowds left that town to begin the ascent toward the Mount of Olives. Wishing to regain his sight, Bartimaeus threw off (*apoballō*) his cloak (*himation*), went to Jesus for healing, and then followed him "on the way" (*en tē hodō*, Mark 10:50–52; cf. 8:27; 9:33–34; 10:32). Being "on the way" (or on the road) reflects not only the journey with Jesus toward Jerusalem but also the journey for all disciples, then and now, of learning the cost of discipleship.[1]

Bartimaeus's cry—"Jesus, Son of David, have mercy on me!" (10:47)—anticipates the shouts of the people as Jesus rides toward Jerusalem: "Hosanna! ["Save now!"] Blessed is the one who comes in the name of the Lord! Blessed is the coming kingdom of our ancestor David! Hosanna in the highest heaven!" (11:9b–10). Comprising a composite quote from Psalm 118:25–26, along with perhaps an allusion to Psalm 148:1, the acclamations reflect the crowd's messianic hopes. Their shouts, together with those of Bartimaeus, suggest their own answer to Jesus' question at Caesarea Philippi, "Who do you say that I am?" (8:27–30).

They have good reason to see Jesus as a messianic savior. The Mount of Olives, where his ride into Jerusalem originated, was more than just a convenient staging area from which to secure provisions. Well before the first century, the Mount of Olives had come to be associated with God's eschatological vindication of Jerusalem and the people of Israel. Across the Kidron valley from Jerusalem, its height afforded military protection to the city. Indeed, Psalm 125:2 links the mountains surrounding Jerusalem with God's protection. The prophet Ezekiel sees "the glory of the God of Israel" (Ezek. 43:1–2) returning to Jerusalem from there, where earlier it had "ascended from the middle of the city, and stopped on the mountain east of the city" (Ezek. 11:23). Zechariah associates the place with the coming of the Day of the Lord: "On that day his feet shall stand on the Mount of Olives, which lies before Jerusalem on the east; . . . Then the LORD my God will come, and all the holy ones with him" (Zech. 14:4a, 5b).

---

1. David Rhoads, Joanna Dewey, and Donald Michie, *Mark as Story: An Introduction to the Narrative of a Gospel*, 3rd ed. (Minneapolis: Fortress, 2012), 68.

By the time Jesus enters Jerusalem (Mark 11:11), people may well have expected a climactic ending to this first-century ticker-tape parade: speeches, applause, and perhaps a dramatic statement from the steps of the temple, with the first-century equivalent of cameras rolling. Not so. While each Gospel writer offers a different conclusion, Mark's ending to the episode is by far the most underwhelming. Jesus enters the temple, but he simply looks around at everything and returns to Bethany with his disciples, because it is already late. To be sure, events will heat up considerably the following day and continue to escalate after that, culminating in a cross, an empty tomb, a stranger, and a message for frightened women. On this day, however, as Jesus walks out of the temple, any hopes the people have for a decisive conclusion are dashed. King or not, where the ways of God are concerned, things do not always turn out quite the way people expect—both here and at the end of Mark's Gospel.

AUDREY WEST

Commentary 2: Connecting the Reading with the World

Most pastors worry, for good reason, that their parishioners will try to skip from the "Hosannas!" of Jesus' triumphal entry into Jerusalem to the "Hallelujahs" of his resurrection on Easter morning. The lectionary remedies this by coupling the Liturgy of the Palms with the Liturgy of the Passion, ensuring that—even if Maundy Thursday and Good Friday services are missed—the people of God will remember that the king who enters Jerusalem is heading to victory only by way of the cross.

Mark clearly has the cross in mind as he tells the story of Jesus' entry into Jerusalem, but perhaps no more than in the writing of the prior chapters, where he consistently tries to convince his disciples that to be the Messiah means to serve and to suffer (Mark 8:27–38; 9:30–32; 10:32–34). One might argue that the story this text tells is of an untriumphal entry. Like the other Synoptics, Mark includes no palms in his account. Palms in the ancient world were thought to be symbols of victory and are included only in John (see the alternate Gospel reading for the day).

Mark's account also has a flow that sets it apart from the other Synoptics; the entry into Jerusalem is treated more like a discrete act in the drama of Jesus' life than as the opening scene of the final act. The other Gospels, at the end of the account of the entry, make some comment about ongoing public reaction that segues it to the next stop of Passion Week. Matthew says that "the whole city was in turmoil" (Matt. 21:10). Luke portrays the Pharisees as chagrined by the shouts of joy and praise, asking Jesus to tamp down the disciples' enthusiasm (Luke 19:39). John has the Pharisees feeling helpless because the "whole world" has "gone after" Jesus (John 12:19). In every Gospel but Mark, the energy around Jesus builds with the Hosannas and seems even to fortify Jesus for his next stop in the passion: on to the temple to throw out the money changers!

In Mark, the energy following the entry dissipates. There is no mention of the city, or the Pharisees, being agitated. Instead we find Jesus, possibly all alone, "looking around" the city and then heading back to Bethany to rest with the disciples because "it was already late" (Mark 11:11). Preachers might ask parishioners to imagine what would happen if the famous Oberammergau Passion Play that has been running for over four hundred years in Germany decided to follow Mark's sequencing and inserted a new scene directly after Jesus enters Jerusalem but before he turns over the tables in the temple.

The scene would open with Jesus dismounted, the donkey returned to its owners, the crowds dispersed. Next we would see Jesus walking around town for a while, quite relaxed, maybe buying a snack, checking out the temple, looking at his watch, deciding it is getting late, and then walking the couple of miles back to Bethany to rest before coming back the next day to carry on. Would not audiences and congregations, eager to see Jesus push his way through to the cross, balk? What makes this scene stand out all the more, for careful readers of Mark, is that his Gospel as a whole is peppered with the word "immediately." The preacher might ask, "Why not Mark's typical sense of urgency?"

William Placher calls the return to Bethany following Jesus' entry an "odd anticlimax."[2] Calvin is so bothered by it that he argues Mark must have made an editing mistake. Mark "afterwards inserts" the story of the money changers being driven out, Calvin theorizes, "though not in its proper place."[3] With all due respect to Calvin, a preacher might find it fruitful to assume Mark's twist in the narrative is intentional. What might we make of it and its implications for our lives?

In twenty-first-century American culture, we tend to value doing over thinking. Looking around or calling it a night are far less likely to be considered world-changing behaviors than condemning rampant corruption or calling out hypocrisy on no sleep. A preacher might consider, however, that the Messiah in this story is not like the Jack Bauer of the television series; he is not confined to twenty-four hours to save the world with no time to think or rest. It might even be the case that Jesus is looking around to determine what his plan is for the next day; that reflection and strategizing are the work of the untriumphant Messiah he is. Perhaps he wants to sleep on his radical plan, just to be sure it is what God is calling him do and not an extension of his own bravado.

In a world in which we spend a lot of time crafting our identities on social media, or by wearing certain clothes, holding certain political views, having particular friends, or even hiring life coaches to help us develop our brand, the preacher of this text might notice out loud that Mark's Jesus, like us, is also interested in managing how he is perceived. Charles Campbell reads this text, in fact, as a story of Jesus presenting who he is by way of a carefully orchestrated "piece of street theatre."[4] Campbell's reading of

the story understands the meticulous instructions Jesus gives his disciples about the donkey not as a sign of his adherence to Zechariah 9:9. Rather, they reflect his "coming out" as a Messiah who defies the prevailing expectations of what a Messiah should be.

From the beginning to the end of Mark's Gospel, Jesus in intentional ways challenges people to contemplate who he is and is quite directive about managing what people think about who he is. When demons recognize him as the Son of God, when a leper is healed, and when Peter correctly identifies him as the Messiah, Jesus tells them not to tell anyone (1:34, 44; 8:30). Once it becomes clear that Peter assumes a "Messiah" cannot suffer, Jesus rebukes him harshly (8:33).

The preacher might lead members of the congregation to reflect on how hard it is for human beings to insist on being known as who we are, rather than succumbing to pressure to become who others want us to be. Attention might be drawn to the world of popular author and psychologist Brené Brown, who has captivated millions on the subject of authenticity and vulnerability in her books and TED talks. What does this story in Mark have to add to contemporary efforts at self-help?

Perhaps the preacher can testify to how Jesus' example in Mark can inspire us to live into the fullness of who we are, even as he has shown us himself. A charge could point out that in a few days we will be asked, again, to stand with a Messiah who is called to suffer. Will we argue with Jesus, as Peter did in chapter 8? Will we fall asleep in the corner of Gethsemane, even though he shakes us awake to pray with him (chap. 14)? The preacher might exhort listeners to prepare themselves to participate in the passion by taking time, tonight, to look around, to think, and to rest. Today we have seen the Messiah, and he is not what we expected. What will he do tomorrow, and how can I let go of my resistance?

CYNTHIA L. RIGBY

2. William C. Placher, *Mark*, Belief Commentary Series (Louisville, KY: Westminster John Knox, 2009), 158.

3. John Calvin, *Harmony of the Evangelists: Matthew, Mark, and Luke*, ed. William Pringle, in *Calvin's Commentaries* (Grand Rapids: Baker Books, 2009), 3:9.

4. Charles Campbell, in *Feasting on the Word, Year B, Volume 2* (Louisville, KY: Westminster John Knox, 2008), 157.

John 12:12–16

¹²The next day the great crowd that had come to the festival heard that Jesus was coming to Jerusalem. ¹³So they took branches of palm trees and went out to meet him, shouting,

> "Hosanna!
> Blessed is the one who comes in the name of the Lord—
>   the King of Israel!"

¹⁴Jesus found a young donkey and sat on it; as it is written:

> ¹⁵"Do not be afraid, daughter of Zion.
> Look, your king is coming,
>   sitting on a donkey's colt!"

¹⁶His disciples did not understand these things at first; but when Jesus was glorified, then they remembered that these things had been written of him and had been done to him.

Commentary 1: Connecting the Reading with Scripture

According to John's account of the triumphal entry into Jerusalem, the whole event is nearly finished before it gets started. It takes almost as much ink to explain how the disciples remembered events later as it does to tell of the parade in the first place, suggesting perhaps that the point of the passage extends beyond the triumphal entry itself.

To be sure, the Synoptics, including Mark's pericope in today's lectionary, give about the same air time that John gives to the actual ride into Jerusalem, including several elements shared with John, such as crowds who wave greenery ("palms" in John only), Jesus riding on a donkey or colt, and shouts of "Hosanna!" In the Synoptics, however, attention lands on details about the preparation for entry into the city. Jesus sends two disciples into a village near the Mount of Olives as an advance team to secure a colt (Mark 11:1–2; Luke 19:29–30; in Matt. 21:2, a donkey and her colt). He gives explicit instructions about where to find the animal and what to say if anybody asks about it, which, in fact, somebody does (Mark 11:5; Luke 19:33). Events unfold as Jesus predicts, and the disciples bring the animal to Jesus.

They put (or throw) their cloaks onto the beast, and Jesus sits on it (Mark 11:7; Matt. 21:7; in Luke 19:35 they "set Jesus" upon it). Still others throw their cloaks onto the ground in front of him like a proverbial red carpet (Matt. 21:8; Mark 11:8; Luke 19:36).

In John, Jesus seeks no assistance from the disciples. Instead, when the crowds come to meet him, shouting and waving palm branches, Jesus "found a young donkey and sat on it" (John 12:14). Here, as throughout the Passion Narrative that follows, Jesus acts autonomously and takes charge, even when it appears that events are happening *to* him. For example, when Judas brings a cadre of soldiers and others to Gethsemane to arrest him, Jesus steps forward to meet them (John 18:4). At his trial before Pilate, instead of remaining silent (see Mark 15:5), Jesus speaks up (John 18:36–37; 19:11). No one forces Simon of Cyrene to carry the cross for him (Mark 15:21; cf. Matt. 27:32; Luke 23:26). Instead, Jesus carries the cross to Golgotha "by himself" (John 19:17). Even on the cross, Jesus seems to be in control of the moment of his death, announcing, "It is finished," before bowing his head and giving up his spirit (19:30). As he had previously told the Pharisees, "No one takes [my life] from me, but I lay it down of my own accord. I have power to lay it down, and I have power to take it up again" (10:18; see vv. 11, 15).

In contrast to the Synoptic Gospels—which mention only one visit to Jerusalem during Jesus' public ministry (Matt. 21:10; Mark 11:11; Luke 19:45)—in John, Jesus had been to Jerusalem several times already (John 5:1; 7:10; 10:22), including two prior Passover festivals (2:13; 6:4). During the first Passover, Jesus made a whip of cords (only in John 2:15) and turned things upside down in the temple. He predicted the temple's destruction and its rebuilding (2:19), which his disciples later understood to be a prophecy about himself (2:22)—not unlike the development in their understanding mentioned in our passage (12:16; see 2:17; 16:4). In contrast to Mark, in which the temple incident fuels murderous plans by the religious authorities (Mark 11:18), no such opposition occurs during that first Passover visit in John. Instead, "many believed in [Jesus'] name because they saw the signs that he was doing" (John 2:23), signs that included those prophetic words and actions against the temple's money changers.

People's belief in Jesus plays a role in the third Passover just as it did in the first. This time, however, unrelenting hostility from the religious authorities casts a deep shadow over the whole episode. Their ire is a consequence of the raising of Lazarus (narrated through most of chap. 11), which had resulted in many Jews believing in Jesus. So, "from that day on they planned to put him to death" (11:53). Repeated reference to those two realities—Lazarus's being raised from the dead by Jesus (12:1, 9, 17) and the menacing stance of the authorities (11:57; 12:10–11, 19)—provides the immediate narrative context of our passage. This foreboding literary frame around Jesus' triumphal entry suggests that any celebration occurring at Jesus' arrival is likely to be short-lived.

The crowd's shouts of "Hosanna!" are acclamations that one might hear at a royal procession. Their words mirror Psalm 118:26, proclaiming "the one who comes in the name of the LORD," with the addition of "the King of Israel" (John 12:13). Others who encounter Jesus in John consider the "coming one" to be the prophet (6:14) or the Messiah (4:25; cf. 7:31; 11:27). Whatever those titles convey about their understanding of Jesus' identity, kingship and its association with Jesus run from beginning to end in John. Nathanael calls Jesus the King of Israel (1:49), but before too long, when people want to make Jesus king by force, Jesus prevents it by withdrawing to a mountain by himself (6:15). In the trial before Pilate, questions concerning the nature of Jesus' kingship appear throughout (18:33, 36, 39; 19:3, 12, 14, 19).

At the entry to Jerusalem, Psalm 118 gives voice to the crowd's desire for a king. The psalm itself is a song of thanksgiving for the enduring love of God, a testimony to God's faithfulness in the past and an expression of hope for the future. As the story unfolds in John, this enduring love of God that connects past and future is found also in the identity of Jesus and whence he came. He is "the true light . . . coming into the world" (John 1:9), sent by the love of God not to condemn the world but to save it. Jesus is the one "who comes from above" to do just that (3:16–17, 31). Jesus knows "where I have come from and where I am going" (8:14); that is, "I came from the Father and have come into the world; . . . I am leaving the world and am going to the Father" (16:28; cf. 5:43; 8:42; 14:3). Twice our assigned passage explicitly identifies Jesus with the one who comes (12:12–13), while a similar reference appears in the fulfillment citation, "Look, your king is coming" (12:15; cf. Zeph. 3:15–16).

The verb "to come" (*erchomai*) links all of these passages and many more to a fundamental identity of Jesus: he is the one who came from God that "they may have life, and have it abundantly" (John 10:10). Like the disciples in 12:16, we might not fully understand what that means or how it will play out as events unfold in the life of the church or in our individual lives. Although we live on this side of Easter, we still live in that space between welcome and rejection, between acclaim and denial, between life and death. From that vantage point, we might recognize Jesus as the one who rescued Lazarus from the bonds of death, while we also wait in hope that he will deliver us and the world from forces that seek to destroy and kill. The promise shared by John's Gospel is that "the one who comes in the name of the Lord" is the same one who came "in order that the world might be saved through him" (3:17).

AUDREY WEST

Commentary 2: Connecting the Reading with the World

In the Synoptic Gospels, Jesus instructs the disciples to fetch the donkey he will ride into Jerusalem, giving them detailed instructions that draw both them and the donkey's caretakers into the fanfare surrounding Jesus' entry. In the Gospel of John, Jesus finds the donkey himself, and only after he is greeted by a palm-waving crowd of people who are shouting "Hosanna!" and calling him "the King of Israel" (John 12:13). John informs us that the disciples are confused –they will not understand what is happening until Jesus later is "glorified" (12:16). They are standing on the sidelines, listening to the "Hosannas," wondering about the donkey, not yet connecting the event to the prophecy in Zechariah (12:15; cf. Zech. 9:9). What is the preacher to make of the disciples' place in this alternate reading of the Palm Sunday story?

Perhaps John is emphasizing that the work of these final days is Jesus' work and not the work of the disciples. In chapter 14, Jesus chastises Thomas for complaining that he does not know the way to where Jesus is going. "I am the way, and the truth, and the life," Jesus tells him, implying that Thomas should stop trying to manage things and instead should trust him to do so (14:6). In chapter 17, on the night he is betrayed, Jesus does not try to get the disciples to wake up and pray with him, as he does so fervently in the Synoptics. Rather, he prays for them—for their faith, their unity, their ministry to others.

The preacher might suggest that some will find it difficult, in the week ahead, to bear witness to the unfolding narrative. We may want to manage it, to change it, or at least to find Jesus a more suitable donkey. It is better to give than receive, we like to say, but receiving a gift is often more difficult, especially when it is a gift that comes at great cost to someone we love. Perhaps we can identify with Peter, who is eager to participate but simply cannot figure out what to do. He tries to show his respect for Jesus by refusing to allow Jesus to wash his feet, but Jesus will have none of it (13:8). He attempts to fight off Jesus' enemies but is chastised (18:10–11). He pledges loyalty to Christ and fails (18:15–27).

In a cultural context in which we value getting involved, making a difference, and working for change, congregants might need to be coaxed into stepping back from the crowds, wondering where Jesus got that donkey, and asking why the people are waving palms and shouting "Hosanna!" ("save us"). We commonly mock the disciples when they seem to know less than we do, but maybe we should instead look to them for guidance about where we should stand in relation to the triumphal entry and the passion. Perhaps, in this regard, the skeptics among us have something to teach the go-getters about the value of not immediately joining in, about the value of first wondering what Jesus is up to now, and then considering what these events might mean for our lives and for the life of the world. What if we were to ask, over and over again this coming week: What is Jesus up to, now? When he washes the disciples' feet? When he talks of going away, and coming again? When he scolds Peter for cutting off that ear?

Theologically, the preacher might also want to reflect on how John manages the relationship between *chronos* ("measured time") and *kairos* ("a favorable time") in the telling of this story, and what his approach has to teach us about engaging the events of the week to come. Clearly John wants us to know that he has—and always has had—the end of the chronological story in mind: Jesus will be "glorified" in the resurrection, and all things will be made clear. John, in this, is like us: we already know how this story ends. We come to church on Palm Sunday morning aware that Jesus is about to alter all worldly conceptions of kingship, triumph, and power. The glory of God has already broken into chronological time (*kairos* into *chronos*), John and we readers know, in the person of Jesus Christ (1:14). However, the disciples, confined by their place in chronological time, have not yet fully absorbed this. The disciples will catch on, after they, like us, know the whole story (12:16).

The preacher might acknowledge that some hearers of this story may be frustrated by the disciples' standoffishness. After all, the crowd of palm-waving, testifying people do not have to understand everything in order actively to participate, so why do the disciples not, like them, simply jump on board? John explains the crowd's following of Jesus by pointing backwards, this time, in the chronology of events. These folks have just witnessed Jesus raising Lazarus from the dead (12:17). Why was this enough to draw them into the Palm Sunday festivities, but not enough to hook the disciples?

The tables might be turned by asking members of the congregation on what basis, if any, they believe Jesus is the "King of Israel." Is it because of particular acts Jesus does in chronological time? Is it because they know where the whole story is headed, including the resurrection at the end? Are they more like the crowds who cheer for him, or the disciples who step back and wonder? What is John saying belief looks like, and how do we get there from here? By joining in each event of the coming week with enthusiasm? By, instead, standing back and wondering what in the world Jesus is up to, and how it all comes together? The preacher might want to remind the congregation that the point of telling any story (including the story of the passion)

is not simply to get to the end. Rather, it is to invite listeners to enter into the details of each scene with the storyteller, so that they can find their way into the story—whether as enthusiasts or skeptics—and be transformed by it.

Reflecting on the church's historical teaching on the incarnation might also be useful. Likely the biblical verse most quoted at the Council of Chalcedon (451 CE), where the church declared that Jesus is fully human and fully divine, was John 1:14: "And the Word became flesh and lived among us, and we have seen his glory . . . ." While members of the congregation will probably identify this with Christmas, they might be encouraged to use it as a lens that focuses on what is happening today and in the coming week. There is the Word—in the flesh—right here, at the festival, with us. We have seen his glory: he just raised Lazarus from the dead!

The incarnation, church teaching insists, is not a thirty-three-year experiment, or the way Jesus got down to earth so he could do the saving work of dying. This Jesus who humbly rides a donkey into Jerusalem is fully divine as well as fully human, even when the world does not know him (1:10). This Jesus who in a few days will rise from the dead is fully human as well as fully divine—every bit as human as that king riding on the donkey, today. The Word made flesh will not leave his flesh behind in that tomb, but somehow will take it along with him, just as he will take his divinity to the cross.

This, John insists, is the good news both for the confused and for the enthusiastic, for the disciples and for the whole world God so loves (see 3:16; 13:1).

CYNTHIA L. RIGBY

Liturgy of the Passion

Isaiah 50:4–9a
Psalm 31:9–16
Philippians 2:5–11

Mark 14:1–15:47
Mark 15:1–39 (40–47)

Isaiah 50:4–9a

⁴The Lord GOD has given me
    the tongue of a teacher,
that I may know how to sustain
    the weary with a word.
Morning by morning he wakens—
    wakens my ear
    to listen as those who are taught.
⁵The Lord GOD has opened my ear,
    and I was not rebellious,
    I did not turn backward.
⁶I gave my back to those who struck me,
    and my cheeks to those who pulled out the beard;
I did not hide my face
    from insult and spitting.

⁷The Lord GOD helps me;
    therefore I have not been disgraced;
therefore I have set my face like flint,
    and I know that I shall not be put to shame;
    ⁸he who vindicates me is near.
Who will contend with me?
    Let us stand up together.
Who are my adversaries?
    Let them confront me.
⁹ᵃIt is the Lord GOD who helps me;
    who will declare me guilty?

Commentary 1: Connecting the Reading with Scripture

This is one of the four Servant Songs in Isaiah (Isa. 42:1–4; 49:1–6; 50:4–9; 52:13–53:12). These four poems had long been thought to have constituted a separate corpus in the extensive scribal processes that yielded the magnificent and complex book of Isaiah as we have it. With the rise of more nuanced literary approaches, the scholarly conversation has moved in a different direction, focusing on ways various sections of Isaiah are woven together through shared motifs

and elaborations of earlier material. The Servant Songs have much in common with other material throughout Isaiah 40–55, including several passages that present "Jacob"—all Israel—as the servant of YHWH.

The Servant Songs describe the commissioning and strengthening of an individual who is to teach about God and work for justice (42:3). Appointed before birth (49:1) and graced with God's spirit (42:1), the Servant is to exercise his prophetic vocation within Israel, calling God's people to return to faithfulness (49:5). He also guides many outside of the covenant community, for his teaching is meant to instruct "the coastlands" (42:4; 49:1) and enlighten "the nations" (42:6; 49:6). In these four poems, a dramatic story unfolds through first-person narration and third-person reflections. The Servant faces fierce resistance to his divinely ordained mission; he struggles with despair (49:4) and is subjected to derision (53:3), unjust imprisonment (53:8), and beatings (50:6; 53:5). A communal voice concludes the story: the Servant has been killed, his torturous death understood by his community as somehow bearing the sins of many transgressors (53:11–12).

The third Servant Song offers much for one who preaches during the Liturgy of the Passion. This poem should not be treated merely as background to the drama of Jesus' suffering. Rather, the preacher can explore the compelling images and voicing in Isaiah 50:4–9a to teach about the habits of faithfulness that sustain believers in times of fear, conflict, and suffering. Two dimensions of our passage may compel the preacher's attention: spiritual listening as essential for those eager to learn the purposes of God, and missional resilience based on trust in God as One who is mighty to vindicate the righteous.

A preliminary textual observation will aid our consideration of the poem. The Servant speaks of the Deity as the Lord God ('*adonay YHWH*, with the Tetragrammaton vocalized as '*elohim*). That name for God is not common outside of the corpus of the Latter Prophets. By far, the densest concentration of instances occurs in Ezekiel (over two hundred times), compared to four instances in the entire Pentateuch, three instances in the Psalter, and eight instances in Isaiah 40–55. Within Isaiah 1–39, this appellation for God is used four times, apart from its occurrence within the military title "Lord God of Hosts." Those four instances are in contexts in which those under threat are to trust in the power of the Lord God to avert destruction or overcome death (see 7:7; 25:8; 28:16; 30:15). This theme is articulated in the Servant Songs as well. Within Isaiah 40–55, "Lord God" occurs

only eight times, always in passages celebrating God's might to redeem (40:10; 48:16; 49:22; 52:4; and four times in this Servant Song).

Noteworthy is the instance of "Lord God" at 48:16, introducing the commissioning of the Servant ("now the Lord God has sent me and his spirit"). Immediately following is this theological claim: "I am the Lord your God, who teaches you for your own good, who leads you in the way you should go. O that you had paid attention to my commandments!" (48:17b–18a). Thus the instances of "the Lord God" in Isaiah underscore God's power to redeem and to teach. YHWH instructs the beloved community (54:13, "all your children shall be taught by the Lord") and teaches those outside the fold of Israel as well (51:4, "a teaching will go out from me, and my justice for a light to the peoples"). The Servant participates in this formational instruction offered by God.

First, then, the preacher might highlight that the Servant listens daily as "one who is taught." It is advisable to ignore the emendation proposed by the NRSV for the first clause of verse 4; the KJV has it right with "the tongue of the learned." The Hebrew text is clear: what the Lord God has given the Servant is the tongue of those who are taught (*limmudim*). The sense is that those who devote themselves to theological learning—disciples in the prophetic tradition, those immersed in Torah—know how to speak eloquently of God in ways that refresh "the weary."

This beautiful aspect of the Servant's formation, too often overlooked, is central to his mission as "a light to the nations" (42:6; 49:6). The preacher could lift up the riches of wisdom and deepened faith that await those who follow the Servant's example. How do we listen? Most Christians realize that prayer is important, but many know little beyond the basics of petition and intercession. Though some may be aware of mindfulness techniques, many are unfamiliar with Christian traditions of spiritual discernment. Unless the preacher is addressing a gathering of monastics, the majority of hearers will not have experienced the intentional practice of waiting in deep interior silence for God. All hearers, from the skeptic to the seeker to the seasoned believer, can be enriched by homiletical guidance on ways in which we can be "taught" by God through prayerful listening.[1]

Second, the preacher could expand on the missional resilience presented by the Servant.[2] Scripture teaches that the prophetic vocation inevitably involves opposition. Moses encounters hostility many times as he leads Israel through the wilderness (see Exod. 16:2–8; 17:1–7; Num. 11:1–12:15; 14:1–35; 16:1–35, 41–50; 20:2–13; 21:4–9). Hosea encounters derision; his opponents cry, "'The prophet is a fool, the man of the spirit is mad!'" (Hos. 9:7). Amos is expelled from his ministry context (Amos 7:10–17). Micah's adversaries try to silence him: "'Do not preach'—thus they preach—'one should not preach of such things'" (Mic. 2:6). Jeremiah bitterly laments the animosity and violence that confront him (Jer. 11:18–12:6; 15:10–21; 17:14–18; 18:18–23; 20:1–18); he is incarcerated more than once, thrown into a muddy cistern (38:1–13), and taken to Egypt against his will (42:15–43:7).

The Servant of YHWH too faces ferocious antagonism, something evident especially in Isaiah 50 and 52–53. Nevertheless, the Servant resolutely trusts in God, acclaimed throughout Isaiah as the Holy One, who redeems the righteous. Seen in the light of God's power, human adversaries are of little consequence: "all of them will wear out like a garment" (50:9b). The Servant gives himself wholly to his mission, demonstrating a spiritual resilience that can be inspiring for all who struggle.

The Gospel reading will show Jesus betrayed by Judas, abandoned by the disciples, denied by Peter, scourged, mocked, and crucified. The third Servant Song constitutes a powerful resource to prepare those who would follow this Savior (Matt. 16:24–26; Mark 8:34–37; Luke 9:23–25; Rom. 6:1–11; Gal. 2:19–20). Prayerful listening and resilient trust in our Redeemer: by the grace of God, these can enable us to follow Jesus even to the cross.

CAROLYN J. SHARP

Commentary 2: Connecting the Reading with the World

Here we are at one of the most countercultural of the church's days. In a sense, the end of Holy Week and the suffering of Christ are against just about everything Americans believe in. No wonder the church forces us to stare at the crucified, to look at what the Servant's service to God has done to the Servant. Here is the God many of us did not expect, the God many of us did not think we needed. We wanted a powerful, high, lifted-up deity who could descend, take charge, and fix what is wrong with us by the skillful application of divine power.

What we got was the Servant who offered his innocent body for the abuse, the scorn, and the spitting. Martin Luther King Jr. fiercely defended the rights of African Americans and attacked the systems of white supremacy. Yet he did so as a servant to the Servant. King acted nonviolently and

demanded nonviolent resistance from his followers. He did not do so as a strategy. He did not commend nonviolent sit-ins and nonresistance to police violence as a savvy political technique. King's nonviolence came from the God whom King worshiped. As a Christian, nonviolence was the only weapon King was given by the Trinity. When King's partners in protest knelt before the fire hoses and the dogs in Birmingham, when they stood up to officially sanctioned violence worked against them, they were doing so in imitation of the way of the Servant.

I know someone who stood up to her employer and told the truth about repeated instances of sexual abuse that had occurred in her company. What was the boss's response? He disregarded her testimony, allowing some of her fellow employees to question her integrity. The denials moved into

1. Resources on prayerful listening include Cynthia Bourgeault, *Centering Prayer and Inner Awakening* (New York: Cowley, 2004); Thomas Keating, *Intimacy with God: An Introduction to Centering Prayer* (New York: Crossroad, 2009); Kay L. Northcutt, *Kindling Desire for God: Preaching as Spiritual Direction* (Minneapolis: Fortress, 2009).

2. Preachers may find helpful Patrick W. T. Johnson, *The Mission of Preaching: Equipping the Community for Faithful Witness* (Downers Grove, IL: InterVarsity Press, 2015).

hostile accusation and vilification of this courageous truth-teller. One of her friends in the company asked her, "Why on earth would you take on this problem? You should have known that these men would lie about what they did. Didn't you know that they would try to drive you out of the company?" She responded, "I have no good reason for my actions other than I am a Christian. Just trying to act like Jesus."

Every Christian is named "Christopher." Each one of us is a "Christ-bearer." That means that servants of the Servant are obligated to look like and act like Jesus, the God we got, rather than the one we wanted.

The Servant in Isaiah asks, "Who will argue with me? . . . Who will bring judgment against me?" (50:8 CEB). The events of this week give answer to the Servant when Jesus' life echoes Isaiah. Who will argue, who will judge against God's Servant? Well, just about everybody: the authorities, religious and political, the screaming mob. In short, all of us. A divided populace comes together this week in unified repudiation of the Servant. We echo this rejection. When asked for a verdict on Jesus of Nazareth and his ministry, we all shout with one voice, "Crucify him!"

"We were a bitterly divided congregation," he said. "Our arguments over issues of sexual orientation, biblical interpretation, a new roof on the parsonage, everything we discussed split us into at least two parties. Then Tom came to us. He was one of the finest Christians I've ever met. He is a quiet, serene peacemaker. He spent hours listening to both parties, trying to see the best in each of them. He patiently taught us and loved us, working night and day to be an attentive, loving pastor to us."

"That's wonderful," I said, "just the sort of leadership required in a fractured, contentious church."

"Right. You want to know our response?" he said. "We crucified him. Some people called Tom weak and ineffective. They complained that he spent too much time patiently listening and too little time fixing our problems. What Tom saw as compromise, people—those on both sides, conservative and liberal—saw as a lack of conviction. They just could not stand that Tom refused to take sides in our debates. His ministry here ended a year after it began."

Once, there was One who came to us with open-handed love. He reached out across our boundaries and called to himself those whom we had excluded. When we wronged him, cursed him, resisted his embrace, we added, "Crucify him!" The Servant responded, "Father, forgive."

We look upon the Servant, and we see who God really is. God is whoever came to us as the Servant, as the Crucified Jesus. As the church has long said, Jesus is the full, perfect, complete revelation of who God is and what God is up to in the world. At the same time, the Servant is not only a window into the heart of God but also a mirror that reflects who we truly are. Scripture both reveals who God is and shows what happens—who we are and what we are up to—when God comes to us as the crucified.

"If you turn the other cheek, when someone strikes you on the cheek, then all that happens is somebody will strike you on the other cheek." How true. In his Sermon on the Mount in Matthew 5, when Jesus urges us to turn the other cheek, I do not believe he does so with a claim that by doing so we will bring out the best in our attacker. There are those who see nonresponse to violence as just an opportunity to bring greater violence.

Remember that scene from the movie *Gandhi*? Protesting Indians are met by British soldiers who order them to disperse. When they do not, the British begin beating the first person in line. When they beat senseless one person, the one behind steps up and receives the blows. Then another. And another. All day long they continue to step up. A reporter on the scene says something like, "Today the British Empire has lost any claim of moral respectability." Those Indians following Gandhi exposed the impotency of the powerful.

When Martin Luther King Jr. led the demonstrations in Birmingham and the city fathers unleashed Bull Connor and his police, King planned the demonstrations early enough in the day so that there was time for the national news to film the scene and play it that evening. Across the country, Americans saw the police state that Birmingham had become. In the days afterward, those who did the beatings were themselves beaten, defeated. Evil was exposed. Good gained the upper hand.

As we stand at the foot of the cross, we look upon a victim of humanity's collective evil. We also are forced thereby to consider ourselves. Who are we? We are those who create and build, who work and achieve, and some of our human achievements have indeed been for the common good. However, to tell the truth, you have not told the full truth about us until you have admitted that we are also those who all got together and, on a dark Friday afternoon, democracy in action just happened to crucify the Son of God.

The one who preached love was silenced. The one who so actively moved in the world in God's name, announcing the advent of God's realm, was shut up in a tomb.

Who is God? The one who hangs upon a cross, forgiving those who have crucified him. Who are we? The ones who nailed the Son of God to the cross.

This is what we have done. The next move is God's. What shall God do with those who have, through our words and deeds, revealed who we really are?

WILL WILLIMON

Psalm 31:9–16

⁹Be gracious to me, O LORD, for I am in distress;
    my eye wastes away from grief,
    my soul and body also.
¹⁰For my life is spent with sorrow,
    and my years with sighing;
my strength fails because of my misery,
    and my bones waste away.

¹¹I am the scorn of all my adversaries,
    a horror to my neighbors,
an object of dread to my acquaintances;
    those who see me in the street flee from me.
¹²I have passed out of mind like one who is dead;
    I have become like a broken vessel.
¹³For I hear the whispering of many—
    terror all around!—
as they scheme together against me,
    as they plot to take my life.

¹⁴But I trust in you, O LORD;
    I say, "You are my God."
¹⁵My times are in your hand;
    deliver me from the hand of my enemies and persecutors.
¹⁶Let your face shine upon your servant;
    save me in your steadfast love.

Connecting the Psalm with Scripture and Worship

The Sunday that stands at the beginning of Holy Week is actually two "days" in the Christian year calendar: Palm Sunday/Liturgy of the Palms and Sunday of the Passion/Liturgy of the Passion. At one time, the two "days" were observed on different Sundays, but twentieth-century revisions of the calendar assigned the two to be celebrated on one Sunday, the Sixth Sunday in Lent. The Revised Common Lectionary appoints separate readings for each of the two observances that reflect the shift from the pomp of Palm Sunday to the pathos of Passion Sunday. The juxtaposition of Palm Sunday and Sunday of the Passion takes the worshipers, if they are willing to go, from the crowded, Hosanna-filled, palm-branch-strewn streets of Jerusalem to the barren, God-forsaken, trash heap of a hill outside of the city, where the drama of the events of Holy Week comes to a power-filled head.

On both Palm Sunday and the Sunday of the Passion the readings from the Gospels drive the day. The other readings, including the selections from the Psalms, have been chosen to supplement the Gospel stories. This is never truer than on Passion Sunday, when the Gospel reading tells of the suffering and death of Jesus. So perhaps it is best to hear or sing or read the psalm selection for Passion Sunday, rather than attempt to compose a full sermon on the psalm text.

Often the Psalms express the praise or even lament of the community, but not today's selection, Psalm 31:9–16; these verses are a prayer of one person. "Be gracious to *me,* O LORD, for *I* am in distress" (Ps. 31:9). "I," "my," or "me"—parts of speech on behalf of the subject—are heard twenty-seven times in these eight verses. The subject is desperate. The only other people mentioned or referred to in the psalm selection are the "adversaries" and horrified neighbors. There is no support, no help from others—even the neighbors and acquaintances turn their backs. The pray-er is in trouble and pleads for the Lord to be gracious and to bring salvation in the time of trouble.

In the midst of such dire straits the psalmist utters the word "but" (v. 14), indicating some sort of shift. Even in the midst of trouble and distress, the psalmist is able to pray, "But I trust in you, O Lord," and to declare complete trust: "My times are in your hand" (v. 15). The psalmist affirms full confidence in God even while experiencing utter despair.

It is interesting that verses 9–16 are about a present situation. Often the words of the Psalms recall how God has acted in the past in an effort to remind God, pray-er, and community that God has been there before and is now called on to act again. The eight verses of Psalm 31 appointed for Passion Sunday do not mention the past. They are about the situation here and now. Misery and wasting away are happening now, and the petition is made for God to do something now.

Psalm 31:9–16 is a fitting prayer to be heard or prayed on Passion Sunday as the worshiping community hears the story of Jesus' last days, though the words of the psalm could just as well be the prayer of someone going through betrayal and trials and even death now. Of course, it is not Jesus' words heard in the prayer of these verses, but juxtaposed with the passion story, worshipers hear the plight of Jesus and others in the words of the psalm prayer. As James Mays states, the verses of Psalm 31 have become "a kind of commentary on the passion of Jesus; Christians read in its description of affliction a witness to the suffering he [Jesus] endured."[1]

So, how might these verses best be heard in worship? Perhaps, since they are a prayer, they could be prayed in unison following the reading of the passion story, when worshipers might hear the voice of Jesus, be led to a reflection of personal times of despair, or remember the plight of others.

Using a contemporary reworking of the psalm as a congregational hymn is possible as well. David Gambrell's setting of Psalm 31 is masterful, as it sustains the individual tone of the psalm and yet employs language that is not too personal for nearly all humans to identify with what is sung. Notice that in stanza five, Gambrell preserves the important turn from despair to hope and trust in God: "And yet I trust in you, O God; your covenant still stands. Redeem me, in your faithful love: my life is in your hands."[2]

As congregations celebrate both Palm Sunday and the Sunday of the Passion, the verses of Psalm 31:9–16 will help worshiping bodies voice the lament of Jesus on the cross, sing their own cries of anguish, and yet proclaim their complete trust in their God.

ERIC T. MYERS

1. James Luther Mays, *Psalms*, Interpretation (Louisville, KY: John Knox, 1994), 142.
2. David Gambrell, "You Are My Refuge, Faithful God," in *Glory to God* (Louisville, KY: Westminster John Knox, 2013), #214.

Philippians 2:5–11

⁵Let the same mind be in you that was in Christ Jesus,

> ⁶who, though he was in the form of God,
>> did not regard equality with God
>> as something to be exploited,
> ⁷but emptied himself,
>> taking the form of a slave,
>> being born in human likeness.
> And being found in human form,
>> ⁸he humbled himself
>> and became obedient to the point of death—
>> even death on a cross.

> ⁹Therefore God also highly exalted him
>> and gave him the name
>> that is above every name,
> ¹⁰so that at the name of Jesus
>> every knee should bend,
>> in heaven and on earth and under the earth,
> ¹¹and every tongue should confess
>> that Jesus Christ is Lord,
>> to the glory of God the Father.

Commentary 1: Connecting the Reading with Scripture

Writing from prison, Paul delivers an incredibly joyful letter to the church in Philippi on the nature of servanthood and gratitude. At the heart of the letter is a call to embrace servanthood by possessing the same mind with one another; such a mind is meant to be the mind of Christ. Paul describes that mind of Christ using words from what probably was a hymn familiar to the early church. This is one of four such likely hymns found in NT (Col. 1:15–20; Heb. 1:2–4; and John 1:1–5). These four hymns are oriented around christological confession and reflection, and all four speak of Jesus as having some level of equality or exaltation with God. At the very same time, they describe Jesus laying aside that lofty status for the sake of humanity.

The hymn's structure fits within Greco-Roman notions of honor and shame. In the ancient world, those of high status hold honor. The members of their household and their slaves take a position of shame. Such shame is not the same as feeling ashamed or abased, which is how we tend to define shame in our time. In the ancient world, shame was more a sense of deference or support for the one being honored. Clearly, the one who held honor received status and acclaim. That status increased with the number of people who showed deference. In turn, the one who held honor was supposed to support the ones who showed deference. Such support would demonstrate their generosity and increase their status.

Often, those who hold honor would describe how their generosity or kindness to those of lesser status was a gift that would make the subordinates' lives better, even as they remained slaves or subservient members of the household. The head of a household would grant more food, freedom, or responsibility to a household member or slave as a gift extending from the superior's honor. At the highest level, the emperor, who held the most honor, would claim to shower benefits on all the citizens of Rome by his kindness or declarations of peace. In such a cultural system, there was a finite amount of honor to go around, so those of highest honor were careful how much they bestowed on others. They went to great lengths to describe the sharing of any honor as an incredible gift.[1]

Paul does not seem to worry about a limited supply of honor. Instead, he describes Jesus emptying his honor completely, using the Greek term *kenōsis*. Jesus takes the form of a slave or servant and is obedient, even to death on the cross. Therefore, God (the one of greatest honor) honors him and exalts his name above all names. Paul upturns the honor/shame culture by proclaiming that emptying oneself for the sake of others is the greatest honor. Jesus does not diminish his supply of honor by his kenotic self-emptying but enhances it by his obedience even to death.

Not only that, but Paul tells the Philippians to behave in this same way toward one another. Apparently, there were some disagreements in this community. We do not know for certain what topics divided them, but clearly each side wanted the upper hand in these disputes. Each side wanted its viewpoint to win out; that is, each side wanted to take the position of honor. As one commentator suggests, the church in Philippi was suffering a paradoxically big problem—pettiness. "Paul's response to pettiness was a big answer: a hymn, a creed, a confession of faith."[2] Paul seems to have little interest in who wins or loses but, rather, interest in how the members of the community treat one another. If they wanted the honor that being right would bring them, they were looking in the wrong place. Honor would be found by emptying themselves for the benefit of one another, just as Christ emptied himself for the benefit of all humanity. In addition, Paul later encourages the community to follow his example and the examples of his fellow workers Timothy and Epaphroditus as well.

In fact, Paul views his own imprisonment as an example of what it means to find honor in emptying oneself. He sees his imprisonment as an opportunity to spread the gospel both to guards and fellow prisoners. He even hopes "that I will not be put to *shame* in any way, but that by my speaking with all boldness, Christ will be exalted" (Phil. 1:20). In other words, his shame or deference will not be to the guards or legal authorities who imprison him, but to the one on whose behalf he suffers: Christ. Hence, Christ will have more status and honor from Paul's willing abasement.

Paul's description of Jesus' self-emptying has an echo in a later NT document, the Gospel of John. John begins with Jesus' laying aside his honor when "the Word became flesh and dwelt among us" (John 1:14). It ends with Jesus' death being an accomplishment. Jesus chooses death and abasement to increase the honor of the God he serves. It is completed (*tetelistai*, 19:30). Jesus' death becomes a triumph of honor stemming from his willingness to give himself up for others.

The inclusion of the Philippians passage in the readings for the Passion Liturgy highlights the relationship between the Passion Narratives and the ways in which the early church appropriated the death and crucifixion of Jesus in the proclamation of the gospel and instruction to the early church. Though the Gospels had not yet been written by the time Paul wrote to the Philippians, he certainly knew the stories of Jesus they narrate. In fact, the cross of Christ and the death of Jesus figure prominently in his letters to the Corinthians, the Romans, and, of course, the Philippians. Christ becomes the one who chooses the shame of the cross for the honor of God.

Clearly, the death of a leader at the hands of the Roman Empire would have been considered shameful and certainly not a badge of honor. Yet in Jesus' act of self-surrender, the early church saw the power of God poured out for their benefit. The one of greatest honor was God. God's honor, and by implication that of Jesus, exceeded that of the emperor. The idea that the ones of greatest honor

---

1. Mark Allen Powell, *Introducing the New Testament: A Historical, Literary, and Theological Survey*, 2nd ed. (Grand Rapids: Baker Academic, 2018), 33–34.

2. Fred Craddock, *Philippians* (Atlanta: John Knox, 1985), 43.

would empty themselves makes them even more powerful, according to Paul and the christological hymn he quotes. No wonder the early church used the title "Lord," a title often used to refer to the emperor, as its earliest creed to describe Jesus. By his obedience, death, and exaltation, Jesus is higher than the emperor, the one who supposedly held ultimate honor. and so is the true Lord. Such a reversal of economies of shame and honor represents a bold confession, a confession Christians today might do well learning anew.

The lessons for this day highlight both Jesus' triumphal entry into Jerusalem and the Passion Narrative that follows. The role of the preacher may be to point out the paradoxical nature in the Liturgy of the Passion. It begins with the crowds—and us—singing praises to our Lord. It ends with the crowds—and us—shouting, "Crucify him!" Such is the paradox of our existence: that we both praise and reject God. Paul tells us that Jesus' obedient choice of a shameful act of death on a cross becomes the paradoxical means of Christ's exaltation to honor. In that honor, Christ bestows the gift of the love of God for all humanity.

STEPHEN SMITH

Commentary 2: Connecting the Reading with the World

This text speaks of a reversal that we struggle to grasp: a humble God. The world is filled with fantasies of a god, what that god should be like and what that god should demand. What joins most of these fantasies is an idea of power, and there are just as many fantasies about what power, especially divine power, should look like as there are god fantasies. We generate these fantasies not because of our sense of the transcendent or some inherent intuition about God's life. We do so because we are *vulnerable*. We are creatures who know that we are subject to the winds of chaos and within the reach of the long arm of death. So we dream of a god who controls what we cannot control and who carries power as we would carry it: banishing all hindrances, casting away the shadows, and never ever being subject to our stubborn all-too-human struggles.

This text destroys god fantasies by bringing us into the real history of God, a history that reveals God's very being. God allows Godself to be revealed in the rugged history of a people called Israel. This is the destroying work that God does, crumbling in our hands the conceptual idols we have molded that present a God of smooth surfaces, a God who as the source of all being is self-contained and satisfied, satiated and finished. God wars against that form of God through the story of Christ Jesus. God struggles against our bad imagining of God. There, between hope and dream, between fear and nightmare, God wrestles away from our hands the image of God's own life.

This passage announces a refusal. God will not be contemplated as existing in a stillness, in a repose that might suggest that the divine life is not actually living. The God known in the history of Jesus is already acting and moving. We come to the scene late, after much has already happened and more is yet to come, and in that flow of action we are being moved from fantasy to reality and turned from speculations of what a god might be able to do or might do, to what God has done, is doing, and will yet do in this world. Most centrally, God will be God. This is not a tautology, because the way God will be God will free us, caught as we are between our vulnerability and our hunger for power.

God's image, displayed in this liturgical fragment, aims to set us free from our captivity by inviting us to share in Jesus' frame of vision. Jesus frames a vision of God that frees us *in* our vulnerability, not *away* from it, and reveals God's power as the only thing that can pull us from the addictive quest for power. In Jesus, we find two forms inconceivably brought together—the form of God and the form of the slave—and between them is an act that only God can do: self-emptying.

Only a humble God can place Godself where no one would ever want to be: subject to slavery and bound to death, even a death fit for a slave. God enters the depths of our vulnerabilities

The Author of Our Justification

The fact, therefore, that at the time appointed, according to the purpose of His will, Jesus Christ was crucified, dead, and buried was not the doom necessary to His own condition, but the method of redeeming us from captivity. For "the Word became flesh" in order that from the Virgin's womb He might take our suffering nature, and that what could not be inflicted on the Son of GOD might be inflicted on the Son of Man. For although at His very birth the signs of Godhead shone forth in Him, and the whole course of His bodily growth was full of wonders, yet had He truly assumed our weaknesses, and without share in sin had spared Himself no human frailty, that He might impart what was His to us and heal what was ours in Himself. For He, the Almighty Physician, had prepared a two-fold remedy for us in our misery, of which the one part consists of mystery and the other of example, that by the one Divine powers may be bestowed, by the other human weaknesses driven out. Because as GOD is the Author of our justification, so man is a debtor to pay Him devotion. . . .

The snares of the wicked, the persecutions of the unbelieving, the threats of the powerful, the insults of the proud are there; and all these things the Lord of hosts and King of glory passed through in the form of our weakness and in the likeness of sinful flesh, to the end that amid the danger of this present life we might desire not so much to avoid and escape them as to endure and overcome them.

Hence it is that the Lord Jesus Christ, our Head, representing all the members of His body in Himself, and speaking for those whom He was redeeming in the punishment of the cross, uttered that cry which He had once uttered in the psalm, "O GOD, My GOD, look upon Me: why have You forsaken Me?" That cry, dearly-beloved, is a lesson, not a complaint. For since in Christ there is one person of GOD and man, and He could not have been forsaken by Him, from Whom He could not be separated, it is on behalf of us, trembling and weak ones, that He asks why the flesh that is afraid to suffer has not been heard. For when the Passion was beginning, to cure and correct our weak fear He had said, "Father, if it be possible, let this cup pass from Me: nevertheless not as I will but as You;" and again, "Father, if this cup cannot pass except I drink it, Your will be done." As therefore He had conquered the tremblings of the flesh, and had now accepted the Father's will, and trampling all dread of death under foot, was then carrying out the work of His design, why at the very time of His triumph over such a victory does He seek the cause and reason of His being forsaken, that is, not heard, save to show that the feeling which He entertained in excuse of His human fears is quite different from the deliberate choice which, in accordance with the Father's eternal decree, He had made for the reconciliation of the world? And thus the very cry of "Unheard" is the exposition of a mighty Mystery, because the Redeemer's power would have conferred nothing on mankind if our weakness in Him had obtained what it sought.

Leo the Great, "Sermon 67," in *Nicene and Post-Nicene Fathers, Second Series*, vol. 12, ed. Philip Schaff and Henry Wace (Buffalo, NY: Christian Literature Publishing, 1895), 179–80.

because vulnerability is inherent to the nature of our God. We learn this through Israel's story, which shows us a God risking with a people, allowing the divine life to be intertwined with human unevenness, caught up in the ebb and flow, the highs and lows of human attentiveness and faithfulness. In Jesus, that God enters the absolute depth of vulnerability, marking the entirety of the journey into those depths with divine presence.

Slavery, however, is a perverse vulnerability, grotesquely presenting the lowliness of the creature before those who position themselves as gods. Whether in the history of ancient Israel or the Roman Empire or the modern colonial period or even today, slavery always speaks of systems of control that turn bodies into commodities. Yet the form of the slave points to a continuum that flows from those held against their will and forced to labor all the way to those who through debt or poverty or violence or trauma are forced into ways of life that call forth death or make them agents of its bidding. Jesus in the form of the slave is God moving at the sites of our captivity, feeling all their machinations on his body as they are felt on ours.

In truth, Jesus was never a slave, never lived a slave's life as a boy or a man, was never turned into just a body in use. Jesus did, however, through story and anecdote, through what he said and how it sounded, constantly place his body next to the condition of enslavement until the night his torture began, the night when that placement would be complete. He would die the way slaves die—in great agony, without regard, without mercy, and without help.

Jesus is the last slave. He enters the form of the slave to end the formation of slaves and destroy systems of enslavement from within, but this quiet revolution often escaped the ears of the church as we, at many times and in many places, have sought to prop up crumbling, deadly slave systems, either because we feared being made an enemy of the empire or because we benefited from those systems. We have too quickly aligned a Christian obedience with a worldly slavery, presenting obedience to Christ as a tool to refine even more deadly forms of slavery, but now woven with a Christian logic and given to those imagined in need of the discipline of bondage.

This is not the mind of Christ that we are called to share. Christians who call themselves slaves to Christ, as the apostle Paul did, are announcing a freedom that has been unimagined: a life bound only to God and no one else. This is the life of Jesus we are invited to enter. This slavery sets captives free, because it returns the creature to life with the Creator. Is it even slavery then? No. It is something new; the word "slave" serves only as scaffolding, a temporary structure intended to fall away as the new forms inside it.

The new has a name, and it is Jesus. Jesus is exalted, and it has been easy to misunderstand that exaltation. The untrained eye and the impatient ear see and hear yet another victor in power, another ruler who found his way to a throne, a presidency, or a dictatorship. The exaltation of Jesus by God is the drawing up of the humiliated, the despised, and all those ground down under the weight of the world. The crucified slave is to be worshiped, because there in the places of our fall, God is with us. We rise with Jesus. We rise to our knees when we acknowledge a victory that is for us.

Does this victory entail a Christian imperialism in which everyone is forced to bow the knee to the Christian God? Some have made it so. Christian imperialism always thrives where the story of God is replaced with the fantasy of a powerful god who always gets their way. The victory of Jesus is not a victory *over* people but a victory *for* people and indeed for the whole of creation. Confession, then, is not a sign of forced faith, but formed faith for those who have joined the journey of Jesus in mind and heart from humiliation to exaltation. We go from down to up.

WILLIE JAMES JENNINGS

Mark 14:1–15:47

¹⁴:¹It was two days before the Passover and the festival of Unleavened Bread. The chief priests and the scribes were looking for a way to arrest Jesus by stealth and kill him; ²for they said, "Not during the festival, or there may be a riot among the people."

³While he was at Bethany in the house of Simon the leper, as he sat at the table, a woman came with an alabaster jar of very costly ointment of nard, and she broke open the jar and poured the ointment on his head. ⁴But some were there who said to one another in anger, "Why was the ointment wasted in this way? ⁵For this ointment could have been sold for more than three hundred denarii, and the money given to the poor." And they scolded her. ⁶But Jesus said, "Let her alone; why do you trouble her? She has performed a good service for me. ⁷For you always have the poor with you, and you can show kindness to them whenever you wish; but you will not always have me. ⁸She has done what she could; she has anointed my body beforehand for its burial. ⁹Truly I tell you, wherever the good news is proclaimed in the whole world, what she has done will be told in remembrance of her."

¹⁰Then Judas Iscariot, who was one of the twelve, went to the chief priests in order to betray him to them. ¹¹When they heard it, they were greatly pleased, and promised to give him money. So he began to look for an opportunity to betray him.

¹²On the first day of Unleavened Bread, when the Passover lamb is sacrificed, his disciples said to him, "Where do you want us to go and make the preparations for you to eat the Passover?" ¹³So he sent two of his disciples, saying to them, "Go into the city, and a man carrying a jar of water will meet you; follow him, ¹⁴and wherever he enters, say to the owner of the house, 'The Teacher asks, Where is my guest room where I may eat the Passover with my disciples?' ¹⁵He will show you a large room upstairs, furnished and ready. Make preparations for us there." ¹⁶So the disciples set out and went to the city, and found everything as he had told them; and they prepared the Passover meal.

¹⁷When it was evening, he came with the twelve. ¹⁸And when they had taken their places and were eating, Jesus said, "Truly I tell you, one of you will betray me, one who is eating with me." ¹⁹They began to be distressed and to say to him one after another, "Surely, not I?" ²⁰He said to them, "It is one of the twelve, one who is dipping bread into the bowl with me. ²¹For the Son of Man goes as it is written of him, but woe to that one by whom the Son of Man is betrayed! It would have been better for that one not to have been born."

²²While they were eating, he took a loaf of bread, and after blessing it he broke it, gave it to them, and said, "Take; this is my body." ²³Then he took a cup, and after giving thanks he gave it to them, and all of them drank from it. ²⁴He said to them, "This is my blood of the covenant, which is poured out for many. ²⁵Truly I tell you, I will never again drink of the fruit of the vine until that day when I drink it new in the kingdom of God."

²⁶When they had sung the hymn, they went out to the Mount of Olives. ²⁷And Jesus said to them, "You will all become deserters; for it is written,

'I will strike the shepherd,
    and the sheep will be scattered.'

²⁸But after I am raised up, I will go before you to Galilee." ²⁹Peter said to him, "Even though all become deserters, I will not." ³⁰Jesus said to him, "Truly I tell

you, this day, this very night, before the cock crows twice, you will deny me three times." ³¹But he said vehemently, "Even though I must die with you, I will not deny you." And all of them said the same.

³²They went to a place called Gethsemane; and he said to his disciples, "Sit here while I pray." ³³He took with him Peter and James and John, and began to be distressed and agitated. ³⁴And he said to them, "I am deeply grieved, even to death; remain here, and keep awake." ³⁵And going a little farther, he threw himself on the ground and prayed that, if it were possible, the hour might pass from him. ³⁶He said, "Abba, Father, for you all things are possible; remove this cup from me; yet, not what I want, but what you want." ³⁷He came and found them sleeping; and he said to Peter, "Simon, are you asleep? Could you not keep awake one hour? ³⁸Keep awake and pray that you may not come into the time of trial; the spirit indeed is willing, but the flesh is weak." ³⁹And again he went away and prayed, saying the same words. ⁴⁰And once more he came and found them sleeping, for their eyes were very heavy; and they did not know what to say to him. ⁴¹He came a third time and said to them, "Are you still sleeping and taking your rest? Enough! The hour has come; the Son of Man is betrayed into the hands of sinners. ⁴²Get up, let us be going. See, my betrayer is at hand."

⁴³Immediately, while he was still speaking, Judas, one of the twelve, arrived; and with him there was a crowd with swords and clubs, from the chief priests, the scribes, and the elders. ⁴⁴Now the betrayer had given them a sign, saying, "The one I will kiss is the man; arrest him and lead him away under guard." ⁴⁵So when he came, he went up to him at once and said, "Rabbi!" and kissed him. ⁴⁶Then they laid hands on him and arrested him. ⁴⁷But one of those who stood near drew his sword and struck the slave of the high priest, cutting off his ear. ⁴⁸Then Jesus said to them, "Have you come out with swords and clubs to arrest me as though I were a bandit? ⁴⁹Day after day I was with you in the temple teaching, and you did not arrest me. But let the scriptures be fulfilled." ⁵⁰All of them deserted him and fled.

⁵¹A certain young man was following him, wearing nothing but a linen cloth. They caught hold of him, ⁵²but he left the linen cloth and ran off naked.

⁵³They took Jesus to the high priest; and all the chief priests, the elders, and the scribes were assembled. ⁵⁴Peter had followed him at a distance, right into the courtyard of the high priest; and he was sitting with the guards, warming himself at the fire. ⁵⁵Now the chief priests and the whole council were looking for testimony against Jesus to put him to death; but they found none. ⁵⁶For many gave false testimony against him, and their testimony did not agree. ⁵⁷Some stood up and gave false testimony against him, saying, ⁵⁸"We heard him say, 'I will destroy this temple that is made with hands, and in three days I will build another, not made with hands.'" ⁵⁹But even on this point their testimony did not agree. ⁶⁰Then the high priest stood up before them and asked Jesus, "Have you no answer? What is it that they testify against you?" ⁶¹But he was silent and did not answer. Again the high priest asked him, "Are you the Messiah, the Son of the Blessed One?" ⁶²Jesus said, "I am; and

'you will see the Son of Man
seated at the right hand of the Power,'
and 'coming with the clouds of heaven.'"

⁶³Then the high priest tore his clothes and said, "Why do we still need witnesses? ⁶⁴You have heard his blasphemy! What is your decision?" All of them condemned him as deserving death. ⁶⁵Some began to spit on him, to blindfold him, and to strike him, saying to him, "Prophesy!" The guards also took him over and beat him.

⁶⁶While Peter was below in the courtyard, one of the servant-girls of the high priest came by. ⁶⁷When she saw Peter warming himself, she stared at him and said, "You also were with Jesus, the man from Nazareth." ⁶⁸But he denied it, saying, "I do not know or understand what you are talking about." And he went out into the forecourt. Then the cock crowed. ⁶⁹And the servant-girl, on seeing him, began again to say to the bystanders, "This man is one of them." ⁷⁰But again he denied it. Then after a little while the bystanders again said to Peter, "Certainly you are one of them; for you are a Galilean." ⁷¹But he began to curse, and he swore an oath, "I do not know this man you are talking about." ⁷²At that moment the cock crowed for the second time. Then Peter remembered that Jesus had said to him, "Before the cock crows twice, you will deny me three times." And he broke down and wept.

¹⁵:¹As soon as it was morning, the chief priests held a consultation with the elders and scribes and the whole council. They bound Jesus, led him away, and handed him over to Pilate. ²Pilate asked him, "Are you the King of the Jews?" He answered him, "You say so." ³Then the chief priests accused him of many things. ⁴Pilate asked him again, "Have you no answer? See how many charges they bring against you." ⁵But Jesus made no further reply, so that Pilate was amazed.

⁶Now at the festival he used to release a prisoner for them, anyone for whom they asked. ⁷Now a man called Barabbas was in prison with the rebels who had committed murder during the insurrection. ⁸So the crowd came and began to ask Pilate to do for them according to his custom. ⁹Then he answered them, "Do you want me to release for you the King of the Jews?" ¹⁰For he realized that it was out of jealousy that the chief priests had handed him over. ¹¹But the chief priests stirred up the crowd to have him release Barabbas for them instead. ¹²Pilate spoke to them again, "Then what do you wish me to do with the man you call the King of the Jews?" ¹³They shouted back, "Crucify him!" ¹⁴Pilate asked them, "Why, what evil has he done?" But they shouted all the more, "Crucify him!" ¹⁵So Pilate, wishing to satisfy the crowd, released Barabbas for them; and after flogging Jesus, he handed him over to be crucified.

¹⁶Then the soldiers led him into the courtyard of the palace (that is, the governor's headquarters); and they called together the whole cohort. ¹⁷And they clothed him in a purple cloak; and after twisting some thorns into a crown, they put it on him. ¹⁸And they began saluting him, "Hail, King of the Jews!" ¹⁹They struck his head with a reed, spat upon him, and knelt down in homage to him. ²⁰After mocking him, they stripped him of the purple cloak and put his own clothes on him. Then they led him out to crucify him.

²¹They compelled a passer-by, who was coming in from the country, to carry his cross; it was Simon of Cyrene, the father of Alexander and Rufus. ²²Then they brought Jesus to the place called Golgotha (which means the place of a skull). ²³And they offered him wine mixed with myrrh; but he did not take it. ²⁴And they crucified him, and divided his clothes among them, casting lots to decide what each should take.

²⁵It was nine o'clock in the morning when they crucified him. ²⁶The inscription of the charge against him read, "The King of the Jews." ²⁷And with him they crucified two bandits, one on his right and one on his left. ²⁹Those who passed by derided him, shaking their heads and saying, "Aha! You who would destroy the temple and build it in three days, ³⁰save yourself, and come down from the cross!" ³¹In the same way the chief priests, along with the scribes, were also mocking him among themselves and saying, "He saved others; he cannot save himself. ³²Let the Messiah, the King of Israel, come down from the cross now, so that we may see and believe." Those who were crucified with him also taunted him.

³³When it was noon, darkness came over the whole land until three in the afternoon. ³⁴At three o'clock Jesus cried out with a loud voice, "Eloi, Eloi, lema sabachthani?" which means, "My God, my God, why have you forsaken me?" ³⁵When some of the bystanders heard it, they said, "Listen, he is calling for Elijah." ³⁶And someone ran, filled a sponge with sour wine, put it on a stick, and gave it to him to drink, saying, "Wait, let us see whether Elijah will come to take him down." ³⁷Then Jesus gave a loud cry and breathed his last. ³⁸And the curtain of the temple was torn in two, from top to bottom. ³⁹Now when the centurion, who stood facing him, saw that in this way he breathed his last, he said, "Truly this man was God's Son!"

⁴⁰There were also women looking on from a distance; among them were Mary Magdalene, and Mary the mother of James the younger and of Joses, and Salome. ⁴¹These used to follow him and provided for him when he was in Galilee; and there were many other women who had come up with him to Jerusalem.

⁴²When evening had come, and since it was the day of Preparation, that is, the day before the sabbath, ⁴³Joseph of Arimathea, a respected member of the council, who was also himself waiting expectantly for the kingdom of God, went boldly to Pilate and asked for the body of Jesus. ⁴⁴Then Pilate wondered if he were already dead; and summoning the centurion, he asked him whether he had been dead for some time. ⁴⁵When he learned from the centurion that he was dead, he granted the body to Joseph. ⁴⁶Then Joseph bought a linen cloth, and taking down the body, wrapped it in the linen cloth, and laid it in a tomb that had been hewn out of the rock. He then rolled a stone against the door of the tomb. ⁴⁷Mary Magdalene and Mary the mother of Joses saw where the body was laid.

Commentary 1: Connecting the Reading with Scripture

In fairy tales and folk legends, stories of heroes abound. The plots usually unfold in similar fashion: a person who is poor and overlooked at the beginning of the story ends up as the unlikely hero, strong, admired, and victorious. Young Arthur, raised as an illegitimate child, manages, with the help of the wizard Merlin, to pull the sword from the stone and is crowned the king of England. Cinderella, the abused stepsister, is, with the help of the fairy godmother, transformed into a beauty who marries the prince and becomes a celebrated princess.

The plot of Mark, puzzlingly, moves in the opposite direction. The Gospel begins with Jesus, the strong man, the "hero," engaged in a dazzling display of messianic activity. He boldly announces that the kingdom of God had drawn near (Mark 1:15). He calls disciples, casts out demons, heals the sick, confronts religious authorities, preaches to the enthralled

multitudes, stills a storm at sea, feeds throngs in the desert, raises a little girl from death, and enters Jerusalem to the crowd's hosannas.

Then, the plot turns downward. The hero of the story is betrayed, abandoned, arrested, tried, condemned, and executed. He dies in anguish, with a loud cry and an unanswered prayer. He was proclaimed Messiah and Son of God at the beginning of Mark (1:1), and the mystery of that Gospel is that the *way* Jesus is Messiah and Son of God is through the ignominy of the cross.

The centerpiece of this spiral downward is the passion story in Mark 14–15, the text for this day. This long passage can be treated as a collection of smaller texts, but it is the impact of the whole Passion Narrative that is crucial. As Eugene LaVerdiere writes, "Mark's story of the passion-resurrection, like an oriental rug or tapestry, is tightly knit. . . . Every unit, large and small, contributes to the whole."[1]

---

1. Eugene LaVerdiere, *The Beginning of the Gospel: Introducing the Gospel according to Mark*, vol. 2 (Collegeville, MN: Liturgical Press, 1999), 217.

Here are some of the contrasts between the first part of Mark's Gospel and the Passion Narrative:

The Disciples: From Followers to Deserters.

At the beginning of Mark, Jesus is seen calling his disciples to follow him. He calls Peter, Andrew, James, and John, and they leave their nets and boats and follow him "immediately" (1:16–20). He calls Levi, a tax collector sitting at the tax booth, and "he got up and followed him" (2:13–14).

Now, those who moved toward Jesus are abandoning him. Judas betrays Jesus with a kiss (14:45), Peter denies him three times (14:66–72), and "all of them deserted him and fled" (14:50).

The Crowds: From Astonishment to "Crucify him!"

Earlier, Jesus is in great favor with the crowds. He is, Mark says, famous in Galilee (1:28). So many people seek him that at one point he can no longer travel freely because "people came to him from every quarter" (1:45). However, that was in Galilee; that was at the beginning.

Now, at the end of the story, the festival crowds in Jerusalem have turned hostile. They ask Pilate to release Barabbas, an insurrectionist and murderer, instead of Jesus, whom they demand to be crucified. The governor buckles and gives them what they want.

The Powers of Death: From on the Run to in Charge.

In the beginning of Mark's Gospel, Jesus is portrayed as putting the demons and the powers of death to flight. He goes into the synagogue in Capernaum, and the demonic spirit in a man who is there screams out, "What have you to do with us, Jesus of Nazareth? Have you come to destroy us?" Indeed, he has. Jesus rebukes the man's evil spirit, and unceremoniously casts it out (1:21–28). Jesus forgives the deathly power of sin (2:5), tells a chaotic tempest on the sea to shut up and "be still" (4:35–41), and drives into a herd of swine the demons tormenting a frenetic man in a graveyard (5:1–13). In Mark, Satan may be the strong potentate of death and destruction, but Jesus is the even stronger Son

of God who has come to bind Satan and release the captives (see 3:22–27).

Here in the Passion Narrative, though, the agents of death seem to be in charge. A key term in this narrative, which appears several times, is the verb *paradidōmi*, "to hand over." Judas hands Jesus over to the temple militia (14:41–44), the temple authorities hand Jesus over to Pilate (15:1), and Pilate hands Jesus over to be crucified (15:15). The Jesus who seemed so in command is now passed freely from evil hand to evil hand.

This descending, tragic plot in Mark's Passion Narrative provides at least two points of connection for the preacher:

1. The Character of God's Power. The very first verse of Mark's Gospel tells us that this story of Jesus is "good news," and in the first scene of the Gospel, John the Baptizer proclaims that "the one who is more powerful than I is coming" (1:7). What has happened? Here at the end, has the good news turned bad? Has the power of Jesus been drained away? No, the good news told by Mark is that *God's power is not like human power.* Jesus is no Rambo who combats evil with violence and military might. God's might is displayed in redemptive suffering, and God's power shines most radiantly in the cross. Jesus is the true Messiah, but not the one popular sentiment expected: the new David who would roll into Jerusalem on a war chariot. No, "the Son of Man came not to be served but to serve, and to give his life a ransom for many" (10:45). If we want to see God's power at work in the world, do not look at May Day military parades but in those Golgothas in life where disciples of Jesus pick up their crosses and follow (8:34).

2. The Character of Jesus. The last time we see Jesus in Mark's Gospel, his dead body is being taken down from the cross and buried by Joseph of Arimathea.[2] Nevertheless, even though the Jesus who began his ministry proclaiming the nearness of God's reign ends up a crucified criminal in Jerusalem, it would be a deep misunderstanding of Mark to see Jesus as a tragic victim. It is a good exercise to read

---

2. I assume, as do most Markan scholars, that the original ending of the Gospel was at 16:8.

through the Passion Narrative focusing on Jesus himself, noticing what he says and does.

On the surface, he looks like one being manhandled by the powers of darkness, but he walks confidently, faithfully, obediently. He knows who he is ("Are you the Messiah, the Son of the Blessed One," the high priest scoffs. "I am," Jesus says; 14:61–62), and he knows what he has come to do (Jesus prays in Gethsemane, "Abba, Father, . . . not what I want, but what you want"; 14:36). Hell, spit, and fury rain down on him at the end, but he is not a pathetic victim. He is, through it all, an obedient Son who has come to offer his life for many.

Notice also that this true character of Jesus is not perceived by the raging priests, cowardly Pilate, the bloodthirsty crowds, the mocking soldiers, or the head-shaking passersby. No, the act of deep discernment belongs to a woman with an alabaster jar, who anoints Jesus with costly perfume for burial. She sees who Jesus is and what he has come to do. Wherever the gospel is preached, Jesus says, she will be remembered (14:3–9).

THOMAS G. LONG

Commentary 2: Connecting the Reading to the World

Mark's Gospel is noted for its rapid pace of storytelling. Almost every commentary makes note of the author's frequent use of the adverb *euthys* ("straightway, immediately, forthwith"), and the fact that narrative passages fleshed out in greater detail in the other Synoptic Gospels are here presented with great economy. For example, Jesus' baptism and temptation in the wilderness are described in a mere five verses (Mark 1:9–13). The reader gets swept up in a race toward the narrative's inevitable conclusion—the passion of the Christ—when, by design, time slows down for both the reader and the Gospel's protagonist, Jesus.

Given its placement within the narrative arc of the text, Mark's passion is not only the climax of the story but also the Gospel's very raison d'être. Not surprisingly, it has become the focus of the liturgy on the Sunday before the start of Holy Week for Christians around the world. In Year B of the Revised Common Lectionary, it is read on Palm (now Passion) Sunday in an intentional recovery of an ancient Christian Lenten practice of reading the passion accounts and thus reminding believers of the self-sacrifice and spiritual discipline demanded of catechumens prior to baptism. Consequently, a Gospel distinguished for its sense of urgency and spare description spends its closing chapters describing the final three days in the life of Jesus in agonizing detail.

Arguably, Mark's passion is the bleakest of the four canonical accounts of the suffering and death of Jesus. The author offers a window into the last days of Jesus framed by images of the Suffering Servant in the prophet Isaiah. In this way, Mark transposes the mockery and insult aimed at the nation of Israel as the Servant of the Lord onto the man Jesus of Nazareth, whose life becomes "an offering for sin" and an "intercession for the transgressors" (Isa. 53:10, 12). Given that Jesus and his disciples gather to celebrate the Passover meal in Jerusalem (Mark 14:1), the emphasis on the lamb prepared for ritual sacrifice (v. 12) underscores Jesus' messianic mission, even if the disciples do not yet comprehend what is to come. Consequently, despite differing chronologies in the Synoptic Gospels, what matters most for understanding the passion is that it takes place in the context of the Passover meal, Israel's commemoration of God's intervention in human history to free them from slavery in Egypt.

It is natural for many Christians, reinforced by centuries of liturgical performance, to interpret the passion through a eucharistic lens, especially given the narrative emphasis on Jesus' Last Supper with his disciples. However, without diminishing or undervaluing the sacrificial dimension of this ritualized meal, it is also important to affirm the passion as a highly politicized narrative. In other words, no interpretation of the messianic expectations projected onto Jesus is complete without making sense of the subversive political context in which Mark's

Gospel was written and in which Jesus appears as a potentially dangerous political player.

Ched Myers has argued that the proper context for reading the story of Jesus is the perspective of an occupied people under imperial domination.[3] Biblical scholars and historians usually date the composition of Mark's Gospel to the time around the First Jewish-Roman War (66–70 CE), a war in which a Jewish insurrection led to a retaliatory, scorched-earth Roman campaign that culminated in the destruction of the temple in Jerusalem. Mark reflects this context when Jesus says, "Do you see these great buildings? Not one stone will be left here upon another; all will be thrown down" (13:2).

The early church found itself in conflict with the dominant culture of Rome—especially the emperor cult—and Christians were often accused of political subversion. Myers makes the case that "gospel" as a literary form was identified with the political propaganda of the Roman Empire in justifying its expansionist policies by promoting the image of Rome as a benevolent paternal figure. Such propaganda focused on the deification of the emperor by marking his birth, ascension to power, legal proclamations, and military victories as *euangelion* ("good news" or "glad tidings"). The fact that Mark 1:1 began by saying, "The beginning of the gospel [*euangeliou*] of Jesus Christ," leads Myers to conclude, "Mark is taking dead aim at Caesar and his legitimating myths. From the very first line, Mark's literary strategy is revealed as subversive."[4] It thus makes sense to read Mark's Passion Narrative as a snapshot of the political tensions between Jesus' nonviolent movement and the authoritarian forces of Rome and the Sanhedrin.

The earliest Christians recognized the political implications of following Jesus, given that they faced persecution from the Roman conquerors. Following the destruction of the temple in Jerusalem in 70 CE, Rome soon represented everything wrong in the world, evidenced by the labeling of Rome as "the beast" (Rev. 13:11–18) and "the whore of Babylon" (Rev. 17:5) in

John's Apocalypse. Mark's passion reinforces this by showing how Jesus was executed for the crime of political sedition under the authority of the Roman regional governor, Pontius Pilate, as made evident by the sarcastic inscription of the charge against him: "The King of the Jews" (Mark 15:26).

What Pilate got wrong is that while Jesus resisted Roman aggression, he was not a political seditionist. The writer of Mark's Gospel makes this point by contrasting Jesus to Barabbas, a rebel "who had committed murder during the insurrection" (15:7). Furthermore, while Jesus made many political enemies in the Sanhedrin, it was Joseph of Arimathea, "a respected member of the council" (15:43), who made sure Jesus received a proper burial. By contrast, Mark goes to great lengths to bring to the fore the extent of Roman cruelty in gory detail. Despite being beaten, tortured, ridiculed, and spit upon (15:15–20), Jesus endures his torment in silence (15:4), another allusion to Isaiah's Suffering Servant, thereby modeling nonviolent resistance to political tyranny.

There is no way of knowing how many Christians were killed during the Roman persecutions. We can, however, be certain about the impact the stories about these persecutions had on some Christians. The *Acts of the Martyrs*—texts describing the trials of the Christians before the governing authorities—parallel the trial of Jesus before Pilate and his execution as a common criminal. Eventually, these martyr narratives—alongside Mark's passion—became manuals for the Christian life.

The concepts of virtue and character become vital lenses for reinterpreting martyrdom. *Askesis*—a Greek term at the root of our word "asceticism" and understood by the apostle Paul as "training" or "exercise"—and the concept of *aretē*, meaning "virtue" or "excellence" (see Phil. 4:8), bolster the notion that the persecuted church understood itself as a school of virtue.[5] By drawing on the theological virtues of faith, hope, and love (1 Cor. 13:13) to differentiate

---

3. See Ched Myers, *Binding the Strong Man: A Political Reading of Mark's Story of Jesus*, 20th anniversary edition (Maryknoll, NY: Orbis Books, 2008).

4. Myers, *Binding the Strong Man*, 124.

5. See Robin Darling Young, *In Procession before the World: Martyrdom as Public Liturgy in Early Christianity* (Milwaukee: Marquette University Press, 2001).

Christians from their surrounding culture, the early church nurtured and equipped believers for the Christian life in the midst of religious and political persecution by emphasizing fidelity to the revealed Word of God in Christ. Though death is not demanded of every believer, every believer is expected to live a life for others: "Let them deny themselves and take up their cross and follow me" (Mark 8:34).

RUBÉN ROSARIO RODRÍGUEZ

Mark 15:1–39 (40–47)

[1]As soon as it was morning, the chief priests held a consultation with the elders and scribes and the whole council. They bound Jesus, led him away, and handed him over to Pilate. [2]Pilate asked him, "Are you the King of the Jews?" He answered him, "You say so." [3]Then the chief priests accused him of many things. [4]Pilate asked him again, "Have you no answer? See how many charges they bring against you." [5]But Jesus made no further reply, so that Pilate was amazed.

[6]Now at the festival he used to release a prisoner for them, anyone for whom they asked. [7]Now a man called Barabbas was in prison with the rebels who had committed murder during the insurrection. [8]So the crowd came and began to ask Pilate to do for them according to his custom. [9]Then he answered them, "Do you want me to release for you the King of the Jews?" [10]For he realized that it was out of jealousy that the chief priests had handed him over. [11]But the chief priests stirred up the crowd to have him release Barabbas for them instead. [12]Pilate spoke to them again, "Then what do you wish me to do with the man you call the King of the Jews?" [13]They shouted back, "Crucify him!" [14]Pilate asked them, "Why, what evil has he done?" But they shouted all the more, "Crucify him!" [15]So Pilate, wishing to satisfy the crowd, released Barabbas for them; and after flogging Jesus, he handed him over to be crucified.

[16]Then the soldiers led him into the courtyard of the palace (that is, the governor's headquarters); and they called together the whole cohort. [17]And they clothed him in a purple cloak; and after twisting some thorns into a crown, they put it on him. [18]And they began saluting him, "Hail, King of the Jews!" [19]They struck his head with a reed, spat upon him, and knelt down in homage to him. [20]After mocking him, they stripped him of the purple cloak and put his own clothes on him. Then they led him out to crucify him.

[21]They compelled a passer-by, who was coming in from the country, to carry his cross; it was Simon of Cyrene, the father of Alexander and Rufus. [22]Then they brought Jesus to the place called Golgotha (which means the place of a skull). [23]And they offered him wine mixed with myrrh; but he did not take it. [24]And they crucified him, and divided his clothes among them, casting lots to decide what each should take.

[25]It was nine o'clock in the morning when they crucified him. [26]The inscription of the charge against him read, "The King of the Jews." [27]And with him they crucified two bandits, one on his right and one on his left. [29]Those who passed by derided him, shaking their heads and saying, "Aha! You who would destroy the temple and build it in three days, [30]save yourself, and come down from the cross!" [31]In the same way the chief priests, along with the scribes, were also mocking him among themselves and saying, "He saved others; he cannot save himself. [32]Let the Messiah, the King of Israel, come down from the cross now, so that we may see and believe." Those who were crucified with him also taunted him.

[33]When it was noon, darkness came over the whole land until three in the afternoon. [34]At three o'clock Jesus cried out with a loud voice, "Eloi, Eloi, lema sabachthani?" which means, "My God, my God, why have you forsaken me?" [35]When some of the bystanders heard it, they said, "Listen, he is calling for Elijah." [36]And someone ran, filled a sponge with sour wine, put it on a stick, and gave it to him to drink, saying, "Wait, let us see whether Elijah will come to take him down." [37]Then Jesus gave a loud cry and breathed his last. [38]And the curtain of

the temple was torn in two, from top to bottom. ³⁹Now when the centurion, who stood facing him, saw that in this way he breathed his last, he said, "Truly this man was God's Son!"

⁴⁰There were also women looking on from a distance; among them were Mary Magdalene, and Mary the mother of James the younger and of Joses, and Salome. ⁴¹These used to follow him and provided for him when he was in Galilee; and there were many other women who had come up with him to Jerusalem.

⁴²When evening had come, and since it was the day of Preparation, that is, the day before the sabbath, ⁴³Joseph of Arimathea, a respected member of the council, who was also himself waiting expectantly for the kingdom of God, went boldly to Pilate and asked for the body of Jesus. ⁴⁴Then Pilate wondered if he were already dead; and summoning the centurion, he asked him whether he had been dead for some time. ⁴⁵When he learned from the centurion that he was dead, he granted the body to Joseph. ⁴⁶Then Joseph bought a linen cloth, and taking down the body, wrapped it in the linen cloth, and laid it in a tomb that had been hewn out of the rock. He then rolled a stone against the door of the tomb. ⁴⁷Mary Magdalene and Mary the mother of Joses saw where the body was laid.

Commentary 1: Connecting the Reading with Scripture

Deceit, desertion, denial, betrayal, abuse, ridicule, and agony—these are words that describe Mark's Passion Narrative. Mark's account of Jesus' arrest, trial, and crucifixion has the most gloomy and depressing tone of the four Gospels. For example, while the crucifixion in Luke ends with Jesus' words of confidence, "Father, into your hands I commit my spirit," and in John, Jesus triumphantly declares, "It is finished," in Mark Jesus' only words from the cross are the dire declaration from Psalm 22:1: "My God, my God, why have you forsaken me?" (Mark 15:34). For three hours, Mark reports, darkness covered the land, magnifying this pessimistic tone (v. 33). Why this somber presentation? To answer this question, we must examine Mark's Passion Narrative in the context of his Gospel as a whole.

Mark's Narrative Strategy. Mark's Gospel can be outlined simply into two halves, both focusing on Christology (1:1–8:29; 8:30–16:8). The central theme of the first half of the Gospel is *the authority of the Messiah* (1:1–8:29). Mark's opening line announces Jesus' identity: "the beginning of the gospel of Jesus the Messiah, the Son of God" (1:1 NIV). This identity is confirmed at Jesus' baptism, as the heavens are "torn" open, the Spirit descends like a dove, and the voice of the Father from heaven resounds, "You are my Son, whom I love; with you I am well pleased" (1:11 NIV).

Jesus' authoritative words and deeds confirm his identity as Messiah and Son of God. He heals the sick, casts out demons, calms the storm, feeds the multitudes, walks on water, and even raises the dead. He is "lord of the Sabbath" and has the authority to forgive sins. The question that pervades the Gospel's first half is the one raised by the disciples as they stand in awe at Jesus' ability to command the forces of nature: "Who is this? Even the wind and the waves obey him!" (4:41 NIV). This question finds its initial answer at Peter's confession, the center point of the Gospel. While accepting Peter's confession, Jesus begins to teach the disciples that "the Son of Man must suffer many things . . . and that he must be killed and after three days rise again" (8:31 NIV). Jesus here redefines the role of the Messiah. His mission is not to conquer the Roman legions but to suffer and die.

Peter's confession marks a decisive turn in the narrative. If the first half of Mark's Gospel is about *the authority of the Messiah*, the second half concerns *the suffering role of the Messiah*. Over the next three chapters, Jesus will repeatedly predict his coming death (8:31; 9:31; 10:33–34). Each time, the disciples will respond with some act of pride or spiritual immaturity (8:33; 9:33–34; 10:35–41). Jesus then follows with teaching concerning servant leadership (8:34–38; 9:35–37; 10:42–45). These three cycles reach their climax in 10:32–45, when for a third time Jesus predicts his death and then defines Christian leadership: "You know that those who are regarded as rulers of the Gentiles lord it over them, and their high officials exercise authority over them. Not so with you. Instead, whoever wants to become great among you must be your servant, and whoever wants to be first must be slave of all" (10:42–44 NIV). In short, the Messiah's role is not to crush the Roman legions. It is to "give his life a ransom for many" (10:45) and in this way accomplish the salvation of the world. True leaders serve for the good of others.

The Passion of the Messiah. Mark's Passion Narrative (chaps. 14–15) begins with the plot by the Jerusalem religious leaders to kill Jesus (14:1–2). Jesus is fully aware of his destiny and moves intentionally toward it. When a devoted follower anoints him with costly perfume, he identifies it as the preparation for his burial (14:3–11). At the Passover meal, Jesus predicts that one of his own disciples will betray him and that all will desert him. The institution of the Lord's Supper is to be in memory of his coming sacrificial death (14:22–24). In Gethsemane, Jesus agonizes over his coming death and pleads for a reprieve. Yet he remains faithful to his task (14:36).

If Jesus is a model of faithfulness, his disciples are the opposite. Judas betrays Jesus, leading a mob from the high priest to Gethsemane. The other disciples cannot even "watch and pray." At Jesus' arrest, everyone abandons him. While once boasting that he would never fall away, Peter three times denies that he even knows Jesus (14:53–54, 66–72).

The rejection of Jesus intensifies at his trial. The religious leaders bring false accusations against him. When Jesus admits that he is the Messiah, the high priest accuses him of blasphemy, and the whole council calls for his execution (14:62–64). Jesus is mocked, beaten, spit upon. The crowds, though once amazed at his miracles, now call for his crucifixion. Pilate,

though convinced of Jesus' innocence, ignores justice and turns him over to be crucified.

During the crucifixion Jesus is mocked and ridiculed by everyone, even the criminals crucified beside him! Just as "darkness came over the whole land" (15:33), so darkness descends over the Gospel narrative. Jesus dies in agony, apparently forsaken even by his Father in heaven (15:34).

Victory through Apparent Defeat. Yet this is not the end. Those with faith who have followed the story from the beginning know that these events are not the tragic fate of a false prophet or a messianic pretender. They are rather God's plan to bring salvation to a lost world. Jesus has moved intentionally toward this climax, repeatedly predicting his death and explaining its meaning as a "ransom for many" (10:45), an atoning sacrifice for the sins of the world. Jesus' blood, "poured out for many," inaugurates a covenant between God and humanity (14:24).

Two events that occur at Jesus' death confirm this significance. First, the curtain of the temple is torn from top to bottom (15:38), indicating how Jesus' death mediates God's presence in a strikingly surprising way. The curse of the cross becomes the path for God's self-revelation. Second, the Roman centurion directing the crucifixion sees how Jesus dies and shouts, "Surely this man was the Son of God!" (15:39 NIV). It is the most unlikely of characters— a Roman soldier and pagan Gentile—who recognizes that *through his suffering and death* Jesus confirms his identity as the Son of God and Savior of the world!

The Gospel's Message of Hope. The Gospel's paradoxical theme of success through suffering provides rich applicational possibilities for the preacher. For those facing trials, suffering, persecution, and even death, Jesus' divine authority and victory over death provide confidence that, no matter what the circumstances, those who are willing to "take up their cross" and follow him will indeed find life (8:34–35).

While Mark's Gospel has particular application for those suffering for their faith, it reminds all believers that the standards of success and achievement of this world are not the same as the upside-down values of the kingdom of God. In a world where so often the strong oppress the weak, injustice prevails, and evil appears to win, the paradoxical message of the kingdom is that

to live, you must die (to yourself) (8:34–37); to lead, you must serve (9:35; 10:35–45); to become first, you must be last; and God's victory is accomplished through apparent defeat.

MARK L. STRAUSS

Commentary 2: Connecting the Reading with the World

It is difficult to think about preaching Mark 15 without noting that it follows Mark 14, which includes Jesus' anointing by "a woman," unnamed, who prepares him for his burial. Jesus responds to her anointing by saying that when the gospel is preached, "what she has done will also be told, in memory of her" (14:3, 9 NIV). It is difficult to preach chapter 15 without Mark 14's Last Supper, at which Jesus predicts that someone at the table with him will betray him (14:18). It is just as difficult to do so without noting Jesus' prediction that Peter will deny him (14:29–30). Mark 14 is also where Jesus' arrest occurs, where Jesus is betrayed by Judas's kiss, and where we get a hint of at least one reason why he might have been arrested, when Jesus asks, "Am I leading a rebellion . . . that you have come out with swords and clubs to capture me?" (14:48 NIV).

These details help frame how those planning for worship using Mark 15 might approach singing, prayers, and preaching alike. After all, unmoored from the text's political reality, it becomes easy for worshipers to move past the clash between Jesus' mission and the Roman Empire. When Jesus stands before Pilate, the charge is first and foremost political: "Are you the King of the Jews?" (15:2). If, as has happened so often in some North American churches, we rush to what we think the religious significance of the trial and crucifixion is, we might actually miss the horror of it all. We might give these imperial authorities a pass and decide political power has nothing to do with how we ought to remember the trial, death, and

burial of Jesus. It is important to remember that Jesus has been arrested for political reasons as a possible insurrectionist.

According to Mark's Gospel (cf. Matt. 27:11–24; Luke 23:1–24; John 18:28–19:6), Pilate asks the people whom he should release "according to custom" (15:8–12). This oddity does not reflect any custom that scholars are able to find. These texts have been used to accuse Jewish people of killing Jesus, fomenting antipathy toward Jewish people and Judaism. Christian churches have not fought such antipathy robustly enough, though some efforts have been helpful advances. Vatican II sought to counter the damage of anti-Semitic readings of the Gospels. Fifty years later, Pope Francis has spoken again to try to address anti-Semitism among Roman Catholics, and Jewish scholars and rabbis have reflected on this history in a report on Judaism and where the Christian church is now on these pressing questions.[1] Protestant preachers also must push back against such rhetoric regarding our Abrahamic kin. Songs, prayers, and sermons must push against a false doctrine of deicide. Unfortunately, many commentaries written in the twentieth century bolster such dangerous thinking.

If the church is both to reclaim Jesus' Jewish roots and to try to understand its own beginnings, then pastors and worship leaders will need to confront the church's historic anti-Semitism and any latent prejudices within themselves. Examining songs typically sung at the passion with an eye toward anti-Jewish sentiment thus becomes an imperative. Perhaps musicians and

1. https://www.ajc.org/sites/default/files/pdf/2017-09/AJC_and_Nostra_Aetate_IN_OUR_TIME.PDF. For other resources leading Christians away from anti-Semitic readings, see Ronald Allen, *Preaching the Gospels without Blaming the Jews: A Lectionary Commentary* (Louisville, KY: Westminster John Knox, 2015). I also recommend Amy-Jill Levine and Marc Zvi Brettler, eds., *The Jewish Annotated New Testament* (Oxford: Oxford University Press, 2015), and Brooks Schramm and Kirsi I. Stjerna, eds., *Martin Luther, the Bible, and the Jewish People: A Reader* (Minneapolis: Fortress, 2012), among many others.

lyricists will find themselves writing new verses to old songs that will counter the impulse to "blame the Jews" for Jesus' death.

Beyond congregational worship settings, ecclesial communions have to face their own histories regarding this challenge, since anti-Semitism shows up subtly *and* blatantly in some of our creeds, our sermons, and our liturgies.[2] Thinking of Jesus as a Jew may help us as we read these texts. It might help listeners to know that Jesus' accusers used a combination of religious disputes, Roman law, and Roman custom to falsely arrest and crucify him. Reading the world in front of the text, preachers might also think of any number of recent examples in which innocent folks have been imprisoned, even executed; we may also remember that too few of them have lived to experience vindication. In the United States, those examples might be seen most clearly through the lens of this country's history of racial violence, since an inordinate number of non-white people have been harshly punished, even as we see efforts like those of the Innocence Project try to disrupt systems of (in)justice.[3]

Moreover, Mark 15's allusions to Psalm 22 can lead hearers and readers to understand that Jesus was a falsely accused, innocent man. What we see in Psalm 22 and in Mark 15 is an innocent person assailed by imperial power. Are there songs already in our repertoire that will speak to such misuse of power and might help us lament how all too willing we are to participate, either actively or passively, in someone's execution? As Peter denied Jesus, how all too easy it is for us to back away from following Jesus when it may cost us our reputations, our jobs, or even our lives? The church's musicians must write such songs so that we might more faithfully and truthfully approach the Passion Narratives.

Jesus, the unjustly condemned man, led through a kangaroo court, resonates in the African American church tradition. I was asked to present a necklace to a woman that had a cross on it as she was being ordained. I said to her, "Wear this cross to remind yourself that your Savior, the one you follow, was executed for challenging religious authority and empire oppression. Let this necklace weigh you down with the burden to always choose justice, even if it costs you your life." The congregational members gasped, but that is precisely what I think the cross is.

It is what James Cone teaches us in his *The Cross and the Lynching Tree* (Maryknoll, NY: Orbis, 2013). If American Christians cannot discern the connection between the cross and the lynching tree, Cone would argue, then they do not understand the horror of either. Mark 15 describes the humiliation Jesus experienced, from being mocked to being spat on to being stripped naked in full public view (15:16–20). As with lynching, others are compelled to join in the spectacle—like Simon, who was pressed into carrying Jesus' cross (v. 21). Churches must lean into the horror, so they may let themselves *feel* it and not just speak about it. The Passion Narrative should make us recoil at humanity's ability to be cruel, then and now. It should lead us to consider how we might advance a different vision of the world for Christ's sake.

As leaders act out the passion from trial to crucifixion, as they remember the people named and unnamed who witnessed it, the most faithful outcome would be a people transformed and mortified to the point that they collectively say, "Even if God answered Jesus' unjust killing with resurrection, we must say 'never again' to such state-sanctioned cruelty." The opportunities to transform violence, to resist oppressive imperial policies, and to live a different kind of life in God's name are more than possible; they are a promise God has made to us.

VALERIE BRIDGEMAN

2. See "Christian Churches and Antisemitism: New Teachings," https://www.facinghistory.org/holocaust-and-human-behavior/chapter-11/christian-churches-and-antisemitism-new-teachings.

3. See The Innocence Project at https://www.innocenceproject.org/.

Holy Thursday

Exodus 12:1–4 (5–10), 11–14
Psalm 116:1–2, 12–19

1 Corinthians 11:23–26
John 13:1–17, 31b–35

Exodus 12:1–4 (5–10), 11–14

¹The LORD said to Moses and Aaron in the land of Egypt: ²This month shall mark for you the beginning of months; it shall be the first month of the year for you. ³Tell the whole congregation of Israel that on the tenth of this month they are to take a lamb for each family, a lamb for each household. ⁴If a household is too small for a whole lamb, it shall join its closest neighbor in obtaining one; the lamb shall be divided in proportion to the number of people who eat of it. ⁵Your lamb shall be without blemish, a year-old male; you may take it from the sheep or from the goats. ⁶You shall keep it until the fourteenth day of this month; then the whole assembled congregation of Israel shall slaughter it at twilight. ⁷They shall take some of the blood and put it on the two doorposts and the lintel of the houses in which they eat it. ⁸They shall eat the lamb that same night; they shall eat it roasted over the fire with unleavened bread and bitter herbs. ⁹Do not eat any of it raw or boiled in water, but roasted over the fire, with its head, legs, and inner organs. ¹⁰You shall let none of it remain until the morning; anything that remains until the morning you shall burn. ¹¹This is how you shall eat it: your loins girded, your sandals on your feet, and your staff in your hand; and you shall eat it hurriedly. It is the passover of the LORD. ¹²For I will pass through the land of Egypt that night, and I will strike down every firstborn in the land of Egypt, both human beings and animals; on all the gods of Egypt I will execute judgments: I am the LORD. ¹³The blood shall be a sign for you on the houses where you live: when I see the blood, I will pass over you, and no plague shall destroy you when I strike the land of Egypt.

¹⁴This day shall be a day of remembrance for you. You shall celebrate it as a festival to the LORD; throughout your generations you shall observe it as a perpetual ordinance.

Commentary 1: Connecting the Reading with Scripture

The night of the first Passover was dramatic. Preachers who know the book of Exodus backwards and forwards should keep in mind how startling this story will be for those who do not know it well. Just as the Israelites waited for deliverance from One whom they barely remembered (Exod. 3:13), many in the pews today have not been steeped in the scriptural traditions that teach us who God has been in the ancient past. Indeed, at the core of the Passover reading is precisely this potential loss of religious memory: the passage tells of divine

deliverance in a way that will ensure its liturgical remembrance for future generations.

The venerable Abraham had obeyed a mysterious deity calling him out of Chaldea (Gen. 12:1–3). Abraham's son Isaac had been too terrified to speak of God (see Gen. 22:1–14), so the Deity had become known not only as "God" (*'Elohim*) and "God Most High" (*'El 'Elyan*, Gen. 14:19; Ps. 78:35) but also as "the Fear of Isaac" (*Pakhad Yitzhak*, Gen. 31:42). Ancestor Jacob had revelatory dreams of the Holy One (Gen. 28:10–17) and had even wrestled with God (32:22–28).

But the old traditions had been all but forgotten; enslavement in Egypt had left no energy for the cherishing of tradition. Then Moses exhorted his people in the name of YHWH, who had thundered from a bush alight with flame but not consumed. Contests unfolded between Moses and the Egyptian diviners. Water into blood, frogs, fiery hail, a darkness beyond dark—a cosmic battle was unfolding before the eyes of the astonished Israelites.

Now Moses announces something new: an annual feast, beginning that very evening, to be celebrated with roast lamb and bitter herbs. The Israelites are to mark their door frames with lamb's blood to prove they are keeping the new festival. Death will sweep through all the households that do not observe the feast.

For the Thursday of Holy Week, the Christian preacher may weigh two choices for how to work with the Passover festival announced in Exodus 12. Ancient and beautiful is the tradition that the first Passover may be read as a foreshadowing of Christ. The Gospel reading for Holy Thursday is from John 13, focused on the ritual of footwashing. However, in the Synoptic Gospels, the beginning of the Passover festival is the time of Jesus' Last Supper with his disciples. The theological connection of Jesus' impending crucifixion with the sacrifice of the Passover lamb is clear (see Matt. 26:17–29; Mark 14:12–25; Luke 22:1–23). The preacher could offer that redemption has been effected for the entire cosmos by the blood of the Lamb that was slain, with saints and angels singing in ceaseless praise, "Worthy is the Lamb that was slaughtered" (Rev. 5:11–13). With Matthew, Mark, Luke, and rank upon rank of Christian theologians from the early church to today, the preacher may reflect on the symbolic valences of the Exodus narrative as pointing to Christ.

A second homiletical possibility too may be rich with meaning. Instead of moving immediately to the theme of christological deliverance, the preacher could explore the spiritual drama of this night within the arc of Israel's story. Exodus 12 offers a marvelous opportunity for believers to reflect on the liminal moment in which the enslaved Israelites find themselves after darkness has fallen. Any of three foci might be fruitful for the preacher: contesting the claims of empire, waiting for God, and glimpsing the holy through sacred time.

First, the preacher might explore this terrifying "passover of the LORD" (Exod. 12:11) as the culmination of a series of plagues in which YHWH decisively defeats the power of imperial Egypt. No other plague narratives are read in any year of the Revised Common Lectionary, so believers who do not read the Bible on their own may have only dim memories of the plagues from Sunday school curricula or films, some recalling Charlton Heston as Moses in the 1956 Cecil B. DeMille epic *The Ten Commandments*, others remembering the 1998 DreamWorks animated musical *The Prince of Egypt*. The preacher might frame the plagues as cosmic battle, ancient testimony to the power of the Creator to bring down worldly empires. In the tenth plague, the Lord delivers the oppressed by wreaking havoc on those who trust in the "the gods of Egypt" (v. 12).

The preacher may offer this display of divine force as an expression of covenantal fidelity: "the Israelites groaned under their slavery" and "God heard their groaning, and . . . remembered [the] covenant with Abraham, Isaac, and Jacob" (2:23–24). Hearers could be invited to see the preparation of the Passover lamb as a celebration of God's power over the cruelty of empires in every age.

Second, the preacher might evoke what it may have been like for the Israelites, readying themselves for escape and eating this feast in haste, as they waited for God to deliver this people from centuries of enslavement (12:40; see Gen. 15:13). Ancient Hebrew prose is famously spare in its narration of emotion; all we learn is that the Israelites obey when Moses relays the Passover instructions, bowing and showing reverence (Exod. 12:27). The elliptical nature of Hebrew narrative need not constrain the preacher, who can help hearers imagine what that night would have been like for the Israelites, their "loins girded and . . . sandals on [their] feet" (v. 11), as they waited for death to scythe their path to freedom.

The preacher could invite hearers to stay present to those dread-filled hours before Pharaoh released the Israelites (12:31–34). In this way, believers may be encouraged to stand in solidarity with those who wait for God in present-day

Employ Our Gifts and Graces

Consider well His thoughts and His deed. He knows and thinks of it that He is Lord God over all; that in less than one day the devil shall have accomplished what he can, and that thereafter all His enemies shall be vanquished and His Christians be at ease. Now turn to His deed, and what is it? Why, this very Lord performs now a task which is commonly done by the servants of the house; He washes the feet of His disciples.

Christ desires us to learn from this occurrence to humiliate ourselves, and not to abuse our position and our power by insolence and arrogance toward our fellow-men, but to help and serve them with our means as much as we can, even as He Himself, the Lord of glory, became humble and of low estate, yea, even the servant of His disciples. Jesus Himself explains the meaning of the feet-washing when He says: "Know ye what I have done to you? Ye call me Master and Lord: and ye say well; for so I am. If I then, your Lord and Master, have washed your feet; ye also ought to wash one another's feet. For I have given you an example, that ye should do as I have done to you. Verily, verily, I say unto you, the servant is not greater than he that sent him. If ye know these things, happy are ye if ye do them." Here we see what this feet-washing really means, and that this story is told us that we might imitate its precepts with care and diligence. . . .

It is evident that our Lord, by His action in the Gospel, did not intend to teach us the outward washing of feet, which is done by means of water; for then it would be obligatory to wash the feet of all; or rather, which would certainly be more serviceable, to prepare a regular bath for the people, in which they could wash their whole body. This of course cannot be the meaning of Christ's command in this regard. He simply gave us by His example an important lesson, that we should be humble, and properly employ the gifts and graces which we have, to the advantage of our brethren, and that we should despise no one, but rather excuse the shortcomings of our fellow-men, and help them to become better.

In this sense, the washing of feet must be practiced not merely upon this day, but every day of our life, and we must not grow weary in well-doing towards our fellow-men. For such a purpose, and for such a foot-washing, Christ sets us the example which we are now considering. Let us remember this.

Martin Luther, "Thursday before Easter: Jesus Washes the Feet of His Disciples," in *Sermons on the Gospels for the Sundays and Principal Festivals of the Church-Year*, vol. 2 (Columbus, OH: Schulze and Glassmann, 1871), 28–29, 31.

circumstances of subjugation, honoring the sure prospect of deliverance even in times of darkest terror, knowing that God's covenantal fidelity does not erase the reality of suffering but responds to it with a mighty and emancipatory love. On this night before Good Friday, the preacher could suggest that the Beloved Community must always prepare for a long journey through wilderness terrain into freedom.

A third possible focus has to do with liturgy. The preacher on Holy Thursday could illumine ways in which the lives of believers are infused with glimpses of the holy through liturgical festivals as expressions of sacred time. In Exodus 12, the instructions about preparing the lamb evoke the majestic, ordered world of the Israelite priestly imagination, with its understanding of the importance of sacral time for formation of believers in faithfulness. Markers of holy time abound in this passage: we hear about "the first month of the year" (v. 2), "the fourteenth day of this month" (v. 6), "twilight" (v. 6), night and morning (vv. 8, 10), and "a day of remembrance . . . a festival to the LORD . . . a perpetual ordinance" (v. 14). Sacred time prompts us to reflect on the mystery of divine presence as we move through days, weeks, and seasons, experiencing joy and fear and hope in the textures of our daily living.

However the preacher works with Exodus 12, a troubling ethical problem should be engaged. In this story, the Creator mercilessly slaughters the firstborn of every Egyptian household and kinship group. Terrible loss comes at a stroke to countless human families and groups of animals across Egypt, from the palace of Pharaoh to prison cells to livestock pens (12:29). Whether the preacher focuses on the tenth plague as subverting the claims of empire, dramatizes waiting for God, or lifts up sacred time, it is imperative to address this issue. Such violence ought not to be enshrined in the theology of believers called to love our enemies (Matt. 5:44; Luke 6:27).

CAROLYN J. SHARP

Commentary 2: Connecting the Reading with the World

For four hundred years, we languished in Egyptian slavery. Prayers were offered, no doubt, for divine intervention. "Please, God, save us from the pharaoh!" Powerless, under the heel of the most powerful empire in the world, what hope had we but God?

Then one night God moved to deliver us. Passover.

In college, they made us read Beckett's revolutionary play *Waiting for Godot*. Two disheveled men sit on a park bench waiting for a man to arrive. They sit there, they think about leaving, but they stay. The man never comes. The play ends without resolution. "Get it?" asked a professor of mine. It is really *Waiting for* God—the God who never shows up, the life of eternal waiting and anticipating but never being fulfilled. That was the enslaved children of Israel. That is us. So much of life is spent waiting for God.

"I believe in the power of prayer; but the timing is hard," she said to me. How true. God answers prayer, but sometimes we receive an answer we do not want. Perhaps an even bigger problem is that often the response is so slow in coming that we lose heart. "God is good," I have heard churches led in response. "All the time, God is good." Yes, but sometimes the time of God's goodness is the challenge. The waiting is hard, the long night vigils, the endless train of days. Waiting for God is difficult.

"Please, God, save us from the pharaoh!" "Please, God, let the therapy be successful." "Please, God, melt their hard hearts so that they will accept me." "Lord, I am going down for the third time. I need you, please help." Such are the anguished prayers of those in wait for the Lord.

I know someone who has been beseeching God for thirty years—thirty years!—for help with her family's drug addiction. As of this date, she has received no noticeable response from the Lord. Waiting for the Lord to move, to save, to come and help, is difficult. Then, what if the Lord should come?

That is what happens at Passover. At last, about four hundred years late, God shows up and begins giving directions. Get a lamb. Mark the doorposts. Eat this specifically prescribed food on the run. Get ready to be liberated.

So much of church life is spent waiting, spent on the verge. One day we are enslaved to the moment, killing time, hanging out, and waiting. Then God shows up, and things start moving. Are we ready to move? Be honest. Life can be easier on the verge, when we are waiting, anticipating. There is a kind of comfortability in saying, "One day, someday, this problem will be fixed. Not today, of course, but someday." You can relax, cultivate your patience, and anticipate that future time when God will come and you will be called to move. Such is life on the verge.

What happens when there is response to your prayer, when the God who has been only anticipated and expected becomes undeniably present? What then? I know someone of whom it was said, "She enjoys poor health." She had been ill for as long as anybody in the congregation could remember with a variety of complaints, unable to participate in most church activity, prohibited by her rather vague illness from regular church attendance, listed on our "homebound" registry. Then she was given a clean bill of health by her doctor. She made the mistake of sharing that professional certification of good health with a couple of folks. "That is wonderful," said one of her friends. "Now you can attend church more often. You are now able to be a fully functioning member." We marveled. All those years waiting to be whole and then, once she got healthy, her newfound health was an onerous assignment! She was forced to find another alibi.

I know a church that was in decline for many years. They were a "neighborhood church" whose fortunes rose as the suburban neighborhood was being built and then declined when the suburbs became urban. They prayed for renewal. A couple of pastors ago, they tried some programs for evangelism. Nothing worked. Their decline continued unabated. "Lord, please give us a way to reach out to our new neighbors and grow," was an often-repeated prayer.

Then the bishop sent a new pastor to the dwindling church. She was in her late twenties. There had been a day when no pastor with so little age and experience would have been sent to that church, but that was yesterday. They received their new, young pastor with a sigh.

Wonder of wonders, the congregation began to grow. A wave of new, young families moved into the neighborhood. For some reason—maybe it was the cheerful young pastor, or perhaps they were attracted by the older women in the congregation who were glad to serve as surrogate grandmothers for their children—they found a new home in the congregation. Now the church that was dying became the church that was growing. Their decaying building required refurbishing. The empty Sunday school rooms had to be refitted for the children's nursery and kindergarten. A new sound system was required for the band that now led worship. "We need everyone to step up and increase your giving," said the pastor one Sunday.

While it was wonderful to see their church growing, new life in the congregation brought new challenges. "It was sure a lot of easier to be a member of a dying church than one that is growing," said one of the longtime members.

At Passover, the prayers of the slaves were answered. God came for them. The moment of divine intervention arrived. At last! The time of deliverance had come. Immediately, Exodus 12 moves from divine action to human responsibilities. This is the way it often is with divine deliverance. God acts and then immediately enlists us to respond.

Every act of divine deliverance carries with it an assignment. I am reminded of Exodus 3. Moses is hiding out in Midian. He has killed a man back in Egypt. A bush bursts into flame. The bush speaks! "I'm the God of your forebears. I have heard the cries of my people. I have come down to deliver them. Now you go and tell Pharaoh to let my people go!" Although the text does not include these words, surely Moses spoke them: "What was all that 'I heard, I have come down to deliver . . .'? How come you need me?" Sorry, Moses. This is the way this God works. This God works typically not by descending from above and working solo. This God works through vocation, enlistment, recruitment of ordinary women and men like Moses.

Too often, contemporary theology renders God into an allegedly compassionate, caring, and considerate—but also impotent, inactive, noninterventionist—deity. God is said to care, but then we are squeamish about denoting *specific ways* that God actually cares. We believe that God is love, but then we are not too sure that God is love in action. Passover is one of those dramatic, climactic moments in Scripture when God not only loves and cares but also acts, moves, intervenes to liberate and to free. The challenge of proclaiming Passover is to assert an activist God who actively works in behalf of the slaves, a just God who judges and punishes the empire and those who serve imperial interests. Passover asserts a more interesting God than many modern Americans believe in.

WILL WILLIMON

Psalm 116:1–2, 12–19

¹I love the LORD, because he has heard
   my voice and my supplications.
²Because he inclined his ear to me,
   therefore I will call on him as long as I live.
. . . .
¹²What shall I return to the LORD
   for all his bounty to me?
¹³I will lift up the cup of salvation
   and call on the name of the LORD,
¹⁴I will pay my vows to the LORD
   in the presence of all his people.
¹⁵Precious in the sight of the LORD
   is the death of his faithful ones.
¹⁶O LORD, I am your servant;
   I am your servant, the child of your serving girl.
   You have loosed my bonds.
¹⁷I will offer to you a thanksgiving sacrifice
   and call on the name of the LORD.
¹⁸I will pay my vows to the LORD
   in the presence of all his people,
¹⁹in the courts of the house of the LORD,
   in your midst, O Jerusalem.
Praise the LORD!

Connecting the Psalm with Scripture and Worship

Much happens as the church gathers on Holy Thursday. The Revised Common Lectionary appoints the story of Jesus washing his disciples' feet from John as the Gospel reading for the evening. The epistle reading is always the institution of the Lord's Supper as received by the apostle Paul in 1 Corinthians 11:23–26. The Old Testament reading recounts the institution of the first Passover celebration as recorded in Exodus 12. The readings for this day help us remember significant times when God has provided for God's people. There is much to remember on this holy day: Jesus' washing of the feet, the Lord's Supper, God delivering the people of Israel from the land of Egypt. Remembering all that God has done prompts us to give our praise and thanksgiving as individuals and as the gathered community together.

A portion of Psalm 116 is the psalm for Holy Thursday. An individual song of thanksgiving, Psalm 116 is one of the Hallel Psalms (Pss. 113–118), a grouping of thanksgiving psalms recited on festival celebrations, particularly Shavuot, Sukkot, and Pesach (Passover). The recitation of this group of psalms takes place at various points throughout the celebration meals. Psalm 116 is recited or sung after the meal. The practice is ancient and would have been part of the Passover observance known by Jesus. Some scholars contend that when the Gospels tell of Jesus and his disciples singing a hymn at the conclusion of the Passover celebration, the hymn sung could very well have been Psalm 116.

Of course, Psalm 116:1–2, 12–19 works well as a response to the reading from the Hebrew Scriptures heard on Holy Thursday evening.

Exodus 12 gives directions for the Passover celebration: assembled congregation, roasted lamb, unleavened bread, bitter herbs—all as sign of God's deliverance of God's people from the oppressive Egyptian hand. Because the people remember the plight of their forebears, they respond with great thanksgiving. "I will lift up the cup of salvation" (Ps. 116:13). "I will offer to you a thanksgiving sacrifice" (v. 17). "I will pay my vows to the LORD" (v. 18).

Psalm 116:1–2, 12–19 begins with a succinct summary as to why the psalmist is responding with extravagant praise and thanksgiving. "I love the LORD, because he has heard my voice and my supplications" (v. 1). A voice cried out to the Lord, God heard the cry. Verses 3–11, omitted from the psalm selection for Holy Thursday, flesh out how the Lord responded to the cries of the psalmist. The threat of death, distress, and anguish was all around, but the Lord was gracious and delivered the one who cried out. The psalmist was close to being separated from God through death (Sheol) but cried out for help, and God responded with protection and salvation. Therefore, the psalmist is moved to offer thanksgiving to God.

Remembering God's provisional care prompts the psalmist to ask, "What shall I return to the LORD for all his bounty to me?" (v. 12). Here, "bounty" is a summary term encompassing all God has done, including bringing the psalmist back to the "land of the living" (v. 9) from near death (v. 8). In other words, how can I say thank-you to God for all that God has given to me or done for me? Verses 12–19 answer that question: "I will lift up the cup of salvation. . . . I will pay my vows to the LORD. . . . I will offer sacrifice. . . . I will pay my vows to the LORD."

An amazing thing happens as we hear the stories of the exodus and Passover deliverance and join with the psalmist's and the people's exclamations of thanksgiving. Somehow their story becomes our story, and their plight becomes our plight. Their deliverance becomes our deliverance, then and now. So it is only fitting that we join in the song of gratitude. The song of the individual becomes the song of the community and our voices sing, "Praise and thanksgiving to the God who heard our cry." Those gathered on Holy Thursday cannot hear phrases such as "cup of salvation" and "thanksgiving sacrifice" and not be reminded of the cup of blessing of Jesus' Passover meal with his disciples in the upper room. There God's love abounded, as Jesus spoke of the giving of himself so the love of God would be known. The bounty of God's love is remembered, and great thanksgiving is our response.

A pairing of a portion of Isaac Watts's paraphrase of Psalm 116 with an African American spiritual tune is found in several contemporary hymnals and song collections as "I Love the Lord, Who Heard My Cry." This hymn might be used in a responsorial reading or chanting of the psalm for the day, or sung before and after verses 12–19 are read.[1]

ERIC T. MYERS

---

1. Isaac Watts, "I Love the Lord, Who Heard My Cry," in *Glory to God* (Louisville, KY: Westminster John Knox, 2013), #799.

1 Corinthians 11:23–26

²³For I received from the Lord what I also handed on to you, that the Lord Jesus on the night when he was betrayed took a loaf of bread, ²⁴and when he had given thanks, he broke it and said, "This is my body that is for you. Do this in remembrance of me." ²⁵In the same way he took the cup also, after supper, saying, "This cup is the new covenant in my blood. Do this, as often as you drink it, in remembrance of me." ²⁶For as often as you eat this bread and drink the cup, you proclaim the Lord's death until he comes.

Commentary 1: Connecting the Reading with Scripture

Writing to the Corinthian church, Paul deals with an incredible diversity. There are factions (see 1 Cor. 1 and 11:17–19), consisting of people with allegiances to different church leaders. There are people of obviously different status and wealth (11:20–22). There are people with divergent understandings of freedom in Christ, and different attitudes about what foods are lawful or not (chap. 9). All these factions and perspectives seem to be erupting in conflict and disagreement.

Paul calls for unity using three interlinked appeals. The first is an appeal to the unity that may be found in the celebration of the Lord's Supper, the community gathered to honor Jesus' command to celebrate in remembrance of him. Paul transforms this celebration into a metaphor of the church as a body. A body may have many diverse parts, but all are needed for the full functioning of the body (1 Cor. 12). Finally, he shows a "more excellent way" (12:31), by calling on the Corinthians to treat each other with self-denying, *agapē*, love (chap. 13). The three appeals are not separate but build on one another.

Paul begins with the Lord's Supper. At this early juncture in the church's life, the Lord's Supper had not taken on fully the connotations Christians today associate with the Eucharist or Holy Communion. Nevertheless, it is obvious from Paul's words that the bread represents the body of Christ and the wine his blood. This gathering for a meal by the Corinthians is not what

we might call a potluck or a shared, communal dinner. It was meant to be a symbolic event representing the presence of the Lord. This conflicted church seems to be missing that point.

Apparently the Corinthian celebration of the Lord's Supper has deteriorated into something that looks like little more than a meal, and not necessarily a shared one at that. Paul accuses them of coming together to eat as factions, with groups or families sitting down to their own food. Those with little food go hungry, and some with an abundance even get drunk. Paul says that if people are just coming together and eating in the same room, without regard for one another, then they might as well eat at home (11:21–22).

Paul then quotes a formula that predates him, and says that what was told to him were the very words of Jesus: "That on the night he was betrayed. . . ." This formula will appear in almost identical form in the later Gospels of Mark, Matthew, and Luke. It will become the basis for eucharistic services across the centuries (vv. 23–26). However, at this point, Paul's concern is for the Corinthian community, not necessarily the church across time. He is trying to bring them together as a group to remember the Lord's Supper. It is a simple formula, a shared meal of bread and wine in which all partake. The bread and wine become central to that meal, and all other references to food or dining fade away. In the end, Paul emphasizes the importance of perceiving the body of the Lord in this shared meal and that failing to perceive the body of the Lord brings judgment and in some cases can even be fatal (vv. 27–31).

Though Paul emphasizes perceiving the body of the Lord, we are still a long way from transubstantiation and debates over the real presence of Christ in the Eucharist. That would come much later in the history of the church. Yes, this meal is about recalling Jesus' Last Supper and proclaiming his presence revealed in continued remembrance. For Paul, the Lord's Supper becomes a jumping-off point for the metaphor of the church as the body of Christ (chap. 12). The body Paul hopes the Corinthians will perceive is not just the presence of the Lord in the bread, but also the body of Christ, that is, the church. Though it is made up of many members (presumably with many different opinions, potential factions, and on a more positive note, different gifts), the church is still meant to be one body. The judgment that comes on the Corinthians for not perceiving the body of the Lord is the one with which Paul has already admonished them: the fact that they came together for the Lord's Supper to eat separately, as separate groups, rather than coming together as a community. Paul then goes on in detail to describe the church like a human body, ascribing various gifts to various limbs or parts, all working together for the good of all, a point the Corinthians seem to keep missing.

Finally, Paul concludes this appeal for unity with his "more excellent way," describing the meaning of self-sacrificing love (chap. 13). This segment is not removed from the previous two appeals for unity (the Lord's Supper and the metaphor of the body) but is rather the conclusion to them. If the Corinthian community comes together for the Lord's Supper, they will discover a shared meal that brings them together in the presence of the Lord. Being together in perceiving the body of the Lord leads them to an understanding of the gathered community as an extension of that body, the church. When the body works together for the benefit of all,

then its members will act out of love, the same love demonstrated by Jesus when he gave himself "on the night he was betrayed" (11:23b). Though we may perceive this only dimly, eventually love will abide over all (13:12–13). From the collection of material that makes up 2 Corinthians, we can determine that Paul's appeals to unity did not meet with great success. Conflict and dysfunction persisted.

Nevertheless, the church has repeated his words for centuries: "For I received from the Lord what I also handed on to you, that the Lord Jesus on the night he was betrayed took a loaf of bread. . . ." At almost every wedding, we read 1 Corinthians 13 and remind ourselves of Paul's call to community that concludes with living out the love of God.

Using this reading on Maundy Thursday in conjunction with the footwashing lesson from John 13:1–17 points toward Paul's threefold appeal for unity. The shared meal of communion is remembered, but so are its implications: that we see the church as the body of Christ, and if the body, then a community that calls for us to love one another as Christ loves us. We read of the shared meal that represents the presence of the Lord, but we also get called to the humility of footwashing, of bowing ourselves before others for their benefit. In so doing, we perceive the body of Christ, the church.

A sermon on this text might introduce the Triduum: that movement from Maundy Thursday through Good Friday to the joyous celebration of Easter. The preacher might appeal to Paul's call for unity while at the same time reminding us of our failure to live it out. Just like the Corinthians, we may fall into our own traps of functionalism, classism, theological differences, and, in our day, the evils of racism, sexism, and exclusion. The call for unity is one that cannot be achieved without a savior, a savior who loves us enough to take our sins of conflict and division upon himself, yet also rises triumphant in new life. Our unity then comes from the one who loves us all and offers us the hope of new life.

STEPHEN SMITH

Commentary 2: Connecting the Reading with the World

These words demand repetition. Like only a few other words of Scripture, these words belong to the "again." Spoken or sung or whispered in intimate spaces, they rarely are weakened in translation, because they always bring a story and solidify a promise. The story they tell brings us to screams, cries, and shouts of desperation and many hands all reaching, straining to touch Mary's son and God's Beloved. Jesus is in the midst of the crowd—pushing, shoving, yelling—all trying to get to him and get from him what they need. The repetition begins with him and the constant cries: "Help me, Jesus" or "Son of David, have mercy on me." Oftentimes, the crowd exhausts Jesus—never enough time, never enough energy, never enough of him to go around. His disciples fear that they will tear him into pieces, so the disciples place their bodies between the body of Jesus and the crowd, hoping that they can keep him safe from the overwhelming hunger of the multitude for help.

Somewhere on the journey, a tired Jesus began to see a connection between his body and bread, his blood and wine. Maybe he saw it as he gave thanks for the bread and wine he ate for his sustenance. Maybe he heard the connection in the words spoken in thanks and praise to God for the mighty acts done through Jesus' own hands. Maybe it is even simpler than this. He saw himself as one with the earth, joined to the land as his people were joined to the land, learning from the land and from animals the way life gives life from seeds and dirt, from branches and birds, from flowers and rain. Regardless of how it came about, the connection was made. Just as the earth brings forth life, just as that life is shaped and molded to form bread and wine, just as it will be given daily for the sake of the creature who needs it daily, just as it is received with joy and thanksgiving, so too does Jesus give his body. The disciples who worked so diligently to protect his body from the hungry crowd now must offer his body to that same eager multitude.

These famous words speak of the sure knowledge that Jesus gained—the creature hungers and the first act of love that God demands of God's child Jesus is that he feed the creature,

first with his words, then with his mighty acts, and finally with his own body, all of it woven in relentless compassion. The disciples must eat him because they are in the midst of a self-giving that is the logic of Jesus' very life. All love begins with feeding and eating; every creature that lives knows this. This is why starvation for any cause, whether of war or inequalities or poverty or neglect, is always the deepest signature of hatred and rebellion against God. God wills the creature to eat, and God meets us in our hungers.

In Jesus, holiness meets hunger, yielding to it and caressing it in the divine embrace. Too often, we have turned hunger into the enemy of a holy God, but nothing could be further from the truth of God or of the creature. God joins us in our hungers, exposing and loving us in them. This is the truth that the disciples must carry forward into the future. God wants to be eaten, consumed in the fire of our needs, our longings, and our desperate cries for help.

There is an exactness to these words that witnesses the uniqueness of the God of Israel. This God and no other offers God's own body to be eaten. This is what must be repeated now and into eternity. This is the tradition that makes possible the tradition, the eucharistic word that makes possible all words of praise and thanksgiving to the triune God. The outrageous scandal of these words is only heightened by the betrayal that marks their institution.

Self-giving often meets betrayal, and the church has not always handled this meeting well. We have either met betrayal and not taken it seriously—using forgiveness like a credit card that is not ours, ignoring those who have been betrayed, and lazily thinking that God's grace covers treachery rather than exegeting it. Or we have met betrayal with an exaggerated seriousness—bending our faith toward scapegoating, always looking for those who fail, and confidently anticipating faithlessness. Yet Jesus meets betrayal with a new word: he is greater than any betrayal. It was indeed a night of betrayal that set the stage for this self-giving, but it was the self-giving that frames the betrayal. Betrayal is never our last word, and never the word that contextualizes holy word.

A holy work is found in this word. Jesus is joining his body to bread through his own words of thankfulness to God. He inserts himself into the repetition of a blessing said countless times by him and his people, thanking God for the everyday of food for life, and now the everyday belongs to Jesus, taken up in bread and wine marking a new commitment of God to God's people. Yet the new commitment does not negate the old. It only intensifies the faithful actions of Israel's God moving further into the life of the creature, down into the body, all the way to blood and bone and flesh. This covenant will be swallowed from a never-ending cup. His body will be the meal in the meal, enfolding all eating, aiming for all hungering, and ever inviting. This repetition must be remembered.

It seems misdirected that churches yet argue over how to understand the body of Jesus in relation to the bread and wine. How could there not be a tangible presence in and with these earth-formed elements, given their real history in the life of Jesus—his feet having touched the dirt, his hands having held wheat and grape, his senses all filled with the taste and textures of bread and wine, and his voice joined to other voices in thanksgiving to God for this meal. Jesus remembers the meal. It is in him. He remembers his joining to bread and wine. He is in them. At the sound of a word that remembers his death for the sake of life, his self-giving that will end our hunger, there and then he is revealed in the touching and through the eating. He is present at the meal urging us to remember a death that will end all death.

This is, however, thick remembering, not only of mind but of mouth. God forms the body to remember, and God holds our bodies in God's own sure memory. The mouth remembers the bread and wine—even as a child or an elderly person—and every eating of this bread and drinking of this wine reminds us that God remembers us, God will not forget, even if and when our memories fade. The remembering is not our effort at historical reconstruction. It is our response to God's invitation to remember with God. The bread and the wine answer a plea for help before it is articulated, a plea for guidance in the remembering and the living. God guides us in how to remember and how to live. This is the bread from heaven come down who feeds and guides, guides and feeds, now and into eternity.

WILLIE JAMES JENNINGS

John 13:1–17, 31b–35

¹Now before the festival of the Passover, Jesus knew that his hour had come to depart from this world and go to the Father. Having loved his own who were in the world, he loved them to the end. ²The devil had already put it into the heart of Judas son of Simon Iscariot to betray him. And during supper ³Jesus, knowing that the Father had given all things into his hands, and that he had come from God and was going to God, ⁴got up from the table, took off his outer robe, and tied a towel around himself. ⁵Then he poured water into a basin and began to wash the disciples' feet and to wipe them with the towel that was tied around him. ⁶He came to Simon Peter, who said to him, "Lord, are you going to wash my feet?" ⁷Jesus answered, "You do not know now what I am doing, but later you will understand." ⁸Peter said to him, "You will never wash my feet." Jesus answered, "Unless I wash you, you have no share with me." ⁹Simon Peter said to him, "Lord, not my feet only but also my hands and my head!" ¹⁰Jesus said to him, "One who has bathed does not need to wash, except for the feet, but is entirely clean. And you are clean, though not all of you." ¹¹For he knew who was to betray him; for this reason he said, "Not all of you are clean."

¹²After he had washed their feet, had put on his robe, and had returned to the table, he said to them, "Do you know what I have done to you? ¹³You call me Teacher and Lord—and you are right, for that is what I am. ¹⁴So if I, your Lord and Teacher, have washed your feet, you also ought to wash one another's feet. ¹⁵For I have set you an example, that you also should do as I have done to you. ¹⁶Very truly, I tell you, servants are not greater than their master, nor are messengers greater than the one who sent them. ¹⁷If you know these things, you are blessed if you do them. . . .

³¹ᵇ"Now the Son of Man has been glorified, and God has been glorified in him. ³²If God has been glorified in him, God will also glorify him in himself and will glorify him at once. ³³Little children, I am with you only a little longer. You will look for me; and as I said to the Jews so now I say to you, 'Where I am going, you cannot come.' ³⁴I give you a new commandment, that you love one another. Just as I have loved you, you also should love one another. ³⁵By this everyone will know that you are my disciples, if you have love for one another."

Commentary 1: Connecting the Reading with Scripture

In each of the Gospels, the events of Jesus' betrayal, arrest, trial, and crucifixion are preceded by a symbolic meal that Jesus shares with his disciples (Matt. 26:17–30; Mark 14:12–26; Luke 22:1–38). This passage presents John's distinctive recollection of that "last supper."

The Passover setting of John 13 recalls the paradigmatic deliverance of Israel from slavery recorded in Exodus 12–15. As with the first Passover, so with this one: the blood of a lamb will effect a glorious salvation that both rescues a people from bondage and also sets them apart for life with God (see, e.g., John 1:29, 36; 3:16–17). Jesus, we are told, is fully aware of this as the following scene unfolds.

John 13:1 refers to the "hour" of Jesus' glorification. John has been leading readers for the entire Gospel to anticipate this climactic "hour," in which the love of God is revealed on the cross (e.g., 2:4; 4:21–23; 12:23, 28). John also knows that the great deliverance through Jesus' death will not result in an immediate restoration. Jesus will return to the Father; the disciples will continue in discipleship after Jesus is physically absent. John sets up the footwashing narrative to show the love of Jesus for his disciples as he condescends to serve them and to display the nature of Christian community. The closing phrase of verse 1 emphasizes the extent of the love that is on display.

Verses 2–4 are set at the meal. These verses consist of one long sentence in Greek that emphasizes Jesus' awareness of his vocation and his impending betrayal. The discrete actions of Jesus ("he rose . . . took off . . . wrapped himself") work on two levels. First, they describe Jesus taking the initiative to serve his disciples, even as he is fully aware of the significance of the moment in terms of both his identification with the Father and Judas's betrayal. Second, they serve as a metaphor for Jesus' entire life, in which the Word of God has taken initiative, set aside any divine prerogative to be aloof to creation, humbly become flesh, and willingly died. In the New Testament, clothing is often representative of a person's identity (e.g., Gal. 3:27; Rev. 3:4–5). At his crucifixion, Jesus will be stripped by Roman soldiers as a sign of his innocent suffering (John 19:23–24). In John 21:18 Jesus predicts Peter's death and says that Peter's inability to clothe himself will signify his being led where he would rather not go.

Jesus' actions in verse 5 subvert expectations for service and humility. A rabbinic source states that footwashing is a task too menial for a Jewish slave to perform on another Jew.[1] Peter's words reflect his visceral rejection of Jesus' humiliating actions. Verses 6–8 might be translated: "You—you would wash my feet?!? . . . You will never, ever wash my feet!" Peter's words here stand in close parallel to his rebuke of Jesus' need to suffer in Mark 8:29–33 and Matthew 16:20–23 (absent from John). Instead of the sharp rebuke of Peter that Jesus delivers in the Synoptics, here Jesus insists that Peter will understand "later" (that is, "after these things")

and that being washed by him is necessary in order to have a share with him.

This points to the symbolic nature of the footwashing: accepting the humility of Jesus as he washes his disciples' feet is representative of an ability to receive the gospel as a whole, which requires accepting God's condescending self-revelation in the profound frailty of "sheer humanity."[2] The cross is the most vivid embodiment of this condescension. Peter is eager to keep his share with Jesus, so he blurts out that if washing is required, then not only should his feet be washed but his hands and head too. In the exchange that follows, Jesus brings Peter back to the moment at hand. It is the willingness to accept footwashing that is necessary at this point. Insofar as the disciples belong to him, they are clean (John 13:10). The exception is the disciple whose belonging is superficial and treacherous (vv. 10–11).

With the act of footwashing completed, Jesus interprets it in verses 12–17. His question, "Do you know what I have done for you?" is a summons to reflection. In verses 13 and 14 Jesus reminds his hearers that he has acted as the one whom they call "Teacher and Lord" in order to provide an example to imitate. Both "teacher" and "lord" were titles used of rabbis in John's time, but the term "Lord" is multivalent, and at the climax of the Gospel, Thomas will confess Jesus as "my Lord and my God" (20:28). The Gospel does not make this explicit, but it would have readers ponder how the cross and the footwashing reflect the identity of the Lord. The word for "example" in 13:15, *hypodeigma*, is borrowed from the language of moral instruction. Jesus has given his disciples "a definitive prototype."[3] The aim of the action is to inspire the disciples toward their own expressions of humble, self-giving love. The proverbial saying in verse 16 occurs in Matthew 10:24 and Luke 6:40. Like John 13, those passages are concerned with the character of faithful discipleship.

The lectionary omits verses 18–31a, a passage in which Jesus identifies Judas as his betrayer and dismisses him from the meal. As readers turn to

1. *Mekhilta De-Rabbi Ishmael*, trans. Jacob Z. Lauterbach (Philadelphia: Jewish Publication Society, 2004), 3:358 (Exod. 21:2).

2. Rudolf Bultmann, *The Gospel of John: A Commentary*, trans. G. R. Beasley-Murray (Philadelphia: Westminster, 1971), 63.

3. Heinrich Schlier, "ὑπόδειγμα," in *Theological Dictionary of the New Testament*, vol. 2, ed. Gerhard Kittel, trans. Geoffrey Bromiley (Grand Rapids: Eerdmans, 1965), 34.

verses 31b–35, they should remember that Jesus washed the feet of his betrayer; selfless love is not an insurance policy against bitter rejection. It is, however, a display of God's character and, thus, God's glory. Judas's departure initiates a series of events that will lead inexorably to Jesus' death. With the betrayal now in motion, Jesus calls his disciples to see in his suffering a display of God's glory. (The term "glorify" occurs four times in vv. 31–32.) The disciples are to look past the shame and humiliation of a crucified Galilean rabbi and to recognize in that figure God's willingness to rescue his people not through a dazzling display of might but through a humble identification with the plight and sin of the world.

The lection ends with Jesus' presentation of a new commandment (Lat. *mandatum novum*): "Just as I have loved you, you also should love one another" (v. 34). This commandment repeats and deepens the "just as . . . , so . . ."

pattern that John uses to present believers as people whose lives take shape in direct response to the character of Jesus (see 20:21). Along these lines, Jesus' closing statement in verse 35 makes mutual love a witness to the disciples' identification with Jesus.

In John, "love" is not a vague or sentimental term but a fully involved, others-oriented, and often costly commitment to a person's flourishing according to the will of God. John comes back to this teaching in 15:12–17. First John 3:18–24 and 4:7–21 implore the church to concrete expressions of the love commandment. In its context here, Jesus' new commandment looks back on the footwashing as an act of humble service, forward to the complete humility and love revealed on the cross, and further forward to the way in which believers will witness with their lives to the glory of God in actions of humble, self-giving love.

CHRIS BLUMHOFER

Commentary 2: Connecting the Reading to the World

Matthew's Jesus encapsulates his teaching with two great commandments: "You shall love the Lord your God with all your heart, and with all your soul, and with all your mind," and "You shall love your neighbor as yourself" (Matt. 22:37–38). In the preaching of Jesus, the love of God is inescapably intertwined with the love of neighbor, and as regards the neighbor, his words are clear: "Love your neighbor as yourself." Yet in the Gospel of John, Jesus qualifies that commandment in a surprising and important way.

This reading for Holy Thursday from John is unique among the Gospels. Unlike the Passion Narrative in the Synoptics, the Last Supper with the disciples as described by John *is not* the Passover meal, as evidenced by the fact that the representatives from the high priest Caiaphas refused to enter Pilate's palace the next day "so as to avoid ritual defilement and to be able to eat the Passover" (John 18:28). Yet perhaps the most striking difference between the accounts of the Synoptics and John is the account of the footwashing in the latter. Jesus—whom the disciples called Rabbi (John 1:38, 49; 3:2; 8:4;

9:2; 11:8, 12, 21; 13:13–14) and Lord (6:68; 11:3, 32, 34; 13:6, 9, 13, 14, 25; 21:15–24)—kneels before them as a servant, with a towel tied around him and a basin of water in hand, and washes the feet of the disciples.

The always obtuse (if well-intentioned) Peter even tries to stop Jesus, "You will never wash my feet," to which Jesus replies, "Unless I wash you, you have no share with me" (13:8). Providing your guests with a basin for footwashing or even instructing a servant to wash your guests' feet was likely a customary hospitality in antiquity (see Luke 7:44), but to place yourself, as master of the household, in the role of menial servant is something beyond the norm of hospitality. The writer of John's Gospel clearly seeks to amplify the act's importance by making *the footwashing*, rather than the Passover meal, the central focus of this Last Supper narrative.

Within the Christian tradition and often as part of Holy Thursday worship services, some communions have embraced ritual footwashing as a meaningful symbol of service and love for one another and as a means of embodying

Christ for each other, through a sacramental act described in 1 Timothy 5:10 as washing the feet of the saints. Ultimately, the symbolism behind ritualized footwashing is an expression of our Christian commitment to follow Jesus' example of humble, self-giving service.

Other Christian communions choose not to interpret Christ's command literally but instead view it figuratively as moral instruction for cultivating the appropriate attitude—that of a servant living for others—that comes with living the Christian life. In other words, what we find in John's Gospel is further elaboration of the radical discipleship, present throughout all the Gospels, that calls Christians to be the servants of all (e.g., Mark 10:43–44), just as Jesus lived among us "as one who serves" (Luke 22:27). Implied in such passages, but made explicit in John 13, is the idea of humble service toward those whose status is lower than one's own. Jesus speaks through action by serving the disciples on his knees, then follows it up with an unequivocal interpretation of his actions: "Do you know what I have done to you? You call me Teacher and Lord—and you are right, for that is what I am. So if I, your Lord and Teacher, have washed your feet, you also ought to wash one another's feet. For I have set you an example, that you also should do as I have done to you" (John 13:12–15).

In other words, a vital part of the narrative describing the passion and death of Jesus Christ is this compact drama of the washing of the feet, which summarizes for believers how the followers of Jesus are to live and what they are to do. Without question, Jesus has given the disciples a concrete example they are to emulate in their own lives, an example that goes beyond good deeds for the neighbor in need and that is best characterized as a radically new orientation: "I give you a new commandment, that you love one another. Just as I have loved you, you also should love one another. By this everyone will know that you are my disciples, if you have love for one another" (13:34–35). So, if the two greatest commandments in the Torah are to love God and to love our neighbor as ourselves, why is Jesus now speaking a *new* commandment?

Twentieth-century theologian Paul Tillich defines faith as "the state of being grasped by an ultimate concern, a concern which qualifies all other concerns as preliminary and which itself contains the answer to the question of the meaning of life."[4] What Tillich means by "ultimate concern" is that which is most important in an individual's or a society's life, what gives that life meaning and sustains it. The danger with Tillich's definition is that when human desires are distorted by sin, we tend to focus our devotion on the wrong concerns. Such misguided devotion, when absolutized, becomes a false god. Ask any drug addict. For the hard-core heroin addict, the all-encompassing, ultimate drive that relativizes all other concerns is the desire for the next fix. To quote the rock singer Lou Reed, "Heroin, it's my wife and it's my life."

Therefore, when Jesus tells us to love our neighbor as ourselves, this assumes that we are well-adjusted (not self-destructive) individuals who understand the meaning of love. Therein lies the problem. The human condition is rife with distorted self-love. Some of us are serial adulterers, others of us struggle with gluttony, others of us do not value ourselves highly enough, and still others remain trapped in cycles of addiction and substance abuse. In other words, as sinners, we are unable to save ourselves, so are wholly reliant on God's saving grace. Therefore, even if we wanted to obey Jesus by loving our neighbor as we love ourselves, we are so far from knowing how to properly love ourselves that it is next to impossible to know how to properly love our neighbor, which is why Jesus provides us with a new commandment.

Notice his words: "I give you a new commandment, that you love one another. Just as I have loved you, you also should love one another" (13:34). Of what does this new commandment consist? Not that we love our neighbor as ourselves. That is as old as the Torah itself (Lev. 19:18). Rather, what is new is that we are now to love one another *as Christ has loved us.* In other words, the commandment to love our neighbor according to the standard of self-love found in Matthew and Leviticus is inadequate for the simple reason that we are

---

4. Paul Tillich, *Systematic Theology* (Chicago: University of Chicago Press, 1963), 3:4.

sinners. Therefore, Jesus in his wisdom has gone to great lengths to demonstrate for us proper love for neighbor, even if we have yet to master a healthy self-love. Jesus does not define love of neighbor in terms of feelings or emotions but concretely, in terms of actions done for the sake of the other as key to our own well-being. Most challenging of all, we are expected to serve even our enemies—while being careful not to enable their abuse and exploitation—as attested by the betrayer Judas, whose feet Jesus also washed.

RUBÉN ROSARIO RODRÍGUEZ

Good Friday

Isaiah 52:13–53:12
Psalm 22

Hebrews 10:16–25 and Hebrews
4:14–16; 5:7–9
John 18:1–19:42

Isaiah 52:13–53:12

^{52:13}See, my servant shall prosper;
    he shall be exalted and lifted up,
    and shall be very high.
¹⁴Just as there were many who were astonished at him
    —so marred was his appearance, beyond human semblance,
    and his form beyond that of mortals—
¹⁵so he shall startle many nations;
    kings shall shut their mouths because of him;
for that which had not been told them they shall see,
    and that which they had not heard they shall contemplate.
^{53:1}Who has believed what we have heard?
    And to whom has the arm of the LORD been revealed?
²For he grew up before him like a young plant,
    and like a root out of dry ground;
he had no form or majesty that we should look at him,
    nothing in his appearance that we should desire him.
³He was despised and rejected by others;
    a man of suffering and acquainted with infirmity;
and as one from whom others hide their faces
    he was despised, and we held him of no account.

⁴Surely he has borne our infirmities
    and carried our diseases;
yet we accounted him stricken,
    struck down by God, and afflicted.
⁵But he was wounded for our transgressions,
    crushed for our iniquities;
upon him was the punishment that made us whole,
    and by his bruises we are healed.
⁶All we like sheep have gone astray;
    we have all turned to our own way,
and the LORD has laid on him
    the iniquity of us all.

⁷He was oppressed, and he was afflicted,
    yet he did not open his mouth;
like a lamb that is led to the slaughter,
    and like a sheep that before its shearers is silent,
    so he did not open his mouth.
⁸By a perversion of justice he was taken away.
    Who could have imagined his future?
For he was cut off from the land of the living,
    stricken for the transgression of my people.

⁹They made his grave with the wicked
    and his tomb with the rich,
although he had done no violence,
    and there was no deceit in his mouth.

¹⁰Yet it was the will of the LORD to crush him with pain.
When you make his life an offering for sin,
    he shall see his offspring, and shall prolong his days;
through him the will of the LORD shall prosper.
    ¹¹Out of his anguish he shall see light;
he shall find satisfaction through his knowledge.
    The righteous one, my servant, shall make many righteous,
    and he shall bear their iniquities.
¹²Therefore I will allot him a portion with the great,
    and he shall divide the spoil with the strong;
because he poured out himself to death,
    and was numbered with the transgressors;
Yet he bore the sin of many,
    and made intercession for the transgressors.

Commentary 1: Connecting the Reading with Scripture

Known as the fourth Servant Song, this text poses several interpretive possibilities. Within the poem itself we hear two voices: the voice of Yahweh and the voice of the Servant, who may be an individual or perhaps ancient Israel. Isaiah 52:13–15 opens with the voice of Yahweh confidently claiming that Yahweh's Servant will prosper. However, arriving at this prophetic future entails traveling through difficult circumstances. The circumstances themselves are not given in detail, but in heartfelt poetic language: "so marred was his appearance, beyond human semblance, and his form beyond that of mortals" (Isa. 52:14b). The disfigurement of the Servant is a surprise to the nations. It is unexpected and will cause those who are powerful (kings) to be silenced.

We hear another voice beginning in the new chapter, a voice asking questions concerning God's revelatory movement in the form of this "despised and rejected" Servant. The suffering of the Servant is intense—and silent. Has justice been perverted in the suffering of the Servant? Is the Servant suffering for the "transgressions of my people"? The poet of the fourth Servant Song offers a poignant yes.

This text is part of what is commonly known as Second Isaiah, the part of the book of Isaiah likely written toward the end of the exile of the southern kingdom of Judah, the remnant of ancient Israel. Most of the scholarly community agrees that the book of Isaiah is likely three different bodies of literature, formed at different moments in ancient Israel's history. As Walter Brueggemann explains,

> According to critical consensus, chapters 1–39 are linked to Isaiah of the eighth century B.C.E. in the context of the Assyrian Empire between 742–701. Chapters 40–55 are commonly dated to 540, just at the moment when the rising Persian Empire displaced the brutal and hated domination of Babylon. And chapters 56–66 are dated later, perhaps 520, when Jews who had returned from exile went about the critical and difficult task of reshaping the community of faith after its long exilic jeopardy.[1]

That this text is a reflection of ancient Israel in exile gives a particular poignancy to the suffering of the Servant, because exile was the second

---

1. Walter Brueggemann, *Isaiah 40–66*, Westminster Bible Companion (Louisville, KY: Westminster John Knox, 1998), 3.

powerful hinge of ancient Israel's history. If the *exodus* account gives hope and imagination to ancient Israel as the beginning of its covenantal relationship with God and its nationhood (the first hinge), the *exile* unravels this imagination and gives despair to ancient Israel in the second hinge. This unraveling has its seeds in 1 Samuel, when God's covenant people reject the form of government God had intended (1 Sam. 8:4–6). God claims that such a rejection is a repudiation of the Divine: "And the LORD said to Samuel, 'Listen to the voice of the people in all that they say to you; for they have not rejected you, but they have rejected me from being king over them'" (1 Sam. 8:7).

Once that decision was made, the united kingdom—and subsequently the divided northern and southern kingdoms of Israel and Judah—had a series of kings, some who "did what was right in the sight of the LORD" (1 Kgs. 15:11), but most who "did what was evil in the sight of the LORD" (15:26), until this fateful decision led to both kingdoms' destruction and entry into exile. What does that reality do to the imagination of the prophetic and poetic voice? Our text gives pathos to that voice and returns us to an interpretive question: is Isaiah's Suffering Servant an individual or the whole people of ancient Israel?

This is a question that vexes many commentators. The language of the Servant Songs is poetic, and the language of poetry does not depend on literal facts or even narrative that we might associate with biography. Because the language of the Servant Songs is poetic, with the beauty of its symbolic language giving pathos to the voice of the Servant, perhaps we must ask a different question. Paul Hanson suggests that this dichotomy of whether the Suffering Servant is an individual or ancient Israel misses an important point:

> Is the Servant an individual or a people? To make this the central focus of the study of the Servant Songs seems fruitless, and it easily degenerates into Jewish-Christian polemic. The central point is, rather, the redefinition of power that occurs in the Songs.

The power that can annul the wages of sin and restore human beings and their communities to health is not the power that worldly potentates wield. It is, rather, the power with which God has endowed the Servant, the power to place God's will over selfish desire and thereby to become an instrument of God's healing.[2]

This redefinition of power gives the preacher an interesting interpretive entry point as the Isaiah text interacts with the other lectionary texts for Good Friday. The sense of forsakenness from the opening line of Psalm 22 turns into praise for the great reversal that God has brought forth: "The poor shall eat and be satisfied; those who seek him shall praise the LORD. May your hearts live forever" (Ps. 22:26). Hebrews draws from Jeremiah's claim that instead of God mediating God's laws through human leaders (such as Moses), God will write the law on hearts and minds; human iniquity is thus forgiven—an echo of Isaiah. The writer of Hebrews begins to make the connection to Jesus' sacrifice, which offers a "new and living way" (Heb. 10:20a), which then provokes his followers to love and do good deeds. The lectionary texts for this Good Friday include the passion story from the Gospel of John, and perhaps Hanson's suggestion that the Isaiah text challenges us to redefine power finds voice in the exchange between Jesus and Pilate. Pilate asks, "Are you the King of the Jews?" Jesus' enigmatic, power-redefining answer is, "My kingdom is not from this world" (John 18:33, 36a).

Isaiah's description of the Suffering Servant has been appropriated into the Christian tradition through the suffering of Jesus. Jesus' own life and ministry, as testified to by the Gospels, have also redefined power. In John's account of the passion story, human power is embedded in the figure of Pilate, an arm of the Roman Empire. Jesus reminds Pilate that this power has been given to Pilate not by the emperor but "from above" (John 19:11). As in the text in Isaiah, that power will be used to cut the Servant off from the "land of the living" (Isa. 53:8b), yet the Servant will "make many righteous, and he shall bear

2. Paul D. Hanson, *Isaiah 40–66*, Interpretation (Louisville. KY: John Knox, 1995), 166.

their iniquities" (53:11b). Power is redefined and is located in the pain and suffering of the Servant and of Jesus. Power is now redefined as the power to heal both the individual and the community. This power to heal becomes embodied in the return from exile for ancient Israel, and it becomes embodied in the resurrection of Jesus for the New Testament community.

The Isaiah text for Good Friday begins with the exaltation of the Servant and then journeys through the pain and suffering of the Servant. The text ends with the claim that the suffering one will bring many into righteousness. To a people bearing the pain of exile, this text must have given them hope for a future restoration of their communal life with God in the land once promised to them by God—a hope that has come out of a hard journey of loss.

KRISTA KIGER

Commentary 2: Connecting the Reading with the World

The Suffering Servant has been beaten down, humiliated, and crushed. Isaiah looks forward to the vindication of the Servant's suffering. A redemptive, just, and righteous God forges a link between suffering and vindication, between Good Friday and Easter.

It had been a stormy meeting. I was seated in the church office the morning after, going over in my mind the fierce words said, the contentious actions taken, and the raw feelings expressed. Never had I been so wounded in all my six years of ministry. What did I do wrong? I should have not allowed the issue to be debated so soon. I should have spent more time listening to the critics. Why did I not poll the members beforehand in order to be forewarned of the debacle? Why did I let them put it to a vote? Ringing in my ears were the words one member spoke to me in the parking lot afterwards: "After tonight, you maybe ought to look for another church. Your ministry here is in doubt." That was followed by helpful words from another: "Son, this is only one defeat. You will be able to recover from this. I hope. Remember, at least I still love you."

I am the worst Methodist pastor in the world, I concluded. I do not know anything about how to manage a church. How could I have been so dumb? To think, I looked on myself as a good leader! I ceased my self-flagellation long enough to look at the upcoming lections. Holy Week was staring me in the face. Five sermons in seven days. I had better lay my suffering aside and get busy.

My eyes fell on a portion of Isaiah 53, the assigned lection for the dark, violent Friday we call "Good." "He was despised . . . appeared disfigured . . . pierced . . . wounded." On reading those words, it was if the heavens opened, a dove descended, and the voice of the Holy Spirit whispered in my ear, "Now what about the word 'cross' do you not get?" I realized that I had been guilty of thinking, in effect, "I'm a better leader than Jesus." He preached in the power of the Spirt, showed courage mixed with compassion, and how did his ministry culminate on that fateful Friday? A cross.

Of course, the church has from earliest days applied Isaiah 52–53 to Jesus. Christ is *the* Servant, the one who was obedient to God, even unto death. The Suffering Servant is Jesus, not me. Still, the text at least implies that those who follow the Servant walk in his way of suffering, the way to the cross. Was he not upfront with us on a number of occasions, that each of us must take up the cross? Did he not tell us that if we follow him, there will be smiting, rejection, crisis, and pain? How did we ever get in our heads that the way of Jesus is the way of prosperity, blessing, and glory? Good Friday, along with the texts for this day, is a stinging rebuke to the notion that the cross is optional equipment for Christians. I think it was Father Daniel Berrigan who said, on his way to jail, "If you follow Jesus, you better look good on wood."

Yet please note: if the suffering of the Servant applies to us and our sufferings for righteousness' sake, then so does the rest of Isaiah 52–53. The

Servant's suffering is ultimately vindicated. Sure, it is Friday now, but take heart. Easter is coming.

By the way, that stormy meeting was not the end of my ministry at that church. What I feared would be the end actually became the beginning. As someone told me a year later, "Son, you were five years ahead of us. You had to give us time to catch up to where you were. Thanks for how you are leading us. You are as good a pastor as we have ever had."

First the suffering, the humiliation and degradation, and then God vindicates. First Good Friday, then Easter. We cannot get to Easter except by way of the cross. Easter, when we arrive there, is not just the resuscitation of a dead body; it is the vindication of the crucified Jesus. No one had ever been raised from the dead except the crucified, Suffering Servant Jesus.

As C. S. Lewis said, "the Christian religion is, in the long run, a thing of unspeakable comfort. But it does not begin in comfort; it begins in the dismay I have been describing."[3] Easter does not leave us there. Christianity is a way toward abundant life, but it is a way that passes through death. God vindicates the Suffering Servant on Good Friday by raising crucified Jesus on Easter.

Presumably, there are gods who get what they want through battles with other gods, by swooping down from heaven and forcing good to get done. This God, the one who hangs there on the cross on Good Friday, wins through suffering love. By implication, our victories will come the same way. I believe in righteousness. I am willing to work for justice. Am I willing to suffer for it? Not that all suffering is immediately vindicated. Jesus prayed in Gethsemane that his "cup," his suffering, be bypassed. "Nevertheless, thy will be done."

I know someone who has given her life to working against mass incarceration in America. Her son was jailed for life after his third conviction of drug dealing. She has organized others, sent out appeals, crafted petitions. She has tirelessly lobbied her legislatures, sleeping in her car in Washington when she met with her state's senators. She has worked night and day for justice. Sadly, her hard, self-sacrificial work has converted few among the powerful. She got no laws passed, no wrongs set right. Most people, I am told, considered her somewhat of a nut. Because of her exhaustion, her overwork, her total commitment and self-sacrifice, her health was broken. At least that is the way I see it. Last month, I attended her funeral. Her imprisoned son was not allowed to come stand by the grave.

I wish that God had vindicated her suffering so all could see that she, and the cause she cared about, were divinely vindicated. How I pray that she had lived long enough to realize even one of her goals for the elimination of mass incarceration.

Yet on the basis of Isaiah 52–53, which I believe to be true, we can have hope that the way of the Suffering Servant and those whom he calls to suffer for righteousness' sake shall be vindicated. Maybe not today, but someday. I did not say that this suffering servant, this tireless advocate for social justice, was just like Jesus. I say she walked the way of Jesus, the way of the cross. She shall be vindicated. Her way shall be shone to be God's way—someday.

Those who put themselves at the disposal of a good, righteous, and just God and who suffer for it shall be vindicated. Those who have been crushed down because they committed themselves to the accomplishment of God's will shall rise. They shall shine like the sun, because that is what the God of Israel does for righteous sufferers.

Isaiah 52–53 says it. I believe it. That settles it. Take heart! It is Good Friday. This is the day of unspeakable suffering. Yet be well assured: vindication is coming.

WILL WILLIMON

---

3. C. S. Lewis, *Mere Christianity* (New York: HarperOne, 2001), 32.

Psalm 22

[1]My God, my God, why have you forsaken me?
    Why are you so far from helping me, from the words of my groaning?
[2]O my God, I cry by day, but you do not answer;
    and by night, but find no rest.

[3]Yet you are holy,
    enthroned on the praises of Israel.
[4]In you our ancestors trusted;
    they trusted, and you delivered them.
To you they cried, and were saved;
    in you they trusted, and were not put to shame.

[6]But I am a worm, and not human;
    scorned by others, and despised by the people.
[7]All who see me mock at me;
    they make mouths at me, they shake their heads;
[8]"Commit your cause to the LORD; let him deliver—
    let him rescue the one in whom he delights!"

[9]Yet it was you who took me from the womb;
    you kept me safe on my mother's breast.
[10]On you I was cast from my birth,
    and since my mother bore me you have been my God.
[11]Do not be far from me,
    for trouble is near
    and there is no one to help.

[12]Many bulls encircle me,
    strong bulls of Bashan surround me;
[13]they open wide their mouths at me,
    like a ravening and roaring lion.

[14]I am poured out like water,
    and all my bones are out of joint;
my heart is like wax;
    it is melted within my breast;
[15]my mouth is dried up like a potsherd,
    and my tongue sticks to my jaws;
    you lay me in the dust of death.

[16]For dogs are all around me;
    a company of evildoers encircles me.
My hands and feet have shriveled;
[17]I can count all my bones.
They stare and gloat over me;
[18]they divide my clothes among themselves,
    and for my clothing they cast lots.

[19]But you, O LORD, do not be far away!
    O my help, come quickly to my aid!

²⁰Deliver my soul from the sword,
   my life from the power of the dog!
      ²¹Save me from the mouth of the lion!

From the horns of the wild oxen you have rescued me.
²²I will tell of your name to my brothers and sisters;
   in the midst of the congregation I will praise you:
²³You who fear the LORD, praise him!
   All you offspring of Jacob, glorify him;
   stand in awe of him, all you offspring of Israel!
²⁴For he did not despise or abhor
   the affliction of the afflicted;
he did not hide his face from me,
   but heard when I cried to him.

²⁵From you comes my praise in the great congregation;
   my vows I will pay before those who fear him.
²⁶The poor shall eat and be satisfied;
   those who seek him shall praise the LORD.
   May your hearts live forever!

²⁷All the ends of the earth shall remember
   and turn to the LORD;
and all the families of the nations
   shall worship before him.
²⁸For dominion belongs to the LORD,
   and he rules over the nations.

²⁹To him, indeed, shall all who sleep in the earth bow down;
   before him shall bow all who go down to the dust,
   and I shall live for him.
³⁰Posterity will serve him;
   future generations will be told about the Lord,
³¹and proclaim his deliverance to a people yet unborn,
   saying that he has done it.

Connecting the Psalms with Scripture and Worship

Psalm 22 begins, "My God, my God, why have you forsaken me?" (Ps. 22:1). The psalmist asks a drastic question. Followers of the Crucified One cannot hear these first words of Psalm 22 without hearing the words of Jesus from the cross as recorded in Matthew's (27:46) and Mark's (15:34) Passion Narratives. The words are heard every Good Friday as the church gathers around the foot of the cross. Interestingly, the Revised Common Lectionary appoints not the narrative from Matthew nor Mark but the story from John's Gospel as the version heard in the shadow of the cross. Also of interest,

though Matthew's and Mark's passion stories are not heard on Holy Thursday, many Holy Thursday liturgies conclude with the reading of Psalm 22 as the worship space is stripped of its appointments.

A song of personal lament, the whole of Psalm 22 is the appointed psalm for the Liturgy of Good Friday. The thirty-one verses can be divided into two sections. Verses 1–21 are a crying out to God in misery, as the psalmist is overtaken with the feeling of being forsaken by God and attacked by enemies all around. Verses 22–31 comprise an expression of thanks to God for having rescued the psalmist, as the psalmist bids the community to join in praise.

The thrust of the psalm is expressed in verse 1: "My God, my God, why have you forsaken me? Why are you so far from helping me?" Verse 2 continues, "I cry . . . , but you do not answer." The psalmist's cry is one of desperation and loneliness. One of the wonderful gifts of the lament psalms is that as we hear the plight of the one praying the words of the psalm, we are given permission to voice our own desperate pleas to God as well.

The remaining verses of the first section (through v. 21) are smaller units alternating between affirmations of who God is and what God has done and units that give detailed description of the psalmist's situation and bring to voice the desperation felt. Interestingly, each of the affirmation units begins with the conjunction "yet" or "but." "My God, I cry by day, but you do not answer" (v. 2) is followed by "Yet you are holy" (v. 3). "All who see me mock at me" (v. 7) is followed by "Yet it was you who took me from the womb" (v. 9). Then, in an extended section the psalmist uses metaphoric animal language to describe being closed and attacked by those around, only to affirm, "But you, O LORD, do not be far away! . . . come quickly to my aid!" (v. 19).

Even in the midst of despair, the psalmist voices affirmation that the God of the ancestors, the God of Israel, has helped before and must be able to help once more. Even in the midst of an overwhelming sense of abandonment or forsakenness, the psalmist is able to cry out to God. God is the object of the psalmist's pain—or maybe even the source, according to the words of the psalm—yet God is also the source of the psalmist's relief, the psalmist's hope.

In verses 1–21a the psalmist cries out for help: "do not be far from me" (vv. 11, 19), "come quickly to my aid" (v. 19), "deliver my soul" (v. 20), and "save me" (v. 21). The need is now. The psalmist affirms that God is God and that God has acted in the past, but the psalmist

needs God to act *now*. Then somehow prayers are answered. In verse 21b the psalmist states, "From the horns of the wild oxen you have rescued me." We do not know what is meant by "wild oxen." We just know that whatever was the reason for the desperate cry for help, salvation has come.

The remaining verses (vv. 22–31) express praise and gratitude for deliverance. "[God] did not hide his face from me, but heard when I cried to him" (v. 24). The psalmist voices individual praise but then calls for all of creation and all the peoples of the earth (even the dead) to join in the praise. Thus, future generations will know about the God who hears desperate cries and acts, even now.

In the congregation I serve as pastor, more people attend worship services on Good Friday than on Holy/Maundy Thursday. Many reflect about how stirring it is when the gathered community joins together to sing the spiritual "Were You There When They Crucified My Lord?" Others remark how the ancient, yet fresh words of the Solemn Intercessions and the Solemn Reproaches of the Cross are moving and still speak today. "My God, my God, why have you forsaken me?" is the psalm refrain for the evening as worshipers witness the Savior of the world hanging on the cross. As Psalm 22 is heard or chanted or sung or read, all the world's sufferings and pains are gathered up in the words, "My God, my God . . . ," as the congregation, on behalf of the world, identifies with the separation, the God-forsakenness of the cross.

Maybe that is why they come—because in coming they hear the story. In hearing Psalm 22 and the passion story, they hear the good news of the gospel: that our God is a God who enters into our world and becomes one of us, even in our sufferings, even in our separateness from God, even in our death. Somehow the hope of the world is there before us as we hang on to the promise of new life, trusting that the one forsaken is the very one suffering—and yet the one able to do a new thing.

ERIC T. MYERS

Hebrews 10:16–25

[16]"This is the covenant that I will make with them
    after those days, says the Lord:
I will put my laws in their hearts,
    and I will write them on their minds,"

[17]he also adds,

"I will remember their sins and their lawless deeds no more."

[18]Where there is forgiveness of these, there is no longer any offering for sin.
  [19]Therefore, my friends, since we have confidence to enter the sanctuary by the blood of Jesus, [20]by the new and living way that he opened for us through the curtain (that is, through his flesh), [21]and since we have a great priest over the house of God, [22]let us approach with a true heart in full assurance of faith, with our hearts sprinkled clean from an evil conscience and our bodies washed with pure water. [23]Let us hold fast to the confession of our hope without wavering, for he who has promised is faithful. [24]And let us consider how to provoke one another to love and good deeds, [25]not neglecting to meet together, as is the habit of some, but encouraging one another, and all the more as you see the Day approaching.

Hebrews 4:14–16; 5:7–9

[4:14]Since, then, we have a great high priest who has passed through the heavens, Jesus, the Son of God, let us hold fast to our confession. [15]For we do not have a high priest who is unable to sympathize with our weaknesses, but we have one who in every respect has been tested as we are, yet without sin. [16]Let us therefore approach the throne of grace with boldness, so that we may receive mercy and find grace to help in time of need. . . .
  [5:7]In the days of his flesh, Jesus offered up prayers and supplications, with loud cries and tears, to the one who was able to save him from death, and he was heard because of his reverent submission. [8]Although he was a Son, he learned obedience through what he suffered; [9]and having been made perfect, he became the source of eternal salvation for all who obey him.

Commentary 1: Connecting the Reading with Scripture

The Letter to the Hebrews is neither a letter nor is it directed necessarily to a Hebrew audience. We know very little about the original readers, but given the constant references to the Old Testament, we may presume they knew something of the stories of Melchizedek (see Heb. 5:6, 10; 6:20–7:17). They would have also known the accounts of the wanderings in the wilderness.

The author assumes they had some knowledge of the temple in Jerusalem and the role of the priest in entering the Holy of Holies. Beyond that, we cannot be sure who the audience was or what they were expected to know.

In the first century, there were plenty of God-fearers (Gentiles who were interested in and attended synagogue worship). If they attended synagogue, they would have become familiar with the stories of Abraham (including his encounter with Melchizedek), the stories of wilderness wanderings, and references to tabernacle worship. God-fearers who later became Christians may have been the target audience of Hebrews, or the first audience may have been Jews who recognized Jesus as the Messiah. Either way, they would be quite aware of all the biblical references.

In the split reading from portions of three different chapters assigned for Good Friday, we encounter all of the items mentioned above: the story of Melchizedek, the tabernacle in the wilderness, and the Holy of Holies.

Let us begin with Melchizedek. Other than a brief reference in the Psalms (Ps. 110:4), Hebrews is the only book of the Bible that mentions Melchizedek, outside of Abraham's encounter with him in Genesis. Hebrews refers to him by name eight times.

Melchizedek was the priest and king at Salem (perhaps a reference to the future site of Jerusalem). His name means "righteous king" in Hebrew, but he is also called a priest. After Abraham wins a military victory, he is blessed by Melchizedek. In turn, Abraham offers this priest a tithe of his spoils of war (Gen. 14:1–20). The author of Hebrews uses this knowledge to raise the priesthood of Melchizedek above that of the inherited Levitical priesthood. After all, the Levitical priesthood is passed down from generation to generation. The priesthood of Melchizedek predates Abraham. Abraham shows deference to Melchizedek with a tithe. We never hear of Melchizedek's death, and Psalm 110 refers to him as a "priest forever."

So the author of Hebrews presents Melchizedek as the ultimate, eternal model for priesthood. Never mind that Psalm 110 is actually a victory psalm dedicated to the king. If anything, it is giving the king assumed in the psalm the combination of priestly and kingly roles in Melchizedek. Hebrews takes just the one phrase about being a priest forever out of context and emphasizes the idea of eternal priesthood (Heb. 5:6–7). Melchizedek is thus the model of eternal priesthood, of which Jesus becomes the prime example.

Hebrews then compares Jesus to this model. Since Jesus is described early on as the imprint of God's very being and thus eternal (1:3–4), he is like the eternal Melchizedek. At the same time, Hebrews emphasizes the humanity of Jesus (4:15; 5:7–9). We are told he offers his tears and prayers for deliverance and learns obedience through what he suffers. Jesus is said to be a priest who can sympathize with our weakness and struggle. Though the doctrine of the Trinity will come much later, Hebrews does not seem to have any problems describing Jesus as the eternal imprint of God or his being an eternal priest while at the same time being fully human.

In a theological connection to the sacrificial practices of Second Temple Judaism, the author describes Jesus' death in the language of sacrifice for sin. This makes Jesus both the eternal priest and a sacrificial offering at the same time. Hebrews argues that, unlike the Levitical priests, who offer sacrifices day after day that cannot take away sin, Jesus is offered once, as the perfect sacrifice (10:11–12). The metaphor is carried even further when Jesus' blood is seen as the blood sprinkled for the sins of all. To add even more metaphorical connections, his body is equated with the curtain that divides the Holy of Holies from the rest of the temple. So, by implication, we pass through Jesus (the curtain) to get to the presence of God. Though Jesus is the imprint of God, Jesus is also human. That reality is meant to give us confidence to approach this metaphorical image of the temple, or tabernacle in the wilderness, with hope and a clean conscience.

According to Hebrews, all of this takes place in the midst of God's people's being on a journey from this world to the heavenly hope. Hebrews claims it is the journey everyone from Abraham to Moses and everyone in between has been on and is still on. In our journey of faith, we are surrounded by these witnesses, as we all press on with the race that is set before us (chaps. 11–12). God accompanies us on this journey, just as the tabernacle in the wilderness accompanied the people and reminded them of the presence of God. Now we have the addition of one who is both high priest *and* sacrifice, one

Wash Him with Your Tears

But, lo, the traitor advances with the impious crowd behind him; Judas offers the kiss; they lay hands on Jesus; they hold their Lord fast bound; they manacle those dear hands of His. Who could endure it? Pity, I know, fills all your heart now, and zeal inflames all your inmost parts. Let Him alone, I pray you; let Him suffer; He is suffering for you. Why do you want a sword? why does your anger burn? why are you filled with indignation? For if, like Peter, you cut off an ear of one of them; if you draw the sword and sever a foot from its limb, He will restore everything; nay, should you even kill one of them, without doubt He will raise him to life again.

No; better follow Him to the high-priest's palace, and that loveliest face of His, which they besmear with spittings, wash, O wash it with your tears.

See with what pitiful eyes, with what a merciful and what an efficacious glance He turned and looked on Peter, now for the third time denying Him; and Peter turning back to Him, and returning into himself, wept bitterly. O, good Jesus, would that that dear eye would look on me, that have so often denied Thee by the worst of actions and of desires at the voice of a pert serving-maid, my flesh.

And now, for it is morning, He is delivered up to Pilate, before whom He is accused and holds His peace, for He was led as a sheep to the slaughter. Mark Him, how He stands before the governor, with Head bent down, with Eyes turned to the ground, with Face all peace; He speaks little and seldom, He is ready for insults, and goes all eagerly to be scourged. You cannot bear more of this, I know; you cannot bear to see there before your very eyes that dearest Back furrowed by the thongs, that Face bruised with blows, that sensitive Head crowned with thorns; that Right Hand, which rules heaven and earth, dishonoured with a reed. But see, they are leading Him out; the scourging is over; He wears a crown of thorns, and a purple garment; and Pilate cries, "Behold the Man!" Man in very truth, who can doubt it? Witness the stripes the rods have made, the livid wounds, the filthy spittings.

Know now, at last, thou Devil, that He is a man. "I grant you," you say, "He is a man." But yet you say, "What is He?" Ay, what is He? For amid so many injuries He is not angry, as a man would be; He is not moved, as a man would be; He is not indignant against His torturers, as a man would be. Then surely He is more than man. But if so, who owns more than man? He is owned, I grant, as man in His endurance of the judgments of the wicked of the earth; He will be owned as God when He comes to pass judgment. Too late, O Devil; you have found it out too late. Why have tried to work by Pilate's wife to procure His discharge? You spoke not quick enough. The judge is on the bench; the sentence is pronounced already.

Anselm of Canterbury, *Book of Meditations and Prayers*, trans. M. R. (London: Burns and Gates, 1872), 212–14.

who gives us access to even the inner sanctuary and the direct encounter with God's presence. All of this theological narration is meant to provoke us to good deeds and to encourage us in gathering together as a community.

This process of interpretation used in Hebrews is called midrash. It was a common approach among Jews, interpreting new ideas by appealing to already known texts of Scripture. For example, the Gospel of Matthew undertakes a similar process as it cites the Hebrew Scriptures many times to describe how the coming of Jesus fulfills

ancient prophecy. Hebrews is trying to place an understanding of Jesus and his role in salvation history in the context of known scriptural passages: passages about Melchizedek, the tabernacle in the wilderness, and temple sacrificial rites. To readers today, the exegesis of Hebrews may appear to be little more than theological gymnastics. However, Hebrews uses what was then a common interpretive technique, to make a case for the Christ who is both priest and sacrifice; not only that, Jesus is also a priest forever, just like Melchizedek.

It may be difficult to explain in any one sermon all the intricacies of how midrash and all its interpretive efforts work, let alone to define who Melchizedek was and why he is an important example for making the case that Jesus is both priest and sacrifice. In fact, the plethora of metaphors makes this a difficult passage on which to preach. Choosing one metaphor and then connecting it to the other lessons may be the best course of action. The idea that Jesus, though the imprint of God, also suffered as a human being may fit well with the Suffering Servant passage from Isaiah and the suffering detailed in Psalm 22. This would create a sermon about the depth and power of Jesus' sacrifice.

Jesus as both priest and sacrifice may meld well with John's Passion Narrative, leading to a sermon on the one who died for us as also the priest who mediates the presence of God to us. The metaphor of journey may fit with the overall theme of Holy Week, as the biblical texts travel from the triumphal entry to the crucifixion. The journey is difficult, but God is with us, even to the point of suffering and death.

STEPHEN SMITH

Commentary 2: Connecting the Reading with the World

The God who gives life has given God's own life. This is the surprise lodged in the heart of Christian faith. We worship a giving God, one who offers up the divine life daily to us, permeating our senses, and drawing us to prayer and a shared communion that would bind us together in love and hope. God's giving of life is the first and most important meaning of sacrifice. God is the sacrifice. God has done this for the sake of Israel and the long history of God's relentlessly drawing close to them. The covenant speaks divine desire, the same desire out of which creation itself came, the same desire that bound God in faithfulness to Israel, and the same desire that God forever seeks to weave into the heart of the creature.

In Jesus, that weaving works. The will of God is one with the flesh of Jesus. The will of God is found in his heart and intoxicating his mind. He is divine law embodied and love of God made manifest. Jesus is not some shiny new penny in the world, free of mud-bound existence or the nicks and bruises of actual bare life. He is one with the story of his people Israel, sharer in their suffering, joint heir with their oppression and their longing for Israel's political and social restoration. He knows their temptations to be the temptations of the creature and of all peoples seeking food, shelter, safety, and significance. They are tempted to despair and tempted by desperation to a wayward life that traffics in hate and violence and greed and callousness to the vulnerable even in their midst: the widows and orphans, the aliens and estranged kin.

Jesus will face these temptations and overcome them, not by might or power, but through the weaving enacted in him through the Spirit of God. Jesus will yield to the Spirit and not give himself over to these temptations, and this too is the sacrifice. Too often, Christians have narrowed the sacrifice of Jesus to his death on the cross and thereby lost sight of the full range of the divine self-giving. From a life lived in his mother's "Yes" to God, through a journey of faithful service in the midst of frustration with religious leaders, to an agonizing prayer in a garden for strength to do the divine will, Jesus is offering himself to God for us. So the cross becomes important, not because it is a cross, but because of who is on the cross: this child of Israel who embodies the will of God.

Jesus is put on the cross because he has exposed our wayward life. He has revealed our propensity to violence, especially the violence woven in the machinations of statecraft. He has cast light on our faulty forms of judgment that criminalize the innocent and use torture and murder with a hubris that is nothing less than idolatry. That hubris allows us to imagine that we, like God, can recreate the world in our own image if we punish or destroy those who stand in the way of our prosperous futures. Christians have always been susceptible to this hubris and the illusions that come with societies' shifting constructions of morality and the law. We have often blindly followed those who spoke the language of morality and of what is right and wrong, believing that their speech matches the gospel, when in point of fact, it is far removed from the good news.

Our good news begins with the fact that we worship a criminal. Christianity begins in crime with a transgressing people pushing against theological and political borders and against cultural and social boundaries and placing themselves in the dangerous place of being seen as traitors and insurrectionists. Indeed, we have always been tempted to wrap ourselves inside morality structures and legal conventions of various nations and cultures, in order to stay out of trouble and appear to the world to be not only threat-less but patriots. Yet this text speaks of a people and to a people who have not achieved such safety. Individually and collectively, they are tempted with the same temptations Jesus knew so well and through which Jesus learned an obedience hard won and now freely available to all who would touch his sacrifice.

The book of Hebrews, however, reads sacrifice through Jesus and not Jesus through sacrifice. We are not allowed to isolate sacrifice as a purpose or a practice and then try to fit the logic of God's life or our life into such a schema. Too often, sacrifice in the Scriptures has been read as though it is intelligible apart from the story of a giving God and thereby made to render a fiction—a vampire God who thirsts for blood and who is always looking for bodies to be used as slaves or surrogates. Such a god needs death as a servant, an agent of justice. This is not the God found in Jesus, who has revealed death to be the enemy and justice to be always aimed at eliminating death, not using it.

Our God has rendered the final word to death: Jesus is the last sacrifice. After him, what it means to give is to receive. We give him our needs, our burdens, our moments when the temptations seem too great to resist, our failures and blunders, our tormenting regrets; he gives us the grace we need to live and flourish, the grace that is his life. Yet our living now is formed in confession, and the logic of this confession oftentimes escapes some contemporary Christians. This confession is not first of sin and personal failings nor does this confession mark a Christian exclusivity. We confess the giving God revealed in Jesus and his final sacrifice.

Jesus has opened a way forward through his own body. Our task is to hold fast to this way and hold one another to it. What we give to God we must also give to one another—a confession that echoes the sacrificial life of God. We owe to one another for the sake of Jesus a holy provocation, a pressing one another to love, to deeds of mercy, and to encouragement even in the face of oppositions both political and personal, both economic and psychic, both individual and familial. We offer this aware that we live in the bodily knowledge of our Savior, whose loud cries, tears, anguish, and pain went ahead of our own, making a way to a God who fully and deeply understands our struggle, and giving us a confidence in divine empathy that will not yield.

We speak to one another, therefore, not in religious slogans but in and through the depth of shared knowledge of a sympathetic God who draws us to communion. Confession is the sacrifice we Christians make to God and to one another, offering up words of love or encouragement or even rebuke, always recognizing we follow the offering God gives through Jesus and by the Spirit. This is the weaving of a covenant in our hearts and the inscribing of a new law in our minds that binds us in love to one another forever. This is life already on the other side of death, life that merges the present with the future through the promise of a faithful God who turned the cross of Jesus from a last word to a first word: finished.

WILLIE JAMES JENNINGS

John 18:1–19:42

¹⁸:¹After Jesus had spoken these words, he went out with his disciples across the Kidron valley to a place where there was a garden, which he and his disciples entered. ²Now Judas, who betrayed him, also knew the place, because Jesus often met there with his disciples. ³So Judas brought a detachment of soldiers together with police from the chief priests and the Pharisees, and they came there with lanterns and torches and weapons. ⁴Then Jesus, knowing all that was to happen to him, came forward and asked them, "Whom are you looking for?" ⁵They answered, "Jesus of Nazareth." Jesus replied, "I am he." Judas, who betrayed him, was standing with them. ⁶When Jesus said to them, "I am he," they stepped back and fell to the ground. ⁷Again he asked them, "Whom are you looking for?" And they said, "Jesus of Nazareth." ⁸Jesus answered, "I told you that I am he. So if you are looking for me, let these men go." ⁹This was to fulfill the word that he had spoken, "I did not lose a single one of those whom you gave me." ¹⁰Then Simon Peter, who had a sword, drew it, struck the high priest's slave, and cut off his right ear. The slave's name was Malchus. ¹¹Jesus said to Peter, "Put your sword back into its sheath. Am I not to drink the cup that the Father has given me?"

¹²So the soldiers, their officer, and the Jewish police arrested Jesus and bound him. ¹³First they took him to Annas, who was the father-in-law of Caiaphas, the high priest that year. ¹⁴Caiaphas was the one who had advised the Jews that it was better to have one person die for the people.

¹⁵Simon Peter and another disciple followed Jesus. Since that disciple was known to the high priest, he went with Jesus into the courtyard of the high priest, ¹⁶but Peter was standing outside at the gate. So the other disciple, who was known to the high priest, went out, spoke to the woman who guarded the gate, and brought Peter in. ¹⁷The woman said to Peter, "You are not also one of this man's disciples, are you?" He said, "I am not." ¹⁸Now the slaves and the police had made a charcoal fire because it was cold, and they were standing around it and warming themselves. Peter also was standing with them and warming himself.

¹⁹Then the high priest questioned Jesus about his disciples and about his teaching. ²⁰Jesus answered, "I have spoken openly to the world; I have always taught in synagogues and in the temple, where all the Jews come together. I have said nothing in secret. ²¹Why do you ask me? Ask those who heard what I said to them; they know what I said." ²²When he had said this, one of the police standing nearby struck Jesus on the face, saying, "Is that how you answer the high priest?" ²³Jesus answered, "If I have spoken wrongly, testify to the wrong. But if I have spoken rightly, why do you strike me?" ²⁴Then Annas sent him bound to Caiaphas the high priest.

²⁵Now Simon Peter was standing and warming himself. They asked him, "You are not also one of his disciples, are you?" He denied it and said, "I am not." ²⁶One of the slaves of the high priest, a relative of the man whose ear Peter had cut off, asked, "Did I not see you in the garden with him?" ²⁷Again Peter denied it, and at that moment the cock crowed.

²⁸Then they took Jesus from Caiaphas to Pilate's headquarters. It was early in the morning. They themselves did not enter the headquarters, so as to avoid ritual defilement and to be able to eat the Passover. ²⁹So Pilate went out to them and said, "What accusation do you bring against this man?" ³⁰They answered, "If this man were not a criminal, we would not have handed him over to you." ³¹Pilate

said to them, "Take him yourselves and judge him according to your law." The Jews replied, "We are not permitted to put anyone to death." ³²(This was to fulfill what Jesus had said when he indicated the kind of death he was to die.)

³³Then Pilate entered the headquarters again, summoned Jesus, and asked him, "Are you the King of the Jews?" ³⁴Jesus answered, "Do you ask this on your own, or did others tell you about me?" ³⁵Pilate replied, "I am not a Jew, am I? Your own nation and the chief priests have handed you over to me. What have you done?" ³⁶Jesus answered, "My kingdom is not from this world. If my kingdom were from this world, my followers would be fighting to keep me from being handed over to the Jews. But as it is, my kingdom is not from here." ³⁷Pilate asked him, "So you are a king?" Jesus answered, "You say that I am a king. For this I was born, and for this I came into the world, to testify to the truth. Everyone who belongs to the truth listens to my voice." ³⁸Pilate asked him, "What is truth?"

After he had said this, he went out to the Jews again and told them, "I find no case against him. ³⁹But you have a custom that I release someone for you at the Passover. Do you want me to release for you the King of the Jews?" ⁴⁰They shouted in reply, "Not this man, but Barabbas!" Now Barabbas was a bandit.

¹⁹:¹Then Pilate took Jesus and had him flogged. ²And the soldiers wove a crown of thorns and put it on his head, and they dressed him in a purple robe. ³They kept coming up to him, saying, "Hail, King of the Jews!" and striking him on the face. ⁴Pilate went out again and said to them, "Look, I am bringing him out to you to let you know that I find no case against him." ⁵So Jesus came out, wearing the crown of thorns and the purple robe. Pilate said to them, "Here is the man!" ⁶When the chief priests and the police saw him, they shouted, "Crucify him! Crucify him!" Pilate said to them, "Take him yourselves and crucify him; I find no case against him." ⁷The Jews answered him, "We have a law, and according to that law he ought to die because he has claimed to be the Son of God."

⁸Now when Pilate heard this, he was more afraid than ever. ⁹He entered his headquarters again and asked Jesus, "Where are you from?" But Jesus gave him no answer. ¹⁰Pilate therefore said to him, "Do you refuse to speak to me? Do you not know that I have power to release you, and power to crucify you?" ¹¹Jesus answered him, "You would have no power over me unless it had been given you from above; therefore the one who handed me over to you is guilty of a greater sin." ¹²From then on Pilate tried to release him, but the Jews cried out, "If you release this man, you are no friend of the emperor. Everyone who claims to be a king sets himself against the emperor."

¹³When Pilate heard these words, he brought Jesus outside and sat on the judge's bench at a place called The Stone Pavement, or in Hebrew Gabbatha. ¹⁴Now it was the day of Preparation for the Passover; and it was about noon. He said to the Jews, "Here is your King!" ¹⁵They cried out, "Away with him! Away with him! Crucify him!" Pilate asked them, "Shall I crucify your King?" The chief priests answered, "We have no king but the emperor." ¹⁶Then he handed him over to them to be crucified.

So they took Jesus; ¹⁷and carrying the cross by himself, he went out to what is called The Place of the Skull, which in Hebrew is called Golgotha. ¹⁸There they crucified him, and with him two others, one on either side, with Jesus between them. ¹⁹Pilate also had an inscription written and put on the cross. It read, "Jesus of Nazareth, the King of the Jews." ²⁰Many of the Jews read this inscription, because the place where Jesus was crucified was near the city; and it was written in Hebrew, in Latin, and in Greek. ²¹Then the chief priests of the Jews said to Pilate, "Do not write, 'The King of the Jews,' but, 'This man said, I am King of the Jews.'" ²²Pilate answered, "What I have written I have written." ²³When the soldiers had crucified Jesus, they took his clothes and divided them into four parts, one for each soldier. They also took his tunic; now the tunic was seamless, woven in one piece from the top. [24]So they said to one another, "Let us not tear it, but cast lots for it to see who will get it." This was to fulfill what the scripture says,

"They divided my clothes among themselves,
  and for my clothing they cast lots."

[25]And that is what the soldiers did.

Meanwhile, standing near the cross of Jesus were his mother, and his mother's sister, Mary the wife of Clopas, and Mary Magdalene. [26]When Jesus saw his mother and the disciple whom he loved standing beside her, he said to his mother, "Woman, here is your son." [27]Then he said to the disciple, "Here is your mother." And from that hour the disciple took her into his own home.

[28]After this, when Jesus knew that all was now finished, he said (in order to fulfill the scripture), "I am thirsty." [29]A jar full of sour wine was standing there. So they put a sponge full of the wine on a branch of hyssop and held it to his mouth. [30]When Jesus had received the wine, he said, "It is finished." Then he bowed his head and gave up his spirit.

[31]Since it was the day of Preparation, the Jews did not want the bodies left on the cross during the sabbath, especially because that sabbath was a day of great solemnity. So they asked Pilate to have the legs of the crucified men broken and the bodies removed. [32]Then the soldiers came and broke the legs of the first and of the other who had been crucified with him. [33]But when they came to Jesus and saw that he was already dead, they did not break his legs. [34]Instead, one of the soldiers pierced his side with a spear, and at once blood and water came out. [35](He who saw this has testified so that you also may believe. His testimony is true, and he knows that he tells the truth.) [36]These things occurred so that the scripture might be fulfilled, "None of his bones shall be broken." [37]And again another passage of scripture says, "They will look on the one whom they have pierced."

[38]After these things, Joseph of Arimathea, who was a disciple of Jesus, though a secret one because of his fear of the Jews, asked Pilate to let him take away the body of Jesus. Pilate gave him permission; so he came and removed his body. [39]Nicodemus, who had at first come to Jesus by night, also came, bringing a mixture of myrrh and aloes, weighing about a hundred pounds. [40]They took the body of Jesus and wrapped it with the spices in linen cloths, according to the burial custom of the Jews. [41]Now there was a garden in the place where he was crucified, and in the garden there was a new tomb in which no one had ever been laid. [42]And so, because it was the Jewish day of Preparation, and the tomb was nearby, they laid Jesus there.

Commentary 1: Connecting the Reading with Scripture

It is Friday night, with no sign of Sunday. Friday night, when even the most even-tempered of Jesus' followers might balk at the bright assertion that everything will work together for good (Rom. 8:28). Friday night, when the only path to solidarity with the suffering world requires leaving behind domesticated understandings of Christian hope.

It is Friday night, and John has resurrection in mind. So does John's Jesus, who is confident and self-sufficient. There is no struggle of wills the night before his death (e.g., Luke 22:41–44);

no compulsion to shake the disciples awake for companionship (Matt. 26:40–41); no piercing cry of forsakenness (Ps. 22:1; Matt. 27:46; Mark 15:34). Jesus is in full command at all times. He identifies himself as the giver of "living water" that will quench our thirst forever (John 4:11–15), "the light of the world" who will guide us out of the darkness (8:12), "the good shepherd" who lays down his life for his sheep (10:11), and "the way, and the truth, and the life" through whom we will enjoy fellowship with God the Father (14:6).

John recounts Jesus' final day of earthly life with a tone of triumph, casting no doubt on anything Jesus has already told us he is and stands for. His arrest, trial, crucifixion, and burial, far from being events that throw us into confusion about Jesus' identity, are meant by John to assure anyone paying attention to his "open" teaching (18:19–20) that Jesus has accomplished his mission exactly as planned, every detail in place. "It is finished," he says (19:30), after expressing his thirst "in order to fulfill the scripture" (19:28).

When Pilate is confused about Jesus and truth, Jesus suggests he would not be if he would only listen to Jesus' voice (18:37). This sounds a lot like the guidance he gives Nicodemus (chap. 3), the Samaritan woman (chap. 4), and Thomas (14:5–7). In John, whenever anyone expresses confusion about matters spiritual or philosophical, Jesus directs them back to himself. Jesus is the "Word [that] became flesh," after all; he has been sent by God to reveal "his glory" to the world (1:14) "in order that the world might be saved through him" (3:17).

John portrays Jesus as the good shepherd who wants his sheep to know his voice but finds ways to include in the one flock even those who do not recognize him (10:14–16). Skeptics are included, as we see when Nicodemus visits Jesus by night (3:2). So is a secret disciple, like Joseph of Arimathea, who joins Nicodemus to embalm and bury Jesus' body (19:38–42). The preacher might contrast the Gospel of John, where Jesus has a clear identity and an expansive mission, with the Gospel of Mark, where Jesus is enigmatic and only the centurion at the cross has clarity about who Jesus is (Mark 4:12; 15:39).

It should be noted, however, that biblical scholars commonly identify John as the most "anti-Jewish" of any New Testament book (e.g., John 8:44). Noting that John 18–19 offers an "unequivocally negative portrayal of the Jews," Marianne Meye Thompson tries to reconcile this with John's inclusive vision, suggesting John believes that "if the saving love of God the Father is revealed in the death of the Son as the king of those who have most deeply betrayed him . . . then nothing can stop this love from reaching all people in the entire world."[1]

Consistent with this centered and saving portrayal of Jesus is his insistence on protecting, instructing, and exhorting to service those whom the Father has given him (18:9), for whom he has just prayed (chap. 17). He barters with those who come to arrest him, insisting his disciples be released (18:8). He will not let Peter fight (18:10–11), explaining he will drink "the cup that the Father has given" him. Jesus continues to recognize Peter as a leader of the church (chap. 21) even after Peter's denials (18:17, 25–27). He trusts the "disciple whom Jesus loved" to take care of his mother after his death (19:25–27), and he expects his disciples to serve one another as he served them by washing their feet (13:14–17).

The sufferers depicted in Isaiah 52–53 and Psalm 22 share much with the persona of John's Jesus. The Servant is "exalted and lifted up" (Isa. 52:13), even as the crucifixion, in John, marks the triumphant end to Jesus' ministry on earth. In Psalm 22, as well as in John's account, others "divide [the sufferer's] clothes among themselves" (Ps. 22:18; John 19:23–24).

The idea that kings and nations would be "astonished" and would "contemplate" what they see and hear in Jesus is certainly true of Pilate, though Pilate nonetheless flogs Jesus (John 19:1) and releases him to be executed. In Isaiah and in Psalm 22, however, the astonishment is elicited less by the individual's willingness to suffer than by the insidious injustice of the suffering itself. "By a perversion of justice he was taken away," Isaiah marvels: "Who could have imagined his future?" (Isa. 53:8). The sufferer himself seems astonished at his fate: "I can

1. Marianne Meye Thompson, *John: A Commentary* (Louisville, KY: Westminster John Knox, 2015), 398.

count all my bones. They stare and gloat over me," he laments (Ps. 22:17).

This Good Friday the preacher might want to ask listeners what they are most astonished by. Is it Jesus' eloquence and willing sacrifice? Is it the intractable injustice he experiences—that which makes majestic things hideous and the unimaginable normal? John's seamless, self-giving, inclusive Jesus reminds us of how things should be, and this should make the world's pain less bearable. Our witness to Jesus' triumph should deepen our horror before the distortions that rob the world of abundant life (John 10:10).

When we are clear enough about truth to be devastated by injustice, we will inevitably be undone by our complicity in systemic distortions. Our lectionary reading from Hebrews 10 celebrates forgiveness by way of a hope that is not contingent on triumphing over ugliness. Rather, it implies we will not have to choose between a majestic understanding of Jesus and an uncomely one. For Jesus' voluntary service on our behalf did not simply culminate on the cross, as the author of Hebrews understands it. Rather, it came to a full stop there as an unimaginable, ugly, violent, thing happened: Jesus shed his blood, precisely as the victorious

suffering one (Heb. 10:19). He entered a dark Friday night and comforted us by being tested just as we are, "yet without sin" (4:15).

While John's crucifixion punctuates the truth of everything Jesus is and does, Jesus in Hebrews is perfect because he continues to learn through obedience and, possibly, even through suffering. Anyone preaching about this must of course be clear about the ways in which the claim that suffering improves us can be used to justify and perpetuate injustice.

There are other ideas that can also do damage. If we follow John's triumphant account of the cross exclusively, for example, imagining Jesus had no doubts, no struggles, and no need for help, we risk forgetting John's greatest insight. "The Word became flesh," he testifies at the beginning of his account (John 1:14). This truth he holds is no less applicable on Good Friday than it is on Christmas. Preachers might want to press John a bit, asking him why, at times, Jesus seems to hover slightly above our worldly cares. How might we "abide" in the suffering Christ (chap. 15), loving and serving one another even on this Friday night?

CYNTHIA L. RIGBY

Commentary 2: Connecting the Reading to the World

Our reading provides rich sermon material for the homilist, while creating the challenge of what story to make the focus of one's preaching. Granted, the preacher cannot lose sight of the overall Passion Narrative, with its christological claims and careful unfolding of God's salvific plan; but a sermon that attempts to cover the entire arc of Jesus' final day risks diluting the impact each carefully crafted scene contributes to the overall account. The ideal would be a series of sermons, but for the homilist who has only one opportunity to preach on this passage, one issue demands attention: the troubling, anti-Semitic interpretations of this text throughout history and still today.

Over the years, many scholars have critiqued John's Gospel for its anti-Semitism, citing how "the Jews" are singled out by Jesus, who calls

them deceivers and liars (John 8:44), slaves of sin (8:31–38), and children of the devil (8:44), despite the fact that Jesus and his disciples were themselves Jewish, that only John explicitly proclaims "salvation is from the Jews" (4:22), and that in the very passage we are considering, John goes out of his way to affirm that Jesus was buried "according to the burial custom of the Jews" (19:40).

Most incriminating is the fact that, however exegetes nuance the term, in John, "the Jews" represent the opponents of Jesus who press Pilate to crucify him (19:12, 15). Consequently, John quickly came to be used to justify the widespread, erroneous, deadly belief that Jews as a whole were responsible for Jesus' death, as well as the hateful violence perpetrated by Christians against Jews during the Crusades, the Spanish Inquisition, the Russian pogroms, and the Holocaust. This is a pressing issue for all Christians, given the historical and contemporary prevalence of anti-Semitic hate crimes. So a careful reading of John's passion is needed that once and for all destroys the hateful belief that "the Jews" killed Jesus.

Rabbi A. James Rudin once published a plea aimed at Christian preachers in which he confessed to attending Good Friday services incognito and all too often hearing the painful, distressing perpetuation of the hateful "Christ killer" myth. When he confronted these preachers afterwards, the Christian clergy responded by saying, "Rabbi, why didn't you tell me you were coming to the Good Friday service?" Rabbi Rudin responded, "Would that have changed your preaching?" They inevitably defended themselves with this pathetic plea: "Knowing a rabbi was present would have made a real difference. I would have changed my message, so I didn't offend you." Rudin then challenged every Christian preacher to preach as if "Jews, the kinsfolk of Jesus, are physically present at all your services, not just on Good Friday."[2] Taking Rabbi Rudin's plea seriously, what can we do to put an end to anti-Semitic messages in our Good Friday sermons and every sermon after too?

We begin by not merely glossing over the text's troubling context. John presents a complex, carefully worded tale in which every detail is rife with meaning. For instance, by distinguishing the Last Supper from the Passover meal, and then emphasizing the guards' efforts to remain pure for the Passover (18:28), only to have the priests deny God in order to ensure Pilate executes Jesus (19:15), John narratively heightens the contrast between Jesus and the established religious order. In the end, the priests' rejection of Jesus by rejecting God serves to bring Jesus and God together on the same side, over against priests whom John narrates as corrupt and hypocritical. In this way, John reinforces christological themes that Jesus is the Word of God (and thus equal with God, 1:1), God incarnate in human form (1:14), and

God's one and only Son (3:16–18). All of this reinforces the need for Christians to approach this text with caution, lest John's identification of the Jewish religious leaders as the enemies of Jesus lead preachers down the path of anti-Semitism. It is time for homilists to adopt in their preaching the guiding mantra of contemporary historical Jesus scholarship that Jesus was "a Galilean Jew within Judaism within the Roman Empire."[3]

The Gospel does not contain a wholesale rejection of Judaism, for John presents Jesus as a faithful Jew who worships in the temple and cites the Torah and the prophets. Furthermore, given that the majority of Jesus' followers in John are Jewish, it is inaccurate to interpret the phrase "the Jews" (*Ioudaioi*) as demarcating a distinct ethnic and religious community, over against followers of Jesus. Even when Jesus interacts with Gentiles and they become his followers—the Samaritan woman at the well (4:7–42) or the Roman official whose son is dying (4:46–54)—the evangelist is careful always to locate Christ's mission within the messianic expectations of Judaism. In fact, it is the Samaritan woman who reiterates, "Salvation is from the Jews" (4:22).

While later Christians have employed John to justify a supersessionist theology, such an accusation ought not to be made against the author of John's Gospel, who was most likely himself Jewish. By identifying "the Jews" as the political enemies of Jesus, the author is not scapegoating the priests as "Christ killers." John makes it clear that not all Jews opposed Jesus, and not all Jewish religious leaders condemned him. Two prominent leaders, Joseph of Arimathea and Nicodemus, asked Pilate for permission to take the body of Jesus, which he granted (19:38). Together, they prepared his body for burial and laid him in a new tomb. Had it been John's intention to paint all Jews as enemies and opponents of Jesus, then the Passion Narrative would not have ended with such a pious and loving act carried out by two respected members of the Sanhedrin.

2. A. James Rudin, "Let's Drop the Anti-Semitic Messages This Good Friday," *Sojourners* (March 26, 2015). https://sojo.net/articles/lets-drop-anti-semitic-messages-good-friday.

3. John Dominic Crossan, "Jesus and the Challenge of Collaborative Eschatology," in *The Historical Jesus: Five Views*, ed. James K. Bielby and Paul Rhodes Eddy (Downers Grove, IL: InterVarsity Press, 2009), 105.

These details remind us that Christ became incarnate at a particular moment in human history: Jesus was a Jew from first-century Galilee interpreting God's Word in a way (according to John) which brought him into opposition with the ruling powers and authorities, Jewish *and* Roman. As the Latin American liberation theologian Jon Sobrino writes, "The most historical aspect of the historical Jesus is his practice and the spirit with which he carried it out. By 'practice' I mean the whole range of activities Jesus used to act on social reality and transform it in the specific direction of the Kingdom of God."[4] Sobrino's point is that we cannot fully understand the earthly ministry of Jesus without accounting for his first-century political reality—for example, by recognizing Jesus was involved in nonviolent resistance to Roman political tyranny—and then incorporating that dimension of his public ministry into our understanding of the Christian life.

Under the shadow of anti-Semitic violence in the past and present alike, Christians once again need to accept responsibility for our history of anti-Semitism and intolerance. Too many Christians have tolerated anti-Semitism, enabled by preachers spouting anti-Jewish readings of the Gospel; even more, too many have then tolerated barely veiled anti-Semitic drivel from the mouths of politicians. It is time we heed the plea from Rabbi Rudin and embody the love and compassion of Jesus by learning to affirm the sacred image of God in all human beings, regardless of race, religion, or gender.

RUBÉN ROSARIO RODRÍGUEZ

---

4. Jon Sobrino, *Jesus the Liberator: A Historical-Theological View*, trans. Paul Burns and Francis McDonagh (Maryknoll, NY: Orbis Books, 1993), 239.

Easter Day/Resurrection of the Lord

Isaiah 25:6–9
Psalm 118:1–2, 14–24
Acts 10:34–43

John 20:1–18
1 Corinthians 15:1–11
Mark 16:1–8

Isaiah 25:6–9

⁶On this mountain the LORD of hosts will make for all peoples
   a feast of rich food, a feast of well-aged wines,
   of rich food filled with marrow, of well-aged wines strained clear.
⁷And he will destroy on this mountain
   the shroud that is cast over all peoples,
   the sheet that is spread over all nations;
⁸he will swallow up death forever.
Then the Lord GOD will wipe away the tears from all faces,
   and the disgrace of his people he will take away from all the earth,
   for the LORD has spoken.
⁹It will be said on that day,
   Lo, this is our God; we have waited for him, so that he might save us.
   This is the LORD for whom we have waited;
   let us be glad and rejoice in his salvation.

Commentary 1: Connecting the Reading with Scripture

One of the great eighth-century prophets, Isaiah was a contemporary of Amos, Hosea, and Micah. His prophecies combine oracles of judgment with visions of hope and redemption. The book of Isaiah contains material compiled over two centuries (the latter half of the eighth to the latter half of the sixth century BCE).

Isaiah is often broken into three segments that reflect various historical periods. First Isaiah (Isa. 1–39) dates from the eighth century BCE in the southern kingdom of Judah. Second Isaiah (chaps. 40–55) dates from the time of the exile in Babylon in the sixth century BCE. Third Isaiah (chaps. 56–66) was most likely written after 538 BCE, when the Persian ruler, Cyrus, gained a victory over the Babylonians and allowed the Jewish exiles to return to their homeland.

In Second Isaiah the prophet beseeches the people to return to Jerusalem from Babylon, making a broad appeal for repentance. He promises that God, creator and lord of history,

will redeem Israel through a figure known as the Servant of the Lord. Many scholars identify this figure as a collective representation of the community. Through the suffering of the Servant, the nation will be saved. The so-called Servant Songs (Isa. 42:1–4; 49:1–6; 50:4–9; 52:13–53:12) became an interpretive key for early Christians reflecting on the significance of Jesus' death and resurrection.

Third Isaiah is a collection of oracles that decry idolatry and insist on repentance and justice for the poor. The theme of hope in God's forgiving, recreating goodness, central to Second Isaiah, remains an important theme in these last chapters of Isaiah.

First Isaiah was probably produced in the first half of the eighth century BCE, when Judah, the southern kingdom, faced the combined opposition of Syria and Israel. King Ahaz turned to the Assyrians to protect the nation, a move opposed by Isaiah. Isaiah's context shaped his theological themes: the holiness of Yahweh,

179

the coming Messiah of Yahweh, the judgment of Yahweh, and the necessity of placing one's own and the nation's trust in Yahweh, rather than in any earthly movement, leader, or nation.

First Isaiah recounts the prophet's call in a mystical experience in the temple (Isa. 6:1–6). Then follows the prophecy that his words will not be well received by the faithless people to whom he is being sent. Jesus echoes this realistic perspective in Mark 4:10–12. Not everyone will understand his words, take them to heart, and amend their lives.

First Isaiah is the context for two well-known prophecies, that of the "young woman" who will conceive and bear a child and that of a stump from the shoot of Jesse. When Syria and Israel join forces against Judah, Isaiah challenges King Ahaz's reliance on the protection of the Assyrians rather than on Yahweh. He prophesies a sign of Yahweh's faithfulness to the covenant people: "Look, the young woman is with child and shall bear a son, and shall name him Immanuel" (7:14). Later, when Assyria begins to seek to control Judah, he prophesies that "a shoot shall come out from the stock of Jesse" (11:1), a messianic figure from the lineage of David.

Chapters 13–23 consist of oracles of judgment against nations that are oppressing and threatening Judah. Chapter 24 prophesies a worldwide catastrophe in which a city will be destroyed, its inhabitants scattered. This time will be marked by the end of all joy. "All joy has reached its eventide" (24:11b).

While chapter 24 is largely doom and gloom with a brief respite of hope, chapter 25 is largely hopeful, with a brief foray into judgment (25:10b–12). The chapter begins as an individual hymn of praise: "O Lord, you are my God" (25:1) By the ninth verse it has morphed into a collective affirmation of faith: "Lo, this is our God" (25:9a). The prophet begins by praising God, using phrases that echo the Psalms (Pss. 31:15; 40:5; 118:28). Says Walter Brueggemann, "Israel keeps a ready stock of remembered miracles at hand, ready to recite, reaching all the way back to the Exodus."[1]

The prophet emphasizes the faithful, reliable nature of the plans for the salvation of the people God has made: "plans formed of old, faithful and sure" (Isa. 25:1b). Says Brueggemann, "This first verse . . . situates the present moment in the context of Yahweh's most trusted, transformative fidelity."[2] As Christians, reading this text on Easter Day, we both remember and experience the miracle of the resurrection of Jesus Christ from the dead, a sure and certain sign of God's fidelity in this life and into the next.

The city referred to in verse 2 could be Babylon, but it more likely represents a concentration of power hostile to God that God has plans to one day destroy.[3] This city is a place where the needy and vulnerable are neglected and disgraced. They are without resources and vulnerable to the whims of the ruthless, selfish powers that be. Their only hope is Yahweh, who will not disappoint them. The promises of protection the prophet makes in Isaiah 25:4–5 echo those of Psalm 121:6: "The sun shall not strike you by day, nor the moon by night."

In verse 6 the vision of the ruthless city God has reduced to a heap (25:2) disappears, giving way to that of a feast on "this mountain," Mount Zion, the opposite of the ruthless city. The nations make a pilgrimage to Zion, where Yahweh will set the very best before them. The notion of the salvation of the nations, which comes to the fore in Second Isaiah's Servant Song (49:6), is an undercurrent here. Eventually the nations will come to recognize the sovereignty of Yahweh, and Yahweh's own people will, after a cleansing judgment, return to faithful worship. All will join in the eschatological banquet alluded to in Luke's version of the parable of the Great Feast (Luke 14:15–24). For Christians, the celebration of the Eucharist is a foretaste of this banquet that is to come, spread before us in this present moment.

In chapter 24 the end of joy is the hallmark of the desolate city (Isa. 24:11b). The vanquishing of death is the hallmark of the mountaintop feast. God will remove the shroud of death, sadness, and loss that has covered mourning faces and the entire world. Death is a reference not primarily

---

1. Walter Brueggemann, *Isaiah 1–39*, Westminster Bible Companion (Louisville, KY: Westminster John Knox, 1998), 197.
2. Brueggemann, *Isaiah 1–39*, 197.
3. Otto Kaiser, *Isaiah 13–39*, Old Testament Library (Philadelphia: Westminster, 1974), 198.

to mortality, but to the active, negative force that diminishes human life and community in relation to God and one another. By ourselves, we are powerless to resist it. We need God to "swallow it up," destroying it forever. We get the image of God taking death in the divine jaws, crushing it, chewing it up, and spitting it out. Once death is dead, there is no more call for tears. The disgrace that the people have felt for centuries, at being simultaneously God's chosen people and under the heel of cruel rulers, is removed. For the host of this mountaintop banquet, the Holy One

of Israel, summons them to faith and promises them comfort.

It is no wonder that details of this vivid depiction of the death of death are borrowed by New Testament authors. Says Paul in 1 Corinthians (15:54), "Death has been swallowed up in victory." The author of Revelation assures us that "God himself will be with them; he will wipe every tear from their eyes. Death will be no more; mourning and crying and pain will be no more, for the first things have passed away" (Rev. 21:3b–4).

ALYCE M. MCKENZIE

Commentary 2: Connecting the Reading with the World

Science-fiction movies like the *Star Wars* series, *2001: A Space Odyssey*, and *Black Panther* provide snapshots of the larger social imagination. Sci-fi provides space to display humanity's desire to envision its future. It explores the consequences of current actions when carried to their fuller extent. It would not be a surprise to conclude that the distant planets and alien worlds that populate the content of sci-fi are, in imagination and manifestation, interpretative keys to our current reality.

The third eschatological section of the book of Isaiah operates in ways similar to the genre of sci-fi. Isaiah 25:6–10a comprises an apocalyptic scene that confronts the common sense of oppression that filled the minds of a downtrodden and exiled people. The scene consists of a sacred mountain called Zion and the preparation of a lavish feast by the creator of the universe. It portrays that same creator's salvific efforts to destroy the shroud of death that covers all nations and their peoples, and to tenderly comfort all those who have been delivered. This alternate imagining of the future reveals a harsh critique of the current order of the world, and a hope, both theological and material, that there is another way to live in relationship. The evidence of this right relationship is "a feast of rich food," a refutation of scarcity and systemic lack. The outworking of the current order of things within the shroud or sheet mentioned in Isaiah 25:7 operates within an imagination of tears, death, and disgrace.

These texts yield insights seemingly as rich as the meals of bone marrow, and as enjoyable as the well-strained wines celebrated in verse 6. The possibilities for spirited and authentic preaching on this passage are enlivened when the preacher can step into the Near Eastern world between 540 and 425 BCE and interpret the ancient apocalyptic sci-fi literature that discloses insights into our present realities and possibilities.

According to Isaiah, the future of all nations and their peoples was headed for perpetual death and shame, due to a "veil" "cast over" them. The word *massekah*, translated here as "sheet" (v. 7), can refer to how molten metal is poured, especially for making idols or graven images as mentioned in Exodus and Deuteronomy. The children of Israel would periodically make gods of molten metal, fashioned in images that served their immediate desires and material needs. The image of the golden calf represented a system of thought, action, sacrifice, and understanding of human value that was contrary to God's intention for the children of Israel. A golden calf does not merely appear in the wilderness. It must be imagined by a group with its every detail planned and executed. Idolatry is hard work. This is the veil of darkness covering humanity and ensnaring its collective imagination.

African American sociologist W. E. B. Du Bois was inspired by aspects of the prophetic tradition of Hebrew and Christian Scripture and would often engage in a similar prophetic role at the turn of the twentieth century in America. Channeling the poetic sensibilities observable in Isaiah 25, Du Bois in 1903 explored the concept of the "veil" regarding white supremacy and racial justice with his landmark work *The Soul of Black Folks*. He accurately forecast that the dominant issue of the twentieth century would be what he called "the color line." The metaphor of the color line would express the adverse relationship to power and resources African Americans would experience. The belief of white racial superiority and its corollary belief in the innate inferiority of blacks would become the veil or imagination that would support and empower all manner of repression of African Americans, including the violent and perverse practice of lynching. Du Bois wrote at a time when lynchings, throughout the nation but particularly in Southern states, were so common that, for African Americans, it seemed like a racial apocalypse.

Isaiah's confidence in God's destroying the veil and swallowing death evokes a familiar trope in sci-fi, where the future of the universe is at risk as an evil force seeks to conquer it. The shared imagination of conquest by any means places the universe at risk in fiction and in real life. The impulse to conquer and the deformed imagination to exploit may change form over time, but their outcomes are the same: the imaginative distortion of relationships between self, God, and neighbor. Isaiah identified the veil in his time, and Du Bois identified the veil for our time. The ominous outcome of the veil's logic requires a vision for the future both theological and material.

The church as an institution must engage in the necessary work of combating the works of the shroud of imagining that populates the consciousness of the people of all nations. Yes, Isaiah is clear, God will destroy this shroud and save us. The applicable "us" for preaching is the church, both institutional and the larger body of Christ. Acting as God's body in the world means engaging the principalities and powers of this world and not relenting in the presence of spiritual wickedness in high places, which the epistle writer discusses in Ephesians 6:12–14.

It would be little surprise to see the destruction of a collective idolatrous imagination occur on a holy mountain. Zion is the site of God's liberation. God is truly the master of the high places, both in literal and in imaginative outcomes. God not only destroys death but tenderly consoles with the gentlest of touches those who were oppressed. The church and those who compose its mission and membership must seriously engage the simultaneous work of destroying the idols poured out on our age, but also of consoling those who are harmed and under persistent threat by the death impulse active within society.

The church and the individual believer can draw strength and imaginative fodder for the cosmic fight for our souls through the alternate reality of the Table. The eucharistic overtones are pronounced and essential to future imaginings of relationship in a new world. Jesus, when facing his impending state-sponsored execution, took the meagerness of bread and wine and offered his disciples the richness of Isaiah's feast. The bread, representing the body of Christ, is a more extravagant food than marrow because it was broken for us. The wine, maybe not strained for dross, cleanses our hearts from sinful sediments.

God's hand (Isa. 25:10) will serve us this meal and save us from our sins. This meal is not of the instant or microwavable variety. In fact, it is a vision, a meal for the soul, that is prepared while God's people wait. The people wait for "that day." This nondescript period in the future is the object of human hope, the goal of often futile planning, and the mirror to our collective souls. Imagining justice on "that day" means we cannot passively accept injustice today. The disgrace of death and the distortion of the human imagination are not permanent. The movie of our existence does not have to end in a puff of dystopic ash, as the natural outworking of a white supremacist imagination becomes progressively encoded into the programming of our cloud-based world. In fact, according to Isaiah, it will not. It is the Table of Communion, the eucharistic moment, where we, the children of God, gain strength to be God's body in the world with the goal of making "that day" this day.

MARK ANDREW JEFFERSON

Psalm 118:1–2, 14–24

¹O give thanks to the LORD, for he is good;
   his steadfast love endures forever!

²Let Israel say,
   "His steadfast love endures forever."
. . . .
¹⁴The LORD is my strength and my might;
   he has become my salvation.

¹⁵There are glad songs of victory in the tents of the righteous:
"The right hand of the LORD does valiantly;
   ¹⁶the right hand of the LORD is exalted;
   the right hand of the LORD does valiantly."
¹⁷I shall not die, but I shall live,
   and recount the deeds of the LORD.
¹⁸The LORD has punished me severely,
   but he did not give me over to death.

¹⁹Open to me the gates of righteousness,
   that I may enter through them
   and give thanks to the LORD.

²⁰This is the gate of the LORD;
   the righteous shall enter through it.

²¹I thank you that you have answered me
   and have become my salvation.
²²The stone that the builders rejected
   has become the chief cornerstone.
²³This is the LORD's doing;
   it is marvelous in our eyes.
²⁴This is the day that the LORD has made;
   let us rejoice and be glad in it.

Connecting the Psalm with Scripture and Worship

The language of Psalm 118 is certain and sure. "Let Israel say . . ." is explicitly stated only in verse 2, but the poetry throughout bids the people to respond to what is heard and seen. It sits with ease and poise in the lectionary for Easter Sunday.

In the appointed texts for the day, this psalm follows four short but similarly stirring verses from Isaiah 25, a vision of God's future, ending with a present exhortation like the psalmist's: *Let us be glad and rejoice.* As if on cue, the psalmist picks up with a call to worship, and indeed, this psalm's language easily finds its way into our liturgies. The church often gathers with the greeting in verse 24, and the psalm's patterns and rhythms lend themselves to the calls and responses that are worship's natural conversation. In the case of Easter worship, its vibrancy and boldness make it a natural response to the Isaiah text and to the whole resurrection story that we know, tell, and retell.

The psalm is easily adapted for liturgical use. Forgiveness might be declared with words drawn from verses 18 and 21:

Reader 1: God does not give us over to death, but answers us with salvation.
Reader 2: Hear and believe the good news: in Jesus Christ, we are forgiven.

A Great Thanksgiving might move from dialogue to salvation story with verses 1, 14, and 17:

Reader 1: O God, we give thanks to you: you are good and your love endures forever.
Reader 2: You are our strength and our salvation. With joy we recount your mighty deeds . . .

The Lord's doing is marvelous in our own sight (Ps. 118:23); it may also be evident when others look into our eyes and see the hope and joy of an Easter people. We are certain what Easter worship will be and sure of what awaits us: songs and sounds and sights that rightly overflow with exuberant gratitude for this central act of God.

That exuberance is much less clearcut in the Gospel Easter stories. Jesus is resurrected yet mysterious, present yet elusive. Hearts are slow, yet they burn. Wounds are still visible and touchable. The women approach the tomb faithfully but sorrowfully. Disciples flee in fear. Where is Psalm 118's mighty language for these Easter people?

The truth is that they—and we—do not always feel like Easter people. What does a bold and vibrant song like Psalm 118 offer us—and them—in those moments? Perhaps this psalm is not just a vibrant response to the news of life, but a bold affirmation of faith *in* new life, a faith song in the face of death. It is not so difficult to say or sing when the Easter story is bright and clear and we are feeling joyful. It is far less easy to sing or say when shrouds are cast over us, when a sheet seems spread over community or nation or world. In predawn places, this psalm

may not be a loud song, but it may be a strong one, even when voices crack or whisper or when words come only as silent sighs.

In C. S. Lewis's novel *The Lion, the Witch, and the Wardrobe*, Aslan the lion returns from death and recalls what "deeper magic" had foretold: that "death itself would start working backwards." Perhaps Psalm 118 works backwards on the Easter morning told by the Gospel writers. The women awake in lament and despair, yet they make a quiet prayer: *This is the day the Lord has made; let us rejoice and be glad in it.* They come to a tomb, see a stone thrust aside, and recall a hymn: *The stone that the builders rejected has become the chief cornerstone.* The tomb stands open; is it the gate of the Lord? Has Jesus, the righteous one, reentered the world through it? When they tell what they have seen, they say a creed and end with thanksgiving: *I shall not die, but I shall live. O give thanks to the Lord, for he is good; for his steadfast love endures forever!*

Verses 1 and 19–29 of this same psalm come to us a week before Easter, on Palm/Passion Sunday. There, the language of gates opening and the righteous entering is assertive, even defiant: the Blessed One, who comes in the name of the Lord, enters a city of death, a week of sorrow. What has happened since then? What has been opened, entered, done, forgiven?

In the face of all that seems closed, powerless, death-dealing, or death-ridden, Psalm 118 sings—shout or silence, word or music, commanding or quivering. It may be our response to the story of new life, or it may carry us toward the story. We may come to the story through gates of splendor or through doors that groan on hinges long rusted.

Whatever else the day may be, it is still the day that God has made. It is the conviction of a bright, blooming Easter and the faith of a gray, bare Easter—the restored *Alleluia* of Easter morning and the never-absent *Alleluia* that makes our song at the grave, in sure and certain hope of the resurrection to eternal life, through Jesus Christ.

ERIC WALL

Acts 10:34–43

³⁴Then Peter began to speak to them: "I truly understand that God shows no partiality, ³⁵but in every nation anyone who fears him and does what is right is acceptable to him. ³⁶You know the message he sent to the people of Israel, preaching peace by Jesus Christ—he is Lord of all. ³⁷That message spread throughout Judea, beginning in Galilee after the baptism that John announced: ³⁸how God anointed Jesus of Nazareth with the Holy Spirit and with power; how he went about doing good and healing all who were oppressed by the devil, for God was with him. ³⁹We are witnesses to all that he did both in Judea and in Jerusalem. They put him to death by hanging him on a tree; ⁴⁰but God raised him on the third day and allowed him to appear, ⁴¹not to all the people but to us who were chosen by God as witnesses, and who ate and drank with him after he rose from the dead. ⁴²He commanded us to preach to the people and to testify that he is the one ordained by God as judge of the living and the dead. ⁴³All the prophets testify about him that everyone who believes in him receives forgiveness of sins through his name."

Commentary 1: Connecting the Reading with Scripture

Peter's brief sermon to those gathered in Cornelius's household refers to two kinds of knowing: *possessing* information and *processing* it, having data and grasping the significance of that data. This should not be surprising for a narrative that begins with a purpose statement centered on ensuring that its audience understands accurately the significance of the events about which they had already been informed (Luke 1:1–4).

Peter begins by declaring that he now *understands* God's perspective: "God shows no partiality, but in every nation anyone who fears him and does what is right is acceptable to him" (Acts 10:34–35). He then turns to what his audience *knows*, which turns out to be the briefest sketch covering the high points of the gospel narrative: "That message spread throughout Judea, beginning in Galilee after the baptism that John announced: how God anointed Jesus of Nazareth with the Holy Spirit and with power; how he went about doing good and healing all who were oppressed by the devil, for God was with him" (10:37–38). (Curiously, the NRSV moves the verb "to know" from its position at the beginning of 10:37 to the beginning of 10:36. The translation of 10:36 in the CEB

is better on this point: "This is the message of peace he sent to the Israelites by proclaiming the good news through Jesus Christ: He is Lord of all!") As it turns out, what Peter proclaims to Cornelius's household depends on God's having raised Jesus from the dead, which he mentions explicitly in 10:40. Clearly Jesus' resurrection is not simply a datum recited in the church's creed but plays a pivotal role in God's plan to bring salvation to all.

Let us begin with *what Peter comes to understand*. His abbreviated message culminates a series of scenes that begins with 9:32, with the interactions recounted in 10:1–33 plainly choreographed by God. Throughout, Peter is on a journey, with his movement measured both in geographical terms (further and further away from Jerusalem and its temple [see 1:8], to Lydda, to Joppa, and to Caesarea) and in socio-religious terms (further and further away from concerns with religious purity as he interacts with the sick, the dead, and a tanner [9:32–43]; experiences a vision in which he is told to eat unclean foods [10:9–16]; and sets aside a ban against entering Gentile homes [10:25–28; see 11:2–3]).

God Is the Conqueror

This is the Easter Faith: God is the conqueror. Outside and beyond the bounds of this life, in a way we cannot pretend to comprehend, his creative power conquers our decay. What sin has rotted and age has atrophied, he will make again a new man: new, and yet the same. He will bestow on this new man the fellowship of all the saints and the vision of his own face. And our faith in this miracle is to overcome the evidence of our senses—we are to look on the utter destruction, the blank non-entity of death, and see through to the miracle of resurrection on the other side, on a shore we have never observed nor can even point to, for it is neither up nor down nor before nor behind. And to this miracle we must look, not merely as our comfort in the face of death, but as the mark by which we are to strain our whole aspiration. And of the truth of this, God has given us our only sufficient pledge: what he will do for all in the end and out of this world, he did for Jesus in this world and as it were by anticipation.

Austin Farrer, "Physical Faith," in *The End of Man* (London: S.P.C.K, 1973), 15.

Along the way, though, we observe Peter's difficulty in processing what God is doing. The apostle was "greatly puzzled about what to make of the vision that he had seen" (10:17), he mulled it over in his mind (v. 19), and he apparently required clarification from Cornelius: "Now may I ask why you sent for me?" (v. 29). For Peter, the pieces fall into place, finally, when Cornelius, a Roman army officer, bears witness to God's work. In short order, Cornelius attests his exemplary piety, reports on his visionary experience, and, in a truly astounding claim, affirms God's presence in his (a Gentile's!) residence (vv. 30–33). Only now, in the light cast by Cornelius's testimony, does Peter grasp and affirm truly that God exhibits "no partiality, but in every nation anyone who fears him and does what is right is acceptable to him" (vv. 34–35).

Although Jesus had spoken of a mission "to all nations," indeed, "to the ends of the earth" (Luke 24:47; Acts 1:8), the far-reaching implications of Jesus' words seem only now to sink in. Recognizing that Cornelius and his household are neither Jews nor Christ-followers, we might say that they are the recipients of what the Wesleyan tradition calls *prevenient grace,*

God's gracious work prior to conversion, enabling faithful response. Cornelius thus proves instrumental in Peter's own transformation, helping Peter to grasp more deeply the ramifications of his faith. For the first time in the narrative of Luke–Acts, we hear the astonishing confession "Jesus is Lord of all" (Acts 10:36).

Using terminology familiar to readers of Luke's Gospel, Peter goes on to outline *what was apparently common knowledge*: the work of John the Baptist and Jesus' Spirit-empowered ministry (10:37–38; see Luke 3:1–23; 4:16–21; 13:10–17). In doing so, Peter presses the point that the Jesus story marks the turning point in redemptive history. Both when covering familiar territory and when adding information from what "we" have witnessed, Peter summarizes the relatively limited scope or reach of Jesus' mission: God sent good news *to the people of Israel*; news of John spread across *Judea*, beginning in *Galilee*; Jesus was from *Nazareth*; these events happened in *Judea* and *Jerusalem* (10:36–39).

Even Peter's commission to preach, he claims, was directed to "the people," using words (*ho laos*) that, in Luke's narrative, typically signify "the Jews." This underscores the extraordinary nature of Peter's subsequent breathtaking claim that a movement and message defined so narrowly explodes with universal significance: "in *every* nation *anyone*" (v. 35), "Lord of *all*" (v. 36), and "*everyone* who believes" (v. 43). Peter thus recognizes and proclaims a truth not always understood: God's agenda knows no bounds. The reaches of God's grace are not walled off or controlled by human concerns, commitments, conventions, or categories. What matters is God's capacious graciousness and, then, the human response it engenders—with the latter exemplified in Cornelius's exemplary religious practices (vv. 2, 30, 35) and identified in Peter's affirmation of the importance of faith, that is, of declaring one's fundamental allegiance and entrusting oneself to the Lord (v. 43). Indeed, quite apart from any plan or prompting on Peter's part, the Holy Spirit interrupts this scene, falling on those gathered (v. 44). What could more powerfully effect and symbolize the message sent to Israel, that Jesus is Lord of Jew and Gentile (see 11:17–18; 15:7–9)?

Peter's final sentence—"All the prophets testify about him that everyone who believes in him receives forgiveness of sins through his name" (10:43)—uses the words "forgiveness of sins" as shorthand for the totality of *salvation*, as Luke often does (see Luke 3:3; Acts 2:38; 3:19; 5:31; 10:43; 13:38; 15:9; 22:16; 26:18). The logic of this claim, together with that of the other universalizing declarations in Peter's sermon, works only in relation to Jesus' resurrection. The prophets (like the Old Testament as a whole) do testify concerning forgiveness but identify the Lord, Israel's God, as the one who offers pardon (e.g., Jer. 31:34; 33:8).

How is it that prophetic testimony concerning YHWH is transferred to Jesus? The answer can only be that, according to the view that pervades the Acts of the Apostles, Jesus was confirmed as Lord on account of his resurrection (Acts 2:32–36). This does not mean that Jesus *became* Lord at his resurrection and ascension; after all, he is proclaimed as Lord already at his birth (Luke 2:11). Moreover, during his ministry in Luke's Gospel, Jesus exercises God's authority to forgive sins (see 5:17–26; 7:47–50). However, just as his execution on a Roman cross seems to counter any notion that he is God's agent of salvation (24:19–21), so his resurrection confirms his status. Indeed, according to Peter's sermons at Pentecost and here, on account of Jesus' having been raised up by God, he now serves as coregent with God, as "judge of the living and the dead" and as exercising the divine prerogative to administer the benefits of salvation to all who call on his name (Acts 2:21, 32–36; see also 3:13–16). In short, Jesus' resurrection serves as the basis of Peter's confession and proclamation: Jesus is Lord of all, Jew and Gentile.

JOEL B. GREEN

Commentary 2: Connecting the Reading with the World

It can be a challenge for preachers to find something fresh to say on Easter, especially if preaching on one of the Gospel texts. Here are some possibilities for preaching on this text.

It is part of a larger story in which Cornelius (a centurion of the Italian Cohort, a Gentile) has a vision in which an angel tells him to send men to go collect Peter; and Peter has a vision in which God tells him three times: "What God has made clean, you must not call profane" (Acts 10:15). While both men are puzzled by the meaning of their visions, they pay attention to what God says to them, and both experience transformation. Cornelius, who invites Peter to speak a word of the Lord to Gentiles, is visited by the Holy Spirit and baptized in the name of Jesus. Peter, who accepts the invitation of the Gentiles to tell the good news of Jesus Christ, is changed in his thinking about the relationship between Jews and Gentiles, and with the presence of the Holy Spirit baptizes new Gentile believers.

How does the preacher proclaim the good news of Christ's resurrection so everyone present knows that God is still in the business of resurrection? How does the preacher help the congregation reflect on the resurrection of Jesus not just as a one-time event, but also as an ongoing way of life God offers us?

In 1989 five African American teenagers were wrongly accused and convicted of sexually assaulting a white woman who was jogging in New York City's Central Park. The boys ranged in age from fourteen to sixteen. The miniseries called *When They See Us*, by director Ava Duvernay, chronicles their arrests, convictions, and release from prison when another inmate confessed to the attack. The oldest boy, Korey Wise, sixteen, was tried as an adult and served thirteen years in prison for a crime he did not commit.

Reflecting on his life now, Wise said in a recent interview, "This is life after death. I always say that. . . . There's life after death."[1]

Not everyone has such a dramatic story of life after death, but there will be those present who face illnesses, struggle with addictions, or have relationship difficulties. What does resurrection look like for them?

When Peter speaks to the Gentiles he speaks of Christ's life, death, and resurrection. He gives witness to what he saw himself. He testifies to his own experience of Jesus. Another possibility for preaching this text is to focus on the words "witness" and "testify." Both find their root in the Greek word (*martys*) from which we get the English word "martyr." We often associate "martyr" with someone who dies for their faith or a particular cause. Here we are reminded that to be a martyr is to bear witness, to testify. When someone testifies to something, they give their account of what happened—what they saw and heard, and how they reacted.

Poet Mary Oliver writes about testimony as a way of life. "Instructions for living a life: *Pay attention. Be astonished. Tell about it.*"[2] These are also instructions for being a witness. A preacher could lead the congregation in reflecting on how they might be witnesses in daily life. Invite them to pay more attention to where they encounter the Divine. Ask them to keep a journal of where they see God in their experience; take time at the end of the day to write down one place they experienced God that day. No event or encounter is insignificant. Perhaps even take time during the sermon to let people practice paying attention. Ask them to reflect silently on when in the past week they felt God's presence or witnessed God's transformative love in the lives of others.

Last, give them opportunities to tell about it. Some years ago, National Public Radio aired a series called *This I Believe*. People from all walks of life, professions, nationalities, and so on spoke about what they held most dear. It was a personal credo. This sermon could be the launching pad for a similar series in the congregation. For the season of Easter, one person from the congregation could speak for five minutes about how they experience Jesus' presence in their lives. You could even conclude each talk with a verse from the hymn "I Love to Tell the Story."

When Peter spoke to Cornelius and his household, he spoke from his lived experience. He told the story of Jesus' life, death, and resurrection that pointed to the power of God who offers us forgiveness and hope. It was enough. The implications of this form of evangelism for people living in the twenty-first century are clear. There is no need for explanation or defense of Jesus, because you are telling *your* experience of Jesus. Simply tell your story. On Easter you could follow Peter's example for the sermon and tell your own story.

Peter begins his speech to Cornelius and the Gentiles like this: "I truly understand that God shows no partiality." Peter has had a change of heart about who can claim Jesus as their Lord and Savior. The preacher could explore places in our world where the kind of transformation that Peter experienced has been lived out.

Places like the Corrymeela Community in Northern Ireland. The Corrymeela Community was founded by the Rev. Ray Davey and a group of Queens University students. They were concerned about the growing sectarian tensions and violence between the Unionists, those who wanted to remain allied with the United Kingdom and were mostly Protestant; and the Republicans, those who wanted a united Ireland and were mostly Roman Catholic. They were looking to build a community where all people were welcome to come and learn to live together and discover things they had in common. In 1965 that dream became a reality, and the group purchased some land on the north coast of Northern Ireland in Ballycastle.

Over fifty years later Corrymeela is still committed to bringing different people together. The impact of the Corrymeela Community can be found in this story told by American scholar John Appleby from the University of Notre Dame. Appleby was invited to speak at Queens

1. Aisha Harris, "The Central Park Five: 'We Were Just Baby Boys,'" *New York Times*, May 20, 2019, https://www.nytimes.com/2019/05/30/arts/television/when-they-see-us.html

2. Mary Oliver, "Sometimes," in *Red Bird: Poems* (Boston: Beacon Press, 2008), 37 (italics original).

University in Belfast in 2015. He was addressing the question if the work of Northern Ireland's faith-based activism was having any effect on the violence in Northern Ireland. He told a story of a taxi driver whose life was transformed through his connection with Corrymeela.

> The taxi driver who picked him up to take him to the airport was from the Shankill Road. With the naivety that only an American could get away with, he asked the taxi driver if he had ever joined the paramilitaries.
>
> The taxi driver told him, "no," but that his brothers had. Appleby pressed further, and asked why he hadn't.
>
> "Well," the taxi driver told him. "When I was young my mother sent me to Corrymeela. I made friends with Catholics. And after that, it didn't seem to make sense to fight them."
>
> So there it was: the simple story of one life changed through the activism of the group of ecumenically-minded Christians who originally founded Corrymeela, and those who have come after to carry their work forward.[3]

While every Sunday is a little Easter, today is *the* day of resurrection. Tell the story of Jesus and his love, and know it is enough.

PAMELA S. SATURNIA

3. https://www.corrymeela.org/50/50-years-50-stories/1/the-taxi-driver-who-went

John 20:1–18

¹Early on the first day of the week, while it was still dark, Mary Magdalene came to the tomb and saw that the stone had been removed from the tomb. ²So she ran and went to Simon Peter and the other disciple, the one whom Jesus loved, and said to them, "They have taken the Lord out of the tomb, and we do not know where they have laid him." ³Then Peter and the other disciple set out and went toward the tomb. ⁴The two were running together, but the other disciple outran Peter and reached the tomb first. ⁵He bent down to look in and saw the linen wrappings lying there, but he did not go in. ⁶Then Simon Peter came, following him, and went into the tomb. He saw the linen wrappings lying there, ⁷and the cloth that had been on Jesus' head, not lying with the linen wrappings but rolled up in a place by itself. ⁸Then the other disciple, who reached the tomb first, also went in, and he saw and believed; ⁹for as yet they did not understand the scripture, that he must rise from the dead. ¹⁰Then the disciples returned to their homes.

¹¹But Mary stood weeping outside the tomb. As she wept, she bent over to look into the tomb; ¹²and she saw two angels in white, sitting where the body of Jesus had been lying, one at the head and the other at the feet. ¹³They said to her, "Woman, why are you weeping?" She said to them, "They have taken away my Lord, and I do not know where they have laid him." ¹⁴When she had said this, she turned around and saw Jesus standing there, but she did not know that it was Jesus. ¹⁵Jesus said to her, "Woman, why are you weeping? Whom are you looking for?" Supposing him to be the gardener, she said to him, "Sir, if you have carried him away, tell me where you have laid him, and I will take him away." ¹⁶Jesus said to her, "Mary!" She turned and said to him in Hebrew, "Rabbouni!" (which means Teacher). ¹⁷Jesus said to her, "Do not hold on to me, because I have not yet ascended to the Father. But go to my brothers and say to them, 'I am ascending to my Father and your Father, to my God and your God.'" ¹⁸Mary Magdalene went and announced to the disciples, "I have seen the Lord"; and she told them that he had said these things to her.

Commentary 1: Connecting the Reading with Scripture

John, the Fourth Gospel, is not as familiar to the lectionary preacher as are Matthew, Mark, and Luke. One reason is that each of the Synoptic Gospels has its own year in the lectionary: Matthew Year A, Mark Year B, Luke Year C. The lectionary features the Gospel of John somewhat like the way cultural Christians show up at church—primarily at Christmas and Easter!

The Gospel of John also strikes a stark contrast to the three Synoptic Gospels. In John, Jesus' public ministry is three years rather than one. Unlike the Synoptics, most of the narrative takes place in Judea and Jerusalem, as opposed to Jesus' home region of Galilee. Moreover, the Gospel of John is short on parables and moral aphorisms. The Johannine literary style is more often composed of dramatic narratives and lengthy dialogues. Theological meaning emerges from the activity and dialogues of the characters. Jesus' rich and sustained engagements with other characters in the Gospel of John are replete with moral and spiritual import.

The Fourth Gospel's resurrection account captures these characteristics. Mary Magdalene arrives at Jesus' tomb early on Sunday morning to discover the stone removed from the entrance.

She flees to announce what she interprets as a grim discovery. "They have taken the Lord out of the tomb, and we do not know where they have laid him" (John 20:2). Mary assumes that grave robbers have stolen Jesus' corpse, which would be a natural occasion for anguish and distress. In case the reader misses what Mary was thinking, Mary repeats the line in verse 13 when addressing the angels, "They have taken away my Lord, and I do not know where they have laid him."

A prominent theme that emerges from this scene and dialogue is the relationship between seeing and believing. Mary sees the empty tomb, and thus concludes that someone has stolen Jesus' body. In her case, seeing is not believing. The other disciple, possibly John or maybe James the brother of Jesus, sprints to the tomb with Simon Peter. His response runs counter to Mary Magdalene's. The author writes in verse 8 that "the other disciple, who reached the tomb first, also went in, and he saw and believed." Mary and the other disciple see the same scene, but come to two radically different conclusions. They both can see; the difference is one of vision.

It is important to note that the ancients held a different conception of vision than we do. Our modern culture tends to privilege eyesight over all the other senses. Physical sight is the primary source of epistemological certainty. We see to believe, as ocular vision is the ultimate form of veracity. The ancients, however, did not reduce vision to physical sight. Vision, for them, involved intuition, imagination, the mind (rational), and the heart (affective). People can see with their eyes, heart, and even flesh. Many in our contemporary society have come to appreciate this insight from the ancient world.

For instance, all theorists of perception affirm that interpretation has a subjective dimension. What we "see" is informed by our presuppositions. Beliefs inform our interpretations, and personal experiences shape our conclusions about all perceived events. Mary Magdalene suffers the terror of crucifixion Friday, the stress of Roman imperialism, and pain of persecution associated with being a follower of Jesus. These experiences are seared into her mind and upon her flesh. When she views the empty tomb through such lenses of anxiety and fear, her interpretation is understandable. Mary has what

some might consider a visceral reaction, "They have taken the Lord out of the tomb" (v. 2). This is understandable.

The other disciple, however, sees the empty tomb and remembers the teachings of Jesus. Maybe he recalls the experiences and encounters with Jesus that brought together the ignored, the violated, and the vulnerable. Possibly he recalls Jesus' teaching on compassion and empathy as the source of God's power. The preacher would do well to consider all the moments in the Johannine tradition where Jesus disrupts tradition and defies convention on behalf of those people others would otherwise overlook. Jesus' encounter with the woman of Samaria (4:1–41), his healing of the man who had been ill for thirty-eight years (5:1–18), and his treatment of the man born without sight (chap. 9) are fine examples that reflect Jesus' vision of the kingdom of God symbolized by the resurrection.

The writer of Acts conveys this vision of events in the corresponding lectionary text of the week, Acts 10:34–43. Peter delivers a sermon to the assembly about the ways Jesus spread the good news, doing good, and healing all who were oppressed. Peter states, "We are witnesses to all that he did both in Judea and in Jerusalem. They put him to death by hanging him on a tree; but God raised him on the third day" (Acts 10:39–40).

Similarly, the resurrection account in Luke 24:1–12 makes explicit what the writer of John leaves to conjecture. When Mary Magdalene and the other women see the empty tomb, the angel explains, "Remember how he told you, while he was still in Galilee, that the Son of Man must be handed over to sinners, and be crucified, and on the third day rise again" (Luke 24:6–7). There is no such explanation in John. Thus Mary flees to declare Jesus is missing.

It is crucial to refrain from castigating Mary Magdalene for her initial response. Theological commentators have already maligned her character enough through the ages. Mary Magdalene has become synonymous with prostitution or with a woman of ill repute. Part of this has to do with her introduction in Luke 8. Jesus casts out seven demons from inside of her. The mischaracterization of Mary as a prostitute also has to do with an androcentric imagination among male commentators. Highly gendered definitions of sin have reduced women's wrongdoing to sexual vice. There is no biblical reference to support the association of Mary Magdalene with prostitution—not that it would make a difference in this narrative.

What is essential is to note Mary's role among the other disciples. She is the first to arrive at the tomb on Sunday morning. When she races to the disciples, declaring, "They have taken the Lord out of the tomb, and we do not know where they have laid him" (John 20:2), the text intimates that Mary is speaking on behalf of the other disciples. Mary gives voice to all their anxiety and doubt in the moment. Rather than maligning Mary, we might assume that most people in our congregations will identify with her. Many people live under the debilitating weight of anxiety that negatively shapes their perception of reality. Mary Magdalene gives voice to the feelings of doubt that often

coincide with human despair. It matters little what we see when despair takes hold. We will interpret all reality through this prism.

Some may feel that the narrative meets its dramatic conclusion early, in verses 6–8. The writer of the story provides a clue for the beloved disciple, the linen wrappings. Grave robbers would not have removed the linens from around Jesus' body. The only other instance when someone emerged from the tomb involved Lazarus. Lazarus was covered in the linen strips of cloth until Jesus commanded, "Unbind him, and let him go" (11:44). Nobody unwrapped the linen from Jesus' body. God commanded Jesus to rise up from the grave. Like the linen shroud, Jesus left death behind.

In the words of the apostle Paul, "Death has been swallowed up in victory." "Where, O death, is your victory? Where, O death, is your sting?" (1 Cor. 15:54b–55).

JONATHAN L. WALTON

Commentary 2: Connecting the Reading with the World

At the end of John 20, we are told the purpose of the entire Gospel of John: "that you [the readers and hearers of this Gospel] may come to believe that Jesus is the Messiah, the Son of God, and that through believing you may have life in his name" (John 20:31). Indeed, the whole of John 20 is about this believing, and it includes five episodes of people coming to belief: the beloved disciple (vv. 1–10), Mary Magdalene (vv. 11–18), the disciples minus Thomas (vv. 19–23), Thomas (vv. 24–29a), and future generations (v. 29b). Each episode takes a different perspective, and each adds wisdom about belief. For Easter, the lectionary focuses on the beloved disciple and Mary Magdalene, saving the other three episodes for the following Sunday.

The disciple "whom Jesus loved" (v. 2) is the first participant in the Easter event who comes to believe (v. 8), and in John's Gospel "belief" is not a matter of accepting facts about Jesus to be true but, instead, entering into a trusting, abiding relationship with him.

We can discern something about this form of belief by contrasting two paintings of the

resurrection. The first, *Triptych of the Resurrection*, painted by Hans Memling at the end of the Middle Ages, depicts the garden where Jesus was buried. In the background, on the left, we can see three crosses still standing on Calvary's hill; on the right, we see the city of Jerusalem in the distance. Three women are making their way along a road from the city to the tomb. In the center foreground is the resurrection itself. Jesus' tomb is pictured not as a cave but as a sarcophagus. As the Roman guards sleep at its base, an angel lifts the lid from the tomb. Jesus, dressed in a vivid crimson robe and holding a staff with a victory flag, steps out of the sarcophagus, one foot at a time, like getting out of a bathtub.

In Memling's painting, the resurrection is an event in history—a stunning event, to be sure— but an event like others, like the crucifixion or the women visiting the tomb. On Friday Jesus was dead, but on Sunday he was stepping out of his grave full of life.

We see a different understanding in *The Resurrection of the Christ*, by the Renaissance painter

Tintoretto. Like Memling, Tintoretto also portrays mundane history: the women are still making their way toward the tomb, and the guards are still asleep on the ground. Tree branches and thick foliage surround the scene—ordinary nature. However, at the center of this painting we see neither history nor nature, and we do not see a revivified Jesus stepping gingerly out of the tomb. Instead, there is the appearance of a rip, a hole, in the canvas, and in the middle of this aperture we see the risen Christ surrounded in a golden light that is both like the glow of the dawn in the distance and markedly unlike it. Light shines on Jesus; light also shines *from* him. The guards and the women and the foliage—history and nature—are in one time zone, but the risen Christ intrudes into that zone from another reality altogether. The resurrection transforms history and gathers up all of nature, but history and nature cannot contain it. In the resurrection, the transcendent glory of God enters time and space, infusing and redeeming everything.

Oddly, many contemporary worshipers think of the resurrection more like Memling than like Tintoretto, namely, as just one more historical fact. Water freezes at thirty-two degrees, Aretha Franklin recorded "Respect," and Jesus was raised from the dead—all facts to be believed. Doubt creeps in because we can take ice cubes out of our freezers, and we can hear Aretha sing on the radio, but we are called to believe the resurrection simply because the church says so.

John's understanding of belief is more like Tintoretto's. Belief requires a double vision. We see things as they are, but we also discern a rip in the canvas and the light of God streaming through. The believer stands in time and place, in history and nature, but discerns that everything is infused with the glory of God. Belief sees eternity shining in temporality, the Spirit making holy the everyday. So we see Jesus, born of flesh, but also as the eternal Word. On the table we see ordinary bread and everyday wine, but we also see the glory of Christ's body and blood. In other people we see the woman who lives next door or the guy in the next cubicle at work, but we also see the light of glory and the image of God in their faces.

The beloved disciple displays this kind of believing. His belief is not provoked by any convincing appearance of the risen Christ, no slam-dunk theological argument. In fact, he does not even yet know all the persuasive biblical passages (v. 9). What he does know is a loving relationship with Jesus, and all it takes is an empty tomb and some left-behind grave clothes to give him the double vision of faith. Jesus is his friend, but Jesus is also the risen Christ. Jesus was a human being, and yet, through him all history, time, and place have been filled up with God's glory and abundant life.

The episode involving Mary Magdalene intensifies this understanding of belief. Incidentally, ever since Pope Leo in the sixteenth century confused everybody by announcing that Mary Magdalene was the same woman as the sinful woman in Luke 7, Mary has been tainted with the whiff of scandal and defamed as a prostitute. Right after the advent of photography, poor women in England were even manipulated into posing for mildly pornographic "Magdalene photos."[1] Not so in Scripture. In John, she is a heroine, a woman who comes to true belief in a graveyard and then becomes a preacher of hope to the apostles and to the whole church.

We first see Mary as a woman with only single vision: Jesus' body has been stolen, the man she meets is a gardener, and the world is a place of grief and tears. Facts are facts. Then, Jesus speaks her name, and her single vision takes on the discernment of belief. Mary the believer moves in two directions. First, she moves toward Jesus in devotion and love, which is the theme of the undeniably sappy hymn "In the Garden." Yet, as novelist Marilynne Robinson observes,

> [F]or a long time, until just a decade ago, at most, I disliked this hymn, in part because to this day I have never heard it sung well. Maybe it can't be sung well. The lyrics are uneven, and the tune is bland and grossly sentimental. But I have come to a place in my life where the thought of people moved by the imagination of joyful companionship with Christ is so precious that every fault becomes a virtue. I wish I

1. Galen C. Knutsen, "The Feast of Saint Mary Magdalene," *Worship* 71, no. 3 (1997): 206.

could hear again every faltering soprano who has ever raised this song to heaven. God bless them all.[2]

Second, Mary moves, as true believers do, toward the world in joyful witness: "I have seen the Lord." The Mary of the old hymn claims, "And the joy we share as we tarry there, none other has ever known"—but in John, because of Mary's witness, everyone gets to know it.

THOMAS G. LONG

2. Marilynne Robinson, "Wondrous Love," *Christianity and Literature* 59, no. 2 (2010): 203.

1 Corinthians 15:1–11

[1]Now I would remind you, brothers and sisters, of the good news that I proclaimed to you, which you in turn received, in which also you stand, [2]through which also you are being saved, if you hold firmly to the message that I proclaimed to you—unless you have come to believe in vain.

[3]For I handed on to you as of first importance what I in turn had received: that Christ died for our sins in accordance with the scriptures, [4]and that he was buried, and that he was raised on the third day in accordance with the scriptures, [5]and that he appeared to Cephas, then to the twelve. [6]Then he appeared to more than five hundred brothers and sisters at one time, most of whom are still alive, though some have died. [7]Then he appeared to James, then to all the apostles. [8]Last of all, as to one untimely born, he appeared also to me. [9]For I am the least of the apostles, unfit to be called an apostle, because I persecuted the church of God. [10]But by the grace of God I am what I am, and his grace toward me has not been in vain. On the contrary, I worked harder than any of them—though it was not I, but the grace of God that is with me. [11]Whether then it was I or they, so we proclaim and so you have come to believe.

Commentary 1: Connecting the Reading with Scripture

Historical and Literary Context. The letter we refer to as "First Corinthians" was written by the apostle Paul during his third missionary journey, around 55 CE, while he was based in Ephesus and establishing churches throughout the Roman province of Asia (modern western Turkey; Acts 19:10). Paul had established the church in Corinth several years earlier on his second missionary journey (18:1–28). The church struggled in a variety of ways because of various factors: (1) the pagan and idolatrous background of many its members, (2) the influence of Greek religious and philosophical traditions, and (3) the diverse social statuses within the Christian community. While in Ephesus, Paul received reports of trouble in Corinth.[1] He therefore wrote a letter dealing with problems in the church and answering questions from the church.

The greatest problem in the church was disunity resulting from pride and self-centeredness, and Paul takes the first quarter of the book to deal with this issue (1 Cor. 1–4). The problem of disunity was also a factor in a variety of other topics Paul addresses: lawsuits among church members (6:1–11), the debate over whether it was necessary to abstain from food that had been sacrificed to idols (chaps. 8–10), conflict between the rich and the poor during church gatherings, especially when partaking of the Lord's Supper (11:17–34), and pride associated with the misuse of certain spiritual gifts (chaps. 12–14).

Debate and dissension may also be part of the issue Paul addresses in chapter 15: the resurrection of the dead. In 15:12 Paul writes that "some of you" say there is no resurrection, perhaps indicating differences of opinion within the church. Greeks were in general averse to the idea of bodily resurrection. The body was viewed by many as a prison from which the soul could escape at death. Some of the Corinthians were evidently claiming that "there is no resurrection of the dead" (v. 12)—meaning that the resurrection was merely spiritual rather than physical. Paul counters by pointing

---

1. These reports came from "Chloe's people" (1 Cor. 1:11), probably the servants of a businesswoman named Chloe, and from a three-man delegation (Stephanas, Fortunatus, Achaicus, 16:17) from the Corinthian church.

to the reality of Jesus' bodily resurrection, the firstfruits and prototype of our (bodily) resurrection. Paul's theological understanding of the goodness of God's creation and the promises for its restoration (e.g., Isa. 11:1–9) meant a merely spiritual resurrection was no resurrection at all.

In this chapter Paul refutes the false teaching about the resurrection by showing three things: (1) Jesus' bodily resurrection is essential to the gospel message and is confirmed by its many witnesses (15:1–11). (2) If there will be no bodily resurrection of believers, then Christ did not rise from the dead and the Christian faith is meaningless (vv. 12–34). (3) For those Corinthians who mocked the idea of resurrection as a zombie-like reanimation of the body, Paul teaches that the resurrection body will be different from, but related to, our present mortal bodies (as a seed is related to a plant). This new body will be eternal and imperishable and will be received at the return of Christ (vv. 35–58).

Exegesis: Christ's Death and Resurrection as Central to the Apostolic Gospel. Paul begins by calling the Corinthians to remember the gospel he had preached to them, which resulted in their salvation. This salvation is assured, however, only "if you hold firmly to the word I preached to you" (v. 2b TNIV). Paul is not here asserting that believers can lose their salvation (see Rom. 8:28–35; Eph. 4:30). Rather, he is pointing out that the Corinthians' denial of the resurrection is such a distortion of the authentic gospel that he fears they may have "believed in vain" (v. 2c).

The authentic gospel, Paul asserts, is the one he preached to them: "that Christ died for our sins in accordance with the scriptures, and that he was buried, and that he was raised on the third day in accordance with the scriptures" (vv. 3–4). This is the essence of the gospel ("of first importance"), the authoritative tradition that he received from those before him and passed on to the Corinthians.[2] By repeating that both the death and the resurrection were "in accordance with the scriptures," Paul emphasizes that

Christ's work is the culmination of salvation history—God's plan of redemption predicted in the OT Scriptures.

To defend this resurrection claim, Paul reports an impressive list of eyewitness testimony (vv. 5–7): Cephas (Peter), the Twelve, five hundred believers at one time, James the brother of Jesus, all the apostles, and finally Paul himself, "as to one abnormally born" (v. 8 NIV). The Greek term used here (*ektrōmati*) can refer to any "untimely" birth, whether a premature birth, miscarriage, or abortion.[3] Paul is no doubt referring to his Damascus-road experience, which was different in kind and occurred long after these other resurrection appearances.

The statement that follows, "For I am the least of the apostles" (v. 9), could be misunderstood as false humility. It is better seen as the apostle's reminder to the readers of the amazing transformational power of God's grace. The gospel he has been describing transformed him from a violent persecutor of the church to its greatest advocate. His gratitude for this created an overwhelming passion for proclaiming the gospel, so that he "worked harder than any of them [the apostles mentioned in vv. 5–7]." For a glimpse of Paul's work ethic, read his "resume" in 2 Corinthians 11:16–33 and the accounts of his missionary journeys in Acts 13–28. It is without a hint of hyperbole that he can say, "I worked harder than any of them." Yet no sooner does he utter this than he must qualify even this as a gift from God: "Though it was not I, but the grace of God that is with me" (v. 10d).

The Significance of the Resurrection. For Paul the resurrection was the vindication of all that Jesus said and did. Jesus the Messiah and Son of God was indeed "appointed Son of God *in power* by his resurrection from the dead" (Rom. 1:4 TNIV). Yet the resurrection was much more than this. It was the beginning of the end-time resurrection and confirmation that we too will be raised. For Paul, believers can be confident in their salvation because Jesus rose victorious from the grave.

---

2. Many scholars think that this sentence represents an early Christian hymn or confession.

3. Walter Bauer, et al., *A Greek-English Lexicon of the New Testament and Other Early Christian Literature*, 3rd ed., rev. and ed. Frederick William Danker (Chicago: University of Chicago Press, 2000), 311.

Can we know that Jesus' resurrection in fact occurred? Could these accounts be myths and legends that arose over time in the church? Postmodernity has taught us that our apprehension of truth is always contextual and perspectival, colored by the lens of our own culture and worldview. There is no such thing as a purely "objective" observer. Despite this important caution, in real life no one is ready to abandon all claims to objective truth or historical veracity. After all, our courts of law are still in session. Witnesses are still called; testimony is still weighed; credibility is judged and conclusions are reached. Judgments on "what actually happened" are made every day. People go to prison or are set free on the basis of these judgments.

In 1 Corinthians 15, the apostle Paul calls witnesses to the stand to testify to the resurrection of Jesus: Peter, James, the Twelve, the rest of the apostles, five hundred people at one time! He calls on his readers to hear the witnesses, to weigh the evidence, and then proclaim as he does: "He is risen indeed!"

MARK L. STRAUSS

Commentary 2: Connecting the Reading with the World

The questions will come. In fact, they will come later in this chapter when the writer approaches questions that have been posed, that is, "how are the dead raised?" (1 Cor. 15:35); but in the first eleven verses, readers and hearers are invited to proclaim their faith. They also are invited to recognize they stand in a tradition, "according to the scriptures" (vv. 3–4). It seems a push back from any notion that this resurrection religion is "new," devoid of a history. Indeed, they are invited to stand in a community that proclaims faith together. None of the opening to 1 Corinthians is an appeal to individual piety. Every "you" is plural, which indicates that these proclamations need the support and witness of community.

By the time the canon has given us 1 Corinthians 15, it seems doubt—about the message, about their faith—may be creeping in. That supposition may be a good place, liturgically, for those planning worship or prayer in our time. If the passing of time and constant persecution and struggle dismayed the early church, how much more in the twenty-first century might people face doubt about the resurrection, or even about the faith. It would be easy to foster a bunker mentality, but worship has to help the community leave the sanctuary and reenter a world that does not believe in the resurrection, nor see signs of it, and still boldly proclaim the church's tradition.

How might the songs or the prayers offered help to address such doubt? How might the arc of worship bring people back to tradition in a vibrant way, without insisting that the only way to move forward is the way our forebears did? In a world where seeking meaning and significance seems heightened, how might worship lean into the hope that believing is not in vain (v. 2)? Here, in 1 Corinthians, the resurrection is not doctrine, but proclamation. So any worship setting ought to be careful to make this text or its message not about dogma but, rather, about testimony, about communal ritual memory of God's acts in the world through the death, burial, and resurrection of Jesus the Christ. In other words, the confession and profession of faith may be evoked in hope.

The resurrection, as remembered and proclaimed, was expected by this account. These verses put Resurrection Sunday/Easter in the company of witnesses, where the gathered may add their own song and memories to a grand and ongoing history of the church's story. Easter allows us to be "reminded" of the good news. If we take the readings seriously, then we are working on what is "of first importance" (v. 3). Easter Day and Eastertide give us a view into God's intentions in otherwise mundane and stressful times to remember there is a better story than the one we might be living; that there is a cosmic story larger than our own—whether the "our" is personal, communal, or national. Christians, by these standards, are encouraged to embrace again this good news.

If worship strengthens the witness of the church, this text also wants to strengthen the church as a body. For this writer, resurrection is at the core of what it means to be the people of God, or else we may have "come to believe in vain" (v. 2). The witnesses listed in verses 5–8 are paramount to this pleading, because they represent the constituted church; Cephas (Peter) is an important name to invoke throughout 1 Corinthians (1:12; 3:22; and 9:5). The people rallied around him; but the ecclesial band is wide: Cephas, the Twelve, more than five hundred, James, all the apostles, then the one "untimely born," Paul.

This list reminds us that we are not the only witnesses and that circles of disciples and still untimely born apostles also have "seen Christ," though perhaps not in the same way as described of these early believers. Having seen Christ in the world is a requisite for forming and making church. It is, in fact, "of first importance" (v. 3). It is the rallying point for which communions may make decisions: has Christ appeared in this moment, in this decision, and in this stance?

What does it mean to say, in our time, "Christ appeared"? In this text, we might take exception with where Paul begins, that is, with Cephas and the Twelve, given that even the Gospel texts attached to this lectionary cycle are clear that Christ's first appearance after resurrection was to women. Those women are erased in this witness, except in the generic "more than five hundred." As we read the roll call here, we have to ask why? Is it because of male-centeredness, or patriarchy, given that in one of the Gospels, when the women told the men, those men say it sounded to them "an idle tale" (Luke 24:11)? Those women were the first to say, "He is risen." As we read these texts now, and as we proclaim them, I believe it is fair to ask: "Whose witness of God's life-giving work in the world are we currently erasing?" "Whose witness have we made invisible by choosing to focus on the 'acceptable' witness?" "Why do we choose to believe one report of Christ encounter and not another?" "How do we decide who is

a 'credible' witness?" It is disturbing that, not a generation later, the women at the tomb are missing in the message.

This text, read or sung, allows a gathered community to put the resurrection event into a larger context. For example, the preacher might consider how resurrection might be experienced and explained beyond salvation of humans, which limits the Christ event to one species. Here is an opportunity to remind worshipers that death is not the final word, not only for humans, but for the earth.

Nobel Peace Prize winner Wangari Maathai connected environmental degradation and poverty among rural Kenyan women and built a movement that addressed both. By the beginning of the twenty-first century, the organization she founded, Green Belt Movement, was credited with planting more than 30 million trees. The trees stop erosion, replenish firewood supplies, and help clean the air. Her work bears the resurrection impulse, and is a witness I believe any preacher or worship leader could lift to add to the witness that God was present in death to bring life.[4]

Maathai did her work in response to her deeply held Christian beliefs, as well as her ancestral religious practices, in which she connected trees to sacred life. She connected Genesis and Psalm 23 to her belief that we are called to this restorative/resurrection work.[5] As "Mother of Trees," Maathai and her work inspired many conservationists around the world. Her work, as with all resurrection work, testifies that death is not the final word. That God has a "yes" beyond death.

I am sure there are many other generative stories from throughout the world, and from our own neighborhoods, where we might proclaim the resurrection, not as a mystical, far-off event, though the cosmic implications are real and needful, but as an impulse in the world that lives. When death comes for the cosmos, for us, for our testimonies, God's resurrection principle rises.

VALERIE BRIDGEMAN

---

4. "Wangari Maathai, Kenyan Educator and Government Official," https://www.britannica.com/biography/Wangari-Maathai. See also Jeffrey Gettleman, "Wangari Maathai, Nobel Peace Prize Laureate, Dies at 71," *New York Times*, September 26, 2011, https://www.nytimes.com/2011/09/27/world/africa/wangari-maathai-nobel-peace-prize-laureate-dies-at-71.html. You may read her Nobel Prize Acceptance Lecture here, https://www.nobelprize.org/prizes/peace/2004/maathai/26050-wangari-maathai-nobel-lecture-2004/.

5. Judy Valente, "Wangari Maathai Profile," *Religion & Ethics Newsweekly*, https://www.pbs.org/wnet/religionandethics/2007/11/09/november-9-2007-wangari-maathai/4544/.

Easter Day/Resurrection of the Lord

Mark 16:1–8

¹When the sabbath was over, Mary Magdalene, and Mary the mother of James, and Salome bought spices, so that they might go and anoint him. ²And very early on the first day of the week, when the sun had risen, they went to the tomb. ³They had been saying to one another, "Who will roll away the stone for us from the entrance to the tomb?" ⁴When they looked up, they saw that the stone, which was very large, had already been rolled back. ⁵As they entered the tomb, they saw a young man, dressed in a white robe, sitting on the right side; and they were alarmed. ⁶But he said to them, "Do not be alarmed; you are looking for Jesus of Nazareth, who was crucified. He has been raised; he is not here. Look, there is the place they laid him. ⁷But go, tell his disciples and Peter that he is going ahead of you to Galilee; there you will see him, just as he told you." ⁸So they went out and fled from the tomb, for terror and amazement had seized them; and they said nothing to anyone, for they were afraid.

Commentary 1: Connecting the Reading with Scripture

Of the four Gospels, Mark's contains some of the most odd and unusual passages. For example, Jesus tells his disciples that he speaks in parables *so that people will not understand and be saved* (Mark 4:12)! At times Jesus' power seems to be limited. In his hometown, "He could not do any miracles there, except lay his hands on a few sick people and heal them" (6:5–6 NIV; all future quotes NIV). (Ironically, on a "bad" day Jesus heals a few people.) Another time Jesus does not quite get a healing right. After Jesus spits in a man's eyes (an odd healing strategy!) and lays hands on him, the man can see only partially (people look like trees walking around). Jesus then apparently fine tunes the healing, touching the man's eyes a second time so that he can see clearly (8:22–26). Strange characters also show up in the narrative. At Jesus' arrest in Gethsemane, a young man who has never been mentioned before suddenly appears in the story. "Wearing nothing but a linen garment" (14:51), he is seized by the crowd and flees naked, leaving his garment behind. Matthew and Luke either drop or modify all of these unusual passages.[1]

Of all Mark's idiosyncrasies, however, his resurrection narrative is perhaps the most unusual (16:1–8). Three women disciples go to the tomb on Sunday morning after Jesus' death and burial to anoint his body. They wonder on the way how they will roll the large stone from the entrance. When they arrive, they find the tomb has already been opened. A young man dressed in white is inside, sitting to the right. He announces that Jesus of Nazareth, who was crucified, has risen from the dead! The women are told to go and tell his disciples that they will see him in Galilee. Instead, trembling and bewildered, the women flee from the tomb. The Gospel ends with the surprising statement that, "They said nothing to anyone, because they were afraid" (16:8). End of story.

So what happened? Did the women recover and tell the disciples? Did they see Jesus on the way, as in Matthew's Gospel? Did the male disciples subsequently see Jesus alive? In Jerusalem (as in Luke)? In Galilee (as in Matthew)? This abrupt ending is disturbing to most readers.

To be sure, there is a longer ending in many later manuscripts (vv. 9–20), which describes

---

1. While quirky and odd, all of these are understandable when viewed in the context of Mark's narrative strategy. For details, see Mark L. Strauss, *Mark*, Zondervan Exegetical Commentary on the New Testament (Grand Rapids: Zondervan, 2014), 183–86, 244, 354, 645–46.

several resurrection appearances and Jesus' commission to the disciples to take the gospel to the ends of the earth. Yet this ending is no doubt an addition, added by a later editor because of the unusual and abrupt ending. The style of the Greek and the vocabulary used in this section are different from the rest of the Gospel. The transition in verse 9 is awkward, with a participle describing Jesus (*anastas*) but no antecedent naming him (the women are the subject of the previous two sentences). Mary Magdalene is introduced in 16:9 as though the reader does not know her. Yet she has appeared in the previous three scenes (15:40, 47; 16:1)! The theology of this section contains non-Markan elements, with references to picking up snakes, drinking poison, and speaking in tongues (16:17–18)—themes not mentioned elsewhere in the Gospel. The resurrection appearances themselves seem to be a summary of those found in the other Gospels.[2] Finally, there are several other endings that appear in a few other manuscripts. It seems clear that this longer ending was added because Christian scribes were bothered by the abrupt ending.

A point of clarification is important here. Some critics claim that there is no resurrection in Mark's Gospel. This is not true. Mark clearly communicates that the resurrection has taken place. Jesus, who appears in Mark's story as an entirely trustworthy character, four times predicts that he will rise from the dead (8:31; 9:9, 31; 10:34). Similarly, the angel at the tomb, another entirely reliable character, announces that Jesus *has risen* (16:6). The resurrection appearances to the disciples are also a reality for Mark. At the Last Supper Jesus predicts that his disciples will see him in Galilee after his death (14:28). The angel at the tomb also says, "He is going ahead of you into Galilee. There you will see him, just as he told you" (16:7). There is no doubt that the author is certain that Jesus rose from the dead and that his disciples saw him alive.

So why such an abrupt ending? Why are there no resurrection appearances narrated? Scholars are divided over what happened. A small minority think that Mark never had a chance to finish, perhaps because of his arrest or

martyrdom. It seems very strange, however, that Mark would get this far—to the last page—but then fail to finish.

A more widely held view is that Mark finished his Gospel, but the ending was lost. Perhaps the last page became detached from the original before the document was copied and distributed. In this case, the original ending may have been similar to Matthew's, with the disciples going to Galilee where they saw Jesus and received the Great Commission (Matt. 28:16–20). While this "lost page" view is possible, it seems unlikely that a page would be detached so quickly, before the Gospel was copied. Manuscripts certainly wear out and can lose pages over time; but it is improbable that Mark's Gospel was not quickly copied and disseminated. Evidence for its dissemination is the general consensus that both Matthew and Luke used Mark as one of their sources. This would suggest that this Gospel was widely available at an early date.

A more likely view is that Mark intended to end his Gospel this way—with a call for faith over fear. The women have witnessed Jesus' death and burial. They hear the announcement of the resurrection and are shocked and baffled. Will they respond with faith, proclaiming the resurrection to the other disciples? Will they, rather, respond with fear and silence? Throughout Mark's Gospel there has been an implicit call to respond in faith. After calming the storm, Jesus says to the disciples, "Why are you so afraid? Do you still have no faith?" (4:40). He says to the woman with the blood disease, "Daughter, your faith has healed you" (5:34), and encourages Jairus, "Don't be afraid; just believe" (5:36). He marvels at the lack of faith in his hometown (6:6) and says to the father of a demon-possessed boy, "Everything is possible for one who believes," to which the father replies, "I do believe; help my belief!" (9:23). With faith, Jesus teaches, you can move mountains (11:22–24).

Mark's original readers, the suffering church in Rome,[3] are facing suffering, persecution, and even martyrdom. In many ways they are like the women at the tomb. They know the

---

2. Vv. 9–11=John 20:11–18; vv. 12–13=Luke 24:13–35; v. 14=Luke 24:36–43; v. 15=Matt. 28:18–20; v. 19=Luke 24:50–51.

3. This is the traditional view and still the majority opinion among scholars.

announcement of the resurrection. They have been called to faith and endurance. How will they respond? Will they retreat into silence and unbelief? Will they continue to boldly proclaim the message of salvation, whatever the cost? Will it be faith or fear? This is the question every reader of Mark's Gospel must answer.

MARK L. STRAUSS

Commentary 2: Connecting the Reading with the World

The text we see in Mark 16:1–8, from a literary point of view, might seem on first blush to be an unsatisfactory ending. What is the church, that is, the local congregation and its worldwide expressions, to do with fleeing women from an empty tomb, gripped by terror and amazement? What is the church to make of silent witnesses? What is the church to make of the stated reasons for that silence: fear? These questions leap from Mark's telling of the encounter in the tomb, an encounter whose ending is very differently described in the other canonical Gospels. This is the ending we have for worship, and what we have to consider in relation to human longings and striving today. What are we to make of this ending?

In some ways this ending fits the beginning of Mark. This Gospel skips singing angels and swaddling infants, wise men, and shepherds, and leaps headlong into the "beginning of the good news of Jesus Christ," and baptism and temptation. Starting with a grown-up Jesus, Mark is sparse of details we might want, but clear that the goal is "repent and believe" (Mark 1:15) as requisites for the kingdom of God. However, believing is not a strength, even of those who follow him closely. So this ending fits that challenge. Even in the end, they do not believe—or is that true? Is fear the same as not believing? Is silence a sign of disobedience to a young man in a tomb, next to an empty shroud? After all, the women have his word, but in Mark's account, they do not have a direct encounter with the risen savior, at least not in Mark 16:1–8. Is that ending enough?

The ending was not enough for the early church, since at some point a scribe added to the shorter version the following words: "And all that had been commanded them they told briefly to those around Peter. And afterward Jesus himself sent out through them, from east to west, the sacred and imperishable proclamation of eternal salvation." Much later, verses 9–15 were added, syncing the story with other Gospel stories, noting that Mary Magdalene was the one who proclaimed to the (male) disciples who did not believe her, then adding sightings and "but they did not believe them." Finally came verse 14, which reiterates the theme of Mark's Gospel. Dull-witted disciples full of unbelief are reprimanded by the risen Jesus: "Later he appeared to the eleven themselves as they were sitting at the table; and he upbraided them for their lack of faith and stubbornness, because they had not believed those who saw him after he had risen."

For the sake of worship, then, this text does open many possibilities of the ways humans experience loss and grief; the ways humans need ritual to make some sense of that loss; and the ways seeing is not the same thing as believing. Grief submerged in fears can distort one's abilities to comprehend an event as "good news." Mark begins with good news, and even in the presence of the women's fear and amazement, ends with good news, even at this "first ending." After all, the tomb does not hold Jesus' body. Where he is, they cannot comprehend, and perhaps if we did not have centuries of distancing ourselves from these women's grief and terror and amazement, we would not know either. We have the benefit of knowing what happened.

Nevertheless, if the truth is really truth, there are times we are as bereft of the beginning good news as these women, and as astonished at a missing Jesus. These also are the women who stood at a distance as he was being crucified (15:40–41). Maybe something about our connection to them could serve our prayers, our songs, and our spiritual longing. Maybe something about our connection to them can help us face our own fears and terror when the "good news" seems lost in the world's death-dealing realities. I do not know. However, I do know that the church needs to grapple much more with the intersections of "I believe" and "I am afraid" to help people on their spiritual and religious journey.

In addition, I think the work that biblical scholar Michael R. Whitenton provides us on the emotions in the text can help us connect to the emotions I have described above. His reading helps us to see how we have distanced ourselves further from the women in order to assume we are, or would be, somehow different from them; that our feelings would be different and that we would not have kept the encounter of the strange young man to ourselves. When Whitenton notes that Mark's "earliest audiences would have experienced the Gospel narrative through performance,"[4] it gives us some clues on just how performatively we have experienced it and still do. Because we typically read the book devotionally in private, or because we hear it read in snippets in worship settings, we do not have the benefit of the suspense and evocative nature of the reading to help in our interpretation of it. What if we take seriously the drama of the text in the face of our dramas as an interpretative starting point?

While I have focused on the women, I think we need to pay some attention to the young man in the tomb in verses 5–7. It is worth noting that he says words that sound like the angels of other Gospel endings, but he is not an angel. He is dressed in a white robe. Is it a baptismal robe? A burial shroud? Remember, there was a young man in Mark 14:51. He had been following Jesus, and escaped by leaving his clothes as the guards tried to detain him. Is it the same young man? Has he beaten the women to the tomb? Did he help roll away the stone, in Mark's telling?

As we imagine the cultural context the disciples faced, we might also think about whose stories get overlooked as we imagine the liberating and terrifying Gospel stories. Had this young man risked everything to bear witness? Is he so easily overlooked because he is unnamed? Is he a symbol of the many unnamed followers over the years, bearing witness and repeating Jesus' own declaration: He is not here, "just as he told you"? In the end, this "unsatisfactory" ending holds so much potential to demand of us that we pay much more attention to whom we pay attention to, and whom we believe, and why. It offers us a window into our own complex emotional and spiritual responses to God's activities in the world. It reminds us that we stand in a company of people who experience the same. It also offers church communions opportunities to examine when their denomination has acted out of fear, rather than as gospel bearers to the world. When those fear-based policies are reexamined, it offers them the opportunity to change.

VALERIE BRIDGEMAN

---

4. Michael R. Whitenton, "Feeling the Silence: A Moment-by-Moment Account of Emotions at the End of Mark (16:1–8)," *Catholic Biblical Quarterly* 78, no. 2 (2016): 272–89, 274. Another article that helps us see Mark's point of view from a performative angle is by Bryan Nash, "Point of View and the Women's Silence: A Reading of Mark 16:1–8," *Restoration Quarterly* 57, no. 4 (2015): 225–32.

Second Sunday of Easter

Acts 4:32–35   1 John 1:1–2:2
Psalm 133   John 20:19–31

Acts 4:32–35

³²Now the whole group of those who believed were of one heart and soul, and no one claimed private ownership of any possessions, but everything they owned was held in common. ³³With great power the apostles gave their testimony to the resurrection of the Lord Jesus, and great grace was upon them all. ³⁴There was not a needy person among them, for as many as owned lands or houses sold them and brought the proceeds of what was sold. ³⁵They laid it at the apostles' feet, and it was distributed to each as any had need.

Commentary 1: Connecting the Reading with Scripture

Since the second century CE, the author of Luke–Acts has been identified as Luke, a member of Paul's missionary team. Addressed to Theophilus (which can be translated "friend of God"), perhaps a pseudonym for a leading Roman government official, Acts is an invaluable resource for understanding the context of key events referred to in the letters of Paul. It presents a positive depiction of the church, but also opens a window on its squabbling and setbacks. Acts 2:44–47, directly following the account of Pentecost, describes the community sharing goods in common, breaking bread, worshiping together, experiencing goodwill with one another, praising God, and growing in numbers day by day.

A few chapters later, Acts 4:32–35 paints a similar portrait of a harmonious, growing community. Leading up to our passage, Peter has healed a man lame from birth (Acts 3:1–10) and been jailed along with John (4:1–22). Upon their release they gather with friends and supporters and pray, not for the overthrow of their enemies, but for the Holy Spirit's boldness in meeting whatever challenges lie ahead (4:29). The actions of two members of the community (Ananias and Sapphira), recounted in chapter 5, reveal that obstacles to the work of the Spirit come from within the community as well as beyond it. Following 4:32–35, the apostles and other believers redouble their healing and preaching efforts. A pattern emerges that pervades the whole book of Acts: bold witness, retaliation by the authorities, and perseverance by God's presence and power.[1]

The author of Luke–Acts is convinced that the Holy Spirit, at work in the words and work of Jesus, is now unleashed in the world through the growing body of Jesus' followers. Dramatic healings and exorcisms are not the only way the Spirit is made manifest in Acts. The Spirit is at work in the everyday work of building communities, like the one described in Acts 4:32–35.

As it is the Holy Spirit who empowers the apostles' healings, so the Spirit energizes the young community to care for one another and live in harmony. The book of Acts presents a picture of the practices of the early community, rather than a developed ecclesiology. The same is true of the understanding of the Holy Spirit in Acts. There is no nuanced pneumatology but, instead, a focus on the practical manifestation of the Holy Spirit in the community.

The Spirit gave the apostles, "uneducated and ordinary men" (4:13), the extraordinary boldness to face the Sanhedrin and to meet

---

1. Beverly Roberts Gaventa, "Towards a Theology of Acts: Reading and Rereading," *Interpretation* 42 (1988): 155.

Truth above the Reach of Human Reason

The cause of life spiritual in us, is Christ, not carnally or corporally inhabiting, but dwelling in the soul of man, as a thing which (when the mind apprehendeth it) is said to inhabit and possess the mind. The mind conceiveth Christ by hearing the doctrine of Christianity. As the light of nature doth cause the mind to apprehend those truths which are merely rational; so that saving truth, which is far above the reach of human reason, cannot otherwise, than by the Spirit of the Almighty be conceived. All these are implied, wheresoever any one of them is mentioned as the cause of spiritual life. Wherefore when we read that "the Spirit is our life," or "the Word our life," or "Christ our life:" we are in every one of these to understand that our life is Christ, by the hearing of the Gospel apprehended as a Saviour, and assented unto by the power of the Holy Ghost. The first intellectual conceit and comprehension of Christ so embraced, St. Peter calleth the seed whereof we be new born: our first embracing of Christ, is our first reviving from the state of death and condemnation. "He that hath the Son hath life," saith St. John, "and he that hath not the Son of God hath not life." If therefore he which once hath the Son, may cease to have the Son, though it be but a moment, he ceaseth for that moment to have life. But the life of them who live by the Son of God, is everlasting, not only for that it shall be everlasting in the world to come, but because, as "Christ being raised from the dead dieth no more, death hath no more power over him;" so the justified man, being alive to God in Jesus Christ our Lord, doth as necessarily from that time forward always live, as Christ, by whom he hath life, liveth always.

Richard Hooker, "A Learned Discourse of Justification, Works, and How the Foundations of Faith is Overthrown," in *The Works of the Learned and Judicious Divine, Mr. Richard Hooker*, vol. 2 (Oxford: Oxford University Press, 1841), 628.

persecution with energetic courage. The Spirit can also be credited with creating a close sense of fellowship in the early community we see in Acts 4:32–35. When we are told that "great grace was upon them all," the author is reminding us that nothing but the Spirit of God could have enabled the apostles to give such testimony to the resurrection in their midst. Nothing but the Spirit of God could have empowered the other believers to show such generosity.[2]

The author describes the close relationship between the members of the early community in terms Greek readers would have recognized. We are told that "the whole group of those who believed were of one heart and soul [mind]." To say that people were "of the same mind" was a Hellenistic expression for friendship. In Philippians 2:5, Paul admonishes the Philippians to "let the same mind be in you that was in Christ Jesus." The lectionary texts from Psalms and the Gospel of John for this Second Sunday of Easter underscore this theme of unity. Says Psalm 133:1, "How very good and pleasant it is when kindred live together in unity!" In the Johannine version of Pentecost, the resurrected Jesus passes through locked doors to breathe the unifying and energizing peace of the Holy Spirit on his disciples (John 20:19–23).

In addition to being of "one heart and soul," this early community had "everything . . . in common," a Hellenistic expression for sharing among friends. They shared their material goods, but biblical scholar William Kurz points out they also shared their spiritual goods of faith, love, suffering, and the charisms and fruits of the Holy Spirit. He refers to this depiction of common goods and generosity (Acts 4:32–35) and the recounting of the tight-fisted Ananias and Sapphira that follows (5:1–11) as "The Sharing of Goods: Two Contrary Examples."[3]

Acts 4:36–37 presents Barnabas as a model of generosity. He was a Jew from Cyprus, where there was a large Jewish colony, and a Levite, entitled to perform minor duties in the temple.

2. William Neil, *The Acts of the Apostles*, New Century Bible (Greenwood, SC: Attic Press, 1973), 93.
3. William S. Kurz, SJ, *Acts of the Apostles*, A Catholic Commentary on Scripture (Grand Rapids: Baker Academic, 2013), 89.

Barnabas's name conveys his character: "son of refreshment," "son of consolation," or, as the NRSV renders it, "son of encouragement." Here and in Acts 11:22–24, this seems to be an apt description for his role. Later in Acts the church in Jerusalem sends Barnabas to Antioch, where he "exhorted them all to remain faithful to the Lord with steadfast devotion; for he was a good man, full of the Holy Spirit and of faith. And a great many people were brought to the Lord" (11:22–24).

Immediately following this positive portrait of Barnabas is the story of Ananias and Sapphira (5:1–11), who model the opposite of generosity. They withhold a portion of the proceeds from the sale of their land and pay the price with their lives. The callousness of Peter and the extreme nature of their punishment make this text a poor choice to kick off a stewardship campaign! Setting it in the context of the larger book of Acts makes it more understandable, if not more palatable. The church in Acts does not bound from one triumph to another on an onward and upward journey. For every triumph and positive response to their ministry, Jesus' followers face failure and rejection. There is no time for halfhearted commitments. The church's mission is too fragile, and at the same time too critical, to brook the withholding of any resources, spiritual or material, that followers bring to the table.

In today's churches, we often hear the complaint that 20 percent of the people do 80 percent of the work. This passage reminds us that uneven commitment has been the case in the life of churches from the beginning. Rather than reason for discouragement, we can interpret it as motivation to press on.

Angelic rescues and divinely orchestrated earthquakes exist in the world of Acts side by side with arrests (4:1–22), imprisonments (5:18), persecutions (8:1–3), and the deaths of James, Stephen, Peter—and predicted of Paul. Idyllic harmony in the life of the church exists side by side with lack of commitment and painful consequences (Ananias and Sapphira)

In every age the church endures by the power of the Spirit through external and internally imposed pressures. Luke's confidence in the ultimate triumph of God's will for the world and the church's role in enacting it is all the more compelling for the realism with which he depicts its early days.

It reminds us that, no matter what conflicts within and oppositions from without the church faces today, we can be assured that God is at work and will prevail.

ALYCE M. MCKENZIE

Commentary 2: Connecting the Reading with the World

Some occurrences seem to be more miraculous than others. Admittedly, there is something sparkly and mysterious about how blinded eyes receive sight or how weakened legs instantaneously gain years of strength. The spectacular restoration of the human body is a miracle indeed. We inhabit our bodies. We perceive the world in our bodies. We are self-conscious when our earth vehicles bear the marks of imperfection, wear, or abuse. The desire for the healing of our bodies is often the impetus for our persisting prayers, and instant qualifiers for what we might call a miracle. Upon a closer inspection, as with many healing narratives, there is wholeness being offered not only to the individual but to a larger body as well.

We should be alerted to this fact by Acts 4:31, where the group of persons, including Peter and John, was praying. The Holy Spirit was made manifest, shook the dwelling where they gathered, and filled them. The result of this indwelling was their ability to speak the word of God with boldness. The presence of the Spirit often discloses that God is going to establish patterns of being and thinking that disrupt our current world and introduce us to new ways of being. The Spirit is mirroring the healing that occurred in Acts 3:4–10. The man born with weakened feet and ankles was miraculously healed. The mobility of his body was restored and ready to be deployed as evidence to the power of the risen Christ. Peter, in like manner, began preaching with this same power and converting people, in part because of his unlearned and inspired style of testimony.

It is not uncommon for the dominant social order to struggle with how to respond to miracles. Acts 4:3 describes a prison, a system of human confinement and punishment, a place where those who upset the social system are placed. Tidy narratives about how "only the bad people go to jail" or how those in the prison system "are getting what they deserve" are often upended when we pay attention to the biblical record. The New Testament chronicles the prison experiences of Paul, Peter, John, and Jesus of Nazareth. The Old Testament gives the account of Jeremiah, who, though prophesying what God said, found himself beaten and assigned to the imperial penal system. The miracle, the active movement of the Spirit for the healing and wholeness of the body, took place once they were released.

Yes, the man born with weakened lower extremities is a body where we detect a miracle (Acts 3:1–10), but the healing or wholeness of the body of Christ is displayed in Acts 4:32–35. Those individuals who claim the name and operate under the lordship of the risen Christ begin to operate in new patterns of mutual care and wholeness. The people who believed "were of one heart and soul," and from that unity of imagination they did not claim "private ownership" of possessions but held all things in community (Acts 4:32). This fact is truly the miracle of the text. People who are socialized and encouraged to pursue their own interests and make artificial claims of ownership reject the patterns of scarcity and lack.

They make a commitment to modeling a whole body of Christ, one that nourishes itself through mutuality and sharing. These people, existing within a system of Roman exploitation and an economic system of slave and master, live a resurrected life that materially attends to the body of those called out of this world's ways of death. The miracle of healing and wholeness is represented in the man who is restored, but the deeper healing is evidenced in these believers' ability to model life together that daily nourishes one another. Maybe that is why Peter and John were thrown in jail. The seeds of the Spirit's work would challenge the spirit of the age in the bodies of those who define themselves as Christ's servants more than as Roman citizens.

The Rev. Dr. Martin Luther King Jr. found himself in a jail cell in Birmingham, Alabama, on April 16, 1963, seeking to mobilize the larger national body to reject the legal logic of racial segregation and white supremacy. King detected the weakened ability of society to arise to its call and sought to strengthen its weakened extremities. His open letter from the Birmingham jail diagnosed the social malaise of many liberal white ministers and the gradualist instincts and social conservatism of many black ministers.

These ills not only left the body of Christ and the body politic in need of a miracle, but also placed him in jail. Interestingly, a more ideologically mature King would become manifest after this experience. He began to believe God for a larger miracle, not just of racial inclusivity, but of a reimagined economic order—one operating to serve humanity instead of demanding humanity's unyielding servitude to economic forecasts and external assessments. King, reminiscent of Acts 4:34, wanted to see that "there was not a needy person among them," meaning that the poor of the country—those in shorthand called "the 99 percent"—would be fully included and mobilized for productive work.

The role of the church in Acts regarding the purposes of human flourishing became front and center. The people of the text would sell their private possessions and bring the proceeds to the apostles for just administration of the resources. It is in this act that those believers displayed that they were not possessed by their possessions but in fact were possessed by the Spirit who inspired them to share.

The church, both institutional and individual, must take an active role in bearing social witness. The possession of the Spirit is not experienced only in worship on Sunday. No! The possession of the Spirit must be made manifest in every outworking of our lives. God is not only manifest in the breaking of bread and the pouring of wine. God is expressly manifest in the feeding of the hungry, the clothing of the naked, and the attention to the materiality of life.

The ideological climate of the United States today is one in which labels like "capitalism," "socialism," and "communism" cloud the administration of God's mandate. Wrestling with ideas—striving to adhere to a false ideological purity regarding economic concepts or relationships that mobilize resources—often replaces the action of actually attending to God's people. The arresting of our ability to be the church must be healed, and our desire to exist within a body politic that privileges wholeness and mutual care must be enacted. Certainly this would be a miracle. Asking people to rethink and reimagine themselves as not possessed by their possessions seems miraculous, even fanciful and immature.

That vision for life has often placed persons of prophetic orientation in prison, even candidates for public execution.

Nevertheless, the vision persists. Life fights to live. It is this impulse that makes the church the miraculous body it is. The church, both catholic and local, is a site to engage the habits of heart that restrict the "great grace" (4:33) that the Acts church experienced. The church is also a place to experience the mobility provided by the Spirit to move us to care for creation and for our neighbors, who also care for us. Therefore, we can live, thrive, and bless the Lord with this life that we all hold in common.

MARK ANDREW JEFFERSON

Psalm 133

¹How very good and pleasant it is
 when kindred live together in unity!
²It is like the precious oil on the head,
 running down upon the beard,
on the beard of Aaron,
 running down over the collar of his robes.
³It is like the dew of Hermon,
 which falls on the mountains of Zion.
For there the LORD ordained his blessing,
 life forevermore.

Connecting the Psalm with Scripture and Worship

A late-night television monologue: the host, played on stage by the house band, pauses before the audience.

Host: "The community I used to live in was so amazing . . ."
Audience: "How amazing was it?"
Host: "It was so amazing, it was like someone pouring expensive oil over my head."

The band raises a collective eyebrow; audience members glance at each other; the host wonders how that cue card got in there.

Psalm 133 is striking in its graceful and flowing language. Verse 1 is direct; it is clear eyed and clearly worded: "How good and pleasant it is when kindred live together in unity." This elegant description of community and harmony naturally invites the classic audience question: "How good and pleasant is it?" The psalmist anticipates the question and responds, "It is like the precious oil on the head, running down upon the beard." It is a lovely, if slightly less-than-everyday, comparison; it shares the beauty of the entire psalm. Often in musical settings of Psalm 133, verse 1 has a certain primacy because it is a repeated congregational refrain; it gets more airtime. The repetition establishes it as an anchor; the remaining two verses, if sung or spoken by other voices, may pass by more

quickly, with time for little more than a glance at the cue card in verse 2.

The similes and images in verses 2–3, though, are not just agreeable echoes of verse 1. They are like alabaster jars, breaking open the waiting wonder in words like "good" and "pleasant." They are sensory, tactile, generous. They suggest comfort, delight, even enchantment. They invite us to take time to imagine a sensation: the sensual feel and patient glide of oil over one's head. If dwelling together is like that, or like dew-covered mountains welcoming pilgrims home, then this unity—this life together—must be special indeed.

Musical settings may capture some of what the words cannot, when a composer says, in effect, "These sounds are what it is like." In Pablo Sosa's hymn "Miren que bueno" the sound we hear is a dance of delight. At the close of Leonard Bernstein's *Chichester Psalms*, we hear the sound of a serene, rarified chorale. Simile and poetry take description beyond ordinary words; other arts move past words altogether.

This short psalm follows a short text from Acts. Like the psalmist, Luke is giving a description of life together, with tangibles: no private ownership, no one in need, fair distribution of all goods. Oil poured over the head might raise the eyebrows of contemporary hearers; the kind of community described in Acts might raise outright skepticism. Yet there is inescapable rightness in this town: all seems at home here. In this community it is not oil flowing, but grace—"great grace" (Acts 4:33) on everyone.

God's grace and blessing are at the center of both texts. "For there the LORD ordained his blessing, life forevermore" (Ps. 133:3). These special communities are not city council proposals; they are God's life. Perhaps that is why they are so appealing and convincing. They seem almost to defy description, but they do not seem to defy belief. They are both imagination and testimony. In Acts, it is testimony to Jesus and an actual way of life. For the psalmist, the dwelling *is* good and pleasant. In this pairing of texts, reality and simile seem to merge. Even the lectionary order blurs; which text leads, and which follows? If the psalm is what Acts feels like, then Acts might be what the psalm looks like. Each suggests the other.

Twentieth-century North American composer Aaron Copland once said in an interview that one reason he wrote music was to try to describe what it was like to be alive. In 1941 he wrote the score for the film of Thornton Wilder's *Our Town*. The score's plain tune sings, caresses, assures; harmony is open-hearted, gentle, with brush strokes of dissonance that let it glow all the more. Art says to us, *Here—or there—is a world, and this is what it is like.* It captures or releases an elusive yet hyperreal transcendence, the mysterious rightness of life or community or creation. In Acts, it is as though Luke says, *This is our town: fairness, grace, heart, soul.* The psalm is like it: *This is our town: good and pleasant, like oil, like dew.*

What is this place like where kindred dwell together? What might it be like to share things in common? What is it like when grace is poured out like oil? Perhaps there is an unspoken invitation to more similes like the psalmist's. This is our wondrous town. How wondrous is it?

ERIC WALL

1 John 1:1–2:2

1:1We declare to you what was from the beginning, what we have heard, what we have seen with our eyes, what we have looked at and touched with our hands, concerning the word of life— 2this life was revealed, and we have seen it and testify to it, and declare to you the eternal life that was with the Father and was revealed to us— 3we declare to you what we have seen and heard so that you also may have fellowship with us; and truly our fellowship is with the Father and with his Son Jesus Christ. 4We are writing these things so that our joy may be complete.

5This is the message we have heard from him and proclaim to you, that God is light and in him there is no darkness at all. 6If we say that we have fellowship with him while we are walking in darkness, we lie and do not do what is true; 7but if we walk in the light as he himself is in the light, we have fellowship with one another, and the blood of Jesus his Son cleanses us from all sin. 8If we say that we have no sin, we deceive ourselves, and the truth is not in us. 9If we confess our sins, he who is faithful and just will forgive us our sins and cleanse us from all unrighteousness. 10If we say that we have not sinned, we make him a liar, and his word is not in us.

2:1My little children, I am writing these things to you so that you may not sin. But if anyone does sin, we have an advocate with the Father, Jesus Christ the righteous; 2and he is the atoning sacrifice for our sins, and not for ours only but also for the sins of the whole world.

Commentary 1: Connecting the Reading with Scripture

First John lacks the features typical of an ancient letter. For example, there is neither the expected greeting nor the closing words (for comparison, see 3 John), and it reads more like a written sermon. Together, the three "letters" attributed to John address a community of Christian congregations from whom a group has splintered. This communal fracture provides the occasion for 1–3 John. Like 2 John and 3 John, 1 John shows that what we believe about Jesus and the salvation he brings (theology) is integral to how we live in this world (ethics).

The opening of this sermon (1 John 1:1–4) centers on *life*: the life God has revealed and, by extension, the life within which believers find community (*koinōnia*; NRSV "fellowship") with God and each other. The section that follows (1:5–2:29) characterizes those who live in the light. Having been cleansed from sin, Christ-followers live light-filled lives, for God is light (1:5–7). Accordingly, they leave behind their sinful ways (1:8–2:2) and demonstrate in their day-to-day lives that evil and sin no longer exercise power over them (2:12–14); they put God's commands, particularly the love command, into practice (2:3–11); they renounce their allegiance to the ways of the world (2:15–17); and they hold fast to the true faith while resisting false claims concerning Jesus (2:18–29). John's pastoral tone ("my little children," 2:1) should not mask the gravity of his concerns for the faith and unity of the church.

Although John begins with a dizzying discombobulation of words that seem to tumble from his pen (1:1–4), his message is not lost in a disorderly interlacing of phrases. His central claim is nestled in the middle of this section: "this life was revealed" (1:2)—a claim mirrored at the end of 1 John: Jesus Christ, God's Son, is "eternal life" (5:20). Bracketing this initial claim are two closely related affirmations: the life revealed—this is what we witnessed and now proclaim (1:1–2, 3a).

Equally transparent is the twofold aim of John's declaration: "so that you also may have fellowship with us" and "so that our joy may be complete" (1:3b–4). What is at stake, then, is the possibility of genuine *community* grounded in recognizing, embracing, and appropriating the life God has given; and the possibility of *joy*, that is, the communal response of those who are the recipients of and participate in God's saving activity.

Genuine community does not depend on agreement in all things, but the community John envisions is contingent on shared faith—that is, belief that Jesus is God's Son, and allegiance to him (cf. 5:13). The revelation of the word of life, embodied in Jesus Christ and proclaimed concerning him, brings eternal life into the present for those who believe. John fears that some of his audience fail to embrace this word of life, fail to grasp the filial relationship between God and God's Son, and therefore fail to have communion with God and God's people. These failures are tantamount to sharing communion with some other god (or gods), which is the way of idolatry (5:21).

Shifting his emphasis on *life* to *light* (1:5), John drives home the stark nature of the available options: "God is light and in him there is no darkness at all." John thus introduces a universal metaphor, associating *light* with goodness, warmth, and understanding, over against such negative feelings associated with *darkness* as ignorance, evil, and fear. At the same time, John draws on the use of *light* in Israel's Scriptures to signify divine revelation and salvation: "The LORD is my light and my salvation; whom shall I fear?" (Ps. 27:1; see Exod. 13:21–22; Ps. 119:105; Isa. 30:26; 59:9). John not only identifies God with light, but insists on the complete absence of darkness with God. This is not only a statement about God, however; it extends to God's people as well. Using the scriptural metaphor of "walking" to signify "living in such and such a way," he urges that God's people are known by their allegiance to God and conformity to God's ways; they are people of the light just as God is light.

In order to make sense of John's message at this point, it may be helpful to set aside one way of viewing the picture he paints, as though light is found in one container, darkness in another, and people can be divided into one or the other. An alternative would be to think of spheres of influence and allegiance. Here the emphasis falls not on boundaries that separate one group from another, but on the center toward which one is walking (or living). In this case, the direction in which one is moving is more important than one's location. If we adopt this view, we are prepared for John's message about sinfulness in 1:7b–10.

If God is the light and we live in the light, then it follows logically that we are without sin, right? Apparently, this is the view of some, whose beliefs and behavior have led to a fracture in the community of churches John addresses. A claim like this probably results from the relegation of the category of *sin* to really bad behaviors (not envy, gossip, or hoarding wealth, but grand larceny, rape, or murder), a general belief that "we" (as opposed to "they") are the righteous ones (cf. Luke 18:9–14), and/or a wholesale dismissal of the spiritual importance of embodied life in this world. Proclaiming that we are sinless, John contends, is the antithesis of living in the light; it is the consequence of self-deception and proves that we have not appropriated the life God has given.

If community with God and God's people, or living in the light, is not sinless perfection, then what is it? Certainly, John does not countenance willful sin. As Paul would say, "By no means! How can we who died to sin go on living in it?" (Rom. 6:1–2). John writes, "I am writing these things to you so that you may not sin. But if anyone does sin . . ." (1 John 2:1). If (we might say, "when") we sin, we need to confess that sin, depending on the saving intervention of Jesus Christ. Just as denial of sin is rooted in lies, so confession of sin is rooted in truth, and therefore dependent on the work of Jesus Christ.

John develops the latter with two images. The first derives from the world of worship and is concerned with atonement: the resolution of estrangement between two parties, whose relationship has been interrupted or broken by sin, typically is tied in Scripture to sacrifice and mediation. Here, as in Israel's Scriptures, God is the source of atonement—in the OT, by arranging a sacrificial system through which God mediates atonement, here through Jesus' death, understood in sacrificial terms. As in biblical images of the atonement more generally, here the aim of atonement is not to assuage God's anger but to cleanse human beings.

The second image derives from the courtroom, with Jesus portrayed as an advocate who intercedes on behalf of others. As sinners, we cannot plead our own case, but "Jesus Christ the righteous" (2:1) pleads in our stead, doing so on the basis of his faithfulness, his sacrifice that marks our having been forgiven. John's point, then, is that those who claim sinlessness render Jesus' sacrifice as needless; but those who confess their sins appropriate for themselves the life God has given. Christ-followers, then, can live light-filled lives because they have been cleansed from sin's effects and conform their lives to God's own life.

JOEL B. GREEN

Commentary 2: Connecting the Reading with the World

In the opening paragraph of the Epistle of 1 John we find words that strike a familiar chord. Reading this text, we may find ourselves thinking about the opening of the Gospel of John. This makes sense, as tradition claims that John, the son of Zebedee, also known as the disciple whom Jesus loved, is credited with writing both the Gospel of John and the three Epistles of John. While some disagree about the authorship, there is no denying that there are similarities in how these books convey the gospel message. John the Gospel writer refers to the great cosmic beginning at which the Word was present. That Word is Jesus Christ. The writer of 1 John also refers to a beginning that commences with Jesus Christ, the word of life. The Fourth Gospel and 1 John both refer to God and to Jesus as light and contrast that light with darkness.

God is light. Jesus is light. There is no darkness in them. In elementary school science class we learn about photosynthesis, the process by which plants get the light that they need to grow. Without light, plants not only do not grow; they die. One could make the case that, with Jesus the light, we have life and are forgiven our sins; but without Jesus the light, we go down a road that leads to death. What is it that helps the people of God grow? What stifles or stunts our growth? This could be an opportunity to talk about what helps you or others you know grow in faith. What helps the community gathered grow in faith? It can also be a time to own up to the ways that we do not tend to our faith.

For the writer of 1 John, a life of faith is about how we live, about how we respond to the gift of Jesus who is the Word and the light of life. We walk in the light when we are honest about our sin and the ways we miss the mark. As a result, we have fellowship with Jesus and each other. When we walk in darkness, we are untruthful about who we are and the ways we sin that cut us off from fellowship with God and with others. For the writer of 1 John, walking in the light is to be authentic, warts and all, and to repent of the ways we sin.

The author is not so much concerned about *if* we will sin. For him sin is part of the human condition. His thoughts align with those of John Calvin, who wrote: "Original sin, therefore, seems to be a hereditary depravity and corruption of our nature, diffused into all parts of the soul."[1] Even if in our humanness we have the capacity to sin, sin does not define us. We walk in darkness, not when we sin, but when we do not own up to how we hurt God, others, and ourselves. It is true, according to 1 John, that confession is good for the soul.

For the sermon one could reflect on the role in the liturgy of the call to confession, prayer of confession, and the assurance of forgiveness. A common call to confession used in many congregations comes from verses 8–9. It gets at the

---

1. John Calvin, *Institutes of the Christian Religion* 2.1.8, ed. John T. McNeill, trans. Ford Lewis Battles (Philadelphia: Westminster, 1960), 251.

heart of what it means to walk in the light. The call to confession functions as a reminder of the promise of forgiveness in Jesus Christ, whom the author calls the advocate. The advocate is the one who is the atoning sacrifice for our sin and the sin of the world. The call to confession assures the people of God that there is indeed nothing that can separate us from God's love (Rom. 8:39), and nothing that we do is so terrible that it cannot be forgiven. It allows us to be truthful about who we are, the ways we have faltered, and our desire to try again. Of course, the corporate prayer of confession helps us to be honest about our shortcomings as individuals and as a community. It is the honesty to which the writer of 1 John alludes. The assurance of forgiveness once again affirms the promise that in Jesus we have the promise of redemption, which makes it possible for us to walk in the light.

Many years ago, at a workshop with the famed preacher Barbara Brown Taylor, we were asked to participate in an exercise in which we each were given a piece of fruit. We were asked to experience the fruit with all our senses: sight, touch, smell, taste, and hearing. The writer of 1 John seems to be appealing to us to employ our senses as we experience Jesus, the word of life and the light of the world. Perhaps one could reflect on what it is like to experience Jesus through the senses of sound, sight, and touch. When we say Jesus speaks to us, what does that sound like? How does that happen for people? The same questions could be asked of seeing Jesus and touching Jesus. The writer of 1 John might say that when we have fellowship with one another, the words we speak can be heard as Jesus' words, the love we witness can be seen as Jesus' love, and the hands we hold in prayer and comfort can be felt as the touch of Jesus'

hands. What is it like to hear Jesus, to see Jesus, to touch Jesus? When does this happen in our lives? What are some examples?

In the movie *Pleasantville*, walking in the light and walking in the darkness are illustrated through the contrast between living in a world of black and white and living in a world of color. Twins David and Jennifer are living in the 1990s. Jennifer is a social butterfly, and David leads a more interior life, spending much of his free time watching a black-and-white television show from the 1950s called *Pleasantville*. After fighting over a remote, the twins are given a new remote by a repairman, one that transports them into the television show *Pleasantville*.

They become the characters Bud and Mary Sue. David, who knows the show inside and out, tries to brief his sister on the plot, saying that they cannot do anything to alter the life of the people in Pleasantville. Bud seems happy with life in Pleasantville with its rules and boundaries and niceties. Mary Sue, though, breaks all the rules, and as she influences other characters, one by one, people and things begin to appear in technicolor. Not everyone is happy with this change, because in this new light some things are exposed. The high school kids want to know what life is like outside of Pleasantville. Passions awaken for art and for love. Not all that comes to light is good. Living in color exposes the racism that exists in Pleasantville. What is revealed, illumined, is the truth about life in Pleasantville, that sometimes life is not pleasant at all, but stifling, oppressive, and sinful.

The writer of 1 John is concerned with how we deal with sin. Will we own up to it? Will we be truthful about our part in it? Will we repent? What will help us to trust in God's mercy and forgiveness so that we can walk in the light?

PAMELA S. SATURNIA

John 20:19–31

[19]When it was evening on that day, the first day of the week, and the doors of the house where the disciples had met were locked for fear of the Jews, Jesus came and stood among them and said, "Peace be with you." [20]After he said this, he showed them his hands and his side. Then the disciples rejoiced when they saw the Lord. [21]Jesus said to them again, "Peace be with you. As the Father has sent me, so I send you." [22]When he had said this, he breathed on them and said to them, "Receive the Holy Spirit. [23]If you forgive the sins of any, they are forgiven them; if you retain the sins of any, they are retained."

[24]But Thomas (who was called the Twin), one of the twelve, was not with them when Jesus came. [25]So the other disciples told him, "We have seen the Lord." But he said to them, "Unless I see the mark of the nails in his hands, and put my finger in the mark of the nails and my hand in his side, I will not believe."

[26]A week later his disciples were again in the house, and Thomas was with them. Although the doors were shut, Jesus came and stood among them and said, "Peace be with you." [27]Then he said to Thomas, "Put your finger here and see my hands. Reach out your hand and put it in my side. Do not doubt but believe." [28]Thomas answered him, "My Lord and my God!" [29]Jesus said to him, "Have you believed because you have seen me? Blessed are those who have not seen and yet have come to believe."

[30]Now Jesus did many other signs in the presence of his disciples, which are not written in this book. [31]But these are written so that you may come to believe that Jesus is the Messiah, the Son of God, and that through believing you may have life in his name.

Commentary 1: Connecting the Reading with Scripture

After encountering Mary Magdalene, Jesus makes subsequent appearances to his disciples in John 20:19–31. We can infer from the text that word of Jesus' resurrection and appearance to Mary Magdalene and others spread to the broader community. On the evening of "that day, the first day of the week," Jesus' followers huddle in secret in a house "for fear of the Jews" (John 20:19). The context here is important.

First, there is no reason to believe that the writer is referring only to Jesus' closest twelve, save Judas. That Mary Magdalene knew precisely where to find Simon Peter in the first resurrection account suggests a broader network of disciples. The reader should feel comfortable concluding that those gathered in the house represented a larger assembly of the faithful. Jesus' appearing despite the fact that the door is locked speaks to Christ's capacity to show up wherever his followers gather.

Second, readers should be careful how to interpret the phrase "fear of the Jews." The disciples gathered in the house are all Jews. The distinction that the author seeks to draw is between religious officials and authorities in the synagogue, and those Jews who embraced Jesus as the Messiah. The Fourth Gospel employs "fear of the Jews" or "afraid of the Jews" four times (John 7:13; 9:22; 19:38; 20:19). The author aims to illumine the relations of power within the Jewish community. Consider the dialogue surrounding Jesus' healing of the blind boy in John 9:13–41. Here the Pharisees interrogate the boy and his family about the source of his sight. The boy's parents deflect knowledge of who performed the healing because "they

214

were afraid of the Jews; for the Jews had already agreed that anyone who confessed Jesus to be the Messiah would be put out of the synagogue." We should assume that the boy and his family were Jews, as were all of Jesus' earliest followers.

We must be careful, then, not to read back into the text a Jewish/Christian division and the implicit and explicit anti-Semitism that seeped into the Jesus movement in the ensuing centuries. The thoughtful Christian preacher has a responsibility to disabuse Christian theology of its anti-Semitism.

We find a similar intrareligious tension in Acts 5:27–32. When Peter and the apostles of Jesus were brought before the chief priests in that passage, the high priest declared, "We gave you strict orders not to teach in this name, yet here you have filled Jerusalem with your teaching, and you are determined to bring this man's blood on us." It is difficult not to empathize with the priests. Teaching people that Jesus was the Messiah and Savior (*sōtēr*, savior), a term reserved for the Roman emperor, would certainly bring charges of insurrection against Jews in the region. Few Roman officials would take the time to distinguish between the many different dimensions and belief systems within the Jewish community. This dynamic would place religious leaders in a position either to publicly denounce or to silence members of the nascent Jesus movement. Hence, the response of the religious authorities: "You are determined to bring this man's blood on us" (Acts 5:28).

Nevertheless, all religious leaders would do well to heed the moral lesson that Jesus and his followers posed to the religious authorities in the first century. Whenever religious professionals and those living with relative levels of privilege fail to show care and concern for the marginalized, victimized, and ignored within the faith, their particular religion becomes an accomplice in injustice. This is true among Judaism, Christianity, Islam, and other organized faith perspectives. The Johannine miracle accounts and spiritual teachings of Jesus depict Jesus breathing life back into the teachings of the Law and Prophets among those who felt otherwise overlooked. God raises Jesus from the dead, and Jesus immediately encourages his followers to do the same.

In verse 21, the author narrates this exact charge to the community. "As the Father has sent me, so I send you," Jesus says. Then Jesus breathes on his followers, declaring, "Receive the Holy Spirit." The Holy Spirit will empower Jesus' followers to continue the work of Christ. What we witness here is how the two distinct liturgical seasons of Easter and Pentecost are inseparable in the Johannine tradition. The gift of the Holy Spirit, who animates and empowers disciples to fulfill the great commission, is bound up with Jesus' resurrection. Easter is not merely about God's power to raise Jesus from the dead. It is also a story about the Holy Spirit's power to catalyze Jesus' followers to participate in the work of Christ.

The image of Jesus breathing on the disciples in verse 22 points the reader to the creation account and the Hebrew prophets. When God formed Adam out of the dust, God "breathed into his nostrils the breath of life" (Gen. 2:7). Similarly, when Ezekiel prophesied to the valley of dry bones, Ezekiel concluded, "Come from the four winds, O breath, and breathe upon these slain, that they may live" (Ezek. 37:9). The Fourth Evangelist then situates Jesus' resurrection account within this larger Hebrew tradition. Jesus' appearance and invocation of the Spirit inaugurate new life for followers of Christ.

The narrative takes a turn in verse 24 to introduce Thomas, one of the Twelve. When the other disciples tell him that they have seen Jesus, he replies with doubt. That the negative appellation "doubting Thomas" has come to signify all who view life through a lens of skepticism speaks to the power of this story. Nevertheless, this is not a fair reading of Thomas. Thomas's response is no different from that of Mary Magdalene, Simon Peter, and the beloved disciple a week earlier (John 20:1–9). There is even interpretive ambiguity around the beloved disciple who "saw and believed" (v 8). He may have believed in Jesus' teachings, but his belief around the resurrection is not clear. The following clause in verse 9, "for as yet they did not understand the scripture, that he must rise from the dead," is the reason to believe that none of the disciples were confident that Jesus rose from the dead. The Fourth Evangelist seems to employ Thomas as a synecdoche for the broader Johannine community.

Jesus' final words to Thomas take the form of a rhetorical question and commendation: "Have you believed because you have seen me? Blessed are those who have not seen and yet have come to believe." This is not a rebuke of Thomas and the disciples who have seen the risen Jesus. Rather, the Fourth Evangelist is commending subsequent generations who will come to embrace the living Christ without physical evidence. Seeing is not a prerequisite for believing. The Fourth Evangelist foreshadows this entire scene—the resurrection and the commissioning—in Jesus' farewell prayer. "As you have sent me into the world, so I have sent them into the world. . . . I ask not only on behalf of these, but also on behalf of those who will believe in me through their word" (17:18–20). The future of the faith depends on those who are willing to bear witness. This act of bearing witness is why, as stated in verse 30, "Jesus did many other signs in the presence of his disciples." Testimony, not sight, is how others will come to believe.

As Paul writes in the letter to the Romans, "faith comes from what is heard, and what is heard comes through the word of Christ" (Rom. 10:17).

JONATHAN L. WALTON

Commentary 2: Connecting the Reading with the World

John 20 includes five scenes about people coming to belief. The Easter lection supplied the first two of these scenes—about the "beloved disciple" and Mary Magdalene—and now, for the Sunday after Easter, we receive the other three.

In the first (John 20:19–23), the disciples are those who come to belief. Throughout John, believing is not merely accepting facts but, rather, entering into a deep and abiding relationship with the risen Christ. So John does not say straightforwardly that "the disciples believed." He employs relationship language: "they rejoiced when they saw the Lord." Because of their relationship to Christ, they were given both the joy Jesus promised ("your pain will turn to joy," 16:20) and a new way of perceiving. They were able now to see what is seen in heaven, that "Jesus is Lord," that the broken and tragic pieces of history have been gathered up into the glory of God "and of his Messiah, [who] will reign forever and ever" (Rev. 11:15).

This scene may end with hallelujahs, but it does not begin that way. It begins in terror. The disciples have locked the doors out of fear. "Disciples" here probably means the Twelve, minus Judas, the betrayer, and Thomas, who will appear in the next scene, but most scholars think that "disciples" also symbolizes the church—John's

church, our church. What we have theologically, then, is disturbing: a picture of the church *without* the risen Christ. It is a picture of the church locked off from the world, crouching in fear. John says they were afraid "of the Jews," surely reflecting the perilous relationship between John's own community and its powerful synagogue neighbors. Today we should translate this as the church locked away from whatever frightens us, terrified of the powers that be.

What does a church without Christ look like? Insulated, afraid, and powerless. One of the characters in Flannery O'Connor's novel *Wise Blood* is Hazel Motes, a preacher in the church *without* Christ. He says,

> Well, I preach the Church Without Christ. I'm member and preacher to that church where the blind don't see and the lame don't walk and what's dead stays that way. Ask me about that church and I'll tell you it's the church that the blood of Jesus don't foul with redemption.[1]

Sadly, sometimes the church prefers to be without Christ, believing that locked doors keep out, not only the threat of the world, but also the challenge of the risen Christ calling us

---

1. Flannery O'Connor, *Wise Blood* (New York: Farrar, Strauss & Giroux, 2007), 101.

to transformation and to mission. This was, of course, O'Connor's wry and satirical point. "I preach peace," says Hazel Motes. "I preach the Church Without Christ, peaceful and satisfied!"

Renovation of the Church tells the story of a California seeker church that discovered its whole way of being church was more about consumerism than discipleship, that it was, in its own fashion, a "satisfied" church without the risen Christ. Kent Carlson, one of the pastors, tells about a Sunday "seeker" service that had gone particularly well. The music, the drama, were all powerful. People were laughing one minute and moved to tears the next. "From a performance perspective," Carlson said, "we had put together a first-rate product." After the service, Carlson sat down next to the staff member who had planned the service and said, "Wow!"

The staff member responded with dark irony, "You know, we don't even need God to do this."[2]

John reminds us that the risen Christ is not stopped by the church's locked doors. In spite of fear, in spite of false "satisfaction," in spite of smug assurances that the church can be church without God, the risen Christ invades the church, pushing through the locked doors and bringing peace, his own presence, forgiveness, the Spirit, and life abundant.

The second scene in this week's text is about Thomas, who was not present when Jesus appeared to the rest of the disciples. Thomas says that even though all the other disciples have "seen the Lord," he will not believe unless he gets to see and touch the risen Christ for himself. A week after this declaration, Jesus appears and invites Thomas to see and touch, saying, "Do not doubt but believe." "Doubt" is probably not the best translation here, since it comes freighted with contemporary baggage about the plausibility of faith. The Greek is *apistos alla pistos* marking the movement from "lacking belief" to "believing," that is, from lacking an abiding bond to the risen Christ to having a joyful and life-transforming relationship.

The theological heart of this passage is not that Thomas touched Jesus' wounds and

consequently came around as a believer. The text does not say whether Thomas actually touched Jesus. The key, rather, is that the risen Jesus opened himself and his life to Thomas in a way that Thomas could receive him, in a way that Thomas could move from separation to confession: "My Lord and my God" (John 20:28).

This story, then, is first a christological declaration. Jesus comes to people, offering himself in ways that can open their eyes and evoke belief. It is also a guide for the church's mission, that the church is to listen to the needs of people and to offer the faith in ways that respond to those needs.

Michael Mather, a United Methodist pastor, tells about his own transformation on this issue of mission. He was serving in a congregation that was known in the community as the "social service" church. The church had a food pantry distributing government surplus food, and other forms of "charity ministry."

Once Mather preached on Peter's Pentecost sermon in Acts 2, where Peter quotes the prophet Joel, "I will pour out my Spirit upon all flesh." In a sermon feedback session after the service, a woman in the congregation asked, "If what Joel said is true, why don't we treat people that way?" Mather, puzzled, asked what she meant. "When people come to the food pantry," she continued, "we ask people how poor they are, rather than how rich they are. Peter is saying that all people have God's Spirit poured into them."

Mather realized that she was right. The church was ministering to people, all right, but not in the way they truly needed if they were to receive Jesus' gift of abundant life. The church treated people as problems, charity cases, people who lacked, rather than as those possessing God's Spirit. So the church changed. Instead of focusing on what people did not have, the church began to look at people as the gifts they are. Mather writes, "[Now we began to ask] whether people could put up drywall or fix a toaster or knew how to drive a car. 'Do you play a musical instrument?' we asked. 'Do you

---

2. Kent Carlson and Mike Lueken, *Renovation of the Church: What Happens When a Seeker Church Discovers Spiritual Formation* (Downers Grove, IL: InterVarsity Press, 2011), 23–24.

garden?' If so, 'Do you grow vegetables, flowers, or both?'"[3]

In the third scene (v. 31), the houselights go up, and we—the readers of John—are suddenly in focus. Blessed are all who come to believe. Preachers should connect this to the worldwide mission and impact of Christ's church. In a single chapter, John has moved from a tiny cemetery filled with grief and a narrow church locked away in fear, to us today and beyond, to the hopeful picture of Christ's abundant life flowing out joyfully to all humankind.

THOMAS G. LONG

3. Michael Mather, *Having Nothing, Possessing Everything: Finding Abundant Communities in Unexpected Places* (Grand Rapids: Eerdmans, 2018), 14–15.

Third Sunday of Easter

Acts 3:12–19

Psalm 4

1 John 3:1–7

Luke 24:36b–48

Acts 3:12–19

¹²When Peter saw it, he addressed the people, "You Israelites, why do you wonder at this, or why do you stare at us, as though by our own power or piety we had made him walk? ¹³The God of Abraham, the God of Isaac, and the God of Jacob, the God of our ancestors has glorified his servant Jesus, whom you handed over and rejected in the presence of Pilate, though he had decided to release him. ¹⁴But you rejected the Holy and Righteous One and asked to have a murderer given to you, ¹⁵and you killed the Author of life, whom God raised from the dead. To this we are witnesses. ¹⁶And by faith in his name, his name itself has made this man strong, whom you see and know; and the faith that is through Jesus has given him this perfect health in the presence of all of you.

¹⁷"And now, friends, I know that you acted in ignorance, as did also your rulers. ¹⁸In this way God fulfilled what he had foretold through all the prophets, that his Messiah would suffer. ¹⁹Repent therefore, and turn to God so that your sins may be wiped out."

Commentary 1: Connecting the Reading with Scripture

Acts begins with a summary of the Gospel of Luke (Acts 1:1–5), addressed to an official named Theophilus (which can be translated "friend of God"), perhaps a code name for a particular Roman official, perhaps a generic name indicating that the book is for everyone. We are then invited to rehearse the events following Jesus' resurrection: his appearances, his ascension, and the choice of Matthias to replace Judas. After an event-packed first chapter come the author's account of Pentecost (Acts 2:1–13); Peter's address to the crowd; their response; and a description of life among the early believers, featuring repentance, baptism, corporate worship, common meals, and common ownership. Chapter 2 ends with the positive report that "day by day the Lord added to their number those who were being saved" (2:47).

Chapter 3 begins with Peter's healing a man lame from birth (3:1–10). This is the event that precipitates the apostles' persecution and perseverance. That a healing would be cause, not for rejoicing, but for contention, is a familiar plot line from the Gospels. In John 5 Jesus heals a man with a thirty-eight-year illness on the Sabbath (John 5:2–18), and in Luke 6:6–11 (see also Matt. 12:9–14) Jesus heals a man with a withered hand on the Sabbath. Peter's healing of the lame man stirs up that old, familiar fury.

In Acts 3:12–26 Peter addresses those who have witnessed the healing and who are "filled with wonder and amazement" (3:10). The first part of Peter's speech is accusatory (3:12–16). He affirms that the lame man has been healed by the name of Jesus the Messiah, whom his listeners rejected and handed over to death. In verses 14 and 15 he piles up a list of traditional messianic titles to emphasize the magnitude of their error: "Holy and Righteous One," "Author of Life."[1]

---

1. J. W. Packer, *The Acts of the Apostles*, Cambridge Bible Commentary (Cambridge: Cambridge University Press, 1966), 36.

In the second portion of his speech, Peter becomes more conciliatory. In the spirit of Christ himself, who forgave his murderers from the cross (Luke 23:34), Peter emphasizes God's mercy and holds out the assurance of forgiveness on condition of repentance. He underscores Jesus' identity as the Suffering Servant of God (Acts 3:13) witnessed to by the prophet Isaiah. He challenges the chosen people to acknowledge Jesus as fulfilment of ancient promises, and offers them a chance to return to God.

Everything about his speech would have been offensive to them: his laying the blame for Jesus' death entirely at their feet, his claim that the healing was by the power of this resurrected Messiah, his call for them to repent, and his warning of the consequences of ignoring that call. Nothing would have been more irritating to the Sadducees, though, than his announcement of a "universal restoration" foretold by the Hebrew prophets (3:17–26). As the story of Acts unfolds, the Sadducees, who did not believe in the resurrection of the dead, become increasingly threatened by and jealous of these "uneducated and ordinary" companions of Jesus (4:13). How dare they perform "signs and wonders" and preach and heal with the appearance of divine power? They must be silenced. The leaders' disapproval escalates into persecution, and in chapters 6 and 7 we learn of Stephen's arrest, defense, and stoning. The narrative then introduces Saul, his persecution of Christians, and his transformation.

A theme in Peter's speech that threads its way through the New Testament is the inevitability of Jesus' death as an integral part of God's plan to save humankind. The idea of the necessity of Jesus' suffering (often using the Greek term *dei*, "it is necessary") as ordained by God occurs frequently in Luke (Luke 9:22; 17:25; 24:7, 26). This was in part to counter the Jewish objection to Jesus as the Messiah that he died a felon's death and was therefore under the curse of the law (Deut. 21:23; Gal. 3:13). "How could he be the Messiah?" they asked. "God planned it that way," the early church answered. In Isaiah 52:13–53:12 early followers of Jesus saw the crucifixion as being within the plan of God,

discerning there a foundation for an incipient doctrine of the atonement through the death of Christ and a promise of his vindication beyond the cross.[2] In his account of Jesus' struggle on the Mount of Olives (Luke 22:39–46), Luke depicts the anguished decision of his human will, his exercise of human choice to persevere. His death on the cross is a self-offering for us, a gift from the heart of God, not the infliction of divine punishment by the Father on the Son.

A current-day reader cannot help but cringe as Peter blames the Jews for the rejection and murder of Jesus. Passages such as Acts 3:12–19 have been used throughout the centuries to countenance anti-Semitism in a naive, literalist reading of the past into the present with pernicious effect.[3] About two thousand years ago, a particular group of Jewish leaders, in company with representatives of the Roman government, orchestrated Jesus' crucifixion—not the Jewish people as a whole, either then or now. This critical disclaimer needs to accompany preaching on texts that blame "the Jews" for the death of Jesus.

This brief text (Acts 3:12–19) features themes that occur elsewhere in Scripture and that have positive homiletical potential: that Jesus' followers are channels of the Spirit's power, a power that is manifested in a variety of ways. The Spirit does not perform only dramatic healings, prison breaks, and outpourings of the Spirit on people en masse; the Spirit also inspires bold speech in the difficult encounters that seem to accompany every advance of the apostles' mission (4:3, 4). When, as predicted in Luke, the followers of Jesus are arrested and brought before synagogue rulers and authorities, the Holy Spirit aids them in speaking (Luke 12:12) so that their opponents are not able to withstand them (Acts 4:14).

Another key theme of this text is perseverance. While challenges accompany the way of the followers of Jesus, so do the encouragement and presence of the risen, ascended Christ through the Holy Spirit. That realistic assurance comforts and energizes followers in each new age.

Objections to the apostles' ministry both precede and follow this text, yet they press on. Acts 3:12–19, with its fervent affirmation of

2. William Neil, *The Acts of the Apostles*, New Century Bible Commentary (Greenwood, SC: Attic Press, 1973), 85.
3. See also Matt. 23:31–33; 27:25; John 8:38–39.

God's power to resurrect and heal, forgive and restore, inspires perseverance in those who are called to proclaim the good news. In this it joins a chorus of other biblical texts that teach us not to look back once we put our hand on the plough (Luke 9:62), but to "press on toward the goal for the prize of the heavenly call of God in Christ Jesus" (Phil. 3:14), inspired by the example of Jesus, who "for the joy that was set before him endured the cross, disregarding its shame" (Heb. 12:2).

ALYCE M. MCKENZIE

Commentary 2: Connecting the Reading with the World

Human beings are creatures of habit. We are the product of our habits, and they, in turn, shape the boundaries of our world. They can constrict the prospects for thriving in God's creation or they can inspire us to reach for new horizons of possibility. An imagination committed to right relationships with various dimensions of creation can foster a future of hope and mutual flourishing.

Habits that restrict human potential for thriving in God's world, however, must be broken, because those patterns of thought and behavior ensnare and enslave us, reducing the quality and scope of life. God's grace can be experienced as the intervening power of disruption—a disruption of our comfortable but insufficient imaginings of the world. Prophetic preaching, as exhibited by Peter in Acts 3:12–19, works in tandem with God's purposes of liberating humanity by challenging the threat of destructive habituation. To ensure the collective thriving of God's world, prophetic preaching confronts our patterns of habit, spiritually, intellectually, and physically.

The raucous assembly of persons at Solomon's Portico who surround the healing of the man born without the ability to walk would appear to be an unlikely congregation. Peter, the passionate and oft-impetuous disciple of Jesus, bears a searing message condemning the sociopolitical system of the day, while preaching a gospel of fragility and weakness to which he has become a recent convert. Peter brings a prophetic disruption to the habits of the day that accepted Roman domination as all-pervasive. The habits of being and imagination subsumed under the shorthand of the Pax Romana (Latin for "the Roman Peace")—such as state-sanctioned violence, unrelenting economic exploitation, and a rigid system of human enslavement—revealed the power of human potential in an oppressive, self-destructive form.

Peter confronts the death impulse of depraved and deformed human relationships and the power of human potential that has been sinfully habit formed, by telling the crowd that they "killed the Author of life, whom God raised from the dead" (Acts 3:15). How is this even possible? What an indictment indeed! How can finite humans, seemingly limited in capacity, fashion anything that could kill the author, pioneer, and founder of life itself?

Genesis 11:6, a part of the Tower of Babel narrative, is concerned with the power of human potential and with the habits that shape us. When God told humanity to expand and populate the earth after the great flood, those flood survivors traveled a little way and settled in a plain. In their settlement, they formed habits of thought and being that built a singular system of relationship. They shared the thoughts and spoke a language contrary to God's intentions for a flourishing of creation and a diverse expression of humanity. They were so successful that God had to intervene and *confuse* their imagination through the imposing of differing languages in order to *shift* their imaginations. When human beings exercise their power in self-serving ways and seek to lord it over others—this is a situation primed for divine disruption.

Peter disrupts the dominant logic of religious thought and social structure of the day by preaching about the folly of a Suffering Messiah. He names the people's complicity in the current system of injustice, a lethal interplay of ingrained social and religious habits, that rendered Jesus as only another lamb fattened for the biased legal system and processed for the Roman industry of capital punishment. Such habit systems that the people created and sustained represented the potential of human agency and the mechanism by which they "kill the Author of life."

The hope within this text is not merely a theological platitude but, more concretely, a way to break the habits of mind and heart that ensnare down to the most fundamental levels of human existence. Peter calls for systemic and individual repentance. The people enmeshed in the systems needed to repent, which would have the impact of changing the systems wherein they were complicit.

Repentance is not merely a verbal confession, though it is, in part, an audible expression. Repentance is an embodied response to the mystery and power of the resurrection God made evident in the Author of life. God raised Jesus from the dead, and that same power animates us to turn away from our patterns of oppression and our systems of exploitation.

True repentance is an embodied disruption to the forces that distort God's image alive within our neighbor and in creation. Peter's prophetic preaching is embodied because he himself had turned away from ideas he once held that had placed him at such odds with Christ that Jesus commanded him, "Get behind me, Satan!" (Matt. 16:23 and par.). With his course corrected, Peter exemplifies God's interruption to a culture well-tuned to enmity against God, an interruption that also shifts the possibilities of human flourishing by offering a way forward for us as individuals and for the systems we are complicit in sustaining.

What does it mean for a system to repent? What is our culpability in the evil that is committed and sustained for our benefit? Our addictive habits, which minimize our own power and responsibility, drain our systems of vitality and the ability to change course, to repent. A press release is not repentance. A statement of regret is not repentance. Claiming probable deniability is not repentance. Peter preached so that the crowd would understand that their systems needed to repent. If these mechanisms can kill the Author of life, they will certainly devour the humans who fashioned such brutal and effective instruments of death.

The resurrection, the power of life to swallow death, is the impetus for repentance. We are not to turn away from the world as much as we are to turn toward the power of the empty tomb. Peter's preaching, prophetic to the core, challenges systems and the persons of the system. We, as individual persons, must embrace the power of the resurrection as the intervention into our habits of apathy, abnegation, and, ultimately, death. We assume that our micro-encounters are meaningless, but when we live in light of the power of life, we can embrace the world-changing ability that rests within our very being.

Prophetic preaching is often construed as fist-shaking, partisan proclamation that deals in current issues. Peter, in fact, engages public issues theologically. Jesus, the Author of life, was the victim of state-sanctioned violence, and the guilt was on all those who were present. By accepting the gift of the resurrection and the result of that intervention, which is repentance, we can become ourselves personal disruptions to the larger patterns of death. We can become embodied manifestations of the resurrection who bear witness to the manifold power of God.

We cannot persist in imagining a world where we are insignificant and powerless. Our guilt arises from our unwillingness to make the changes that we can. The future is lighted by the power of God's ongoing work: to be present wherever life is fighting for life. This is not the gospel of a militarily strong Messiah who brings peace through earthly tactics and mental manipulation. This is not the gospel of the empire that needs its subjects supple and disempowered. This is the gospel of Jesus Christ, the one who liberates by freeing us to be ourselves in him, raising us up to walk in the newness of life. The gospel makes us all miracles so that we can bear witness to the resurrection deep within us and manifest it everywhere we go.

MARK ANDREW JEFFERSON

Psalm 4

¹Answer me when I call, O God of my right!
You gave me room when I was in distress.
Be gracious to me, and hear my prayer.

²How long, you people, shall my honor suffer shame?
How long will you love vain words, and seek after lies? *Selah*
³But know that the LORD has set apart the faithful for himself;
the LORD hears when I call to him.

⁴When you are disturbed, do not sin;
ponder it on your beds, and be silent. *Selah*
⁵Offer right sacrifices,
and put your trust in the LORD.

⁶There are many who say, "O that we might see some good!
Let the light of your face shine on us, O LORD!"
⁷You have put gladness in my heart
more than when their grain and wine abound.

⁸I will both lie down and sleep in peace;
for you alone, O LORD, make me lie down in safety.

Connecting the Psalm with Scripture and Worship

"Ponder . . . and be silent."

Selah.

In this psalm, this rubric appears twice in four short verses. In verse 2, it follows a complaint: "How long, you people, shall my honor suffer shame? How long will you love vain words, and seek after lies?" Just two verses later, the psalmist comes to the core instruction: "When you are disturbed, do not sin; ponder it on your beds, and be silent."

Selah.

This psalm makes a move towards nonmovement. The fervency of the initial prayer and complaint shifts quickly to a reminder of God's faithfulness, and then it all slows down. Like a yoga or childbirth class, the lights dim . . . the instructor's voice goes low . . . the instructions gently emerge . . . do not sin . . . be silent . . . trust in the LORD . . . lie down . . . sleep in peace. It is as though a composer began with a standard term for "slow" like "adagio" and ended by writing (like Bach or Mahler) its superlative, "adagissimo."

In eight verses, the psalm follows an arc that in some ways is shared by the Acts text that it follows. Both begin with accusation: where the psalmist's complaint is shaming and falsehood, Peter's is the people's complicity in the death of Jesus. There is no Selah in the Acts text, but it is not difficult to imagine a pointed, pregnant pause as Peter rebukes, then teaches:

> . . . you killed the Author of life, whom
> God raised from the dead.
> To this we are witnesses.
> [*Peter holds the moment, scans the crowd, then turns to the one who is healed.*]
> And by faith in his name, his name itself has made this man strong.

Both texts bring a word of assurance, a turn toward restoration. Peter is stern in verses 13–15; his tone broadens in verses 17–19, as he

Make Me Your Sacrifice

O most mighty and most merciful God, who though thou have taken me off of my feet, hast not taken me off of my foundation, which is thyself, who, though thou have removed me from that upright form, in which I could stand, and see thy throne, the heavens, yet hast not removed from me that light, by which I can lie, and see thyself, who, though thou have weakened my bodily knees, that they cannot bow to thee, hast yet left me the knees of my heart, which are bowed unto thee evermore; as thou hast made this bed thine altar, make me thy sacrifice; and as thou makest thy Son Christ Jesus the priest, so make me his deacon, to minister to him in a cheerful surrender of my body, and soul to thy pleasure, by his hands. I come unto thee, O God, my God, I come unto thee, so as I can come, I come to thee, by embracing thy coming to me, I come in the confidence, and in the application of thy servant David's promise (Psalm XLi. 3), *that thou wilt make all my bed in my sickness*; all my bed; that which way soever I turn, I may turn to thee; and as I feel thy hand upon all my body, so I may find it upon all my bed, and see all my corrections, and all my refreshings to flow from one, and the same, and all, from thy hand. As thou hast made these feathers thorns, in the sharpness of this sickness, so, Lord, make these thorns feathers again, feathers of thy dove, in the peace of conscience, and in a holy recourse to thine ark, to the instruments of true comfort, in thy institutions, and in the ordinances of thy church. Forget my bed, O Lord, as it hath been a bed of sloth, and worse than sloth; take me not, O Lord, at this advantage, to terrify my soul with saying, Now I have met thee there where thou hast so often departed from me; but having burnt up that bed by these vehement heats, and washed that bed in these abundant sweats, make my bed again, O Lord, and enable me, according to thy command, *to commune with mine own heart upon my bed, and be still* (Psalm iv.4). To provide a bed for all my former sins, whilst I lie upon this bed, and a grave for my sins before I come to my grave; and when I have deposed them in the wounds of thy Son, to rest in that assurance, that my conscience is discharged from further anxiety, and my soul from further danger, and my memory from further calumny. Do this, O Lord, for his sake, who did, and suffered so much, that thou mightest, as well in thy justice, as in thy mercy, do it for me, thy Son, our Saviour, Christ Jesus.

John Donne, "Devotions: III. Prayer," *The Works of John Donne,* vol. 3 (London: John W. Parker, 1839), 507–8.

---

acknowledges the ignorance in the people's sin and urges their repentance. The psalmist shows us the people who, in their waiting and contemplation, implore newness: "There are many who say, 'O that we might see some good! Let the light of your face shine on us, O LORD!'" (Ps. 4:6).

In its lectionary position, this psalm is not just a commentary or songful distillation of Acts; it is like a liturgical response. Peter calls the people to confession: he names the reality of sin, reminds the people of God's faithfulness and power to heal, and calls for repentance. The psalmist asks God to hear prayer and is unafraid to say how things are, then makes the pivotal move toward stillness, trust, gladness, and blessing.

A confession and pardon sequence for this Third Sunday of Easter might easily flow from these texts:

Reader 1: The psalmist tells us, "When you are disturbed, do not sin,"

Reader 2: but our sin is ever before us.

Reader 1: Trusting that God hears when we call

Reader 2: and that faith in Jesus can bring us health,

All: let us turn to God in repentance and confess our sin.

After a corporate prayer of confession and a period of silence, the presider continues:

Reader 1: God raised Jesus from the dead: to this we are witnesses.

Reader 2: God is able to put gladness in our hearts,

Reader 1: and to bring us to new life in safety and peace.

Reader 2: In the name of Jesus Christ, we are forgiven.

At some 150 words, Psalm 4 might be well suited for a social media post—or not. In a high-tech world of instantaneity—quick shaming, knee-jerk rebuttal, immediate like or dislike—when it is all too easy to strike back at someone simply by hitting "Send," Psalm 4 instructs us in a different way. "When you are disturbed, do not sin. Ponder . . . and be silent." Pray instead of reacting; wait for a word before offering a word; listen before speaking; take a breath; pray some more.

A gift of Psalm 4 is the exhortation to silence—to do it, not just mention it. For the psalmist, silence means trust, peace, safety. Silence takes time. In liturgy, we often give people words to say; we less often give them time to say their own prayers, or time not to say words at all. The words of worship articulate our trust in God; our silence in worship (or lack of it) also speaks volumes about that trust. In silence, the

psalmist finds sleep and trusts in peace and safety. If not in the time of confession, Psalm 4 might invite silence elsewhere in worship: within other prayers, between parts of worship, even during preaching. The space for silence is crucial. However we understand the word *Selah*, it at least suggests that something beyond words is called for.

"Ponder . . . and be silent."

The psalm echoes Aaron's blessing, asking for the light of God's face to shine. Both texts call to mind the faithfulness of God to a chosen people. Peter speaks of the God of ancestors; the psalmist recalls that "the LORD has set apart the faithful." There is time—time to remember who we are and whose we are, to press "Pause" long enough to remember that, whatever may disturb us, we lie down and rise up in the safety, peace, and light of God.

ERIC WALL

1 John 3:1–7

¹See what love the Father has given us, that we should be called children of God; and that is what we are. The reason the world does not know us is that it did not know him. ²Beloved, we are God's children now; what we will be has not yet been revealed. What we do know is this: when he is revealed, we will be like him, for we will see him as he is. ³And all who have this hope in him purify themselves, just as he is pure.

⁴Everyone who commits sin is guilty of lawlessness; sin is lawlessness. ⁵You know that he was revealed to take away sins, and in him there is no sin. ⁶No one who abides in him sins; no one who sins has either seen him or known him. ⁷Little children, let no one deceive you. Everyone who does what is right is righteous, just as he is righteous.

Commentary 1: Connecting the Reading with Scripture

First John 3:1 marks a pivot point in this written sermon. From 1:5 to 2:29, John's message focuses on the characteristics of those who live in the light. Now he turns to a different image, namely, the qualities of those who live as God's children (1 John 3:1–5:13). The primary difference between the sermon's two major segments is one of emphasis, since the topics engaged in this new section are already familiar to anyone reading or hearing the sermon from beginning to end. With relative ease, we can chart the parallel development of these two sections below.

John therefore sketches in 1:18–29 and 3:1–5:13 what it looks like to live in the light or to live as God's children. In 1:5–2:29, though, John targets the beliefs and behaviors of a splinter group that was disrupting the community enjoyed among the network of churches to whom he

addresses the three letters of John. Now, in 1 John 3:1–5:13, his message centers on the theological and moral formation of the faithful.

The lectionary reading set for the Third Sunday of Easter spans the first two of these subunits: 3:1–3 (we are children of God the Father) and 3:4–10 (therefore, we demonstrate in our everyday lives that evil and sin no longer exercise power over us). Although John's sermon is especially concerned to draw out the significance of our status as God's children, it is worth reflecting at the outset on what it means to refer, as John does, to God as Father. Israel's Scriptures identify these characteristics: the father as source or origin of a family who provides an inheritance for children, the father as protector and provider for children, and the father as authority figure to whom obedience and honor

1:5–7	God is light—we live in the light God is Father—we live as God's children	3:1–3
1:8–2:2	leaving sin behind	3:4–10
2:3–11	keeping God's commands, particularly the love command	3:11–24; 4:2–5:4
2:12–14	demonstrating in daily life that sin has lost its power	(3:4–10)
2:15–17	renouncing allegiance to the world's ways	4:1–6
2:18–29	holding fast to the true faith	5:5–13

are appropriately given.[1] In these ways, Scripture depicts God's relationship to God's people, highlights the promise of God's faithfulness and love, and calls Israel to faithfulness. Jesus, of course, addresses God as Father, and teaches his followers to do the same; in doing so, he promises God's faithfulness and love, highlights God's beneficence, and calls for renewed trust in God and love for one's neighbor.

In the present text, John spotlights two elements of the relationship of God and God's children: first, that our status as God's children is God's gift; second, that our status as children has ramifications for our moral formation. John affirms: we are called God's children, and that is what we are! God's love is a gift to us, so that we both are loved and can love. God's love is more than God's disposition toward us (a gift in and of itself); additionally, we come now to embody the gift, so that God's love works in and through us.

In order to reflect fully our status as God's children, though, transformation is needed. On the one hand, the timing of this transformation is eschatological: when we see God fully, then our transformation will be complete (3:2; see John 1:18; 1 John 4:12, 20). On the other hand, now is the time of transformation: "All who have this hope in him purify themselves, just as he is pure" (1 John 3:3). We might have expected John to refer to the cleansing that Jesus' sacrificial death provides (see 1:7; 2:2), but John refers instead to the human side of the equation, emphasizing the role in our transformation of our own thinking, feeling, believing, and behaving. This sets the stage for John's emphasis on renouncing sin.

John's message in 3:4–10 turns on the use of the metaphor of "child" or "children of." Two elements are crucial. First, to be a "child of" someone or something is to share a family resemblance, measured in terms of one's dispositions, allegiances, and behavior. A "child of the devil" is therefore devilish, diabolic; as John observes, children of the devil sin because "the devil has been sinning from the beginning"

(3:8). "Children of God," though, do not sin; they do what is right and they love their brothers and sisters (3:9–10). Pressing even further, John urges, second, that God's children share in God's own nature: "God's seed (*sperma*) abides in them" (3:9), or as the CEB puts it, "God's DNA remains in them." This means that God's children are not simply told to stop sinning; they are actually enabled to do so. The phrase in 3:5, that Jesus came to take away sins, means that Jesus' sacrificial death removed the effects of sin *and also its power*.

Notice the parallelism of 3:4–6 and 3:7–10:

Sin is lawlessness (v. 4)	Sin is diabolic (v. 7)
Jesus came to remove sin (v. 5)	Jesus came to destroy the devil's works (v. 8)
No one who abides in Jesus sins (v. 6)	No one born of God sins (v. 9)

With this symmetry, John underscores the seriousness of sin, explains the aim of Jesus' coming in terms of getting rid of sin's effects and power, and draws out the moral corollary for daily living of Jesus' work. If we have genuinely declared our allegiance to God, if we have appropriated for ourselves the gift of being God's children, how can we keep on opposing God and God's ways? The force of John's message is to press the faithful toward moral excellence, toward lives without sin, toward lives characterized by love of God and others. John's counsel is not that we should simply try harder. On this transformational journey, he maintains, we are not left to our own devices; we are cleansed as a result of Jesus' death and empowered by God, who imparts to us God's own nature.

Even so, for many of us, this portrait of life as God's children—"no one who abides in him sins; no one who sins has either seen him or known him" (3:6)—represents an ideal so far removed from lived experience that we may wonder if John dwells in the land of fantasy.

---

1. See Marianne Meye Thompson, *The Promise of the Father: Jesus and God in the New Testament* (Louisville, KY: Westminster John Knox, 2000), chap. 2.

Moreover, John's expectations here seem out of sync with his earlier claim, "If we say that we have no sin, we deceive ourselves, and the truth is not in us" (1:8). Some interpreters have found help on this point by noting that John's verbs are in the present tense and, therefore, might be understood as "habitual presents"; accordingly, *continuing habitually in sin* would be the problem. Others urge that the sin against which John rails is willful sin; accordingly, the *deliberate practice of lawlessness* is the problem.

Perhaps more to the point, we should remember that John's concern earlier in the letter was the false notion, apparently put forward by a splinter group, that Jesus' atoning death was unnecessary, since they were without sin. Here, John's interests lie elsewhere. He insists that Jesus' atoning death ought to lead to ongoing transformation. Christ-followers demonstrate that they are, in fact, God's children, by mirroring God's purity and justice (3:3, 7). Doing so, they demonstrate in their lives that Jesus' work has broken sin's power.

JOEL B. GREEN

Commentary 2: Connecting the Reading with the World

The author of 1 John makes a transition in chapter 3. He has not completely lost his focus on the meaning of sin, but there is a shift that focuses on God's love for us and our identity as children of God.

Some years ago, the Presbyterian Church published a catechism to help children and youth understand what it means to be a person of faith.[2] As in all catechisms, there are questions and corresponding answers. The first question is "Who are you?" The answer is "I am a child of God." Then, "What does it mean that you are a child of God?" "That I belong to God who loves me." "What makes you a child of God?" "Grace—God's free gift of love that I do not deserve and cannot earn." While the author of 1 John does not explicitly talk about grace, he does say we are God's children because of God's love for us. As God's children we are part of the family of God.

In our life together as communities of faith, we see the outward sign of this love and grace when we administer the sacrament of baptism. We are engrafted, adopted, into the family of God; baptism is the outward sign and seal of the adoption that already happened—God has chosen us as children of God. This is why many Christian traditions practice the baptism of infants and children. Grace is God's free gift of love that no one of us deserves or can possibly earn. It is given to us freely by our loving God.

The love and grace God offers are given just as freely to a newborn as to an adult who has been born again. Infant and adult stand equally loved as children in God's eyes.

Easter traditionally was a time when converts were baptized. After an extensive time of preparation, they would be baptized at the Easter Vigil, dying to their old life and rising to their new life in Christ—their old identity left behind and a new identity claimed as a child of God. It is common to close a service of baptism with the words from 1 John, "See what love God has for us, that we should be called children of God, and that is what we are." Infant, child, youth, adult—we all are children of God. A sermon could focus on what it means to be baptized. What kind of claim does God have on us after we have been baptized? How do we live out our lives as baptized people?

In his contemporary Christian song "Hello, My Name Is . . . ," Matthew West reflects on this question of identity. He begins the first few stanzas of his song, "Hello, my name is regret/defeat." Soon the tone of the stanzas changes as the singer realizes that we are not defined by the things we have done or not done. The resounding answer to all the voices of negativity is "I am a child of the one true King." West goes onto allude to the opening lines of our text from 1 John 3.

A sermon on this text could include taking time to let the congregation think about all the

---

2. *Belonging to God: A First Catechism,* Approved by the 210th General Assembly (1998) of the Presbyterian Church (U.S.A.).

voices of negativity they have toward themselves. A preacher could lead them in a "call and response" naming some of the names we might use to identify ourselves; followed by the congregation responding, "I am a child of God." An additional hands-on approach might involve preprinted name tags that say, "Hello, my name is . . . ." After reflecting on all the voices that we hear that shape who we are, invite worship participants forward to receive a name tag that reads "Hello, my name is Child of God," as a reminder of who they are and how much they are loved by God.

Sometimes we forget who we are. We can get lost in many ways. We hear many different voices telling us who we are or should be. We live with trauma, illness, and grief that can leave us wondering who the person is that we are now. In the classic Disney movie *The Lion King*, Simba, who is a cub born at the beginning of the movie, is the next in line to be the lion king. When his father Mufasa dies and Simba thinks he is responsible for the death, Simba runs away. He lives a life of Hakuna Mattata, a life of no worries and no responsibilities. He grows to become a young adult and has left his life in the lion pride behind. Until . . . until the spiritual leader of the animal kingdom, Rafiki, finds him and helps him to remember who he is. Mufasa tells Simba in a vision, "You have forgotten who you are." Simba realizes he has been running from his past instead of learning from it; and he heads back to the pride to take his place as the leader.

Remember who you are. What are the ways people forget who they are as individuals and as a congregation? When they have forgotten who they are, what or who reminds them they are a child of God?

John reminds us that we are loved by God, and our identity lies with being God's children. This is the essential message Fred Rogers was trying to communicate with the world via his television show *Mister Rogers' Neighborhood*. His foundational message to viewers young and old alike was "Each of us is a beloved child of God." His show ended with the song called "It's Such a Good Feeling," which speaks of how good it feels to be alive and includes a promise that he would return to have another television conversation. After the song, he ended each show with these words: "You always make each day a special day. You know how, by just your being you. There is only one person in the whole world like you. That is you, yourself." Mister Rogers's mantra was: "I like you just the way you are." He understood that each of us is precious and unique and made from love by Love itself. That was his message.

The governor of Pennsylvania declared May 23 to be a day to honor Fred Rogers and his message. The number 143 was an inspirational number for Rogers and the weight he maintained all his adult life. The number stands for the letters in each word of "I love you." May 23 is the 143rd day of the year, so it is fitting that on that day the people of Pennsylvania, where Fred Rogers lived and worked, would show kindness, generosity, and thoughtfulness to one another.

Perhaps a sermon could address the possibility of honoring "143 day" in the community where the church resides or maybe even declare "143 day" as every day. It could be an emphasis to show love and kindness to one another and those who are our neighbors. See what love God has for each of us, that we should be called children of God. See what love God has for us, that we should love ourselves and one another as God loves us.

PAMELA S. SATURNIA

Luke 24:36b–48

[36b]Jesus himself stood among them and said to them, "Peace be with you." [37]They were startled and terrified, and thought that they were seeing a ghost. [38]He said to them, "Why are you frightened, and why do doubts arise in your hearts? [39]Look at my hands and my feet; see that it is I myself. Touch me and see; for a ghost does not have flesh and bones as you see that I have." [40]And when he had said this, he showed them his hands and his feet. [41]While in their joy they were disbelieving and still wondering, he said to them, "Have you anything here to eat?" [42]They gave him a piece of broiled fish, [43]and he took it and ate in their presence.

[44]Then he said to them, "These are my words that I spoke to you while I was still with you—that everything written about me in the law of Moses, the prophets, and the psalms must be fulfilled." [45]Then he opened their minds to understand the scriptures, [46]and he said to them, "Thus it is written, that the Messiah is to suffer and to rise from the dead on the third day, [47]and that repentance and forgiveness of sins is to be proclaimed in his name to all nations, beginning from Jerusalem. [48]You are witnesses of these things."

Commentary 1: Connecting the Reading with Scripture

The twenty-fourth chapter of Luke provides two post-resurrection accounts involving the appearance of Jesus. Jesus appears to two of his disciples on the road to Emmaus, and then to a larger assembly of "the eleven and their companions" (Luke 24:33). This latter narrative, recorded in verses 36b–48, follows a thematic pattern similar to Matthew 28:16–20 and, most notably, John 20:19–31. The disciples express doubt, Jesus provides physical evidence to confirm his bodily resurrection, and he commissions the disciples to spread the good news.

Despite Jesus' initial greeting, "Peace be with you," the disciples receive Jesus in a manner consistent with a theophanous encounter, with fear and trembling. Early twentieth-century theologian Rudolf Otto described this experience of the numinous as *mysterium tremendum*, a frightening and overwhelming sense of unworthiness.[1]

Recall previous examples in Scripture. When God revealed Godself to Moses at the burning bush, Moses "hid his face, for he was afraid to look at God" (Exod. 3:6b). In response to God's call to Isaiah, the prophet declared, "Woe is me! I am lost, for I am a man of unclean lips, and I live among a people of unclean lips; yet my eyes have seen the King, the LORD of hosts!" (Isa. 6:5). In the book of Job, Eliphaz described his response to God as follows: "Dread came upon me, and trembling, which made all my bones shake" (Job 4:14).

In our Gospel text, some of their fear may also be attributed to the fact that they thought Jesus was a ghost. This line appears to have been placed here for at least two reasons. First, it suggests that the disciples misunderstood the resurrection. A phantasmic apparition is different than bodily resurrection. Luke sought to make clear for early followers that Jesus' appearance was the latter and not the former. Second, the line sets the stage for Jesus to confirm his presence: "Touch me and see; for a ghost does not have flesh and bones as you see that I have" (Luke 24:39).

The narrative in verses 37–39 develops the more significant motif of doubt. Like all the

---

1. Rudolf Otto, *The Idea of the Holy: An Inquiry into the Non-Rational Factor in the Idea of the Divine and Its Relation to the Rational*, 2nd ed. (London: Oxford University Press, 1958), 12.

other Gospel accounts (Matt. 28:17; Mark 16:13–14; John 20:25), Luke inserts apprehension as a precondition of acceptance. That the early church allowed for this level of misgiving among Jesus' disciples can serve as a source of comfort for modern hearers. The disciples are neither chastised nor demeaned for questioning Jesus' physical presence. Doubt appears to be a precondition of faith.

What is more, after Jesus provides initial evidence by showing his hands and his feet, the writer states, "While in their joy they were disbelieving and still wondering" (Luke 24:41a). Whether the disciples still believed Jesus to be a ghost or remained skeptical of his bodily resurrection, their demeanors shifted from terror to joy. Though questions remained, their encounter with Jesus led to a positive change in attitude. They certainly recalled the love they had for Jesus, and his love for them. Possibly it was this acknowledgment of love's presence that catalyzed his disciples toward their first step of faith. Similarly, for today's congregants, the presence of love (charity) within a community may not be enough to overcome the persistence of doubt around difficult theological questions, but it may nevertheless foster a sense of joy.

Verse 41 introduces the second piece of evidence that Jesus has risen. He eats with the disciples. Spirits do not eat broiled fish. More importantly, just as the disciples' eyes were opened when Jesus "took bread, blessed and broke it, and gave it to them" (24:30) in the Emmaus account, there is here a eucharistic aspect to the meal. A shared meal is a focal point of Christ's communion with his followers. In both the feeding of fish to the five thousand (9:10–17) and the final meal before his crucifixion (22:14–20), early followers recognized Jesus through his willingness to share this most tender of family rituals. The shared meal signifies Jesus' presence, intimacy, and communion.

During the meal Jesus resumes the teaching that he is most known for in the Gospel of Luke. Verse 45 states, "Then he opened their minds to understand the scriptures." This is the third time in the chapter that the Gospel writer employs the verb "to open." In the Emmaus account, when Jesus ate with the two disciples, "their eyes were opened," just as the writer describes Jesus' teaching along the road as "opening the scriptures to us" (24:31–32).

Jesus' teachings can be difficult to see and interpret, yet they are central to this Gospel. The Gospel of Luke contains the largest number of parables, eighteen of which are unique to Luke. Parables such as the Great Banquet (14:15–24), the Lost Sheep (15:1–7), and the Prodigal Son (15:11–32) invert customary social arrangements by including those who would be excluded according to prevailing cultural dictates. This may be why the Holy Spirit must open our eyes, the Scriptures, and our minds uniquely. Without the intervention of the Holy Spirit, it would be easy for the visible realities of our world to blind us to God's kingdom ethic. It is easier for the logic of injustice and empire to obscure the alternative sources of power via justice, love, and compassion found in Scripture and Jesus' teachings.

Finally, the Christian preacher would do well to pay attention to the language of the text in the context of the earliest followers of Jesus. Note how Jesus cites Hebrew Scripture. While teaching his disciples, Jesus says, "This is what I told you while I was still with you: Everything must be fulfilled that is written about me in the Law of Moses, the Prophets, and the Psalms" (24:44 NIV). Luke's Gospel was tailored for a broader audience of Jews and non-Jews alike. The writer assumed some familiarity with the Hebrew tradition but did not take it for granted. With the above line, the writer locates Jesus and his followers as an extension of this rich tradition.

The language of fulfillment relates to an anticipation of a coming Messiah, or anointed one. Recall the words of Isaiah, "For to us a child is born, to us a son is given, and the government will be on his shoulders. And he will be called Wonderful Counselor, Mighty God, Everlasting Father, Prince of Peace" (Isa. 9:6 NIV). The anti-Semitic Christian theological concept of supersessionism, which contends that Jesus inaugurated a new covenant, where Christians "supersede" the Jews as the covenant people of God, developed centuries later.[2]

---

2. James Carroll, *Constantine's Sword: The Church and the Jews* (Boston: Houghton Mifflin, 2001), 58.

Today's preacher must clarify this distinction. The blood of anti-Semitism covers the pages of the Gospels, due to centuries of such perverse exegesis.

With this distinction in mind, we can more responsibly interpret the ways this narrative underscores the life and teachings of Jesus. He calls into fellowship a community who can bear witness to his presence; instructs them to revive the precious lessons of righteousness, compassion, and care for the vulnerable as recorded in the Hebrew Scriptures; and then commissions these followers to spread the message far and wide. This is our story. If we believe Jesus is risen, we are called to act accordingly.

JONATHAN L. WALTON

Commentary 2: Connecting the Reading with the World

At the heart of this postresurrection appearance narrative are three significant theological themes, all radiating out to the contemporary church and world:

1. The Embodiment of the Risen Christ.

This story, almost to an amusing degree, insists on the physicality of the risen Jesus. ("Come on, I am not a ghost. Look at my hands and feet. Go ahead, do not be shy, touch me. You ever seen a ghost who looks like this? Didn't think so. Anybody here got something to eat? I'll have that piece of broiled fish.")

This emphasis on what the creed will ultimately call "the resurrection of the body" must be parsed carefully. It is not a display of divine fireworks proving how powerful God is; if that were the case, the risen Christ would have appeared to the Sanhedrin and Pontius Pilate, saying, "Want a rematch?" Nor is the embodiment of the risen Jesus an indication that the resurrection is merely a resuscitation, that Jesus was dead as a doornail on Friday, but is back in fine form on Sunday, good as new, polishing off a plate of fish.

The New Testament accounts of postresurrection appearances testify to a risen Christ who is embodied, but in a body both continuous and discontinuous with his "earthly" body. The New Testament conveys this somewhat like riding a bicycle: pushing down the pedal on one side and then pushing down on the other. So, the risen Christ was recognizable to his followers (Matt. 28:9), and yet not (Luke 24:16). He has solid flesh and bones, complete with an appetite (our passage), and yet he passes through locked doors and can vanish in an instant (Luke 24:31; John 20:19). He invites his followers to touch him (our passage) and yet forbids them to cling to him (John 20:17). The risen Jesus is embodied, but his body is different, a glorified body, an eschatological body, an eternal body appearing in temporality.

The main implication of this embodiment is not verification of God's omnipotence or resuscitation of a corpse, but a *validation* of the ways God performs redemption among us in Jesus. Jesus' hands are the hands that reached out to raise a widow's dead son, that lifted Jairus's daughter from death to life, and that blessed little children. His feet are those kissed and anointed by the sinful woman who came in desperation to the Pharisee's house, and the feet that carried him from village to village on his way to the cross. The embodied resurrection is a validation of the whole of Jesus' presence and ministry and also a validation of the ways that people of faith are called to body forth the gospel in the world.

A contemporary writer who wonderfully understood the embodied, even the sacramental, character of the Christian faith was Andre Dubus, who said, "[W]ithout touch, God is a monologue, an idea, a philosophy; he must touch and be touched . . . but in the instant of the touch there is no place for thinking, for talking; the silent touch affirms all that, and goes deeper: it affirms the mysteries of love and mortality."[3]

2. Divine Necessity.
One of Luke's favorite terms is *dei*, a Greek word meaning "must," "bound," or "obliged," which appears forty

---

3. Andre Dubus, "On Charon's Wharf," in *Broken Vessels* (Boston: Godine, 1991), 77.

times in Luke and Acts. When his anxious parents finally find the twelve-year-old Jesus in the temple conversing with the scholars, he says, "I *must* be in my Father's house" (Luke 2:49). Jesus tells an astonished Zacchaeus, "I *must* stay at your house today" (19:5). In our passage, Jesus explains the crucifixion and resurrection to his disciples by saying that "everything written about me in the law of Moses, the prophets, and the psalms *must* be fulfilled" (24:44). The Messiah *had to* suffer and *had to* rise from the dead.

This "must theology" was once seen as a weak point in Luke, a kind of determinism. Allegedly, Luke viewed the Scripture as a kind of rigid script that Jesus was obliged to follow, like Johnny Cash's misguided song about world crises and the book of Revelation, which has the refrain "It's going by the book."

Recently, however, Luke's theology has gotten a fresh look. Luke's "musts" stem not from a mechanical view of Scripture but from a view of providence and human sin. Like a dear friend who travels a thousand miles to be at the funeral of a friend and says, "I *had* to be here," it is the very character of God that obliged God's coming redemptively in Jesus. When that kind of love risks everything in this kind of world, it was inevitable that "the Messiah must suffer"; it just had to be. When the God of life encounters that kind of violence and hatred, it was necessary that the Messiah would "rise from the dead."

A good connection can be found between Luke's theology and Wendell Berry's novel *Jayber Crow.* Jayber is the town barber and gravedigger in Port William, Kentucky, but he is also a wise folk theologian. In college, Jayber says, he was taught to speak of God as the "First Cause" or "Universal Mind" or "Unmoved Mover." Now, as he has gained wisdom about life, such names "explained nothing." He senses the best name for God might be the parental "Father" (or "Mother"), because that name would gather up "the love, the compassion, the taking offense, the disappointment, the anger, the bearing of wounds, the weeping of tears, the forgiveness, the suffering unto death." He asks,

[C]ould I not see how even divine omnipotence might by the force of its own love be swayed down into the world? Could I not see how it might, because it could know its creatures only by compassion, put on mortal flesh, become a man, and walk among us, assume our nature and our fate, suffer our faults and our death?[4]

The Scriptures are wise. They know that when the trajectory of God's restoring love enters into human life and history, it brings a falling and a rising, crucifixion and resurrection.

3. The Ministry of Witness. The passage ends as a kind of ordination service. Jesus has done his work, and it is now time for the disciples— then and now—to do theirs. Jesus sends them into the world, not as soldiers, diplomats, program planners, or celebrities, but as "witnesses" (24:48). It is the thinnest of all portfolios. The church has no weapons, no credentials, no powerful allies, no fancy remedies or quick fixes; it has to offer only what it has seen and heard in Jesus. However, that, of course, is what the world most needs: honest and courageous disciples who will get on the witness stand and tell the truth, the whole truth, and nothing but the truth.

In her poem "Requiem," Anna Akhmatova is standing outside a Leningrad prison during the Stalin era. Her own son is being held there with many other political prisoners, and the families and loved ones gather at the prison gates every day. The mother of another prisoner recognizes Akhmatova, comes over to her, and whispers, "Could you describe this?"

Akhmatova answers her, "Yes, I can."

"Then," she writes, "something that looked like a smile passed over what had once been her face."[5]

There is hope when someone can bear witness to the truth, and the disciples are sent to bear witness to the best truth of all: Christ is risen, forgiveness is offered, hope is everywhere.

THOMAS G. LONG

4. Wendell Berry, *Jayber Crow* (Washington, DC: Counterpoint, 2000), 251–52.

5. Anna Akhmatova, "Requiem," in *The Complete Poems of Anna Akhmatova*, trans. Judith Hemschemeyer, ed. Roberta Reeder (Boston: Zephyr Press, 1997), 384.

Fourth Sunday of Easter

Acts 4:5–12
Psalm 23

1 John 3:16–24
John 10:11–18

Acts 4:5–12

⁵The next day their rulers, elders, and scribes assembled in Jerusalem, ⁶with Annas the high priest, Caiaphas, John, and Alexander, and all who were of the high-priestly family. ⁷When they had made the prisoners stand in their midst, they inquired, "By what power or by what name did you do this?" ⁸Then Peter, filled with the Holy Spirit, said to them, "Rulers of the people and elders, ⁹if we are questioned today because of a good deed done to someone who was sick and are asked how this man has been healed, ¹⁰let it be known to all of you, and to all the people of Israel, that this man is standing before you in good health by the name of Jesus Christ of Nazareth, whom you crucified, whom God raised from the dead. ¹¹This Jesus is

'the stone that was rejected by you, the builders;
    it has become the cornerstone.'

¹²There is salvation in no one else, for there is no other name under heaven given among mortals by which we must be saved."

Commentary 1: Connecting the Reading with Scripture

After Peter, along with John, heals a man with a mobility impairment at the temple gate (Acts 3:1–10), he speaks publicly in Solomon's Portico (3:11–26). He addresses the people, telling them that:

- The Israelites rejected and killed Jesus, but God raised him up.
- The man has been healed by (faith in) the name of Jesus.
- Jesus is the Messiah and prophet whom God sent to restore God's people. Therefore, repent.

Peter's speech highlights God's raising up of the prophet—God's servant ("child," *pais*), which implies the resurrection of Jesus (3:22, 26). This irritates the Sadducees, who apparently deny the resurrection of the dead, so they arrest Peter and John (Luke 20:27; Acts 23:8). Despite their imprisonment, large numbers of believers join the community (Acts 4:4).

On the next day, the power holders (the rulers, elders, scribes, and priestly authorities) interrogate Peter and John, asking about the source and authority for their healing (v. 7). "Luke" (the author of Luke and Acts) himself provides an answer to this question: The apostles received "power" (*dynamis*) when the Holy Spirit came upon them (1:8). This term, which also signifies "powerful deed," is often accompanied with "wonders and signs." Since the apostles and followers of Jesus received the same Spirit and power with which God anointed Jesus (Luke 4:18–19; Acts 10:38), they continue to do exactly what Jesus did: deeds of power, wonders, and signs among the people (Acts 2:22, 43; 4:16, 22, 30; 5:12). Both Luke and Acts describe Jesus and his followers as Spirit-filled prophets (Luke 1:15, 41, 67; 4:1; Acts 2:4; 4:31; 6:3, 5; 7:55; 9:17; 11:24; 13:9). After Jesus is taken up into heaven, he continues to be present in his followers' ministries both in his name and with the power of the Holy Spirit.

The Holy Spirit enables the apostles not only to do powerful deeds but also to proclaim boldly or confidently (Acts 4:8, 31; "the Spirit gave them ability/utterance," 2:4, 14). The boldness (*parrēsia*) of their proclamations is characteristic of such prophetic figures (Acts 2:29; 4:13, 29, 31; 28:31). Powerful deeds, signs, and wonders are performed through the name of Jesus in our passage, and later the apostle Paul and others continue to speak boldly (*parrēsiazomai*) in the name of Jesus (4:30; cf. 9:27–28).

When asked about the source and authority for healing, Peter, filled with the Holy Spirit, gives another public speech similar to his previous one (3:11–26), although this time he addresses the "rulers of the people and elders" (4:8–12):

- The man has been healed ("saved") by the name of Jesus (v. 9).
- The rulers of the people crucified Jesus, but God reversed that injustice by
- raising him from the dead.

The latter point is supported by the quotation of Psalm 118:22 (117:22 LXX), indicating that the stone rejected by the leaders (the "builders") became the cornerstone ("head of a corner") essential to construction (Acts 4:11; cf. Luke 20:17). This building metaphor points to the restoration of the people, as signified in the healing of the paralyzed man.

Luke uses the term "salvation" as broadly meaning physical and spiritual healing and wholeness, as well as deliverance from life-threatening situations and evils (e.g., Luke 8:36, 48, 50; 17:19; 18:42; Acts 4:9; 14:9; 27:20, 31, 34). Salvation, as a both present and future reality, applies to a person, a household, a people, and nations (Luke 1:77; 19:9; Acts 11:14; 13:47).

What is highlighted in Peter's speech is that there is salvation only by the name of Jesus (4:12; cf. 2:21). This statement of "salvation in no one else," along with Luke's charge that the people of Israel killed Jesus, should be understood in the narrative context. First, Luke applies the literary pattern of the Jews' rejection of the prophets to Jesus and his followers; this always results in the gospel's movement toward the Gentiles (13:46).

Luke envisions history as "the time of universal [*pantōn*] restoration that God announced long ago through his holy prophets" (3:21). This restoration of "all" includes the restoration of Israel. Just as the ancient Israelites, especially their rulers, did not listen to the prophets, Luke understands Jesus' death to result from the Jews' rejection of the prophet. However, it is not only the Jews who are responsible for his death, but also Rome's client rulers: "Both Herod and Pontius Pilate, with the Gentiles and the peoples of Israel, gathered together" against Jesus, whom God anointed as the prophet (4:27–28).

Second, there is no other name under heaven that can save humanity. "No other name" demonstrates God's determination to save "all" through Jesus' death and resurrection, despite the evil scheme of human powers. Our other lectionary texts support this reading. John depicts Jesus as the shepherd who laid down his life for us (John 10:11). This good shepherd is compared to the "hired hand," who runs away when he sees the sheep in danger, because the sheep are not his own (John 10:12–13). This shepherd provides protection, restoration, and abundance of life for his flock, in which other sheep are included (John 10:16; Ps. 23). First John 3:16 argues the same: "We know love by this, that he laid down his life for us." The "salvation in no one else" is not a doctrinally exclusive truth claim. Instead, it refers to the singular act of Jesus—laying down his life for the sheep. Jesus is "the Author of life" (Acts 3:15).

Such an act derives from the extraordinarily intimate relationship between God and Jesus (John 10:15, 17–18): "For this reason the Father loves me." There is no other way for Jesus to express his love for God than giving his life to save all people whom God loves. There is no other way for God who loves God's only child besides raising him up again. The expressions "salvation in no one else" and "no other name under heaven" do not mean to present the superiority of Christianity over other religions. Instead, they testify to God's exceptional commitment to humanity through the singular act of Jesus, based on the love between God and the Son. In short, the authority inscribed in Jesus' name, which manifests God's unconditional love for all, generates healing power and brings salvation.

God's love manifested in Jesus' death and resurrection compels believers to love one another. "Laying down our lives for one another," as Jesus did, is a difficult commandment to practice (1 John 3:16). Yet it can start with helping a brother or sister in need (1 John 3:17). Also, loving others in truth and action includes speaking boldly to powers that question and refuse to heal the sick and to free the oppressed (1 John 3:18; Acts 4:9–10, 16–18). As Jesus was rejected by the religious and political establishments, the radical love that his followers imitate may meet resistance. However, like Peter speaking out, those who boldly proclaim and act through God's abiding love in Jesus have boldness (*parrēsia*) before God (1 John 3:21).

On this Fourth Sunday of Easter, believers continue to reflect on the meaning of Jesus' death and resurrection. Salvation, which includes healing the whole person and the restoration of God's people, has been extended to all in the name of Jesus, whom God raised up from the dead in power. When Jesus' followers witness to the resurrection power today, Jesus continues to be at work through the Holy Spirit.

JIN YOUNG CHOI

Commentary 2: Connecting the Reading with the World

At this point in the Easter season the tulips and lilies we have taken home from the sanctuary have been planted in the ground by hopeful hands, or perhaps some are beginning to wilt in their pots. Spring gestures to us as signs of new life surround us at each step into the hot summer. These signs of new life often make their way into makeshift mugs and plastic cups filling empty spaces in our houses. To this day, I am amazed by my daughter's relentless attention when it comes to picking flowers. We cannot go anywhere without her stopping to pick flowers along the road or in our front yard after I have just planted some tender shoots. Usually they are a handful of weeds with the roots hanging off, and she gives them to me saying each time, "I know you love flowers." Her offering reminds me of the grace conveyed in the words "He is risen."

We are a few Sundays out from celebrating the resurrection, where we find ourselves in the middle of the first instance of conflict between Jesus' witnesses and the local authorities in the book of Acts. At this moment, Peter and John have fully healed "a man lame from birth" (Acts 3:2), and it has caused a stir among the people who are watching the man who once begged for alms at the Beautiful Gate now "walking and leaping and praising God" (3:8). Positive reception for Peter's public proclamation (3:11–26) riles the temple authorities, prompting them to arrest Peter and John (4:1–4).

This comes shortly after the followers of Jesus have witnessed his departure and received the gift of the Holy Spirit. They are trying to sort out this new reality—what their histories mean in terms of how they occupy the present and how they orient themselves to the future. The lines that clearly demarcate these realities are beginning to be undeniably fuzzy. On the one hand, they continue as denizens of the Roman Empire, even as they are tied genealogically and traditionally to Israel. On the other hand, they are now followers of the Messiah Jesus—marked and sealed by the fire of his presence.

For this reason, the scene that is set up in this text illustrates the intersection of these colliding realities in the early church: Peter and John stand as new followers of Jesus in the midst of the council to give testimony before the "rulers, elders, and scribes," as the carceral language of "prisoners" indicates the Roman imperial context. It asserts the liminality of their position, which is an in-between space that provokes the authorities to question, "By what power or by what name did you do this?" (4:7).

The religious leaders' question of power is a question not only of authority, but one of intelligence and legitimacy, as these new followers of Jesus tell stories that make no sense to the empire and little sense to the current religious establishment. Who is this Jesus? What does it mean to follow Jesus? How do these followers fit in?

What is now the role and place of these followers in this community even as they seem intent on disrupting the status quo? In response, perhaps as a precursor to the apologetics employed by Paul (26:2) as he makes his defense in a trial speech to Festus and Agrippa, Peter, "filled with the Holy Spirit," simply speaks to them.

Not only does Acts 4:5–12 resonate with Luke 12:11–12 in language and tone; it also accurately foresees how Jesus' followers will respond. Peter is "filled with the Holy Spirit" (4:8) and answers in a way that the narrative ultimately calls "boldness" (4:13, *parrēsia*).

The rationality of power that is operational in this context is one of sovereignty over death. Giorgio Agamben claims that biopower and sovereignty are fundamentally integrated to the extent that "it can even be said that the production of a biopolitical body is the original activity of sovereign power."[1] In other words, sovereignty's first act is the political management of life through death by instrumentalizing the bodies of its citizens in order to make them instruments that ultimately reproduce empire.

However, when Peter and John enact the curative power of the Holy Spirit by healing the paralyzed man who has his place in the empire, it threatens the system. It is apart from and against empire. The only political remedy is to capture it—"so they put them in custody" (4:3)—and contain it by asking them the source of this power in order to possess it or destroy it. Peter's bold response is not simply a defense but an offense. It is meant to be offensive, because he rejects the terms of life and death as shaped by the current political order.

He says, "Let it be known to all of you, and to all the people of Israel, that this man is standing before you in good health by the name of Jesus Christ of Nazareth, whom you crucified, whom God raised from the dead" (4:10). Rather than speak directly about power in the way the leaders demand of him, Peter invokes the name of Jesus, thereby rejecting the definition of power according to their systems. Instead, he tells a story of healing: "someone who was sick . . . this man has been healed" (vv. 9–10). In other words, true power is not about replicating empire through a language of credibility or capacity, but about restoring bodies to wholeness. Its source is that which is fugitive: the name of Jesus, that is, a word that signifies a way of living and being that falls outside of the life-death/death-life opposition. Being an instrument of care and healing is precisely what is unkillable.

The power in the Acts of the Apostles is about life, and life restored—life renewed, life recovered. The other lectionary texts for this Sunday provide us with a similar picture: Psalm 23 gives us a Shepherd whose power results not in coercion or manipulation but presence, in tender care, in nourishing attention, in feeding and anointing, and a space to breathe. Likewise, the text from John's Gospel in chapter 10 tells us about the good shepherd, the one who is trustworthy because he possesses the loving power to lay down his life for his beloved sheep. For the followers of Jesus, power is not only about life over death, but trusting the one who has survived both life and death and gives us the power to do so through the Holy Spirit.

In November 2015 in Paris, France, 130 people were killed by a series of coordinated terrorist attacks. A heart-wrenching video of a French father reassuring his young son about the massacre has been shared more than 11 million times on Facebook. The father and son were standing next to one of the memorials as the son expressed poignant concern about the "baddies," and the guns, and the power of these guns to take away life, to which the father responded, "They have guns. But we have flowers. Look, everyone is laying flowers here." The father told a different story, and named a different power—one that seems on the surface to be fragile and vulnerable, but one that is meant to be a radical sign of new life.

MIHEE KIM-KORT

---

1. Giorgio Agamben, *Homo Sacer: Sovereign Power and Bare Life* (Stanford, CA: Stanford University Press, 1998), 6.

Psalm 23

¹The LORD is my shepherd, I shall not want.
  ²He makes me lie down in green pastures;
he leads me beside still waters;
  ³he restores my soul.
He leads me in right paths
  for his name's sake.

⁴Even though I walk through the darkest valley,
  I fear no evil;
for you are with me;
  your rod and your staff—
  they comfort me.

⁵You prepare a table before me
  in the presence of my enemies;
you anoint my head with oil;
  my cup overflows.
⁶Surely goodness and mercy shall follow me
  all the days of my life,
and I shall dwell in the house of the LORD
  my whole life long.

Connecting the Psalm with Scripture and Worship

While it is the Gospel reading that grounds the texts for this week in the image of Jesus as the good shepherd, the assembly will likely recognize, by the proclamation of Psalm 23, that it is Shepherd Sunday. The images of shepherd found in the psalm and in the text from the book of Acts emphasize the shepherd as the one who brings life, healing, and salvation. These gifts are closely associated with the name of Jesus. In the contemporary Easter context, it is possible to make the connection to baptism, in which Christians experience life, healing, and salvation, in the name of the Father, Son, and Holy Spirit.

At both the center and the margins of Christianity, Psalm 23 is most often associated with funerals. Members of the assembly may find that the proclamation and musical settings of this psalm evoke memories of loved ones and of loss. In this way, personal memories of death are carried into the more universal Easter hope of resurrection. Biblical scholar J. Clinton McCann suggests that although this psalm is often associated with consolation in the face of death, it can also "be read and heard as a psalm about living, for it puts daily activities, such as eating, drinking, and seeking security in a radically God-centered perspective that challenges our usual way of thinking."[1] It may be this very life-affirming security that makes the psalm such a popular choice for prayer during difficult times.

As a response to the text from the Acts of the Apostles, Psalm 23 focuses on the saving activity of God that is continued through the ministry of the early church. Someone who was ill has been healed. The connection between salvation and human healing is made manifest "by the name of Jesus Christ of Nazareth" (Acts 4:10). As one theologian has pointed out, "one of the

---

1. J. Clinton McCann, "Psalms," in the *New Interpreter's Bible* (Nashville: Abingdon, 1996), 6:767.

primary Christian metaphors for what God has done for humanity in the person and mission of Jesus of Nazareth is salvation, a medicinal concept sharing the same Latin root *salus* (health), with salve, a healing ointment."[2]

There is thus a clear link between the healing of the person who is sick and the proclamation in Acts 4:12 that "there is salvation in no one else" but Jesus Christ. Perhaps less obvious is the connection to verse 3 of Psalm 23. Here McCann suggests that "restores my soul" might be better translated that God "keeps me alive,"[3] thus underlining the trajectory between the necessities of daily life (rest, water, and security) mentioned in verse 2, and the sustaining and salvific presence of God, who leads the psalmist "in right paths for [God's] name's sake" (Ps. 23:3).

In the liturgical context of the Fourth Sunday of Easter, verse 3 of the psalm, emphasizing the name of God, will be heard to echo the language of Acts, in which Peter is asked, "By what name did you do this?" (Acts 4:7). He replies that "this man is standing before you in good health by the name of Jesus" (v. 10). Peter concludes that "there is no other name under heaven given among mortals by which we must be saved" (v. 12). The repetition of the word "name" here echoes the psalm and emphasizes that it is God who continues to bring healing and salvation through human actions that are undertaken in "the name of Jesus."

Preachers and assemblies might reflect on this trajectory in the work of Christians today. In the lectionary context, the physical healing in Acts is thus underlined by the broader proclamation of salvation that is in keeping with Psalm 23's depiction of a God who "keeps me alive."

In the text of Acts, both the physical healing and the overarching promise of salvation can also be heard in more Trinitarian language. Peter, who is "filled with the Holy Spirit" (Acts 4:8) heals "by the name of Jesus Christ of Nazareth . . . whom God raised from the dead." The invocation of God as Trinity is a powerful means of healing and salvation in the early community. This Trinitarian framework may also be heard in the Easter season in resonance with the baptismal liturgy in which the individual is often both received by her or his personal name and is baptized in the name of the Father, Son, and Holy Spirit. In the Roman Catholic tradition, for example, the *Rite of Baptism for Children* moves from asking about the name of the individual, "What name do you give your child?" to claiming the child for Christ with the sign of the cross "in the name of the Christian community," to anointing the individual with "the oil of salvation in the name of Christ our Savior," to the water baptism in the Trinitarian formula. Baptismal rites could thus also be a source for reflection on the significance of naming and acting in the name of someone else (Christ or the Christian community) for the purposes of salvation and healing.

RHODORA E. BEATON

2. Bruce Morrill, *Divine Worship and Human Healing: Liturgical Theology at the Margins of Life and Death* (Collegeville, MN: Liturgical Press, 2009), 5.
3. McCann, "Psalms," 767.

1 John 3:16–24

[16]We know love by this, that he laid down his life for us—and we ought to lay down our lives for one another. [17]How does God's love abide in anyone who has the world's goods and sees a brother or sister in need and yet refuses help?

[18]Little children, let us love, not in word or speech, but in truth and action. [19]And by this we will know that we are from the truth and will reassure our hearts before him [20]whenever our hearts condemn us; for God is greater than our hearts, and he knows everything. [21]Beloved, if our hearts do not condemn us, we have boldness before God; [22]and we receive from him whatever we ask, because we obey his commandments and do what pleases him.

[23]And this is his commandment, that we should believe in the name of his Son Jesus Christ and love one another, just as he has commanded us. [24]All who obey his commandments abide in him, and he abides in them. And by this we know that he abides in us, by the Spirit that he has given us.

Commentary 1: Connecting the Reading with Scripture

The theme of this passage is human love in community (1 John 3:13–18), but such love does not stand alone. Christ is its source, and God is its end. On the one hand, this love comes as a natural but necessary response to Christ's love (v. 16), and on the other, such love leads to confidence before God (3:19–24). It is through concrete acts of love in the community—not just words (v. 18)—that reassurance comes to the community that they are "from the truth." Believers already deeply know this—"we know" or "we will know" (*ginōskō*, 3:16, 19, 24; *oida*, 3:14–15) occurs five times in verses 14–24—but such knowledge is not a human achievement. Confidence that they are "of the truth" is ultimately established by God, whose knowledge exceeds human reasoning or thought (v. 19).

Undergirding the affirmation that believers are "of the truth" is the peculiar Johannine dualism: those who are "of the truth" stand in stark contrast to those not of the truth. We have seen this dualism before in the contrast between light and darkness (2:9, 11), between those who love God and those who love the world (2:15–17), and between the "children of God" and the "children of the devil" (3:1–3, 10).

Here the author employs similar ideas through a dramatic contrast: between Cain, the first murderer (3:12; cf. Gen. 4:9), and Jesus, who died on behalf of the guilty (3:16). Cain murdered (3:12) because he sprang from the devil (also called "the evil one," 2:13–14; 5:19). In contrast, the children of God "love one another" because their deeds spring from God and God's righteousness. Unlike Cain, they should not meet hate with hate, but with a love that formed them as God's children.

Jesus as God's Son is not only the source of the community's love but also their example. Rather than turning life into death (as Cain did), Jesus brings people from death to life, through his own sacrifice. Supporting this idea of Jesus as model, the author presents versions of the confession "Jesus is the Christ, sent by God in human form" (see 4:2). Even though this dual divine-human formula was used in the christological deliberations of later councils, the writer of 1 John did not intend this claim as a systematic theology or even as a separate topic. The goal here in confessing Christ both as from God and in human form was to reestablish the community's beliefs (3:23), to encourage its commitments, and to orient it toward loving action.

Jesus "laid down his life for us" (v. 16). This language is peculiarly Johannine (cf. John 10:11, 15, 17; 13:37–38). The emphasis falls not merely on Jesus' death but on Jesus' volition in dying for others. Jesus died voluntarily and on behalf of others, not as an accident of history. Here again, Jesus is the example. Believers should act toward others with the same compassion and effort seen in Jesus (1 John 2:6; 4:11; see John 15:12–17).

Just as Christ compassionately met the fundamental needs of humanity by laying down his life, so too Christ's followers who see (*theōrein*, better translated "observe" or "perceive") others in need (3:17) should "lay down" their lives (3:16). What does this look like? Often it takes the form of giving one's own material goods (*ton bion tou kosmou*, "the goods of this world," 3:17) to those in need. Such practical giving actualizes godly love for others and stands in contrast to Cain's deeds, which were evil because he was of the evil one (3:12). Freely giving to others marks believers as the children of God. Rather than taking life, they preserve it, expressing their full faith in Christ as God's Son. This kind of love is compassionate but not a matter of sentiment alone. It comes not merely from human emotion but from God's actions in Christ. It puts God's commandment into action, since it entails "truth and deeds" and not simply speech (3:18).

Even so, performing acts of love will not always overcome self-critical scrutiny, which can lead to doubt that one is born of God. The author counters by arguing that human knowledge, however persuasive, is not as great as God's knowledge, and God has not condemned those who live by the confession of love (3:19–22).

When the author uses the phrase "and by this" at the beginning of verse 19, it is not entirely clear what "this" means. It could refer to the acts of love mentioned in verse 18. If so, then what believers *do* would be evidence of their status before God. However, the grammar of the passage more likely points forward to

The One Lesson He Has to Give Is Himself

Christ is the way out, and the way in; the way from slavery, conscious or unconscious, into liberty; the way from the unhomeliness of things to the home we desire but do not know; the way from the stormy skirts of the Father's garments to the peace of his bosom. To picture him, we need not only endless figures, but sometimes quite opposing figures: he is not only the door of the sheepfold, but the shepherd of the sheep; he is not only the way, but the leader in the way, the rock that followed, and the captain of our salvation. We must become as little children, and Christ must be born in us; we must learn of him, and the one lesson he has to give is himself: he does first all he wants us to do; he is first all he wants us to be. We must not merely do as he did; we must see things as he saw them, regard them as he regarded them; we must take the will of God as the very life of our being; we must neither try to get our own way, nor trouble ourselves as to what may be thought or said of us. The world must be to us as nothing.

George MacDonald, *Unspoken Sermons, Second Series* (London: Longmans, Green, and Co., 1885), 252.

verse 20, which describes the greatness of God. Because God is great and compassionate, even if one's heart condemns, one has confidence not in what we do but in *the one who knows us fully*. Perhaps, though, the ambiguity here was purposeful, reflecting the author's insistence that status before God is a function of God's mercy and acting mercifully is a demonstration of one's trust in God's mercy.

Since God's knowledge is greater and more merciful than our hearts, believers can be confident before God, now and in the future. The believer is freely known to God, and since, in sending God's Son, God has fully expressed God's reality to humans (4:9, 10, 14; cf. Rom. 5:9–11; 8:1–17), the believer can be free and bold before God. The term "boldness" in verse 21 (*parrēsian*; also 2:28; 4:17–18; 5:14) implies full openness, which is also a result of obedience to God, that is, behavior consonant with an understanding of God's actions in Christ. This includes prayer, which is an articulated desire to align one's will with the will of God. Since "whatever we ask" (3:22) is in accord with the will of God, one can be confident that it will occur.

The author summarizes all this by naming God's one commandment: "believe in the name of his Son Jesus Christ and love one another" (3:23). This is consistent with the Johannine view that there is only one commandment: "to love as Jesus has loved" (John 13:34; 15:12). Believing and doing, believing and loving, are woven together Believing and doing—the commandment combines belief in Jesus as the Christ with a life that reflects the love demonstrated through Christ's death.

Confessing Jesus Christ and living communally by his example is yet another expression of a major theme in John: believers "abiding in God" and having God abide in them (3:24). In the Gospel of John, Jesus explains that those who follow him "love me [and] will keep [*tēreō*] my word and my Father will love them, and we will come to them and make our home with them" (John 14:23; also 15:1–7, 9–17). Jesus then immediately refers to the Spirit, who will be sent as a guarantor of this relationship. Here in 1 John too, the Spirit is given to assure the believers that Christ abides in them (1 John 3:24). The Spirit is another proof that God abides in those who love one another and God, since the Spirit's presence individually and corporately marks their incorporation into the family of God (4:1–6, 13; 5:6; Rom. 5:5; 8:12–17; 1 Cor. 12:12–13).

STEVEN J. KRAFTCHICK

Commentary 2: Connecting the Reading with the World

Love, in John's letter, is not something you define; love is something you do. So what does love look like? To describe love, the letter points back to John's Gospel, as does the lectionary for the Fourth Sunday of Easter, often called Good Shepherd Sunday. In addition to 1 John 3, the liturgical context includes the Fourth Gospel's famous "I am the good shepherd" discourse. The connections here are rich, and John's "letter," without a recipient or a greeting, reads like a sermon, expounding on the Gospel and translating the truth of the story into instructions for the community. As Jesus commanded the disciples to love one another to the point of death, 1 John calls its readers to lay down their lives for one another.

This call for sacrificial love mirrors the criteria for a "noble death" in Greco-Roman literature. An ancient "noble death" is one where the hero dies in an act of their own volition, embracing their own suffering for the benefit of others. In John's story, Jesus does not ask to escape his death (John 12:27–28) but moves knowingly toward it. Jesus claims to be the good shepherd whose life and death will be for the benefit of the "sheep" who follow him (John 10:10–11). He contrasts himself with "hired hands" who do not care for their sheep and would not risk or sacrifice for them. John draws on messianic expectations from the Hebrew Bible that God would one day act on behalf of God's people (Ezek. 34:11–14). In a mixed metaphor, Jesus is both the gate to safety and provision and the good shepherd who sacrifices his own life to bring salvation to God's people. This, John's letter claims, is how we know love. We come to know love in this story of incarnation and sacrifice. We come to know love when we see that God did not leave humanity on its own, but joined humanity in the form of Jesus, who gave his life so that God's love might be demonstrated. Jesus' death is noble, since he lays down his life for the benefit of others. John's letter challenges its readers to let Jesus' sacrificial love move them to love in similar ways.

Jesus' claim that he has the power to lay down his life and take it up again (John 10:17–18) echoes another scene from John's story. Just before giving the new commandment, Jesus is with his disciples at supper. The text says that he *lays down* his cloak to take up a towel and wash their dirty feet. While we may think of footwashing in terms of symbolism and ceremony, picture the context of ancient Palestine. In a desert climate where most travel was on foot, washing someone's feet was no small task.

In fact, this task was saved for servants and slaves of the lowest ranks. It was a humble job, but it was also essential. Diners reclined at the table to eat, one guest's feet resting next to another guest's plate. To wash someone's feet was to recognize them as a welcome guest, to remove any barriers that might keep them from the table.

To wash someone's feet was to recognize the need of another and to use one's own effort and resources to meet that need. John's letter makes this connection between sacrifice and hospitality. The author calls for love that moves beyond words to truth, beyond speech to action. If we fail to recognize our own resources, if we neglect the needs around us, then how can God's love abide in us (1 John 4:16)?

Tangible, economic need is a reality in today's world, and in the United States the need is highlighted by income disparity. According to the Kairos Center for Religions, Rights, and Social Justice:

> At least 46.5 million people in the US, including 1 of every 5 children, are living in poverty. . . . 97.3 million people are officially designated as low income. Taken together, this means that 48% of the US population, nearly one in every two people, is poor or low income. . . . The top 1% of the population own 43% of the nation's wealth; the top 5% own 72% of wealth and the bottom 80% are left with just 7% of wealth. At the same time, racial and gender inequality remains as deep as ever.[1]

Nonprofit, parachurch, and activist organizations often have a keen vision for what active love looks like in the face of such needs. In 1967 Dr. Martin Luther King Jr. gathered leaders from over fifty multiracial organizations in Atlanta, Georgia, to launch the Poor People's Campaign. In addition to planning a march on Washington, the campaign developed a platform and advanced an Economic Bill of Rights that included annual appropriation of funds to fight against poverty, congressional passage of employment and income legislation, and construction of low-cost housing units. Unfortunately, these efforts were cut short, due in part to the assassination of Dr. King. Recently, on its fiftieth anniversary, the Poor People's Campaign was revived, uniting tens of thousands of people across the country to challenge the evils of systemic racism, poverty, the war economy, ecological devastation, and the nation's distorted morality[2]—ills laid bare all the more in the context of a global pandemic. The renewed campaign began with an audit assessing the conditions and trends of poverty over the past fifty years in the United States. The ongoing work combines theological reflection with calls for artistic engagement and activism.

In Christian contexts, we often focus on "spiritual" needs to such a degree that we neglect tangible needs. Consider the story of Mary of Bethany anointing Jesus with expensive ointment in John 12, of Judas rebuking her for wasting money that could have been given to the poor, and of Jesus' answer, "The poor you always have with you." I for one have heard this phrase used to justify apathy in the face of poverty and to criticize movements that work for systemic change. Judas does not actually care about the poor. He is stealing from the common purse.

It is compelling how John "flips the script" here, as he is fond of doing. The provocative woman is praised for her indecent generosity; the powerful man from Jesus' own inner circle is called out for the misuse of his privilege. This story reminds us to be like Mary, to give in unreasonable measure. It also presents the good news that when we find ourselves in need or when we are deemed poor in certain ways, we also have surprising resources to share. Those of us with much privilege and access to financial resources should take caution, lest we congratulate ourselves for how we look in comparison to Judas. Too often, when those of us who have resources talk about the poor, we are not doing so in order to comfort those in need. We are doing so to ease our own guilt.

1. "Building a Poor People's Campaign for Today," Kairos: The Center for Religions, Rights, and Social Justice; http://kairoscenter.org/poor-peoples-campaign-concept-paper/.
2. The Poor People's Campaign: A National Call for Moral Revival; https://www.poorpeoplescampaign.org/.

This portion of John's letter invites us to make these connections between Jesus' sacrificial death and our own call to love. It invites us to experience love as we lay down our lives, relinquish our resources, and put down our privilege for the benefit of others. It calls us to see the tangible needs around us and respond with a love that is true, a love that takes action. As we do this, God's love will continue to be made known in the world.

LINDSEY S. JODREY

John 10:11–18

¹¹"I am the good shepherd. The good shepherd lays down his life for the sheep. ¹²The hired hand, who is not the shepherd and does not own the sheep, sees the wolf coming and leaves the sheep and runs away—and the wolf snatches them and scatters them. ¹³The hired hand runs away because a hired hand does not care for the sheep. ¹⁴I am the good shepherd. I know my own and my own know me, ¹⁵just as the Father knows me and I know the Father. And I lay down my life for the sheep. ¹⁶I have other sheep that do not belong to this fold. I must bring them also, and they will listen to my voice. So there will be one flock, one shepherd. ¹⁷For this reason the Father loves me, because I lay down my life in order to take it up again. ¹⁸No one takes it from me, but I lay it down of my own accord. I have power to lay it down, and I have power to take it up again. I have received this command from my Father."

Commentary 1: Connecting the Reading with Scripture

The lectionary readings for the Fourth Sunday of Easter, often called Good Shepherd Sunday, portray trust in God and Jesus as the good shepherd caring for sheep in a pastoral, nonurban setting.

When Jesus declares emphatically in John 10:11, "I am the good shepherd," the writer of the Fourth Gospel is using a metaphor to describe Jesus as the good shepherd who saves, addresses, calls, protects, feeds, and leads the sheep back home. The sheep in turn hear, follow, recognize, and benefit from the shepherd's voice, since they find pasture and still water. The good shepherd gives his (or her[1]) life for the sheep, because leaders protect and assume responsibility for the sheep; sheep know and trust their leaders. The hired hand, in contrast, flees when danger threatens in the shape of a predatory wolf, leaving the sheep exposed, vulnerable, and likely to die, since his loyalty is not to the sheep, whom he neither cares for nor protects.

By using an adjective "good," John also invites readers or hearers of the Gospel to view the shepherd metaphor through the lens of honor and shame, two important values in the social milieu of Jesus' time. In the Greek version of John 10:11 and 14, the shepherd leader is called *kalos*—a term that connotes someone or something good, honorable, or noble. Its opposite is "shameful," or "bad." Since the shepherd gives his life for the sheep at whatever cost, and knows them, the shepherd is good, or honorable.

The mutual knowledge of sheep and shepherd is similar to the relationship between Jesus and the Father, as verse 15 states, "just as the Father knows me and I know the Father. And I lay down my life for the sheep." The Father knows the Son through election and adoption; so the Son acknowledges and accepts the Father's revelation and will. "Knowing" in John's Gospel is relationship: to know the Father is to be in relationship to the Father. Jesus' voluntary death on behalf of others occasions the Father's love (John 10:17–18) as a sign of approval. So the shepherd is both courageous and honorable, since he protects the sheep, whereas the hired hand acts shamefully, because he thinks only of himself. The sheep do not matter to him. Jesus' behavior as the good, honorable shepherd is presented as a model of honorable even salvific behavior to be emulated by others; in John 15:13, Jesus exhorts the disciples, "No one has greater love than this, to lay down one's life for one's friends."

---

1. In Sardis, at the Artemesion, our tour group saw a woman shepherd with her flock in 2013.

John 10, the chapter in which Jesus identifies himself as the good shepherd, belongs to a sequence in the Gospel that begins with the story of Jesus and the disciples encountering a blind man (9:1–3) and ends with those across the Jordan who believe in Jesus (10:42). We cannot understand the good shepherd metaphor apart from this context. Into this narrative the reader is placed and invited to identify Jesus through actions and metaphors as healer, door, gate, and shepherd, rather than with the judgments of the antagonistic Jews (Judeans)/Pharisees. Indeed, there is even a wider context: filtered through the perspective of the Johannine community, the Jesus encountered in John 9–10 as healer, gate, door, and shepherd of the sheep is also the resurrected Jesus and the Word (Logos) of John 1, existing with God in the beginning, incarnate flesh, pitching a tent amongst us.

The Pharisees/Jews on one side and the man born blind on the other model disbelief and belief in their attempted dialogue in John 9. The former "did/do not believe" that the man has been blind, and has received his sight, in contrast to the healed man, who hears Jesus' voice before he sees Jesus and who comes through dialogue and gradually deepening insight to worship him, saying, "Lord, I believe" (9:38). For the blind man, for Lazarus whom Jesus also called (11:43–44), and then us, hearing is crucial.

Jesus' identity can be secured only through insight, which the healed man has by the end of chapter 9. Although cast out from worship in the synagogue, he is found by Jesus, whom he comes to worship. So while disciples, Pharisees, and the man born blind hear Jesus' words in John 9 and 10, the Pharisees and Jews (Judeans) are not able to see, that is, to recognize Jesus' origin, identity, and potential. Indeed, a failure to understand leads to further division and misperception: "he has a demon" (10:20–21), while the truth is the complete opposite, as we see in Jesus' declaration: "The Father and I are one" (10:30).

If John 9 and 10 are indeed a narrative sequence, why does Jesus choose the imagery of the gate and the good shepherd to interpret the healing of the man born blind, now one of Jesus' sheep? Perhaps because toward the end of his life, in John 18, Jesus will be the gate of the sheepfold, standing between and going out from the disciples, who are safely in the garden, toward the threatening soldiers outside the garden, who have come to arrest him. Embodying God's love is making a conscious decision not to act in domination or coercion, but instead in sacrificial self-giving.

The good shepherd metaphor draws on biblical imagery, including that found in Psalm 23: "The LORD is my shepherd." This shepherd provides food, water, and protection for each sheep, whose worth is not determined by a search for them. "He restores my soul" is another way of saying, "He brings me back." At the psalm's ending we are not followed, but chased and pursued, by goodness and kindness every day of our lives; where I am, there God will be my whole life long.

Who are shepherds, and what do they do? From ancient Greece to Persia, to parts of Africa and the Middle East, good shepherds protect their flocks. Biblical shepherds like Moses (Exod. 3:1) and David (2 Sam 5:2) lead Israel. The image of a shepherd describes God's watchfulness, care, and benevolent devotion in Ezekiel 34, Isaiah 40:11, and Psalm 23. Presbyters in 1 Peter 5:4 are encouraged to behave by the thought of the returning chief shepherd. Chief shepherds exercise authority, responsibility, and oversight over the shepherds and the flocks. It is up to them to see to it that the flocks are grazed in the best pastures, that shepherds are remunerated, and that the animals entrusted to their care are returned.

In biblical tradition, office holders called pastors are required to exercise watchfulness and continual care for the sheep, providing food, guiding the movements of the flock (Num. 27:17; Ps. 80:2), leading them to pasture (2 Sam. 5:2; Isa. 40:11; Ezek. 34:15; Pss. 23; 95:7), keeping the sheep from dispersing and bringing back the strays (1 Kgs. 22:17; Isa. 53:6; Zech. 11:16; 13:7; Ps. 119:176), defending them against savage beasts (Exod. 22:13; 1 Sam. 17:34; Amos 3:12; Isa. 31:4) and thieves (Gen. 31:39; Job 1:17). Much courage and self-denial is therefore necessary in a "good shepherd" who seeks only the well-being of the flock. The mission in John is wide, since "God so loved the world" (John 3:16); there are other sheep not of this fold (10:16) to whom the disciples will be dispatched (20:21).

DEIRDRE GOOD

Commentary 2: Connecting the Reading with the World

What makes Jesus the good shepherd? As we discover in this passage, Jesus truly knows the sheep of his flock, and he is willing to lay down his life for them. In his classic work *To Know as We Are Known: Education as a Spiritual Journey*, Parker Palmer describes both knowing and being known as emanating from love. He notes that the kind of love that shapes our knowing and being known is not a "soft and sentimental virtue, not a fuzzy feeling of romance." For Palmer, this love is the "connective tissue of reality" that makes a bold claim on our lives. It implicates us in the web of life and wraps both the knower and the known in compassion. Palmer says this knowing results in an "awesome responsibility as well as transforming joy; it will call us to involvement, mutuality, and accountability."[2]

Recent surveys on our current culture describe a stark contradiction. Despite a myriad of social media platforms to connect with one another, steadily rising numbers of Americans report feeling more isolated. Psychologists are reporting an epidemic of loneliness. People want to know others and to be known by others.

Jesus' claim that he is a good shepherd because he knows his sheep is good news for today, and the preacher would do well to describe the malady of loneliness and isolation that many are experiencing, and then to expound on the proclamation that Jesus first and foremost knows each of us with all of our accomplishments and failings and hopes and despair. While this news is good for many, others will wonder exactly how they are to be known by Jesus the good shepherd. Here the preacher must show the worshiper what it means to be a part of the church, the body of Christ.

One of the most important and powerful things a preacher can do is to describe ways that the church is helping persons to be known. Begin by telling how the church is helping others to know they are known. It may be through a medical mission partnership or through a recent youth or intergenerational mission trip. It may be through support of mission coworkers across the country or across the world. Begin by extending the sheepfold widely beyond one's community to expand the worship space beyond the walls that surround you.

Do not leave the image of the church being only "out there." Turn the congregation's view closer to home. Hold up a proverbial mirror before the congregation. Help them see what they are doing to know others and to help others be known.

Show in the mirror all ages and stages of life. Several weeks ago, a young family was visiting our church. They had a reluctant four-year-old who was not at all sure she wanted to be in this strange place, and the parents decided to take her to the Sunday school class. They were not at all sure this was going to work out. As the little girl was holding tightly to her mother's leg, they stepped into the room. Emma, who was five, saw the little girl and ran up to her and took her by the hand and blurted out, "You're going to be my new friend! I'm Emma! What's your name?" The little girl was both surprised and delighted. She said her name was Annabelle. Emma exclaimed, "That's a beautiful name! Come on, Annabelle, let's go play!" The next month, the family joined the church.

In this age of loneliness and isolation, to be known by God through the body of Christ is a remarkable gift. Jesus knows his sheep, and his sheep know him. First and foremost, this is what makes him the good shepherd.

The second commitment that makes Jesus the good shepherd is that he is willing to lay down his life for his sheep. He contrasts his deep commitment with that of the hired hand, who runs away when a wolf threatens the sheep. Good shepherds are willing to give their all, even their lives.

Recently while driving, I saw a pickup truck with a bumper sticker in its rear window that read: "When the going gets tough, the tough go fishing." True to form, the back window had a gun rack, but instead of guns, there were fishing rods. This driver was serious about his love for fishing. Jesus' bumper sticker would read differently. His would read something like: When the going gets tough, I am all-in.

---

2. Parker Palmer, *To Know as We Are Known* (San Francisco: HarperSanFrancisco, 1993), 9.

All-in. That's what it means to be a good shepherd. A good shepherd is not in it for the money, like the hired hand. A good shepherd is willing to make the ultimate sacrifice for the sheep. He is willing to give up his life for the sheep.

Recently while officiating a wedding, I led the couple in reciting vows that each one had composed for the other. They did not know what the other was going to say until the words were spoken in the midst of the marriage ceremony. When Jared said his vows to Eryn, he told her how much he loved her and how much he looked forward to their life together, no matter what it might bring. He told her how she had already made him a better person and how he was going to strive every day to love her and honor her. Then he ended his vows with four words: "I am all-in." Before God and Eryn and family and friends, Jared said unequivocally that he was completely committed to being married.

Preachers would do well to invite the congregation to reflect on their own commitments and on what they are willing to sacrifice. Again, engage in the practice of holding up a mirror for the congregation. Tell the congregation of the retired schoolteacher, now housebound, who continues in her ministry of writing letters and cards as a way of helping each person know they are known through her faithfulness and diligence. Tell the congregation of the young mother who for four years has volunteered to sit with the same child at a school across town and read every Thursday mid-morning. Busy with her own children and many commitments, this mother wanted to be part of a community that was very different from her own and a school that was very different from the schools her children attend. Remind the congregation that being all-in involves risk and sacrifice and commitment.

American anthropologist Margaret Mead is famous for saying: "Never doubt that a small group of thoughtful, committed citizens can change the world; indeed, it's the only thing that ever has."[3] Mead reminds us that even though few in number, the thoughtfulness and, most importantly, the commitment of persons can change the world.

The good shepherd demonstrates such an extraordinary commitment that he is willing to give up his life. In these Eastertide days, the good news of the empty tomb resounds as we rejoice that the one who is risen is the good shepherd who knows each of us, even as he knows God, and who loves with such love that he is willing to give up his life for us.

RODGER Y. NISHIOKA

3. Nancy Lutkehaus, *Margaret Mead: The Making of an American Icon* (Princeton, NJ: Princeton University Press, 2008), 261.

Fifth Sunday of Easter

Acts 8:26–40

Psalm 22:25–31

1 John 4:7–21

John 15:1–8

Acts 8:26–40

²⁶Then an angel of the Lord said to Philip, "Get up and go toward the south to the road that goes down from Jerusalem to Gaza." (This is a wilderness road.) ²⁷So he got up and went. Now there was an Ethiopian eunuch, a court official of the Candace, queen of the Ethiopians, in charge of her entire treasury. He had come to Jerusalem to worship ²⁸and was returning home; seated in his chariot, he was reading the prophet Isaiah. ²⁹Then the Spirit said to Philip, "Go over to this chariot and join it." ³⁰So Philip ran up to it and heard him reading the prophet Isaiah. He asked, "Do you understand what you are reading?" ³¹He replied, "How can I, unless someone guides me?" And he invited Philip to get in and sit beside him. ³²Now the passage of the scripture that he was reading was this:

> "Like a sheep he was led to the slaughter,
> and like a lamb silent before its shearer,
> so he does not open his mouth.
> ³³In his humiliation justice was denied him.
> Who can describe his generation?
> For his life is taken away from the earth."

³⁴The eunuch asked Philip, "About whom, may I ask you, does the prophet say this, about himself or about someone else?" ³⁵Then Philip began to speak, and starting with this scripture, he proclaimed to him the good news about Jesus. ³⁶As they were going along the road, they came to some water; and the eunuch said, "Look, here is water! What is to prevent me from being baptized?" ³⁸He commanded the chariot to stop, and both of them, Philip and the eunuch, went down into the water, and Philip baptized him. ³⁹When they came up out of the water, the Spirit of the Lord snatched Philip away; the eunuch saw him no more, and went on his way rejoicing. ⁴⁰But Philip found himself at Azotus, and as he was passing through the region, he proclaimed the good news to all the towns until he came to Caesarea.

Commentary 1: Connecting the Reading with Scripture

As the number of the disciples increased in the Jerusalem church, the community became diversified. Acts 6:1–7 describes tension between the Hebrews (Jews who speak primarily Aramaic) and the Hellenists (Diaspora or Jerusalemite Jews who speak exclusively Greek). This tension arose around the issue of daily distribution in which the Hellenist widows were discriminated against. As a result, the twelve apostles appoint the seven men to serve (*diakonein*) the table so that the apostles were able to focus on the service (*diakonia*) of the word.

Stephen and Philip are among those seven who represent the Hellenists. While their task of serving the table looks secondary, they are depicted as the same as the apostles in what they actually do: they preach and do powerful deeds, miracles, and signs among the people (Acts 6:8; 8:6). Just like Peter and John, they confront persecutions while being filled with the Holy Spirit.

After giving a prophetic speech, Stephen is martyred (7:54–60). His death results in a severe persecution against the church in Jerusalem and then the scattering of the believers, except the twelve apostles (8:1; 11:19). Although Luke often describes challenges in and outside of the community, the conflicts, persecutions, and dispersion bring about the progress of the word: "Now those who were scattered went from place to place, proclaiming the word" (8:4).

The great persecution against the church in Jerusalem is contrasted to great joy in Samaria as the result of Philip's ministry (vv. 1, 8). Philip goes to Samaria, where he does signs and miracles of healing as well as proclaims the good news about the kingdom of God (vv. 5–8, 12–13). The Samaritans accept the word of God and are baptized in the name of Jesus. Peter and John visit them and pray for them to receive the Holy Spirit (vv. 14–16). The success of Philip's ministry in Samaria is a part of the fulfillment of Jesus' programmatic prophecy: "But you will receive power when the Holy Spirit has come upon you; and you will be my witnesses in Jerusalem, in all Judea and Samaria, and to the ends of the earth" (1:8). The Samaritans were regarded not as Gentiles but as akin to Jews. Yet Samaria functions as a transition to the Gentile mission.

The movement of the Spirit continues. God's angel directs Philip to "go toward the south to the road that goes down from Jerusalem to Gaza" (8:26). On this road in a desert he encounters an Ethiopian eunuch, a high-ranking official serving for the Ethiopian queen wealthy enough that he possesses an Isaiah scroll (v. 27). In contrast to his high socioeconomic status, the eunuch, both as a foreigner and as emasculated, is a non-Jewish outsider (see Deut. 23:1).

However, the eunuch appears to be committed to Jewish faith, probably as a God-fearer, because he has worshiped in Jerusalem and on the way home he is reading a passage from the prophet Isaiah. Following the Spirit's guidance, Philip joins him in the chariot. Starting with the Scripture, he proclaims the good news of Jesus (cf. 3:18, 21). The text, Isaiah 53:7–8, that the eunuch was reading might originally have referred to a righteous exilic sufferer in general, but for Luke, the Suffering Servant is Jesus. Then how does it become good news to the eunuch?

What if the eunuch and Philip unrolled the scroll of the prophet Isaiah a bit further and found what the prophet says about the eunuch (cf. Luke 4:17)? Isaiah 56:3 says, "Do not let the foreigner joined to the LORD say, 'The LORD will surely separate me from his people'; and do not let the eunuch say, 'I am just a dry tree.'" Isaiah's prophecy continues with God's promise that God will give them "an everlasting name that shall not be cut off," despite the fact that a eunuch's progeny is cut off (Isa. 56:5). God will gather outcasts of Israel and others such as foreigners and eunuchs to God's house. This prophecy includes: "My house shall be called a house of prayer for all peoples" (Isa. 56:7; cf. Luke 19:46). He has already gone to worship God at the Jerusalem temple, and now he might understand that the promise about his inclusion in God's people has been fulfilled in him through the Suffering Servant, Jesus. It is indeed good news for him (Acts 8:35).

The eunuch immediately requests baptism: "Look, here is water! What is to prevent me from being baptized?" (v. 37). Philip and the eunuch find water in the desert and stop the chariot, and Philip baptizes him. While Luke does not provide details of the eunuch's baptism, a simple structure of the second half of our story can be observed:

> Philip proclaims to the eunuch the good news about Jesus (v. 35).
>> Philip and the eunuch go along the way (v. 36).
>>> They go down into the water (v. 38).
>>> They come up out of the water.
>> The eunuch goes on his way (v. 39).
> Philip proclaims the good news to all the towns (through Azotus to Caesarea) (v. 40).

The scattering of the believers due to the persecution in Jerusalem resulted in the proclaiming of the good news (v. 4). Philip proclaimed the good news in Samaria, which is followed by baptism, and then Peter and John joined him in proclaiming the good news (vv. 12, 25). Now the good news about Jesus has been proclaimed on the road in the desert for the eunuch, regarded as an outsider to God's covenant people. We do not know if the eunuch received the

Holy Spirit, but the eunuch, even though he does not see his baptizer anymore, goes on his way "rejoicing" (v. 39).

The Spirit's snatching of Philip immediately after the eunuch's baptism has significance for both of them. The eunuch's new faith is neither tied up with a place—Jerusalem as the center of both Jewish identity and the Jesus movement— nor is who gave him baptism important (see 1 Cor. 1:12–15). His journey home, full of joy, implies that the good news may be proclaimed in his own country. Philip also continues to go his own way, a way that started from Jerusalem, to Samaria, through wilderness and towns, and to Caesarea.

It is the Holy Spirit who makes the gospel freely move forward across cultural and geographical boundaries: from Jerusalem to Samaria and from the city to the wilderness. The eunuch's hearing the good news and his baptism may be viewed as an accidental event in an unexpected

place, but God does not want him to say, "I am just a dry tree" (Isa. 56:3). Instead, he is a branch from the true vine, Jesus; and God is the vine-grower (John 15:1). He is both a foreigner and a eunuch, but he will not be cut off from God's abiding love through Jesus.

Imagine a person or a people—a tree branch that cannot bear fruit (John 15:2). Who is this person or people? What if the person responds to the good news, "What is to prevent me from being baptized?" The one who loves God cannot prevent this baptism but must perform it. The one who loves God cannot hate brothers and sisters who also abide in God's love (1 John 4:20). God sent Jesus as the Savior of the world to deliver "a people yet unborn" (1 John 4:14; Ps. 22:31). God's abiding love in Jesus and the Holy Spirit's work have no limits and transcend all bounds.

JIN YOUNG CHOI

Commentary 2: Connecting the Reading with the World

For about half a year I had volunteered in the kitchen or at the hospitality desk at the Shalom Community Center, which provides resources for the homeless and displaced population in our town. The work was meaningful, but I often struggled to see beyond the borders of their clothing and the fringes of their unraveling shirts or Salvation Army sweatshirts. I saw what I had been conditioned by global capitalistic structures to see, and this meant that I saw people who were economically unviable. Homeless. Jobless. Maybe this translated to faithless too, or untrustworthy or lazy or weak. In other words, I saw people I would normally ignore and avoid on a regular basis, but also judge, and who justified my privileged existence.

These barriers are present not only in the form of closed doors, walls, and fences, but also in terms of regional or national borders, racial/ethnic categories, and language. In Acts, we begin to see the emergence of these borders and the negotiation of those borders among the various groups. In the first seven chapters of Acts, the narrative highlights this Christ

movement in Jerusalem (Acts 1:12–8:1a), including an early conflict within the group along "ethnic" lines (6:1). It is in this section that we learn of two subgroups within the Jerusalem Christ community, the Hellenists (likely Greek-speaking Jews) and the Hebrews (likely Hebrew/Aramaic-speaking Jews). To refer to a Jew as a "Hellenist" was one way of identifying someone who accepted and participated in Greek culture, some aspects of which were offensive to more traditional Jews. In some ways we might understand these two groups representing two distinct liturgical groups, each worshiping in the language with which they were most comfortable. At the same time, we already see how porous these lines of definitions have become with the advent of the Holy Spirit, as well as the response of those who dug in their heels a bit because they were anxious about their place in the kingdom.

After a few passages about the increasing persecution of those who profess Christ, we get a glimpse here of the ways God is determined to keep expanding those borders. The story from

Acts 8 begins with Philip answering the angel's call to go south on the road from Jerusalem to Gaza. We encounter Philip numerous times in Acts: he was one of the seven chosen to care for the poor of the Christian community in Jerusalem; he had witnessed the conversion of many Samaritans (8:9–25), and then the Ethiopian eunuch. Later he lived in Caesarea Maritima with his four daughters, who had the gift of prophecy, where he was visited by Paul the apostle.

The text highlights the dramatic encounter with the Ethiopian eunuch, which resulted in a powerful conversion. Philip heard the eunuch reading the prophet Isaiah and asked him, "Do you understand what you are reading?" (8:30). The eunuch invited him into the chariot and asked, "About whom, may I ask you, does the prophet say this, about himself or about someone else?" (v. 34). This question opened up the world for the eunuch, and it also opened up the good news to the world. The story of Jesus and the gift of the Holy Spirit would come not only to those associated with Jerusalem, but even to the Samaritans (in the passage prior to this text in chap. 8), and then to the Gentiles, where even a Roman centurion would become a part of the household of God (Acts 10). The particular encounter between Philip and the Ethiopian eunuch shows how the center is expanding and crossing surprising and unexpected borders, even into those places that seemed impossible.

This expansion produces a different orientation to the structures of knowledge and power and who or what provides that authority. Sometimes these borders are clearly delineated between people groups based on national or state borders, but theories of deterritorialization from the Global South give us ways to account for subjugated peoples within the borders. In other words, borders are not simply associated with lines on a map or fences and walls. Other types of marginalization can emerge in the most surprising lives. Borders are inscribed on particular bodies and not simply on geography and regions. In other words, this kind of deterritorialization is meant to disrupt those boundaries we rely on to understand who belongs and who is outside, and all the other ways that power structures relationships—ethnically *and* economically.

The Ethiopian eunuch was not simply an example of one of the first non-Jewish converts, but someone who fell outside of the familiar Jewish-Gentile dichotomy, the Other of others. Remarkably, the Holy Spirit commanded Philip to go to *him*, to this particular Other to engage in the good news of Jesus. It was a different image, a reading of a specific passage in Isaiah, that would meaningfully shape a radical theology that would exceed the current philosophical categories—a Christology grounded in both the human and the divine. So the eunuch's question opened the way Philip understood Jesus' role and work in the history of salvation and gave space to see and articulate this beautiful part of the redemptive narrative.

In a way, this story is less a story about how Philip converted the Ethiopian eunuch and more about how the eunuch converted Philip. It is a glimpse of how certain power structures go sideways, crumble, and fall when we encounter and listen to those who stand at the intersection of marginalized realities. The liberative moment was mutual: "As they were going along the road, they came to some water; and the eunuch said, 'Look, here is water! What is to prevent me from being baptized?' He commanded the chariot to stop, and both of them, Philip and the eunuch, went down into the water" (vv. 36–38). They both experienced a transformation, participating in a shift initiated by the Holy Spirit.

Likewise, Willie Jennings writes about this passage in terms of Gloria Anzaldúa's *mestiza* consciousness: "the consciousness of the *mestiza* is one of ambivalence and contradiction, ready to embrace change or create new paradigms of family and society. The *mestiza* by her very nature is willing to travel into the unknown, allowing mystery to be revealed in each step."[1] Philip and the eunuch are in that strange new unknown that surrounds divine presence. The good news means that we occupy a different space, a different orientation to power, and abide in relationships in a radical way. Then John 15 and the parable of the vine, which uses

---

1. Willie Jennings, *Acts* (Louisville, KY: Westminster John Knox, 2017) 84.

the language of residence, location, and abiding, and 1 John 4, which uses language like that of the John passage about love and what it means that "God abides in those who confess that Jesus is the Son of God, and they abide in God" (1 John 4:15), make sense in light of the dissolution of these borders. Likewise, the proclamation of Psalm 22 that "the poor shall eat and be satisfied; those who seek him shall praise the LORD" (Ps. 22:26) echoes that it will be all—but especially the poor, the marginalized, the Others of Others—who will see and be filled.

MIHEE KIM-KORT

Fifth Sunday of Easter

Psalm 22:25–31

[25]From you comes my praise in the great congregation;
   my vows I will pay before those who fear him.
[26]The poor shall eat and be satisfied;
   those who seek him shall praise the LORD.
   May your hearts live forever!

[27]All the ends of the earth shall remember
   and turn to the LORD;
and all the families of the nations
   shall worship before him.
[28]For dominion belongs to the LORD,
   and he rules over the nations.

[29]To him, indeed, shall all who sleep in the earth bow down;
   before him shall bow all who go down to the dust,
   and I shall live for him.
[30]Posterity will serve him;
   future generations will be told about the Lord,
[31]and proclaim his deliverance to a people yet unborn,
   saying that he has done it.

Connecting the Psalm with Scripture and Worship

Well into the Easter season, we encounter Psalm 22, perhaps the most famous of the psalms of lament. A longer portion of this psalm (Ps. 22:1–31), including the portion for today, was proclaimed on Good Friday. We also find that the passage that the Ethiopian is studying (Isa. 53:7–8) in this week's reading from the Acts of the Apostles is part of the Good Friday first reading, from Isaiah 53. Thus, on this Fifth Sunday of Easter we hear the echo of the Good Friday readings recapitulated in a more hopeful key. This week's psalm includes only the concluding seven verses, which constitute the praise section, and Philip proclaims "the good news about Jesus" (Acts 8:35) in light of the text of the Suffering Servant from Isaiah.

J. Clinton McCann observes that biblical scholars regard Psalm 22 as unique among the psalms for its "intensity and inclusiveness" and for the extended "two part" praise section.[1] In contrast to other psalms of individual lament, Psalm 22 begins with the individual, but quickly moves to "the poor" (Ps. 22:26), "the ends of the earth" (v. 27), "the families of the nations" (v. 27), the dead, or "those who go down to the dust" (v. 29), and even "future generations" (v. 30) and "a people yet unborn" (v. 31). The first part of the praise, of which we have only one verse (v. 25) in this week's reading, is the individual's praise. The second part (vv. 26–31) "draws everyone— living and dead alike—into God's reign."[2] It is this second section that forms a most appropriate response to the reading from Acts, in which the early church begins to understand the call to evangelization, as well as the gift that "the nations" can contribute to the worship of God.

In keeping with this focus on worship, the beginnings of both readings reference temple

---

1. J. Clinton McCann, "Psalms," in the *New Interpreter's Bible* (Nashville: Abingdon, 1996), 6:762.
2. McCann, "Psalms," 762.

liturgy. The powerful Ethiopian court official has been to Jerusalem "to worship." He is returning home in his chariot with some challenging spiritual reading. The psalmist also references the temple, praising God in "the great congregation" (Ps. 22:25) and paying vows before those who fear God. The paying of such vows might have involved an offering of thanksgiving or a sharing in a sacrificial meal. McCann suggests that this meal would have been shared with "the poor," who "shall eat and be satisfied" (v. 26). Thus "the afflicted psalmist, having been assured of God's presence in his or her affliction, becomes a source of life for other sufferers."[3] Hope and compassion emerge out of affliction.

In a parallel manner, one could see Philip's Spirit-motivated generosity in continuity with his experience of the death and resurrection of Jesus. Having been afflicted by confusion himself, he is eager to help another. Thus, from the foundation in temple worship, all three figures seek to expand their outreach and experiences. The psalmist turns his thoughts to "all the ends of the earth," "and all the families of the nations" (Ps. 22:27); Philip willingly sets out "to the south" (Acts 8:26); while the Ethiopian ponders a challenging passage in the book of Isaiah on his way home. All have looked beyond their original geographic settings to seek God's work in the wider world.

In the Easter context, the psalm's movement from the individual, to the ends of the earth, to the people yet unborn, invites reflection on the Ethiopian as a model of contemporary seekers who have considered or received baptism in the Easter season. Like many people today who become interested in Christianity, this well-educated Ethiopian begins to study a text privately. When Philip, prompted by the Holy Spirit, offers companionship, the Ethiopian asks a series of questions. The first, in verse 31, is a rhetorical one that invites Philip's company and advice. The second, in verse 34, is an astute question about the text. The third, in verse 36, is a request for baptism. This individual, who has authority in the world and is "in charge of [an] entire treasury" (v. 27), finds happiness in companionship and a discussion of texts. He is hospitable and open to a conversation with a stranger who must seem to him to be of a lower social status. After his baptism, the Ethiopian "went on his way rejoicing" (v. 39), thus providing an image of the Easter joy that the newly baptized bring to the assembly, especially in the Easter season.

The preacher or liturgist might make this connection five Sundays after the Easter Vigil, in order to follow up with the recently baptized and remind the larger assembly of the ongoing presence of neophytes, or as a way of continuing the mystagogical process.

Finally, as the Easter season moves closer to its conclusion and the feast of Pentecost appears on the horizon, the texts this week invite attention to the role of the Holy Spirit, who first moved Philip to outreach and later "snatched [him] away" (v. 39) for a new task. In light of the text from Acts, we can see the Holy Spirit's role in the church's proclamation of the good news. The resulting praise extends to "the nations," such as Ethiopia in these early days of the church, and to generations "yet unborn," such as those who gather around the world in assemblies today. Our praise of God is in continuity with the hopes of the psalmist and the rejoicing of the Ethiopian. We are energized in this praise by the Holy Spirit, whose feast we approach.

RHODORA E. BEATON

---

3. McCann, "Psalms," 764.

1 John 4:7–21

7Beloved, let us love one another, because love is from God; everyone who loves is born of God and knows God. 8Whoever does not love does not know God, for God is love. 9God's love was revealed among us in this way: God sent his only Son into the world so that we might live through him. 10In this is love, not that we loved God but that he loved us and sent his Son to be the atoning sacrifice for our sins. 11Beloved, since God loved us so much, we also ought to love one another. 12No one has ever seen God; if we love one another, God lives in us, and his love is perfected in us.

13By this we know that we abide in him and he in us, because he has given us of his Spirit. 14And we have seen and do testify that the Father has sent his Son as the Savior of the world. 15God abides in those who confess that Jesus is the Son of God, and they abide in God. 16So we have known and believe the love that God has for us.

God is love, and those who abide in love abide in God, and God abides in them. 17Love has been perfected among us in this: that we may have boldness on the day of judgment, because as he is, so are we in this world. 18There is no fear in love, but perfect love casts out fear; for fear has to do with punishment, and whoever fears has not reached perfection in love. 19We love because he first loved us. 20Those who say, "I love God," and hate their brothers or sisters, are liars; for those who do not love a brother or sister whom they have seen, cannot love God whom they have not seen. 21The commandment we have from him is this: those who love God must love their brothers and sisters also.

Commentary 1: Connecting the Reading with Scripture

Earlier in 1 John, the author discussed two big theological concepts: *love*—how believers who have experienced Christ's love can express that love to others, and *knowledge*—how believers can "know God" and "know [*ginōskomen*] the spirit of truth" (1 John 4:6). In this passage, these two themes are intertwined. Love entails knowing God, and knowing God is demonstrated by active love for one another.

Verse 7 clearly announces the theme: "Beloved, let us love one another, because love is from God; everyone who loves is born of God and knows God." The logic is apparent: since love is "from God" (v. 7a), then those "born from God" (v. 7b) are necessarily characterized by love. Conversely, those who do not love others cannot know God, even if they profess love for God (v. 8), because "God is love," that is, the origin and reality of all love, human and divine.

What does it mean to "know God"? Here it means remembering that the love of God (in the subjective sense of God's love for us) precedes and defines our love of God (in the objective sense). Knowing God is not primarily a speculative activity—human beings trying to figure out the nature of God. Rather, it is a discovery of how God has acted lovingly toward us. God sent the Son as a revelation of love (the grammar of v. 9 stresses God's initiative, see 1:2; 3:5). Love is not known because we first love God, but because God first loved us, by sending the Son as atoning sacrifice (4:10).

Coming to know the God who is love involves at least three elements. First, it means *acknowledging what God has done*, that is, the loving act of sending "the Son into the world" (v. 9). The verb "sent" appears only in chapter 4 (vv. 9, 10, 14), recalling language found in the Fourth Gospel

(John 3:16–17; 5:36). Why was this sending an act of love? Each use of "sent" adds a different nuance. First, Christ was sent "so that we might have life" (v. 9; see 1:2; 2:25; 3:14–15; 5:11–13). Second, he was sent as an offering for our sins (v. 10; see 2:2). Finally, he was sent as "the Savior of the world" (v. 14; see John 4:42).

Second, coming to know the loving God means *recognizing the scope of what God has done*. The first two expressions of "sent" refer only to the children of God, but the third (v. 14) is much wider. It refers to all of God's created reality. The benefits of Christ's death are total, the ultimate salvation of the social and created world.

Third, coming to know the loving God means *confessing the uniqueness of the Son*. In verse 9, Jesus is described as the "only Son" (*monogenēs*, used only here in 1 John, but see John 1:14, 18; 3:18). While there are many children of God, there is only one Son.

In verse 11 (as in 4:1, 7), the addressees are called "beloved," which implies not only that they are loved but that they are those who should love. Love of one another is not a hypothetical, but a necessary reflection of God's initiating love, a sign of abiding in God (v. 12).

Abiding in God has been noted before (2:14, 24, 27; 3:9, 15, 17), but here it is connected to confessing Christ as the Son of God (vv. 14–15; cf. 3:24). God abides in those who confess that Jesus is the Son of God and they in God. Confession of Jesus is a requisite of the children of God, but it is validated only when enacted in one's loving relationships with others.

No one has ever seen God (v. 12a), and proof of a loving God cannot be directly validated. However, human love can be observed, and when it occurs, it implies its origin. One loves the unseen God, whose love is manifested in acts of love for others (which can be seen). The presence of God's love is proved through the presence of love within God's community (see 2:4).

This is the essence of fellowship with God and with one another (2:5; 1:3–4), referred to as the "love of God" perfected in us (v. 17). The "in us" echoes the claim that God remains "in us." The verb "to perfect" is used twice more (vv. 17, 18), with regard to complete/full love

as assurance of future existence with God (cf. 2:24; 3:2–3, 19–22). No one has "seen God," but the addressees "have seen" (v. 14) what God has done through the sending of the Son. It is this to which they testify, thus joining other witnesses to the truth, so that the "you" are now incorporated into fellowship as a "we." The presence of the Spirit itself, which has been given to us (see 3:24; 4:1–6), corroborates this, a claim further explored in 5:6–8.

"Perfected love" is also proof of abiding in the one who is love (v. 16), and the basis for bold confidence (see 3:21) on the day of judgment (see 1 John 2:28; 5:14; Rom. 5:1–5, 9–11). The author once more presumes that God's love precedes the human response (made explicit in v. 19) and is foundational for the entirety of one's life before God. God's act of love demonstrates God's desire for full relationship with humanity, hence there is no fear of God, either now or at the end of human history (v. 17). Had God not acted in love, the "punishment" for disobedience would loom over all reality (v. 18). However, since God has sent the Son as the atoning sacrifice (v. 10) and the "we" responded with their own love—for God and for one another—they abide in perfect relationship with God, and fear of existence without God is "cast out" (v. 18).

Once again, believers are to witness to God's love through mutual love (v. 19). The phrase "we love," which is a declaration, can also mean "let us love," which is a command. The ambiguity is hard to resolve, but in effect, the exhortation and the declaration are equivalent: loving is the essence of believing. The verb has no direct object, so whether the sentence declares "we love" or exhorts "let us love," the love invoked is an absolute, defining the community's ethic and mission and witness—that is, to love in obedience to the One who is love (v. 10).

The section ends by pointing once again to the contradictory nature of any response to God except mutual love (v. 20). Since God is love, and believers are the children of God, the nature of God dwells in them; so love must be expressed among them. To break these connections is to lie about God's nature by acting against it. Hence the commandment language, because the nature of God is love; to love aligns one with God (see 2:7–8; 3:23). Typically, the commandment to love is associated with Jesus in the Johannine tradition (John 13:34; 14:15, 21–24; 1 John 2:7–11; 3:23–24), but here the commandment comes "from him," likely referring to God, whose love has made itself fully known in Christ. Love is not seen as a human force or power, but the very nature of God, and to love is not obedience to a statement, but full allegiance and trust in the one who has acted on behalf of all humanity. This is the basis for all full human existence, and so the author has referred and will refer to it as the conquering of the world (5:1–5).

STEVEN J. KRAFTCHICK

Commentary 2: Connecting the Reading with the World

By the time a reader gets to the fourth chapter of 1 John, the love theme begins to sound as if it is on repeat. It is interesting, though, that this outpouring of love follows some harsh and divisive language. The author speaks of "us" and "them," revealing a split in the community (1 John 2:18–28). All texts reflect the situations surrounding their writing. First John reflects a community in conflict. The writer speaks of a group within the community who separated themselves and challenged the validity of the other community members. The writer calls these people deceitful and "antichrists." What he probably means here is that these people lack true anointing (the word "christ" means "anointed"). The dispute was at least partially based on doctrinal differences. The writer hints that those separated were not holding up traditional beliefs that Jesus was both human and divine. The writer does not spend much time discussing these false doctrines. Rather, he challenges the opponents' claim to determine who is "in" and who is "out."[1]

This section of John's letter includes striking connections to the famous story of Nicodemus in John's Gospel. Jesus explains to Nicodemus that he must be born again (John 3:3, 5). The Greek word used here, *anōthen*, can mean "again" in terms of a rebirth, and it can also mean "from above." Here 1 John avoids the ambiguity, opting instead for "born of God." "Born from above" recalls the incarnation of Jesus. As a Jewish resident of the Roman Empire, Jesus was part of a social minority and politically oppressed group. The invitation to be born again is an invitation to take up residence with those who are marginalized. Nicodemus cannot fathom such a rebirth, which for him would mean abandoning his privileged identity as one of the religious elite (John 3:1). In John's letter, we find the opponents in a similar situation, securing their own elevated status by challenging whether some people belong.

Our churches and society are no strangers to conflict and the drawing of boundary lines. In much of his work, James Baldwin disrupts the notion of "stranger" that has become so central to American identity, at least or especially among the privileged in this country. An alleged "outsider" himself (a black gay man from Harlem), he was one of the most erudite social critics in modern American history. He challenges the privileged in the United States to consider why we need the "other" in the first place.

Those in privilege too often create these categories when they/we use privilege to decide who gets to cross a border line, when we decide who gets access to health care and education and housing, when we decide who gets a voice—whenever we decide who is in and who is out. From the point of view of privilege, there is an inescapable cost to letting go of our construction of the "other." Nicodemus's identity is wrapped up in his position; so, when asked to be reborn among the vulnerable, he responds with disbelief. The opponents in John's letter must discredit the others in the community to establish their own authority. Those of us in positions of privilege face the same challenge. As James Baldwin says in his book *Nobody Knows My Name*, "Any real change implies the breakup of the world as

---

1. William Countryman, "The Johannine Letters," in *The Queer Bible Commentary*, ed. Deryn Guest, Robert E. Goss, Mona West, and Thomas Bohache (London: SCM Press, 2006), 737–46.

one has always known it, the loss of all that gave one an identity, the end of safety."[2]

How can our churches today avoid the mistake of Nicodemus, who resisted vulnerabilities? How can we avoid the "us-and-them" mentality that divides? The lectionary links this passage to one of the most striking boundary-crossing conversion stories in the Bible. This is an important connection, because it helps us to recognize the agency of those who have been pushed to the margins. The Ethiopian eunuch can be labeled an "outsider" based on race and ethnicity and nontraditional gender identity. Traveling to Jerusalem for worship and reading a Greek translation of Isaiah, this person appears to be interested in the Jewish religion. However, given their status as a eunuch, circumcision, the mark for inclusion in the faith of Israel, would be impossible. The Torah presents a clear boundary; someone like this eunuch was an outsider (Deut. 23:1).

During the course of the story, the eunuch moves from a place of helplessness ("How can I understand unless someone guides me?" Acts 8:31) to a place of curiosity ("About whom does the prophet say this?" Acts 8:34). If we use our exegetical imaginations, we might picture the eunuch seeing themselves as they read in the text of Isaiah. The prophet describes a figure who is "like a root out of dry ground," "despised," "held of no account," "struck down by God," and "cut off from the land of the living" (Isa. 53:2–4, 8). Perhaps, seeing themselves in this description of the Suffering Servant, the eunuch begins to see that the boundary is not the final word. After all, in the same chapter these afflictions are called a "perversion of justice" and the eunuch reads about a future hope (Isa. 53:8–11). Perhaps the eunuch kept reading, finding the world of Scripture joining their own push against these boundaries.[3]

In the first major individual conversion story in the story of the early church, this person whom the Old Testament deems "out of bounds" becomes the exemplar. Those with identities that challenge the systems of power in the world are particularly equipped to do the work of the gospel. The Ethiopian eunuch reminds us that the Christian church was founded on the community's ability to recognize where existing boundaries restricting who could belong in the people of God needed to be pushed against. The connection to 1 John can remind us to continue that initiative to resist any criteria that create the categories of "us" and "them," and instead to embrace the criteria of love for one another.

These stories we see reflected in John's letter, in John's Gospel, and in Acts open a space for us to imagine how the lines of "us" and "them" are drawn in our own contexts. They also invite us to recognize the wealth of perspectives and life experiences of those in groups labeled "other." In his writings and interviews, activist Darnell Moore shares about what he calls "black magic," the unique resourcefulness, depths of powerful love, and resilience he witnessed growing up in a black family and community.[4] Where have you seen resourcefulness, hope, and compassion in the midst of oppression or in communities pushed to the margins? If you find yourself othered, what resources have you experienced in your own community?

Look to the places where our culture may not expect to find power, meaning, and abundant life. I have found this sort of magic in a group of queer seminarians developing resources for the church, and among immigrant families who demonstrate true hospitality even while enduring mistreatment from the US government. Look around. Where do you find this boundary-breaking magic?

LINDSEY S. JODREY

2. James Baldwin, *Nobody Knows My Name* (New York: Dial Press, 1961), 117.

3. See Isa. 53:5–8 for an especially hopeful message for the eunuch. For these connections, I am indebted to Mona West, "The Story of the Ethiopian Eunuch," in *The Queer Bible Commentary*, 572–74.

4. Darnell Moore, "Self Reflection and Social Evolution," recorded for *On Being*, August 18, 2019, https://onbeing.org/programs/darnell-moore-self-reflection-and-social-evolution/#transcript.

John 15:1–8

[1]"I am the true vine, and my Father is the vinegrower. [2]He removes every branch in me that bears no fruit. Every branch that bears fruit he prunes to make it bear more fruit. [3]You have already been cleansed by the word that I have spoken to you. [4]Abide in me as I abide in you. Just as the branch cannot bear fruit by itself unless it abides in the vine, neither can you unless you abide in me. [5]I am the vine, you are the branches. Those who abide in me and I in them bear much fruit, because apart from me you can do nothing. [6]Whoever does not abide in me is thrown away like a branch and withers; such branches are gathered, thrown into the fire, and burned. [7]If you abide in me, and my words abide in you, ask for whatever you wish, and it will be done for you. [8]My Father is glorified by this, that you bear much fruit and become my disciples."

Commentary 1: Connecting the Reading with Scripture

In John 13–17 we find Jesus' discourses to the disciples after the footwashing in chapter 13. Only in John do we find Jesus so wordy. Earlier dialogues with outsiders and disciples like Nicodemus and the woman at the well have fallen away. The Logos has the last word.

Jesus' speeches in John 13–17 take place at the Last Supper. Jesus' farewell to the disciples before the Passion Narrative promises how the Johannine community will function internally as a group and externally to the world. This is John's notion of how the Johannine community continues. Jesus bequeaths many services to the grieving community: metaphors of connection both to the group and to God; help of the Paraclete, the Spirit of truth, who will cause them to remember all things so as to foster a more complete understanding of Jesus' earthly words.

Images, metaphors, and allegories of Jesus as the good shepherd (John 10) and true vine (John 15) express a sense of mystical union, spreading from God and Jesus, that now encompasses the disciples. The image used of Jesus as true vine here draws specifically on the depiction of Israel as God's vine in Hebrew Scripture in, for example, Hosea 10:1–2, Isaiah 5:1–10, and particularly Psalm 80:8–11 ("You brought a vine out of Egypt; you drove out the nations and planted it . . ."), with the result that God's care ensures

a thriving vineyard, Israel, spreading from the Mediterranean Sea to the river Euphrates.

Metaphors of vines in Israel's Scriptures convey God's love and deep care for Israel to ensure fruitfulness, connectivity, unity, but also pruning and judgment; in Isaiah 5:1–7 Israel is judged for its failure to produce fruit. Here, the essentially relational connections of the vinedresser, God; the true vine, the Son; and the disciples, the branches, are spelled out, but not in a logical way. Understanding of the images of Jesus as the true vine and disciples as branches, together with the repetition of "remain" or "abide," is intuitive and mystical. A vine, for example, is not separate but rather indistinguishable from its branches, and as the branches in turn may be cut off, their whole identity is nevertheless in the vine. Branches are never independent but always rooted and growing in Jesus. The metaphor, "I am the true vine" encourages meditation on ways Jesus lives on after departure, for example, in eating and drinking Jesus' flesh and blood (John 6:56), as well as in the law-abiding and justice-seeking practices of disciples and followers (15:10).

John 15:1 is Jesus' last declarative "I am" followed by a predicate noun. The list of these statements in John's Gospel is short but significant: in John 6:35 and 48 Jesus says, "I am the bread of life"; in 8:12 and 9:5, "I am the light of the world"; in 10:7, "I am the gate for the sheep"; in 10:11 and 14, "I am the good shepherd"; in 11:25–26, "I am the resurrection and the life"; in 14:6, "I am the way, and the truth, and the life." Use of the definite article "the" indicates that the predicate noun points to what alone merits the designation. This grammatical observation supports the understanding that in declaring, "I am the true vine," Jesus claims to be distinct from Israel (and the branches), but also the embodiment and thus fulfillment of imagery used of the nation of Israel.

In John 15:2–8, Jesus explains to the Johannine community (every "you" in the English text is plural in Greek) how the grapevine, branches, fruit, and actions of the vine-dresser describe the relationship of the community to the Father and Jesus. The use of the verb "to abide" ten times stresses the importance of disciples' mutual dependence on the vinegrower in order to be fruitful. Without the vinegrower, the vine will not grow and flourish; in turn, the vinegrower needs the vine to produce as it is meant to do. The force of the aorist imperative indicates what it means to abide in Jesus (15:4). Repetition of mutual abiding functions on both a descriptive and a meditative level; its meditative truths console and sustain a community likely traumatized by exclusion from a local synagogue for belief in Jesus as Messiah and Son of God (9:22) and by Jesus' death. Having been separated from their community of origin, John's community is here given to understand that community relationships are restored to them along with an intimate connection to God.

Verse 2 emphasizes the discipline of production and pruning as part of a living relationship

The Bond of Union

It is of the essential idea of love, that whoever loves wishes the good of the object loved. But God wishes His own good and the good of other beings; and in this respect He loves Himself and other beings.

It is a requisite of true love to love the good of another inasmuch as it is his good. But God loves the good of every being as it is the good of that being, though He does also subordinate one being to the profit of another.

The essential idea of love seems to be this, that the affection of one tends to another as to a being who is in some way one with himself. The greater the bond of union, the more intense is the love. And again the more intimately bound up with the lover the bond of union is, the stronger the love. But that bond whereby all things are united with God, namely, His goodness, of which all things are imitations, is to God the greatest and most intimate of bonds, seeing that He is Himself His own goodness. There is therefore in God a love, not only true, but most perfect and strong.

Thomas Aquinas, *Of God and His Creatures*, trans. Joseph Richaby (London: Burns and Oates, 1905), 67.

with God and Christ. In John 13:2 Judas's actions indicate to John that the disciple Judas acted in concert with the devil to hand Jesus over (or "betray" him); in 13:27, Satan enters into Judas Iscariot.

There may be a word play in verse 3 between the word "clean" and the word "prune" in verse 2, since these words derive from the same root.[1] John Ashton proposes that Jesus' explanation in 13:10, "one who has bathed does not need to wash, but is clean all over," may be "a symbolic anticipation to 15:3 with the full founding of the community outlined in the allegory of the vine."[2]

In verses 4–5, disciples see that because they do not act by themselves, but rely instead on the strength from vine and the vinegrower, greater works are possible. One commentator explains that "the love of which John speaks and which Jesus wants to see in the disciples is not a passion that is designed to possess, that is intended to take possession of a thing or a person, but is that

---

1. Colleen Conway, study note on John 15:2–3, in *The New Oxford Annotated Bible NRSV with the Apocrypha*, 5th ed. (Oxford: Oxford University Press, 2018), 1944.
2. John Ashton, *The Gospel of John and Christian Origins* (Minneapolis: Fortress, 2014), 37.

self-abnegation that Jesus illustrates in the foot-washing."[3] In verse 6, disciples see that without connection to a source of life, flourishing life does not exist but ends in despair, even though it might look externally successful. Disciples are encouraged to ask for anything, on the basis of their relationship of dependence and trust, and in circumstances where they will no longer see the true vine.

In verse 8, "glory" connotes splendor, particularly of God. Preachers might be interested to note that John's Gospel also depicts ways Jesus' followers witness to Jesus' manifestation of glory. Jesus' mother is present at the start of his ministry as a witness to Jesus' revelation of his glory (2:11) and at the end of his life, the last revelation of glory. She embodies abiding with Jesus through witnessing his life and death, and she is the catalyst for the miracle in this story. When Jesus' mother speaks to Jesus in 2:3 about the lack of wine, she asks nothing explicit of him, but Jesus' response in 2:4 makes clear that her words contain an implied request. Jesus' words are an important assertion of Jesus' freedom from all human control. Verse 4 insists that Jesus' actions will not be dictated by anyone else's time or will. His mother's response indicates that she understands this. She does not leave but remains to tell the servants with utter confidence that Jesus will do something. Jesus' mother embodies a presence of discipleship and a witness to glory: she trusts that Jesus will act and allows him to act without coercion in freedom.

DEIRDRE GOOD

Commentary 2: Connecting the Reading with the World

Central to this lectionary reading is our relationship with God through Jesus Christ. In fact, eight times in these verses Jesus invites his followers to abide in him. Jesus uses familiar viticultural imagery of a vine and its branches to teach his followers not only about the spiritual practice of abiding in Jesus, but also for understanding their place in God's kingdom.

In 1847, while suffering from tuberculosis, Scottish Anglican Henry Francis Lyte composed the profound hymn "Abide with Me." As its title suggests, the hymn's central theme comes from our lectionary passage, which involves Christ's call to abide in him. Indeed, this connection between the hymn and the biblical text can offer preachers a creative way to link this central theme to current life simply by alternating between singing a verse of the hymn, reading from the passage, and preaching the sermon.

> *Abide with me: fast falls the eventide.*
> *The darkness deepens; Lord, with me abide!*
> *When other helpers fail and comforts flee,*
> *help of the helpless, O abide with me.*[4]

These are such powerful themes. Both in Jesus' words and in this first verse, we find powerful themes that are familiar to all human beings. People everywhere know what it means to feel alone, abandoned, and helpless. Perhaps here an invitation can be extended to the congregation to remember moments when hope seemed lost and abandoned by those close to them. Moreover, the preacher may want to have the congregation connect with people they know who are feeling lost and alone. Draw out the personal experiences of those in the congregation, and connect them to those beyond the walls of the church who are helpless and who are calling out for someone to abide with them. Beyond their immediate social circles, the preacher can direct the congregation to other vulnerable populations in the world who struggle to find a trustworthy and vibrant community and who are victims of systems of injustice. Remind the congregation that as part of the body of Christ, the church is called to abide with those abandoned, alone, and oppressed outside of its immediate faith context.

3. Ernst Haenchen, *John 2: A Commentary on the Gospel of John Chapters 7–21*, trans. Robert Walter Funk, Hermeneia (Philadelphia: Fortress, 1984), 131.

4. Henry Francis Lyte, *Abide with Me* (Boston: Lee and Shepard, 1878), 1–2.

Swift to its close ebbs out life's little day;
earth's joys grow dim; its glories pass away;
change and decay in all around I see.
O thou who changest not, abide with me.

God as the vinegrower moves through the vineyard, and where there is decay, where branches are not bearing fruit, God prunes away these branches so that fruit may be borne and the branch may grow stronger. With God's pruning, the focus is less on that which is lost and more on the new life that this process creates. The hymn reminds us that even as one's life appears to ebb, God nurtures and seeks that which ultimately gives new life.

In a similar way, the preacher can shift the gaze of the congregation away from that which is being lost to that which is emerging, by naming new opportunities for ministry, like caring for persons with cognitive disabilities and their caregivers or providing groceries for immigrant families, especially those suffering the loss of a family member detained and deported. Members of the congregation might accompany families when they visit a loved one in immigration detention. What other new ministries could the church consider that would bring it new life? Invite the congregation to see this by illustrating fruit that is being produced in the world right now through specific examples of ministry. Then invite the congregation to be fearless in imagining new ways the Holy Spirit is calling the church to be in the world, as heaven's morning is breaking as in life and in death, Christ abides with us all.

I need thy presence every passing hour;
what but thy grace can foil the tempter's power?
Who, like thyself, my guide and stay can be?
Through cloud and sunshine, Lord, abide
with me.

There is a marvelous play on words between the Scripture passage calling us to stay in Christ and Lyte's naming God as guide and stay. Even as we seek to stay with Christ, Christ is himself our stay. Even as we are to stay in him, he, remarkably, chooses to be our guide and stay. Too often, after a high moment, we fall into a depression of sorts. When the moment of joy has passed, we see that little if anything has

changed. Even with Christ's conquering death, we still see and encounter death all around us. We encounter poverty, racism, sexism, classism, heterosexism, and we wonder if anything has really changed.

Connect this passage with the world in naming the truth that the world is not yet what God desires, and temptations abound. When faced with declining resources, we are tempted to turn inward and focus only on our self-preservation. Faced with the consumerism of our age, we are tempted to make church convenient and comfortable. These temptations are real. The world still is broken. That is why we cling to the vine.

I fear no foe, with thee at hand to bless;
ills have no weight, and tears no bitterness.
Where is death's sting? Where, grace, thy victory?
I triumph still, if thou abide with me.

This is the gift of abiding in Christ. While it is true that apart from Christ we can do nothing, the opposite is also true. In Christ, through Christ, and with Christ, we can do all things, not because of us but because of Jesus Christ. Connect this passage to the world in testifying to this truth: we triumph not only when we abide with God, but we triumph because God abides with us. This is the message of hope for the whole world—that our abiding in Christ is what enables us to share Christ with the world. This message calls the congregation to be fearless by considering the pain and suffering of those beyond its walls of comfort. The church in the world is freed to be courageous signs of hope as we show Christ's love to all.

Hold thou thy cross before my closing eyes;
shine through the gloom and point me to the
skies.
Heaven's morning breaks, and earth's vain
shadows flee;
in life, in death, O Lord, abide with me.

Jesus closes with a powerful promise here. Because we abide in him and he abides in us, whatever we ask will be given. This promise is certain, because as we remain in him, we grow more and more into his likeness. As we grow more and more into his likeness, what we desire will be more commensurate with what he desires. That is the result of abiding. That is what the hymn means when we sing "Hold thou thy cross before our closing eyes." We come to see as God sees. As our desires align more faithfully with God's desires, we bear the kind of fruit that honors and glorifies God.

Connect this passage to the world by claiming the promise that because we abide in Christ, all that we ask and desire will resemble everything that Christ asks and desires—a world that is just and righteous for all of creation.

RODGER Y. NISHIOKA

Sixth Sunday of Easter

Acts 10:44–48

Psalm 98

1 John 5:1–6

John 15:9–17

Acts 10:44–48

⁴⁴While Peter was still speaking, the Holy Spirit fell upon all who heard the word. ⁴⁵The circumcised believers who had come with Peter were astounded that the gift of the Holy Spirit had been poured out even on the Gentiles, ⁴⁶for they heard them speaking in tongues and extolling God. Then Peter said, ⁴⁷"Can anyone withhold the water for baptizing these people who have received the Holy Spirit just as we have?" ⁴⁸So he ordered them to be baptized in the name of Jesus Christ. Then they invited him to stay for several days.

Commentary 1: Connecting the Reading with Scripture

Our lection describes what happens as Peter speaks to a Roman centurion named Cornelius and his folks in Caesarea (Acts 10:34–43). The encounter of Peter and Cornelius begins with their visions and ensuing acts of hospitality. Going back to the stories of Peter's raising up Aeneas from paralysis in Lydda, and then the widow Tabitha from death in Joppa (9:34, 40–41), these events, which recall Jesus' resurrection, result in many new believers in the regions. Peter stayed in Joppa at the house of a tanner named Simon, whose role is just to provide hospitality for Peter (10:6, 18, 23, 32).

Tanner was a despised occupation, due to the uncleanness from contact with the skins of dead animals. Receiving hospitality from Simon the tanner, Peter plays the role of host as soon as he receives Cornelius's people as guests (v. 23). Here, a guest becomes a host. The hospitality a tanner offers to a stranger, Peter now extends to another guest.

Cornelius is a Roman official and, along with his household, is a devout God-fearer. He is a righteous man, recognized by "the whole Jewish nation" (v. 22). In a vision, an angel of God says that his prayers and alms of mercy toward Rome's colonized people have arisen as a remembrance to God (vv. 4, 31). Following the angel's direction, Cornelius sends three men, including a soldier, to Peter in Joppa (vv. 3–6).

In view of the overall role of Roman soldiers in Acts, these messengers are viewed not only as Gentiles but also as enemies.

Peter's vision confirms Cornelius's vision (10:9–16; see 9:3–6, 10–16). As Cornelius's men approach the city, Peter falls into a trance while praying and sees a vision in which God orders him to kill and eat unclean animals. While resisting the order three times, he hears the voice, "What God has made clean, you must not call profane" (10:15). Hearing what these men say about Cornelius's vision, Peter receives them as guests (v. 23).

After the guests stay one night at the tanner's house, Peter goes with them and some believers to meet Cornelius in Caesarea. In this initial encounter, Cornelius, despite his position as a Roman official, falls at Peter's feet and worships him. Peter refuses to receive such honor, highlighting that he is a fellow human being. Peter explains how his vision has changed him. While the purity law prohibits a Jew from "associating" (*kollasthai*) with a Gentile or a person from another tribe, God has broken the boundary by making all clean (v. 28). Luke uses the same word for how Philip "joined" (*kollēthēti*) the Ethiopian eunuch in his chariot (8:29). Now Peter hears directly from Cornelius about his vision. Listening to each other, it is clear that not only have Cornelius's prayers and his alms

All Are Neighbors One of Another

God is love, and in every living creature He has set this faculty of love, but especially in man. It is therefore nothing but right that the Lover who has given us life and reason and love itself should receive His due tribute of love. His desire is to all He has created, and if this love be not rightly used, and if we do not with all our heart and soul and mind and strength love Him who has endowed us with love, then that love falls from its high estate and becomes self-ishness. Thus arises disaster both for ourselves and for other creatures of God. Every selfish man, strangely enough, becomes a self-slayer.

This also I have said, "Love thy neighbour as thyself." Now although in a sense all men are neighbours one of another, yet the reference is especially to those who habitually live near each other, for it is an easy matter to live at peace with one who is near at hand for a few days only, even though he be unfriendly; but in the case of one who has his dwelling near you, and day by day is the cause of trouble to you, it is most difficult to bear with him, and love him as yourself. But when you have conquered in this great struggle it will be more easy to love all others as yourself.

When man with all his heart, mind, and soul loves God, and his neighbour as himself there will be no room for doubts, but in him will be established that Kingdom of God of which there should be no end, and he, melted and moulded in the fire of love, will be made into the image of his heavenly Father, who at the first made him like Himself.

Sadhu Sundar Singh, *At the Master's Feet* (New York: Fleming H. Revell, 1922), 21–22.

---

been remembered before (*enōpiōn*) God, but also he and his household are in the presence (*enōpiōn*) of God (10:4, 31, 33).

Thus Peter announces that God does not discriminate according to who they are, but accepts anyone who fears God and does righteousness, regardless of his or her race, ethnicity, or nationality (v. 34). Hearing Jesus Christ's good news of peace proclaimed to the people of Israel, the Roman official may realize that this peace is different from the Pax Romana brought by the empire. The Roman emperor is not the lord. "Jesus Christ—he is Lord of all" (v. 36). Peter's speech summarizes the good news of Jesus Christ (vv. 34–42) as follows: (1) God's anointing Jesus with the Holy Spirit and with power; (2) Jesus' earthly ministry of liberation; (3) Jesus' death, resurrection, and post-Easter appearances; (4) his commission of the disciples to preach about Jesus as the coming judge; (5) for everyone who believes in him, forgiveness of sins through his name (v. 43).

While Peter is still preaching the gospel, the Holy Spirit falls on all who hear the word. Just as the Holy Spirit suddenly came on those Jewish followers of Jesus in Jerusalem on the day of Pentecost (2:1–4), here the Gentiles receive

the same gift. The same phenomenon of speaking in tongues evidences this gift. Before this event, the Gentiles in Samaria had accepted the word of God and received baptism; then they received the Holy Spirit as Peter and John laid their hands on them (8:16–17).

What Cornelius and his household experience is unique in that they first receive the Holy Spirit with the undeniable evidence of speaking in tongues, and then are baptized in the name of Jesus. No one can defy the sign of the Holy Spirit working across these socioreligious boundaries. If one "hinders" the Gentiles' baptism and thus their inclusion in God's people, he or she "hinders" God (8:36; 10:47; 11:17). After receiving baptism, Cornelius provides hospitality for Peter and his Jewish colleagues from Joppa. Peter's role changes again from a host to a guest. Such fellowship with the "uncircumcised" becomes the source of criticism in Jerusalem (11:3).

As is Luke's pattern, followers of Jesus like Peter continue to do what Jesus did. Just as Jesus was criticized because he welcomed tax collectors and sinners and ate with them (Luke 15:2), Peter is critiqued for staying with the Gentiles and eating with them. In Acts, Luke often describes in detail that after staying or abiding at one another's houses, the gospel moves forward with the guidance of the Spirit (e.g., 21:4, 10; 28:12, 14). Those hosting missionaries participate in mission. In our story, the Gentiles who believe in Jesus Christ, as well as the unclean tanner, are equal partners in the gospel.

Luke depicts the good news of peace expanding across ethnic and geographical boundaries through the Holy Spirit (cf. 1:8). Our story witnesses that a Roman official, who serves an empire that claims to bring peace and security to the world, accepts the good news of Jesus and becomes part of the kingdom of God. This dramatic event exhibits the lordship of Jesus Christ, who rules over the world with peace and equity.

Similarly, the psalmist proclaims the Lord's victory. While God is still faithful to the house of Israel, God's righteous rule stretches to the end of the earth. All the nations will join in praising God with joy, anticipating the coming of Jesus Christ, who will judge the world with righteousness (see Ps. 98:9). First John 5:1–6 relates the victory of God to that of believers: everyone who has faith in Jesus Christ is born of God and thus conquers the world. Baptism in the name of Jesus and with the Spirit is the proof of this faith.

In the end, God's victory, Jesus' authority, and the Spirit's power must not be understood in triumphalist or imperialist terms. God conquered the world by way of having God's Son lay down his life for the world. In John 15:13–14, Jesus says that he lays down his life for his friends. Only this greatest love can conquer the world. Jesus' ultimate hospitality, accepting us not as servants or inferiors but as friends, is the true source of our love for others. In turn, if we keep this commandment of love for one another, we will abide in his love as Jesus abides in God's love. The love that flows from God through Jesus Christ encourages us to live the resurrection belief by providing love and hospitality to those who are viewed by mainstream society as not deserving God's love.

JIN YOUNG CHOI

Commentary 2: Connecting the Reading with the World

"Then the singing enveloped me. It was furry and resonant, coming from everyone's very heart. There was no sense of performance or judgment, only that the music was breath and food."[1]

For a campus-wide dinner church one evening we read from Acts about the life of the early church. Inspired by Emily Scott of St. Lydia's Church in Brooklyn, a number of different ministries came together around a liturgy of sharing soup and breaking bread, which spoke to the deep hunger of these communities. In that time, I offered a meditation on Luke's familiar passage in Acts 2 that narrated these seeming idyllic days—how the faithful would sell their possessions and shared what they had with their sisters and brothers in faith so that there was not a needy person in their midst. Whenever communities gather to break bread and share the cup as a way to embody this abundance, we embody the meaning of resurrection—not only the reality of life thwarting the clutches of death and destruction, but that our lives are tied up together.

At the center of this entanglement is the resurrection and the power of God countering annihilation and insignificance, grace countering sin, reconciliation countering estrangement, and the highest and most important, love dispelling hate. The text from Acts 10 is a direct extension of these earlier images of community from Acts 2; it invites us to see once again not a mandate or moral prescription for church life but a description. We see an image of what community looks like when we gather at the Communion table together. When we come together on a regular basis in the midst of our shared fragility and vulnerability, our brokenness and neediness, we get a glimpse of that kingdom-come, heaven-on-earth that we ask for in the Lord's Prayer.

Yet it is not our commonalities that are the substance of this joining together, but the reality that we can come together rooted in our

1. Anne Lamott, *Traveling Mercies: Some Thoughts on Faith* (New York: Random House, 1999), 48.

differences and even disagreements. The miracle of our life together is that we are foreign and strange to one another, but in the same way God came to us—we who are so Other to God. It is at this table that we come to each other and experience the love that will not let us go, the love that will not give up on us.

The text also shows us how the Communion table is intimately entangled with baptism by water, and so this passage fleshes out this identity for the community even more. "Peter said, 'Can anyone withhold the water for baptizing these people who have received the Holy Spirit just as we have?' So he ordered them to be baptized in the name of Jesus Christ" (vv. 47–48). The new life as exhibited by the baptism is not meant to be experienced in isolation. It is always about and for each other. It is about our lives being inextricably connected, intertwined, and joined together.

So this passage today is a story not simply of inclusion and multiculturalism, but of the dissolution of boundaries across numerous levels. Earlier in the chapter we encounter a centurion from the Roman Cohort named Cornelius, a pious and God-fearing person with his entire household, giving many alms to the people and praying often to God (vv. 1–2). Likely, Cornelius was a patron for Jews and non-Jews alike and a practitioner of Jewish piety, though not a full convert to Judaism. Thus, Cornelius has not undergone the traditional Jewish (boundary-crossing) ritual of circumcision, nor does he follow the traditional Jewish customs pertaining to clean and unclean food. He is what we have come to refer to as a God-fearer. According to Willie Jennings,

> Cornelius is a man of war, bound to the Roman state. He is a master, an owner of slaves. He is a ruler, a leader of men. He is what so many men and women in this world aspire to be and what so many peoples want to be defined as—a strong self-sufficient people who look to the world like one unified, strong, self-sufficient man. Cornelius is an aspiration, but he is also an anomaly.[2]

One day, during afternoon prayer, Cornelius has a vision in which he sees an angel who instructs him to send for Peter, who is staying in the nearby town of Joppa (vv. 4–6). He sends his servants to Peter, who is the middle of his own vision of God's kingdom, specifically, a depiction of what it means to choose abundance in the midst of scarcity and fear, of the old ways of living, loving, and belonging. Peter realizes that he needs to see Cornelius and follows the servants to his house, where he preaches the good news to all who are gathered there, and we arrive at this, another Pentecost moment. The Holy Spirit descends, people speak in tongues, there is a baptism, and people share time and space together. That it happened among these particular Gentiles signifies that our life with one another goes beyond languages, bodies, and economies and yet requires a posture toward the Other as our source of belonging and identity, and that this is rooted in abundance.

Mike Mather, pastor of Broadway United Methodist Church in Indianapolis, explains how abundance has shaped his community by asking questions about cultivating gifts, rather than focusing on what they were lacking in their church: "We created a new account and called it 'The Abundance Fund.' We don't use money from this fund to pay utility or rent bills. We use The Abundance Fund to pay people to share their gifts with others."[3] In other words, this community understood that being baptized, anointed, and invited into the fellowship of the Holy Spirit meant belonging to an abundance that ran deeper than any endowments or capital investments. They lived out a different kind of community and identity. It changed how they shared, how they gave, and how they lived with each other.

The other lectionary passages, from Psalm 98, John, and 1 John, touch on the relationship between Communion and baptism through images of water and the sea, as well as what it means to abide in love and friendship. So I am back at Jesus, again thankful for the way God comes to us over and over as Emmanuel,

---

2. Willie Jennings, *Acts* (Louisville, KY: Westminster John Knox, 2017), 102.

3. "Excerpt: Having Nothing, Possessing Everything," *Faith & Leadership*; https://www.faithandleadership.com/excerpt-having-nothing-possessing-everything.

God-with-Us, who showed us the way to participate in this salvation: he shared his life with the disciples, he shared his life with us, he shares his life with all of humanity through the Holy Spirit, so we can taste and see the ever-present possibility of risen life and life made new. In doing so, he gives us the capacity to summon the courage, in Brennan Manning's words, "to say yes to the present risenness of Jesus Christ,"[4] to feel and participate in that life shared and given for us in every moment of the day, to live and love in the abundance of that goodness now and always.

MIHEE KIM-KORT

---

4. Brennan Manning, *Abba's Child: The Cry of the Heart for Intimate Belonging* (Colorado Springs, CO: NavPress, 1997), 80.

Psalm 98

¹O sing to the LORD a new song,
    for he has done marvelous things.
His right hand and his holy arm
    have gotten him victory.
²The LORD has made known his victory;
    he has revealed his vindication in the sight of the nations.
³He has remembered his steadfast love and faithfulness
    to the house of Israel.
All the ends of the earth have seen
    the victory of our God.

⁴Make a joyful noise to the LORD, all the earth;
    break forth into joyous song and sing praises.
⁵Sing praises to the LORD with the lyre,
    with the lyre and the sound of melody.
⁶With trumpets and the sound of the horn
    make a joyful noise before the King, the LORD.

⁷Let the sea roar, and all that fills it;
    he world and those who live in it.
⁸Let the floods clap their hands;
    let the hills sing together for joy
⁹at the presence of the LORD, for he is coming
    to judge the earth.
He will judge the world with righteousness,
    and the peoples with equity.

Connecting the Psalm with Scripture and Worship

Psalm 98 is a psalm of enthronement that is both a triumphant response to the "marvelous things" (Ps. 98:1) that the Holy Spirit has worked among the Gentiles in Acts and also a resounding echo of God's victory over the Egyptians in the book of Exodus. In the Easter season, these echoes of Exodus refer assemblies back to the Genesis and Exodus readings at the Easter Vigil. This backdrop frames the celebration of creation and salvation in the gifts of the Holy Spirit. These gifts are spread through the preached word and culminate, in the Christian context, in the sacrament of baptism, which is offered to all who seek it.

Biblical scholars note the similarity between Psalm 98 and the second reading, from Exodus, which holds a central (and sometimes disconcerting) place in the Liturgy of the Word of the Easter Vigil. J. Clinton McCann points out these parallels between the language of the psalm and the language of Exodus 15. First, the psalm exhorts hearers to "sing to the LORD a new song" (v. 1). In Exodus, Moses, Miriam, and the Israelites are depicted similarly as singing to God on the shore of the Red Sea, after being rescued from the Egyptians by means of God's power acting in the waters (Exod. 15:1, 20–21). In both cases, the song of thanksgiving is in response to "victory" over enemies, which is associated with God's "right hand" and "holy arm" (Ps. 98:1; Exod. 15:6).

The focus in both texts is a proclamation of God's authority over the whole world. As the psalm puts it, "all the ends of the earth have seen the victory of our God" (Ps. 98:3). In similar fashion, as McCann reminds us, "the stated purpose of the exodus was that the Egyptians might know God's sovereignty."[1] These songs of praise to God the "divine warrior"[2] can be understood as a kind of public proclamation of the strength and power that God exercises on behalf of a particular people, and yet also offers to "the nations" (Ps. 98:2) and "the Gentiles" (Acts 10:45) through the working of the Holy Spirit. This exercise of power is directly related to the "steadfast love and faithfulness" (Ps. 98:3) that is characteristic of the God of Israel.

The psalm's images of the roaring sea (v. 7) and the floods that are exhorted to "clap their hands" (v. 8) evoke the furious waters of the Red Sea that brought victory and salvation to the Israelites. They may also suggest the "wind from God [that] swept over the face of the waters" (Gen. 1:2) in the Easter Vigil's first reading from the book of Genesis. In the Easter context these images also point to the waters of the font that welcome the new Christian through death and rebirth. As a response to the text from Acts in which Peter asks, "Can anyone withhold the water for baptizing these people?" (Acts 10:47), the psalm underlines the image of powerful forces of nature cooperating with God for the purposes of praise and salvation. McCann notes

that the images of creation and the exodus are the reasons for the NRSV decision to use "victory" instead of "salvation" in the translation of the psalm.[3] In the lectionary context, the "marvelous things" can be heard to refer to the working of the Holy Spirit. The victory-clinching waters of the Red Sea are represented by the baptismal waters, which are also the waters of new creation; the Acts reading suggests that no one can hold these life-giving waters back from those who have already received the Holy Spirit.

Finally, Psalm 98 can also be understood as a psalm about singing and making music; it is a musician's psalm. Beginning with an exhortation to sing "a new song" (Ps. 98:1), followed by the call to "all the earth" (v. 4) to "make a joyful noise to the LORD [and] break forth into joyous song and sing praises," the psalm overflows with the energy of a thriving music ministry. Various musical instruments are mentioned: the lyre (v. 5), trumpets, and horns (v. 6). The floods "clap" to keep time, and even "the hills sing together for joy" (v. 8). For choirs and musicians who have worked especially hard in their ministries during the Easter season, this psalm could be experienced as an expression of joy and thanksgiving to God for the gift of music in and for communities. While the music ministers deserve credit for their work, if the hills can sing, so also might reluctant members of the assembly be exhorted to add their voices in praise of God.

RHODORA E. BEATON

---

1. J. Clinton McCann, "Psalms," in the *New Interpreter's Bible* (Nashville: Abingdon, 1996), 6:1072.
2. McCann, "Psalms," 1072.
3. McCann, "Psalms," 1072.

1 John 5:1–6

[1]Everyone who believes that Jesus is the Christ has been born of God, and everyone who loves the parent loves the child. [2]By this we know that we love the children of God, when we love God and obey his commandments. [3]For the love of God is this, that we obey his commandments. And his commandments are not burdensome, [4]for whatever is born of God conquers the world. And this is the victory that conquers the world, our faith. [5]Who is it that conquers the world but the one who believes that Jesus is the Son of God?

[6]This is the one who came by water and blood, Jesus Christ, not with the water only but with the water and the blood. And the Spirit is the one that testifies, for the Spirit is the truth.

Commentary 1: Connecting the Reading with Scripture

This passage picks up once more some of the familiar themes readers have encountered in 1 John: believing, the love of God, and love in the community. Verses 1 and 5 serve as a frame for the passage and together express its basic meaning: the love of God requires love for fellow believers, and this love is the lived confession of Jesus Christ, the Son of God (1 John 5:1–5). This passage continues the theme of proper love and confession begun in 4:7–21, but with a difference. Earlier the author used negative examples to define the relationship of human love to divine love, but now the examples employed are positive.

Before, the author advanced the negative example of Cain and Abel (3:11–12) to show that human relationships do not naturally result in love. Because of this, a relationship of love must be a deliberate choice, one that is dependent on one's relationship to God. To demonstrate this, now a positive example is used: parent and child. Starting with the colloquial maxim that if one loves the parent, one will love the child, the author infers that if one claims to love God, then one will choose to love God's children. The metaphor of believers as the children of God is strong. Earlier the author used biological, "begetting" language regarding members of the community formed by God (2:29; 3:9; 4:7, see also 5:1, 4).

In verse 3, this positive parent-child image is extended into the arena of obedience. When a command is given in business or the military, it can be onerous, but not when the command comes from a loving parent to a responsive child. In such a relationship, God's "commandments are not burdensome." Some of the grammar in verse 3 is difficult, but the ultimate meaning is not obscured. The problem comes in knowing what the author means by the phrase "by this" in verse 2a. What exactly is "this"? One clue comes in what follows: "by this" believers know that they love fellow believers. That suggests one possibility, that "this" refers backward to the parent-child analogy of verse 1. Since everybody knows that those who love the parent also love the child, then "by this" analogy we know that those who love God love God's children.

However, we can also read forward, and if we do, "by this" refers not to what lies behind but to what comes next. Taken this way, what the author is saying is that we know we love the children of God when we "obey [God's] commandments" (v. 2b). In other words, we discover our love for God's children by actually getting out there and doing what God has commanded.

Either way, it comes out much the same. Loving and doing are bound together, both in our relationship with God and our relationship with others. In Greek, verse 2 speaks of "doing" the commandments and verse 3 talks of "keeping" them. The NRSV translates both verbs "obey," thereby blurring the author's aim to show that interior decisions ("keeping") must become exterior expressions ("doing") if belief is to be genuine. Earlier (2:6) the author showed this by using the verb "to walk," indicating that believing is not simply inner illumination but, instead, leads to a pattern of behavior.

The second positive image for the relationship between belief and action is borrowed from the battlefield: the victorious conqueror. The author has been discussing the relationship between God's love and ours, and now, with verses 4–5, we see that this love is tied to the specific belief that God has sent the Son as the liberator and as an agent of salvation. Jesus is the risen Christ who now subjugates all cosmic powers, freeing people who trust in Christ. "Who is it that conquers the world?" the author asks (5:5a). Obviously, it is Christ who conquers, but it is also "the one who believes that Jesus is the Son of God" (v. 5b).

This victory is broader than just the company of believers. "Whatever is born of God conquers the world" (v. 4a). The noun here is neuter rather than the masculine (i.e., "everything," not "everyone"), stressing the comprehensiveness of Christ's victory in creation and over the cosmos. To believe, then, is far more encompassing than holding on to an idea. It is rather understood as trust in and visible commitment to Jesus as the Son of God, that is, living one's whole life by the claim that Christ has overcome the world.

This is underscored by the three different perspectives that 1 John brings to the concept of "victory" (*nikaō*), of conquering. First, 1 John employs "victory" in a way that is shared elsewhere in the New Testament (see Eph. 4:5, 13; 6:23; Col. 1:23; as well as 1 Tim. 1:2; 3:9; 4:1), namely, as the great eschatological conquest, won by the atoning, salvific death of Christ (2:13–14; 4:4), in which Christ fills up the cosmos and becomes all in all. This is the "victory [*nikē*] that conquers the world, our faith" (5:4). The use of the noun "faith" (*pistis*) here—rather than the verb "to believe" (*pisteuō*)—is atypical in the Johannine material; the noun is found

only here in that literature. Faith now takes on the same meaning as *the* gospel story, the cry of victory that arises from the battlefield.

The second way 1 John uses the concept of victory is as a fundamental truth claim that guides the actions of the community. Verses 4 and 5 speak of a completed act that overcomes the world. The world is passing away (2:8, 17), and it is this knowledge that governs how the community lives out its life in the world. Despite appearances to the contrary, the world's forces for division and hate are not all-powerful. Indeed, they have been incapacitated through the overcoming of death in God's raising of Jesus. The powers of this world may appear to be in charge, but they are actually a defeated force—hence, the emphasis on "all" in verse 1 ("everyone" NRSV) and "everything" in verse 4 ("whatever"), anticipating the eschatological moment when God's redemption reveals the "all" spoken of in 3:1–3 (see also 5:11).

The third way "victory" is expressed has to do with the means of conquest, specifically the water, the blood, and the Spirit (vv. 6–7). The confession in verse 5 that believers are conquerors leads to a series of two declarations concerning how that victory took place. It took place, first, "by water and blood" (v. 6). The meaning of this is ambiguous and has been taken to mean (1) the physical realities connected with human birth, (2) the sacraments of baptism and Eucharist, and (3) Jesus' own baptism and death, among others. The third of these seems most likely, given the author's insistence that confession of Jesus as the Christ must involve confessing Jesus' full humanity (see also John 19:34–35). The fully human Jesus experiences all that humanity involves, from birth to death, and this involvement in humanity is the means by which the victory of Christ occurs. Second, the victory happens through the testimony of the Spirit: "the Spirit is the one that testifies, for the Spirit is the truth" (v. 6). The Spirit's testimony is that "God gave us eternal life, and this life is in his Son" (5:11), and because believers have this "testimony in their hearts" (v. 10), they are bold conquerors.

STEVEN J. KRAFTCHICK

Commentary 2: Connecting the Reading with the World

Believing is perhaps the most significant theme in the Johannine literature. The Greek verb *pisteuō* appears eight different times in this short letter, and almost ninety times in John's Gospel. Compare this to seven times in Matthew, fifteen in Mark, and nine in Luke. Acts comes a bit closer with sixty-four. Even when including the noun form, *pistis* ("faith" or "belief"), fewer than twenty occurrences appear in each of the Synoptic Gospels and Acts. Here in 1 John 5:4, we find the only occurrence of the word *pistis* in 1 John, a noun that never appears in John's Gospel. For John, one does not *have* faith. Rather, one believes. It is something that you do, a muscle that you exercise. John cannot conceive of disembodied, inactive "faith." Demanding action, John's Gospel and letters call readers to believe.

First John says that believing is the key to being "born of God." In the ancient world, many works of literature focused on one single hero followed a set of rhetorical topics to outline the hero's life. These are called *encomiastic topics*, or topics for a speech of praise, and included the hero's origin, training, noble deeds, and noble death. John's story of Jesus corresponds to this pattern. Particularly interesting for the connection to 1 John is the topic of origin. Rather than a birth story or discussion of Jesus' ancestry (as we see in the Gospels of Matthew and Luke), John presents Jesus as the Word who was with God in the beginning, even before the creation of the world. The Word who was with God in the beginning gives those who believe in him the power "to become children of God." Though these believers come from different earthly and physical family lines, the Fourth Gospel introduces a new family "not of blood or of the will of the flesh or of the will of man, but of God" (John 1:13), and a new birth, from above (John 3:3, 7) or "of the Spirit" (John 3:5). As Jesus is the "Son of God" (John 1:34, 49; 3:18; 11:4,

27; 19:7; 20:31), those who believe become children of God (John 1:12; see 14:1–2; 20:17).

This family theme is also present in the letters, where readers are reminded that they are children of God, born of God (1 John 2:29; 3:1, 10; 4:4; 5:2, 19). Believing is the means by which Jesus' followers are brought into this divine family. Believing brings humans into unity with God, and enables humans to join Jesus' work in completing God's mission.[1] In the Gospel, Jesus is asked an important question, "What must we do to perform the works of God?" (John 6:28). The answer? Believe. "Believe in him whom God has sent," Jesus says (John 6:29). John's prologue revealed that Jesus' work in the world was to lead the way to God, to show the world the God they had not been able to see—a mission that was possible only because of Jesus' complex and mystical unity with God (John 1:18).[2] Before his ascension, Jesus tells the disciples, "As the Father has sent me, so I send you" (John 20:21). Now those who follow Jesus are called to fulfill the mission to show the world the God they would not otherwise be able to see. First John 4:12 echoes John 1:18, and the comparison shows the connection between Jesus' mission and our own:

> No one has ever seen God. It is God the only Son, who is close to the Father's heart, who has made God known. (John 1:18)

> No one has ever seen God; if we love one another, God lives in us, and God's love is perfected in us. (1 John 4:12)

In order to fulfill God's mission of love for the world, in order to make God's love perfect, the children of God must love.

If there is another contender for the most significant theme in the Johannine literature, it is love. It appears thirty-nine times in the

---

1. Karl Weyer-Menkhoff, "The Response of Jesus: Ethics in John by Considering Scripture as Work of God," in *Rethinking the Ethics of John: Implicit Ethics in the Johannine Writings*, Wissenschaftliche Untersuchungen zum Neuen Testament 291 (Tübingen: Mohr Siebeck, 2012), 164.

2. Definitions of *exēgeomai* in Henry George Liddell, Robert Scott, and Henry Stuart Jones, *A Greek-English Lexicon*, 9th ed. (Oxford: Clarendon, 1996), 593, include "to lead," "to show the way to," "to expound," "to tell at length, relate in full." There are various interpretations for the complex phrase *monogenēs theos*. However it is interpreted, this description emphasizes Jesus' unity with God as the reason he could be the revealer of God. See Rudolf Bultmann, *The Gospel of John: A Commentary*, trans. George R. Beasley-Murray (Philadelphia: Westminster, 1971), 81–83; Frederick Dale Bruner, *The Gospel of John: A Commentary* (Grand Rapids: Eerdmans, 2012), 40–41.

Gospel. In 1 John, it could hardly be more emphasized, appearing twenty-six times in just five short chapters. It seems as if believing is the first step, and love is the follow-through (3:23). First John makes clear that without love, one cannot claim to know God (2:5; 4:7–8) or to be "in the light" (2:10). God's love is the basis for being included in God's children (3:1; 4:7), but it is love for others that proves one to be a child of God (3:10). If one does not love others in tangible and sacrificial ways, they cannot claim to love God (3:16–18; 4:20–21). The command to love is the ultimate command, from Jesus to his disciples and in the early Christian community (3:11). Love is an indication that one truly has abundant life.

James Baldwin, an activist and author, wrote this reflection on the intersection of his Christian faith tradition and pressing social issues: "It is for this reason that love is so desperately sought and so cunningly avoided. Love takes off the masks that we fear we cannot live without and know we cannot live within."[3] In the context of 1 John, the community is experiencing division; one group is claiming the exclusive rights to religious authority, and there are battles over important points of doctrine. Rather than providing a list of criteria for authority or setting the doctrine straight, the author of 1 John perhaps surprisingly but quite clearly calls the community simply to love. Sometimes in the midst of conflict, we tend to reach for masks of certainty or authority or power. Love calls us to real vulnerability, even in the midst of conflict.

James Baldwin knew his share of oppression. He was a gay black man in the United States who lived and wrote before and during the civil rights era. Despite his own social location and the harm that he experienced because of hatred and bigotry, he saw love as intricately woven into the fabric of faith. "What was the point," he asked, "the purpose, of *my* salvation if it did not permit me to behave with love toward others, no matter how they behaved toward me?" He speaks of love "not merely in the personal sense but as a state of being, or a state of grace." This difficult call is nonetheless possible, because in believing we are initiated into a unity with God's mission for the world, given a new identity as children of God, and empowered by God's Spirit. Love is not only what we have to do. It is how we do it. We love because God first loved us.

LINDSEY S. JODREY

---

3. This quote and the excerpts below are from James Baldwin, "A Letter from a Region in My Mind," *New Yorker*, November 17, 1962, 59–144.

John 15:9–17

[9]"As the Father has loved me, so I have loved you; abide in my love. [10]If you keep my commandments, you will abide in my love, just as I have kept my Father's commandments and abide in his love. [11]I have said these things to you so that my joy may be in you, and that your joy may be complete.

[12]"This is my commandment, that you love one another as I have loved you. [13]No one has greater love than this, to lay down one's life for one's friends. [14]You are my friends if you do what I command you. [15]I do not call you servants any longer, because the servant does not know what the master is doing; but I have called you friends, because I have made known to you everything that I have heard from my Father. [16]You did not choose me but I chose you. And I appointed you to go and bear fruit, fruit that will last, so that the Father will give you whatever you ask him in my name. [17]I am giving you these commands so that you may love one another."

Commentary 1: Connecting the Reading with Scripture

Scholars have identified John 13–20:31 as the Book of Glory. This section of John is characterized by a slowing down of the Gospel's momentum, and the careful and lengthy reporting of all the events and discourses that Jesus shares with his disciples on their final evening together (John 13–17). In this section John draws together the theme of love (in the love command of 13:34, repeated in 15:12 and 15:17) into the theme of Jesus' bringing to perfection the task given to him by the Father (especially in the account of the footwashing and the gifts of the piece of bread in John 13) in the double use of the commandment to love (15:12–17 and in the words of v. 17) comprising both a legacy and a last will and testament. The love theme and love words also appear as dialogues among Jesus and his disciples in John 14:15 and 16:26–27. John's Jesus acts out a demonstration of love in John 13 and speaks of it again in John 15.

John 15:12–17 completely determines our understanding of the love command in this part of the Gospel. In the prayer of John 17, love is at the heart of Jesus' final evening with his disciples. If so much space is given to this account of the final evening of Jesus and the disciples, it is clearly significant for the author of John's Gospel. At the very center of John's account of Jesus' final evening with his disciples is the love command, including the stipulation that disciples are no longer Jesus' servants or slaves but friends, and he has chosen them so that they might love one another as he has loved them. Explicit language of love and friendship increases in the second half of the Gospel, after Jesus' public ministry is over and when he turns to address his teaching to the community of the beloved disciples.

John 15:10 records Jesus' instruction to the disciples: "if you keep my commandments, you will abide in my love, just as I have kept my Father's commandments and abide in his love." What are these commandments that disciples must keep in order to abide in God's love? The heart of the discourse, 15:12–17, provides the answer. In John 13:1–7, Jesus has already shown his love in the footwashing. He now tells them of the need for their response to that love, built on his prior love for them. Disciples are enjoined to exercise this charge while Jesus is still with them. The disciples are to love one another with a love that is continuous and unconditional. In order to show this, the love commandment is expressed in the present tense.

A crucial element of Jesus' teaching is the frequent use of the Greek verb *menō*, as in

John 15:1–10. Here, the disciples are to keep the Father's commandments in order to abide (*menō*) in the love with Jesus and fullness of joy. Abiding is a distinctive description of enduring fellowship and mystical union between God and Jesus, and between and among God, Jesus, and the disciples.

In Greek, John 15:10 takes the form of a conditional sentence in the third class, denoting a more probable future condition; that is, "if you keep my commandments," Jesus says, then it is assured that "you will abide in my love." Jesus clarifies what this one commandment entails: love of one another. First stated in 13:34, the command is a repetition and clarification of 13:34 by the addition of 15:13: "No one has greater love than this, to lay down one's life for one's friends." Jesus' love models sacrifice of life itself for friends as a description of Jesus' disciples. In John's circle we do not see different offices allocated to disciples, such as those of apostle, leader, deacon, or elder. The term *philoi*, friends, in the Hellenistic world at the time of Jesus and Paul describes court counselors to leaders like Alexander the Great and kings like Darius. John 19:12 recognizes this usage.

Some years ago, Wayne Meeks made a strong case that the Gospel of John has no value for moral formation.[1] John, he argued, offers no explicit moral instruction and limits the command to love to showing love for friends, namely, those in the circle of John's followers. The Gospel includes no models for human behavior, and finally, the discourses of Jesus in which the love injunction is located are couched in mystical rather than rational language, which cannot be taken as the basis for ethics.

Responses since then have argued that John's narrative form does in fact provide critical reflection on behavior. Through characters in the Gospel and words of instruction, certain forms of belief and action are commended. Taking the role of a slave, Jesus washes the disciples' feet and indicates to the disciples that this is an example for them to imitate (13:15). If Jesus is the good shepherd, he also entrusts responsibility for shepherding to someone else (21:15–19). Jesus'

command to "love one another as I have loved you" is crucial to this discussion. Rather than understand that this imperative creates boundaries within the Johannine community, interpreters have proposed that while the command focuses on the community, it stresses that such love is also an external orientation, since it is integral to Johannine witness to the world. This argument relies on acceptance of the premise that for John, the world has become in the course of the gospel alienated from God, and yet it remains the object of divine love (3:16).

Jesus conveys love through actions meant as examples for the disciples. Jesus washed the feet of all the disciples, including those of the betrayer Judas. This action intimates that acts of love are to be extended to one's enemies, thus breaking down the distinction between those in John's community and those in the world. The addition of 15:13 to verse 12 makes it clear that the disciples as Jesus' friends are expected to do what Jesus commands them. As friends and not slaves, the disciples are in some sense equal to Jesus. In the end, love is only one factor in shaping human actions. Jesus' love for Lazarus shows God's love for the world and God's desire for life. By extension, Jesus' followers will also seek to bring life and love to the world through concrete actions.

We must note, in regard to love, that anti-Judaism in the Fourth Gospel reaches to the core of John's proclamation and is intrinsically oppressive rather than revelatory. Repeated use of the description "the Jews (or Judeans)" is not later redaction of the words of Jesus to be regarded as unacceptable from a Christian point of view. Nor can one excise them from the Gospel to save the healthy core of the message. Yet it is true that Scriptures themselves are not the only place or the end of divine revelation. The author of John was a sinful human being. Nor can the Gospel be reduced to its anti-Jewish elements. It projects an alternative world of all-inclusive love and life that transcends its anti-Judaism, and this world of the text rather than the world of the author is a witness to divine revelation.

DEIRDRE GOOD

1. Wayne A. Meeks, *The Moral World of the First Christians* (Philadelphia: Westminster, 1986), 109.

Commentary 2: Connecting the Reading with the World

"The brightest and best" was the phrase that sent shivers down my spine. I was attending a workshop on youth ministry, and the presenter was talking about the best strategies to grow our youth group. He said, "First, you go for the brightest and best. You look for the athletes, the cheerleaders, the student government leaders, the most popular and the best-looking kids—the kids everyone wants to be like. You go after them and get them to join your youth group, and then all the kids who want to be like them, which, to be honest, is pretty much everybody else—they will join too."[2] He was serious.

There is nothing about the brightest and best in this reading. There is everything about love. It sounds both simple and incredibly profound. Everything about being followers of Jesus Christ has to do with love. Love is the motivation for everything. God's love for Jesus is what motivates Jesus to love us. If we are obedient to what Jesus has commanded, then we abide in his love, just as Jesus has been obedient, doing what God commanded, and abides in God's love. Then, to be clear, Jesus tells us what the commandment is. He speaks about his commandment as if there is no other. Love others as Jesus has loved us. Then he tells us what this love looks like. This love is sacrificial. This love causes Jesus to give his life for us.

Jesus' strategy is contrary to the strategy to get "the brightest and best" first, because everyone else will follow. Jesus' strategy is different. Love! Love as I have loved you. Love so much that you would lay your life down for others.

Remind your hearers that Jesus is speaking to his followers; in that same way, we who are his church are hearing his words to us. We are to be characterized by how we love one another. That is what builds the community. That is how we embody Christ, not by seeking first "the brightest and best" but by loving one another, no matter who they are, because that is how Jesus loved.

Then, in an extraordinary naming, Jesus says that those who love as he loved are his friends.

Imagine that! To be a friend of Jesus Christ! He is helping his disciples know and understand what will mark this community of believers. We will be friends of Jesus Christ as much as we love one another. In loving one another, our community will be characterized by this love, and we will be friends among friends as well. What is striking in this community is the lack of distinctiveness. The passage avoids any naming of gifts, so common in Paul's descriptions of the community of believers. There is no hierarchy here. The only true measure of a Christian community is to love as Jesus loved, and all are equally accountable to this one standard. The distinctiveness that marks this community is how it loves, not who its members are or what they bring to the community itself. There is only one calling, and that is to love one another, so that the community bears lasting fruit. This image of lasting fruit alludes to the fact that loving as Jesus loved is neither fleeting nor episodic. Loving as Jesus loved is both sustaining and enduring.

The danger in this passage is to view Jesus' call to love one another as insular and focused only on the community. Even the final verses in this reading could be read this way. Is the bearing of fruit only for the community? An easily overlooked message is Jesus' call to go and bear fruit. This going moves the community to love beyond itself. It is also worthy to note that when communities love, truly love, they are attractive.

The situational television comedy *Friends* ran for ten years and during nearly all of its seasons was the most-watched television show, especially among American youth and young adults. The show about six twentysomething young adults struggling to survive in Manhattan remained popular because, time and again, young people said they wished they were part of a group of people who loved one another as they did. The Christian community that spends time with one another, listens to one another, shares with one another, and walks with one another is compelling and attractive, because it embodies exactly what Christ is calling us to.

2. Kyle Tauber, "Doing Contact Work to Grow Your Youth Group" (workshop, Youth Specialties National Conference, Cincinnati, OH, June 1998).

Connect this reading with the world by helping the church know and understand what it means to love one another as Christ loved us. Help the church see that just as Christ transgressed the deeply stratified social-class boundaries of his day, we who follow Christ are called to do the same. Further, help the church to understand that we do this, not for our own self-preservation, but because the ethics of our faith call us to do what is right and just.

I was speaking at a youth conference, and after my talk, one earnest young man came up to me and said, "You really believe all this stuff, don't you?" When I told him I did, he asked, "But what if you are wrong?" I smiled and paused, then replied, "If I am wrong, then I am assured that I am in great company. Because in the church, I have met some of the finest people I will ever know."

With all of our faults and foibles and shortcomings, we are still the church, Christ's body here on earth. In the moments when we are at our Holy-Spirit-enabled best, we shine like no other.

Last Easter, a thirty-seven-year-old man and his wife and their three boys visited church. They had not been in church in years. The father had recently been diagnosed with an aggressive brain cancer, and he was going through chemo and radiation therapy. They started coming regularly. Then six weeks later his health went from bad to worse. The family called the pastor and asked if he could come see them. When he arrived, he was shocked to see the man's condition. It was clear he was dying. They asked if they could join the church; the pastor called for an elder, and together in their home they welcomed the family into the church. The next week, the man died.

They set the funeral for the following Sunday afternoon. The pastor asked the congregation to attend. He told the story of the family and said that even if the congregation did not know them, they were part of them and to please come support the family. At the service, the sanctuary was packed, with standing room only. When the family entered the crowded sanctuary, they were surprised to see so many people. When the pastor stood up to begin the service of witness to the resurrection, he told the young widow and three boys that they were part of the family of God, and this is how families love one another.

Preachers will do well to recall for the congregation times when the church has truly been the church. Being the church takes us beyond our walls, loving all. The central mark of the church is how it loves. When the church loves as Christ loved, then fruit is borne that is lasting, even beyond the walls and the life of the church itself, all for the glory of God.

RODGER Y. NISHIOKA

Ascension of the Lord

Acts 1:1–11
Psalm 47 or Psalm 93

Ephesians 1:15–23
Luke 24:44–53

Acts 1:1–11

¹In the first book, Theophilus, I wrote about all that Jesus did and taught from the beginning ²until the day when he was taken up to heaven, after giving instructions through the Holy Spirit to the apostles whom he had chosen. ³After his suffering he presented himself alive to them by many convincing proofs, appearing to them during forty days and speaking about the kingdom of God. ⁴While staying with them, he ordered them not to leave Jerusalem, but to wait there for the promise of the Father. "This," he said, "is what you have heard from me; ⁵for John baptized with water, but you will be baptized with the Holy Spirit not many days from now."

⁶So when they had come together, they asked him, "Lord, is this the time when you will restore the kingdom to Israel?" ⁷He replied, "It is not for you to know the times or periods that the Father has set by his own authority. ⁸But you will receive power when the Holy Spirit has come upon you; and you will be my witnesses in Jerusalem, in all Judea and Samaria, and to the ends of the earth." ⁹When he had said this, as they were watching, he was lifted up, and a cloud took him out of their sight. ¹⁰While he was going and they were gazing up toward heaven, suddenly two men in white robes stood by them. ¹¹They said, "Men of Galilee, why do you stand looking up toward heaven? This Jesus, who has been taken up from you into heaven, will come in the same way as you saw him go into heaven."

Commentary 1: Connecting the Reading with Scripture

Ascension Sunday presents the preacher with the challenge of making sense of an event far removed from our cultural experience—Jesus' ascent into heaven. These eleven verses restate the close of Luke's Gospel (Luke 24:36–53). They offer the preacher at least four explanations for the significance of Jesus' ascension.

The repetition of material from the last chapter of Luke's Gospel suggests more than a literary connection between Luke and Acts. It suggests the need to address some issues troubling those addressed by Luke–Acts. The preacher might use these explanations to address the circumstances of congregants who live in between the time of Jesus' ascension and return.

Significant to this ascension story is that it accounts for the absence of Jesus. The Gospel rightly makes much of Jesus' resurrection. Luke's resurrection narrative (Luke 24) is much longer than those of Matthew and Mark. Jesus has overcome the worst that Roman power could do. Rome was not able to keep him dead, but despite Luke's accounts of the risen Jesus appearing to disciples, he is no longer around.

Where is Jesus? Why is he not bodily present? The preacher's attention to Jesus' absence will resonate with some hearers who struggle to know divine presence.

In the ancient world, accounts of ascension into the heavens—and its variation of postmortem apotheosis—involved powerful, prestigious, and divinely blessed men. These men included Rome's founder Romulus, Julius Caesar, emperors like Augustus and Titus, and Jewish figures Enoch and Elijah. The understanding was that powerful men were translated into the heavens and the realm of the gods. This act reflected and revealed the person's special standing with the gods and the gods' acclaim for his outstanding achievements. Jesus' ascension associates him with such figures and God's sanction.

Verses 1–4 refer to some of the great things Jesus accomplished as God's representative: healings and feedings, teaching, choosing apostles, suffering, being raised and appearing to his followers with proofs and teachings, and eating with disciples. The reference in verse 2 to Jesus' being "taken up to heaven" recognizes these accomplishments and shows his special standing as approved by God as God's agent (Luke 1:32–33; 4:18–19).

Verse 1 also indicates that Jesus is not on vacation. We can translate verse 1: "all that Jesus *began to* do and teach." What Jesus did in his ministry was only the beginning, and it is not finished. Jesus is still at work, even though he is not physically present.

The sermon can provide hearers with reassurance of Jesus' ongoing work in their lives, in the church, and in the world. It can also encourage hearers to look for such signs of Jesus' presence in continuing actions and teachings. The passage assures that he has not abandoned us to despair and disappointment, nor is he absent from us.

A second explanation for the significance of Jesus' ascension addresses another question a sermon might engage: how is Jesus continuing what he began to do and teach? Jesus ascends to God to send the Holy Spirit to his followers. Jesus declares this plan in Luke 24:49. In Acts 1:4 he repeats the instruction to wait in Jerusalem for the Spirit. In verse 8, he tells them that the Spirit will empower them to be witnesses to him.

Jesus' postresurrection bodily presence with the disciples limits his ability to be present with them. His departure to be with God means he can send the Spirit to be present with every disciple. In Acts 2:33, Jesus is "exalted at the right hand of God," from whom he has received the Spirit. The exalted Jesus "pours out" the Spirit "that you both see and hear" at Pentecost. The preacher might remind congregants that Jesus continues his work and teaching through the Spirit and the Spirit-endowed community of believers, the church.

The preacher can develop a third explanation for the significance of Jesus' ascension, namely, the purpose of the ascended Jesus'

sending the Spirit to believers. Verse 4 calls the Spirit "the promise of the Father." So the events of Pentecost are a sign of God's faithfulness and reliability in keeping God's word (Acts 2). The Spirit also empowers disciples for mission, enabling believers to bear witness to Jesus and to God's workings and purposes for good life for all (1:8).

The sermon can pose questions and provide pointers concerning the church's mission. The locations named in verse 8—Jerusalem, Judea, Samaria, the ends of the earth—provide an agenda for the ever-expanding mission of the church throughout Acts (chaps. 1–7; 8–12; 13–28). That pattern of expansion provokes the contemporary church to consider its circles of mission. The preacher might lead the congregation in recognizing that we do not exist for ourselves, in identifying current mission work, in inviting participation in those programs, and in challenging hearers to expand mission work at both personal and community levels.

Another of the lections assigned for today develops this emphasis on the Spirit's role in equipping believers for mission. The writer of Ephesians prays that God "may give you a spirit of wisdom and revelation as you come to know him" (Eph. 1:17–18). This knowledge and understanding are not inconsequential or static. They lead to knowing or experiencing the "working of his great power" that raised and exalted Christ to reign over "all rule and authority and power and dominion" (Eph. 1:19–21). The preacher can elaborate on the mission of the church as participating in and actualizing that victory over all in our world that is contrary to God's good and life-giving purposes.

The sermon might also attend to a fourth significance of Jesus' ascension. Jesus' ascension to be with God is his current dwelling until he returns to establish God's purposes in their fullness. In verse 6 the disciples ask Jesus if he will at this time "restore the kingdom to Israel." The question reflects a prophetic and apocalyptic expectation, centered on Israel, concerning the establishment of God's reign over the nations. Psalm 47, assigned for this day, also celebrates God's reign over all nations. This reign is not spiritual or an inner reality alone. It is also societal and political. Its full establishment is the end of Rome's empire even as it reinscribes imperial universal rule. Jesus deflects the question about timing by appealing to God's exclusive knowledge (Acts 1:7). Then he commissions his disciples to mission empowered by the Spirit (v. 8).

Immediately Jesus is taken up toward heaven; clouds commonly symbolize divine presence and power. This is a sacred moment. His ascent is watched by the disciples (vv. 9–10a). Two men/angels appear and rebuke them for staring into heaven. They announce that Jesus "will come in the same way as you saw him go into heaven" (v. 11). The importance of the angels' rebuke and announcement is to link Jesus' ascension with his future return as the Son of Man to complete God's purposes. This figure, described in Daniel 7, establishes God's dominion over all people and nations.

The preacher can develop implications of the rebuke and time frame. The church exists "in between" Jesus' ascension and his return. It is empowered by the Spirit, derived from Jesus' ascension, and turned toward his return, when Jesus establishes God's reign in its fullness. In this in-between time of hope and anticipation, Jesus' followers are not to be passively staring into heaven but undertaking the mission committed to them. Empowered by the Spirit, our mission is to make known God's good, gracious, and just purposes for all people. The preacher can challenge us to specific actions that engage this mission.

WARREN CARTER

Commentary 2: Connecting the Reading with the World

In the opening passages of Acts, its author is interpreting the church's transitions—from Jesus' first followers, to the Jewish Christians gathered in Jerusalem, to a Gentile church—as the fiery outpouring of the Spirit. These transitions are initiated by the resurrection of Jesus, but what is unleashed is a power that moves far beyond the historical Jesus. Institutional Christianity has tended to be leery of the Spirit or to imagine it enjoys sole possession of the Spirit. However, the Spirit does not belong to us. She invites us to belong to her; to share her work for healing, justice, and beauty all through the wide world. The promise of the Spirit is that God will be ever-responsive to the challenges and possibilities the world offers.

In her book *Dancing with God,* Karen Baker-Fletcher describes this as "dancing with God," the holy perichoresis that is a "liberative dance in a world of crucifixion . . . . [This dance] courageously changes its movement and style in liberative response to ever-shifting challenges of oppression. It is a dance of life. It defies the dance of the walking dead."[1] The book of Acts pictures the Spirit as walking abroad, inviting Christians into the power of her creativity, zest, and courage.

The promise of the Spirit comes after the heartbreaking departure of Jesus. The ascension celebrates our confidence that the life of Jesus did not end in inglorious agony but in vindication. What was most desecrated is now most honored. This is the sacred seed of our faith. Jesus' glorification promises us that divine goodness will transform suffering and defeat. The ascension is also the acknowledgment that Jesus no longer dwells among those who love him. He will no longer be here to teach, empower, and guide. We know him as an absence and love him like a woman who pines for a lover who has sailed to a far and distant land, from whom no love letters are expected to come.

In his last teaching, Jesus leaves followers with obscure clues concerning what the dance with the Spirit might look like. His followers ask hopefully whether the "promise of the Father" means that the kingdom of Israel will be restored. Does the resurrection augur an end to the nightmare of Rome's violence and injustice? Will the longheld dream of a peaceable kingdom be fulfilled? Jesus disabuses them of this hope, saying that it is not for us to know the Father's timetable. In promising the coming of

1. Karen Baker-Fletcher, *Dancing with God: The Trinity from a Womanist Perspective* (Danvers, MA: Chalice Press, 2006), 48.

the Spirit, he suggests that they will be empowered to live out a countervision within the world as it is. Leaving them with no more than this unsettling promise, "a cloud takes him" and he is gone.

Jesus sounds a bit like Mrs. Whatsit in *A Wrinkle in Time*, who prepares Meg for her struggle against evil by giving her only the gift of her faults. Like Mrs. Whatsit, Jesus has no illusions about historical evil. He does not offer a fantasy in which tyrannical powers or embedded oppressions are extinguished. He does not promise the apostles that they will not make mistakes—even terrible, shocking ones. Paul's zealous ministry will splinter the church, contributing to catastrophic enmity between Jews and Christians. The loyal women who followed Jesus, suffered with him, provided for him, and consoled him will be forgotten or recast as penitent prostitutes. The "absence" of women disciples has relegated women to perpetual silence. Gender diversity still registers in many denominations as subhuman and anti-Christian. If we are disappointed in the church, we might remember that there is little in Jesus' closing words to sustain our hope that the church will embody a divine kingdom.

What Jesus does promise is a baptism of the Spirit. In his absence, a Spirit will come. Pentecost, celebrated two weeks hence, represents a fulfillment of this promise, a picture of what this dramatic baptism meant to the early readers of Luke's story. In this opening passage, we find ourselves between ascension, Pentecost, and the divine kingdom. Indeed, we still find ourselves there. What signs are there that teach us how to dwell in this liminal space here and now, in the light and power of a spiritual baptism? How do we recognize the Spirit at work in the church and in all of creation? What does the dance of the Spirit look like if she is ordained to move about in a church and a history continually resistant to compassion, beauty, equity, adventure?

One outpouring of the Spirit might be the brilliance and power of Lin-Manuel Miranda's musical *Hamilton*, which must almost be seen to be believed. The story is, as the work of Spirit tends to be, multivalent. It is the story of a child born out of wedlock on the scruffy side of town in rough-and-tumble St. Croix. Reared in poverty, orphaned by twelve, he made his way to New York, and through his sheer brilliance, courage, and maniacal hard work, envisioned much of what has become the bedrock of the nation. Miranda tells this story to illuminate the underside of our national history: a story of immigrants and slaves, visionaries and laborers, whose courage and hard work made possible one of history's most extraordinary, if imperfect, experiments in human liberty. "Who lives, who dies, who tells our story."[2]

The Spirit moves in the lives of immigrants, orphans, children of abandoned women, and from them creates beautiful visions of what might be. The Spirit moves in great artists who tell stories that have been hidden and obscure. Through them, she inspires us to take up the dream and reject discouragement or disillusionment. The book of Acts does not encourage us to imagine this work will be easy, unambiguous, or ever completed. The Spirit keeps blowing, She keeps the spark alive.

The Spirit revels also in creation itself: "I am that living and fiery essence of the divine substance that glows in the beauty of the fields. I shine in the water, I burn in the sun and the moon and the stars."[3] This green beauty, the shining water are now traumatized by ecological violence. It is not clear whether or in what form our planet, with its complex ecosystems and thousands of vulnerable species, will survive the predations we inflict upon it. This assault on nature endangers us all; it also defrauds us of the nurture of its beauty. Contemplating climate change, the dance becomes a dirge.

Jesus' ascension is a promise of vindication, but the Spirit resides with us in the continuing crucifixion of life. The Spirit is not merely passive endurance, she is an invitation to live differently, to allow ourselves to be refreshed by the greening around us and to reorder our

---

2. Lin-Manuel Miranda and Jeremy McCarter, *Hamilton the Revolution* (London: Little, Brown, 2016), 280.

3. Hildegard of Bingen, quoted in Umberto Eco, *Art and Beauty in the Middle Ages*, trans. Hugh Bredin (New Haven, CT: Yale University Press, 1986), 47.

lives so that we participate less in the rapaciousness of our society. As Mark I. Wallace states, she invites us to "feel the erotic passion of the Spirit's love for this place and all other places she has made and sustained . . . [to feel] God's greening, earthen presence pulsing through the glassy water, dense foliage, and sheltering animal life."[4] In lament, in action, and in celebration, we feel the movement of the Spirit who dwells with us in the absence and anticipation of the Christ.

WENDY FARLEY

4. Mark I. Wallace, *Finding God in the Singing River* (Minneapolis: Augsburg Fortress, 2005), 155.

Psalm 47

¹Clap your hands, all you peoples;
 shout to God with loud songs of joy.
²For the LORD, the Most High, is awesome,
 a great king over all the earth.
³He subdued peoples under us,
 and nations under our feet.
⁴He chose our heritage for us,
 the pride of Jacob whom he loves.

⁵God has gone up with a shout,
 the LORD with the sound of a trumpet.
⁶Sing praises to God, sing praises;
 sing praises to our King, sing praises.
⁷For God is the king of all the earth;
 sing praises with a psalm.

⁸God is king over the nations;
 God sits on his holy throne.
⁹ The princes of the peoples gather
 as the people of the God of Abraham.
For the shields of the earth belong to God;
 he is highly exalted.

Psalm 93

¹The LORD is king, he is robed in majesty;
 the LORD is robed, he is girded with strength.
He has established the world; it shall never be moved;
 ²your throne is established from of old;
 you are from everlasting.

³The floods have lifted up, O LORD,
 the floods have lifted up their voice;
 the floods lift up their roaring.
⁴More majestic than the thunders of mighty waters,
 more majestic than the waves of the sea,
 majestic on high is the LORD!

⁵Your decrees are very sure;
 holiness befits your house,
 O LORD, forevermore.

Connecting the Psalm with Scripture and Worship

Perhaps the most neglected festival day of the Christian year, at least in contemporary practice, the Ascension of the Lord is closely related to a central doctrine of the Christian faith: the sovereignty of God. The psalms appointed for this day help us to grasp the significance of this unsung celebration and make important contributions to our understanding of God's sovereignty.

Psalms 47 and 93 are among a number of enthronement (or "kingship") psalms; others include Psalms 96–99. Some biblical scholars, notably Sigmund Mowinckel, have asserted that such psalms were used in the worship of ancient Israel at a new year festival commemorating God's triumph over other divine (or demonic) forces. According to this interpretation, these psalms would have been sung as part of a symbolic annual recoronation of the Lord (represented by the person of the human king), including a ceremony of ascent to the throne.[1] Later scholars have suggested that this hypothesis makes too much of parallels to other religious traditions in the ancient world and fails to account for the emphasis on God's eternal sovereignty and covenant loyalty in the Hebrew Scriptures. Regardless of their original ritual application, the theological message of these psalms is unmistakable: "The LORD is king" (Ps. 93:1).

Psalm 47 envisions God's sovereignty through vertical metaphors, the images of ascent to the throne and elevation above the earth. These images support the theory of a cultic commemoration of the Lord's dominion over cosmic forces. However, the psalm also lifts up themes that are specific to Israel's history: the conquest of Canaan (Ps. 47:3), the heritage of Jacob (v. 4), and the children of Abraham (v. 9). As a hymn of victory, Psalm 47 reads like a musical score, beginning with the invitation to "clap your hands" (v. 1), punctuated with a "*selah*" (v. 4), centered around the blast of a trumpet (v. 5), and concluding with a fivefold exhortation to "sing praises," four of which occur in a single verse (vv. 6–7).

Psalm 93 was added to the texts previously assigned to the Ascension of the Lord in the process of amending the 1983 Common Lectionary to form the 1992 Revised Common Lectionary. As a commentary on the lectionary explains: "While Psalm 47 captures themes of the Ascension, Psalm 93 (new to RCL) presents water images that relate to baptism language in the Acts reading, and it has a less vertical cosmology."[2] This decision reflects two recent and ongoing concerns: first, an effort to develop liturgical language that is more consistent with a scientific understanding of the universe, and second, an ecumenical movement for sacramental renewal, particularly with respect to the baptismal identity and mission of Christians.

Indeed, as Psalm 47 resounds with singing, Psalm 93 is saturated with water. Three references to rising rivers (or surging floods) in the central verse (Ps. 93:3) spill over to the following one, where God's threefold majesty is likened to "mighty waters" and the "waves of the sea" (v. 4). In place of the vertical images of lordship, we find other symbols of sovereignty: robe, throne, and palace (vv. 1, 2, 5). With all the water imagery, and without explicit mention of Israel's history (as in Ps. 47), this psalm offers stronger support for the hypothesis of a cultic commemoration of God's victory over other cosmic contenders, represented by the chaotic floods.

As responses to the first reading, Acts 1:1–11, both psalms address the same topic Jesus discussed with his disciples when he was "appearing to them during forty days and speaking about the kingdom of God" (Acts. 1:3). Interestingly, while the psalmists praise the "already" of divine sovereignty, the disciples seem to lament the "not yet": "Lord, is this the time when you will restore the kingdom to Israel?" (v. 6). This is precisely the theological tension set before us by the feast and doctrine of the ascension. Christ has risen to reign, yet we still await the consummation of God's realm of righteousness, justice, and peace. Therefore, with generations of faithful disciples, we watch for the day when Jesus

---

1. Sigmund Mowinckel, *The Psalms in Israel's Worship* (Oxford: Basil Blackwell, 1962; Grand Rapids: Eerdmans, 2004), 121–23.
2. "Consultation on Common Texts," in *The Revised Common Lectionary, 20th Anniversary Annotated Edition* (Minneapolis: Fortress, 2012), 79.

We Whom He Embraces

The great event that we commemorate to-day was no doubt something very different to the disciples at that time from what it is to us. They had hardly recovered from the stunned condition into which His death had thrown them; they had hardly come to realize calmly their pain at His separation from them; at least, they had certainly not yet learned to look at it in the right way, for they regarded it as the ruin of His whole work on earth—when His joyful resurrection took them by surprise, comforting them and setting them right. But now when He was withdrawn from their eyes while they gazed up to heaven, it was more tranquilly and wisely, and certainly with a greatly lightened sorrow, as one looks at the close of a full and completed life, that they regarded the end of the relations in which they had hitherto stood with their beloved Lord and Master. For us, on the contrary, this event stands as the beginning of that relation of Christ to His people which has continued ever since then—the only relation which we know by direct experience. Hence, while we can, it is true, sympathise with the sorrow of the disciples, we cannot feel it directly as our own; and it would be unnatural in us to try to work ourselves up into such a state of feeling, as if we missed something by the personal, visible presence of the Saviour being denied to us. But we may profitably inquire today whether we thoroughly appreciate all the good and beauty of the relation that has subsisted between the Saviour and His people since He ascended from the earth, and enjoy it, as He intended, in all its fulness. The Saviour certainly brought that good very thoroughly into view in the comforting promises that He gave to His disciples as often as He already in spirit saw Himself exalted to the right hand of the Father. If, in a general way, there is little or nothing, even of what Christ said to His disciples in their most intimate intercourse, that might not also be applied to us; if we share with them almost all the privileges that He bestowed on them, as well as all the duties He imposed on them; how much more may we apply to ourselves what He said for the purpose of preparing them for the position which we have in common with them. If we take all the utterances, ever becoming more clear and intelligible, concerning the spirit and manner of His kingdom; the tender outpourings of His glorious love in the presaging sense of His departure; the earnest warnings and exhortations addressed to their hearts not yet fortified against danger;—if we regard all this as said to us also, whom He embraces in the same love, and for whom He prayed, even as for those through whose word we believe; how much more may we claim a share in the elevating promises by which He sought to comfort the disciples for their loss, and to make them fit for their new position.

Friedrich Schleiermacher, "The Parting Promises of the Saviour," in *Selected Sermons of Schleiermacher,* trans. Mary F. Wilson (New York: Funk & Wagnalls, 1890), 423–24.

will come again in glory, "in the same way as you saw him go into heaven" (v. 11).

As suggested above, the vertical imagery of Psalm 47 lifts up the account of Jesus' ascension in Acts 1:9, whereas the water language of Psalm 93 claims the baptismal promise of Acts 1:5. Similar connections may be made with the other readings appointed for this day. Like Psalm 47, the second reading, Ephesians 1:15–23, underscores the elevation of Christ in glory, raised from death to the "heavenly places" (Eph. 1:20), above all other powers and names (Eph. 1:21), with all things under his feet (Eph. 1:22–23). Echoing

Psalm 93, the Gospel reading, Luke 24:44–53, is steeped in baptismal themes—dying and rising with Christ (Luke 24:46), repentance and forgiveness of sin (Luke 24:47), and the gift of the Holy Spirit (Luke 24:49). Furthermore, the images of God's robe (Ps. 93:1) and being "clothed with power" (Luke 24:49) evoke the baptismal garment worn by new believers in the early church.

With this broad array of images and themes in mind, what are we to make of the ascension of the Lord in Christian preaching and worship? How might Psalms 47 and/or 93 illuminate our proclamation and celebration? Liturgical theologian Laurence Hull Stookey provides four possibilities. He identifies the following theological implications of the ascension: (1) the completion of God's saving work through Jesus Christ, (2) the raising up of the whole fallen creation, (3) the embrace of human experience at the very heart of God, and (4) the liberation of the risen Christ from the constraints of time and space.[3]

Consider how the psalms for the day relate to each of these points: (1) both psalms acclaim the eschatological accomplishment of God's mighty acts; (2) Psalm 93 celebrates the lifting up of creation into God's sovereign care; (3) Psalm 47 rejoices in how the beloved people are drawn into God's embrace; and (4) together, the psalms suggest how God's saving work is both incarnate within human, historical experience (Ps. 47) and yet ultimately transcends it (Ps. 93).

Of course, it is rare for congregations to hold services on the sixth Thursday of Easter to commemorate the ascension of the Lord. Some communities instead observe this festival on the following Sunday, the seventh Sunday of Easter. An even better idea would be to contemplate the implications of the ascension over a longer arc of time. Like the doctrine of Christ's resurrection, it is difficult to do justice to the ascension on a single Sunday morning or Thursday night. These theological themes are so critical to the gospel that they can and should be proclaimed throughout the Easter season and at other times of the year.

With the psalmists, we affirm that the Lord is sovereign. With the disciples, we affirm that Jesus is Lord. In Jesus, we have come to know God with us, God among us, God *for* us. This is the uplifting message of the ascension: God's sovereignty is not only *over* humanity and creation; it is—above all—*for* human salvation and the life of the world.

DAVID GAMBRELL

---

3. Laurence Hull Stookey, *Calendar: Christ's Time for the Church* (Nashville: Abingdon, 1996), 65–72.

Ephesians 1:15–23

¹⁵I have heard of your faith in the Lord Jesus and your love toward all the saints, and for this reason ¹⁶I do not cease to give thanks for you as I remember you in my prayers. ¹⁷I pray that the God of our Lord Jesus Christ, the Father of glory, may give you a spirit of wisdom and revelation as you come to know him, ¹⁸so that, with the eyes of your heart enlightened, you may know what is the hope to which he has called you, what are the riches of his glorious inheritance among the saints, ¹⁹and what is the immeasurable greatness of his power for us who believe, according to the working of his great power. ²⁰God put this power to work in Christ when he raised him from the dead and seated him at his right hand in the heavenly places, ²¹far above all rule and authority and power and dominion, and above every name that is named, not only in this age but also in the age to come. ²²And he has put all things under his feet and has made him the head over all things for the church, ²³which is his body, the fullness of him who fills all in all.

Commentary 1: Connecting the Reading with Scripture

The lectionary text from Ephesians 1 is part of Paul's larger prayer, which begins in verse 3.[1] Verses 3–14 offer a blessing to God who has blessed us with "every spiritual gift" (Eph. 1:3). Paul's blessing is effusive and theologically rich. We learn about God's intentions and sovereign choice (vv. 4–5), the manner in which God establishes redemption through Jesus (v. 7), and the long list of benefits for those who have been reconciled with God (vv. 8–12). Throughout, there is a lavish abundance to God's grace and redeeming work in Christ. As indicated by the repetition of a similar phrase three times in this paragraph (vv. 6, 11, 14), the intended result of God's saving work is the "praise of his glory." The frequent invitation to praise God in Psalm 47:1, 6, and 7 mirrors this emphasis in Ephesians 1.

In Ephesians 1:15, Paul focuses his prayer on the Ephesians. While he does not specify how, Paul has heard of the Ephesians' reputation for faith/fulness and love. Without getting into the technical and often fraught debate about the meaning of *pistis* ("faith" or "faithfulness") here and elsewhere in Paul's letters, the fact that Paul has heard about the Ephesians' *pistis* should

inform our understanding of it here. While it may include certain invisible convictions or beliefs about Christ, it is certainly not limited to them. Rather, the Ephesians' *pistis* is active and observable. We can think of this visible *pistis* as a commitment to an identity and way of life rooted in Jesus Christ.

Paul has heard of their love for all the "saints" as well. Paul does not explain what this love consists of, but again we can infer that it is a tangible, observable behavior. Elsewhere in Ephesians, love looks like exercising humility, gentleness, and patience while bearing with one another (4:2); it is a characteristic of Christian speech (4:15); it is the stuff that sustains and builds up the body of Christ (4:16); it mirrors the self-giving love of Christ that takes on flesh whenever Christians give of themselves for the sake of others (5:2). Elsewhere in Paul's letters, love is held up as the most important Christian virtue (1 Cor. 13; Col. 3:14), that which limits Christian freedom (Rom. 14:15; Gal. 5:13), and that toward which Christians should constantly grow (1 Thess. 3:12). The combination of faith/fulness and love, sometimes with the

---

1. Many modern NT scholars doubt the Pauline authorship of Ephesians. For the sake of convenience, I refer to the author of Ephesians as "Paul" in this article.

addition of "hope," serves almost as a shorthand reference for the ideal shape of Christian life together (see, e.g., Gal. 5:6; 1 Thess. 1:3; 3:6; 5:8; Phlm. 5). The Ephesians' reputation leads Paul to unceasing thanksgiving whenever he remembers them in his prayers.

Paul's thankfulness leads to further intercession for the Ephesians. In a long and complicated clause that stretches through verse 19, Paul prays that God would grant the Ephesians an even deeper knowledge of God through a "spirit of wisdom and revelation." The combination of wisdom and revelation occurs only here in Paul's letters. In 1 Corinthians 1–2, Paul speaks frequently of wisdom, especially of the "wisdom of God" (1 Cor. 1:21, 24, 30; 2:7) that stands in contrast to the "wisdom of the world" (1 Cor. 1:20; 2:5–6, 13; 3:19). Wisdom refers to more than the acquisition of knowledge; it speaks to applied knowledge, a way of being in the world, a practical insight that is shaped by the life of Jesus and embodied in the lives of his followers. "Revelation" signifies the uncovering of things previously hidden. Paul can speak both of revelation in reference to God's redeeming action in Christ (Rom. 1:17; Eph. 3:5) and of ongoing revelations of divine insight delivered to himself (Gal. 1:12; 2:2; 2 Cor. 12:1, 7) and to members of the gathered community (1 Cor. 14:6, 26). Taken together, wisdom and revelation underscore the perpetual process of knowing God. There is no end to this searching for, discerning, articulating, and responding to the deep and "inscrutable" wisdom of God.

If "wisdom and revelation" are the means of knowing God more deeply, verses 18–19 outline what Paul hopes the Ephesians will know about God. A set of parallel phrases identifies three things: the hope to which God has called them, the riches of God's glorious inheritance, and the immeasurable greatness of God's power. With hope and calling, Ephesians 1 speaks more clearly to a reality that is only hinted at in Psalm 47. While Psalm 47 initially limits God's choice and promised inheritance to "the pride of Jacob" (Ps. 47:4), the end of the psalm imagines the "princes of the peoples" gathering together as the "people of the God of Abraham" (Ps. 47:9). Ephesians celebrates this reality in

the joining of Gentiles and Jews in the worship of the one God (Eph. 2:11–22).

Paul has the most to say about the third item in the list, power, indicated by the long relative clause that stretches from verse 20 through verse 23. This surpassingly great power of God for believers is the same power activated in God's raising Jesus from the dead, seating him at the right hand, putting all things under his feet, and establishing him as the head of the church. God's resurrection and session of Jesus at God's right hand is fundamental to the early Christian message (Acts 2:22–35; 5:30–31) and axiomatic to much of the New Testament writings (see, e.g., 1 Cor. 15:20–28; Heb. 8:1; 1 Pet. 3:22).

Paul's explanation of God's power evokes the ascension of Jesus. Luke and Acts contain narrative accounts of Jesus' ascension, and the two distinct accounts are included in this week's lectionary readings. Both texts say relatively little about Jesus' ascension. In Luke 24:44–53, Jesus spends time teaching and commissioning the disciples (Luke 24:44–49) before blessing them at Bethany (Luke 24:50). Only a portion of one verse mentions that Jesus "withdrew from them and was carried up into heaven" (24:51). Similarly, Acts 1:3–8 describe Jesus' final conversations with the disciples. Suddenly in verse 9 Jesus is "lifted up" and a cloud takes Jesus out of their sight. Then, in verse 11, two mysterious men direct the disciples' attention *away* from Jesus' ascension: "Why do you stand looking up toward heaven?" Instead of focusing on his ascension, the two messengers direct the disciples' attention to Jesus' promised return.

There is a tension between the men's question, "Why do you stand looking up toward heaven?" and the focus of Ephesians 1:15–23. In many ways, the prayer in Ephesians is a literary and liturgical "looking up" to heaven. Paul seeks to focus the Ephesians' identity and attention on heavenly realities—the purpose of God, the blessings of God, and the rule of Christ. Taken together, the lectionary texts capture the "already" and "not yet" of Christian confession. Ephesians 1 imagines the subjection of all things under the feet of Christ as a present reality, much like the psalmist's view of God's kingship in Psalm 47. Acts redirects our attention to the return of Jesus, when his rule will become a visible, tangible reality on this earth. The lectionary texts beckon us to both praise God for all that has been completed through Christ and yearn deeply for Christ's return.

CHRISTOPHER T. HOLMES

Commentary 2: Connecting the Reading with the World

In the small rural church where my faith was planted and lovingly tended, the Apostles' Creed was a nonnegotiable element in the order of worship. Each Sunday we would rise together and in one voice "say what we believed." As my knowledge of the material world advanced in grade school, those words and I began to struggle a bit.

The sixth article of the tightly parsed Apostles' Creed proclaims Christ's ascension to the right hand of God. It is one-twelfth of the faith, as it were. The problem is that I did not believe it. I still do not—that is, "believe" in the common sense of affirming the literal, historical fact of the account. Since Yuri Gagarin was first to rocket beyond the dome of the sky and behold the vastness of space, we know with demonstrated certainty that God and the ascended Jesus are not there. Ascension made spatial sense in the ancient world, where beyond the dome of the sky that holds the waters of creation at bay, reigned God and the heavenly hosts. It is comforting to think of God so close and the power of God so palpable. Unlike the situation today, in the ancient world the ascension narrative made cosmological sense.

The Ascension of the Lord is the church holy day that I have most often chosen to ignore. The great tradition, however, perceives Christ's ascension to be an essential component of the faith. One can avoid the challenge by not saying the creed —an option often taken by contemporary "liberal" Christians. I am thankful that the tradition tends to find its way, regardless. For example, the most striking architectural features of the last two churches I have served have been dramatically rendered stained-glass "Ascension" windows. Each Sunday for fourteen years, towering over the limp words of my sermon, the light of Christ's ascension fell on the pulpit in spite of me — and of course it was not my pulpit to begin with, but the pulpit of our risen Lord, who is seated at the right hand of God.

If I were to practice what I preach, I would admonish myself that just because I do not believe a thing, my unbelief does not make a thing not true, nor God not still God. Neither am I—as a steward of the tradition—free to ignore an essential part of what has been handed on to me. Ignoring the ascension has been an act of personal unfaithfulness. The creed and tradition are not mine to edit; rather, I have been called to pass on what I have received (1 Cor. 11:2).

Fortunately, the faith is wiser and deeper than I am; it has been tested and searched for thousands of years by sharper minds than mine. There is astonishing grace in this gift. A thing not "believed" may be meaningless at one moment in our lives, but will have peculiar resonance and power in another. I have come to teach doctrines and creeds, then, not as lists of certainties that one must affirm, but rather as mysteries, lines of questioning, places that inspire meaningful conversation and witness.

The Christian faith, from its first breath, is witness that the birth, life, death, resurrection, and ascension of Jesus are God's saving work and reveal, as fully as we can know, the character of God and God's will for us. Moreover, the story of Jesus, contained in Scripture, has essential contours without which the faith would be diminished. As we read Scripture, the Apostles' Creed and other elements of the tradition hold these contours in place. The ascension, according to our ancestors, is one such essential.

We recognize, however, that our ancestors' knowledge of the material world was more limited than our own. Their witness to their encounter with Jesus of Nazareth could be expressed only within the earthen vessels of their hearts and minds, in their thought world, in their moment in time. It is impossible in reading their witness to separate that limitation from what they would want us to see. To compound the challenge of reading, in ancient writing, history, poetry, interpretation, imagination, and rhetoric are intermixed freely in ways that challenge our scientific objective rationality. Perhaps, though, there is a way forward.

We assume (1) that the text's witness and our faith have the same subject: God as made known in Jesus Christ; and (2) that the rendering of Jesus Christ in the text faithfully reveals the nature and will of God as fully as the tradition attests. So, we will allow the text its own world. We will read the text and tradition on their own merits and let our ancestors speak to us and teach us about God. In places like the ascension, their language appears more imaginative to us than historical, but that imagery is a gift of the inspiration of the Holy Spirit. Let us assume by faith that there is something essential in the church's depiction of Christ's ascension, and ask what the ascension tells us about God and our humanity. The epistle lesson appointed for this Sunday is remarkably helpful in this task, because this is exactly what the author does.

These verses are a prayer of thanksgiving and encouragement that the recipients' hearts may be opened to the hope that comes from knowing the great power of God. This power was revealed at work in the resurrection and ascension of Jesus, and this power continues to be present in Christ's church. Presented in the image of Christ's presence at the right hand of God, this power is greater than any earthly power that may assail us. This is a straightforward and compelling interpretation of the gospel. It is hope for the powerless, but power is a tricky thing.

The human tendency is to image this glorified Jesus in our own image and seat ourselves at the right hand of God as well. The result has been the sad wreckage of Christian triumphalism, colonialism, racism, and bigotry. The power we perceive to be Godlike is the power we covet; it is power over, a power to impose our will upon one another. In the deep narrative of Scripture, it is the kind of power our God rejects. In the very beginning of the text, the Bible predicts our behavior in a tower called Babel (Gen. 11:1–9).[2] Babel is an image of the repeated attempt at ascension by the human being seeking Godlike power.

When humanity gives birth to an "ism," we put one particular image of ourselves in the heavens and rank everything lower as lesser. Colonial racism puts the white male at the top; rationalism puts reason alone at the summit, fundamentalism certainty; homophobia reproductive sex, and so on. Every once in a while, God comes down and throws the whole thing to the ground, which is exactly where we are supposed to be. This is where the power of God came and comes today, in a face of a poor, childless, middle-aged day worker turned failed rabbi.

This crucified one is the one risen, ascended, and head of the church. The genius of the ascension as an image of the great power of God is that it insists that the power at work in us and in the world is Jesus Christ. A power, as Paul said, made perfect—come to its completion—in a love that loves every creature that has breath.

MARK F. STURGESS

2. Jonathan Sacks, "The Dignity of Difference," in *The Dignity of Difference* (London: Continuum, 2003), chap. 3.

Luke 24:44–53

⁴⁴Then he said to them, "These are my words that I spoke to you while I was still with you—that everything written about me in the law of Moses, the prophets, and the psalms must be fulfilled." ⁴⁵Then he opened their minds to understand the scriptures, ⁴⁶and he said to them, "Thus it is written, that the Messiah is to suffer and to rise from the dead on the third day, ⁴⁷and that repentance and forgiveness of sins is to be proclaimed in his name to all nations, beginning from Jerusalem. ⁴⁸You are witnesses of these things. ⁴⁹And see, I am sending upon you what my Father promised; so stay here in the city until you have been clothed with power from on high."

⁵⁰Then he led them out as far as Bethany, and, lifting up his hands, he blessed them. ⁵¹While he was blessing them, he withdrew from them and was carried up into heaven. ⁵²And they worshiped him, and returned to Jerusalem with great joy; ⁵³and they were continually in the temple blessing God.

Commentary 1: Connecting the Reading with Scripture

This passage depicting the ascension of the resurrected Jesus brings the story of his embodied presence and ministry in Luke to a fitting conclusion and connects it to the story of his ongoing presence and work through the Holy Spirit in Acts.

The resurrection appearance stories that immediately precede this text are focused on the issue of *recognition*. Is it really Jesus who is appearing? In the case of the two disciples he meets on the road to Emmaus, this is a complicated question. Although their hearts "burn" (Luke 24:32) within them as Jesus lays out the case for his suffering and glorification as fulfillment of the Scriptures (vv. 25–27), they nevertheless fail to recognize him until he is revealed to them at last in the act of blessing and breaking bread (vv. 30–31, 35). Later that same night in Jerusalem, recognition is the focus once again. Jesus appears to the eleven and their companions, but this time he is mistaken for a "ghost" (v. 37) until he shows them his "flesh and bones" (v. 39) and eats fish as a sign that it is really him.

In this Sunday's reading, the focus shifts from recognition to *commission*. Now when he interprets Scripture for them, it is not only confirmation that this Jesus must "suffer and rise"

(v. 46), but also a charge that "forgiveness of sins is to be proclaimed in his name" (v. 47). Seeing that it is really Jesus, they are now given a mandate to spread this news and the forgiveness it brings. Both of these aspects are captured in the word "witnesses" (v. 48). They have passively witnessed these things; now they must actively bear witness "to all nations, beginning from Jerusalem" (v. 47).

Interpretations of the resurrection tend to emphasize one of these themes at the expense of the other. Conservative interpreters have gravitated toward *recognition* and focus on the objective reality of the resurrection: "He is risen! It is really him!" At its best, such faith takes seriously the text's insistence that what was happening with Jesus in resurrection came as a shock and a surprise to his followers. The testimony of these stories is that the resurrection of Jesus has an objective quality; it was not merely the self-comforting projection of traumatized minds longing for things to return to the way they were before. Luke testifies that the resurrected Jesus is present to his followers not as a fond memory, but in a challenging new way that confounds (vv. 31–32), and terrifies (v. 37), and delights (v. 41). At its worst, an emphasis on recognition can become a bid for certitude and control that pretends to know too much about a mystery that confounds ordinary human experience. When the objective and the bodily are emphasized exclusively, resurrection is reduced to resuscitation, and we are left with a doctrinal claim about the past and very little to say or do that matters in the present.

Progressive interpretation has emphasized the resurrection as a *commission* to embrace the reign of God and carry on with the agenda of inclusive justice and love that Jesus preached and lived. At its best, such faith takes seriously the text's insistence that what is happening with Jesus in resurrection is experienced subjectively as challenging and transformative. These stories point toward resurrection as a profoundly affecting experience—not just an objective fact that calls for intellectual assent. At its worst, an exclusive emphasis on resurrection as commission may reflect modern embarrassment at the claim that God vindicated Jesus in an extraordinary way. Without the hope of real vindication, the commissioned are powerless in the face of evil and are vulnerable to despair.

The conclusion of Luke's Gospel resists this tendency toward interpretive bifurcation. As noted above, Luke's testimony to resurrection involves the juxtaposition of both kinds of resurrection story, and these accounts are carefully constructed to frustrate oversimplification. The Jesus who is raised bodily with flesh, bones, and an appetite for fish nevertheless appears in their midst in an unusual way that is described as "startling" (v. 37). When the resurrected one insists "These are my words that I spoke to you while I was still with you . . ." (v. 44), we are confronted with a Jesus who is narrated as somehow both present to them as one who speaks and yet not present to them as he was before, when he was "still with" them. Most striking, perhaps, is the contorted construction "disbelieving for joy and wondering" (v. 41)—a phrase that strains at the limits of categories like objectivity and subjectivity.

More importantly, Luke's account of the ascension points toward a paradox that holds recognition and commission, objective reality and subjective experience in productive tension. At first, it may appear that ascension represents a move away from the objective. After all, the ascended Jesus is no longer accessible to them as before, and they are left to carry out a daunting task without access to his embodied presence. Nevertheless, the claim of Luke–Acts is that the very same Jesus they experienced bodily is still very much with them. In fact, the implied argument of this narrative is that Jesus must leave them in order to be truly with them; he ascends to the Father as the precondition of a new and more powerful mode of presence that will make his mission and theirs fully possible. As Luke Johnson has observed, "when Jesus is not among them as another specific body, he is accessible to all as life-giving Spirit."[1]

This becomes clear when we consider that the last word of the embodied Jesus to his followers is that in order to fulfill their commission to the inclusive work of proclamation "to all nations," they must first wait in the city of Jerusalem until the coming of what the Father has promised (v. 49). This promised gift is described somewhat ambiguously in Luke as "power from on high," but when this story is retold in Acts (1:8), this power is none other than the Holy Spirit of the risen one. Throughout the Gospel, Luke has compared Jesus to the prophet Elijah, especially in relation to the ascension. On the mount of transfiguration, Elijah appears and speaks with Jesus "about his departure, which he was about to accomplish at Jerusalem" (9:31). Elijah too, of course, was taken up into heaven (2 Kgs. 2:11), leaving behind "a double share" of his spirit on his disciple and successor—a reality represented by the passing on of an article of literal clothing (2 Kgs. 2:13–14). When Jesus ascends, his Spirit passes with multiplied effect to his followers, whom he describes as "clothed with power from on high" (Luke 24:49).[2]

So, all that Jesus "began to do" (Acts 1:1) when bodily present will come to fruition through his continuing work as a living Spirit. The program of testimony to all nations beginning in Jerusalem (Luke 24:47; Acts 1:8) will be carried out to the letter in the book that describes the Acts

1. Luke Timothy Johnson, *The Gospel of Luke*, Sacra Pagina (Collegeville, MN: Liturgical, 1991), 406.
2. Johnson, *The Gospel of Luke*, 406.

of the Apostles, but more accurately the Acts of the Spirit of the Risen One. In this sense, Jesus is fully recognized as himself only in the fulfillment of the commission to preach forgiveness to all. His resurrection becomes fully objective, perfectly embodied, consummately real in the work of the ones he left with a blessing as he was carried up into heaven (v. 51).

LANCE B. PAPE

Commentary 2: Connecting the Reading with the World

Ascension Day was once one of the great feasts of the church, on par with Christmas, Easter, and Pentecost. To say it has fallen on hard times is to risk understatement. Ask an average parishioner when Ascension is. Ask them *what* it is. This lack of general knowledge is a bonanza for the preacher. Imagine if you got to explain Easter to someone for the first time: their look of disbelief, the saucer-like eyes, the thought dared . . . could this be *true*?

After forty days with his disciples after his resurrection, Jesus gathers for one final Bible study. We look over his shoulder as he reads the entirety of the Law, the Prophets, and the Psalms with reference to himself, his suffering and rising, his forgiveness of sins for all nations. Then he goes. Bodily. Into heaven. As he withdraws, he blesses them (Luke 24:50). No, he blesses us. All of us. God's work in the world is one of blessing. Think of the infinite gentleness of that tiny gesture: hands out, offering blessing. So much faith is so angry. We understand why. The world is so broken.

He rises, broken but repaired, and he calls a people to be broken, repaired, repairing, as he blesses us forward. That gesture of blessing is a good place to begin a sermon. God is not angry—except at the way we hurt ourselves and others. God wants our thriving, our flourishing, the world's mending, everyone's blessing. Anytime the Bible goes out of its way to give us a gesture as tactile and specific as Jesus' hands in these verses, zero in, focus, draw their attention to it: God's pierced palms are raised in blessing.

There has been a general embarrassment about the near-mythical nature of this story. It seems to confirm the three-tiered universe that Rudolf Bultmann made his career railing against, a critique that John Spong popularized in the United States. Is heaven really "up"? Did Jesus actually float up there? Our B-grade sci-fi movies have better special effects than this! However, the story gets at a serious and difficult question: where is Jesus' resurrected body now? The creed professes he is "at the right hand of the Father"—a place of honor, of power. Bultmann famously opined that Christ "rises into the kerygma," that is, into our faith, with no metaphysical implication.

The Protestant reformers knew better. Their debates over the nature of the Eucharist revolved around the physical body of Jesus and its potential availability to us now. Martin Luther took Jesus at his word when he said, "This is my body." He is there, in, with, and under the elements of bread and wine. The "right hand of the Father" means Jesus is everywhere the Father is. He is "even in your pea soup," Luther said. What is different about the Eucharist then? Well, Christ is present everywhere. He is *da* in German, but he's not *der da*, he is not "there *for you*." He promises to be savingly present to those who eat and drink with faith. Luther's younger colleague and frenemy John Calvin disagreed. Jesus' presence "at the right hand of the Father" means he is not bodily available to be in the elements of the Eucharist. Calvin professed to believe in a sort of "spiritual real presence," in which by the power of the Holy Spirit the church is lifted up for a vision of Christ in his heavenly rule. For Calvin, Christ is not in your pea soup, bodily speaking, and he is not in the elements; he is, by the power of the Spirit, *in* the church, which looks forward to his coming again.[3]

---

3. David Steinmetz told this story so often in all his classes at Duke that I cannot specify one. He retells some of the story in "Christ in the Eucharist," in *Taking the Long View: Christian Theology in Historical Perspective* (Oxford: Oxford University Press, 2011), 215–26.

These Reformation debates, which carried on fairly acrimoniously for centuries, show the importance of the body of Jesus, its physical nature, its availability to the church now. We might want to add that Christ promises to be present in his poor in a way more dramatic and provable even than his presence on the altar table (Matt. 25:31–46). Scripture sounds all of these themes. He is absent (ascension). He is present (the Eucharist, the poor). He is coming again (the entirety of the New Testament). This is a moment for the preacher to rear back and wonder, marvel aloud with the congregation. Jesus' body is amazing. It walks through walls, it eats a fish, it offers grace, it floats to heaven, it is on the altar, it is in your neighbor (especially the one you do not like), it is in the next needy person you see, it is in the mirror. Bultmann's and Spong's mistake is to think faith ever meant to be understandable. It is not. It is a mystery. Ask a world enthralled with epic impossible tales like *Star Wars* and *Lord of the Rings* and *Harry Potter* whether it longs for rationalistic tales. No. It longs for true and beautiful ones. We have the truest and most beautiful. Do not critique it. Marvel at it, as the disciples do here. Shane Claiborne says the gospel does its best work not by force but by fascination.

The ascension also has a political element. Rome claimed to be in charge of the world— and its claim was verifiable. Caesar ruled every corner of the world known to the biblical writers. His face was on every coin, his image broadcast in every ancient medium, citizens expected to pinch incense to his genius. You did not need faith in the claim that Caesar was lord—you had proof. Just look around—whose soldiers are those? Whose laws are these? Who can put whomever they want on crosses? By contrast ancient Christians claimed Jesus is Lord. Where is your evidence? Where is his image? Where are his legions or his crosses?

We do not have those. He has ascended into heaven. What do we have? One another, a church, gathered in his name, being made over into his likeness, doing the things he did in the world by his Spirit. The early church had to have faith that Jesus is Lord—and that faith won out over the "proof" that ancient Romans had for Caesar's lordship. The ascension points to Jesus' rule over every power and authority. They are all pretenders and will all fade. The one ascendant this day actually reigns, despite all evidence to the contrary.

It is striking that Jesus recedes from our sight. David Cunningham points out that the ascension leaves us with no Jesus to gaze upon or listen to as the first disciples had.[4] Instead, we have a world to gaze on, listen to, serve, and preach to. Jesus withdraws from our presence, he literally makes space, so the church can be driven out by the Spirit in mission. Jesus' giving way is faithful to the triune nature of God. In the life of the Trinity each person "makes space" for the other, deferring to the other, directing attention to the other. God is no needy God. God makes space—first in the triune life, and then for all creation, us included. A sermon could run far down these tracks of the giving-way God.

JASON BYASSEE

---

4. David S. Cunningham, "Theological Perspective" on Luke 24:44–53 in *Feasting on the Word: Year B, Vol. 2: Lent through Eastertide*, ed. David L. Bartlett and Barbara Brown Taylor (Louisville, KY: Westminster John Knox, 2008), 522. He cites Douglas Farrow and Rowan Williams in this regard.

Seventh Sunday of Easter

Acts 1:15–17, 21–26
Psalm 1

1 John 5:9–13
John 17:6–19

Acts 1:15–17, 21–26

[15]In those days Peter stood up among the believers (together the crowd numbered about one hundred twenty persons) and said, [16]"Friends, the scripture had to be fulfilled, which the Holy Spirit through David foretold concerning Judas, who became a guide for those who arrested Jesus— [17]for he was numbered among us and was allotted his share in this ministry." . . .
     [21]"So one of the men who have accompanied us during all the time that the Lord Jesus went in and out among us, [22]beginning from the baptism of John until the day when he was taken up from us—one of these must become a witness with us to his resurrection." [23]So they proposed two, Joseph called Barsabbas, who was also known as Justus, and Matthias. [24]Then they prayed and said, "Lord, you know everyone's heart. Show us which one of these two you have chosen [25]to take the place in this ministry and apostleship from which Judas turned aside to go to his own place." [26]And they cast lots for them, and the lot fell on Matthias; and he was added to the eleven apostles.

Commentary 1: Connecting the Reading with Scripture

Jesus has told the church to wait for the coming of the Spirit. Between Jesus' ascension and the awaited Pentecost Spirit that will empower the disciples for worldwide mission, what is the church to be about?

The group that witnessed Jesus' ascension returns to Jerusalem as he instructed them to do (Acts 1:4). Verse 14 constructs the gathered group as "united" in "devoting themselves to prayer." The preacher might reference one of the other lections (John 17:11, 21) where Jesus prays to his Father that his followers "may be one, as we are one." The church waits in unity and prayer before the Spirit comes to empower them to mission (Acts 1:8). The preacher might highlight the interaction of prayer and mission as crucial for the church's life.

Now a development occurs (1:15). From this time of prayer comes Peter with a proposal to replace the deceased Judas. The circle of twelve must be completed again as the nucleus of this expression of the people of God. The Twelve

function as the leaders for a group that now numbers some one hundred and twenty persons. The preacher might draw attention to how Luke–Acts opens by offering assurance or security about God's workings among this group (Luke 1:4).

Peter outlines Judas's failings (Acts 1:16). Judas guided those who arrested Jesus; Peter references the scene in Luke 22:47–54. Peter does not repeat the Gospel's claims that attributes motives to Judas. According to Luke 22:3–6, the devil inspired his betrayal, and he was rewarded with money. Another appointed lection, Psalm 1, starkly contrasts the wicked who perish with the righteous who prosper.

Peter underscores the depths of Judas's fall and betrayal. He was "numbered among us," the group of Twelve. He "was allotted his share in this ministry" commissioned by Jesus and comprising exorcizing, healing, preaching, and, in the future, ruling Israel (Acts 1:17). He has "turned aside" from "this ministry and apostleship" (1:25). It is this circle and mission entrusted to him by

Jesus that Judas betrays. He was both apostle and apostate.

Yet Peter makes sense of Judas's death, not his action of betrayal, within the purposes of God. Precision is needed by the preacher at this point. What does Peter claim the Scriptures said concerning Judas? The psalms are not quoted until verse 20, separated from the reference to Judas's betrayal in verse 16. The quotes follow the description of the field Judas has bought and the graphic account of his death. In this sequence, Peter now reads Psalms 69:25 and 109:8 in relation to Judas, particularly his loss of possessions and position.

Judas's life and death—as constructed here by Acts—provide the preacher opportunity to discuss sin and failing in the church. Parts of Acts seem to idealize the early church and provoke some to call for an impossible return to the halcyon days of the early church (2:43–47). This section does not do so. There were no glorious early days. Failure and frailty existed from the outset. Preachers might observe that the one who speaks here about Judas's failure is one who also miserably failed his master (Luke 22:54–62). Scandals and sinfulness among us are not new.

The preacher might reflect on the humanness of this community that God has called into being. It is divinely summoned, entrusted with sacred work, but it is never immune to sinfulness. This inevitability, of course, does not mean turning a blind eye to sin in our midst, as some leaders have done in recent years. Nor does it mean not calling members continually to faithfulness or not holding forth forgiveness. This recognition does mean, though, that there is no room for the church to assume superiority in relation to any sinful and unjust situations. The church goes on its way always being reformed.

Peter's reference to the death of Judas mutes his suicide. "Everyone knows" Judas commits suicide, an act the church has often condemned and thereby has intensified the pain of those who have suffered the suicide of a loved one. The preacher might point out, however, that while Judas clearly commits suicide in Matthew 27:5, it is not so clear that he does so in Acts 1:18. Does "falling headlong" signify an act of self-destruction (jumping from a height), or an accident (or was he pushed)? Muting Judas's

suicide indicates it is not the issue here. The Acts narrative evokes his death because Judas's death creates a problem of math.

Jesus had chosen Judas to be among the inner group of *twelve* male apostles (Luke 6:12–16). The *twelve* men are authorized to undertake a mission of repair that comprises exorcizing, healing, and preaching (Luke 9:1). In the future, Jesus declares, they will sit on thrones and rule over the *twelve* tribes of Israel (Luke 22:28–30). The number *twelve* represents the nucleus of an expression of the people of God.

Judas's death, however, has disrupted the group of twelve. Now there are eleven, listed by name in verse 13. One more is needed to replace Judas.

The narrative, though, exposes a problem of gender. The male apostles are present, but so too are "certain women" who have followed Jesus from Galilee and witnessed his ministry and resurrection (Luke 8:2; 23:49, 55; 24:10–11). While eleven men are named in verse 13, only one woman, Mary, is named in verse 14. When it comes to replacing Judas, the women become invisible. Peter declares that the short list of candidates can be peopled only by "one of the men" who accompanied Jesus (Acts 1:21). The women arbitrarily become ineligible for the group of twelve, even though women meet the criterion of accompanying Jesus in his ministry.

The sermon could invite hearers to reflect on the church's continuing challenges to be an inclusive community in matters of gender, but also in all sorts of other categories of exclusion: social status, ethnicity, national origin, sexual orientation, and so forth. Why in our multicultural global village does difference frighten us so much? In terms of inclusiveness, this community is certainly a work in progress

The section finishes with the selection of Matthias to complete the circle of twelve male apostles (vv. 21–26). There are two candidates, prayer, and the casting of lots. The preacher might foreground the section's attention to the quality of being an eyewitness (1:21–22). On the positive side, being an eyewitness means being a witness to Jesus' activity throughout the time from his baptism to his resurrection and ascension. What is at stake here is continuity and reliability. The Acts narrative continues the work of the Gospel in providing assurance or certainty about God's workings (Luke 1:4). The subsequent narrative will show that responsiveness to the Spirit, itinerancy, and flexibility will also be needed (Acts 1:8). Fundamentally, leaders in the Jesus community are to be grounded in and represent significant experiences in and understandings of Jesus.

Yet the preacher might also reflect on the difficulty of prioritizing this criterion of being a male eyewitness. These verses certainly do not prescribe gender as *the* criterion for choosing contemporary church leaders. The account gives no attention to the character of the two candidates, Joseph and Matthias. Nor is there any consideration of leadership experience or standing among the one hundred and twenty. Certainly, no attention is given to inclusivity of ethnicity, gender, sexual orientation, or social status, given the dismissal of the women who accompanied Jesus through his ministry. Leadership must reflect the diversity of the community and embody the all-inclusive grace of a loving God.

WARREN CARTER

Commentary 2: Connecting the Reading with the World

The reading for today is as interesting for what it leaves out as for what it includes. Acts is a Gentile's story of the transition of the Jesus movement from Jerusalem to Rome, from Peter to Paul. The Twelve symbolize the recapitulation of the twelve tribes of Israel, reconstituted in the leadership of the Christian community. The lot falls to Matthias, not because of his special significance. The story allows readers to trust that the evolution of the Jesus movement from the direct teachings of Jesus to a predominantly Gentile mission is trustworthy and that the elect community is symbolically complete.

What is missing from the lectionary is the memory of the broader community that gathered in the aftermath of the ascension, as well as a discussion of the puzzling matter of Judas's betrayal. The disciples return to the Mount of Olives, where they pray with great intensity with "the women and with Mary the mother of Jesus and with his brothers" (Acts 1:14).[1] We have a picture here of the reuniting of an inner circle. The symbolic twelve (now eleven) disciples rejoin the women disciples and Jesus' family. This represents a different kind of completeness, not only symbolic leadership but Jesus' intensely devoted intimates. These women are the ones who stayed with Jesus to the bitter end of his death on the cross and who were the first to know of his resurrection. Of his brothers, we know only of James, who became a leader of the Jerusalem church and whose death grieved Jews and Christians alike. What happens if we understand the symbolic completeness of the Christian community to include these intimates?

Church history and theology tempt us to think of "the church" in terms of its leadership and its canonical voices, but if we include what the lectionary excised, a different picture of the church emerges. Who are "the women"? The Mount of Olives is where Bethany lies, the home of Mary and Martha, the sisters who had opened their home to Jesus in the past and remained such close friends to him. Does this geography suggest that they are among the women who are keeping vigil in the terrifying and unsettling aftermath of crucifixion and resurrection? The Gospel of Luke tells of a group of women who "had come with him from Galilee" (Luke 23:49) and remained with him until his death.[2] These same women followed the body "and saw the tomb and how his body was laid" and then went to prepare spices for its proper burial (Luke 23:55–56).

Luke 24 opens with these women returning to the tomb with their spices. Some of them now have names: the Magdalene woman, Mary; Joanna; Mary, the mother of James. Luke reports that when they returned to tell that they had learned of Jesus' resurrection, they were dismissed

---

1. David Bentley Hart, *The New Testament: A Translation* (New Haven, CT: Yale University Press, 2017), 221.

2. Hart, *New Testament*, 164.

by the eleven, as their story seemed nonsense. Nevertheless, Acts returns to these same women.

We are offered a glimpse of women who are at the very edge of our stories of gospel and church, their presence in those heady, Spirit-filled days excised by the lectionary, but their marginal presence, hardly more than a whisper, belies their intense, passionate commitment. They accompanied Jesus on his travels, providing for him from their own means (Luke 8). Martha provided him shelter in her home, respite from his harsh travels (Luke 10). A loose-knit group of women stood by Jesus to the very end, keeping vigil during the prolonged agony of the cross. In the opening of Acts, sandwiched between the ascension and Pentecost, we find them again, in an upper room devoting "themselves constantly to prayer, with a shared intensity of feeling" (Acts 1:14).[3]

Outside the limelight, but in the very heart of Jesus' ministry, women were present to support and console Jesus, to listen to his teachings, to keep vigil, to be awestruck by his resurrection, and to carry the sacred good news to his followers. In honor of today's reading, which symbolically completes the Christian community through the grafting on of Matthias, congregations might consider other names that symbolize the completeness of Christian leadership.

Melania the Elder founded a monastery and practiced radical compassion and charity during the tumultuous theological conflicts of the fourth century. She was deeply committed to a peaceful and tolerant Christianity, even as conflicts tore the early church into hostile factions. She was a spiritual counselor to Evagrius Ponticus, who on her advice entered a monastery and become an influential teacher. His writings remain important today.

Julian of Norwich provided spiritual counsel to the spiritual seekers of her town that suffered traumas of plague, warfare, and the rise of the English inquisition. The tenderness and compassion of her counsel and her writings continue to console.

Sojourner Truth, an escaped slave, was the first black woman to successfully sue a white man when he had illegally sold her five-year-old

son away south. After her conversion to Christianity, she spent the rest of her life campaigning for the abolition of slavery, equal rights for black and white women, prison reform, and land grants to freed slaves.

Mamie Till Mobley pulled the mask off racial violence by holding an open casket funeral, revealing the mutilated body of her lynched son, Emmett Till.

The Reverend Janie Spahr worked for decades as a traveling evangelist for inclusion and hospitality to LGBTQ+ Presbyterians. She recognized in Christianity the good news of radical love and sacred worth of all persons. Her delightful kindness and generosity helped open the doors of many churches to those previously abandoned and driven away.

These and countless others have remained invisible or their work and wisdom dismissed as "nonsense." As we await the kingdom, the Spirit vindicates them and keeps their dreams alive.

The other missing passage in this lectionary reading (vv. 18–20) is an attempt to make sense of the presence of Judas in Jesus' inner circle. The author of Acts imagines an appropriately horrible ending for him, and yet there is an indication that these events happened according to a divine plan, (obscurely) foreshadowed in the Psalms.

Perhaps it is consoling to imagine evildoers coming to nasty ends. It might also be useful simply to sit with the disturbing mystery that, even in a Spirit-infused understanding of Christianity, treachery and destruction can infiltrate the very heart of the inner circle of the Christian community. The seemingly endless litany of sexual abuse and harassment committed by clergy of every denomination reminds us how closely connected treachery and leadership can be. Alliances between Christianity and all forms of oppression are well known: the German Christians, the Afrikaans Protestant Church, the connections between Latin American death squads and religious leaders, the denominational splits over slavery, women's ordination, and gender diversity.

Christianity continues to harbor traitors to the gospel at its table. The implication of today's readings suggests that somehow this is contained

3. Hart, *New Testament*, 221.

in a divine plan, governed by the Holy Spirit—who inspires Scripture and is embodied in the church and the world. It is unlikely that the moral ambiguity of the church will ever disappear. How can one discern the movement of the Spirit, when it is not always written as clearly as Judas's outpouring entrails? How do we make peace with conflict and bitter disagreements about the way to live out the gospel in different times and places? How do we discover a spirit of reconciliation that will make "a field of blood" unnecessary to make right what has gone wrong?

WENDY FARLEY

Psalm 1

¹Happy are those
   who do not follow the advice of the wicked,
or take the path that sinners tread,
   or sit in the seat of scoffers;
²but their delight is in the law of the LORD,
   and on his law they meditate day and night.
³They are like trees
   planted by streams of water,
which yield their fruit in its season,
   and their leaves do not wither.
In all that they do, they prosper.

⁴The wicked are not so,
   but are like chaff that the wind drives away.
⁵Therefore the wicked will not stand in the judgment,
   nor sinners in the congregation of the righteous;
⁶for the LORD watches over the way of the righteous,
   but the way of the wicked will perish.

Connecting the Psalm with Scripture and Worship

"Like the foundation in a house, the keel in a ship, and the heart in a body,"[1] so stands Psalm 1 in relation to the rest of the Psalter, according to Basil the Great (330–79), a fourth-century bishop of Caesarea. The First Psalm serves as a fitting overture for this book of praise and prayer by describing the deep blessing of a faithful life—and the dire consequences of sin.

One might think of this psalm as an extended beatitude. In fact, the beatitudes of Matthew and Luke echo the opening words of this psalm in the Greek Septuagint: "Happy" (*makarios*) or "blessed is the one . . ." (Ps. 1:1; cf. Matt. 5:3, Luke 6:20). In a manner characteristic of the Wisdom literature of the Hebrew Scriptures, Psalm 1 establishes a strong opposition between the way of the righteous and the folly of the wicked.

The primary metaphor is that of "trees planted by streams of water, which yield their fruit in its season" (Ps. 1:3), an image resonant with the tree of life found at the beginning and the end of the biblical canon (Gen. 2:9; Rev. 22:2). The counterpart to this symbol of a faithful, fruitful life is the image of chaff—empty husks of grain—rootless and worthless, dried up and driven away by the wind. The implication is clear: those who "delight . . . in the law of the LORD" and "meditate day and night" (Ps. 1:2) on God's word will surely prosper.

As a response to Acts 1:15–17, 21–26, Psalm 1 reflects the stark contrast between the treachery of Judas (Acts 1:16) and the faithfulness of those who remained as witnesses to the resurrection (Acts 1:22). Alas, Judas was one who chose to "follow the advice of the wicked, or take the path that sinners tread, or sit in the seat of scoffers" (Ps. 1:1). As revealed in the gruesome details of his demise (mercifully omitted by the lectionary), Judas was "like chaff that the wind drives away" (Ps. 1:4). The rest of the apostles, on the other hand, are depicted in Acts as those who have stood beside Jesus "beginning from the baptism

---

1. *Ancient Christian Commentary on Scripture, Old Testament VII, Psalms 1–50*, ed. Craig A. Blaising and Carmen S. Hardin (Downers Grove, IL: InterVarsity Press, 2008), 2.

of John" (Acts 1:22); they are indeed "like trees planted by streams of water" (Ps. 1:3).

Another way to juxtapose the words of this psalm with the reading from Acts is to consider them as criteria for discernment, insights for the eleven as they sought a suitable replacement for Judas. Joseph (also known as Barsabbas or Justus) and Matthias are identified as faithful disciples and qualified candidates, worthy to stand "in the congregation of the righteous" (Ps. 1:5). Ultimately Matthias is chosen through prayer and the casting of lots.

It may be helpful to know that one of the omitted verses in this passage, Acts 1:20, quotes two psalms, neither of which is Psalm 1. Peter cites Psalm 69:25 and Psalm 109:8 as biblical harbingers of Judas's fate. This is why Peter's remarks begin: "Friends, the scripture had to be fulfilled, which the Holy Spirit through David foretold concerning Judas . . ." (Acts 1:16). As is evident from numerous references to the Psalms in the Gospels and epistles, the earliest Christian communities considered these ancient hymns to be prophetic preludes to the events surrounding Jesus' life, death, and resurrection.

Additional connections may be found between Psalm 1 and the other readings for the Seventh Sunday of Easter. The second reading, 1 John 5:9–13, draws a sharp distinction between those who believe and have eternal life and those who do not (1 John 5:10–12), a division reminiscent of the duality found in the psalm. In the Gospel reading, Jesus asks God to protect the disciples who "have kept your word" (John 17:6) and prays: "Sanctify them in the truth; your word is truth" (John 17:17). As the psalmist might have said of such disciples, "their delight is in the law of the LORD" (Ps. 1:2). This Gospel passage also makes a subtle reference to

Judas and Peter's interpretation of the psalms: "Not one of them was lost except the one destined to be lost, so that the scripture might be fulfilled" (John 17:12).

The lectionary texts for the Seventh Sunday of Easter present an opportunity for reflection on the role of faithful discipleship and leadership in the life of the church. Those who follow and model the way of Jesus are called to be like the trees of Psalm 1: rooted in the promise of God's word, watered by the grace of their baptism, bearing good fruit in the world. Preachers might apply these insights to the church's rites of baptism, confirmation, ordination, and/or installation, perhaps to be celebrated the following week at Pentecost.

As the great fifty days of Easter draw to a close, it is not too late to sing joyful hymns of resurrection. "Now the Green Blade Rises" (*Glory to God* #247), "Because You Live, O Christ" (*Glory to God* #249), and "In the Bulb There Is a Flower" (*Glory to God* #250) all complement the botanical themes of the psalm. Brian Wren's "Christ Is Risen! Shout Hosanna!" (*Glory to God* #248) would be another excellent choice, with its imagery of "a spreading tree" (Ps. 1:3), "gladness in the morning" (Ps. 1:2), and a "grim, demonic chorus" (Ps. 1:1).[2] All of these hymns proclaim the transforming power of Christ's resurrection in the lives of the people of God.

Surely it is no coincidence that Basil's analogies for the book of Psalms—a house, a ship, a body—are also common metaphors for the church. Like Matthias, as witnesses to the resurrection, we are called to take our own places in the mission and ministry of Christ's church (Acts 1:25), devoting ourselves to the life-giving law of the Lord.

DAVID GAMBRELL

---

2. *Glory to God: The Presbyterian Hymnal* (Louisville, KY: Westminster John Knox, 2013), #248.

1 John 5:9–13

⁹If we receive human testimony, the testimony of God is greater; for this is the testimony of God that he has testified to his Son. ¹⁰Those who believe in the Son of God have the testimony in their hearts. Those who do not believe in God have made him a liar by not believing in the testimony that God has given concerning his Son. ¹¹And this is the testimony: God gave us eternal life, and this life is in his Son. ¹²Whoever has the Son has life; whoever does not have the Son of God does not have life.

¹³I write these things to you who believe in the name of the Son of God, so that you may know that you have eternal life.

Commentary 1: Connecting the Reading with Scripture

The reading from 1 John starts in the middle of a paragraph that, at least in several modern translations, begins in verse 5. As a result, verses 9–13 should be considered in light of verses 5–8. The transition between paragraphs in 1 John 5 is not entirely clear, nor is the author's progression of thought, as is often true of 1 John. What seems to matter most, however, is that verse 5 insists that the one who "overcomes the world" is the one who believes that Jesus is the Son of God.

The identity of Jesus, the significance of his death, and the consequences of both for those who gathered in his name seem to be on trial throughout 1 John and much of the Gospel of John. This is clearly indicated by the frequent use of the verb *martyreō* ("to bear witness, testify"), which occurs six times in 1 John and thirty-three times in John, and the noun *martyria* ("witness, testimony"), which occurs six times in 1 John and fourteen times in John. In John 5, Jesus points to several witnesses that attest to his identity: John the Baptist (John 5:33–35), his own signs (John 5:36), the Father himself (John 5:37–38), and Scripture (John 5:39).

Likewise, 1 John opens with reference to the "testimony" (1 John 1:2, 3) of what has been experienced concerning the "word of life." In 1 John 5:6–8, the author names three additional witnesses to the identity of Jesus: the water, the blood, and the Spirit. The text of 1 John provides no further explanation, and there is some uncertainty among interpreters about exactly what these three witnesses refer to. The exact significance of each need not concern us here. What matters for 1 John 5:9–13 is that these three witnesses agree (v. 8) and that they all witness to the identity of Jesus as the Son of God (v. 5). The identity of Jesus, and the implications of that identity for the community addressed by the epistle, dominate the remainder of the paragraph.

First John 5:9–12 focuses on two ideas mentioned above: testimony and life. The language of testimony and witnessing is concentrated in the first three verses. Verse 9 functions like a thesis statement for verses 9–12: the testimony of God is greater than that of human beings; it is the highest in an ascending list of witnesses. The contrast between "human testimony" and the testimony of God recalls Jesus' own reluctance to accept human testimony in John 5:34. For both the Gospel of John and 1 John, human testimony only prepares for or confirms the testimony of God.

The author insists that the superior testimony of God is confirmed by the experience of the addressed community. Those who believe Jesus is the Son of God have the testimony of God themselves; their belief indicates that they receive and keep the testimony of God (v. 10). Verse 11 functions like a hinge, connecting verses 9–10, which are dominated by witnessing language, and verses 12–13, which are filled with references to life. The addressed community's reception of the testimony of God enables them to experience "eternal life" in the Son. Eternal life is the consequence for those who receive and accept the testimony about Jesus. In the dualism typical of both the Gospel and the letters of John, those who do not believe in Jesus do not have the testimony in themselves (v. 10) and thus do not have life (v. 12).

Verse 13 marks the beginning of the concluding section of 1 John, and it reiterates the author's purpose for writing: that those who believe in the name of the Son of God—those addressed by the letter, those who continue to gather together, unlike those who have "gone out" (1 John 2:19; 4:1; 2 John 7)—may know that they have eternal life. In this way, 1 John 5:13 echoes the ending of the Gospel of John, which says that the events it records have been presented as written witnesses so that those who receive the testimony "may come to believe [or keep believing] that Jesus is the Messiah, the Son of God, and that through believing you may have life in his name" (John 20:31).

Psalm 1 resembles the understanding of (eternal) life in 1 John, while reflecting the impulse of much of the wisdom tradition: the righteous experience good things (Ps. 1:3), while "the way of the wicked will perish" (v. 6). The image of "trees planted by streams of water" (v. 3) applies just as easily to the experience of those who have received and hold fast to the testimony of God about Jesus (1 John 5:11–12) as it does to those who delight in and meditate on the law of the Lord (Ps. 1:2).

The lectionary text from Acts 1 aligns with the emphasis on testimony and witnessing in the writings of John. In Acts 1:16, Peter interprets the significance of Judas's treacherous actions and insists that Judas must be replaced

O What a Changed People We Would Be

O careless sinners! that you did but know the love that you unthankfully neglect, and the preciousness of the blood of Christ which you despise! O that you did but know the riches of the gospel! O that you did but know, a little know, the certainty, and the glory, and the blessedness, of that everlasting life, which now you will not set your hearts upon, nor be persuaded first and diligently to seek. Did you but know the endless life with God which you now neglect, how quickly would you cast away your sin, how quickly would you change your mind and life, your course and company, and turn the streams of your affections, and lay your care another way! How resolutely would you scorn to yield to such temptations as now deceive you and carry you away! How zealously would you bestir yourselves for that most blessed life! How earnest would you be with God in prayer! How diligent in hearing, and learning, and inquiring!—How serious in meditating on the laws of God! How fearful of sinning in thought, word, or deed; and how careful to please God and grow in holiness!—O what a changed people you would be! And why should not the certain word of God be believed by you, and prevail with you, which, openeth to you these glorious and eternal things?

Richard Baxter, *A Call to the Unconverted* (York: Wilson, Spence, and Mawman, 1795), xv–xvi.

by another. Peter explains the requirements for consideration: Judas's replacement must have accompanied the other disciples during "all the time that the Lord Jesus went in and out" among the disciples (Acts 1:21), beginning with the baptism of John and ending with the ascension of Jesus (v. 22). In Acts 1:22, Peter names Judas's replacement a "witness" to Jesus' resurrection. Acts frequently identifies the apostles and the followers of the Way as "witnesses" (*martyres*) to Jesus' life, death, and resurrection (see Acts 1:8; 2:32; 3:15; 5:32; 10:39, 41; 13:31; 22:15, 20; 26:16). Through its collection of speeches, Acts narrates several iterations of "testimony" about Jesus, not unlike the one that 1 John seeks to instill and reinforce in the addressed community. This testimony is perhaps narrower in 1 John, as it focuses primarily on the identity of Jesus as the Son of God and on the actuality of his coming in the flesh and dying.

The reading from John 17 reminds us of the relationship between the disciples' testimony about Jesus and Jesus' own words about himself. While praying, Jesus says that he has given to the disciples the very words that God gave him (John 17:8), and the world hates them as a result (v. 14). Just as God sent Jesus into the world, so Jesus sends the disciples into the world (v. 18).

The coalescing of God's word, Jesus' word, and the word of the disciples stands in some contrast to the testimony of the witnesses in Acts. From beginning to end, the acts of witnessing in Acts remain *human words* about God's actions in and through Jesus Christ. These testimonies look back on experiences of God's activity in the world and offer interpretations of those experiences for members of the Way. Of course, the narrative of Acts insists that those who reject the testimony of human witnesses ultimately are rejecting God and God's ways (e.g., Acts 13:46), but there is no equation of these human testimonies with the very words of God.

The Johannine writings press further, however. Not only does 1 John claim decisive testimony from those who experienced the "word of life." It also claims particular access to the very testimony of God. Maybe the tension between witnessing in 1 John and Acts reflects the mystery of the preaching moment, when writings covered in human fingerprints become "the Word of God for the people of God."

CHRISTOPHER T. HOLMES

Commentary 2: Connecting the Reading with the World

John Wesley privileged the letter of 1 John, calling it a compendium of the faith and the deepest part of the Scripture. The fourth chapter especially holds a pride of place in Christian theology. Verses closely preceding this Sunday's lection soar in simplicity and power. "God is love, and those who abide in love abide in God, and God abides in them" (1 John 4:16b). "We love because God first loved us" (4:19). It is difficult to think as Christians and not hear these words. Living them is another matter.

Today's reading, on first hearing, is not appealing. In fact, outside of the discipline of reading the whole letter or following a lectionary, I am not sure what might draw me to this part of the text. We no longer live in a time where we can count on a worshiper being present each Sunday. Dropping into these few verses as if listening for the first time, we hear the word "testimony" five times and a warning not to make God a liar. When read as the last in a sequence of readings, however, the final verse of this passage sounds like a conclusion (not unlike the last verses of chapter 20 of the Gospel of John): "I write these things to you who believe in the name of the Son of God, so that you may know that you have eternal life." This verse offers a solid ending; that may be a clue where to begin.

The gift of the gospel of Jesus Christ and the purpose of a sermon on this or any other Sunday are that we may have eternal life. This is the testimony: that in Christ we have eternal life (5:11). These words, read aloud, serve to gather the whole. Even a marginally churched Christian hearing a reader's cadence concluding here is reminded of the most famous verse in this literature: John 3:16, "For God so loved the world that he gave his only Son, so that everyone who believes in him may not perish but may have eternal life." After years of preaching I have found that if our subject is eternal life, it is very difficult even for lifelong Christians, or those who have received our teaching only in caricature, to hear anything other than the evangelical guarantee or purchase of eternal life, providing that we believe or affirm the right set of facts. This makes the faith a matter of right thinking, not right living.

In the Gospel of John and in this letter, however, eternal life is present now in Christ, and right thinking about God cannot be separated from right living with one another. Eternal life is life lived in mutual love of God and one another. Trust, a relational term, is in fact the primary definition of belief in the ancient world. A sermon on this text might connect here: where our fear of death meets our life together. The caricature of the faith with which we have to contend is one where the content of our ideas purchases through Christ's sacrifice a place in the afterlife. It is a flimsy hope. It cannot stand against the abyss of death. The least appealing characteristic of this letter may be the most poignant for us. It is essential to hear and teach the faith correctly.

Eternal life is a quality of living, now; whatever life beyond death may or may not be, the Johannine community is intent on the invitation into this life of abiding with one another and with God in Christ. The only salve, or assurance, of freedom from death I have known is the taste of eternity experienced in love. The Johannine literature returns to this theme again and again. In fact, there is only one commandment: that you love one another. To love the Son is to know the Father, and to know this life is to abide in the love of one another: for we are called to love that which God loves, and God so loves *the world*. That this is so difficult that it comes to us as a command—again, in John *the only* command—should give the reader and hearer pause.

It is far easier to deny that the life of faithfulness is about our relationship with one another, than contend with the day-to-day challenge of our neighbor, our fellow Christian, the stranger, the opinion of our "friend" on social media. The fact that this is challenging was apparently as true in the first century as it is today, or we would not have the epistle literature of the New Testament. We see God in the face of the other. "Those who say, 'I love God,' and hate their brothers or sisters, are liars; for those who do not love a brother or sister whom they have seen, cannot love God whom they have not seen" (4:20). It may be that the Johannine community focused this love inward toward their "brothers and sisters"; however, placing our reading in the context of the whole tradition, it is clear that we are called to love every human that has breath, most especially those that have not been so loved (see Matt. 25:31–46).

This brings us to this text's peculiar obsession with the word "testimony." It seems to many readers as if the occasion of this letter is a dispute about Christology, whether or not Jesus was fully human (1 John 4:2–3). Reconstructing the nature of this dispute is challenging, but it is easily noted that even today folks tend to fall into two camps: those who assume Jesus was only an exemplary human being or those who believe that Jesus was God in a way that removes him from the human frailties and limitations that each of us carry. The challenge of the "testimony" then and now is that in Jesus we behold the divine life fully human. The vocabulary just before this lection draws us once again to the cross, to behold our divine life loving and suffering in our flesh and blood: "This is the one who came by water and blood, Jesus Christ, not with the water only but with the water and the blood" (5:6). This is exactly the testimony beheld at the foot of the cross (John 19:34–35).

What is at stake here in the insistence that Christ, eternal life, and the divine life were, and are, about life enfleshed? Today's sermon may do well to explore that question. Being Christian is inseparable from our treatment of the enfleshed one before us, whom God in Christ lived and suffered for. Any sermon on this subject will drive to the heart of the faith and the joy and challenges of being human. A final word from John Wesley:

> *And this commandment have we from him*—Both God and *Christ; that he who loveth God, love his brother*—Every one, whatever his opinions or mode of worship be, purely because he is the child and bears the image of God. Bigotry is properly the want of this pure and universal love. A bigot only loves those who embrace his opinions, and receive his way of worship: and he loves them for that, and not for Christ's sake.[1]

MARK F. STURGESS

1. John Wesley, *Explanatory Notes upon the New Testament*, Fourth American Edition (New York: J. Soule and T. Mason, 1818), 665.

John 17:6–19

6"I have made your name known to those whom you gave me from the world. They were yours, and you gave them to me, and they have kept your word. 7Now they know that everything you have given me is from you; 8for the words that you gave to me I have given to them, and they have received them and know in truth that I came from you; and they have believed that you sent me. 9I am asking on their behalf; I am not asking on behalf of the world, but on behalf of those whom you gave me, because they are yours. 10All mine are yours, and yours are mine; and I have been glorified in them. 11And now I am no longer in the world, but they are in the world, and I am coming to you. Holy Father, protect them in your name that you have given me, so that they may be one, as we are one. 12While I was with them, I protected them in your name that you have given me. I guarded them, and not one of them was lost except the one destined to be lost, so that the scripture might be fulfilled. 13But now I am coming to you, and I speak these things in the world so that they may have my joy made complete in themselves. 14I have given them your word, and the world has hated them because they do not belong to the world, just as I do not belong to the world. 15I am not asking you to take them out of the world, but I ask you to protect them from the evil one. 16They do not belong to the world, just as I do not belong to the world. 17Sanctify them in the truth; your word is truth. 18As you have sent me into the world, so I have sent them into the world. 19And for their sakes I sanctify myself, so that they also may be sanctified in truth."

Commentary 1: Connecting the Reading with Scripture

This lection is taken from the middle of the intercessory prayer (John 17) Jesus offers at the conclusion of a lengthy discourse (chaps. 13–16). The language of the prayer may strike a contemporary reader as somewhat stilted, ranging from the overtly didactic to the tautological (v. 7), with Jesus even referring to himself in the third person by name and title at one point (v. 3).

What appears at first as an unrealistic depiction of prayer—or even a strangely condescending way to address the Deity—makes sense as a narrative device that allows for theological explication, even as it shows us the intimate relationship between Father and Son in action. Like an earlier moment in the Gospel, when Jesus lifted his eyes to heaven and spoke (11:41b–42; cf. 17:1), this prayer is offered in order to be overheard by the disciples, and by extension the reading community that identifies with them. As his "hour" (v. 1) approaches, Jesus supplies the fullest interpretation of his mission among them by directly addressing the one who has sent him (v. 3) and to whom he will soon return (v. 13). Drawing together multiple themes from the prologue and earlier discourses, this chapter has been called the theological climax of the book of John.[1]

Readers familiar with the Synoptic accounts of Jesus at the end of his life will be struck immediately by the different quality of the relationship between Jesus and God depicted in this prayer. The anguished prayer from the Mount of Olives (Luke 22:42, 44) and the cry of abandonment from the cross (Mark 15:34) are a world apart from the unbridled confidence of this Jesus, who speaks of his imminent

---

1. Gail O'Day, "The Gospel of John," in the *New Interpreter's Bible* (Nashville: Abingdon, 1995), 9:787.

glorification in death and resurrection as the inevitable ratification of his preexistent destiny (John 17:5). He is so certain of the outcome that he can speak as if it is all already accomplished—as if even in the act of praying he is leaving the world and coming into the very presence of the Father (v. 11a).

The prayer simultaneously describes and performs the perfect oneness (v. 11b) of a Father and Son who do all the same things. Both are described as "glorifying" (vv. 1, 4), as "sanctifying" (vv. 17, 19), as possessing together the community of believers (v. 10), and as protecting that same community (vv. 12, 15). Their unity is also strongly implied when Jesus speaks of making the "name" of God known (v. 6) and even claims it as his own name, given to him by God (vv. 11, 12). This calls to mind the language of the prologue, where the preexistent Word is simply identified with God (1:1), and the several occasions throughout the Gospel when Jesus takes the divine name ("I AM," Exod. 3:14) on his own lips (e.g., 6:35; 8:12; 10:11; 14:6). (The final and climactic instance will come soon after this prayer at 18:6, where Jesus will declare, "I am," and the soldiers who have come to the garden to arrest him will fall to the ground as if struck down by a wave of divine power.) In all of this we are shown a Son who has come close, indeed, to the Father's heart (1:18). In the Gospel lection for Ascension of the Lord from Luke (24:44–53), the resurrected Jesus is depicted ascending into the clouds to be spatially close to God. Here, without any special effects, arguably an even greater relational closeness is achieved with surprising evocative power, simply through the language of an overheard prayer.

Perhaps this passage is a challenge for preaching because the Jesus it shows us is not the highly identifiable figure with whom we have become most comfortable. We may be more at ease with the fraternal Jesus—Jesus our intrepid sibling, who goes before us on the path of faith despite the doubts, the anxieties, the fears and finitude he shares with us all. However, this passage wants to show us something else that is also true about Jesus.

At this crucial moment of full disclosure about his ministry, the Jesus John shows us is not angsty and fraternal, but rather competent and parental. In the discourse that precedes this prayer, Jesus refers to the disciples as his children (13:33) and promises that he will not leave them orphaned (14:18). Now he is shown interceding for them as vulnerable children. Indeed, the community of believers overhearing this prayer can be compared to children overhearing their parents talking together and making plans to provide for the well-being of the offspring they share, and know, and love together.

Primarily this provision is a matter of "protection." Up to this point, the disciples have been protected and guarded (17:12) by Jesus. Now Jesus will be leaving, and he prays that the Father will continue protecting them in his absence. The disciples—and by the logic of narrative identification the community of believers that reads this Gospel—require this protection because of "the world." This term simultaneously describes both the context they inhabit—which Jesus has entered and is soon leaving—and a threatening power at work within it that holds animosity toward them as the believing community (v. 14). As long as they are in the world, they are in danger from the evil one (v. 15), who is its ruler (16:11). The world is ignorant of and therefore antagonistic to the Son's mission (1:10–11). Indeed, it would make no sense for Jesus to pray on behalf of the world *as* the world (17:9).

For all these reasons, this is a text that has sometimes funded a sectarian understanding of Christian faith. A close reading, however, leads to a more nuanced understanding. The Father loves the world (3:16) and sent the Son into the world to save rather than to condemn it (3:17). Now the believing community is likewise sent (17:18) into that same world so that it may come to believe (vv. 20–21). The community must be protected *within* the world precisely because it is not God's will that they should be removed *from* the world.

It should not surprise us that a story about the animosity of "the world" for Christian faith has been distorted by some in ways that lead to self-congratulatory sectarianism and engender animosity toward the very world God loves. How difficult it is to speak honestly of hatred without giving in to it! For this reason, it is tempting to simply admit that this category of "the world" has outlived its usefulness for preaching.

However, Christian preaching that wants to take the testimony of the Fourth Gospel seriously must risk saying something about the hostility of the world. There is no way to think along with this story without speaking explicitly of its chief antagonist. Only by wrestling with the tragedy of the world's misunderstanding and antagonism can the true identities of the Father, the Son, and the community be narrated in all their beauty and pathos. Ultimately, it is for the sake of a great love—the Father's, the Son's, and the believing community's—that the dangers of the world must be risked. The Son and the Father are loving parents, but they will not remove their children from the dangers of the world. They will not, because an even greater love—an inclusive love that risks everything—refuses to abandon the world to its hate.

LANCE B. PAPE

Commentary 2: Connecting the Reading with the World

An innovative movie some years back had for its script the entire Gospel of John, verbatim, no additions or subtractions. Something about hearing every word in this prolix Gospel, with no option to skim, made my wife ask, "Will Jesus ever shut up?"

This passage comes from what scholars call Jesus' high-priestly prayer. Like Israel's priests of old, Jesus prays on behalf of the people in ways they could not for themselves, but that they need, both for its benefits and for the model it offers for how to pray for others. These particular verses focus on the disciples' "protection" (John 17:11–15). Jesus will not be around to do it as their good shepherd, so God has to (v. 11). Of course, Jesus has also predicted his people will be cast out of God's house and killed, as he himself is about to be (16:2). It is an odd notion of protection he calls for then. Most of my prayers for my children are for their protection. I treat God as a sort of talisman, to cast a spell of defense around my family. There is nothing wrong with praying for protection. Jesus asks for something similar here for his, but the passage shows the protection sought and offered by a crucified Messiah is protection from "stumbling" (16:1), from distance from or antagonism to God, not from physical harm.

Jesus also seeks the "sanctification" of those for whom he prays (17:17–19). That is, he prays they will be holy. The word does not conjure up warm associations, due especially to its history among US evangelicals, where too often holiness has meant merely not doing certain things (drinking, smoking, chewing, cussing, in some places dancing, playing cards—the goalposts seem infinitely movable). In biblical parlance, to be holy, to be sanctified, is to be set apart by God to be a blessing for the world.[2] God chooses Israel to be his surprising, counterintuitive means to repair what we human beings have ruined. Jesus prays for the church to be part of this God-given means to make right everything we have made wrong.

Consider all the ways God might have healed his beloved creation. God could have done it instantly, by fiat. God could have destroyed it all and started over (to read Gen. 6–9, God tried that once!). To listen to advocates for liberal democracy and capitalism, God could have chosen a political party to usher in the kingdom. Instead, God chooses a people. Not the likeliest or best people—to read Israel's Scripture, quite the opposite actually.

God chooses an ordinary, stiff-necked, difficult, self-involved, and self-important people through whom to bless and repair all things. Jesus likewise chooses sinners through whom to bless the world. There are no non-sinners available! Piously minded Christians sometimes speak as though they will be "better" than their neighbors, and this will be a sign of holiness. Jesus makes clear those claiming to be religiously "better" are often guilty of the worst sins—pride,

---

2. David Cunningham, "Theological Perspective" on John 17:6–19, in *Feasting on the Word: Year B, Vol. 2: Lent through Eastertide*, ed. David L. Bartlett and Barbara Brown Taylor (Louisville, KY: Westminster John Knox, 2008), 548.

self-importance, hypocrisy, presumption. So he gathers around himself a batch of sinners so ordinary that no one could think them "better" than anyone else—and he prays for them. Blesses them. Prepares them for his departure.

He also radically identifies with them. Most religions describe a God who stands aloof from humanity.[3] Not the God of the Bible. He makes himself radically one with human beings. Not the best human beings, but as sorry a batch as has ever been. All of these Twelve will deny, abandon, betray, desert. He knows they will. Yet he still identifies with them. With us, that is. He joins them with his prayer, vouching for them (vv. 9–10). They have God's own Word, or *Logos*, as Jesus does in John 1 (vv. 6, 14). Like Jesus they do not belong to the world—it hates them (vv. 14, 16). They are sent into the world, as Jesus was (v. 18). This is no aloof God, concerned to remain unsullied, distant from us. This is a God who is in our flesh, so radically one with us our theology has yet to catch up with this blazing insight, millennia later—but not only that.

Jesus is also one with God, the One who sent him. He has the authority to pray in a way that effectively orders God around. He gives knowledge of God straight to the people, as any prophet does, but more so (vv. 6–8). He confidently announces plans to return to God with his death (v. 11). He can ask for God's anointing, sanctifying, holiness-making goodness over those who in no way deserve it. He who is one with God asks God to be one with us (v. 11). The ancient church, which spoke of the Son being everything God is, and also being everything we are, was simply reading their Bible well. Not that we have any idea what either of those claims means.

Just as God does not stay aloof, removed, unsullied by the world, so here Jesus sends his people into the world (v. 15). All religion has within it an impulse to remove its adherents from a miserable world. The pietist Christians I mention above are not wrong to avoid sins; they just have a narrow list of such sins (and ask any recovering alcoholic whether teetotaling is a good idea). Monks and nuns in Orthodox and Catholic Christianities and in other faiths are quite right to see the harm done in the world and seek to opt out. The world needs people to pray for it, Lord knows, and that is a monastic's main job. Jesus here sets apart the entire church, represented in the witless and hapless disciples for whom he prays. Yet he does not ask for their removal from the world. He asks that they be sent back into the world in a new way (v. 18).

It is not clear we Christians have ever figured this balance out—to be in but not of the world. Christians who overemphasize the "in" part end up falling in altogether, looking no different from their neighbors. Christians who overemphasize the "not of" part can look down their nose with disdain on their neighbors. The Gospel of John presents Jesus as falling into neither trap. He loves the world (John 3:16). He eats and drinks and befriends and teaches and luxuriates in all the goodness of creation, for which he will die and which he promises to make new.

He is so radically different from the world, such a stark challenge to its ways, that we cannot stand him, and all of us—religion and law and culture and all the rest—team up and string him up to die so that he will leave us alone—but he does not stay dead. He keeps on praying for us. He is determined to make us holy, to make all the world holy, that is, so full of him and his divine life that all there is is life, more life, and nothing but life.

JASON BYASSEE

3. I am indebted here to George Ramsey's "Exegetical Perspective" on John 17:6–19, in *Feasting on the Word, Year B, Vol. 2: Lent through Eastertide*, ed. David L. Bartlett and Barbara Brown Taylor (Louisville, KY: Westminster John Knox, 2008), 547.

Day of Pentecost

Acts 2:1–21
Psalm 104:24–34, 35b
Romans 8:22–27

John 15:26–27; 16:4b–15
Ezekiel 37:1–14

Acts 2:1–21

¹When the day of Pentecost had come, they were all together in one place. ²And suddenly from heaven there came a sound like the rush of a violent wind, and it filled the entire house where they were sitting. ³Divided tongues, as of fire, appeared among them, and a tongue rested on each of them. ⁴All of them were filled with the Holy Spirit and began to speak in other languages, as the Spirit gave them ability.

⁵Now there were devout Jews from every nation under heaven living in Jerusalem. ⁶And at this sound the crowd gathered and was bewildered, because each one heard them speaking in the native language of each. ⁷Amazed and astonished, they asked, "Are not all these who are speaking Galileans? ⁸And how is it that we hear, each of us, in our own native language? ⁹Parthians, Medes, Elamites, and residents of Mesopotamia, Judea and Cappadocia, Pontus and Asia, ¹⁰Phrygia and Pamphylia, Egypt and the parts of Libya belonging to Cyrene, and visitors from Rome, both Jews and proselytes, ¹¹Cretans and Arabs—in our own languages we hear them speaking about God's deeds of power." ¹²All were amazed and perplexed, saying to one another, "What does this mean?" ¹³But others sneered and said, "They are filled with new wine."

¹⁴But Peter, standing with the eleven, raised his voice and addressed them, "Men of Judea and all who live in Jerusalem, let this be known to you, and listen to what I say. ¹⁵Indeed, these are not drunk, as you suppose, for it is only nine o'clock in the morning. ¹⁶No, this is what was spoken through the prophet Joel:

¹⁷'In the last days it will be, God declares,
that I will pour out my Spirit upon all flesh,
    and your sons and your daughters shall prophesy,
and your young men shall see visions,
    and your old men shall dream dreams.
¹⁸Even upon my slaves, both men and women,
    in those days I will pour out my Spirit;
        and they shall prophesy.
¹⁹And I will show portents in the heaven above
    and signs on the earth below,
        blood, and fire, and smoky mist.
²⁰The sun shall be turned to darkness
    and the moon to blood,
        before the coming of the Lord's great and glorious day.
²¹Then everyone who calls on the name of the Lord shall be saved.'"

Commentary 1: Connecting the Reading with Scripture

What can the preacher say about Pentecost beyond the usual "birthday of the church" approach with its singing of "Happy Birthday," decorating with red banners and balloons, and eating red cake?

The assigned Acts 2 reading narrates the Spirit's coming (Acts 2:1–4), the responses of questioning (v. 12) and sneering (v. 13) of those who hear them speaking in other languages (vv. 5–13), and Peter's sermon (vv. 14–21). Peter explains, using the prophet Joel, that the scene is not the consequence of public drunkenness but God's gift of the Spirit (vv. 14–21).

Here, I identify four dynamics in Acts 2 that the preacher might develop.

The sermon, or part thereof, might focus on the interplay of tradition and new experience. The preacher might explain that Acts 2 makes sense of the coming of the promised Spirit by appropriating language and concepts from the biblical tradition. The clearest example of this comes in the setting for this event at Pentecost (2:1). The significance of this Pentecost festival changes over time through the tradition, but one thing remains constant: it is associated with God giving good gifts.

At first, Pentecost was a festival of weeks or firstfruits that occurred seven weeks after Passover. It celebrated the harvest and expressed thanks for God's faithfulness in supplying the harvest for the whole household—sons and daughters, male and female slaves, strangers, orphans, and widows (Exod. 23:16; Deut. 16:9–12). Then the significance of Pentecost changed. It came to be associated with the gift of the Ten Commandments as instructions for faithful living in the covenant (Exod. 19).

Now, in a third meaning, Pentecost is associated with God's giving the gift of the Spirit. God provides harvest, instruction for faithful living, and the Spirit that manifests God's presence and empowers faithful witness. God gives what God's people need.

The preacher can ask congregants to supply additional meanings of Pentecost. What good gifts does the Spirit bring into the lives of the congregation? What do folks need today that they might receive from God? In other words, how might the circumstances and experiences of the folks interact with this tradition of God supplying good gifts at Pentecost?

A second dynamic available to the preacher is the gift of divine presence. Attention to divine presence can be a challenge for preachers and a concern for some contemporary believers, who often find God's presence to be elusive. In the Acts 2 narrative, there is not much mystery. The Spirit's coming is seen and heard; it is like wind and fire, symbols of God's presence. Moses encounters God in the burning bush. In the exodus, the people encounter God in the cloud by day and the pillar of fire by night.

The preacher can explore the wide variety of encounters with God throughout the biblical tradition. Sometimes divine presence is obvious, other times very elusive (Job), other times disruptive, confrontational, gentle, reassuring, oppressive, even absent: "My God, my God, why have you forsaken me?" (Matt. 27:46).

This interplay of divine presence and absence offers preaching possibilities. The sermon could highlight how the scene makes God's presence so clear and evident. Yet some of us know that divine presence is much more mystifying, much more difficult to discern, and much more difficult to experience. Some of us know much more about the experience of divine hiddenness or absence than divine presence, of God as an oppressive rather than a comforting presence. The challenge for the preacher is to engage the narrative's confident assertions of divine presence along with the biblical record of and personal struggles with divine absence.

The preacher might pursue a third dynamic, the interplay of silence and speech. Speaking is a crucial part of this Pentecost account. The declaration of the risen Jesus orients the narrative; the Spirit will empower "witnesses in Jerusalem, in all Judea and Samaria, and to the ends of the earth" (Acts 1:8). The Pentecost story delivers on Jesus' promise of power for witnessing and speaking.

The first sign of this empowered speaking comes in verse 4. Filled with the Spirit, they "began to speak in other languages, as the Spirit gave them ability." The assembled folks "hear them speaking in [their] native language[s] . . . about God's deeds of power" (2:6, 11).

The preacher can point out, though, that after verse 11 things quiet down as speech gives way to silence. By verse 14, everyone is silenced except for one person. Peter alone gets to talk as he preaches his Pentecost sermon.

Yet it gets stranger in verses 17–18. Peter quotes the prophet Joel: "I will pour out my spirit upon all flesh," namely, sons and daughters, young and old men, male and female slaves. The Spirit equips everyone to speak about God's deeds of power, regardless of gender, ethnicity, and social status.

If we read on through the book of Acts, however, this vision of everyone speaking for God disappears. Silence takes over. We do not see in Acts women and slave preachers; male witnesses do most the speaking.

One of the other lections emphasizes the Spirit's roles in bearing witness, convicting the world, and teaching all followers (John 15:26–27; 16:4–13). The preacher can invite congregants to be talkers about God's deeds of power. Since the Spirit equips all to speak, how many talkers of the good news of God's deeds of power do we have among us? What structures or strategies do we need to enable folks to speak the good news? How do we make space for the Spirit to turn our frequent silence into healing speech?

Fourth, the preacher might engage the interplay of Scriptures with new circumstances evident in Peter's sermon. In verses 17–21, Peter interprets the Scriptures of Joel 2 in relation to

the Pentecost experience. The preacher might highlight how Scriptures that had spoken to folks over centuries in different contexts in different ways are now interpreted in relation to this event. The fit, though, is not exact. Joel refers to cosmic signs, but they are absent here. Peter selectively uses this passage to interpret the community's speaking or prophesying in other languages as a sign of the last days marked by speaking.

In Romans 8:22–27, Paul similarly links the Spirit to the last days. He anticipates the future renewal of creation and redemption of bodies of which the Spirit's presence now is the firstfruits or guarantee.

Subsequently, Peter will interpret Psalms 16 and 110 in verses 25–31 and 34–35 in a similarly selective and perspectival manner that focuses on Jesus and the gift of the Spirit. In Psalm 16, the psalmist expresses confidence and trust in God to protect him and keep him alive in difficult circumstances. Peter reinterprets the psalm as referring to God's resurrecting power that brought Jesus out of death. God's raising of Jesus matters, because in verses 34–35 Peter reads Psalm 110 also in relation to Pentecost. He declares that the risen Jesus enthroned with God gives the Spirit. The preacher could point out that the same process of reinterpretation continues to this day, week by week, as we read the Scriptures in relation to our own lives and make meaning of our experiences.

The Pentecost sermon might develop several of these interplays in inviting us to reflect on our own experiences of the Spirit in our churches, lives, and world.

WARREN CARTER

Commentary 2: Connecting the Reading with the World

As the postresurrection followers of Jesus attempt to form community in his absence, Luke narrates a fiery baptism that inaugurates the gift of the Spirit to the members of the fledgling community. Luke places this event fifty days after Passover, to coincide with the Jewish festival of Shavuot. As Jews celebrate the gift of Torah, Christians will celebrate the coming of the Spirit. The author further links

Jewish and Christian communities by emphasizing that the prophecy from the book of Joel is for all humanity, for people from every land, and on "all who call upon the name of the Lord" (Acts 2:21; Joel 2:32).

Christians have sometimes heard these promises as applying only to them, going so far as to suggest they supersede the ancient promises made to the Jews, or simply ignoring that

Jews are also recipients of the divine presence. The generosity of the Spirit instead invites us to celebrate with our Jewish siblings the variety of gifts God gives the world and to tune our spiritual senses to the unimaginable creativity of the Spirit moving throughout creation.

Our Jewish friends identify something like the inbreaking of the Spirit as "God's presence in history." This awareness "can be defined at its starting point as an abiding astonishment. The . . . religious person . . . abides in wonder. . . . [T]he current system of cause and effect becomes, as it were, transparent and permits a glimpse of the sphere in which a sole power, not restricted by any other, is at work."[1] Abraham Heschel amplifies the ethical dimension of this wonder: "In exposing ourselves to God we discover the divine in ourselves and its correspondence to the divine beyond ourselves. That perception of correspondence, our discovering how acts of human goodness are allied with transcendent holiness, the sense of the sacred context of our candid compassion—is our most precious insight."[2] Weaving Jewish wisdom into our understanding of Pentecost, we may remember the raw wonder at the root of faithfulness, as well as the holiness of all acts of goodness.

Protestants often find the Divine uniquely in our Scriptures, but Pentecost challenges us to embrace with courage life with the Spirit. What might this look like today?

The most dramatic sign of the Spirit is the miracle of mutual understanding. Women and men, slaves, free, Jews, Gentile proselytes, and people from every known land and ethnicity participate in the gift of the Spirit. A miracle of recognition transpires: across impossible boundaries of class, ethnicity, and religion, people joyfully communicate. It is as if they are intoxicated—as they are, but not with wine.

It is significant that the primary sign of the inspiration of the Spirit, the founding event of the new Christian community, is the ability to speak to and understand a diversity of people. What are ways we today can learn to understand people from different lands and backgrounds?

As we struggle with a national crisis regarding the mistreatment of immigrants and refugees, as well as patterns of racial and ethnic profiling, a dramatic rise in hate crimes and white supremacist acts of violence, Christians may turn to this text as a reminder that the fruit of the Spirit is understanding across cultural boundaries. This allows us to recognize the human faces of other peoples, and therefore the face of the Spirit in all the wretched of the earth—and also in faces tortured by hatred and rage.

Looking beyond the confines of the church, we see that the Spirit is active in new visions of justice and liberation. In the Black Lives Matter movement, the Women's March, #metoo, and crusades for environmental justice, we witness the fierce love the Spirit has for this troubled world. Where many of us begin to grow discouraged, the Spirit continually inspires new visions of flourishing. She demands we join her in recognizing the sacred in all human beings and in the beauty and fragility of creation. Social movements are never perfect; they never embody or achieve the kingdom of God. Nevertheless, newly energized social movements reenvision how we can cherish the world, delight in its beauty, and heal its hurts.

Womanist theologian Karen Baker-Fletcher puts it this way:

> My work is always about what God does in creation and in the midst of all peoples. Without God who loves us into loving God, there is no hope for this world. Therefore, I write about God's persuasive, inviting, ever-present loving activity. . . . It is about the loveliness and beauty of the dance of God in the midst of this "ball of confusion." It is about God's love and compassion for this earth with all its creatures and for us human creatures with our beautiful and ugly ways.[3]

The celebration of Pentecost may not tell us how the church actually practiced, but it does remind us of the endless energy of the Spirit to infiltrate our hearts and our communities, and

1. Martin Buber, quoted in Emil L. Fackenheim, *God's Presence in History* (New York: Harper Torchbooks, 1970), 12–13.

2. Abraham Joshua Heschel, "To Be a Jew: What Is it?" in *Moral Grandeur and Spiritual Audacity: Essays*, ed. Susannah Heschel (New York: Farrar, Straus & Giroux, 1996), 5.

3. Karen Baker-Fletcher, *Dancing with God: The Trinity from a Womanist Perspective* (Danvers, MA: Chalice Press, 2006), xi–xii.

invite us to reinvigorate our steps as we practice the steps of her ever-creative dance of life.

The Spirit moves not only in the liberative dance of justice, but in all the ways we humans encounter the Divine. Whenever we are encouraged to be joyful or awakened to the delight in the flourishing of others, we sense the wonder of the Spirit. We might glimpse traces of the Spirit in the recovery of interior spirituality within several Protestant denominations. In seminary classes on religious formation, church parlors, retreat centers, centering prayer circles, and spiritual direction sessions, Protestants are exploring the connection of their interior depths to their beliefs and actions. Remembering—re-membering—the writings of the desert ascetics, medieval contemplative women and men, Golden Age Spanish mystics, poets, African American spirituals, and memoirs opens rooms that have fallen into disuse.

Protestants are finding new ways to find spiritual nurture and to connect modern psychology with ancient Christian wisdom. Contemplative practice highlights the possibilities of liberation from inner demons and destructive habits. It can deepen capacities for amazement, radical compassion, resilience, and delight. For some, this is a way to deepen their already vibrant faith. For those wounded by the church, contemplative practices provide the good news that Christianity offers more than they had imagined. For those flirting with "spiritual but not religious" possibilities, Christian spirituality eases the either/or between institutions and interior practice.

Peter alludes to the coming of the Lord's day, both terrifying and redemptive, but the apocalyptic expectations of early Christians were not realized. The end times did not come with their dark sun and bloody moon. The church quickly realized that a Spirit-led community could be very unruly. The cautionary tale of Ananias and Sapphira indicates how hard it is to throw one's whole self, with all of one's possessions and social standing, into a communitarian egalitarianism (Acts 5:1–11). The irresolvable conflict between the vision of discipleship of Peter and James and that of Paul shows how fragile the unity of movement was. We return to the stirring events of Pentecost, not to bemoan the impossibility of its vision, but to cleanse our hearts and our eyes so we may be more sensitive to ways the Spirit is moving within and beyond the church—always more amazing than our imagination can fathom.

WENDY FARLEY

Psalm 104:24–34, 35b

²⁴O LORD, how manifold are your works!
　In wisdom you have made them all;
　the earth is full of your creatures.
²⁵Yonder is the sea, great and wide,
　creeping things innumerable are there,
　living things both small and great.
²⁶There go the ships,
　and Leviathan that you formed to sport in it.

²⁷These all look to you
　to give them their food in due season;
²⁸when you give to them, they gather it up;
　when you open your hand, they are filled with good hthings.
²⁹When you hide your face, they are dismayed;
　when you take away their breath, they die
　and return to their dust.
³⁰When you send forth your spirit, they are created;
　and you renew the face of the ground.

³¹May the glory of the LORD endure forever;
　may the LORD rejoice in his works—
³²who looks on the earth and it trembles,
　who touches the mountains and they smoke.
³³I will sing to the LORD as long as I live;
　I will sing praise to my God while I have being.
³⁴May my meditation be pleasing to him,
　for I rejoice in the LORD.
. . . .
^{35b}Bless the LORD, O my soul.
Praise the LORD!

Connecting the Psalm with Scripture and Worship

Where does one find the first "hallelujah" in the Bible? It is the last word of Psalm 104—in English, three words: "Praise the Lord!" (Ps. 104:35b). What a fitting word for the final Sunday of the great fifty days of Easter.

Psalm 104 is a grand anthem of praise for God's creative work and providential care. Biblical scholars have identified connections between this psalm and a number of other ancient texts, including the hymn to the Aten (Egypt, fourteenth century BCE), the priestly account of creation (Gen. 1:1–2:4a), and the

Lord's first theophany to Job (Job 38:1–39:30). In its entirety, Psalm 104 presents a panoramic view of the cosmos, praising God's might and mercy in every facet of heaven and earth. No wonder it concludes with a great hallelujah!

The psalm evinces a peculiar preoccupation with animal behavior, astronomical phenomena, and agricultural rhythms. It chronicles the activities of creatures great and small—wild asses, birds, cattle, goats, rabbits, lions, and even the sea monster, Leviathan—indicating how God has provided for their hunger, thirst, shelter, and play. It refers to the cycles of the earth, moon, and sun that mark out the patterns of our years, months, and days. Verse 15 points to the harvest of three significant crops: grapes for wine (in August/September), olives for oil (in October), and grain for bread (in May/June).[1] The third of these is related to the Jewish feast of Weeks (Shavuot), a harvest festival observed fifty days after Passover, from which Christians have derived the commemoration of Pentecost (Greek for "fiftieth day").

Only the final section of the psalm (vv. 24–34, 35b) is assigned for the Day of Pentecost in the Revised Common Lectionary. These verses comprise a recapitulation of the themes of the psalm—divine creation and providence—and a concluding doxology that is both universal and introspective (note the first person singular in vv. 33–35). This portion of Psalm 104 does double duty in the lectionary for the Day of Pentecost, serving primarily as a response to Acts 2:1–21, but also (potentially) a response to the alternate first reading from the Hebrew Scriptures, Ezekiel 37:1–14 (in the case of Year B).

In relation to the Acts reading, this passage from the psalm echoes the peoples' praise of "God's deeds of power" (Acts 2:11; cf. Ps. 104:24, 31). It answers the prophecy of "portents in the heaven above and signs on the earth below, blood, and fire, and smoky mist" (Acts 2:19) with earthquakes and smoking mountains (Ps. 104:32) and sounds an alarm for the coming day of judgment (Acts 2:20; Ps. 104:35). As a response to Ezekiel, this selection from the psalm reads like a dispatch from the valley of dry bones: "when you take away their breath, they die and return to their dust" (Ps. 104:29). It praises the transforming power of God's speech and action, on which all life depends (vv. 27–28).

For either reading, the key line on the Day of Pentecost is this: "When you send forth your spirit, they are created; and you renew the face of the ground" (v. 30). This verse evokes the outpouring of the Holy Spirit upon the believers in Jerusalem, as reported in Acts. It also reflects God's promise of restoration for Israel, as envisioned by Ezekiel. Indeed, there is a sense in which the Acts and Ezekiel readings are two sides of one coin: the former proclaiming the power of resurrection in prophetic speech, the latter embodying it through symbolic action. The psalm helps us to grasp the connection between them, and illustrates the role of the Spirit in the unity of word and sacrament.

In the everyday events of congregational life, the "most joyous span" (*laetissimum spatium*, Tertullian) of Easter has a tendency to peter out by the seventh Sunday of the season, with the breath of the Spirit at Pentecost coming in as a last gasp of joy. We need to reverse this way of thinking. Pentecost ought to be understood as the dramatic culmination of the season of resurrection, with a long crescendo leading up to this great day. Just as the Lord's Day is sometimes called the "eighth day" of the week—a day of new creation—the Day of Pentecost ought to be celebrated as the Eighth Sunday of Easter, a glorious commendation of God's life-giving, faith-shaping, world-changing work.

What would this look like in Christian worship? It might take the form of banners or fabric installations that grow and expand across the fifty days, adding swaths of white and gold week by week, and then flashes of red at Pentecost. It might include special processions of the choir or children, or both. It might involve the exploration of new (actually old) traditions, such as the celebration of weekly Eucharist or standing for the Gospel reading. It might mean scheduling baptisms, confirmation, and/or the reception of new members on the Day of Pentecost, with a process of preparation taking place during the Easter season.

What would it sound like? Many churches have the tradition of suppressing or burying their alleluias during the season of Lent. We often forget the other side of the equation: extravagant, exuberant alleluias *throughout* the season of Easter. These might be added in gathering songs, acclamations for the Scripture readings, communion anthems, and responses to the blessing and charge, so that—at the consummation of

---

1. "Psalm 104," in *The Jewish Study Bible, Featuring the Jewish Publication Society Tanakh Translation*, ed. Adele Berlin and Marc Zvi Brettler (New York: Oxford University Press, 2004), 1397–98.

the fifty days—the Day of Pentecost resounds with the loudest alleluias of all. If nothing else, congregations might reprise Handel's "Hallelujah Chorus" on the Eighth Sunday of Easter.

How can we honor and bless the God of heaven and earth, the Lord of abundant life, the Spirit of new creation? Let Psalm 104 have the last word. Hallelujah!

DAVID GAMBRELL

Romans 8:22–27

²²We know that the whole creation has been groaning in labor pains until now; ²³and not only the creation, but we ourselves, who have the first fruits of the Spirit, groan inwardly while we wait for adoption, the redemption of our bodies. ²⁴For in hope we were saved. Now hope that is seen is not hope. For who hopes for what is seen? ²⁵But if we hope for what we do not see, we wait for it with patience.

²⁶Likewise the Spirit helps us in our weakness; for we do not know how to pray as we ought, but that very Spirit intercedes with sighs too deep for words. ²⁷And God, who searches the heart, knows what is the mind of the Spirit, because the Spirit intercedes for the saints according to the will of God.

Commentary 1: Connecting the Reading with Scripture

The lectionary texts for Pentecost Sunday all convene on the power and presence of the Spirit. The text from Acts recalls the first Pentecost: gathered in a house together, the disciples experience a disruptive, violent wind that fills them with the Holy Spirit (Acts 2:2). With tongues of fire, they begin to speak in a fury of different languages (v. 4), causing those around them to wonder at this unexpected behavior (vv. 6–13).

Ezekiel 37 likewise calls attention to the animating power of the Spirit. In Ezekiel 37:5, the Lord speaks to dry bones: "I will cause breath to enter you, and you shall live." The NRSV reflects the ambiguity of the Hebrew word *ruach*, which can be translated as "breath" or "wind" or "spirit." With the advent of the breath/spirit, the dry bones experience life. While Ezekiel 37 recalls the Lord's original life-giving work at creation, in which God's breath animates the dust to create humanity (Gen. 2:7), Ezekiel's prophecy envisions resurrection, the opening of graves and bringing forth of inanimate bodies from them (Ezek. 37:13). The life-giving power of the Spirit is upheld in the psalm text as well. Not just humans, but all created things arise from the sending of God's spirit (Ps. 104:30), and they cease to exist when God takes away their breath/spirit (v. 29).

Much of Romans 8 focuses on the powerful and revivifying power of the Spirit. In Romans

1–7, Paul talks a lot about sin and the death that it brings about. Death, like sin, is personified. Death reigns over humans, subjecting all of humanity to its demands (Rom. 5:12–17; 6:20–23). Death in Romans is not only a physical thing, the cessation of respiration or brain activity. Death impinges upon human life *now*, so much so that Paul's rhetorical "I" cries out, "Wretched man that I am! Who will rescue me from this body of death?" (7:24).

If the early chapters of Romans create a connection between sin and death, Romans 8 connects the Spirit and life. The Spirit undoes what sin and death have brought about. The Spirit brings a new law that releases humanity from the law of sin and death (8:2). Set free, humanity is able to live "according to the Spirit" (v. 4), set their minds on the "things of the Spirit" (v. 5), and experience "life and peace" (v. 6). Even though the body is dead because of sin, the Spirit's indwelling power brings life (v. 10). As the Spirit brings life to dry bones in Ezekiel, Romans 8:11 says that the Spirit gives life to mortal bodies, to bodies that are prone and subjected to death. What is more, the Spirit enables humans to put an end to the death-bringing practices that previously characterized their existence (v. 13).

All of this sounds quite positive, even triumphal, but Paul's reflection on the Spirit in

Romans 8 does not end in verse 13. It is not all easy living, now that the Spirit has come. Rather, while the Spirit indicates that we are God's children and coheirs with Christ, we also share in the sufferings of Christ (vv. 16–17).

Even with the revivifying power of the Spirit, the reality of human suffering remains. Paul links humanity's suffering and the earth's bondage to decay (v. 21). Paul insists that *all of creation* longs for redemption from decay. Paul likens the "whole creation" to a mother in labor, experiencing the excruciating birth pains that come as something new is brought into existence. The metaphor of labor reminds us that this pain is productive; it is ultimately leading somewhere. Yet, if we read this text in the context of the first-century world, we realize the precarious nature of birthing new things. The mother's birth pains signaled both the advent of new life and the very real possibility of losing her own. Painful, productive, and precarious—creation groans as it awaits God's new thing.

Humanity groans along with the created order. We groan as we "wait for adoption, the redemption of our bodies" (v. 23). Yes, the Spirit marks humanity's adoption, enabling us to cry out to God, "Abba!" (v. 15); the indwelling Spirit testifies that we are God's children (v. 16). Yet we groan to experience this adoption more fully. Paul links this waiting for adoption with the redemption of the body. For all that the Spirit's advent has done, it has not removed the reality of the body's own bondage to decay.

Romans 8 imagines another form of Spirit-speak, an additional Pentecost experience. If the Spirit in Acts enabled foreigners to hear the good news in their own tongue, the Spirit in Romans 8 gives voice to the whole created order's longing for redemption. While Western culture spends billions of dollars on ad campaigns and beauty products that promise to slow the process of aging, Paul's reflection on the Spirit calls for a sober assessment of the reality of decay in the natural world and in our own. Melting ice caps and rising sea levels, violent tropical storms and pervasive drought are poignant reminders of the earth's own "bondage to decay," much of which has been brought about by humanity's tendency to domination and greed. Our bodies too are prone to decay, evidenced by crippling mental illness, cracking joints, the diminishment of the brain's executive functions, and the gradual loss of movement.

Romans 8 reminds us that Christian existence is one of hopeful waiting. The realities of the earth's and humanity's bondage to decay can easily lead to the desperate plea of the Israelites in Ezekiel 37:11: "Our bones are dried up, and our hope is lost; we are cut off completely." If we had only our own resolve and reality to depend on, perhaps the cry of the Israelites would be unavoidable. However, the very animating, life-giving Spirit meets us in our weakness, in our experience of decay. She prays for us. She wraps up our weakness and our cries of desperation, not in neat packages of religious platitudes tied with bows of piety. The Spirit groans for and with us. She joins her voice to our own sobs and pleas, and she "intercedes with words too deep for words" (v. 26). As the Spirit enables us to share in the life and suffering of Christ, so too the Spirit shares in our own experience of suffering. She shows solidarity with human suffering. Because the Spirit groans and suffers with us, and because God knows the "mind of the Spirit" (v. 27), we can be confident that God too knows and hears our sighs.

Balanced with the other Pentecost texts, Romans 8:22–27 makes space for us to name and acknowledge that all is not yet right. It reminds us that, even after all that God has done for us in and through Christ and the sending of the Spirit, we still experience the realities of our bondage to decay. Romans 8:22–27 makes room for lament at Pentecost, a lament for the brokenness of our bodies and our body politic, of the breakdown of our environment and the fabrics of our society. This passage reminds us that groaning and sighing are not impious responses to our lived realities. They are Pentecost moments. In places of deep pain, places between the promise of new life and the risk of death, God's Spirit meets us, reminds us that we are children of God, and inhabits our speech with sighs too deep for words.

CHRISTOPHER T. HOLMES

Commentary 2: Connecting the Reading with the World

I have been fortunate to serve churches in close proximity to the Pacific Ocean. I take evening walks on the beach, and I am awed by the vast beauty of that wilderness. Yet each tide leaves behind a fresh array of trash. One July day, I looked down to find a Christmas ornament decorating the kelp. I left it there, indifferent. Tomorrow's tide would return it to sea and replace it with another selection of discarded plastic. Nothing I could do would make a visible dent in that pollution. That indifference is a failure of faith; hope that is seen is not hope (Rom. 8:24).

Faith is best understood, I have come to understand, not as a cognitive affirmation of "beliefs" but rather in the ancient Hebrew sense of *hesed*: steadfast loyalty, faithfulness, an unshakable persistence in loving God and neighbor. Yet how can our own faithfulness be sustained in the face of overwhelming evidence to its futility? A sermon on these verses of Romans on the day of Pentecost is an opportunity to explore this question. Romans is Paul's magnum opus to the faithfulness of God. Pentecost is the church's commission to faithfulness.

Creation suffers, as do we. The love, goodness, and beauty that humanity breathes into the world every day is an astonishing testament to the abundance of God; yet this gift, like our pollution of the roiling sea, is marred every day by suffering, hatefulness, and brutality without end. It is true, to paraphrase an ancient rabbinical saying, that our place is not to finish the work—that task is God's alone—but we are indeed called, anointed on the day of Pentecost, never to desist from it. When today's epistle lection is read in worship, suffering is plain, but the most essential word I hear in the text is hope. Faith needs hope to sustain it.

In the week-to-week preaching task of the pastoral ministry, I find Paul's genius to be his focus on the core virtues of Christian life: faith, hope, and love. These astonishing gifts of the Spirit—simple in speech, infinite in depth—manifest in peace or *shalom*: right relationship with God and one another. In practice, however, I find that Christians of the former Protestant establishment speak glibly of faith, too

easily of love, and peace—personal or communal—is desperately hard to come by. It may be that we speak too little of hope. "For in hope we were saved" (8:24).

When I was a freshman in seminary, a major percentage of the senior class failed a theology ordination exam. The question was a pragmatic case study: a congregation member asks you—you the Master of Divinity—a question about the book of Revelation. Students became lost in reflections on the rapture, dispensationalism, and the like. The systematic theology faculty took this badly. The next year the lesson was made plain to us—repeatedly—that if you ever get a question on apocalyptic literature, the answer is hope!

In the years since, I have been grateful for my colleagues' misfortune. The lesson is remarkably helpful. On this side of the veil of tears that separates heaven and earth, every person is fighting a battle. It is a special kind of suffering that suffers without hope. Hope is not only the spiritual longing crying out from apocalyptic texts; it is, I believe, the *cantus firmus*, the ground basis of the Christian faith itself.

The resurrection of Jesus Christ is, after all, only the penultimate sign of our ultimate hope: that in the end all things are in the hands of whatever it is that we gesture at with the word "God." This God—as made plain in the life, death, and resurrection of Jesus Christ—is faithful. On the last day, our God of hope (Rom. 15:13) will wipe every tear from our eyes and make all things new (Rev. 21:3–5). Today is likely that day: ours is not to complete the work, but neither are we to desist from it.

The rhetoric of the majestic eighth chapter of Paul's letter to the church in Rome drives forward, through the suffering of creation, toward the one thread that remains for me when all else is doubtful: "For I am convinced that neither death, nor life, . . . nor things present, nor things to come . . . nor anything else in all creation, will be able to separate us from the love of God in Christ Jesus our Lord" (8:38–39). Until the last day, we live in this hope, hope that even in the narrative Scriptures seems as fragile gossamer, yet is a promise stronger than death itself.

A sermon on this text has the opportunity to penetrate the deepest longing and anxieties of our troubled lives and proclaim the most astonishing Word we know.

Like those seminary students floundering in Revelation, however, I am not sure that, as modern Christians, we know what hope means. We take lesser versions as gospel. Our hope passes for faith in progress and our desires for wishful thinking. With the world drawn close in the information age, division, prejudice, violence, and racism of all varieties are instantaneously apparent and virulent in whatever news feed or social media platform we subscribe to. It is certainly the case that if we seek hope in what is seen, that hope is dashed in the news cycle of the day.

Sometimes one is helped to know a thing by establishing some clarity on what it is not. Hope is not wishful thinking, and our hope is not to be found in the advance of technology and knowledge. When I was a child, I absorbed modernity's confidence in itself by watching mid-century science fiction repeats after I came home from school. I watched the original *Star Trek* TV show again and again, imagining myself in the captain's chair, science station, or at the helm. I was inhabiting a world where science, logic, and technology rid the earth of hunger, war, poverty, even money—something often at issue in a preacher's kid's home. I had no doubt that this was where human history was headed.

For some of us, our spirituality followed the same pattern: "liberal" Protestant Christians were so confident in themselves that the mainline Protestant newsmagazine that went into production at the dawn of the twentieth century was titled *The Christian Century*. Obviously, that was not the case; and sadly, perhaps, I have never been part of a Christian community that did not see its best days as past days. Hope is that confidence in the future that remains when faith in progress and faith in our own control of our world are exhausted.

At one point or another, like every human being, I have struggled with anxiety. Contending with this, I came upon a practice called breath prayer. I take walks, simply breathing in deeply and breathing out, "All will be well." Invariably this brings me calm; though sometimes it is a long walk. Intellectually, we are tempted to think this is cliché. Spiritually, we know it is the essence of prayer: opening ourselves to the presence of a God who endures our suffering with us. My guess is that, for the first followers of Jesus in the moment of his crucifixion, their work and ministry together appeared as fruitless as tending to one piece of "God with Us" on a vast shore of pollution. That, of course, was not the last word, or we would not be reading and preaching this text today. Hatred and death will never, ever be the last word. That Word is God's. This is hope.

MARK F. STURGESS

John 15:26–27; 16:4b–15

15:26"When the Advocate comes, whom I will send to you from the Father, the Spirit of truth who comes from the Father, he will testify on my behalf. 27You also are to testify because you have been with me from the beginning. . . .

16:4b"I did not say these things to you from the beginning, because I was with you. 5But now I am going to him who sent me; yet none of you asks me, 'Where are you going?' 6But because I have said these things to you, sorrow has filled your hearts. 7Nevertheless I tell you the truth: it is to your advantage that I go away, for if I do not go away, the Advocate will not come to you; but if I go, I will send him to you. 8And when he comes, he will prove the world wrong about sin and righteousness and judgment: 9about sin, because they do not believe in me; 10about righteousness, because I am going to the Father and you will see me no longer; 11about judgment, because the ruler of this world has been condemned.

12"I still have many things to say to you, but you cannot bear them now. 13When the Spirit of truth comes, he will guide you into all the truth; for he will not speak on his own, but will speak whatever he hears, and he will declare to you the things that are to come. 14He will glorify me, because he will take what is mine and declare it to you. 15All that the Father has is mine. For this reason I said that he will take what is mine and declare it to you."

Commentary 1: Connecting the Reading with Scripture

Like last week's Gospel lection, this reading is part of the lengthy final discourse (John 13–17) that Jesus addresses to his disciples just before his arrest, crucifixion, and resurrection. In these chapters, he speaks with such prescience, clarity, and boldness about the future that it is as if the disciples—and by extension the community of believers who overhear these words—are being addressed directly by the risen one. This is why lections from this lengthy discourse are especially appropriate during the season of Easter.

In 15:26, Jesus once again (see also 14:16, 26) promises the coming of the Holy Spirit, described as the Paraclete (NRSV "Advocate"). This way of naming the Spirit points toward its role of pleading the community's cause in the face of opposition. This understanding of the Spirit's work is consistent with passages in the Synoptic Gospels (Matt. 10:20; Mark 13:11; Luke 12:12) that promise that the Holy Spirit will come to the community's aid, giving them the appropriate words to say when they are handed over and tried for their beliefs.

The situation that will call for an advocate is made explicit in 16:1–4a, verses that have been omitted by the Revised Common Lectionary, but which provide context that is essential to understanding the passage as a whole. The community that first received the Fourth Gospel was caught up in an intramural conflict within Judaism concerning belief in Jesus. This passage anticipates that conflict, depicting Jesus as speaking directly to a situation in which his future followers will be excommunicated from the synagogues and even killed (16:2) on account of their faith in him. In the midst of such trials, the Spirit will come to plead their case.

Strikingly, the role of the Spirit is not to advocate in ways that will exonerate the community or keep it from harm, but rather to make sure that they faithfully tell the truth about Jesus and his mission. This focus on true testimony about Jesus is prevalent in the Fourth Gospel. The witnesses include the Samaritan woman (4:39), John the Baptist (5:33), the Father (5:37), and Jesus himself (18:37). In continuity with this line of true testimony, Jesus promises that the "Spirit of truth" will testify on his behalf (15:26). This assurance is then immediately followed with the injunction that his followers should also testify. In other words, the work of the Spirit will be to inspire the believing community to join its voice to this chorus of witnesses.

Consistent with the theme of the Gospel lections from the two previous weeks (Luke 24 and John 17), Jesus is depicted here as anticipating a future in which his absence will cause a crisis for the community. Especially reminiscent of its effect in Luke 24, Jesus' departure may cause sorrow (John 16:6), but it is necessary as the precondition for the coming of the Spirit (16:7), who will continue his missional agenda in a way that would not be possible, were he to remain physically present.

As noted above, the work of the Spirit is surprisingly unconcerned with keeping the community safe from conflict. Contemporary readers may be inclined to misinterpret the disciples' sorrow as concern for their own well-being, and the Spirit's help as a promise to shelter them and keep them safe from harm, but this passage emphasizes that the Spirit's work is actually focused on helping them in the sense of taking their side, so that the truth will be told fearlessly and persuasively. If we think in terms of the metaphor of a trial, the Spirit-Advocate is not so much presented as defending the community, but rather as prosecuting their enemies. In view of the community's intramural conflict with Judaism, the Spirit's presence with them will help them make the case ("prove," 16:8) that those who cast them out of the synagogues are wrong—wrong, in the first place, about "sin, because they do not believe in me" (v. 9).

This recapitulates a claim that the Fourth Gospel argues in narrative form in chapter 9, namely, that sin is not a matter of immoral conduct, but rather of rejecting Jesus as sent from God. Second, they are wrong about *dikaiosynē* (NRSV "righteousness," but here in the sense of "being right"), because Jesus will be vindicated by resurrection and go to be with the Father (v. 10). Finally, they are wrong about "judgment" (v. 11), because though they judge the community that believes in Jesus, it is the "ruler of this world" who has deceived them

and who will therefore be "judged" (NRSV "condemned").

Perhaps the most fascinating section of this passage for contemporary Christian preaching comes in 16:12–15. Jesus states that there are things that he needs to say, but he cannot say to them "now" (v. 12). The "now" of this statement is the time depicted in the narrative, that is, during the earthly ministry of Jesus. The text anticipates a future moment in which the believing community will be in a new situation that will enable and demand new words. The role of the Spirit will be to speak that future truth—words that Jesus himself would have said if he were present in that new moment with its new demands. What we have here in narrative form is an exposition of the contextual limits of linguistic truth. In this story, it is presented as a limit about oral language, but for us, mutatis mutandis, it suggests also the limits of authoritative texts.

In a sense, the Fourth Gospel is simply admitting that it would have been impossible for the earthly Jesus to have said all that the community would ever need to hear about how to think and feel and act in every conceivable new situation. In fact, the Fourth Gospel itself functions as an example of new teachings, new words of and about Jesus that needed to be spoken in the new situation faced by the community that first read it at the end of the first century CE. This is the role of the Spirit—to interpret new situations and to speak afresh into those new situations in ways that are consistent with the identity and mission of Jesus. For us, the implications are profound. The "new" words of the Fourth Gospel are no longer new to us, and the situations faced by believing communities today will call for new interpretations and new words—words borne by the Spirit of the risen one, who is still articulate in our midst, saying new things in order to remain faithful to the work that began so long ago.

True fidelity demands novelty. Sometimes fidelity to the spirit of old words may require that we even "push back" against those old words at the Spirit's urging. For example, this text's polemical description of the hatred, ostracization, and violence suffered by the believing community that first received it—a community that had very little power—may now function in some contexts to inspire new hatred, ostracization, and violence.

For this reason, this text cries out for reconsideration in a new context, with a different power structure. What new words—words that the community that first read John could not possibly understand or "bear"—might the Spirit be trying to say to us in this new moment? To take very seriously the specific issue raised by this passage: in the wake of the atrocities of the Holocaust and the recent resurgence of the death-dealing ideology of white supremacy, what would it mean for the Spirit to "guide" the contemporary church "into all the truth" (v. 13) about its disposition toward and debt to Judaism?

LANCE B. PAPE

Commentary 2: Connecting the Reading with the World

The challenge of preaching Pentecost is different from the challenge of preaching Christmas or Easter. Christians in the US know these holidays matter; the market has taught them that. However, the market has not yet figured out how to profit off Pentecost. Something about the babe in the manger and the bunny (!) in springtime makes for sales and shopping. The fire and the strange tongues and the mission-to-all-nations . . . yeah, that does not seem to move product—at least not yet.

Perhaps like me you have preached through a few Pentecosts. You know the challenge now of trying to convince folks for whom this is just another Sunday that it is actually one of the great celebrations of the church year. Those Western Protestants who are already dodgy on the Holy Spirit are supposed to make nice with a person of the Trinity about whom their Pentecostal neighbor speaks with entirely too much frequency and familiarity. You have plumb worn out that Acts 2 text. If that is your story, preacher, cheer up. This lection from John is for you.

The Spirit is spoken of here in John as the Paraclete. We immediately bump up against issues of translation. The NRSV renders this as the "Advocate," legal terminology that is appropriate. It can ignite a sermon on what it means to have a powerful attorney on our side of the courtroom, a muscle-bound protector to keep the bullies away. When I was a seminary intern, I was in a minor car wreck that totaled my vehicle. The insurance company tried to stiff me the few hundred bucks that for them was nothing, but for me was the ability to do my work and live my life. An attorney in the congregation made a phone call and suddenly a check was cut. I had an advocate who normally made more in an hour than my car was worth, whose pro bono advocacy got me back on the road.

How much more an Advocate who is one with the Father? The New Testament loves this courtroom language: our defense attorney here is the Holy Spirit. Who accuses us? Only Christ. A district attorney who is entirely on our side. Who judges? The God merciful enough to make and redeem all in love. We have nothing to fear.

Of course, none of this worked out well for Jesus. He is bound for his own mock trial and unjust conviction. He gets the legal treatment we fear and gives us the legal treatment he deserves. The trade at the heart of the gospel is immeasurably generous on God's part. Most of the time we go on as if nothing remarkable has happened. Preaching sounds a trumpet. Look! See! Here is what God has done for us! Here is who God *is* for us! My favorite description of the Holy Spirit is as God *in* us—in our hearts, our living rooms, moving furniture around, making a home. This contrasts with Christ as God *for* us, working on our behalf, making right what we made wrong but could never repair.

Another translation of Paraclete is as the "Comforter," a translation as venerable as the King James Version. This passage does come up at funerals, when we reach, above all, for comfort. My worry is that the image in English is altogether too placid, restful. Celtic Christians have long imagined the Holy Spirit as a wild goose—loud, demanding, aggressive if necessary, but not at all calm or quiet. Of course, comfort is empty if it comes from someone who can do nothing about our circumstances. The Spirit, according to Paul, is the one who raises

Jesus from the dead, the one who makes all creation holy, the one who transfigures us from one degree of glory to another. This may be a different sort of comfort than what I reach for with Netflix and ice cream. It is the comfort of One who will get the world God wants, despite whatever opposition or temporary victories are won by death.

One hallowed image for the Holy Spirit in the life of the church is that the Spirit is the very love shared by the Father and the Son. Since the Father and the Son are both eternal, the love between them is too—a sort of third thing. Think too of whatever relationship you are in that matters to you. There is you, the other person, and then the relationship between you is almost its own entity. Augustine gave us this analogy: the lover, the beloved, and the love between them. In the divine life we capitalize that *L* and say it is God's own person all over again. Critics have worried that the image risks relegating the Spirit to barely their status, as if not a "person" in his own right. Of course, the church has always recognized that "person" barely fits for what there is three of in God, but we have yet to find a suitable substitute. Advocate, Comforter, Love: these are remarkably fresh words for God. As Christians, we should think of God as a powerful defender, a tender conciliator, the glue that attracts within relationship. Indeed, we have good news to tell.

Sarah Coakley, a theologian at Cambridge, speaks of the way Pentecostals pray. When we get quiet enough, we may hear another praying within us. Prayer is joining a conversation long in progress, a dialogue of love between the Spirit and the Father. The Son is creation being deified. We never start prayer, we only join it, long since in progress. Pentecost says there is no person, no living thing, no particle of creation that is not prayed for by God. When we pray, we join in the heartbeat of the universe, the glory of Love that makes all things what they are, and not only that, but what they will be in God's good time—glorious, resplendent, unimaginably beautiful (John 16:14–15).

Another powerful image for the Spirit in these verses is as the teacher (vv. 8–13). Think of the best teacher you ever had. That person could read from the phone book and you would be entranced. They would give a lecture about quarks, and you would turn up and take notes. We choose teachers not for the content of their material, but because of their character, their person, something that attracts us to learn more. The Holy Spirit is all that and more. This is hard to see, because we in the church get in the way and distort. Nevertheless, despite our occlusion, the Holy Spirit still burns through, bright as the sun, shining in whatever is fair.

That might be the most frightening thing about the Spirit, Wild Goose that she is. Not just that the Spirit drives us to speak in languages and to people who are unfamiliar, whom we would not have chosen, who might even be enemies. Not just that the Spirit advocates muscularly, or comforts with her talons, or teaches his guts out. The Spirit makes us and all things holy. Transfigures us into saints. Like it or not, that is the destiny toward which humanity is headed. It will not be linear, direct, or easy. There is lots of resistance left in us, in others, in all things, but the Spirit, you may have heard, is powerful indeed, Power itself, and will have the world God wants.

JASON BYASSEE

Ezekiel 37:1–14

¹The hand of the LORD came upon me, and he brought me out by the spirit of the LORD and set me down in the middle of a valley; it was full of bones. ²He led me all around them; there were very many lying in the valley, and they were very dry. ³He said to me, "Mortal, can these bones live?" I answered, "O Lord GOD, you know." ⁴Then he said to me, "Prophesy to these bones, and say to them: O dry bones, hear the word of the LORD. ⁵Thus says the Lord GOD to these bones: I will cause breath to enter you, and you shall live. ⁶I will lay sinews on you, and will cause flesh to come upon you, and cover you with skin, and put breath in you, and you shall live; and you shall know that I am the LORD."

⁷So I prophesied as I had been commanded; and as I prophesied, suddenly there was a noise, a rattling, and the bones came together, bone to its bone. ⁸I looked, and there were sinews on them, and flesh had come upon them, and skin had covered them; but there was no breath in them. ⁹Then he said to me, "Prophesy to the breath, prophesy, mortal, and say to the breath: Thus says the Lord GOD: Come from the four winds, O breath, and breathe upon these slain, that they may live." ¹⁰I prophesied as he commanded me, and the breath came into them, and they lived, and stood on their feet, a vast multitude.

¹¹Then he said to me, "Mortal, these bones are the whole house of Israel. They say, 'Our bones are dried up, and our hope is lost; we are cut off completely.' ¹²Therefore prophesy, and say to them, Thus says the Lord GOD: I am going to open your graves, and bring you up from your graves, O my people; and I will bring you back to the land of Israel. ¹³And you shall know that I am the LORD, when I open your graves, and bring you up from your graves, O my people. ¹⁴I will put my spirit within you, and you shall live, and I will place you on your own soil; then you shall know that I, the LORD, have spoken and will act, says the LORD."

Commentary 1: Connecting the Reading with Scripture

The book of Ezekiel begins with the throne of YHWH flying from the temple in Jerusalem to Babylon. The opening image captures the thoroughly exilic concerns of the book. In response to the pressing question of the historical moment, Why have we lost our land, our temple, and our nation? Ezekiel is emphatic. The people are completely responsible for the destruction God decided to bring upon them. In image after image and diatribe after diatribe, Ezekiel justifies the divine decision to punish an Israel who freely, consistently—even wantonly—made one bad choice after another (see, e.g., Ezek. 18). Therefore, in the context of the book, the turn to hope that begins with oracles of restoration in Ezekiel 34 and 36 comes as a

surprise. Perhaps not surprising, however, is that restoration is possible only because of God (it has nothing to do with any good thing the people may or may not have done). God's decision to restore the people is rooted not in God's love for the people (cf. Hosea) or in God's pathos (cf. Jeremiah), but in God's desire to demonstrate God's own power.

For Christians, Ezekiel 37:1–14 is a beloved text because it appears to support the Christian doctrine of resurrection. While this is true to some degree, at least poetically, the images in this text do not reflect a resurrection of individuals. Rather, the hope is for the resurrection and restoration of the people Israel to the land of Israel.

When God leads Ezekiel with God's own hand (*yad*), a word that can also mean "power," to the valley of the dry bones, the fate of the people appears to have been sealed (37:1). In a vision, Ezekiel sees the bones of his people lying desiccated and exposed in the valley. This is the equivalent of a tour of hell. The tragedy here is not merely that these formerly living, breathing humans will never again have life, but that their bones are lying in a heap in some unnamed Babylonian valley, uncared for and haphazardly dispersed outside of a family tomb. In the Old Testament, a fulfilled life concludes with one's descendants gathering one's bones into a collective repository to "sleep with his fathers," to be revered and remembered as the ancestors of the living. This vision would have seemed an abomination to the ancient audience.

Further, their bones are languishing outside the land of Israel. This text speaks to the rich connection between people and their homeland, and reminds us of something many Christians in the West have been socialized out of acknowledging, namely, that place matters. For ancient people, whose selves were formed in a particular landscape, place was constitutive of identity. Imagining that a meaningful Israelite afterlife could take place outside of the land would be akin to sketching a vision of heaven in which one's loved ones are absent. For many, that simply would not constitute a hopeful view of an afterlife.

The description of the valley in verse 2 is a staccato attempt to capture the stammering, horrifying incompleteness of this vision. In the span of this one verse, there are three repetitions: "around, around" (*sabib sabib*), "look . . . look" (*hinneh . . . hinneh*), and "very . . . very" (*meod . . . meod*).

In response to God's question about whether the dead are truly dead, Ezekiel stammers: "My Lord, YHWH, you, you know" (v. 3b). The additional second-person pronoun here ("you") could be for emphasis, but it could also express that he is dumbfounded by the question (something along the lines of "God only knows!"). God then tells Ezekiel to prophesy to the bones, telling them to "hear the word of YHWH" (v. 4). The content of the message is revealed in verse 5, where God says that he will bring breath

(*ruakh*) into the bones and the bones will live. This recalls the preface to creation in Genesis 1, where the spirit (*ruakh*) sweeps over the waters in anticipation of bringing form and shape to the formlessness and void of the primordial world (Gen. 1:2). The breath of God will transform the formlessness of the bones in order to form a living people. Also recalled here is Genesis 2, in which YHWH breathes breath (*ruakh*) into the creature (*'adam*) he shapes from the dirt (*'adama*) in order to animate it (Gen. 2:7). Ezekiel 37 is, at its core, about God's creative activity and God's decision to bring breath and life into lifeless places and breathless people.

The prophecy recalls an incantation; Ezekiel drums out the words of life, surrounding the enfleshed corpses with breath and life:

> breath and life (v. 5a)
> sinews, flesh, and skin (v. 6a)
> breath and life (v. 6b).

Even before he has finished speaking, Ezekiel begins to hear a noise. The NRSV's translation of the Hebrew word *ra'aš* as "rattling" (other translations have "rustling") seems a bit tame, given this sound is elsewhere associated with the thundering noise of an earthquake (1 Kgs. 19:11; Isa. 29:6; Zech. 14:5) or the din of an approaching army (Isa. 9:4; Jer. 47:3; Nah. 3:2).

The bones on the battlefield thunder as they come together, bone to bone. Ezekiel blinks and sees that they are covered with skin and sinews and flesh, but creepily, they are lacking *ruakh* ("breath" or "spirit"). As they stand zombie-like, midway through the process of transformation, God tells Ezekiel to prophesy to the *ruakh*, commanding it to "come from the four winds [*rukhot*]" to breathe into the slain ones (v. 9). A form of the word *ruakh* appears here four times and builds to the final word in the verse: *weyikhyu*, "that they may live."

The incantation-like prophecy works. The whole house of Israel ("a very, very great multitude," *gadol meod meod*) stands revived, filled with *ruakh* and life, before Ezekiel. However, they still despair. Plaintively they moan that their bones are dry, their hope is destroyed, and they are "cut off." There is a shift in the meaning of the word "bones" here. Of course, bones can simply refer to the individual calcified elements

When the Holy Spirit Is Poured Out

But you ask: "How shall I know that the Holy Spirit is come upon me?" I cannot tell how you will know, but you will know. No description has been given us of the personal sensations and emotions of the disciples at Pentecost. We do not know exactly how they felt, but we do know that their feelings and behaviour were somewhat abnormal, because people seeing them said they were intoxicated. . . .

When the Holy Spirit is poured out upon God's people their experiences will differ widely. Some will receive new vision, others will know a new liberty in soul-winning, others will proclaim the Word of God with power, and yet others will be filled with heavenly joy or overflowing praise. "This . . . and this . . . and this . . . is that!" Let us praise the Lord for every new experience that relates to the exaltation of Christ and of which it can truly be said that "this" is an evidence of "that." There is nothing stereotyped about God's dealings with His children. Therefore we must not by our prejudices and preconceptions make a water-tight compartment for the working of His Spirit, either in our own lives or in the lives of others. . . .

We must leave God free to work as He wills, and to give what evidence He pleases of the work He does. He is Lord, and it is not for us to legislate for Him.

Watchman Nee, *The Normal Christian Life* (Peabody, MA: Hendrickson, 2007), 86–87, 90.

of the skeleton, but they can also refer to the deepest or most essential part of the self (see Gen. 2:23). Thus, in the lament psalms, the psalmist cries out that their bones are wasting away (Ps. 31:10), shaking (Ps. 6:2), or burning like a furnace (Ps. 102:3).

Why do they lament? What more could these people who have been brought back to life en masse want? The final prophecy suggests that God knows precisely what the problem is: they are still "in graves" (the plural noun appears four times in vv. 12–13). They may look alive, but "cut off" from their land, they remain entombed. In the final four verses (vv. 11–14), the language of death, bones, and graves alternates with that of *ruakh*, life, and land. The house of Israel must be placed back in the land for the "resurrection" to be complete. God vows to open their graves and bring them up from their graves and return them to the land (*'adama*) of Israel because God recognizes that life lived outside of their land is no life at all.

Once God has revived the people and returned them to their land, then they will know that Ezekiel has channeled the speech of YHWH and that the power behind and in that speech can be trusted. What YHWH says, YHWH will do. This is consistent with a refrain in the book, that Israel and the nations will come to know that YHWH is the true God (7:27; 11:10; 13:23; 20:44).

AMY ERICKSON

Commentary 2: Connecting the Reading with the World

This is a perfect passage for Pentecost. It may not have fire, but it surely has breath or spirit. Ten times, "breath" or "spirit" is emphasized, grabbing the reader's attention—but what the Spirit does may not be what is expected. This passage offers preachers the chance to explore the work of the Spirit in a different context than what is normally noted or often considered. Many times, the Spirit is linked to celebrations,

joy, and ecstatic moments. From the beginning of Ezekiel's vision, it is important to remember that he was brought out by "the spirit of the LORD" and set down "in the middle of a valley; [and] it was full of bones."

This is unexpected for Pentecost. Usually, people get excited about Pentecost because they think about the celebration of the multilingual, multiethnic diversity of the church and the explosive power of God across the world on all flesh. Through the lens of Ezekiel, the reality is that sometimes the Spirit brings us to valleys of dry bones, not mountaintop peaks or upper rooms. This is holy honesty in the face of existential hell. Israel is in exile and says, "Our hope is lost." This too is a genuine part of the Christian life in the power of the Spirit. The Spirit works in and leads us to unlikely domains.

The Spirit leads Ezekiel to a place of death and contamination, not away from hard situations and histories. The Spirit leads one to domains of death and death-wielding realities. This vision of Ezekiel may provide an opportunity for congregations to grapple with understandings of the work of the Spirit that do not include prosperity and joy, because the Spirit will cause people to encounter death, lament, and hopelessness, even before any experience of hope or resurrection. In other words, you have to die before you live. This too is faithful discipleship. Christians may want to avoid tough times, but the Spirit will not allow a struggle-free life. If we are honest, it is unavoidable.

The dry bones of human existence are prominent today, just as the image of bones is the most prominent metaphor in this passage. To encounter the bones of the dead meant to risk contamination (Ezek. 39:15–16; cf. Num. 19:16–18). Without a doubt, this text challenges us to face death by speaking of bones, "graves," and the "slain." If we are listening closely, we may hear the spiritual, "Dem bones, dem bones, dem dry bones / Dem bones, dem bones, dem dry bones / Dem bones, dem bones, dem dry bones / Now hear the word of the Lord." Dem bones in Ezekiel offers possibilities to consider historical atrocities when real human bones were laid waste by vast destruction: the Holocaust for Jews, the Trail of Tears for Native Americans, and the enslavement of Africans, to name a few. Ezekiel and the Spirit will not allow us to forget these realities of death that still stink up the earth. The stench of these dry bones soaks the soil of the earth.

The Spirit leads to death. Ezekiel sees death. If we ignore these realities, we ignore what the Spirit might be wanting to do in and through us, and we reveal how we are dead to reality. The Spirit keeps it real and dry.

Beyond the horrific histories of "slain" people, this imagery could also be the door to helping people, in general, deal with the reality of physical death. In his book *Being Mortal*, Atul Gawande, a practicing surgeon, reveals the limits of medicine at the end of life and demonstrates and argues for a quality of life and dignity for all dying patients and their families in order to provide a good end. We all die. We all dry up. How do we prepare for death and handle it when faced with it in the Spirit, because it is inevitable? Do we plan our funerals? What do we think about palliative care? The Spirit makes us deal with our mortality, for we are mere mortals like Ezekiel.

Though death is a reality that the Spirit leads us toward, one should not think that death overwhelms the hope. Throughout the passage, the Spirit is also linked to life as we hear, "You shall live." There is still hope in the valley of dry bones, and the Spirit works through words or prophesying, affirming that words do things and have formative power. Ezekiel possesses the gift of powerful speech. Words should not be taken for granted, because they even spark a resurrection of the bones. Ezekiel reminds the reader that we are stewards of words, because words can hurt and help.

Not only do we see the inspired words of Ezekiel and their effectiveness, but there have been powerful words throughout the world that have shaped the imagination of nations. President Abraham Lincoln's Gettysburg Address is a classic example of the power of words to impact a nation through generations. Dr. Martin Luther King Jr.'s "I Have a Dream" speech altered the imagination of a nation during a time of the social death of racial segregation. When the Spirit is at work through words, there should be no surprise that these words live on, because words create new worlds.

This is not to say that we should be naive and think resurrections can be rushed. They cannot, and only God knows if the bones can live. The truth is that sometimes what may occur is only a semblance of resurrection and not the real thing. Resurrection is on God's watch, whether it is three days or three years. From the outside sometimes, it may look like resurrection, but it is only a zombie shell, because there is no breath or Spirit evident. When Ezekiel prophesies at one point, there is noise, rattling; bones come together; sinews, flesh, and skin emerge; but "there was no breath in them." This image can speak to the way there may be well-manicured structures in place but still no Spirit breathing life into an organization or people. It could be governmental agencies, nonprofits, churches, schools, or other organizations. A public educational system can be in place, but certain schools can still lack the resources to provide proper and adequate education to young people. It is a system or structure, but there is no breath in it. When a prison system becomes a huge profit-making business rather than aims to restore human beings to society, there is no breath.

The challenge of the Spirit is to always ask, "Where is the breath?" If there is no life, no breath, we are in the zombie zone. This also raises the question, "How are we stewards of breath in whatever sector of society we work?" In what ways are we facilitating life and breath or spirit through our lives and vocations? To be in the Spirit is to be on the side of life and through every activity implicitly declaring, "You shall live." Life is the goal. Hope is the telos, and newness does come as the passage reveals, but it takes time, God's time, and one may have to go through a valley to reach the mountaintop. Yet, there will be new worlds and open graves. Bones will live again. How and when, only God knows.

LUKE A. POWERY

Contributors

RHODORA E. BEATON, Associate Professor of Sacramental and Liturgical Theology, Aquinas Institute of Theology, St. Louis, MO

CHRIS BLUMHOFER, Visiting Assistant Professor of New Testament, Fuller Theological Seminary, Pasadena, CA

RYAN P. BONFIGLIO, Assistant Professor in the Practice of Old Testament, Candler School of Theology, Emory University, Atlanta, GA

ANNA M. V. BOWDEN, Lecturer in Religious Studies, Nazareth College, Rochester, NY

VALERIE BRIDGEMAN, Associate Professor of Homiletics and Hebrew Bible, Methodist Theological School in Ohio, Delaware, OH

JASON BYASSEE, Butler Chair in Homiletics and Biblical Hermeneutics, Vancouver School of Theology, Vancouver, British Columbia

WARREN CARTER, LaDonna Kramer Meinders Professor of New Testament, Phillips Theological Seminary, Tulsa, OK

DIANE G. CHEN, Professor of New Testament, Palmer Theological Seminary of Eastern University, St. Davids, PA

JIN YOUNG CHOI, Professor of New Testament and Christian Origins, The Baptist Missionary Training School Professorial Chair for Biblical Studies, Colgate Rochester Crozer Divinity School, Rochester, NY

DAVID DARK, Associate Professor of Religion and the Arts, Belmont University, Nashville, TN

MIGUEL A. DE LA TORRE, Professor of Social Ethics and Latinx Studies, Iliff School of Theology, Denver, CO

O. C. EDWARDS JR., Professor Emeritus of Preaching; Former President and Dean, Seabury-Western Seminary, now a part of Bexley-Seabury Seminary located at Chicago Theological Seminary, Chicago, IL

AMY ERICKSON, Associate Professor of Hebrew Bible, Iliff School of Theology, Denver, CO

WENDY FARLEY, Rice Family Chair of Spirituality, Graduate School of Theology, San Francisco Theological Seminary, University of Redlands, San Anselmo, CA

LINCOLN E. GALLOWAY, K. Morgan Edwards Associate Professor of Homiletics, Claremont School of Theology, Claremont, CA

DAVID GAMBRELL, Associate for Worship, Office of Theology and Worship, Presbyterian Church (U.S.A.), Louisville, KY

DEIRDRE GOOD, Instructor, Stevenson School for Ministry, Diocese of Central Pennsylvania, Harrisburg, PA

JOEL B. GREEN, Professor of New Testament Interpretation and Associate Dean for the Center for Advanced Theological Studies, Fuller Theological Seminary, Pasadena, CA

ANN HIDALGO, Mary P. Key Diversity Resident Librarian for Teaching and Learning, The Ohio State University, Columbus, OH

CHRISTOPHER T. HOLMES, John H. Stembler, Jr. Scholar in Residence and Director of Biblical and Theological Education, First Presbyterian Church, Atlanta, GA

MARK ANDREW JEFFERSON, Assistant Professor of Homiletics, Virginia Theological Seminary, Alexandria, VA

WILLIE JAMES JENNINGS, Associate Professor of Systematic Theology and Africana Studies, Yale Divinity School, New Haven, CT

LINDSEY S. JODREY, Associate Director of Digital Learning, Princeton Theological Seminary, Princeton, NJ

JOHN KALTNER, Virginia Ballou McGehee Professor of Muslim-Christian Relations, Rhodes College, Department of Religious Studies, Memphis, TN

KRISTA KIGER, Executive Director, Community Missions Corporation, St. Joseph, MO

MIHEE KIM-KORT, PhD student in Religious Studies, Indiana University, Bloomington, IN

STEVEN J. KRAFTCHICK, Professor of the Practice of New Testament Interpretation, Candler School of Theology, Emory University, Atlanta, GA

THOMAS G. LONG, Bandy Professor Emeritus of Preaching, Candler School of Theology, Emory University, Atlanta, GA

ALYCE M. MCKENZIE, George W. and Nell Ayers Le Van Professor of Preaching and Worship; Director, The Perkins Center for Preaching Excellence at SMU, Perkins School of Theology, Southern Methodist University, Dallas, TX

ERIC T. MYERS, Pastor, Frederick Presbyterian Church, Frederick, MD

RODGER Y. NISHIOKA, Senior Associate Pastor, Village Presbyterian Church, Prairie Village, KS

LANCE B. PAPE, Associate Professor of Homiletics, Brite Divinity School, Texas Christian University, Fort Worth, TX

LUKE A. POWERY, Dean of Duke University Chapel and Associate Professor of Homiletics, Duke University Chapel, Duke Divinity School, Durham, NC

CYNTHIA L. RIGBY, W. C. Brown Professor of Theology, Austin Presbyterian Theological Seminary, Austin, TX

RUBÉN ROSARIO RODRÍGUEZ, Professor of Theological Studies, Saint Louis University, St. Louis, MO

PAMELA S. SATURNIA, Pastor, First Presbyterian Church, Muscatine, IA

CAROLYN J. SHARP, Professor of Homiletics, Yale Divinity School, New Haven, CT

GARY V. SIMPSON, Associate Professor of Homiletics, Drew Theological School; Leading Pastor, The Concord Baptist Church of Christ, Brooklyn, NY

SHANELL T. SMITH, Associate Professor of New Testament and Christian Origins; Director, Cooperative Master of Divinity Program, Hartford Seminary, Hartford, CT

STEPHEN SMITH, Rector, St. Patrick's Episcopal Church, Dublin, OH

MARK L. STRAUSS, University Professor of New Testament, Bethel Seminary, St. Paul, MN

MARK F. STURGESS, Lead Pastor, Los Altos United Methodist Church, Long Beach, CA

JERRY L. SUMNEY, Professor of Biblical Studies, Lexington Theological Seminary, Lexington, KY

DAVID A. VANDERMEER, Minister of Music and Fine Arts, First Presbyterian Church, Ann Arbor, MI

KIMBERLY R. WAGNER, Assistant Professor of Homiletics, Axel Jacob and Gerda Maria (Swanson) Carlson Chair of Homiletics, Lutheran School of Theology at Chicago, Chicago, IL

ERIC WALL, Assistant Professor of Sacred Music and Dean of the Chapel, Austin Presbyterian Theological Seminary, Austin, TX

JONATHAN L. WALTON, Dean of Wake Forest University School of Divinity, Presidential Chair in Religion and Society, and Dean of Wait Chapel, Wake Forest University, Winston-Salem, NC

AUDREY WEST, Visiting Associate Professor of New Testament, Moravian Theological Seminary, Bethlehem, PA

WILL WILLIMON, Professor of Christian Ministry and Director of the Doctor of Ministry Program, Duke Divinity School, Durham, NC

Author Index

Abbreviations

C1	Commentary 1	G	Gospel
C2	Commentary 2	OT	Old Testament
E	Epistle	PS	Psalm
FR	First Reading (when not from the Old Testament)	SR	Second Reading (when not from the Epistles)

Numerals indicate numbered Sundays of a season; for example, "Lent 1" represents the first Sunday of Lent, and "Easter 2" the Second Sunday of Easter.

Contributors and entries

Rhodora E. Beaton	Easter 4 PS, Easter 5 PS, Easter 6 PS
Chris Blumhofer	Holy Thursday G C1
Ryan P. Bonfiglio	Ash Wednesday OT C1, Lent 1 OT C1, Lent 2 OT C1
Anna M. V. Bowden	Lent 3 E C2, Lent 4 E C2, Lent 5 E C2
Valerie Bridgeman	Liturgy of Passion G C2, Easter Day E C2, Easter Day G C2
Jason Byassee	Ascension G C2, Easter 7 G C2, Pentecost G C2
Warren Carter	Ascension FR C1, Easter 7 FR C1, Pentecost FR C1
Diane G. Chen	Lent 3 G C1, Lent 4 G C1, Lent 5 G C1
Jin Young Choi	Easter 4 FR C1, Easter 5 FR C1, Easter 6 FR C1
David Dark	Lent 3 G C2, Lent 4 G C2, Lent 5 G C2
Miguel A. De La Torre	Ash Wednesday OT C2, Lent 1 OT C2, Lent 2 OT C2
O. C. Edwards Jr.	Ash Wednesday G C1, Lent 1 G C1, Lent 2 G C1
Amy Erickson	Ash Wednesday OT C1, Lent 2 G C1, Pentecost OT C1
Wendy Farley	Ascension FR C2, Easter 7 FR C2, Pentecost FR C2
Lincoln E. Galloway	Ash Wednesday G C2, Lent 1 G C2, Lent 2 G C2
David Gambrell	Ascension PS, Easter 7 PS, Pentecost PS
Deirdre Good	Easter 4 G C1, Easter 5 G C1, Easter 6 G C1
Joel B. Green	Easter Day SR C1, Easter 2 E C1, Easter 3 E C1
Ann Hidalgo	Ash Wednesday E C2, Lent 1 E C2, Lent 2 E C2
Christopher T. Holmes	Ascension E C1, Easter 7 E C1, Pentecost E C1
Mark Andrew Jefferson	Easter Day OT C2, Easter 2 FR C2, Easter 3 FR C2
Willie James Jennings	Liturgy of Passion E C2, Holy Thursday E C2, Good Friday E C2
Lindsey S. Jodrey	Easter 4 E C2, Easter 5 E C2, Easter 6 E C2
John Kaltner	Lent 3 OT C1, Lent 4 OT C1, Lent 5 OT C1

Scripture Index

OT PSEUDEPIGRAPHA